Health Psychology

M. Robin DiMatteo
University of California, Riverside

Leslie R. Martin
La Sierra University

Allyn and Bacon

Boston • London • Toronto • Sydney • Tokyo • Singapore

For Gia, Mike, Mom, and the memory of my Dad.

m.r.d.

For Larry and Shirley, my wonderful parents.

l.r.m.

Executive Editor: *Carolyn Merrill*
Senior Marketing Manager: *Caroline Croley*
Editorial-Production Administrator: *Michael Granger*
Editorial-Production Service: *Walsh & Associates, Inc.*
Composition and Prepress Buyer: *Linda Cox*
Manufacturing Buyer: *Joanne Sweeney*
Cover Administrator: *Kristina Mose-Libon*
Electronic Composition: *Publishers' Design and Production Services, Inc.*

Copyright © 2002 by Allyn & Bacon
A Pearson Education Company
75 Arlington Street
Boston, MA 02116

Internet: www.ablongman.com

Library of Congress Cataloging-in-Publication Data
DiMatteo, M. Robin.
    Health psychology / M. Robin DiMatteo and Leslie R. Martin.
        p. cm.
    Includes bibliographical references and index.
    ISBN 0-205-29777-3
    1. Clinical health psychology.   2. Health promotion.   3. Health behavior.   4. Social medicine.   I. Martin, Leslie R.   II. Title.
    R726.5.D553 2001
    610'.1'9—dc21 2001033677

Photo credits appear on page 594.

Printed in the United States of America
10 9 8 7 6 5 4 3 2   06 05 04 03

CONTENTS

P A R T   T W O   Health and Behavior

PART THREE   Becoming Ill

7 The Process of Illness   241

PREFACE

In writing this book, *Health Psychology*, our goal has been to examine the effects of people's thoughts, emotions, motivations, and actions on their health. We focus on achievement and maintenance of health, on the experience of illness, and people's attempts to cope with the challenges of disease and the acquisition of medical care. Throughout these pages, we review extensive scientific findings regarding the deep intertwining of psychological factors with issues of health and healing. An important goal of the book is to help students to understand, predict, explain, and ultimately change health-related behavior.

Our book presents health issues as they are strongly grounded in interdisciplinary study. We focus on a broad-based approach to psychosocial issues in health, illness, and medical care, as well as on the new research on the etiology, diagnosis, control, and cure of disease. Our approach is rooted, as is the entire field of health psychology, in many areas of inquiry including clinical, social, personality, cognitive, developmental, and physiological psychology, as well as public health, medical sociology, and health outcomes and health policy research. We incorporate methodologies, theories, and substantive topics from these many related areas because of our own training and expertise and the complex nature of the discipline.

Health Psychology is written for undergraduate psychology and nonpsychology majors and graduate students new to the field of health psychology. Our approach and style are designed to be appealing and engaging to students, interspersing clinical case examples with both classic and recent literature. We focus on an individual, patient-oriented perspective with which students can identify and that can help prepare them to be future psychologists or health professionals. This individual approach focuses on human beings coming to terms with health and illness in their own lives and in the lives of their loved ones and emphasizes what they think, how they feel, what they do, and why. This approach centers attention on individual psychology, as well as on interpersonal relationships and on individuals within social structures, cultural settings, societal institutions, and systems of medical care. The individual perspective is supplemented with simultaneous examination of the organizational changes that have recently occurred in healthcare—in particular, how managed care affects individual patient issues. We have used a few personal examples to add a sense of intimacy with us as authors and with the subject matter, and we have attended to making our writing style accessible and enjoyable to students. Our focus on methodological issues teaches students to appreciate and critically examine health-related research and illustrates for them the role of scientific methodologies in arriving at important and applicable findings. In addition to a thorough treatment of Western medicine, we also discuss non-Western philosophies of and approaches to healing in the context of holism and a greater focus on mind-body issues. We include professional development issues for students and examine how they can relate the material in the book to their futures in psychology, medicine, nursing, dentistry, public health, and the allied health professions or to their further study of health psychology in graduate training in health, clinical, or counseling psychology.

Health Psychology provides a comprehensive coverage of a large set of important topics of concern in the field of Health Psychology. In Chapter 1 we begin with an examination of the field of health psychology, its definitions, early research literature, and common methodologies. We examine the process of medical care, laying the groundwork for the field with examination of the mind-body connection, and contrasting the biomedical and biopsychosocial models of illness. The basics of medical terminology are made clear for the student. The patient's perspective is examined in the context of what is known about psychological factors in illness and disease. In Chapters 2 and 3, the process of healthcare delivery is examined, including both instrumental and socioemotional communication in the medical encounter, as well as empathy, nonverbal communication, and the elusive concept of "bedside manner." The lives of medical professionals in training and practice are considered in Chapter 4, and the effects of professional stress and burnout, among other issues, are studied as they affect clinical decisions. The role of the contemporary U.S. healthcare system, insurance, access, and managed care are examined as they affect health professional-patient communication and the process of caring for patients.

In Chapter 5 we deal with the meaning and assessment of physical health, and with individuals' efforts to attain and maintain their health through preventive behaviors such as exercise, healthy diet, and the avoidance of smoking and alcohol/drug abuse. In Chapter 6, psychological theories are examined that help to elucidate the choices that individuals make to follow or ignore health advice. The many factors that affect patient adherence to recommended treatment regimens are presented and examined in the context of patients' lives.

Chapters 7 focuses on an individual's becoming ill—the factors that affect self-definitions of illness and perceptions of pain and symptoms. Theories of pain are then examined in Chapter 8, as are the newest findings of research on pain and its treatment/control. Chapter 9 deals with the psychosocial phenomenon of stress and its effects on health, and examines the field of psychoneuroimmunology. Psychophysiological disorders as they relate to stress are considered, as are concepts of coping and social support. Research findings on numerous methods for coping with stress are presented and discussed in Chapter 10.

Chapter 11 focuses on the patient's perspective in facing serious and life threatening conditions, and in Chapter 12 the challenges of chronic illness, disability, and aging are examined. In Chapter 13, we focus on the ordeal of facing terminal illness in oneself or a loved one. The experiences of bereavement and grieving, and their powerful effects on physical and psychological well-being, are also considered. In

Chapter 14, our book concludes with an examination of some issues relevant to health services and policy research including morbidity versus mortality, cost containment and variations in care, women's health, healthy aging, genetics and health, and health outcomes research. An appendix provides a "crash course" in anatomy and physiology for students who have not had the material in other classes.

In writing this book, we have drawn on our combined experience of over three decades teaching health psychology and conducting research in areas such as personality and illness, physician-patient relationships, physician stress, patient adherence, health promotion and disease prevention, aging, and women's health. We have worked in a variety of settings—psychological research in the laboratory and the field, hospital-based clinical studies, policy research, large-scale survey methods, and with large longitudinal databases. These experiences have provided a rich source of information and methodology for our wide coverage of the field of Health Psychology.

This book contains certain important features that make it especially accessible to advanced undergraduates and beginning graduate students in health psychology, as well as to students in the health sciences. The material does not require previous courses in psychology or in the health sciences. Technical terms in medicine, health services, and psychology are explained as they are encountered. This book has a section on medical terminology and helps students to develop essential skills for reading and working in the health professions. We focus considerable attention on explaining the etiology, prognosis, and treatment of diseases that are related to the psychological issues under consideration. One goal is to help the student of health psychology who has no medical background to become comfortable with issues in medicine that are essential to understanding health and illness. Likewise, we explain research and methodological issues throughout the book for the student who does not have a research background, and we emphasize and clarify the interplay of physiological and psychological factors in health and illness for all students.

Pedagogical features of this book include three types of boxes: (1) "Research Close-up" boxes, which deal with specific research approaches and provide example studies from the health psychology literature; (2) "Hot Topic" boxes, which involve interesting, recent, relevant findings in health psychology, and their "real-world" applications; and (3) "Across Cultures" boxes, which examine cross-cultural issues in health, illness, and medical care. Each chapter contains figures, drawings, tables, photos, detailed summaries, glossaries, and questions for "Thinking Critically." A notable feature of the book is the presentation of case studies in each chapter that provide important clinical stories that illustrate the complexity of applying knowledge of health psychology to real people.

We would like to acknowledge our editor, Carolyn Merrill, as well as the following reviewers, whose recommendations have been invaluable to us in our revisions of earlier drafts: Christopher R. Agnew, Purdue University; Lynette Bassman, California School of Professional Psychology at Alliant University; Lynne H. Durrant, University of Utah; Richard Dwore, University of Utah; Gloria Hamiliton, Middle Tennessee State University; Charles F. Kaiser, College of Charleston; Sara J. Knight,

Northwestern University; Scott F. Madey, Shippensburg University; Mary Meagher, Texas A & M University; Peter C. Trask, University of Michigan; Douglas J. Wessel, Black Hills State University; Josephine F. Wilson, Wittenberg University; and David A. Wittrock, North Dakota State University. We also thank students Desiree Bivens, Joe Harrell, and Michelle Perry for their assistance and colleagues David Madison, Cynthia Palmer, and Paul Wanlass for their support. We dedicate this book to our families.

CHAPTER

1

Introduction

In 1936, in India, an astonishing experiment was conducted on a prisoner who was condemned to death by hanging. The condemned man agreed instead to permit himself to be exsanguinated (have his blood let out), because such a death would be gradual and painless. So, the convict was strapped to a bed and blindfolded, and unbeknownst to him, containers filled with water were set up at each of the four bedposts and the water was allowed to drip into basins on the floor. The skin on the convict's four extremities was only lightly scratched, and the water was set to drip into the basins, first rapidly and then slowly. As the dripping of water stopped, the healthy young man's heart stopped also. He was dead, having lost not a drop of blood. (Lown, 1996)

Consider the case of a young psychiatrist, called to care for a patient who was suddenly paralyzed by a severe neurological disorder.

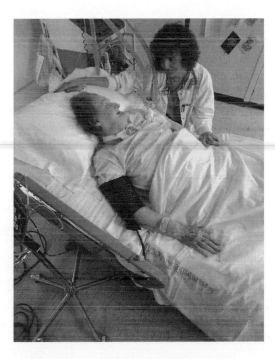

"I am called to see Mr. L because the staff in the intensive care unit are worried about his will to live . . . When I meet him, I see a helpless, locked-in, cachectic man . . . I greet him warmly . . . His eyes glaze over, and he goes a million miles away." (Halpern, 1993, p. 160)

The first case presents an amazing demonstration of the role of the mind in affecting the body and is an example, though somewhat extreme, of a common phenomenon known well to researchers and health professionals, alike—that powerful emotions can affect health.

Most physicians can tell stories of patients who became so enraged over something that they had heart attacks, or of people who were so saddened by a loss that they died of a "broken heart." In our own experience, we may hear a person say that he or she is "lighthearted," or has a "heart full to bursting," or has something "weigh heavily on the heart." We know that when we are under stress, we are more likely to get sick, and that people who become depressed and give up their will to live are more likely to die than those who are optimistic and fight to survive.

The second case is another example of how emotions are related to health. Here, the physician must work to develop *empathy* with her patient, to see the world through his eyes, and in viewing his care in the hospital from his perspective, try to lessen the pain and terror of his illness experience.

As we will see in this book about the fascinating field of health psychology, psychological factors play an important role in health and illness, as well as in the process of medical care, from the perspectives of both physician and patient alike.

The Field of Health Psychology

Until recently, nearly all psychologists have dealt fairly exclusively with issues or problems concerning "the mind." In the field of psychology, "illness" has traditionally referred to cognitive and emotional phenomena such as schizophrenia, anxiety, or depression. In the past forty years, however, psychologists have studied "illness" as it relates to the physical body. Health psychologists have begun to recognize the potentially far-reaching implications of their work for the achievement and maintenance of physical health and well-being. They have become particularly aware of the interplay of theory, research, and practice in the prevention and treatment of disease and in the understanding of illness. As healthcare itself has evolved, opportunities for psychologists to contribute to the healthcare process are constantly increasing (Cummings, 1996; Newman & Reed, 1996). As we will see later in this chapter, the common types of illness today are quite different from those experienced a century ago. Further, the ways in which people obtain medical care have also changed dramatically. These changes have been brought about by tremendous advances in the biological sciences and in technology, as well as in response to various social pressures. In turn, these changes have expanded the field of healthcare and have created professional niches for health psychologists to fill.

In the past, a select number of psychotherapists worked with medical patients in private psychotherapy practices and in teaching hospitals. The goals they pursued included evaluating their patients' mental status and attempting to control their patients' troublesome or self-destructive behaviors. For example, a patient who responded to cancer surgery with severe depression might have been referred to a psychotherapist. This referral may have come in response to the frustration of the patient's physician and family who feared the patient would commit suicide. Or, a hospital staff psychiatrist might have visited a hospitalized patient whose hostility had become a source of great distress to the nurses. The goals may have been to diminish the patient's troublesome behavior and to keep the hospital running smoothly.

Definition of Health Psychology

In the past three decades, the field of "health psychology" has emerged. This field involves research and practice dealing with the role of psychology in health and illness. Health psychology has as its goal a deeper understanding of psychological processes as an aid to improving physical health outcomes for individuals. Health psychologists subscribe to a biopsychosocial model, which is a philosophical point of view that posits the importance and interrelatedness of biological, psychological, and social/societal factors in determining health. Thus, health psychology is concerned with many different topics, such as:

1. Why and how people develop certain health habits (bad habits such as smoking and good habits such as exercising).
2. What factors determine whether a specific intervention will be effective in changing a person's health behavior.
3. What makes people get sick, and why people who are all exposed to the same environmental factors (stress, viruses, toxins) do not all experience the same outcomes.
4. Why different people respond differently to disease and illness.
5. How responses and coping styles can affect the course of a disease or illness.

This is certainly not an exhaustive list of the things that health psychologists study, but it does give an idea of just how broad the field has become.

Miriam is an 88-year-old woman who is recovering from breast cancer. She had one breast removed and is currently undergoing radiation therapy. When meeting Miriam for the first time, you can't help but notice that she seems to have a lot of energy. She smiles a lot and talks briskly. She walks briskly, too, and some of her friends say that they have a hard time keeping up with her. She works in her vegetable garden almost every day, cleans her own house, and belongs to several clubs that raise money for charity and take trips for education and entertainment. Bernice is also 88 years old, and recovering from breast cancer. Her situation, according to her doctor, matches Miriam's exactly—that is, they both had the same kind of cancer, both had a breast removed, and are both undergoing the same radiation therapy regimen. In terms of their measurable physical health, they are equal. Bernice spends most of her time sitting in a reclining chair, however, and rarely goes outside. She says that she has very little energy, and has "lost her pep." She no longer cooks for herself and requires help to keep her apartment clean. She has stopped playing bridge with her friends, and rarely does anything more than watch television. Why do Miriam and Bernice act so differently, when, objectively, their medical situations are so similar?

Health psychologists might address this question from a variety of different angles. They might examine previous behaviors: How active, physically and socially, was Miriam before her diagnosis and surgery? How active was Bernice? How did each woman come to develop these habits? Health psychologists might look at personal preferences and personality characteristics in order to determine what kind of program would be best for getting Bernice to be more active and more engaged in life. They might examine the social support systems that each woman has and talk with family and friends in an effort to strengthen weak areas in each woman's social network. They might look for subtle "rewards" that might be reinforcing Bernice's helpless behavior and then try to remove some of these and replace them with rewards for other, more proactive behaviors. All of these things would represent an effort to increase Bernice's "health," since her quality of life is lower than Miriam's even though her physical status, in terms of the details of her disease, may be equal.

The definition of health, itself, is fundamental to health psychology because the goal of health psychology is to foster health in its broadest sense. Health psychologists do not simply want to help people to be free of disease; they also want to help them maintain a state of mental and psychological health and an ability to do the things that are meaningful to them in their lives. Being "well" and "healthy" certainly depends, to a great degree, on one's physical health status. It is more than that, however. The World Health Organization (WHO) recognized the complexity of "health" more than fifty years ago when it defined health as "a complete state of physical, mental, and social well-being and not merely the absence of disease or infirmity" (WHO, 1948). Later in this chapter, we will further examine the role of health psychology in medicine and describe the ways in which health psychology is different from other fields such as psychosomatic medicine and behavioral medicine.

Early Research Literature

Throughout history, a few physician educators have had opinions about the need to understand the patient's psychology in order to care for his or her physical needs. In the fourth century BC, for example, Hippocrates wrote about how the physician's demeanor can engender a patient's trust and encourage a patient's will to live: "The patient, though his condition is perilous, may recover his health simply through his contentment with the goodness of the physician" (Hippocrates, 1923 translation). In 1904, Sir William Osler, a famous medical educator, lectured to medical students that they should listen to the patient because the patient's own words may reveal the diagnosis (Osler, 1904). Another famous physician, Frederick Shattuck (1907) argued that medicine is an art as well as a science.

In the 1950s, articles appeared in the research literature with titles such as "Choosing and Changing Doctors" (Gray & Cartwright, 1953) and "Why Do People

Detour to Quacks?" (Cobb, 1954). These early articles, written by medical practitioners as well as by psychologists and sociologists, attempted to deal with the complex questions that surrounded the rather widespread dissatisfaction of patients with their medical care professionals. Such papers appeared in the literature in the fields of medicine, psychiatry, nursing, psychology, sociology, pharmacy, hospital administration, medical economics, social work, and anthropology. They pointed to the need for medical professionals to recognize and deal effectively with the psychological as well as the physical aspects of clinical care.

The psychology of physical health and illness, as a field of study, was initially limited in several ways. First, the literature was quite sparse. Few journals carried more than one or two articles a year on the psychological and social aspects of physical illness. Second, the early research was not programmatic (i.e., systematically based on previous work). Researchers tended to carry out isolated studies and failed to build a body of knowledge about a particular topic by improving on the mistakes of earlier work. Third, much of the early work was primarily clinically based. The work of psychoanalysts on the expression of emotional illness through physical disorder is an example. Often, research was done using a clinical population, and then the results were generalized to nonclinical groups. Fourth, the early work was time-bound. That is, writing on health psychology issues often failed to examine general principles and instead dealt with prevailing social conditions. The fifth limitation, which we will examine in more detail later in this chapter, is that the research methods used in the early work on the psychology of health and illness were rather unsophisticated. As a result, in many cases findings remained inconclusive and clinical applications were tentative and sometimes incorrect.

Current Research Literature

The late 1970s saw tremendous progress in research on the psychology of health, illness, and medical care. Psychologists across the country who were interested in medical issues formed an organization. Scholars, researchers, and clinicians who had once been isolated in their work on health issues found the opportunity to share ideas and encouragement. In 1978, the Division of Health Psychology (38) was formed in the American Psychological Association. Division 38 is devoted to promoting health maintenance and illness prevention, as well as to identifying correlates of health, illness, and dysfunction through specific scientific, educational, and professional contributions from the field of psychology (Matarazzo, 1980). Scientists and professionals within Division 38 come from many different types of backgrounds, but all have in common an interest in promoting health.

Currently, there are thousands of psychologists who keep in touch with each other's work through newsletters, journals, and meetings. Other organizations have also sprung up, such as the Society of Teachers of Family Medicine and the Society of Behavioral Medicine. All of these organizations have facilitated dialogue among teachers, researchers, and clinicians and have provided outlets such as *The Journal of Behavioral Medicine, The Annals of Behavioral Medicine,* and *Health Psychology* for the publication of research. Such journals help to centralize the literature on the psychological aspects of health, illness, and medical treatment. Psychologists working in the field now compile their work into edited books (such as *Health Psychology Through the Life Span* (Resnick & Rozensky, 1996)), textbooks (such as the one you are presently reading), and reference volumes (such as the *International Encyclopedia of the Social and Behavioral Sciences* (Smelser & Baltes, in press)).

In the 1980s and 1990s, we saw tremendous growth in this exciting field. With thousands of psychologists focused on issues of health, illness, and medical treatment, there has been a virtual explosion of information regarding both effective psychological care for ill patients and specific psychological interventions that assist in people's attempts to stay healthy. The inauguration of the field of health psychology has encouraged both the development of theory on which to build future research and systematic examinations from which to develop clinical applications. In the 1990s, psychoneuroimmunology emerged as an important factor in health psychology research (discussed in greater detail in Chapter 9). Psychoneuroimmunology combines behavioral science, immunology, and neuroscience and attempts to better understand how psychological factors influence health and disease through the immune system (Kemeny et al., 1992). This represents a distinct change in focus from traditional immunological research, which looked at the immune system as an autonomous system that could not be affected by psychological processes. Take, for example, a colony of monkeys that lives in a psychological laboratory. The laboratory technicians have noticed that these monkeys seem to have more than the usual number of illnesses. They sanitize the cages thoroughly, clean the animals' fur, and begin paying special attention to the quality of the food the animals eat. This makes no difference, however, and the animals continue to get sick. A traditional immunological approach would say that perhaps there is a unique pathogen that hasn't been identified yet, or that the animals have some kind of low-grade infection that is making them sick. A psychoneuroimmunological approach, however, would suggest that perhaps there is something about the social environment that is influencing the monkeys' health. For instance, there may be an unusual level of stress in the colony because of overcrowding or because some of the males are particularly aggressive and fight a great deal. These things may, in turn, impair the functioning of the immune systems of the monkeys, making them more susceptible to illness. It is becoming increasingly clear that all bodily systems, including the immune system, are in constant interaction with psychological systems. Mind and body are not separate and independent entities, but rather function together to maintain homeostasis. As this view becomes more popular in the scientific community, the contributions of health psychology become more and more important.

The Individual Perspective

The focus of this book is primarily on individuals in the context of health, illness, and the experience of medical care. It attends to what people think, feel, and do (and why) when they are trying to achieve health or to deal with illness and suffering. With this perspective, this book is concerned with cognition, emotion, motivation, and action. In

Many teenagers begin smoking cigarettes because they are heavily influenced by peer pressure.

it, we examine how these aspects of the individual's psychology influence his or her responses to illness, to the threat of illness, and to the possibility of avoiding illness through health promoting practices. Because we have chosen the individual perspective, we are less concerned with the roles of social structure, societal institutions, or the system of medical care in issues of health and illness. Although these are addressed briefly, we focus mostly on the individual person and on how and why that person acts and interacts in an attempt to achieve health-related goals.

Consider this example: It is estimated that in the United States, over 400,000 people die prematurely each year because they smoked cigarettes. Cigarette smoking is the direct cause of 80 percent of lung cancers and a strong contributing factor in the occurrence of heart attacks and strokes. This statistic means that every day, well over 1,000 people die because of cigarettes. If the same number of people died every day in airplane crashes, how enthusiastic do you think people would be about air travel? If we were to take a societal perspective, we might look at this statistic and consider issues such as the following: Why aren't there laws against manufacturing and selling cigarettes? Why does the U.S. government subsidize the tobacco industry? Why do magazines display cigarette advertisements? What can psychologists do in their communities to improve the situation? These are interesting questions, but they fall into the arena of politics and ethics, as well as of disciplines that take a societal perspective on health issues.

In this book, we will be presenting the individual issues that relate to healthcare. For example, why would a person who knows the dangers of cigarettes continue to smoke, and what is the role of the individual's beliefs regarding susceptibility to and seriousness of lung cancer? We will examine why a person might believe that the benefits of quitting smoking do not outweigh the costs and consider the emotional factors that might cause a person to shut out thoughts of the dangers and continue to smoke. We will look at the specific actions a person must take in order to overcome this physical and psychological addiction and analyze people's actions in light of their needs and desires. With an individual perspective, we will examine not only health behavior but illness behavior as well and consider when and why people come to define themselves as ill. We will study the effect that illness has on people's lives, including the adjustments it forces them to make in their life plans and the consequences that illness has for their self-image. We will see how illness can influence their ability to face their lives with a sense of purpose and meaning and consider how illness transforms their relationships with the people they care about.

Box 1.1 presents an outline of the additional issues and approaches that will be covered in this book in the boxed sections.

BOX 1.1

On Boxes Called "Hot Topic," "Research Close-up," and "Across Cultures"

In this and each of the other chapters throughout this book, you will come across three types of text boxes. These boxes are intended to supplement the information about health psychology that you learn in the text. We encourage you to read these boxes carefully and hope that you will find each one interesting and thought provoking. We have organized these boxes into three types: "Hot Topic," "Research Close-up," and "Across Cultures." The Hot Topic boxes are intended to convey information about recent issues you may have heard about in the news, topics that are currently "hot" areas of research, or other matters that are simply relevant to your life. For instance, in this chapter the Hot Topic involves the latest on the treatment effectiveness of chiropractic care, once an alternative medical treatment and now quite mainstream. In Chapter 2, the Hot Topic involves physician behavior and how it is altered by patient assertiveness. In Chapter 5, the Hot Topic is skin cancer and the complexities of preventing it.

The "Research Close-up" boxes are intended to guide you in understanding more about in-depth research-related issues and methodologies; these boxes analyze the research approaches used in various studies, and the information can be tied directly to the chapter material but is presented in much greater detail. For

instance, the Research Close-up for Chapter 8 involves a discussion of twin research on pain and its links to genetic and behavioral factors. The Research Close-ups for Chapters 11 and 12 respectively examine the role of social support in illness and the effects of psychoeducational counseling on outcomes for patients with serious chronic diseases.

The "Across Cultures" boxes are intended to guide you to a better understanding of cultural issues as they relate to the field of health psychology. We consider international health topics as well as health issues that are affected by cultural variations among patients in the United States. In this chapter, for example, we present a comparison of the differences in healthcare spending across twenty-three nations. In Chapter 3, we examine differences between doctors and patients of different cultures in their nonverbal styles of interacting with each other. In Chapter 10, we consider religious subcultures in the United States and their influences on health behaviors, and in Chapter 13, we examine differences among cultural and ethnic groups in the conduct and nature of the funerals they hold. We trust that you will find these boxes enjoyable breaks from the text reading and that they will inform and sometimes even entertain you.

Conducting Research in Health Psychology

Now, let us turn to a discussion of the process of research in health psychology. The issues of research design and measurement are central to the conduct of optimal research in the study of health, illness, and medical care, and it is on scientific research evidence that sound interventions and clinical applications are based. A solid understanding of the details of design and measurement serves an important purpose for the health psychologist. His or her understanding and evaluation of existing research findings on any particular topic are always dependent upon the ability to evaluate critically the methodology used to arrive at those findings. Was the approach taken by the researchers appropriate given what they attempted to discover? Were the correct comparison groups employed and the right measurements utilized? Was the outcome brought about by the intervention, or caused by some entirely different phenomenon that is yet to be understood?

Conducting research on the psychology of health, illness, and medical care can be difficult because of the nature of the topics studied in this field. The issues are not simply and easily defined, causality is often difficult to determine, and people's expectations can influence the phenomena under study. The people affected by illness (for example, the patient, the physician, and the family) are embedded within a complex social structure, and absolute precision in answering research questions can often be very difficult to achieve. Let's look at one example. The connection between our responses to stressful situations and our health suggests that we may have some control over what happens to us ("mind over matter," if you will). We hope that if we have the right thoughts and emotions, we can triumph over disease. Such hopes may lead people to accept these possibilities as facts and the trends as clear causes. But the issue is not nearly that simple. When diagnosed with a cancerous tumor, it is not enough to simply "will" the tumor to disappear. If it were that easy, we would not need medical technology at all! As we will see in detail later in this book, the idea that the character of one's thinking may play a role in one's health *is* supported by some current scientific findings. There is evidence that maladaptive responses to stress may have the power to make us sick. Maladaptive responses may include punishing ourselves emotionally when something goes wrong instead of figuring out what we can do to fix it, as well as having feelings of self-blame for bad situations and a sense of hopelessness for the future (Peterson & Seligman, 1987; Peterson et al., 1988). Such thinking might, via complex mechanisms, lead to physical problems and emotional depression. There is some evidence, though not conclusive, that such thinking can lead to depression of the responses of the immune system (Kamen-Siegel et al., 1991). Such findings have prompted the popular press to offer such convincing and provocative headlines as "Worrying Can Make You Sick." Some have touted relaxation as the sole means to eliminate cancerous tumors. These claims have been premature, however. Before an illness phenomenon can be completely understood, a great deal must be learned about the complex mechanisms involved.

Another very important point we must make is that, in some realms of health psychology, causality simply cannot ever be determined by the methods available. The only scientific method that can determine a cause-effect relationship is the "true experiment" (which we will discuss shortly). A true experiment may be impossible to carry out, however, because of its prohibitive difficulty or lack of ethical justification. Researchers may need to settle for much less direct methods of studying the complex ways in which thoughts influence health. These less direct approaches leave a great deal of room for alternative explanations, and, as a result, controversies arise.

Despite the complexities of research, clear errors are avoidable, however. Common pitfalls can be overcome with awareness and thoughtfulness in research design. As students of health psychology, you will learn to exercise this awareness effectively. It is important to keep in mind, of course, that research need not be perfect in order to be valuable. Most research is flawed in some way, and nearly every study involves some compromises. It is critically important to know what can be logically concluded from a study as it was carried out and what cannot be concluded. A clinician who hopes to apply research findings to the treatment of patients must learn to design the best possible studies to answer research questions with as much accuracy as possible. The goal must be to rule out alternative explanations for the findings and to avoid logical errors in attempts to arrive at the truth.

In the next section, we will examine the major points of research design as they pertain to health psychology. This section does not provide an extensive synopsis of all possible research methodologies and designs; such comprehensiveness can be found in a research methods textbook. We will, however, examine the most common research flaws and consider how certain methodologies can lead us to correct conclusions and can form the basis for wise clinical decisions. Table 1.1 presents a description of the two most common research designs in health psychology, the true experiment and the correlational method. The goal of research in all areas of psychology is to determine the causes of phenomena and to be able to assess degrees and types of causality as ethics and practicalities allow.

TABLE 1.1   True Experiments and Correlational Methods

True Experiment

Goal is to determine whether one behavior causes another behavior or outcome

Measures behavior after introducing an intervention

Examines the differences in behavior or outcome between groups of people (all but one group receives some form of the intervention)

Correlational Method

Goal is to determine relationships among behaviors and between behavior and outcomes

Measures behaviors and outcomes in order to assess relationships

Identifies the direction and strength of relationships

Research Designs

The True Experiment. The **true experiment**, or what in medical circles is called the **randomized clinical trial**, is a type of study from which a researcher can safely draw conclusions about causality. A statement that one phenomenon probably causes another is a **causal inference**. (A phenomenon is measured by a **variable,** which is a measurable characteristic of people, objects, or events that may change or vary.) If a researcher is justified in drawing a causal inference about two phenomena, he or she can conclude with a high degree of certainty that VARIABLE A causes VARIABLE B. Thus, if there is a causal relationship between relaxation training and the control of tension headache pain, it is the case that the implementation of relaxation through training *causes* a reduction in the severity and frequency of tension headaches. In order to be able to draw such a conclusion, the researcher would have to assign experimental subjects on a random basis to one of two treatment conditions: the **experimental group**, which receives the intended treatment, and the **control group**, which does not. **Random assignment** means that a random process (such as the toss of a coin) has been used to determine whether any given subject receives the experimental treatment (in this case, the relaxation training) or the control treatment (simply some attention). After administration of the treatments, measurements would be made to determine how many tension headaches were experienced by subjects in the experimental and control groups and how severe those headaches were judged to be by the subjects. The two groups of subjects in the experiment are assumed, by virtue of their random assignment, to have been equal in headache frequency and severity before the administration of the treatment. Thus, any differences between them after administration of the treatment are presumed to be the result of relaxation training.

Methodologically, this is the ideal design. The researcher has control over what happens to subjects. Differences between the experimental and the control group are known to be due to the treatment administered and not to the factors that differentiated the groups before the study began (such as the desire to relax). It is known which variable is the "cause" and which is the "effect." (See Chesney & Shelton, 1976, for an actual experimental study of relaxation and biofeedback in reducing the incidence of tension headaches.) True experiments are particularly useful for testing the efficacy of specific interventions or treatments. If a researcher wants to know whether a particular drug, medical procedure, or psychological intervention really works, the best bet is to conduct a true experiment. Then one can be sure that the treatment is what brought about the results.

Correlation and Causation. A correlation between two variables tells nothing about their causal relationship. This is probably one of the most important facts in the methodology of psychological research, yet it is one of the most easily forgotten. A **correlation** refers simply to an association between two variables. If the correlation is positive, when scores on one variable go up, scores on the other variable go up as well. For example, the more stress a person experiences during a given time period, the more illness she or he reports having sustained during that time period. If the correlation is negative, when the measure of one variable goes up, the measure of the other comes down. For example, the more depression a person experiences, the less compliant he or she is with hypertension medication. It is fairly tempting, though incorrect, to conclude that two variables found to be correlated are in fact causally connected, that is, that one causes the other.

If two variables are correlated, it is just as possible for VARIABLE A to cause VARIABLE B as vice versa. Illness might just as easily cause stressful life events as be caused by them. For example, an undiagnosed illness might bring about tremendous fatigue, mental confusion, and a distortion in emotional reactions. Such upsets in day-to-day functioning might lead an individual to experience stressful life events, such as job loss, divorce, and foreclosure on the mortgage. If the illness is later diagnosed, it may appear that the stressful life events caused the illness, although, in fact, they resulted from it. Or, there might be a third variable that caused both stress and illness. The individual's personality style may have led him or her to act in certain ways that brought about the problems perceived to be stressful life events. Perhaps this person is very irresponsible and, as a result, fails to make regular house payments, which ultimately leads to foreclosure. Perhaps this individual cannot face emotional distress and instead translates it into real or imagined physical symptoms. The patient's personality style might account for both a disordered life and poor health. Further, it is possible that an undiagnosed, slow-growing brain tumor has caused the disturbing personality characteristics that in turn have caused both the stressful life events and the illness. The possibilities for explanation of a correlation are many. Thus, when two phenomena correlate or **covary**, they change in relation to one another. They are connected somehow, though not necessarily in a direct causal relationship.

Correlational studies do not allow the researcher to draw causal connections between the variables under study because he or she did not make a controlled comparison as is done in a true experiment. However, correlational studies do have value. They can, and often do, provide very useful information. First, they determine whether two variables are even related to each other—that is, whether they covary. Second, sometimes the possibility of causality can be entertained because one variable precedes another in time and is therefore more likely a cause than an effect. Evidence can be used to eliminate explanations that compete with the causal one, and the researcher can provide evidence for logical pathways by which the variables might be connected to one another.

Figure 1.1 illustrates one way in which a correlational study done at two points in time can establish a causal relationship between stressful life events and illness. A large sample of subjects is assessed on the same measures at Time 1 and at Time 2, two years later. At both points in time, subjects report on the stressful life changes they have experienced over the previous two years (the measure of STRESS) as well as on precisely what their health status has been during those two years (the measure of ILLNESS). In Figure 1.1, stress at Time 1 is positively correlated with illness at Time 2, and the other correlations (particularly that between illness at Time 1 and stress at Time 2) are close to zero. The correlations in the figure show that stress and illness do not occur simultaneously. Rather, stress at Time 1 is related to illness at Time 2, but

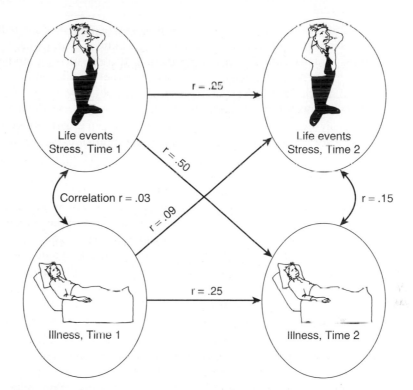

FIGURE 1.1   Hypothetical simple causal model linking stress and illness.

not to illness at Time 1. This suggests that the experience of stressful life events may result in subsequent illness. This type of analysis is referred to as a **cross-lagged correlation** because one of the variables is viewed as a lagged value of the outcome variable.

Prospective versus Retrospective Studies.   Down syndrome (also known as mongolism or trisomy 21) is a genetic condition caused by chromosomal abnormalities that occur at conception. Down syndrome produces mental retardation, abnormal facial features, and, often, serious physical abnormalities such as heart disorders. It is obvious at birth that children with Down syndrome are not normal. The risk of giving birth to a Down's baby is related to the age of the mother, and the risk goes up significantly after the maternal age of 35. Although it is now known that faulty division of chromosomes is responsible for Down syndrome, it was once believed that Down syndrome was caused by maternal anxiety (Brown, 1974). The research that concluded this involved interviewing mothers of normal babies and mothers of Down's babies soon after the birth. Mothers were asked to describe their pregnancies, particularly their feelings during pregnancy. Not surprisingly, mothers of Down's babies described their pregnancies in much more anxious terms than did mothers of healthy babies, leading the researchers to their erroneous conclusions.

This study used a method known as **retrospective data collection**. Subjects were asked to report on something in the past and to recall what happened and how they experienced it. One major problem with retrospective studies is that present events in a person's life tend to influence his or her recollection of past events. A phenomenon called **state-dependent memory** (Fischer, 1976; Fischer & Landon, 1972) partly accounts for the unreliability of retrospective reports. People tend to remember most easily the events of their past that are connected with the same emotional state they feel at the time of recall. If someone is highly anxious, she or he will recall best the instances in which the overriding emotion was anxiety. Thus, retrospective reports are biased, systematically, by emotions.

In order to avoid selective recollection, a researcher must conduct studies prospectively. **Prospective research** requires that the predictor measure (in the above example, maternal anxiety) be assessed well in advance of the outcome (in this case, the child's health status). In practice, prospective research can be quite difficult to carry out. In the case noted above, one would have to design a study in which, throughout the course of pregnancy, the anxiety levels of pregnant women would be measured with questionnaires or interviews. The measures would then be saved and analyzed months later in relation to the birth outcomes of the women in the study—that is, whether their babies had Down syndrome. Of course, the incidence of Down syndrome is relatively low, and so the total sample of mothers participating would have to be quite large. Since this study would not be a true experiment, but only correlational,

Down syndrome is caused by faulty division of chromosomes. On the basis of retrospective research, however, it was once believed to be caused by maternal anxiety.

we would not know for sure whether there was a causal relationship. We could determine whether Down syndrome and maternal anxiety correlate, however, and if they did we might undertake an attempt to suggest possible causality on the basis of the timing of the measures. A true experiment, of course, would be unethical.

Longitudinal versus Cross-Sectional Research. Compared with younger adults, medical patients who are considerably older tend to be more passive in their interactions with their physicians. Older patients ask few questions of their doctors and rarely speak up if they are dissatisfied with their medical care. An important research question is the following: Does assertiveness in medical situations tend to decrease with age? **Cross-sectional research** on this phenomenon would involve measuring assertiveness in groups of people of different ages, for example, people in their 20s, 40s, 60s, and 80s. Various aspects of the subjects' interactions with their physicians might be assessed along with attitudes that these patients hold on the subject of asserting oneself with one's doctor. Suppose that in cross-sectional research one finds that 20- and 40-year-olds ask more questions of their doctors, interrupt their doctors more, and state more opinions on recommended treatments than do 60- and 80-year-olds. Does this mean that as people get older they become less assertive with their medical professionals? Perhaps they do, but the present study does not show this. In fact, the present study demonstrates simply that people in the older age groups are less assertive than are people in younger age groups. The difference might be due to factors other than age. Perhaps their passivity is due to their growing up at a time when no one questioned physician authority. The period of time in which they were born, or their **age cohort**, may be the most important determinant of their actions.

The only way to find out what happens to people as they age is to assess them as they age. This would be a **longitudinal study**, a study conducted over time. An excellent example of a prospective, longitudinal study is the Framingham Heart Study. This is a major, longitudinal investigation of the risk factors for coronary disease. In Framingham, Massachusetts, 2,282 men and 2,845 women who were initially free of coronary heart disease (CHD) have been followed biennially since 1949 for the development of CHD. In addition to data from medical assessments, the researchers on this huge project have collected extensive information about each subject's life history, habits, physical and emotional stresses, personality, and psychosocial states. This research has shed considerable light on the role of many physical and psychological variables in the development of heart disease. Because of its longitudinal nature, this study is able to show the clear relationship between heart disease and such factors as cigarette smoking, weight, cholesterol level, diet, exercise, and the management of stress. (See Haynes et al., 1978, for an example of one of the psychosocial studies conducted within the Framingham Heart Study.) Again, because of its correlational nature, researchers cannot determine the actual cause-effect relationship between these factors.

A researcher's choice of method can be as critical in studies of the psychology of health and illness as it is in other areas of the medical field. Avoiding errors in the design of research is crucial, and drawing appropriate conclusions has particular importance in this field. The results of research in health psychology are often applied directly to patient care. Erroneous conclusions could lead to misunderstanding of the whole picture of a patient's illness and, when applied clinically, could do more harm than good.

The Field versus the Laboratory.   Where a research study is conducted can have important implications for its results and interpretation. Sometimes studies are conducted in a laboratory setting, hence the name **laboratory study**. Usually, true experiments are laboratory studies, although not all laboratory studies are experiments. Laboratory studies have the advantage of increased experimental control, which means that the person running the study can keep many elements constant and thereby minimize the effect that these elements have on the phenomenon under study. In a laboratory study, for example, everyone can be tested at the same time of day and in the same situation. In this way, the experimenter can hold constant the distractions that might affect the accuracy of participants' answers. In a laboratory situation, the experimenter knows that subjects are not being interrupted and that their responses are not being affected by such things as noise or the opinions and emotions of others. While no researcher can control subjects' distracting thoughts, the environment can be held constant in the laboratory. The disadvantage of a laboratory study, of course, is that it does not seem like "real life" for participants. They are very much aware that they are participating in a study. Other investigations, which are conducted in more natural settings, are called **field studies**. These might involve experimental manipulations, but when they do, the manipulation is less obvious to the participants than in the laboratory. In the field, subjects are in their own environments, and their reactions may therefore be more genuine. Some field studies are purely observational, which means that no manipulation takes place at all and instead natural behavior is observed and recorded. The obvious disadvantage of this type of study is the lack of experimental control. Health psychologists use each of these approaches to gather their data and answer their research questions. Often, the research question will be investigated in one of these domains at first (for example, naturalistic observation), and then a modification of the study will be carried out in the other (such as a laboratory experiment). If the results from both types of studies are consistent, the researcher gains confidence that an answer, and not just an artifact of the research method, has been found.

Being a Health Psychologist

The health psychologist has many options available for involvement in matters of health and illness, and the medical care delivery system can benefit greatly from the expertise of the psychologist. In today's medical care arena, many psychologists function as independent clinicians and as consultants to the entire health care team. They are often indispensable in evaluating the psychological aspects of patient care. They work directly with patients or in consultation with the medical team to design treatments that are suited not only to the patient's physical needs but to the patient's psychological needs as well. The psychologist might work with the patient to help him or her evaluate the life-plan changes that are required to accommodate the limitations of illness and to adjust to the treatments necessary to maintain optimal functioning. The psychologist might also work with the patient's family members to assist them in coming to terms with the changes in their own lives that result from the patient's condition. The psychologist might support their attempts to assist the patient in coping with the illness. Many health psychologists with considerable clinical training work with clients whose emotional concerns are influenced by the complications of illness. In this capacity, the clinical health psychologist must be extremely knowledgeable about current research on the connection between mind and body and remain constantly up-to-date on the latest findings relevant to the connection between physical health and psychological processes.

Some health psychologists do not work directly with patients at all. Rather, they are concerned solely with research on the various psychological issues that affect health and illness. Many researchers never provide direct patient care, yet the clinical application of their research findings might vastly improve the treatment of many thousands of patients. For instance, despite having never left the laboratory, a researcher who discovers the connection between emotions and the functioning of the immune system may find the secret to better health for millions of people. Some psychologists are involved in health promotion programs in schools, in communities, and even in the mass media. Through their research, these psychologists learn the most effective ways to communicate information about health promoting lifestyles. By implementing their findings, they develop media messages that have maximum impact on recipients. Psychologists designed many of the health messages you see today on television and

Health psychologists are often included on the healthcare team to provide broad-based psychosocial care of patients.

elsewhere in the media. These include, for example, messages to quit smoking aired by the American Cancer Society. These messages implement what has been learned about how to motivate people to take action toward better health.

In whatever capacity the health psychologist is working, the issues with which he or she is concerned are quite complex and are critically important to the welfare of human beings, both healthy and ill. For the health psychologist, there are many opportunities for work that is meaningful and rewarding, professionally and personally. Today, most health psychologists are trained according to the *scientist-practitioner model*, which views both science and practice as vital elements of psychological expertise. Health psychologists are instructed in the biological, cognitive, psychological, and social bases of health and disease. They also receive rigorous training in measurement, research methods, and statistics, as well as ethics and other professional issues. After doctoral work is complete, it is not uncommon for health psychologists to spend several additional years in postdoctoral training (Belar, 1997). Postdoctoral positions usually combine empirical research with internships or other applied work, providing health psychologists with invaluable opportunities for learning how to function efficiently in various healthcare settings.

While not all graduate schools offer a formal program of study in health psychology, this does not mean that one cannot receive good training in health psychology at these graduate schools. What it does mean is that during graduate school one will have to make a special effort to receive training in health-related areas and possibly to design a program of study that demonstrates expertise in health psychology. Many health psychologists did not receive their training in a health psychology program per se; their degrees may be in areas such as cognitive psychology, social psychology, physiological psychology, psychoneuroimmunology, or developmental psychology. What these individuals share is a desire to apply psychological principles to the study of health.

Basic Issues in Medical Care

One essential element of the medical world, and a necessary component in the study of health psychology, is medical terminology. For some readers of this book, medical terms are second nature and are all too familiar. For others, medical terms truly represent a "foreign language." The Research Close-up presents a quick crash course for those who are not familiar with the material and a refresher course in medical terminology for those who wish to review.

A second essential component of any textbook in health psychology is a review of the systems of the body—basic anatomy and physiology. This review appears in Appendix A at the end of your book. This appendix should be reviewed in detail if this material is not fresh in your mind, for it is essential to know as we examine the field of health psychology. In Appendix B you will find a listing of some of the important and commonly used measurement tools for those doing research in health psychology. These will be of interest to you because we will mention many of them as we describe studies throughout this book. You may also find them useful as you work on

---

BOX **1.2**
Research Close-up

The Scientific Vocabulary of Medicine

Conducting research or practice in health psychology without a working knowledge of medical terminology is like trying to travel in a country without knowing the language. You may be able to get from one place to another, but you will not get the most out of the experience. You may become quite lost and miss opportunities to do the things you desire. Problems will also occur for health psychologists who know little or nothing about medical terminology. They will likely fail to understand some important issues regarding the meaning and the implications of certain diseases for patients' physical and psychological health. They will not be able to communicate effectively with medical professionals, and they will always seem like outsiders in the medical setting. Their access to the relevant medical literature will also be limited.

Medical terminology can probably be learned most effectively by learning the meaning of various word components (roots and stems) and then combining these components into medical words. Analyzing their component parts can help one to arrive at the definitions of most medical terms. The most important step in building a medical vocabulary is to learn categories of words that pertain to external and internal anatomical parts, body fluids, substances, and numerals and by learning prefixes and suffixes. Almost all medical words derive from Latin and Greek (especially the latter, which is particularly adaptable to the formation of compounds). This is true for words that pertain to anatomy (study of the structure of the body), physiology (study of the normal functions and activities of the body), pathology (study of disease), histology (microscopic study of the structure, composition, and function of normal cells and tissues), the signs and symptoms of disease, and diagnostic procedures.

The vocabulary of medicine does not remain stagnant. New words are added often, to reflect the proliferation of diagnostic tests and treatments and the identification of new diseases and disease syndromes. Except for proper names in which a disease or sign/symptom is named after the individual who first described or identified it (e.g., Crohn's disease), most new medical terms will make sense within the framework already learned. Some interesting characteristics of medical names may be noted. For example, many anatomical names for parts of the body are derived from the shape or configuration of some object. The Greeks and Romans named some anatomical structures after familiar objects when they had no better ways to identify them. Except for the words used in anatomy, most medical terms are derived not from a single Latin or Greek word but from a combination of two or more roots, each of which has a distinct meaning. For example, appendicitis means inflammation (*itis*) of the appendix. Another example is osteoarthritis (inflammation *itis* of the bone *oste* and joint *arthr*). Here is a list of some common root examples:

hepat (liver)	*derma* (skin)	*gastr* (stomach)
nephr (kidney)	*arthr* (joint)	*oste* (bone)
card (heart)	*col* (colon, large intestine)	*pulm* (lung)
pleur (lining of the lung)		

The types of surgical operations and their roots are the following: *plasty* (repair); *stomy* (artificial or surgical opening); *otomy* (incision); *ectomy* (excision); *centesis* (puncture). Can you figure out the meaning of the words: colostomy and gastrectomy? *Oma* is a suffix that often refers to a tumor or neoplasm (with some exceptions, such as glaucoma). Translation of the root tells

(continued)

B O X **1.2**   **(Continued)**

you the location of the neoplasm. For example: neuroma (on a nerve), hemangioma (on a blood vessel), lipoma (in the fatty tissue). Another suffix you will often see is *osis*, which usually refers to a morbidly serious condition. For example: arteriosclerosis (thickening of artery walls), nephrosis (damage to the filtering units of the kidneys).

Some common prefixes used in medical terminology are the following:

a: (without, lack of) as in anemia (lack of blood).

anti: (against) as in antisepsis (prevent infection).

de: (away from) as in dehydrate (remove water from).

dia: (through, completely) as in diagnosis (complete knowledge).

epi: (upon, on) as in epidermis (on the skin).

hyper: (over, above, excessive) as in hypertension (high blood pressure).

hypo: (under, below, deficient) as in hypoglycemia (low blood sugar)

pro: (before) as in prognosis (foreknowledge).

retro: (backward, located behind) as in retrolingual (behind the tongue).

trans: (across) as in transection (cut across).

A few important Greek and Latin derivatives are the following:

algia: (pain) as in neuralgia (nerve pain).

caus: (burn) as in causalgia (burning pain).

centesis: (puncture, perforate) as in amniocentesis (puncture of amniotic sac).

dynia: (pain) as in mastodynia (breast pain).

edem: (swell) as in lymphedema (swelling of lymph nodes).

iatro: (treat, cure) as in pediatrics (treatment of children).

logy: (study) as in histology (study of tissues).

lysis: (breaking up, dissolving) as in glycolysis (breaking up of glucose or sugar by the body).

palpit: (flutter) as in palpitation (fluttering feeling in the heart).

phobia: (fear) as in claustrophobia (fear of close places).

plegia: (paralyze) as in paraplegia (paralysis of lower limbs).

therap: (treat, cure) as in chemotherapy (treatment with chemicals).

Once you have mastered the language described above, it becomes fairly simple to identify the various medical specialties. Here is a list of some of the most frequently encountered medical specialties:

Anesthesia is delivered by an anesthesiologist ("an" meaning "not" and "esthesis" meaning "feeling").

Cardiology is devoted to the study of diseases of the heart.

Dermatology is the study of diseases of the skin.

Endocrinology is devoted to the study of the endocrine glands and their hormonal secretions.

Geriatrics is devoted to the study of diseases of the aged and is also a relatively new branch of medicine.

Gynecology is devoted to the treatment of diseases of the female reproductive system.

Internal medicine is involved in the treatment of diseases of the internal organs by a physician called an internist (who should not be confused with an intern, who is a graduate medical student receiving training in a hospital prior to licensing).

Obstetrics is the branch of surgery that deals with pregnancy, labor, and delivery.

Ophthalmology is devoted to diseases of the eye.

Otolaryngology is the branch of medicine that deals with diseases of the ear (*oto*) and the larynx and related structures.

Pediatrics is devoted to curing the diseases of children. (It derives from *pedia*, meaning child.)

Physical Medicine (or *Physiatry*) is a relatively new branch of medicine concerned with physical therapy in the treatment of disease.

Psychiatry (*psych* meaning mind) is devoted to the study of diseases of the mind.

Radiology is a branch of medicine devoted to the study of structures of the body by means of x rays and the treatment of such diseases as cancer with x-ray.

Surgery is the branch of medicine that treats diseases by operative procedures.

Urology is devoted to diseases of the urinary tract.

---

a class paper or project, or as you explore particular areas of health psychology in more depth.

The remainder of this chapter will focus on the early foundations of the field of health psychology, beginning with the development of medicine as a discipline, and will investigate the conceptual models that have dominated the exploration of health, illness, mind, and body, in the field of psychology.

A Brief History of Medicine

Western medicine had its origins in ancient Greece during the time of greatest intellectual development. Then, as throughout most of history, medicine was dominated by a focus on mysticism and superstition. Hippocrates (460–370 BC), the most celebrated of early Greek practitioners, tried to change that and contributed a great deal to existing medical knowledge and beliefs at a time when superstition dominated explanations of illness and healing. He carefully noted the history of his patients' symptoms and examined patients (such as by listening to their heartbeats with ear to chest) and recorded signs such as temperature and respiration rate. He collected data and facts about real phenomena instead of hypothesizing about which god or demon was at work in making people ill. Hippocrates believed that **prognosis** (the forecast of the course of a disease) was extremely important because a patient's expectations influenced his or her emotions and physical condition. Hippocrates charted the courses of various illnesses and prescribed noninvasive, supportive treatments such as baths and massage. He also recommended dietary interventions and a few drugs from India and Egypt.

Claudius Galen (AD 131–200) is considered by many to be the greatest figure in ancient medicine because his work had a lasting influence in Europe until the Renaissance. Galen dissected animals and treated injuries of Roman gladiators and thus learned much about anatomy. He used a Hippocratic foundation to set **diagnosis** (the identification of disease based on the patient's signs and symptoms) on a firm base of anatomy and physiology. While most of "medical practice" around him emphasized the contribution of witches and demons, Galen and his followers throughout the next 1,200 years promoted a scientific approach to health and illness.

In the fifteenth century, the Renaissance brought intellectualism and rationalism to the realm of medicine, and some of the basic tools of medical science were created. Medical scientists pressed on in their attempts to focus attention on the physical aspects of illness, utilizing each new discovery as they built the foundation for modern medicine. In 1590 the microscope was invented by Van Leeuwenhoek and it became possible to view the microorganisms that were later found to play a role in disease. At about that time, Harvey demonstrated with painstaking research that certain mechanical principles applied to the human body. A short time later Sydenham further developed the careful principles of bedside observation and clinical diagnosis that were introduced by Hippocrates. Lavoisier described the nature of respiration, and in 1796 Jenner introduced the practice of vaccination and reduced the incidence of smallpox. In the mid to late 1800s Pasteur and Koch made important discoveries that contributed much to the science of bacteriology. There was a slow but steady widening of knowledge about surgical interventions; in 1846 Morton introduced anesthesia and in 1893 Roentgen discovered x-rays. Considering the long history of the human race, antiseptic surgery on an anesthetized patient is a very new phenomenon.

Around 1900, medicine began to transform into a clinical science. Specific treatments became available, and the physical aspects of illness and injury began to receive considerable attention. Battlefields have often, throughout history, provided rich training grounds and places of discovery for medicine. World War I brought tremendous advances in the treatment of malaria and yellow fever because soldiers fighting in tropical parts of the world quickly became ill and doctors had great incentive to innovate treatments. Further, there were many patients on whom to test their new ideas. World War II brought significant developments in surgical techniques and wound care. Other treatments that we take for granted, such as the intravenous drip, were also perfected during World War II. Prior to this, patients who required fluid replacement and who were unable to drink were given fluids through their colons. Nutrients were often included in the fluid enemas that these patients endured.

It is the twentieth century that has brought the most dramatic changes in medicine and surgery—changes unequaled by any other period in history. Humankind has gone from using leeches to suck patients' blood to procedures such as **dialysis**, which mechanically filters out waste products from the blood. We have progressed from ear-to-chest **auscultation** (listening for sounds within the body) to continuous electrocardiogram monitoring from remote paramedic units to medical centers. Simple **palpation** has given way to computerized axial tomography (CAT), magnetic resonance imaging (MRI), and positron emission tomography (PET), which provide computerized images of sections of organs. Clinicians have a wide variety of pharmaceutical agents that can be prescribed for all sorts of maladies, and patients may choose to participate in clinical trials that test the treatment efficacy of new drugs. Today medical practitioners can probe minute structures buried deep within the human body without scratching its surface. Advances in microsurgery allow transplantation of corneas and the reattachment of severed fingers. New drugs prevent tissue rejection, enabling transplantation of organs from one human being to another. Cloning can be used to create an entire duplicate animal from a single cell of the original, and babies can be conceived in petri dishes. Parents can choose the sex of their child, and fertility can be greatly enhanced so that women can have children well past what have been considered the child-bearing years. These techniques work so well that women can deliver three, four, or more babies. And, although these babies may be born tiny and premature, technological innovations can now keep them alive and often thriving.

Most of the great strides in medicine have taken place in the recent past. It was not until 1943, for example, that penicillin became available for the treatment of bacterial infections. Nearly every day since that time some new physical factor has been discovered in disease or some new specific treatment intervention has been developed. The possibilities seem almost endless. So much has changed so fast that scientific medicine seems to hold infinite promise. Yet, in the search for foolproof technology, medical professionals and laypersons alike have tended to focus so intently on physical factors in illness that they have ignored or rejected phenomena related to the mind. Efforts to avoid the nonscientific approaches that dominated medicine throughout much of history have tended to lead to a single-minded focus of attention on the purely physical aspects of illness. In a sense, the pendulum has swung far from the old days of demons and superstition to a point at which any "mind" phenomena tend to be considered suspicious. In many ways, over the past half century there has been a strong tendency for us to believe that the scientific advances of drugs and surgeries are *all* that are necessary to produce good health.

Western versus Non-Western Traditions

Specialization and specificity, even today, characterize Western medical care. We tend to focus on the minutia of health and illness—microbes and malfunctions. Because of the technological advances we've enjoyed in recent decades, many doctors are specialists in one area or another, and **general practitioners** (physicians trained to deal with a variety of ailments and to care for patients across circumstances and over time) are less common than they were a century ago. In Western medicine, emphasis is placed on the scientific evidence of disease, and on curing the organic problem.

Non-Western medicine is more inclusive and has traditionally focused on promoting health as well as treating illness and curing disease. In this sort of medical practice, cultural traditions and rituals for maintaining health and curing ailments have been largely retained and combined with new advances to create a medical framework in which folk remedies complement scientifically based interventions. Many non-Western interventions are relatively "low-tech" when compared to Western interventions. For instance, herbal therapies, acupuncture, acupressure, and massage are all non-Western approaches for dealing with a variety of diseases and illnesses. Despite their seeming simplicity, however, these techniques are often very effective in relieving symptoms and aiding healing.

Holistic Approaches

A holistic approach to medicine proposes that health is something that can be achieved and is not simply the absence of disease. It combines the best of Western medical technology with the sensitivity and cultural awareness of non-Western traditions, and with aspects of spirituality and psychological functioning. The goal of a holistic approach is to treat the whole person and to be sensitive to the needs of the individual, not just as the container for a disease but as a human being who is experiencing pain or physical distress and a complex array of thoughts and emotions.

Holistic approaches tend to foster care that is sensitive to the psychosocial needs of the patient. Perhaps the best examples come from the processes of birth and death. When a child is delivered in the Western medical tradition, he or she is often delivered with interventions such as forceps or even by cesarean section into the bright lights of the delivery room where the umbilical cord is cut. Several decades ago, it was proposed that a more holistic and effective approach might be to dim the lights and allow the infant a few moments on the mother's stomach prior to cutting the umbilical cord, as well as to massage the child to induce breathing. This method seems to be quite effective, as well as less traumatic for both the mother and the child. Holistic care in the process of dying is also extremely beneficial to patients and their families. It was common, particularly in the 1950s through the 1970s, for cancer to be aggressively treated even when there was no hope of the patient's recovery. Again and again patients would be resuscitated, kept alive on machines, and fed through tubes. Then, in the mid-1970s, the **hospice** movement began as an alternative for dying patients (hospice is discussed in more detail in Chapter 13). The goal of hospice is not to cure the patient, or even to keep the patient alive, but rather to make the patient comfortable and allow him or her to die peacefully. Families are treated as a unit, and professionals are available to help each member of the family, not just the patient, to come to terms with the death. This holistic approach recognizes that death is inevitable and that simply aiding acceptance of it is far preferable to prolonging life at all costs. Holistic approaches recognize that both the mind and the body are important to an individual's well-being and that attempting to separate the two is counterproductive.

Alternative and Complementary/Integrative Medicine

Many holistic techniques fall into the category of "alternative" (also sometimes called "unconventional"), "complementary," and "integrative " medicine. Generally, these approaches to restoring a patient's health are not taught to doctors in medical school. The recent distinction between the terms *complementary/integrative* and *alternative* is that the former are typically used in conjunction with more traditional treatments, whereas alternative treatments are those that are sought in place of traditional care. Both alternative and complementary/integrative treatments are becoming increasingly popular (Boutin et al., 2000; Cowley et al., 1995). In 1990, a national survey found that one-third of respondents had used at least one "unconventional" treatment during the previous year. From this survey of over 1,500 people it was estimated that about 60 million Americans used alternative or complementary treatments in 1990. They made 425 million visits to unconventional care providers compared with only 388 million visits to primary care physicians that same year. In addition, almost three-quarters of these people said that they did not tell their primary care doctor about their pursuit of unconventional treatments (Eisenberg et al., 1993). A recent follow-up to this survey found that alternative medicine use and expenditures have increased dramatically since 1990, with more individuals seeking these treatments than ever before (629 million visits in 1997). The most common therapies sought are herbal medicine, massage, megavitamins, self-help groups, folk remedies, energy healing, guided imagery, homeopathy, chiropractic, hypnosis, and acupuncture. These treatments are most often used for chronic conditions such as back problems, depression, anxiety, and headaches (Eisenberg et al., 1998).

In recent years, there has been increased acceptance of complementary and alternative methods even among conventional medical practitioners. One recent survey found that among general practitioners questioned, more than half had recently been involved in complementary medicine in some way. Twenty-five percent of respondents had referred a patient to a complementary medicine practitioner and 55 percent had endorsed or recommended treatment with complementary medicine during the previous week (White et al., 1997). These doctors rated chiropractic, acupuncture, and osteopathy as the most effective complementary therapies, and a majority felt that costs for these treatments should be included as part of a patient's health care coverage. Box 1.3 examines chiropractic care in detail, citing research evidence of its effectiveness and noting its recent growing acceptance as a mainstay of treatment, particularly for certain chronic conditions.

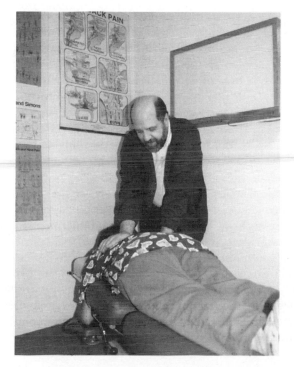

Chiropractic care involves spinal manipulation as well as physical therapies and lifestyle modifications. Its effectiveness for low back pain is superior to that of traditional medical approaches.

BOX 1.3
Hot Topic

Chiropractic

A survey of the United States during the mid-1990s found that up to 46 percent of individuals had used at least one type of complementary health care in the previous twelve months (Eisenberg et al., 1998). Many of these patients went to chiropractors. Chiropractic is a health profession that is focused on diagnosing, treating, and preventing disorders of the musculoskeletal system and their effects on the nervous system and on general health. The word *chiropractic* comes from the Greek meaning "practice (or treatment) by hand."

Chiropractic emphasizes the natural power of the body to heal itself and does not use drugs or surgery. When patients need such services, they are referred to allopathic physicians (MDs) for treatment. Chiropractors focus on the diagnosis, prevention, and chiropractic treatment of biomechanic functional disorders of the spine, pelvis, and extremities. The primary approach to care involves manual treatment, including but not limited to spinal manipulation. Chiropractors use other noninvasive approaches as well, including physical therapy modalities, exercise programs, nutritional advice, and lifestyle modification (Chapman-Smith, 2000).

The chiropractic profession was founded in the United States in 1895 and is established in over seventy countries. There are currently about 65,000 doctors of chiropractic in the United States as well as 6,000 in Canada and 90,000 worldwide. Training involves a minimum of six years of full-time university-level education, including four years at chiropractic college. This is followed by national and state licensing exams and several years of internship, as well as postgraduate specialties in such areas as orthopedics, nutrition, radiology, rehabilitation, and sports chiropractic. Chiropractic education involves the same amount of training in anatomy, physiology, and all the basic sciences as does medicine.

There was once a significant conflict between the professions of medicine and chiropractic, and physicians were forbidden by the American Medical Association to refer patients to chiropractors. In 1987, the American Medical Association was successfully sued by the chiropractic profession for restriction of trade, and today many physicians recognize the importance of chiropractors as members of the healthcare team. In the United States today, over 80 percent of employees in conventional insurance plans and point-of-service plans have full or partial coverage for chiropractic, although the figure is somewhat lower for HMOs. Medicare insurance now covers chiropractic treatment.

In recent years, data from outcomes research has helped the chiropractic profession gain greater legitimacy in the United States. Considerable evidence exists for the efficacy of spinal manipulation in the treatment of a variety of musculoskeletal and other disorders. This research is typically published in the primary research journals of the field, *Topics in Clinical Chiropractic*, the *Journal of Manipulative and Physiological Therapeutics*, and the *Journal of the Neuromusculoskeletal System*, as well as in medical journals such as *Spine*. Chiropractic is now regarded as a first-line approach to treatment for low back pain and has been found to be highly effective (Shekelle et al., 1992). Research has also identified joint and muscle tension in the neck as a major contributor to headache. Cervicogenic headache remained largely unrecognized until 1988; it is as common as migraine and frequently misdiagnosed (Nilsson & Bove, 2000). Studies show that it is dealt with more effectively by treatment with chiropractic manipulation than with any other approach to management. (Nilsson, 1995; Nilsson et al., 1997).

The essential principles of chiropractic are the following:

1. Holism: Health is seen as complete physical, mental, and social well-being, and the purpose of care is not merely to relieve symptoms through conservative, noninvasive methods but also to help the patient by improving nutrition, exercise, and posture, and through advice and counseling on lifestyle. The goal is to help patients understand how their problems developed (e.g., poor posture, poor body mechanics while lifting, too many hours sitting at a computer, overweight, lack of exercise, etc.).

2. Homeostasis: The body has its own inherent healing power and its natural tendency is to return to health.

3. Nervous system regulation: The body's innate recuperative power is affected by and integrated through the nervous system. Mechanical dysfunction in the musculoskeletal system, such as reduced motion and stiff joints or shortened or tense muscles, may disturb the normal regulatory function of the branches of the nervous system.

4. Subluxation: This is the term that chiropractors use for a spinal joint dysfunction. Subluxation is functional—that is, it has to do with abnormal functioning or range of motion in a spinal joint, sometimes with neurological or vascular involvement, and often but not necessarily with some structural displacement of the bone.

5. The neuromusculoskeletal system. Chiropractors identify the close relationship between the musculoskeletal system and the nervous system. For example, limited movement in an arthritic joint can cause pain, and manipulation of the joint produces various reflex effects that can reduce symptoms and affect health.

6. Somatovisceral effects: This is the principle that manual treatment of the body framework (the soma) may influence the functioning of the internal body systems and organs (viscera) through the autonomic branch of the nervous system. There has been less research on this principle than on the issues of back pain and headache. It is not yet established in literature that chiropractic manipulation can be used to treat other chronic conditions, but there is growing clinical evidence in support of this possibility.

In general, for consumers and health professionals interested in complementary healthcare, there are some valuable resources available. Books by Murray (1994) on herbal therapies, by Chapman-Smith (2000) on chiropractic, and by Dr. Andrew Weil (Weil, 1997, 1998) on a variety of alternative/integrative approaches are highly recommended. For more about chiropractic, check out the website where you can read the U.S. Agency for Health Care Policy and Research report on the efficacy of chiropractic care (http://chiropractic.about.com/health/chiropractic/mbody.htm). Also visit the American Chiropractic Association website (http://www.amerchiro.org/) and Chiroweb (http://www.chiroweb.com/archives/ahcpr/uschiros.htm).

Why do patients so often turn to alternative therapies? Sometimes it is because they believe that these are more "natural" and/or less invasive than standard medical treatments. Some pursue these alternatives as a "last resort" when they have tried everything that conventional medicine has to offer. Others try alternative methods on the advice of family or friends. Not surprisingly, the desire for alternative therapies and for treatment by alternative practitioners sometimes derives from patient dissatisfaction with how they have been treated by medical professionals who fail to provide them with sufficient information and emotional support. Many of those who accept alternative therapies are educated patients who place emphasis on personal responsibility and on prevention, especially effective nutrition. These are areas that are often ignored in conventional medical practice. One problem that worries practitioners is that when patients turn from standard medical treatments, particularly for serious illnesses, and do not inform their physicians, they may be exposing themselves to danger. For example, pharmaceutical drugs that are prescribed might interact with herbal remedies. Or seeking alternative treatments may keep the patient from utilizing more focused and appropriate medical technologies. Recent estimates have indicated, however, that only about 2 percent of the population relies solely on unconventional medicine, and approximately 5 percent of cancer patients do so, although far more (10–50%) use nontraditional therapies to *supplement* their conventional medical care (Berrey & White, 2000; Comarow, 1998; Druss & Rosenheck, 1999; Katz, 2000).

Studies show that most patients who use alternative medicine do so for the care of chronic conditions (such as chiropractic for low back pain) for which standard medical care has provided little or no help. Certainly, when used in conjunction with established medical technologies, or as a well thought-out alternative, complementary medicine can be very valuable. Many physicians realize this and are willing to support their patients in the selection of a combination of treatments that best meets their patients' personal needs. This is particularly true of younger physicians (Ernst et al., 1995). Thus, the use of alternative treatments may contribute to a more holistic and comprehensive model of health care. Alternative and complementary medicine is constantly changing and becoming mainstream. Once a treatment's effectiveness has been established, it becomes an accepted form of medical treatment. Medical schools teach about it, hospitals offer it, and insurance companies pay for it. Before this can happen, however, these treatments must be scientifically evaluated. For many years it was argued that the effectiveness of these treatments was due simply to the placebo effect. Recent studies are showing, however, that success of these therapies goes well beyond simple expectations. For example, the effectiveness of chiropractic adjustment for low back pain has been established, and its superiority over other modalities of treatment, including traditional medical approaches of drugs and surgery, has been clearly demonstrated (Shekelle et al., 1992). A recent meta-analysis of the literature on the clinical effects of homeopathy found that effects were not completely due to placebo mechanisms. Although it was not clear that homeopathy was effective for any single disease or condition, the authors of this meta-analysis concluded that homeopathy is, overall, a promising area that deserves further rigorous research (Linde et al., 1998). In 1992 the Office of Alternative Medicine was established by congressional mandate, and in 1998 this office became the National Center for Complementary and Alternative Medicine (NCCAM), one of the twenty-five Centers and Institutes of the National Institutes of Health (NIH). NCCAM supports both basic and applied research into such issues as the safety of herbal remedies and nutritional supplements, the interactive properties of herbal remedies, and the efficacy of complementary and alternative medical treatments such as chiropractic and acupuncture. As more and more research on the healthcare outcomes of alternative/complementary medicine becomes available, truly effective treatments can be expected to move into the mainstream of medical care.

The Mind-Body Connection

In ancient times, it was believed that animating spirits caused everything that happened. If a rock rolled down a hill it was because it was moved by a spirit, if a person walked, it was because of a spirit. This belief, called **animism**, was gradually replaced with physical laws (such as the law of gravity) for inanimate objects, but the idea that people and animals had spirits or "souls" remained. Because no better explanations existed, illness and disease were often attributed to evil spirits or demons. The Greeks were among the first to move from a view of illness as caused by evil spirits to a more biological explanation. Hippocrates and Galen formulated a humoral theory of illness in which an imbalance of the bodily fluids or **humors** (phlegm, blood, yellow bile, and black bile) would result in physical symptoms of disease. These humors were believed to be related to personality characteristics, as well: Phlegm was associated with apathy (phlegmatic), blood with energetic cheerfulness (sanguine), yellow bile with anger (choleric), and black bile with depression (melancholic). These humors could be kept in balance by living healthfully and exercising self-control. Treatments for bringing the humors back into equilibrium, should they become unbalanced, included bloodletting, enemas, diuretics, hot and cold baths, special diets, vomiting, and drugs.

During the Middle Ages, the Roman Catholic Church again emerged as a tremendous influence on people's thinking, and the idea that evil spirits and demons caused illness once again prevailed. Sickness was often seen as punishment from God for some evil thought or act, and people were often tortured in an effort to atone for this evil or to drive out the demons that possessed the body. During this time, religious leaders often served dual roles as medical practitioners, and the Church forbade scientific research on the human body (because the body was viewed as sacred, and such scrutiny was deemed sacrilegious). Illness was dealt with through religious rituals, prayers, and exorcisms. This belief system was not only detrimental to individuals (because they were unjustly blamed for their physical misfortunes), but was also destructive to the progression of medical knowledge.

In the 1600s, René Descartes, a French philosopher and mathematician, argued that the mind and the body were separate entities—that the body was physical (a machine) and that the "mind" or "soul" was distinct. This approach was termed **dualism** because it proposed two independent mechanisms. He also believed, however, that the soul could interact with the physical body. He formalized a model through which he believed physiological processes of the body could be controlled by the mind or soul—that is, a way in which these dual entities might interact. He proposed that the muscles of the body functioned hydraulically (similar to the mechanisms that moved the statues in the Royal Gardens near Paris) with fluid that was pumped through the nerves. The cerebral ventricles in the brain housed this fluid, and the pineal body governed its release by tilting in one way or another. It was at the level of the pineal body that the soul was proposed to exert its influence, although how this occurred was never really explained. Although studying the body was still taboo, Descartes eventually struck a deal with the church leaders: He would be allowed to study the physical body, while the church would maintain purview over people's souls.

Today health psychologists adhere to a view that is more **monistic** than dualistic. Health psychologists believe that the mind and the body cannot be separated and that consciousness and thinking are part of the process of bodily functioning. Although psychologists cannot fully explain consciousness, memory, and other functions of the mind, once the functioning of the body and nervous system are more completely understood, the answers to these questions may be clear, or at least more complete than they are today. Despite the current philosophical trends, health psychologists do not propose that the mind and the body are the *same* thing, but rather that they interact in very important and complex ways. The physical body can be examined in terms of its smallest and most intricate components; for example, tiny muscles, individual cells, and even viruses can be scrutinized. Although the physical brain can also be examined in detail, we do not have the same kind of access to its workings. For example, although we know that memories exist, we cannot *see* a memory being formed or *find* a memory that resides in the brain. As technology advances, this may be possible, but at present we are limited to more abstract observations of mind-related phenomena. So, although the mind resides in a portion of the physical body (the brain), it is more than simply the sum of the physical components as they are currently conceptualized and measured. Instead, the mind and body are synergistic. Understanding the mind requires accurate and detailed knowledge of the structure and physiology of the body (including the physical brain), but that is not sufficient. Conversely, a better understanding of the mind will enable better comprehension of the properties and capabilities of the physical brain and the functioning of the body.

As we saw earlier, the scientific approach to understanding health and disease that emerged with the Renaissance has continued until the present. Descartes conceptualized the body as a machine, and many others contributed as well: Vesalius and Morgagni in anatomy, Leeuwenhoek in microscopy, and Huygens in thermometry. In the nineteenth century Pasteur's discoveries (including a vaccine for rabies) helped to mold **germ theory**, the concept that microorganisms cause disease. As the scientific pursuit of good health accelerated, the mind once again became an important arena for scientific investigation related to physical health, and the field of psychology began to grow.

Particularly important in this regard was Sigmund Freud's work on **conversion hysteria** (mental problems that were "converted" into physical malfunctioning). Freud believed that unconscious psychological conflicts could cause physical symptoms that were symbolic of the underlying psychopathology. This seemed a logical explanation for things such as glove anesthesia (in which the hand feels no sensation but the arm above it is fine)—a condition that cannot be explained physiologically.

Psychosomatic and Behavioral Medicine

The idea that illness and internal conflicts were related to each other continued in the work of Dunbar and Alexander, who linked personality to specific illnesses and whose work laid the foundation for the field of psychosomatic medicine (Alexander, 1950; Dunbar, 1943). Dunbar and Alexander deviated from the Freudian view not only by linking specific personality characteristics to physical illness, but also in their proposal of a mechanism by which this might occur. They proposed that unconscious conflicts caused physiological reactions in the autonomic nervous system, and that these reactions eventually led to bodily damage. They proposed that a number of medical problems such as ulcers, rheumatoid arthritis, asthma, and hypertension were caused by psychological factors. These were termed *psychosomatic diseases*. Psychosomatic medicine, in its original formulation, is not well accepted today because it is recognized that psychological factors are not generally *sufficient* to produce disease. The psychosomatic movement has been very influential, however, in focusing attention on the importance of internal, psychological factors as *contributors* to a variety of physical health issues. These issues are dealt with in more detail in Chapter 7, where we examine the role of emotions in an individual's self-definitions of illness.

Personality factors are now recognized as important contributors to a variety of disease states. One of the best-known personality-disease links is between Type A behavior pattern (discussed in more detail in Chapter 9) and coronary heart disease. Individuals with a Type A personality are often stressed out and are constantly trying to do more and more things in less and less time. They are usually quite anxious, hostile, and angry. As research on the Type A personality has progressed, it has become clear that the biggest risk factor is that of hostility. Being a workaholic wouldn't necessarily be damaging to your health, but being a hostile workaholic very well might! A **meta-analysis** (a synthesis of many research studies) of psychosomatic medicine up to the mid-1980s (Friedman & Booth-Kewley, 1987) found that there seems to be a "disease prone personality," which is characterized by negative emotions such as depression, hostility, and anxiety. These negative emotions were linked to the occurrence of several diseases: asthma, arthritis, coronary artery disease, headaches, and ulcers. Of course, it is important to remember that emotions and disease may covary, and it is not necessarily the case that the emotions caused the disease. The causal link may go in the other direction. Early effects of the disease, before it is diagnosed, might very well cause the emotional experience, or something else might be causing both the emotions and the disease. This meta-analysis does highlight what is perhaps the primary way in which the field of psychosomatic medicine has been changing, however. There is now less emphasis than in the past on linking a particular personality trait to a specific disease. Instead, researchers are searching for patterns among personality characteristics, lifestyles, and varying states of health and illness.

Behavioral medicine is distinct from psychosomatic medicine in that it involves the application of behavioral science knowledge and techniques to medical care with the goal of improving physical health. The concept of behavioral medicine emerged in the 1970s, and was formalized during a conference in 1977 which was cosponsored by

Yale University and the National Institutes of Health's National Heart, Lung, and Blood Institute. At this conference, several important components of this new discipline were defined: 1) that behavioral medicine involves the application of behavioral theory to physical health problems, 2) that the practice of behavioral medicine requires the collaborative efforts of behavioral and biomedical scientists, as well as practicing physicians, and 3) that psychosis, neurosis, and substance abuse were to be addressed in behavioral medicine only as they related to physical health endpoints (Schwartz & Weiss, 1977). More recently, however, behavioral medicine has widened its scope to include general issues of substance abuse problems. Behavioral medicine techniques, such as biofeedback, are useful in modern medicine and are often coupled with advanced technology to produce optimal outcomes for patients. Behavioral medicine techniques, as they are used in the treatment of pain, are examined in Chapter 8.

Health psychology, as we have seen, is a general term for a number of research and practice areas that combine psychology and medicine. Health psychologists draw from and contribute to both psychosomatic medicine and behavioral medicine, as well as to traditional medical and mental health care. Health psychologists also participate in the fields of health outcomes research and the study of the delivery of health services. The goal of health psychology is to utilize psychological knowledge of all types to improve all domains of physical and mental health and functioning.

Medicine Today: The Meaning and Impact of Managed Care

Until about 1920, people were generally responsible for their own medical care. There were some church organizations and charities that did what they could to provide health services for those who could not afford them, but most healthcare needs were handled by the family or by the family doctor who was paid (or bartered with) on an individual basis. Following the Great Depression, however, health insurance became increasingly popular, and by the 1960s over half of the U.S. population had some kind of health insurance (Falk, 1964). Medicare (for the elderly) and Medicaid (for low-income individuals) were instituted during the 1960s in an effort to make healthcare even more accessible to everyone. The resulting increase in availability and usage caused healthcare costs to skyrocket. In fact, national spending on healthcare increased over 400 percent from 1960 to 1990 (VandenBos, 1993). By 1997, the costs of medical care accounted for nearly 14 percent of the Gross Domestic Product (GDP) of the United States, and it is projected that if current practices continue, these expenditures will account for about 18 percent of the GDP by the year 2005 (Anderson & Poullier, 1999; Burner & Waldo, 1995). As discussed in Box 1.4, medical care costs in the United States are substantially higher than in other industrialized countries.

Until quite recently, very little attention was paid to prevention, or to the financial aspects of healthcare. People went to the doctor when they were sick or otherwise in need of care, and insurance companies paid for this care on a fee-for-service basis. That is, they reimbursed providers for services rendered. As healthcare costs rose,

BOX 1.4

Across Cultures

Healthcare Spending across the Globe: Expenditures and Outcomes

It may come as no surprise that healthcare costs in the United States are extremely high, and, despite efforts to curb them, they continue to rise. How does our national spending on healthcare compare with that of other industrialized countries, and what do Americans get for their healthcare dollars? Every year, the Organization for Economic Cooperation and Development (OECD) publishes data on healthcare systems in industrialized countries. In a recent analysis of these data, a comparison was made among 23 nations for the years 1960 to 1998 (Anderson et al., 2000). The goal was to determine the amount of money each nation spent on healthcare per capita, the percent of its Gross National Product (GNP) spent on healthcare, the distribution of that spending, and health-related outcomes. Results showed that the United States spent considerably more per capita than the other 22 countries (in 1998, $4,720 for the United States, compared with $2,000 for the median of the other 22 countries studied); Switzerland had the next highest spending per capita ($2,740). In 1998, the United States spent 14 percent of its GNP on healthcare, whereas the median country spent 8 percent. Germany and Switzerland were the only other countries, besides the United States, that spent more than 10 percent of their GNPs on health services.

Where is the United States putting its healthcare dollars? The data suggest that most of this money goes to technology and to physicians' incomes. Physician services account for 19.9 percent of healthcare spending in the United States, compared with a median of 15.2 percent in the other countries. The United States has approximately the same number of physicians as the median country, but their incomes are much higher. One example of the differences in technology is the fact that in the United States, there are approximately sixteen magnetic resonance imaging (MRI) units per million individuals. Compare that rate with the median of only 2.8 units per million people in the comparison countries.

Do these healthcare dollars result in more positive patient outcomes? First, one must decide what patient outcomes to examine. In terms of life expectancy and infant mortality, the United States is in the bottom half of the 23 countries studied (although education and economic status also affect these outcomes). If one examines more specific effects, such as cancer survival rates, it appears that the United States does indeed have better outcomes. The United States has the highest breast cancer survival rate of all the countries studied (although the data suggest that this rate is only slightly higher than those of Japan, Australia, and Sweden, which spend significantly less on healthcare). Another measure involves waiting times for coronary artery bypass graft (CABG) surgery, a variable that does influence mortality. The data show that the United States has the shortest estimated waiting time, which is a very positive sign.

Overall, the United States spends more on healthcare than other industrialized countries in the world, but only some health outcomes seem to benefit. These issues are very complex, however, and the comparison of healthcare spending trends and outcomes is one task of the fields of health services research and health policy, which are areas of study within the field of public health. The important question is: Are the dollars we spend on healthcare being put to their best use? Its answer is not easily achieved.

Research on this and other topics in the fascinating field of health services research may be found in such journals as *Medical Care*, *Health Services Research*, *Health Affairs*, and the *American Journal of Public Health*.

however, insurance premiums also rose. The fee-for-service system created an atmosphere in which service providers had no incentive for providing preventive care. Quick and efficient, early-stage preventive interventions were typically not reimbursed or were reimbursed at a relatively low level. Instead, providers had incentives to deliver more complex services, many of which were expensive and some of which were unnecessary or even dangerous to the patient (Scarpaci, 1988).

Then, in 1973, Congress passed the HMO (Health Maintenance Organization) Act, which required employers with more than twenty-five employees to offer an HMO option for their employees and provided $325 million for the development of new HMOs (DeLeon et al., 1991). Corporations were now allowed to function as HMOs, providing for-profit medical care. This resulted in a speedy shift in the way services were made available. Suddenly, the focus was on how to control costs and minimize utilization of health services, although early on at least, less than ideal attention was paid to preventing the need for treatment in the first place (R. Friedman et al., 1995).

Recently this focus has begun to change, however. There are now so many HMOs and PPOs (Preferred Provider Organizations) in existence that competition for the business of the medical care consumer has become an important factor in their operation (see Figure 1.2). Providers that do not offer quality services focused on "keeping people healthy" are likely to lose customers and, ultimately, to lose money. Also, many systems are based on **capitation**, in which all health needs are provided at a fixed monthly (or quarterly) price per person. In this type of system, there is a strong

FIGURE 1.2   **The public perception of some managed care organizations is that they focus too much on the "bottom line."**

incentive to keep people well and healthy so that they do not have to come in and "spend" the money that has already been paid to the HMO for them. People who are in good health, and who rarely use available services, bring about larger profits for the company than those who seek care because they pay the same amount of money "up front" for services but do not use them. Finally, because litigation is common today and large settlements and bad publicity can be very problematic, HMOs have strong incentives to provide high-quality care in order to avoid lawsuits. These factors are helping to shift the primary focus of healthcare from the treatment of acute and severe illness to prevention and health maintenance.

Psychological Factors in Illness and Disease

Behavioral medicine, psychosomatic medicine, and, in particular, health psychology have all emerged in large part because of the ways in which patterns of illness in the United States (and other first-world countries) have changed over the past century. Acute illnesses, especially infectious diseases, caused the majority of deaths in the first part of this century. Over the decades, better public health measures—including sanitary practices, nutrition, housing, water, sewage disposal, and prenatal care, as well as the introduction of antibiotics and vaccinations—have largely brought these diseases under control. Now the leading causes of death are chronic conditions (such as cancer and heart disease). Psychological and behavioral factors contribute to the incidence and progression of these diseases and, because they are chronic in nature, they can, in turn, exert a continued effect on an individual's psychological well-being. Because of this, the unique skills of those trained in the areas of psychology and health are increasingly in demand.

As technological advances have radically changed the face of medicine, the concept of **illness** (as opposed to **disease**) has become more and more salient. As we will see in greater detail in Chapter 7, a disease is a collection of physical findings and symptoms that, when taken together, form a definable entity. A disease has clear symptoms, a method for diagnosis, and sometimes a course of treatment that is likely to result in a cure, or the elimination of the symptoms. Illness, however, is more abstract. Illness is often, although not always, associated with a disease. Illness involves the person's perceptions of his or her symptoms, his or her reactions to them, and societal norms regarding these symptoms. Physician and anthropologist Arthur Kleinman differentiates the two nicely with his statement, "Illness complaints are what patients and their families bring to the practitioner. . . . Disease, however, is what the practitioner creates in the recasting of illness in terms of theories of disorder. Disease is what practitioners have been trained to see through the theoretical lenses of their particular form of practice" (Kleinman, 1988, p. 5).

The traditional **biomedical model** of illness (and health) that has been the *sine qua non* for centuries is firmly rooted in reductionism and dualism. It is reductionistic because it supposes that any disease process can ultimately be understood by paring it down to its barest essentials, such as an invading pathogen, a damaged cell membrane, or an aberrant electrical impulse. It is dualistic because it does not account for the role that social and psychological processes play in the etiology and progression of disease

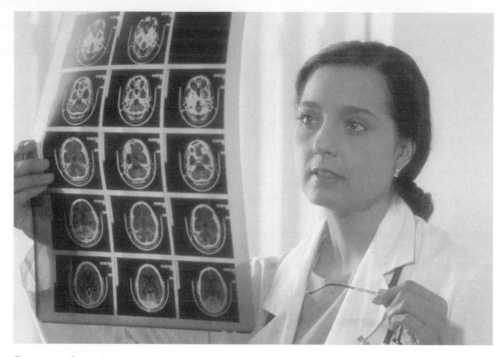

Disease is what practitioners have been trained to see through their particular form of practice.

and illness. Instead, it assumes that physical and psychological factors are independent of one another.

When thinking with a traditional biomedical philosophy, there is little emphasis on health or prevention. The primary focus of medicine is to "find and fix" problems that arise, much as a machine might need to be fixed if it were to malfunction. Of course, certain things may be done to keep the machine functioning at peak levels (such as changing the oil or lubricating the hinges; or if human: exercising or eating a healthy diet). It is easy, however, to ignore these maintenance behaviors when the machine is working as it should. When something goes wrong and the machine begins to malfunction, it's time to rush it in for repairs. Here, physicians who subscribe to the philosophy of the biomedical model intervene by prescribing pills or carrying out surgical procedures. Their goal is to fix the problem and get the person back on track. With this model, the "find it—fix it" approach, nothing else is done for the patient until the next time the body malfunctions!

The **biopsychosocial model**, which was first introduced by psychiatrist George Engel (1977, 1980), proposes not that biomedical factors are unimportant, but that they are not sufficient to understand health and illness. Obviously, certain microorganisms can cause illness, as can dietary deficiencies and various malfunctions in critical bodily systems (for example, the immune system or the cardiovascular system). The biopsychosocial model recognizes, however, that psychological and social factors are important in disease, illness, and health. The name itself, "biopsychosocial," high-

lights the fact that biological, psychological, and social factors are all essential contributors to health (Engel, 1977). As we will see in further detail in Chapter 7, the biopsychosocial model does not attempt to separate mind and body in a dualistic fashion, but
instead requires researchers and clinicians to examine carefully the interplay of mind
and body in order to achieve a full understanding of the individual and his or her
health and well-being. According to this model, health is not simply the absence of disease, but is instead a state of functioning and well-being that encompasses both physical and mental aspects of an individual. This model is reflected in the definition of
"health" adopted by the World Health Organization in 1946, which stated that health
is "a state of complete physical, mental, and social well-being, and not merely the
absence of disease or infirmity."

As we noted above, psychological factors are not independent of the disease
process or the illness experience. Just as being ill can affect one's psychological functioning, an individual's psychological attributes can contribute to their health or disease. There are several ways in which psychological factors and physical health might
be related. First, physical health status might influence psychological status, such as
when a person who has terminal cancer becomes depressed. Second, psychological factors might influence physical health through behaviors. People with certain personality characteristics, for example, might be more likely to do certain things like exercise,
eat healthfully, or abstain from cigarette smoking. Third, psychological factors might
exert an influence on physiological processes, such as when a person who views the
world as a hostile place and who is often anxious has a higher baseline blood pressure
than someone who is more calm and relaxed. And fourth, physical health and psychological factors might be linked through a third variable. That is, physical health and
psychological factors may not be related causally to each other at all, but instead may
be correlated because each is being affected by some other factor. For example, a high
level of autonomic nervous system reactivity might underlie physiological arousal that
makes a person more likely to develop heart disease and might also cause a person to
demonstrate hostility. In this case, hostility might serve as a "marker" for heart disease.
Modifying this psychological variable would do little to change the likelihood of developing the disease.

For many medical conditions today, a cure does not exist. The current leading
causes of death in the United States are heart disease and cancer, which are multifactorial in **etiology** (origin and cause) and treatment. These diseases may be influenced
equally by physical and by psychological and behavioral factors. Consider heart disease.
A person's risk of having a heart attack is greatly increased by leading a sedentary
lifestyle and by smoking cigarettes, two behavioral factors that have very large psychological components. As we will see in this book, a person can significantly reduce the
chances of suffering a heart attack by not smoking and by exercising regularly, but
these kinds of preventive behaviors require psychological commitment and modification of beliefs, attitudes, and behaviors. At present, there is no simple, straightforward
cure for heart disease. There is no single pill and no simple surgery. All treatments
require participation of the whole individual in taking medication and making major
lifestyle modifications, such as changing diet, stopping smoking, exercising, cutting
back on stresses, and relaxing.

Further, a heart attack may affect an individual psychologically because it can be a tremendous assault to a person's self-image. The patient experiences fear and panic and must often implement drastic changes in lifestyle, including modifications of stress reactions, in order to increase the likelihood of survival. A major surgical procedure, called coronary bypass, may be an option for the patient, but it carries high risks and long rehabilitation. The individual must try to manage his or her fear of another heart attack, and adjustments may have to be made in many of his or her activities and habits. Thus, heart disease requires a significant degree of psychological, as well as physical, adaptation.

Cancer is another example of a disease in which prevention and cure affect, and are affected by, the whole person. Unhealthy behaviors figure prominently in the etiology of some cancers. For example, most cases of lung cancer and many cases of throat and bladder cancer are caused by smoking cigarettes. The cure of breast and cervical cancer may depend highly upon early detection, which requires regular preventive screening measures including breast self-exams, mammograms, and Pap tests. Yet for many women, inertia, fear, and other psychological barriers too often stand in the way of early detection. The treatment of cancer may also be heavily influenced by psychological factors. Treatments may involve disfiguring surgery, pain, and discomfort from chemotherapy and radiation, as well as tremendous financial hardship. The patient must work hard to maintain self-image, meaningful involvement in work, and social and family ties throughout the course of treatment. How well the patient accomplishes these psychological tasks may influence his or her physical recovery.

Which is more important to health, physical or psychological factors? There is no simple answer to that question, and any answer will depend on a multitude of issues, including what the disease or illness is and what the important outcomes of "health" are for the individual. In the case of infectious diseases, a clear link can be established between a pathogen and the disease itself. Thus, it might appear that psychological factors are relatively unimportant under these circumstances. A closer look, however, indicates that psychological factors can still be quite important. Let's look, for example, at AIDS (Acquired Immune Deficiency Syndrome).

An individual will not be diagnosed with AIDS unless she or he has been infected with the Human Immunodeficiency Virus (HIV). Certain people may, however, be more likely to become infected with HIV in the first place because of psychological factors such as a tendency to take health risks. Also, HIV has a long incubation period, during which time it is in the body but the individual has no signs of the disease AIDS. People who are stronger and healthier to start with may experience a longer period of good health between the time of infection and the onset of AIDS symptoms (and being physically healthy may be related to psychological characteristics such as the ability to better manage stress). Once a person knows that she or he has HIV or AIDS, his or her emotional response to the diagnosis and the onset of symptoms may affect the course of the disease. Negative expectations regarding HIV have been linked to the onset of AIDS symptoms, and the kind of attributions people make for their illness and their ability to find meaning in it have been shown to affect the rate of immune function decline and even mortality (Bower et al., 1998; Reed et al., 1999; Segerstrom et al., 1996). Additionally, research shows that passive acceptance of one's approaching death may also hasten its arrival (Molassiotis et al., 1997).

At certain points in an illness, psychological factors may be relatively less important than at other times. When one is *experiencing* a heart attack, the physical status of the heart muscle and the speed of medical intervention will be of paramount importance; psychological factors might play a more minor role (perhaps by influencing symptom perception and thereby influencing how quickly the person gets help). Psychological factors have much to do, however, with whether one experiences a heart attack in the first place and the course of recovery following the heart attack. In terms of returning to "health" (that state of well-being that includes physical, mental, and social dimensions) after one has been diagnosed with a disease, psychological factors are crucial.

In this book, we will see that few conditions can be understood or treated in purely physical terms. Illness involves more than disease. We will also see that it is a mistake to imagine that disease can be treated in purely psychological terms. To attempt to do so would be unproductive and perhaps even dangerous, for it would ignore the important advances of modern medical practice that are necessary to combat disease. Psychological techniques cannot replace good medicine, just as medical technology alone is insufficient for encouraging effective health promotion and disease treatment. Together, however, psychology and medicine can elevate the treatment of illness to levels never before achieved.

Summary

1. Until recently psychologists have dealt almost exclusively with the mind. In recent decades, psychological principles have been applied to the arena of health.
2. The definition of "health" is important to defining health psychology. Health is a complete state of physical, mental, and social well-being; it is not simply the absence of illness or disease. Health psychologists are devoted to promoting health, preventing illness, and identifying correlates and predictors of health, illness, and dysfunction.
3. It has long been believed that emotions and mental status interact with physical health. Hippocrates wrote about the physician's demeanor as it affects the patient's will to live. Osler instructed medical students to listen to the patient to find the proper diagnosis.
4. The focus of this book is primarily on individuals in the context of health, illness, and the experience of medical care. There are many intricacies associated with research, particularly in health psychology. Human beings are vastly complex, and issues related to healthcare, healthcare systems, and healthcare delivery are multifaceted.

   - True experiments enable researchers to determine causality, but are difficult, sometimes impossible, to carry out. Correlational studies provide valuable insights, but cannot establish causal relationships.
   - Prospective studies are preferable to retrospective studies because the latter are affected by biases in the ways in which people remember events.
   - Longitudinal studies are usually preferable to cross-sectional studies because they enable us to distinguish patterns of change over time from cohort effects.

- Laboratory studies occur in controlled settings and allow confounding variables to be eliminated, but "realism" may be sacrificed. Field studies provide more natural responses, but extraneous influences are difficult to control.

5. Health psychologists work in various settings as consultants on medical teams, as therapists, contributing to public health promotion programs, and as researchers. Many graduate programs in health psychology exist, but not all health psychologists were formally trained in such programs.

6. The twentieth century is probably the only period in history in which the predominant medical opinion has emphasized a focus on the body and has neglected the mind as a factor in health. During most of recorded history, illness has been attributed to magical and unknowable phenomena such as sinful thoughts, possession by evil spirits, and the will of vengeful gods.

   - Western medicine originated in ancient Greece during the time of greatest intellectual development. Hippocrates built the earliest foundation for rational medicine.
   - Galen is considered by many to be the greatest figure in ancient medicine because he based diagnosis on anatomy and physiology.
   - In the fifteenth century, the Renaissance brought intellectualism and rationalism to the realm of medicine.

7. Around 1900, medicine began to be transformed into a clinical science. Most of the great strides in medicine have taken place in even more recent years.

   - During the time of greatest advances in the technical aspects of medicine, it has been easy to forget the human side.
   - Intense focus on the technical side of medicine has prevented a clear distinction between disease and illness. Disease is the collection of physical findings and symptoms that form a definable disease entity. Illness may or may not involve definable disease, but illness upsets the optimal functioning of the individual. The whole patient may be ignored in an effort to focus on his or her disease.

8. Psychological factors are entwined with physical phenomena. This connection is manifested in many ways presented throughout this book.

   - Psychological factors are as important as physical ones in understanding the etiology of a disease or in carrying out its treatment. There is a delicate interplay between mind and body in the realm of illness.
   - Holistic approaches to healthcare incorporate the mind-body connection and combine Western technology with non-Western traditions.

9. In the mid-twentieth century, Dunbar and Alexander paved the way for the field of psychosomatic medicine linking personality characteristics to specific physical illnesses.

   - Dunbar and Alexander deviated from Freudian ideas regarding some diseases as "converted" from unconscious psychological anxiety. They proposed specific disease-psychology relationships and a physiological mechanism by which personality and illness might be linked.

10. Behavioral medicine emerged in the 1970s as a distinct discipline with the goal of applying behavioral science principles to the maintenance of physical health and the prevention of disease.

11. Because of medical advances, Western society is largely free of many of the diseases of previous centuries; now chronic diseases are of concern. Medical care needs have changed, and there has been a shift in focus from purely biomedical to biopsychosocial frameworks.

THINKING CRITICALLY

1. How do societal versus individual considerations vary when considering cigarette smoking? Are there any issues common to both perspectives?

2. How would you design a laboratory experiment to find out whether experiencing stress increases the tendency to break out in hives? If you had strong laboratory results showing causal relationship, what would you gain by replicating the research in the field? What would you sacrifice? How would you translate your laboratory experiment into a field study?

3. What are some of the challenges encountered by psychologists when working with physicians in a medical setting? What special types of knowledge might a psychologist bring to the collaboration? What knowledge might he or she be lacking?

4. What are some of the ethical considerations of alternative medical treatments?

5. How are ongoing changes in managed care likely to influence the treatment that patients receive? How are they likely to influence medical research? What are some of the positive aspects of a capitation system? What are some of the negative aspects?

6. Imagine that a patient goes to the doctor with a specific complaint (you can be imaginative and decide what that complaint will be). Imagine how the interaction might go if the physician had been trained according to a strict, traditional biomedical model. What kinds of questions might he or she ask? Now imagine that the doctor was trained according to a biopsychosocial model. What changes are likely to occur?

GLOSSARY

Age cohort: A group of people born at the same time who thus share similar experiences (e.g., people born in the late 1940s were young adults in the Vietnam era).

Animism: The belief that every movement (of living or nonliving objects) is caused by animating spirits.

Auscultation: The process of listening for sounds within the human body.

Biomedical model. A model that assumes that illness can be fully accounted for by a person's deviations from the norm on measurable biological variables.

Biopsychosocial model: A model that requires that psychological and social factors be included in any

attempt to understand symptoms and the experience of illness.

Capitation: A system in which all healthcare needs are provided for a fixed monthly or quarterly fee per person.

Causal inference: A definitive statement about the cause of a phenomenon.

Control group: In an experiment, the group that is randomly assigned to receive no treatment.

Conversion hysteria: The phenomenon in which it is believed that unconscious psychological anxiety is transformed into physical symptoms.

Correlation: An association between two variables.

Covary: To correlate, to relate in a specified and predictable way.

Cross-lagged correlation: An assessment of the degree of association between two variables, one of which is viewed as a lagged value of the outcome variable.

Cross-sectional research: Research that compares subjects on one or more variables at a single point in time.

Diagnosis: The identification of disease based on signs and symptoms.

Dialysis: A process of mechanically filtering toxic byproducts from the blood.

Disease: Physical findings and symptoms that form a definable disease entity.

Dualism: The idea that mind and body are separate and independent entities.

Etiology: Cause and origin.

Experimental group: A group or condition in which the participants receive a manipulation or intervention.

Field study: A study that is conducted in a natural setting.

General practitioner: A physician trained to treat a wide variety of diseases.

Germ theory: The idea that microorganisms cause disease.

Hospice: A method of care for the terminally ill in which the goal is not to cure, but to provide comfort and emotional support to the patient and family.

Humors: The four bodily fluids (phlegm, blood, black bile, yellow bile) related to personality; disequilibrium was proposed by the Greeks to result in disease.

Illness: May or may not involve clinical signs, symptoms, and a disease entity. Involves functional impairment as well as effects on cognitions, emotions, and behaviors.

Laboratory study: A study conducted in the laboratory as opposed to the natural environment.

Longitudinal study: Compares subjects on one or more variables over time.

Meta-analysis: A research technique in which the "cases" are research studies; allows researchers to statistically combine all of the findings on a particular topic.

Monism: The idea that the mind and body are one entity.

Palpation: The application of the fingers with light pressure to the surface of the body to determine the consistency of parts beneath in physical diagnosis.

Prognosis: The forecast of the course of a disease.

Prospective research: Research in which the predictor variable is measured in advance of the outcome variable.

Random assignment: A method of sorting participants into experimental versus control group; uses random methods (coin toss, random number table) so that each participant has an equal chance of being chosen for either group.

Randomized clinical trial: In the medical field, the term for a "true experiment."

Retrospective data collection: Data collection method in which participants report past events that they recall (although recall can be biased).

State-dependent memory: The tendency of people to remember most easily the events of the past connected with the emotional state they feel as they report.

True experiment: A type of study in which participants are assigned randomly to either a treatment or control group; groups are assumed to be equivalent prior to the treatment and therefore the researcher can infer causality.

Variable: A measurable characteristic of people, objects, or events that may change or vary.

CHAPTER

2

The Process of Medical Care

The patches of red, flaking skin on Norana's arms and legs had been getting worse for several weeks. Now they looked just awful. She'd tried her mother's hydrocortisone cream, and several home remedies recommended by friends (including the application of mayonnaise!), but nothing had helped. So, she finally decided to stop by the Urgent Care Clinic, a facility she passed every day on her way to work but knew nothing about. She hoped that she could see someone right away and that she could be in and out of the clinic quickly and not have to pay an exorbitant price. These worries were precisely the reasons that she generally avoided doctors and nurses. In fact, she'd not had a medical checkup in many years and didn't have a personal physician. Norana assumed that if she ever got really sick she would just go to the emergency room and be treated by the doctor on call.

Carlos sat in the waiting room of Dr. Li's office. Dr. Li was the internist Carlos had selected to be his primary care physician. He held a clipboard on his lap and busily checked off boxes: "Have you ever been diagnosed with asthma? Bronchitis? Cancer? Emphysema? Gout? Hypertension?" These were only a few of the hundreds of questions on the form. The answers to most of the questions were "no." Carlos was quite healthy. He had recently moved to the area, and after talking to some friends and doing a little research on his own, he had selected the doctor that he

thought would be best for him. Now he was here in the office filling out forms regarding his medical history and soon he would meet Dr. Li, and make a judgment about their compatibility. He already knew that Dr. Li was medically qualified, but it was important to Carlos that he and his doctor be able to communicate. Just as he finished filling out the details of his personal health habits, an assistant opened the door and called Carlos into the office for his physical examination.

Introduction to Medical Professionals, Patients, and the Treatment Exchange

Medical practitioners and patients encounter one another under many varied circumstances. Sometimes they have known each other for years and the patient's illness can be understood readily in the context of the patient's daily life, experience, and personality. Sometimes they are complete strangers, and the physician simply provides a service (a diagnosis, a prescription, or a procedure), and the patient pays the bill. The circumstances of care may also vary. Sometimes the patient can provide a detailed account of, and considerable insight into, the medical problem. Other times, the patient provides no information at all. Sometimes, practitioner and patient have sufficient time to discuss the many implications of the patient's problem. Sometimes, as with some HMOs, they have no more than seven minutes.

Patients vary in their attitudes toward medical practitioners and toward the process of medical care. Some patients, like Carlos above, are knowledgeable about medical matters and hold the physician to be a valuable source of information and experience (Adewuyi-Dalton et al., 1998; Haug & Lavin, 1983). Other patients, like Norana, know very little about their health and they care to learn even less (Krantz et al., 1980). They simply want the problem fixed. Some deny that there is anything wrong with them at all, and believe nothing could threaten their well-being. And, as we shall see in Chapter 7, some patients have high thresholds for discomfort and wait until they have seriously jeopardized their health before they "bother" their doctors. Others regularly turn to medical practitioners for comfort when anxiety overwhelms them or when they need diversion from their unhappy or boring lives (Gardner et al., 2000; Mechanic, 1979).

Medical professionals, primarily physicians, also vary in their attitudes toward patients and toward the character of their role as healers (Mizrahi, 1984; Sangster & McGuire, 1999). Some physicians focus their concerns entirely on the diagnostic puzzle. They see the patient as the bodily container for disease. They view the patient's active mind as a factor that impedes rather than supports the physician's efforts. To such physicians, the best kind of patient is the one with a fascinating disease who keeps his or her mouth shut (West, 1983). Some physicians, on the other hand, prefer to focus on the patient as a person, an individual whose life affects, and is affected by, the disease. Such physicians try to help their patients to achieve happy and productive lives regardless of whether a definitive diagnosis can be reached. Many physicians operate between these two extremes, sometimes acknowledging and attending to, and sometimes forgetting, the patient's mind while treating the patient's body.

The goal of this chapter is to examine in detail what occurs when patients consult physicians and other medical professionals for the diagnosis and treatment of illness. We will examine how the medical consultation affects (and is affected by) several factors: the circumstances of the illness, the circumstances of the medical encounter, and the basic viewpoints (or philosophies) held by practitioner and patient about their roles with respect to one another. Box 2.1 considers one factor that can strongly affect the viewpoints of physician and patient about their relationship—the element of cultural background.

In this chapter, our focus will be on the relationship between medical practitioners and their patients in the healthcare setting. Such a setting will be defined broadly to include everything from office or clinic visits to treatment in the emergency room. And, the relationships described might be between patients and any of a variety of health professionals (physicians, nurses, orderlies, laboratory technicians, paramedics, etc.). It is important to note, however, that the research literature on the medical professional-patient relationships deals primarily with physicians. Although patients rarely interact with only physicians, it is with them that patients carry on the information exchanges that form the basis of the entire diagnostic and treatment process (Cassell, 1985a, 1985b). Of course, many of the findings of research on physician-patient communication apply to other health professionals as well.

In this and the next chapter, we will examine various elements of medical care, including the factors that typically facilitate or hinder the accomplishment of medical goals. In this chapter we focus on the process of medical care: its premises, the basic models of physician-patient relationships, the components of typical interactions between doctors and patients, and some of the outcomes (subjective and objective) of various sorts of interactions. We will continue this theme in Chapter 3 as we delve more deeply into issues of both verbal and nonverbal communication in the medical encounter, including the issues of effective listening, asking questions, emotion, empathy, rapport, and bedside manner.

The Four Premises of Medical Care

The analysis of practitioner-patient interaction in this chapter is based upon several assumptions or premises made explicit by Eric J. Cassell, a physician whose research and theories of physician-patient **communication** have been widely incorporated into medical education. The premises are as follows: (1) [D]octors treat patients, not diseases; (2) the body has the last word; (3) all medical care flows through the relationship between physician and patient; and (4) the spoken language is the most important tool in medicine (Cassell, 1985a, p. 1, numbers ours).

Most medical professionals would probably agree that, in the final analysis, what happens to the patient is what matters most. It's better to have a patient get well and never know precisely what had been wrong with him or her than to make a brilliant **diagnosis** of an obscure condition and have the patient die. It is preferable to communicate with patients in such a way that they are helped to cope with their illnesses, rather than to overwhelm them with technical information that they cannot understand

BOX 2.1
Across Cultures

Does Cultural Background Affect the Doctor-Patient Relationship?

As we will see in this chapter, relationships between physicians and their patients usually fall into one of three basic categories: (1) active-passive (with the doctor making and implementing all of the decisions), (2) guidance-cooperation (with the doctor making most decisions and guiding the patient's actions), or (3) mutual participation (with both doctor and patient working together to make decisions and achieve goals). Do patients freely choose the type of relationship they will have with their doctors, or are they influenced by subtle cultural pressures?

In terms of preferred style of interaction with a physician, there are some interesting differences among ethnic groups, as we will see when we examine the following: Mexican Americans, African Americans, Korean Americans, and European Americans. Mexican Americans and Korean Americans are most likely to have a family-oriented preference when it comes to medical care and medical decision making (Blackhall et al., 1995). This means that in the interaction between the doctor and the patient, the patient will tend to feel comfortable with "family-like" roles. For example, Korean Americans and Mexican Americans are less likely than other groups to feel that a patient should be told if he or she has a terminal illness. Instead, the patient may be "protected" from this knowledge, much as a child might be protected by a parent. This approach is indicative of an active-passive model, or perhaps a guidance-cooperation model.

African Americans and European Americans, however, are more likely to address medical care and decision making from an autonomous perspective, and therefore want to have information about their illness and prognosis. This preference requires that interactions with the physician match a mutual-participation model.

Similarly, African and European Americans are much more likely than the other cultural groups to believe that patients themselves should decide whether to have life-supporting technologies. Korean and Mexican Americans, on the other hand, believe that this decision should be a joint process involving the patient, the doctor, and other family members as well. In medical decision making, particularly about very important matters, Korean and Mexican American patients prefer the physician to have an active role in collaboration with the family, while African and European Americans prefer a more "consumerist" approach and much more autonomy for the patient.

An orientation toward "family" versus "autonomy" is not the only reason for these differences. Research has shown that because of norms regarding social status and respect (such as within the traditional Mexican American culture), a great deal of reverence is shown to physicians, sometimes so much that patients are hesitant to ask questions or to share their concerns (Lipton et al., 1998). This may be coupled with the patient's deference to the opinions and desires of his or her own family. Consequently, the doctor's approach may never be questioned, and the patient's confusions may not be clarified. The patient's own values may not be emphasized to the physician or to the family. Furthermore, if the family's preferences overcome the advice of the physician, the patient might remain noncompliant with the treatment regimen, and the physician might never know why.

Being aware of the effects of cultural values is the first step in making sure that the physician-patient relationship is effective and that family and physician preferences do not overwhelm what is best for the patient as a person. When a patient's concerns are understood, he or she is likely to be much better able to communicate. Cultural values can be used to strengthen the relationship between the doctor and patient. Patients should be asked about their preferences for involvement and these desires should be respected.

or otherwise deal with. The correctness of a diagnosis matters only insofar as it affects the prescribed treatment, the healing of the body, and the patient's psychosocial health. What really matters is that the patient maintains the highest possible quality of life.

The importance of communication in the medical care process is not likely to be entirely clear to all medical practitioners, however. In fact, those who focus on the purely technical aspects of disease might even disagree with the last two premises. But, as we will see in this chapter and the next, considerable research evidence supports the central role of communication in the process of medical care.

Language in Medical Care:
The Role of Words and Gestures

"Your tumor is malignant. I'm sorry to have to tell you that you have cancer." Words are extremely powerful tools in medicine. They establish the reality of suffering. Because of their power, the utterance of words in the medical encounter is a very serious enterprise indeed. Here is a poignant example of the power of words: A woman whose father had just died stood in front of his body, physically protecting him from the physician. She stated that she would not allow her father to be pronounced dead. "When saying something removes all doubt, so long as the truth remains unspoken, reality can be kept at bay" (Cassell, 1985a, pp. 57-58). More evidence for the power of words is that practitioners and patients modify them to establish a more comfortable psychological distance from the illness phenomenon. A breast cancer patient, for example, refers to "the breast," not "my breast," and says, "If you have cancer, you have to follow these treatments." She does not focus on her own experience with treatment, or identify the cancer as her own. Her use of impersonal pronouns helps her to separate herself from her disease. In fact, a medical professional can better understand a patient's feelings about illness by listening to how he or she talks about the disease process.

Of course, medical communication involves more than just words. Medical professionals and patients also communicate with one another using **nonverbal** cues and gestures. We will see that much can be learned about patients by examining their facial expressions, body movements, and tone of voice. Likewise, medical professionals can convey a great deal to their patients with nonverbal cues, particularly when there is limited time to convey verbal messages of support and caring. Thus, a true understanding of interchanges between physicians and patients requires the careful study of both the verbal and nonverbal messages that are central to effective medical treatment (Friedman, 1982; Waitzkin, 1985).

Viewpoint and Skill in Communication

Through the process of communication, practitioner and patient attempt to gain a common understanding of the patient's illness. Each gathers information from, and imparts information to, the other. Each conveys facts as well as the meaning they attach to those facts. Because of the many differences between medical practitioners and patients in knowledge, background, and perspective, communication between the two can be extremely complex.

In 1899, Sir William Osler noted that if physicians would only listen, their patients would tell them the diagnosis. More recently, Roter and Hall (1992) argued that talking is the main ingredient of medical care and that it is the most important means of achieving therapeutic goals. Sophisticated medical tests have their place, of course, but in many and possibly most cases, talking is equally important. These researchers point out that the patient has a story to tell, a story that the physician needs to hear in order to integrate the meaning of the illness and disease. The patient's special expertise regarding his or her own symptoms, as well as physical and emotional experiences, will be reflected in this story. Effective communication combines mutual respect with reciprocity and emotional sensitivity in order to achieve the best possible outcomes from the doctor-patient partnership.

What transpires in the communication between medical professionals and patients depends upon two main factors: (1) what each party is capable of enacting (that is, his or her communication skills), and (2) what each party holds to be true about the therapeutic relationship (beliefs, viewpoints, or philosophies) (DiMatteo, 1979). These two phenomena are interrelated, of course, when people fail to develop the skills to carry out behaviors they do not value, or devalue things they cannot do.

A practitioner's and/or a patient's poor communication skills can cause problems in their relationship. For example, a physician may value listening to patients in a supportive manner but his or her skills fall short of what is needed to achieve these goals. This physician might consistently interrupt patients when they try to speak and dominate all conversations with patients (Irish & Hall, 1995). He or she may fail to recognize how these behaviors affect patients and how shortcomings in communication can limit patient care. If the physician does value listening to patients, he or she may be helped to develop communication skills. Audiotaping or videotaping the medical visit has helped many medical practitioners to see and hear firsthand various aspects of their interactions with patients, including precisely how much they interrupt their patients. Self-awareness has helped many practitioners to correct communication patterns that are less than ideal (DiMatteo, 1985). A patient might also lack the skills to communicate in ways that she or he considers valuable. The patient might fervently believe that patients should have the opportunity to ask many questions of their physicians and might consider patient education to be a central component of the physician's role. However, this same patient may become tongue-tied and passive during the medical visit, experience a flood of anxiety when the physician interrupts, and never assert the desire to ask questions. Thus, although patients may desire and very much value information, they may not actively seek it (Beisecker & Beisecker, 1990).

A physician may give a patient very little opportunity to participate in his or her own care precisely because the physician believes that patient participation is not valuable and certainly not worth the trouble. This physician might be reluctant to depart from the physician's traditional role, with its high degree of power and control (West, 1984). Even when patients are recognized as "experts" regarding their own experience and symptoms, they are not often allowed to play an active role in the integration of this knowledge. Patients tend to be cautious when they give explanations, if they give them at all, and they often seem to downplay their own knowledge in order to maintain the social structure of the interaction. In many cases, patients may be asked to provide facts but not be given the opportunity to analyze those facts and how they relate to the diagnosis and treatment at hand (Gill, 1998).

The effects of uncertainty on physician-patient communication illustrate this point quite well. When a physician is unsure of a patient's diagnosis and/or prognosis, there are several options. He or she can tell the patient what is already known and keep the patient apprised of developments and changes as test results and the reports of consulting specialists become available. Or, the patient can be kept completely "in the dark" until a final, definitive statement can be made. In the latter case, the patient's ignorance may last weeks or months and he or she may be quite distressed, being ill and knowing nothing about what is wrong. By withholding information, the physician maintains a position of power vis-à-vis the patient and saves the time and trouble of keeping the patient informed. The physician-patient relationship may be jeopardized, however, as the opportunity for partnership and building of trust may be foregone.

Several decades ago, it was quite common for physicians to withhold relevant facts from patients until the picture of their illness was quite clear. Physicians often resolved their own uncertainty long before they finally let patients know the truth. In one study from that era, the parents of children who had contracted polio were waiting to hear their children's prognosis (that is, the expected course of disease) (Davis, 1960). They wanted to know whether it was likely that their children would remain crippled for life. For days and sometimes weeks, both physicians and nurses withheld information about prognosis from the parents and gave unclear answers to the parents' questions. These health professionals kept the parents uninformed long after the course of the disease could be predicted. Of course, Davis's study was conducted decades ago when patients were far less assertive and knowledgeable than they are today. While some physicians actually provide their patients with a considerable amount of information under conditions of uncertainty, a great deal of research suggests that many patients feel that their medical professionals intentionally withhold information from them (Phillips, 1996; Shuy, 1976). Many patients are not at all satisfied with the amount of information that is provided to them (Phillips, 1996).

Certainly, some patients welcome the opportunity to be passive recipients of medical care (Benbassat et al., 1998). Their philosophy casts the physician or nurse in the role of parent or caretaker. Such a point of view has many drawbacks, of course. Patients who look to the doctor or nurse to control every aspect of their medical care may actually do little or nothing to contribute to their own well-being. They fail to voice their concerns, they ask no questions, and they allow confusions and misunderstandings to go uncorrected (Taylor, 1979). The degree to which patients prefer active involvement is related to a number of demographic and disease characteristics. A review of the literature on patients' preferences for involvement in medical care indicates that patients are more likely to prefer a passive role when their conditions are more severe, when they are older, when they have less education, and if they are male. Although these are the best predictors of patients' preferences, however, they only explain about 20 percent of the variance. It is important for physicians to ask patients directly about their preferences, because this is really the most accurate way to find out what any particular person desires. The ability to find out patients' preferences and then to respond to these appropriately is an important basic clinical skill (Benbassat et al., 1998).

Although not all patients want to play an active role in their medical care, research suggests that most patients want as much information as possible from their health professionals (Beisecker & Beisecker, 1990; Benbassat et al., 1998; Frederikson, 1995; Waitzkin, 1985). Patient participation in the decision-making process is dependent upon information and is critical to therapeutic effectiveness (Speedling & Rose, 1985). The provision of information to patients increases their satisfaction with their healthcare, enhances their cooperation with treatment, improves their ability to give accurate information to their medical practitioners, and decreases their anxiety (DiMatteo, 1985; Margalith & Shapiro, 1997; Young & Klingle, 1996). Information gives patients an element of psychological control when they are undergoing surgery or stressful medical treatments and improves the outcomes of such procedures (e.g., Egbert et al., 1963; Egbert et al., 1964). As we will see later in this book, patients can often cope much better when they know what they are preparing for than when they do not.

Despite these positive effects, physician-patient communication has been found over decades of research to be characteristically rather poor. Early in this research it was found that as many as 50 percent of patients left their physician's office or clinic with little or no idea of what to do to care for themselves (Ley, 1979; Svarstad, 1976). Most did not even have a rudimentary understanding of their medical problem or its treatment. More recent research has found that about 50 percent of patient complaints and concerns are not addressed in the medical encounter, and about half of the time doctors and patients do not even agree on what the presenting problem really is (Van Der Merwe, 1995). Yet, for a variety of reasons, patients often do not tell their doctors of their concerns and misgivings.

Communication Uncovers Hidden Premises

A patient's illness problem can be dealt with fully only when his or her real concerns have been addressed. For a medical therapeutic interaction to be successful, the patient's and the practitioner's basic **premises** (working assumptions) must either be shared or brought to the forefront and examined. For example, consider a patient who is allergic to dairy products and believes that the antibiotic penicillin is made from dairy products. (It is not.) In an effort to avoid the allergy, the patient fails to follow the prescribed treatment regimen, and in order to determine why this has happened, the physician must learn the premise that underlies the patient's uncooperative behavior. The physician can do this with effective communication (Cassell, 1985b).

A patient's premise might be deeply buried because it causes anxiety. A physician's premise might be deeply buried because it is a fact learned many, many years ago and never questioned. Let's look at what happens when the two come together: A patient has a small, **subcutaneous** (under the skin) cyst. The physician's premise is that this kind of cyst is almost never **malignant** (cancerous) and can be very easily removed. Therefore, the physician reasons that the patient's obvious concern must certainly be over appearance. The physician attempts over and over to reassure the patient that the removal of the cyst will cause, at worst, a very small and barely noticeable scar. The patient knows nothing about this kind of cyst; to the patient any "lump" could be malignant. The patient asks several times, "So, do you think it's okay, doctor?" (It is never specified that "okay" means "not malignant"). The doctor responds with an enthusiastic smile. "You won't see the scar at all. It won't be noticeable . . . really." After a long and unproductive interaction, the patient finally blurts out the fear: ". . . so, uh, you . . . uh . . . you think it's probably benign?" The doctor is taken aback in complete surprise that the thought of malignancy was even an issue. Such a misunderstanding is not at all unusual. Physicians often overestimate the amount of knowledge their patients bring to the medical encounter (Guttman, 1993) and because of this they may fail to provide information that their patients want and need. In fact, in most practitioner-patient interactions the participants have differing views on a number of issues (Waitzkin, 1985). The more central each point is to their entire discussion, the more their attempt to understand and to communicate with one another can be undermined. Sometimes the issues on which patients' and physicians' views differ are very important. For example, in one study healthy college students and outpatients were asked about the seriousness of several symptoms and whether these symptoms required medical attention. A group of doctors was asked about the same thing. For most symptoms, especially common ones, the patients and students significantly underestimated their seriousness compared with ratings given by the physicians (Peay & Peay, 1998). When the symptoms were objectively quite "serious," however, there was somewhat less discrepancy between the physician and lay ratings, and for three of the most serious symptoms (all of which might indicate cancer) lay ratings of the need for medical advice were even higher than physician ratings. This study nicely illustrates the differences between patients and physicians on the most basic of issues, that of whether medical care is even necessary. There are also big differences between what physicians think people should be told about their prescribed medications and what people say they would like to know. This is not to say that patients want to know more than they are told, or that they want to know less, but rather that the types of information that they deem important are not always the same as those of their doctors (Berry et al., 1997).

Patients tend to be more satisfied when their physicians understand and fulfill their needs for the medical visit (Like & Zyzanski, 1987). When physicians accurately recognize their patients' problems, patients are also more compliant, and they have better treatment outcomes (Starfield et al., 1981). When physicians and patients agree on what problems require follow-up, greater problem resolution can be achieved. Both physicians and patients tend to have higher expectations for improvement and perceive the outcomes of treatment to be better when they agree with each other than when agreement is lacking. When physicians are aware of, and agree with, patients' concerns, patients have higher expectations for improvement (Starfield et al., 1979).

Ineffective communication can result in the physician's failing to recognize an important fact about the patient's situation, and perhaps even missing the entire problem. For example, a young woman is experiencing fatigue. The fatigue comes on quickly and overwhelmingly in the afternoon, when her classes are over and just before her workout with the track team. The fatigue is severe and the woman is afraid that she might be suffering from some sort of medical problem, so she makes an appointment with her physician. All the tests run by the doctor show normal results. She tells the patient that there is nothing obviously wrong, that she should perhaps eat more protein, and sends her on her way. The patient feels that the doctor has not really understood how badly she feels, and she departs, annoyed, to find a more satisfactory doctor. The physician in this case *did* miss an important opportunity to help the patient and to win her confidence and satisfaction. The clue to what is really underlying the patient's problem is the track team. The story goes like this: The patient is a talented long-distance runner. She is on an athletic scholarship. But lately she is beginning to feel that her commitments to both schoolwork and track are overwhelming. She has no time for a normal social life. She feels that she must do well in an upcoming track meet, yet she feels conflicted about having to put so much of her energy and time into running with little left for studying. Her emotional response to the daily track workout is overwhelming fatigue. Thus, her problem is not physical. An astute physician would certainly have run the basic tests just to be sure there was no obvious organic problem. But she would then further explore some of the psychosocial issues that the patient herself mentioned and probably make a referral to someone (such as a sports psychologist or trainer) who is well equipped to help the student athlete deal with the pressing demands of a rigorous academic and athletic schedule. She would certainly follow up on the clue: "Just before workout . . ."! Why doesn't the patient simply go to her coach and say, "In two weeks I have to compete in this big race. I'm very conflicted about my athletic and academic responsibilities, and it's starting to take a physical toll on me. What can I do? I can't juggle it all"? It is likely that the patient is not consciously aware that emotional tension is draining her energy. As we will see in Chapter 7, people can unconsciously translate their emotional distress into physical symptoms. A health professional can gain insight into patient beliefs by listening carefully and actively to what the patient says (see Figure 2.1).

Technology and People: Promoting Dialogue

As modern medicine becomes dominated by technology, some medical professionals tend to give less and less attention to practitioner-patient dialogue. Despite the fact that most medical diagnoses can be made on the basis of the information gathered from the patient, some medical professionals consider dialogue with the patient to be irrelevant (Putnam et al., 1985). They find the information about illness produced by clinical tests to be more appealing than the information produced by people. Test data seem to be more direct and succinct than the patient's complex story. What machines can tell about patients is limited in scope, however, and may sometimes even be inaccurate. In fact, about half of all the medical problems that patients present to family practitioners fail to show up on diagnostic tests because these problems have a strong psychological component (Marsland et al., 1976).

Faced with technological obstacles to their mutual understanding, practitioner and patient must take steps to arrive at an explicit consensus on the reasons for the medical visit as well as on their mutual expectations for the visit and for each other. Some researchers have suggested that this be done by having the patient provide the practitioner with a list of his or her concerns and by having physician and patient together generate a list of issues and problems that they agree need follow-up (Starfield

FIGURE 2.1 Communication uncovers hidden premises.

et al., 1981). Providing the patient with a tape recording of the visit has also been suggested and used successfully as a means to help patients remember the issues that were dealt with in the visit and make sense of their discussion with the doctor. In a study of outpatients at the Mayo Clinic, 86 percent of the patients who received a tape recording of their visit said that it improved their healthcare (Butt, 1977). Other technologies can also make the interaction between doctor and patient more efficient and satisfying. Many hospitals and HMOs have interactive voice response (IVR) systems that allow patients to call and hear prerecorded answers to basic health-related questions. In some places, patients who have had diagnostic tests done are given a personal identification number that they can later use to call in and hear their test results and obtain follow-up directions. These kinds of technologies seem popular with patients and are also efficient for doctors and staff members at hospitals and clinics (Borzo, 1994).

The information age has also influenced what the patient brings to the medical encounter. In the past, pharmaceutical companies primarily targeted their advertising toward physicians, who would then prescribe the drugs. Now these companies actively target patients themselves with information and advertising, and many patients request information about these drugs, or even a prescription, from their doctors (Basara, 1995). Many patients have access to the Internet and can easily look up information about their medical conditions, their diet and exercise programs, and their medications (Tyson, 2000). Some of this information is sound, provided by reputable organizations and government agencies (for example, the National Institutes of Health at www.nih.gov, the American Diabetes Association at www.diabetes.org, and the American Hospital Association at www.aha.org) (see also Box 12.1). Other sites provide dubious and even dangerously misleading information, however, so caution must be used when obtaining medical information online. Patients can join online chat rooms and talk to others who have similar conditions or experiences. They can even use their computers to purchase treatments (prescription drugs, exercise equipment, foods meeting special dietary requirements, etc.) conveniently and economically from the

Access to the Internet allows patients more opportunities than ever before to acquire health information.

comfort of their own homes. These factors may influence the perspectives of patients in important ways, and patients might become better informed as a result. They might ask better questions of their health professionals. On the other hand, patients might receive dangerous misinformation from unreliable sources or become unreasonably demanding toward their health professionals. Certainly, technology changes things, but predicting whether the changes will be positive or negative for any individual person is often difficult.

Three Basic Models of the Physician-Patient Relationship

The character of the relationship that a physician and patient develop depends, of course, upon the circumstances that surround their association and upon their beliefs about the appropriate locus of responsibility and power in the relationship. Practitioner-patient interaction is usually seen as taking one of three basic forms (Szasz & Hollender, 1956). The **Active-Passive Model** describes what takes place when the patient is unable, because of his or her medical condition, to participate in care and to make decisions regarding personal welfare. The physician must take over this role. The responsibility for the patient's life is in the hands of the medical professionals who attend to the patient's emergent condition, and the patient has no say in what is done. The following scenario exemplifies this type of doctor-patient relationship:

> The victim was stabbed not far from the hospital. His buddies placed him in the back seat of the car and sped down six big city blocks until they reached the emergency room of the county hospital. If they had waited to call an ambulance, he would have died. Only a few seconds after they arrived, the patient was on a gurney, heading down the hospital corridor to the Trauma Room. In another few seconds, his clothing was ripped off and the severed artery was found and tied. Simultaneously, other physicians and nurses worked to find a vein that had not collapsed in order to put in an intravenous line. Others were pumping oxygen into his lungs. Physicians, nurses, and technicians worked with skill and efficiency. The patient was unconscious, unable to participate in or fight their efforts.

The **Guidance-Cooperation Model** describes what happens when the physician assumes the majority of responsibility for diagnosis and treatment. The patient answers the questions that are asked but leaves the thinking and the decisions to the physician. As we will see later in this chapter and elsewhere throughout this book, it is quite common for the patient who has no input into the initial treatment decisions to have considerable difficulty implementing them. A guidance-cooperation relationship might look like this:

> "Do as I say, Frank, and don't ask so many questions," said the internist who was treating Frank Andersen for his hypertension. "Just take one of these little pills twice a day and you will be just fine." Frank was convinced that pushing for answers to his questions

would be challenging "physician authority," so he went along, figuring the doctor knew best. He couldn't seem to remember to take the pills, though, since he didn't really have any understanding of their purpose. After all, he didn't feel sick. Why did he need pills?

The **Mutual Participation Model** involves the physician and patient making joint decisions about every aspect of care from the planning of diagnostic studies to the choice and implementation of treatment. There is dual input and shared responsibility. Typically, questions and concerns are aired freely. The mutual participation model represents the most effective physician-patient interchange that can occur, because the physician and patient each bring his or her own point of view to the task of achieving the patient's health. They can do this only with clear and effective communication. The following is an example of mutual participation in action:

PATIENT: "I really doubt that I'll be able to eliminate dairy products from my diet immediately. They constitute a pretty large part of what I eat every day."

DOCTOR: "Well, what do you think you can do? Can you gradually change your diet so that you eliminate dairy products more and more each day?"

PATIENT: "Yes, I think I can do this gradually, but it's going to take me a while."

DOCTOR: "What can I do that might help you?"

PATIENT: "Tell me again the precise purpose of the restriction. Also, can you give me a list of things I can substitute for dairy products in my cooking?"

Does this patient seem unusually assertive? Compared to most patients, probably so! But such assertiveness and active involvement in medical care are precisely what is needed in order to form an effective partnership with the physician and ultimately to achieve the outcomes that both doctor and patient desire. Table 2.1 summarizes various models of the doctor-patient relationship that we will examine next.

TABLE 2.1 Models of the Physician-Patient Relationship

Szasz & Hollender (1956)
- The Active-Passive Model
- The Guidance-Cooperation Model
- The Mutual Participation Model

Ballard-Reisch (1990)
- Patient Abdication
- Patient Autonomy
- Collaborative
- Relationship Termination

Roter & Hall (1992)
- Paternalism
- Consumerism
- Default
- Mutuality

Roter, Stewart, Putnam, Lipkin, Stiles, & Inui (1997)
- Narrowly Biomedical
- Expanded Biomedical
- Biopsychosocial
- Psychosocial
- Consumerist

In Box 2.2, we examine recent research on the question of whether physicians' actual medical decisions about patient care are affected by the assertiveness of their patients.

BOX 2.2

Hot Topic

Are Physicians' Decisions Affected by Their Patients' Assertiveness?

An important element of any medical interaction is the treatment plan that is prescribed by the physician. This treatment plan becomes ever more critical the more severe the patient's condition. For instance, the treatment plan for cancer is usually very complex and it is predictive of the patient's survival. Some research suggests that physicians tend to alter their decisions about treatment depending upon their patient's assertiveness.

In Boston, health psychologist Edward Krupat and his colleagues (1999) attempted experimentally to determine how much a physician's treatment recommendations would be affected by the patient's behavior. A sample of 128 physicians was asked to view professionally acted medical interactions between an elderly woman patient and a physician. In these scenarios, the woman presented for treatment of nonmetastatic breast cancer diagnosed from a positive mammogram. The scenarios were varied (and thus acted by different professionals) according to patient age (65 or 80 years of age), race (African American or Caucasian), and socioeconomic status (SES) (upper or lower). Mobility, health, and assertiveness were also varied. The scenarios thus involved combinations of the above characteristics. In one scenario, for example, the patient was white, 65 years old, had higher SES, and was healthy (no other health problems besides the cancer), limited in agility, and assertive. Another involved a patient who was black, 80 years old, had higher SES, and was agile, unhealthy (had other health problems), and nonassertive. Each physician viewed only one scenario and was asked what tests he or she would order and what treatment he or she would

recommend. The physicians did vary in their treatment recommendations. Some physicians recommended full primary therapy consisting of either a mastectomy or a lumpectomy with radiation. Some recommended the use of chemotherapy with or without full primary therapy. Some made additional specific treatment recommendations.

The interesting finding of this research was that physician variation in treatment recommendations was a function of patient characteristics. Although patient assertiveness alone did not directly influence the treatment recommendations made by the physician, patient assertiveness did interact with other patient characteristics in affecting physicians' decisions. For example, physicians recommended more aggressive treatments when an assertive request was made by a black, lower SES patient, or by an unhealthy patient. In addition, assertive younger patients (65 years old) were more likely to have aggressive treatment recommended than were unassertive younger patients. No effect of assertiveness was found for the older (80-year-old) women, however.

These findings suggest that differences in types of therapies ordered may vary according to patient assertiveness level, but in a complex, rather than a simple, way. The authors of this study state, ". . . physicians respond not so much to the behavior per se, but to the behavior as demonstrated by a certain type of patient" (p. 454). Even while treating a life-threatening illness, one in which standards of care might be assumed to be consistent, physicians can be affected by the characteristics of their patients.

Variations of the Three Basic Models
of Physician-Patient Relationships

Since Szasz and Hollender outlined these three basic types of relationships, others have expanded the framework. Ballard-Reisch (1990) defined four relationship options for physicians and patients: (1) **patient abdication** (in which the doctor makes all decisions and the patient relinquishes responsibility; similar to the guidance-cooperation model just described), (2) **patient autonomy** (in which all decisions ultimately rest with the patient; this type of relationship does not have a corollary in Szasz and Hollender's framework), (3) **collaborative** (in which doctor and patient work together to achieve desired outcomes; similar to the mutual participation model outlined above), and (4) **relationship termination** (in which the patient and physician part ways).

Roter and Hall (1992) also described four basic kinds of doctor-patient relationships: (1) paternalistic, (2) consumerist, (3) default, and (4) mutual. A **paternalistic relationship** is one in which the physician has most of the control and the patient has very little. This is most like the patient abdication and guidance-cooperation models. A **consumerist relationship** is one in which the patient wields the power because she or he is essentially buying a service and the physician generally acquiesces to patient demands. This is similar to the patient autonomy model above. A **default relationship** is one in which both parties are relatively uninvolved. Each does the bare minimum required of him or her, and each is reluctant to take responsibility for patient outcomes. A **mutual relationship** is one in which both doctor and patient are highly invested in patient outcomes, and each is actively involved in the medical interaction, from diagnosis to treatment decision. This is essentially the same as what Szasz and Hollender referred to as the mutual participation Model, and what Ballard-Reisch called a collaborative relationship.

Although most models depict four types of relationships, one recent study outlines five different categories of communication that typically occur in doctor-patient interactions: (1) the **narrowly biomedical** type describes an interaction in which the doctor spends most of the time asking closed-ended questions and using a technical, biomedical vocabulary; (2) the **expanded biomedical** type looks very similar to the narrowly biomedical but there is a little bit of psychosocial discussion which occurs; (3) the **biopsychosocial** type is a much more balanced interaction, in which an approximately equal amount of time is spent on biomedical and psychosocial topics; (4) the **psychosocial** type describes an interaction that is primarily psychosocial in nature; and (5) interactions that are consumerist consist primarily of patients asking and doctors answering questions (Roter et al., 1997).

It has recently been suggested that individuals might not exhibit one particular style, but instead might vary depending on various aspects of the situation of their medical care (Lupton, 1997). For instance, a patient might sometimes play the role of consumer, and at other times become passive. He or she might even pursue both goals simultaneously, as emotions and cognitive focus change throughout the medical encounter. Many different factors affect a patient's current desires and behaviors, including past history (Strasser et al., 1993), and it is important for a clinician to be able to assess what the patient wants and expects and what might be best for their relation-ship (Benbassat et al., 1998).

   Mutuality is an element of medical relationships that balances the power between interactants and embodies respect and shared problem solving. Mutuality is common to many models of the effective physician-patient relationship and has consistently been shown to result in the most positive patient outcomes in terms of health, satis-faction, adherence, and cost (Baker & Connor, 1994; Hall et al., 1988; Henson, 1997; Levinson et al., 1997; Stewart, 1995). The achievement of mutuality requires dedica-tion and open-mindedness on the part of the physician and the patient because they must deal with one another as equals with a shared purpose. This approach to the physician-patient relationship requires recognition by both participants that each brings important expertise to the interaction. The physician has considerable medical knowledge and experience gained through years of study and practice. The patient is an expert as well and knows his or her body and its symptoms. The patient also knows what has helped (or not helped) those symptoms in the past, what he or she is willing to do to achieve health, and what constitutes well-being and quality of life. When patients and physician share their expertise in a relationship characterized by mutual-ity, they achieve the best possible outcomes of medical care.

Conflict

Although people generally want to get along with others, and particularly with those they respect, it is probably unrealistic to expect that the physician-patient relationship will be conflict-free. Because physicians and patients have different perspectives and experiences, some have argued that conflict is, in fact, inevitable and that years of tra-ditional, paternalistic medicine have ingrained in us the deep desire to avoid conflict and to be engaged in "pseudomutuality" (Katz, 1984). Wolf (1988) took this argument a step further and suggested that if there was *not* conflict in a doctor-patient relation-ship, something "short of adult collaboration is going on." According to this point of view, disagreements should be seen as evidence of true collaboration and progress, rather than a sign of failure. As such, they should be welcomed, rather than avoided.

   Let us turn now to the research on physician-patient relationships and examine the typical medical care exchange. Research shows that it falls far short of the ideal of mutuality and the Mutual Participation Model described above.

The Medical Care Visit

Whether medical care is delivered in a suburban doctor's office, a storefront medical clinic in a large city, or the emergency room of a university hospital, some basic com-monalities can be found. The medical encounter generally follows a certain course. The medical professional, usually a physician, physician's assistant, or nurse practi-tioner must talk with the patient in an effort to gather information about the charac-ter of the patient's symptoms and the events surrounding their appearance. The medical practitioner then performs an examination of the relevant parts of the patient's body. Finally, the health professional makes a recommendation to the patient either to undergo further diagnostic testing or to follow a certain course of treatment. Obviously, if a patient presents with a condition such as impending childbirth or profuse bleeding, immediate treatment will be instituted. Some of the initial steps will be dispensed with or drastically abbreviated. Usually, however, medical care follows this logical, predetermined course.

Rarely does a patient simply walk into a medical setting, ask to purchase a prescription or procedure, pay the bill, and leave. The usual exchange is quite a bit more complicated. The physician and the rest of the professional medical staff try to find out precisely what is wrong with the patient and determine an appropriate treatment. Although patients can usually describe their symptoms, they rarely have the ability to diagnose or treat correctly. They may have stumbled upon a home remedy that temporarily alleviates their symptoms, but they usually do not have a cure. Typically, patients need medical professionals to diagnose the disease that is causing the symptoms and to recommend a specific, effective treatment.

As detailed below, the medical encounter is divided into three parts (Stiles et al., 1979): (1) history, (2) physical examination, and (3) conclusion (including recommendations). Each part has a particular purpose and is carried out in a specific fashion. There are no time limits for each (although certain institutions may set guidelines for how much total time should be spent on each visit for maximum cost-effectiveness). Each part has a set of goals. For example, during the history, the goal is to learn enough from the patient to guide the physical examination. The information that the patient gives often points the way to certain critical inquiries into the status of the patient's health. Although sometimes what is wrong with the patient is obvious, at other times the practitioner must examine the patient's entire body, hoping that some clear sign will emerge. During the final phase of the visit, the practitioner's goal is to reveal to the patient (perhaps a simplified version of) what has been found and what to do about it. Sometimes plans are made for further follow-up when more is known to guide diagnosis, or when a trial of treatment has been instituted.

Let's use these three parts of the medical visit to organize the considerable research that has been done on practitioner-patient communication.

History-Taking and Interviewing

The patient who presents for care possesses a wealth of information that is critical for the medical professional to collect during the **medical history** and eventually to understand. The history is that part of the medical encounter in which necessary information is elicited from the patient. This information includes such facts as what the symptoms are, when they began, what makes them improve or become worse, and how the patient has tried to overcome the problem before coming to the physician. A useful history helps to determine the physical examination to be carried out, possibly the tests to be ordered, and eventually the diagnosis that is decided upon. The history, therefore, requires that some information be gathered about the patient's past. Has the patient had these symptoms before? What illnesses has the patient experienced? What illnesses currently exist? Have there been any hospitalizations? Are there any drug allergies? What medications are currently being taken? What illnesses have occurred in the patient's parents, siblings, and other close relatives? How does the patient feel emotionally? What impact is the illness having on the patient's day-to-day life?

During the history, the patient tells the story of the illness. Sometimes the physician lets the patient do this in a free and unencumbered manner. Sometimes the story slowly manifests itself in the answers to the dozens of straightforward questions the physician asks the patient: "Do you have pain here, now?" "Did you have a fever last night?" and so on. The goal is to gain as much information as possible from the patient in order to formulate a correct diagnosis and a treatment that the patient can carry out successfully. Many medical professionals are accustomed to asking patients a series of questions, each requiring an answer of one or a few words. The information that is revealed in the first question necessarily leads to the formulation of a second and a third question, and more as necessary. For example:

DOCTOR: Do you drink alcohol?
PATIENT: Yes.
DOCTOR: How much?
PATIENT: About five drinks a week.
DOCTOR: What kind of alcohol?
PATIENT: Beer and wine, but no hard liquor.

And on and on. . . .

The practitioner above asks closed-ended questions. **Closed-ended questions** require answers of one or a few words. They ask for a specific fact or piece of information. Closed-ended questions are best used toward the end of an inquiry because they narrow rather than broaden the area of discussion. However, when used at the outset of the **interview**, they sometimes limit the information that can be gathered. In addition, the patient is left in a more dependent, somewhat constrained position. He or she may feel that the medical practitioner has complete responsibility for the success of the interview, and the patient may fail to do the work of remembering accurately. He or she may suppress ideas and suggestions that could be quite helpful to the investigation. The energy and attention that goes into thinking of new questions may limit the medical practitioner's ability to listen to and understand fully what she or he has been told by the patient (Long et al., 1981).

Open-ended questions invite the patient to talk. They encourage elaboration. For instance the doctor might say: "Please tell me about your use of alcohol these days." The patient has relatively free reign to discuss the forms and extent of his or her alcohol use. Open-ended questions ask for information about an area of concern, but they do not direct the patient to discuss any particular aspect of the issue being examined.

Focused questions are somewhat more narrow than open-ended, but broader than closed-ended questions. For example, Doctor: "Can you describe anything that makes the pain worse?" rather than "Does lying down make the pain worse? How about sitting up?" If the practitioner needs more specific information, he or she can ask the patient a closed-ended question. For example, "How many hours do you tend to sleep before you wake up and can't get back to sleep?"

There are several things that a practitioner can do to improve the quality of the questions that are asked. These are adapted from Cormier, Cormier, and Weisser (1984, p. 134): First, questions should be phrased simply, without **medical jargon** (terms commonly used by health professionals but often unclear to those outside the medical field). Second, questions should be short—that is, phrased concisely. Third, only one question should be asked at a time. Fourth, questions should be phrased in a nonaccusatory way: "Why didn't you take your medication?" may provoke patient defensiveness. "Tell me about how you have been taking your medicine," might be more helpful. Fifth, questions should avoid suggesting anything that influences the patient's answer. Such a leading question might be: "Is your chest pain in the area of your heart?" Better is: "Show me where the pain is."

While gathering a history, the medical professional must listen actively to what the patient has to say. **Active listening** involves giving complete attention to the speaker as well as reflecting back to him or her precisely what is understood. The medical interview also requires that the medical professional provide the patient with privacy, including, of course, the assurance of confidentiality. There must be freedom from interruption and a high degree of *interest* and *concern* on the part of the health professional (Bernstein & Bernstein, 1980). Without this interest and concern, as we will see in the following pages, the quality of communication may fall short of what is necessary for the history, and effective care of the patient may be compromised. It is very important for the medical professional to establish the interview structure during the history portion of the medical visit. In doing so, he or she explains to the patient the purpose of what is being done and tells the patient what to expect from the interview process (Cormier et al., 1984).

The physician might establish the necessary framework in the following way: "Now, Mr. Smith, I need to ask you a few questions about the pain you have been experiencing. Then, I would like to examine you so that we can determine what this pain is all about." This simple step is important because sometimes health professionals are unclear about what they are asking. For example, if the interviewer intersperses friendly personal questions with medical ones, a patient might become confused about their purpose, and straightforward answers may not be forthcoming. The doctor asks, "How's your family?" and then, soon after, "Have you eaten out lately?" in an attempt to rule out hepatitis or some other communicable disease. If the doctor is not clear about the purpose for such apparently "social" questions, the patient might think the doctor is referring to eating out with the family. He then fails to mention that he usually has lunch at the little hot-dog stand near work (which, unbeknownst to him, has been identified as a hazard by the local Health Department). He mentions only the nicer restaurants that he has visited with his family, in an effort to create a good social impression of himself in the seemingly "social" context of the question.

The goal of taking a medical history is ". . . to find out both what is happening in this body—the pathophysiology of the illness—and who the patient is" (Cassell, 1985b, p. 41). Information about both of these issues must be integrated together. When they are, the practitioner can determine how events in the patient's body got him or her into the particular physical and emotional state presenting for care. How long the medical history takes to collect depends upon several factors. If the practitioner knows the patient well, the medical history might be short and deal only with the present illness. On the other hand, if the practitioner is seeing the patient for the first time and will be providing regular care over the coming years, the medical history may be very lengthy. The practitioner might ask about all past illnesses as well as disease conditions in the patient's blood relatives to determine genetic predispositions. In the emergency room, on the other hand, the medical history might be a very rushed affair. There is usually time for collecting only the essential information for treating the emergency condition. In this case, the emergency room physician might, in addition to questions about the current problem, ask only about the following: what medications the patient takes, what allergies (particularly drug allergies) the patient has, whether the patient has ever had surgery or been in the hospital, what illnesses the patient currently has, whether the patient has ever been seriously ill, and when the last time was that the patient saw a doctor for anything. This last question helps to put a patient's problem into perspective. With it, the health professional can evaluate the patient's typical **illness behavior**, that is, how he or she usually responds to the symptoms of illness (see Chapter 7). The patient who has not seen a doctor for five years and who shows up at the emergency room with a headache is someone in serious need of attention. This patient is either facing overwhelming stress in his or her life, or the headache is intensely painful. Perhaps other bodily signals also indicate that this condition is serious enough to warrant immediate attention. The medical history, although limited, provides important information to the emergency room professionals, and the meaning of the illness in the context of this individual patient's life and personality can be illuminated (Cassell, 1985b). This particular headache patient is not one who seeks medical help for trivial matters. In the context of this information about the patient's history, the complaint should be taken very seriously and given strict attention. While this patient may be having a severe migraine or perhaps his first cluster headache, it is also possible that something even more serious is happening. It would be very unwise to dismiss this patient as someone with "just a headache."

Just how good are doctors at eliciting pertinent information from patients? Can anything be done to help them get better at it? What researchers have found might surprise you! First, through the process of going to medical school, doctors-in-training on average seem to lose some of their natural ability to communicate with patients. One study found that medical students in their first year asked more questions, asked fewer leading questions, and elicited more interpersonal information from patients than did fourth-year students. The fourth-year students elicited more factual information about "organic" functioning (Helfer, 1970). Two subsequent longitudinal studies found that interviewing skills increased in the first year or two of medical school, but then began to deteriorate (Barbee & Feldman, 1970; Helfer & Ealy, 1972). Other, more recent studies have demonstrated similar results, showing that residents (in postgraduate training after medical school) tend to obtain less social history information than do interns who are their juniors in the training hierarchy (Griffith et al., 1996; Griffith et al., 1995). One particularly interesting study assessed the effectiveness of a medical school curriculum that was specifically designed to emphasize the skills of interviewing. This study found that during the first and second years of medical school medical students' interviewing skills increased, but that the skills then declined during the third and fourth years (Pfeiffer et al., 1998). These researchers found that while general interviewing abilities and rapport were slightly higher at the end of the fourth year than when students initially started medical school, it was their ability to elicit a *social history* that actually declined over time. Why might this be? The authors of the study have several suggestions. First, the nature of the medical school environment is to train students to focus on "hard" data, and to de-emphasize the psychological and social aspects of the individual patient. Second, students in the fourth year of medical school tended to focus all of their attention on differential diagnosis, and thereby tended not to pay attention to details that they believed would not help them achieve this goal. (Of course, as we will see throughout this book, this was not necessarily a correct assumption.) Third, the students may have been trying to avoid spending too much time with their patients, hoping to move them along through the system efficiently (or in less sympathetic terms, "getting rid of patients" as described by Mizrahi, 1985).

The process of medical diagnosis is based on the assumption that the patient, from whom the history is gathered, is providing accurate and complete information. The health interview, in addition to providing information about the patients' physical condition, also creates a personal connection between the doctor and the patient (Engel, 1997). Thus, the interview provides a foundation for the structuring of the patient history. The medical interview can be problematic, however. It is not a simple, straightforward, foolproof way to gather information from a patient about his or her past (or even current) health status. Asking people questions is not like retrieving information from a computer or a written record. People forget. Sometimes they are so anxious that they misunderstand what is being asked of them. And often they are not particularly motivated to do the work that is required for accurate recall. Extensive research has shown that health interviews can be filled with inaccuracies (Cannell et al., 1977). For instance, healthy subjects were asked to recall various aspects of the medical problems they had in the past. In many cases, the researchers had available the respondents' medical records so that the accuracy of the responses could be checked. Subjects made a number of errors. When asked specifically about past hospital visits, for example, respondents failed to report 12 to 17 percent of documented hospitalizations. Even when interviewed shortly after having a visit with a medical doctor, respondents failed to report 24 to 36 percent of these visits. Respondents also failed to mention at least 50 percent of chronic and acute illnesses that were documented in their medical records. Thus, there was a great deal of underreporting of very relevant information in these health interviews.

Later, we will examine ways in which medical professionals can help patients to report their conditions more accurately. Despite the limitations in the accuracy of the information obtained from the medical interview, the history is the best source of information about what could be wrong with the patient. "Studies have shown that 56 to 85 percent of the diagnoses in internal medicine can be made on the basis of the history alone" (Putnam et al., 1985, p. 74). The search for ways to increase the accuracy of practitioner-patient communication is of obvious value. The manner in which the medical information is "written up" can determine its usefulness to other medical professionals involved in the long-term care of the patient, as well as to the patient him- or herself.

"Handwriting" is an important issue in medicine. Jokes abound regarding the illegibility of physicians' handwriting, but such illegibility is often not a laughing matter. Patients can be given the wrong medicine or an incorrect dosage, sometimes with tragic results. A review of the literature showed that the way written information is presented to patients can drastically affect what they are able to do with it. This review found that patients often receive written information from their doctors that is not legible. They cannot understand it and so they fail to pay attention to, believe, or remember it (Ley, 1998). Serious noncompliance can result (as discussed in Chapter 6).

Physical Examination and Diagnostic Tests

As interactions between people go, the practitioner-patient interaction is a strange one. Fully clothed, the medical practitioner touches, pokes, and prods the body of the patient who is draped, at best, in a flimsy cotton (or even paper) gown. The patient is sometimes asked to assume very uncomfortable or embarrassing positions. And this is often after answering some very personal questions.

Patients are sometimes distressed by the medical practitioner's role as it is manifested during the **physical examination**. There is a discrepancy of power between practitioner and patient, and here is where it clearly shows. Granted, the power is not real, for the physician cannot force the patient to do anything he or she does not want

The physical examination involves a discrepancy of social power and sometimes can be disconcerting to the patient.

to do. But, by virtue of the circumstances in which practitioner and patient relate, the practitioner seems to be the individual in control. Thus, the physical examination is, for some patients, quite an unpleasant experience.

The first visit with a practitioner whom the patient does not know can be emotionally trying and even disorienting. This is why, in many medical offices, a new patient is fully clothed when he or she first meets the doctor. They meet, in a sense, on "equal terms" socially. The history is taken in this manner, and practitioner and patient discuss the factors relevant to the patient's condition. Then, they go on to the examination in the usual manner. In some clinics, medical offices, and HMOs, however, this first step is omitted in an attempt to save time. The patient faces someone he or she has never met wearing nothing but a light cotton or paper smock, and feeling uncomfortable, embarrassed, and possibly even angry. Sociologist Sue Fisher (1986) describes the situation in the following passage from her book on the treatment of women patients:

> On my initial visit [with the gynecologist] a nurse called me into an examining room, asked me to undress, gave me a paper gown to put on and told me the doctor would be with me soon. I was stunned. Was I not even to see the doctor before undressing? . . . How could I present myself as a competent, knowledgeable person sitting undressed on the examining table? But I had a potentially cancerous growth, so I did as I had been told. In a few minutes the nurse returned and said, "lie down the doctor is coming." Again, I complied. The doctor entered the examining room, nodded in my direction while reading my chart and proceeded to examine me without ever having spoken to me. (Fisher, 1986, p. 2)

Imagine a patient who refuses to tolerate this kind of treatment. She might simply refuse to remove her clothing until after she has met the doctor. Despite pressure from a nurse whose job it is to follow established office protocol, the patient might politely insist first on meeting the doctor and discussing her problem, providing the information for the history. Then she might calmly remove her clothing for the physical examination. What effect do you think this deviation from protocol might have? Do you think she would receive better or worse treatment, or that there would likely be no effect? This would be an interesting social situation to examine.

A relationship in which one party can touch and probe the body of the other (but not vice versa), as well as ask all sorts of intimate questions is, as we have noted, an unusual one indeed. One way in which the strangeness of this relationship is dealt with is through the formality and specific decorum of the physician:

> "[The physician must] bear in mind [his] manner of sitting, reserve, arrangement of dress, decisive utterance, brevity of speech, composure, bedside manners, care, replies to objections, calm self-control . . . his manner must be serious and humane; without stooping to be jocular or failing to be just, he must avoid excessive austerity; he must always be in control of himself." (Hippocrates, 1923 translation)

This is a "tall order" interpersonally, if ever there was one!

Besides clinical data for diagnosis of the patient's condition, the physical examination provides additional information as well. The practitioner can learn a great deal from observing the patient's body and the patient's relationship to it. The physician may see in the patient's body things that reflect the patient's history, such as scars, tattoos, malformations, or ways of moving that protect certain parts of the body. Sir Arthur Conan Doyle, novelist and creator of the famous detective character Sherlock Holmes, was trained as a physician. His teacher, Dr. Joseph Bell, taught him the art of careful observation, such as attention to details of the patient's body and behavior. Bell was the original model for the character Sherlock Holmes. Bell was a superb diagnostician and taught Doyle the critical value of precise scrutiny, the commitment of essential details to memory, and deductive reasoning (c.f., Doyle, 1984). Astute observation and excellence at deductive reasoning are just as important for a medical practitioner as they are for a sleuth. Doctors are, in many ways, detectives.

When the history and physical examination have been completed and more information is still needed, the practitioner performs or orders diagnostic tests such as x-rays, blood tests, and urinalysis. Sometimes there may then be a delay before moving to the next stage of the medical encounter. Results from the tests may be needed before any recommendations can be made. In other cases, treatment may be started even while test results are pending.

Medical Recommendations

Once the practitioner has examined the patient and has decided on a diagnosis, or to run further tests at a later time, the practitioner and patient move into the **conclusion** phase of the visit, in which the practitioner makes a **recommendation**. Patients expect practitioners to communicate diagnostic findings and treatment plans during this phase of the medical visit (Leigh & Reiser, 1980). They expect their practitioners to provide them with information necessary to understand and to carry out their treatment (Stiles et al., 1979). Their satisfaction with the entire medical visit can be dependent upon the explanations given by the practitioner in this third phase of the medical visit (Putnam et al., 1985).

Patients are sometimes disappointed, however, as practitioners too often do not provide clear and straightforward recommendations. Instead, they use words that are foreign to the patient (medical jargon, or "doctor-talk" addressed in detail in Chapter 3). Their explanations sometimes convey secrecy and a sense of superiority (Barnlund, 1976). And, when these explanations are unclear, patients often fail to ask questions to clarify their confusions and misconceptions. Furthermore, patients often forget what they have been told (DiMatteo & DiNicola, 1982), even when the information *is* conveyed clearly.

Very often, patients leave the medical encounter with a prescription for medication. In fact, one survey found that prescriptions for medication were given in two out of three medical visits (Rabin & Bush, 1975). Since this is so common, one might expect that communication about medication would be clear and precise. This seems not to be the case, however. When patients are called on the phone by researchers following a doctor visit, they often cannot name their prescribed medications, cannot remember having had side effects explained to them, do not know the cost of their medications, have no information about alternative treatments, and are unclear as to how they should take their medications and what results to expect (Parrott, 1994).

Patients who ask a number of questions and are concerned about their care typically do get more thorough treatment information from their doctors than do those who are passive (Street, 1991). If a patient is to follow treatment recommendations, he or she must understand precisely what is to be done, and often such understanding requires asking questions. The patient must understand why a certain treatment regimen has been chosen and how its fulfillment is likely to lead to eradication (or at least control) of the disease. As we will see in Chapters 5 and 6, the patient must also *believe* in the efficacy of the treatment regimen and must trust that there are negative consequences associated with ignoring the recommendations. The treatment must not conflict with the patient's familial or cultural expectations, and the patient must have the resources (time, money, and the capacity to control his or her behavior) in order to carry out the treatment regimen. Unfortunately, providers often fail to recognize when many of these factors are missing and patients are often reluctant to mention these missing elements to the provider, partly to avoid being reprimanded and sometimes to avoid disappointing the provider. Sometimes providers make recommendations that (perhaps because of limitations in resources) a patient cannot possibly succeed in following (DiMatteo & DiNicola, 1982).

The conclusion phase of the medical visit sometimes gets "stuck"—that is, it drags on rather than concluding efficiently. More than 20 percent of patients typically bring up entirely new concerns at the end of the interaction, when the doctor is trying to finalize things and draw the visit to a close (White et al., 1994). This can be frustrating to the doctor who believes that he or she has already addressed the patient's concerns and then is surprised by new information. Sometimes this new information requires further discussion and explanation and may even change the provider's overall picture of what is wrong with the patient. This situation may also be difficult for the patient, who may have spent much of the visit trying to build up the courage to bring up the new issue. When the patient finally says what is on his or her mind, the provider may appear nervous and pressed for time. Research shows that the introduction of new issues at the end of the encounter happens more often when patients are not given ample opportunity earlier in the encounter to describe all of their symptoms and concerns. It has been suggested that this problem can be minimized by (1) letting patients know at the start of the visit what the general sequence of events within that visit will be, (2) adequately taking patients' beliefs into account, (3) adequately assessing patients' understanding, and (4) recognizing and addressing psychological and emotional issues at the beginning of the encounter (White et al., 1994).

Informed Collaborative Choice

Physician-patient decision making is complex and the communication that occurs (or doesn't) between patients and their healthcare providers is very important (see Figure 2.2). Communication influences many factors, such as satisfaction, adherence, and various physical health outcomes, and a large body of research indicates that when patients take an active role in their own healthcare and maintenance, they benefit greatly (Kaplan, 1991). This concept of "give and take" is important because simply understanding a set of instructions is not enough for a patient. Patients must not only comprehend what it is that they are to do, but they must believe in the treatment protocol, and they must have the resources to carry it out (DiMatteo et al., 1994; Kaplan,

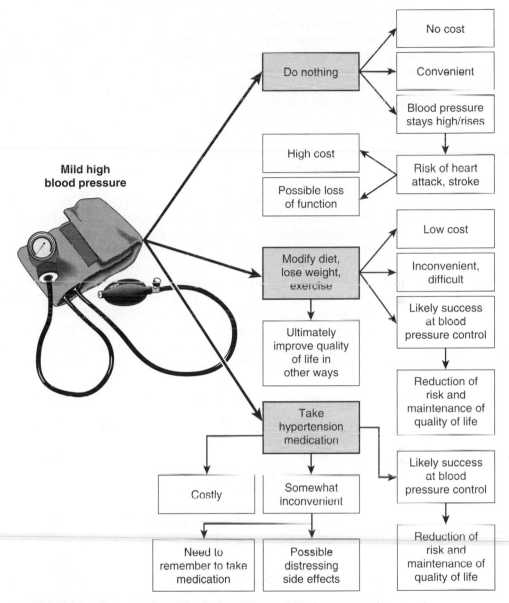

FIGURE 2.2   The complexities of physician-patient decision making in the treatment of hypertension.

1991). In order to meet all three of these criteria, the patient *must* be actively involved in the medical discussion and medical decision-making process.

A structured framework to help patients gather information, weigh the pros and cons of various options, and negotiate the most optimal treatment solution can be very helpful (Ballard-Reisch, 1990). Some researchers advocate the use of a "decision tree" in which patients and healthcare providers lay out each of the available options and discuss the possible outcomes and subsequent options associated with each, similar to what is seen in Figure 2.2 (Speedling & Rose, 1985). This evaluation includes subjective assessments of such issues as quality of life. Of course, these assessments can sometimes be rather complicated. For example, a patient might accept the risks (10% chance of death on the operating table) associated with surgery if there is a 90 percent chance that fifteen pain-free years of life will follow. On the other hand, the patient might reject a treatment with a 99 percent change of living for fifteen more years, although with pain.

One system for structuring collaboration between patients and healthcare providers is the **PREPARED**™ framework (DiMatteo et al., 1994; Gambone & Reiter, 1991). When this system is followed, patients participate in a process of true informed consent, and their medical issues are addressed thoroughly. The word PREPARED is actually an acronym, with each letter standing for a particular step in the process of collaboration and decision making. The first P stands for *procedure* or *prescription* and in this stage the patient is presented with the doctor's suggested treatment. The first R stands for *reason* and it is here that the doctor and patient discuss the reason(s) for the recommended procedure, based on the specific elements of the patient's case. The first E stands for *expectations*, and it is here that goals and expectations for the treatment are discussed. The second P stands for *probability*, and it is at this time that the likelihood of achieving the expected outcomes is evaluated. The A stands for *alternatives*, and here patients discuss various options or alternatives to the recommended treatment. The second R stands for *risks*, and at this point all of the significant risks

It is important for patients—and their parents, in cases of pediatric care—to ask questions of their health professionals and share in making healthcare decisions.

associated with the recommended treatment are addressed. The second E stands for *expenses*; at this time patients weigh the various costs (monetary and otherwise) associated with the recommended treatment. Finally, D stands for *decision*, the time at which the choice regarding treatment is actually made. This system is a very useful tool for helping patients and healthcare providers to communicate effectively and to reach decisions that patients are both committed to and able to carry out.

Box 2.3 suggests an important factor that may affect medical decisions, one about which patients should be aware.

BOX **2.3**
Research Close-up

Men and Women with Angina: Different Care and Different Outcomes

As we have seen in this chapter, the patient and physician interact in many ways during the medical care visit. The physician asks questions, examines the patient, orders diagnostic tests, and recommends treatment. The patient answers questions, allows a physical examination, consents to tests, and contemplates treatment options. At any point during this interaction, assumptions may be made by either participant. One of these assumptions involves the presumed differences between men and women.

Disparities in treatment for men and women suffering from cardiac problems are well documented. Some research shows that women are often undertreated for their heart conditions (Funk & Griffey, 1994; Maynard et al., 1992). Other studies show that although there exist differences in diagnosis, once the diagnosis of coronary heart disease is made, the treatment of men and women is similar (Healy, 1991).

In order to understand the differences in evaluation and outcome between men and women, it is best to examine patients who have not yet received the diagnosis of heart disease and who have not yet had a heart attack. One recent study did take this approach, and examined patients presenting to emergency rooms in Olmsted County, Minnesota (Roger et al., 2000). The study was population-based and utilized medical chart review to obtain relevant data. The researchers hypothesized that women who went to an emergency room (ER) for chest pain would receive poorer care and have worse health outcomes than men who presented with chest pain. Over 2,270 men and women were studied and, on average, these patients were followed for six years after their initial emergency room visit. The researchers examined the following outcomes: mortality, use of cardiac procedures within 90 days of the patients' ER visit, and subsequent cardiac events (cardiac death, nonfatal myocardial infarction, nonfatal cardiac arrest, and congestive heart failure).

A simple comparison between the men and women in this sample showed that the women, on average, were older, were more likely to have a history of hypertension, and were less likely to present with typical angina pain than were the men. After presenting at the ER with angina-related symptoms, the men were more likely within the next 90 days to have noninvasive cardiac tests and cardiac procedures conducted. In fact, the men received 24 percent more of these procedures than the women! While, on average the women in this study were older than the men, after adjusting for age differences, the researchers found that the men had a significantly greater risk for cardiac events. They also had a slight trend toward increased risk of death as compared with the women. Thus, although the women in this primarily Caucasian sample were older than the men and received fewer invasive procedures for their angina symptoms, they had slightly *better* health outcomes!

Reassurance

It is during the recommendation phase of the medical visit that patients expect to receive reassurance. **Reassurance** consists of a hopeful attitude and of specific statements that are designed to allay patients' fears (Leigh & Reiser, 1980). These statements, of course, must be based on data or on the practitioner's experience. Reassurances cannot be superficial or they will not be helpful at all and may alienate the patient. Further, reassurances must go to the source of the patient's fear. They must overturn the patient's incorrect understanding of the disease or of the procedure that he or she dreads (Buchsbaum, 1986). If the truth is indeed grim, the practitioner can provide the patient with accurate information, while emphasizing the more potentially positive aspects of the situation and providing encouragement and emotional support for the patient.

Research suggests that patients are less satisfied with their medical treatment when they receive no reassurance from their physicians (Korsch & Negrete, 1972). Both physicians and patients have been found to rate reassurance as the most desirable type of response a physician can give to a patient (DiMatteo et al., 1985; Linn & DiMatteo, 1983). Reassurance can enhance the treatment outcome, as shown in several studies of surgical patients. In these studies, patients recovered better when they were reassured about what they would experience and were told that various sensations were perfectly normal (Egbert et al., 1963; Egbert et al., 1964; Langer et al., 1975). Reassurance has also been found to enhance the patient's trust in the medical practitioner (Ben-Sira, 1980).

Reassurance, based on the more positive elements of the situation, is particularly necessary when the patient's prognosis is grave or will remain uncertain. In the 1950s and 1960s, it was widely believed by physicians that telling patients "the terrible facts" was bad for them. If their diseases were incurable or forebode a terrible course, patients usually never found out. One patient with inoperable stomach cancer was told by the surgeon that some "cuttin' " was done and the "bad stuff" pulled out, and now "you're gonna be okay" (Cassell, 1985b, p. 148). A patient with blood chemistries that showed a pattern consistent with terminal leukemia was told that his blood was a little weak and he would feel better soon with some pills and a transfusion. Sometimes, until just before they died, patients were led to believe that they were on the road to recovery.

Since the mid-1970s, however, there has been a significant change in the attitudes of medical professionals about reassurance, especially in serious or terminal illness. Most now feel that patients must have information in order to maintain autonomy in the many challenges they face. They need all the facts to make their own decisions. Being truthful with patients has become a moral imperative (Bok, 1978). Of course, telling a patient bluntly, with no element of reassurance, that his or her condition is grave or terminal with no hope of recovery could have devastating consequences. The manner in which the practitioner conveys the information that the illness is very serious can certainly affect how the patient reacts. If done poorly, the patient can become hopeless, depressed, and despairing. Here, too, the practitioner's most important tool is reassurance. The physician cannot always promise recovery or even long-term survival, but he or she can reassure the patient that all possible treatments will be tried if the patient wishes and that the patient will not be abandoned, physically or emotionally. The practitioner might reassure the patient that pain will be controlled, and that he or she will be made comfortable and given all necessary pain medications. (These issues are addressed in more detail in Chapter 13.)

In sum, whether the patient's condition is routine or extremely serious, reassurance is essential in helping to reduce the patient's uncertainty, fear, anxiety, and emotional distress. In Chapter 3 we examine the communication between healthcare providers and their patients in more detail as we consider further some of the more "psychosocial" aspects of care, including the sometimes nebulous issues of bedside manner and rapport.

Summary

1. The goal of this chapter is to examine in detail what occurs when patients consult physicians and other medical professionals for the diagnosis and treatment of illness. It focuses primarily on the *verbal* communication.

   - Communication results in both subjective and objective outcomes. Different points of view, or philosophies, underlie effective and ineffective practitioner-patient communication.

2. The four premises of medical care that are relevant to our analysis are: Doctors treat patients, not diseases. The body has the last word. All medical care flows through the relationship between physician and patient. The spoken language is the most important tool in medicine.

3. Words are extremely powerful tools in medicine; they establish the reality of suffering. Because of their power, the utterance of words in the medical encounter is a very serious enterprise. Through the process of communication, practitioner and patient attempt to gain a common understanding of the patient's illness.

4. A practitioner's and/or a patient's poor communication skills can cause problems in their relationship.

   - A physician may give a patient very little opportunity to participate in his or her own care either because the physician lacks communication skill or believes that patient participation is not valuable and not worth the trouble.
   - Sometimes these two reasons reciprocally affect one another.

5. Communication uncovers hidden premises. As modern medicine becomes dominated by technology, some medical professionals tend to give diminished attention to practitioner-patient dialogue.

6. There are three basic models of the physician-patient relationship.

   - The Active-Passive Model occurs when the patient is unable, because of his or her medical condition, to participate in care and make personal medical decisions.
   - The Guidance-Cooperation Model occurs when the physician takes the bulk of responsibility for diagnosis and treatment.

- The Mutual Participation Model involves physician and patient making joint decisions about every aspect of care.

7. Other model variations (presented by researchers such as Ballard-Reisch, Roter, and Hall) define four or five basic categories. Common to all of them are variations in patient involvement in their care.

8. One important issue in the physician-patient relationship is conflict. Conflict may arise regarding the process of communication and care, and conflict is a good sign that active collaboration between physician and patient is occurring.

9. The medical encounter is divided into three parts.

- The medical history in which necessary information is elicited from the patient; the medical professional must listen actively to what the patient has to say and tell the patient what to expect from the visit.

- Patients and physicians are sometimes uncomfortable with the second part of the medical visit, the physical examination, because of the intimacy of the situation.

- In the third part of the medical visit, the conclusion, the practitioner makes a recommendation. The manner in which this is done can affect patient satisfaction and patient compliance. Reassurance is an important component of the conclusion.

10. Several important problems exist in practitioner-patient interactions. Physicians and patients complain about limited time, and communication problems arise from differences in the perspectives that practitioner and patient have on the illness.

THINKING CRITICALLY

1. How much responsibility do physicians have for patient outcomes? How much of the responsibility belongs to the patient? What role do health psychologists play in answering this question and in implementing a practical response to the answer?

2. Do you think that patients should always be told exactly what their medical condition is? Should they always be fully informed about their prognosis, no matter how bad it might be?

3. Can you think of any times when your doctor used words you did not understand? If so, did you question him or her as to their meaning? Was it difficult to do so? Why or why not?

4. Imagine that you read, on an Internet site, about a new "miracle" cure for the common cold. How would you go about evaluating the reliability of this information?

5. Of the models of physician-patient interaction that are presented in this chapter, where do your interactions typically fall? Is this the ideal type of interaction for you? Why or why not? If not, what can you do to change your interactions with your doctor?

GLOSSARY

Active listening: Giving complete attention to the speaker as well as reflecting back to him or her precisely what is understood.

Active-Passive Model: A model of the practitioner-patient relationship that occurs when the patient is unable, because of medical condition, to participate in his or her own care and to make decisions for his or her own welfare.

Biopsychosocial: A model that incorporates aspects of biological, psychological, and social systems for a fuller understanding of human health and functioning.

Closed-ended questions: Questions that require answers of one or a few words and ask for a specific fact or piece of information.

Collaborative relationship: A relationship in which doctor and patient work together as equal participants to achieve desired medical outcomes.

Communication: A process by which information is exchanged between individuals through a common system of symbols, signs, or behaviors.

Conclusion: The end of the medical encounter, when the practitioner makes a recommendation.

Consumerist relationship: A relationship in which the patient is a consumer, buying a service, and retains decision-making control.

Default relationship: A relationship in which neither the doctor nor the patient are particularly invested in care, and each takes little responsibility for ultimate outcomes; each does the minimum required by his or her role.

Diagnosis: The act or art of identifying a disease from its signs and symptoms.

Expanded biomedical model: A model which predominantly resembles the narrowly biomedical model, but does incorporate some psychosocial elements.

Focused questions: Questions that are more narrow than open-ended and broader than closed-ended questions.

Guidance-Cooperation Model: A model of the practitioner-patient relationship that occurs when the physician assumes primary responsibility for diagnosis and treatment. The patient does not contribute a perspective and leaves all decisions to the physician.

Illness behavior: How an individual responds to the symptoms of illness.

Interview: Foundation for the structuring of the patient history.

Malignant: Cancerous.

Medical history: The part of the medical encounter in which necessary information is elicited from the patient, such as the symptoms, when they began, what makes them improve or get worse, and how the patient has tried to overcome the problem before coming to the physician. The history helps determine the physical examination to be done, diagnostic tests to be ordered, and diagnosis and treatment decisions.

Medical jargon: Medical terms typically used by health professionals that are often not understood by patients.

Mutual Participation Model: A model of the practitioner-patient relationship in which practitioner and patient make joint decisions about every aspect of care. There is joint input from physician and patient, and joint responsibility in the choices made.

Mutual relationship (mutuality): A relationship in which both doctor and patient are highly invested in patient outcomes, and each is actively involved in the medical interaction.

Narrowly biomedical model: A model in which the focus is on purely biological and medical factors, and the physician spends most of his or her time asking closed-ended questions.

Nonverbal communication: Communication without words.

Open-ended questions: Questions that encourage elaboration and invite a patient to talk.

Paternalistic relationship: A physician-patient relationship in which the physician has most of the control.

Patient abdication: When the patient relinquishes responsibility for choices about care and the physician makes all of the decisions.

Patient autonomy: When the ultimate decision-making responsibility rests with the patient.

Physical examination: The part of the medical visit during which the medical professional examines the patient's body to determine possible signs of disease.

Premise: An assumption on which an argument is based.

Psychosocial model: A model in which the medical interaction is primarily focused on psychosocial issues.

Reassurance: Emotional support consisting of a hopeful attitude and of specific statements that are designed to be realistic but also to assist in reducing patients' fears.

Recommendation: The advice that is given to the patient during the conclusion portion of the medical visit.

Relationship termination: When the patient and physician part ways because of an irreparable problem in the relationship.

Subcutaneous: Under the skin.

CHAPTER

3

Communication in the Medical Encounter

Dena had gone to her gynecologist just the week before to have her routine checkup; she had been feeling fine and had no obvious problem. But, a week later, Dena had a message from the doctor on her voice-mail; she needed to make an appointment for another Pap and some follow-up tests. Dena was not particularly concerned because, several years earlier, insufficient cells necessitated a repeat Pap test and everything had gone perfectly well. At her next appointment, however, the doctor walked into the room and his facial expression alarmed Dena. On one level, this expression seemed to make no sense to her, but deep down Dena sensed the reason for how he looked and she guessed the seriousness of what he was about to tell her.

The doctor stood before her, blinking his eyes rapidly and unnaturally as he tried to speak. Before any words came out of his mouth, Dena was already gripped by panic and her heart was beating very fast. She began to feel faint. She had difficulty focusing on the doctor's words, and did not even hear some of them. The doctor told her that her biopsy had shown evidence of cervical cancer. There would be more testing. And then, depending upon how those tests came out, there would be several options for treatment, among them surgery and chemotherapy if necessary. She heard him say, "We'll do the best we can. . . ."

But Dena barely listened. She focused on the tone of his voice and not on the carefully chosen words he spoke. His speech was kind, but halting and controlled. His words were meant to be reassuring, but every other aspect of his communication showed anxiety and distress. His body movements and posture were strained and uncomfortable. He looked away from Dena and his eyes rarely met hers. When they did, they looked frightened. Dena's attention was riveted on the muscles that grew tighter and tighter in her doctor's neck and throat as he spoke to her. In a mental fog, she grappled with the knowledge that he was alarmed, and this terrified her even more.

In this chapter, we will undertake a detailed examination of communication in the medical encounter. We will see considerable evidence for the fact that medical professionals can have a tremendous impact on the ability of patients to withstand the emotional devastation of illness. In this chapter, the terms **medical professionals** and **medical practitioners** include many different healthcare providers, including: physicians, nurses, respiratory therapists, physicians' assistants, nurse practitioners, nurse midwives, phlebotomists, pharmacists, physical therapists, x-ray technicians, medical psychologists, and medical social workers. We will see that through effective communication and interpersonal behavior, medical professionals can make a significant difference in their patients' satisfaction with medical treatment and in their patients' willingness and ability to adhere to recommended medical regimens.

In the first part of this chapter, we examine the practitioner-patient relationship, particularly the role of communication in helping patients to cope and come to terms with illness and its treatment. In the second part of the chapter, we focus on nonverbal aspects of communication between doctors and patients. Finally, we examine the role of empathy and how understanding is conveyed through both verbal and nonverbal communication. Looking ahead, in Chapter 4 we will examine the effects of medical training and treating illness on the emotions of medical professionals and on their communication with their patients. As we will see, medical professionals are indeed affected by their patients' experiences. They often feel personal emotional distress in response to what their patients go through, and health professionals are only sometimes consciously aware of how they are affected by this distress.

Basic Issues in Research on
Practitioner-Patient Communication

For decades, the practitioner-patient relationship has been a topic of concern and analysis among social scientists (e.g., Bloom, 1963; Parsons, 1951, 1975) and physicians (e.g., Balint, 1957; Freud, 1924). Much of the early theoretical writing on this topic, however, dealt with what these theorists believed *should* occur in the physician-patient encounter based on existing theories of society or of the mind. Few examined what actually *does* occur. Normative statements about what *ought* to happen were very prevalent in writings about medical communication, and these statements often reflected the personal experiences and deeply held assumptions of the writer. In the past thirty years, however, more and more research has been empirical, and has tried to identify and examine what actually occurs when practitioners and patients try to communicate with one another (Waitzkin, 1984). Research is finding, for example, that in encounters that do not involve "critical care," much interpersonal work is done during the first-meeting visit to build the relationship between doctor and patient. In the second visit, more time is spent on treatment-related issues than on the relationship itself. It is not usually until the third visit that attention begins to be focused on relevant psychosocial issues such as the patient's job and family (van Dulmen et al., 1997).

When researchers have looked at the kinds of exchanges that occur between practitioners and patients, they have found that there is a lot of similarity across cultures in terms of what is said verbally. Regardless of culture, these dyads typically rely on a fairly defined set of interpersonal exchanges (Stiles, 1996). This makes sense, of course, because all medical interactions are characterized by the presentation of symptoms and the goal of alleviating them and treating or curing the patient. Because the doctor has specialized medical knowledge and the patient knows, and needs to convey, what he or she is experiencing, the interpersonal exchange between the practitioner and patient is bound to follow a structure that is somewhat consistent across medical conditions and cultures. Of course, the verbal exchange is not the only "give and take" that occurs. Much of what is communicated in the medical encounter is done nonverbally, in what psychologist Robert Rosenthal has called a "language without words" (Rosenthal et al., 1974).

Effective communication and a caring therapeutic approach require attention to a number of areas, all of which are potentially problematic in the practitioner-patient relationship. Being effective in the healing relationship requires more than just giving a thorough explanation of a diagnosis and treatment. It depends on more than just smiling or "being nice." Patients' and health professionals' individual characteristics must be taken into account, as must the context of their verbal and nonverbal communications and the unique aspects of the patients' illnesses. Creating an effective medical interaction, therefore, requires attention to a great deal of complexity.

Communication Problems and Solutions in Therapeutic Interactions

"The verbal exchange structure of medical consultations appears consistent across settings and types of medical problems and across countries" (Stiles, 1996, p. 773). By this "exchange," researchers mean that medical practitioners and their patients do more than simply behave or act in one another's presence. They *interact*. In any given interaction, the participants influence one another. Each person's words and actions affect the other person's thoughts, feelings, and behaviors. This "exchange" is particularly clear when something is going wrong in the encounter. Any given problematic element of practitioner-patient communication has the potential to elicit further problematic responses. For example, one person's hostile voice tone is likely to elicit hostility from the other person. Also, since the amount of time available for the interaction is usually limited, when one person talks a great deal the other is able to talk only a minimal amount (Roter, 1984). Thus, the behaviors of the various interactants are mutually influential. So, as we analyze the difficulties in practitioner-patient relationships, we must keep in mind that assigning blame can be quite destructive (and for a health psychologist, quite unscientific). For every practitioner who failed to provide critical information, there was a patient who was not assertive enough to ask for and insist upon receiving it. For every patient who did not understand what she or he was told, there was a practitioner who failed to check that things were clear to the patient in the first place. The medical interaction is (at least) a two-sided enterprise (Stiles et al., 1982).

Time Constraints

Time is very important in the medical visit. Medical professionals don't have enough of it and patients usually want more than they get. In fact, not only is patient satisfaction predicted by longer doctor visits (Chung et al., 1999), but patients are also happier when some time is spent just talking with them. Patients value the relationship itself (Gross et al., 1998). They are, however, not the only ones who are more satisfied with more leisurely visits. Doctors report being more satisfied when they feel that they had enough time to interact with their patients, that they competently addressed their patients' medical issues, and that they communicated effectively (Probst et al., 1997). Physicians often complain that they simply do not have time to spend talking with their patients. Indeed, research suggests that the more time a physician spends with patients, the less money the physician earns (Waitzkin, 1985). Further, physicians tend to underestimate the amount of interaction that their patients desire (Worchel et al., 1995). Even in situations where practitioners could spend more time with their patients, they sometimes fail to do so because they do not recognize their patients' needs.

Patients often cite the failure to take time with them as the cause of their decision to change doctors (DiMatteo & DiNicola, 1982). Of course, while the *objective* amount of time that a physician spends with a patient does influence how much information seeking can take place (Beisecker & Beisecker, 1990), patient satisfaction with the medical visit depends to a great extent upon the patient's *subjective* feeling that enough time was spent to meet his or her communication needs (DiMatteo & Hays, 1980). One survey showed that the average visit with an internist in the United States in the late 1970s took 18 minutes, and with a specialist took 15 minutes (Feller, 1979). Other, more recent studies, indicate that there is a great deal of variability in both waiting time to see a doctor and the duration of the visit with the doctor. One recent study found an average medical visit (with pediatricians and internists) to last 5.5 minutes, while a study at another facility found an average visit time of nearly 18 minutes (Asefzadeh, 1997; Meza, 1998). If no time is wasted in unproductive miscommunication, practitioner-patient encounters can be effective and satisfying in this brief time (Korsch, et al., 1968). But miscommunication is quite common, and it results in patients' feeling that not enough time was spent to satisfy their needs. In the absence of excellent communication skills on the part of all health professionals, brief medical visits have the potential to seriously reduce patient satisfaction and the outcomes of patient care (Beisecker & Beisecker, 1990; Waitzkin, 1985). For full patient participation, information seeking, and question asking to occur, at least 19 minutes may be essential (Beisecker & Beisecker, 1990). Whether a great deal of time is spent with the doctor, successful medical care relies on mutual understanding and the patient's belief that his or her physician is competent and trustworthy (Mechanic & Schlessinger, 1996). As more and more people's healthcare is governed by managed care organizations such as HMOs and PPOs, the issues of trust and competence become increasingly important.

Emerging technology has enabled some aspects of medical care to be accomplished more quickly and may in some ways have decreased the connection that people once felt with their physicians. It has also provided ways to increase patients' trust in their medical care providers. One good example is the computerization of patient records. In one large HMO center that had been using an extensive computerized patient record system for two years, patients revealed that they believed this technology made their doctors more familiar with their medical histories (Churgin, 1995). Thus, although the efficiency of computerization likely makes medical visits a bit shorter, this need not result in patients feeling misunderstood or neglected. Relatedly, teaching doctors to be better communicators does not necessarily mean that they will have to spend more time in their encounters with patients. One seminar, which was designed to improve the communication skills of physicians, led not only to an increase in their ability to address patients' fears and to explain recommendations clearly, but also to increased time efficiency in visits (Clark et al., 1998). Patients also responded more positively to the trained doctors and experienced a reduced need for health services, as they better understood how to care for themselves at home.

The Patient's Perspective

The anxiety of being ill can interfere with the patient's ability to communicate effectively, to say what he or she means, and to hear what is being communicated by the healthcare professional. Research shows that when prior objective information is given to a patient regarding medical examinations and procedures, the patient's negative reactions and anxiety can be reduced considerably (e.g., Campbell et al., 1999; Clark, 1997; Martin, 1996). It is important that this information be geared toward the patient's perspective and that it be accurate. In order to provide clear and concrete information to patients, several factors must be taken into account (Clark, 1997). The patient must be provided with objective information about the details of the procedure, and, once the patient understands it, he or she needs to think about and try to appreciate what the procedure will be like from a personal standpoint. Then the patient will be better prepared for the event, both cognitively and emotionally, than if he or she simply knew the steps of the procedure. Let's consider the example of a patient who is anticipating minor surgery with local anesthetic. In this surgery, a steel pin will be positioned to hold together bones in the hand that were broken in a bicycling accident. The patient will not simply need to know which bones will be pinned, what type of pin will be used, and how long the procedure will take. He or she will also need to be told about the slight tapping that will take place to properly position the pin and the potential for scraping sounds. A squeamish patient might want to bring a tape player with headphones to block out the sounds and may want to keep his or her eyes averted from the procedure.

Communication problems may arise from differences in the perspectives that practitioners and patients have on health and illness. As we saw in Chapter 2, health professionals and their patients often differ in their evaluations of the seriousness of symptoms and the preferred course of action to deal with them. Physicians and patients also tend to differ in their willingness to opt for surgery, for example, and in their preference for medications. Patients do not always agree with their doctors in terms of what constitutes a satisfying interaction (Probst et al., 1997; Wyshak & Barsky, 1995). Although competence and communication are important factors to both patients and doctors, patient satisfaction is associated with things such as waiting time, depression, anxiety, and whether they think the doctor is paying attention. Some of these factors (particularly waiting time and paying attention) tend to be overlooked by physicians when they evaluate the effectiveness of the interaction, leading to relatively low correlations between patients' and doctors' satisfaction and perceptions of the effectiveness of care.

Also, as we see in Box 3.1, communication problems can arise when physician and patient appear to be speaking different languages. Because they bring their own unique expertise to the encounter, it is crucial that each be heard and that any decisions be reached jointly.

Improving the Interview

As we examined in the last chapter, collecting accurate medical history data from patients through the process of interviewing can sometimes be very difficult. Many patients cannot even recall events that are quite recent. Some patients fail to provide correct information because the truth is embarrassing. Many are timid about answering questions regarding certain parts of their bodies or about their sexual behavior. When asked, they may either deliberately lie or simply withhold the complete truth.

BOX **3.1**

Hot Topic

Internal Fleabites

When you ask patients what is ailing them, you can get some pretty strange answers. Consider the patient who says he has a case of "smiling-mighty-Jesus" (spinal meningitis), the patient with "sick-as-hell anemia" (sickle cell anemia), or the one with "fireballs" in her "Eucharist" (fibroids in her uterus). One patient even has to take the medication "peanut butter balls" (Phenobarbital) for a seizure disorder. These examples represent attempts by (perhaps creative) patients to understand "medspeak" (sometimes also referred to as jargon or doctor-talk), the language of the medical profession. Patients develop a language that reflects their understanding. The language is called "patientspeak."

Patients are in foreign territory in the medical setting. "Entering a hospital has now become an internment in an alien culture for most people . . ." (Spaide, 1983, p. 5). They are often anxious, and the logical flow of their ideas may be impaired. Yet, patients work actively to puzzle out and make sense of what they have been told by their physicians. They are often reluctant to ask questions and may convince themselves that they will be able to reason out the meaning of their diagnosis.

Are the incorrect names that patients sometimes settle on simply meaningless "sound-alike" words, or do they tell something about how patients think about their medical problems? Probably the latter explanation is correct.

The patient with sickle cell ("sick-as-hell") anemia most likely does feel extremely sick. The patient who says that the ophthalmologist saw "Cadillacs" (cataracts) in her eyes might suspect that the doctor's income is quite high, or may even be (perhaps unconsciously) distressed at how much money her eye care is costing. The patient who says she has been referred to a "groinocologist" (gynecologist) has chosen an anatomical reference to aid her understanding. Patientspeak may not be simple linguistic misunderstanding. Consider the patient who reports that he has "internal fleabites" (deep vein thrombophlebitis). He may have heard the suffix "itis," which refers to inflammation of the organ preceding it (as in appendicitis—inflammation of the appendix). The patient then reasons that he has a disease of thrombo-phle (pronounced "flea") -bite. . . some kind of fleabite disease. Since there are no apparent external bites and the pain is inside, the patient guesses that "thrombo" must mean "internal," and so the patient guesses "internal fleabites." The patient has had to incorporate common knowledge with linguistic analysis using a kind of creative rationalization. He has worked quite hard to turn medspeak into patientspeak.

We are indebted to Drs. Jim Black and Wendy Haight (personal communication, August, 1983) for some very interesting insights that contributed to this analysis.

Some patients may be embarrassed about their ignorance of medical issues and vocabulary, and so may pretend they understand things that they do not (Korsch & Negrete, 1972). Their primary motivation during the medical visit may be to avoid appearing unintelligent rather than to communicate the necessary information. Sometimes during medical interviews, those asking the questions tend to reinforce their respondents for answering carelessly and even for evading or refusing to answer the question (Marquis, 1970). These reinforcements are typically given with nonverbal cues such as head nods, smiles, and attention. Respondents may also be subtly encouraged to be passive and inaccurate.

Interviewing patients can be made considerably more effective and accurate if these problems are remedied. This can be done in several ways. Patient anxiety can be reduced by making the medical care visit more responsive to patients' emotional needs and by providing patients with the information they wish to have. Since patient passivity and practitioner dominance often contribute to producing unreliable answers, patients who wish to be actively involved in the visit should be given the opportunity to become participants in every aspect of their care (DiMatteo & DiNicola, 1982; DiMatteo et al., 1994). The accuracy of health reporting has been found to increase significantly when respondents make a commitment to provide accurate information to their health professionals. This commitment elicits patient effort and motivation (Cannell et al., 1977). In order to accomplish this, the interviewer tells the patient what kind of information he or she is after and the purpose of the questions (e.g., "Now, I need to ask you some questions about your chest pain . . ." or "Have you experienced any side effects from the medication? By side effects, I mean . . ."). The patient's efforts to be an accurate and responsible reporter must be reinforced (e.g., "Yes, that's the kind of information I need. Tell me what else happened . . ."). Finally, the interviewer must eliminate any possibility that the patient will be embarrassed. The medical practitioner must communicate a completely nonjudgmental attitude about issues that have the potential to embarrass the patient. Physicians who are judgmental or punitive about issues such as sexual behavior, for example, can have a lasting impact on the patient's feeling about his or her body and its functioning.

Medical Jargon

Medical professionals learn a complex language with which to communicate with one another. The purpose of using medical terminology is not simply to say big words when simple ones would suffice. Disease entities, diagnostic tests, and other medical phenomena have particular names. The terms are descriptive and precise, allowing a large amount of information to be conveyed rather efficiently. Yet, the role of medical terminology goes beyond efficiency. The ability to use and to understand medical terminology defines one as a member of the "in group" and as someone "in the know" (Christy, 1979). Doctors and nurses are in the know. Patients are not.

A somewhat more cynical view of medical jargon was provided by the famous heart surgeon, Dr. Michael DeBakey: "Most doctors don't want their patients to understand them! They prefer to keep their work a mystery. If patients don't understand what a doctor is talking about, they won't ask him questions. Then the doctor won't have to be bothered answering them" (Robinson, 1973). Research suggests that sometimes doctors *appear* to use jargon on purpose. A study of patient satisfaction was conducted with 320 patients in four different hospitals and was based not only on patient reports, but also on observations made by the researchers (Phillips, 1996). It was found that patients were most dissatisfied when doctors communicated poorly, seemed insensitive to the patients' symptoms, evaded direct questions, hesitated to give complete information, and appeared to deliberately use medical jargon.

"**Doctor-talk**" (also called "**medspeak**" or medical jargon) is mystifying to patients (DiMatteo & DiNicola, 1982; Phillips, 1996). Doctor-talk is also high sound-ing, formal, and both frightening and exciting to patients (Christy, 1979). Some patients take the physician's use of high-sounding words as a compliment to their intelligence (Korsch et al., 1968); They feel that they will be "taken care of" by a physi-cian who is so obviously competent that his or her words cannot even be understood!

A number of studies show that what doctors communicate is often not well under-stood by their patients (as humorously illustrated in Figure 3.1). One classic study took a list of common medical terms (words that healthcare providers said they would not hesi-tate to use with patients) and showed them to 125 hospitalized patients. The patients told the researchers what they thought each word meant. None was correctly identified by every patient, and there wasn't a single patient who was able to accurately define all of the words (Samora et al., 1961). Patients came up with all kinds of interesting interpretations. For instance, some of the incorrect definitions for "appendectomy" were "cut rectum," "rupture of the appendix," "pain in the stomach," "taking off an arm or leg," "something like an epidemic," and "something to do with the bowels." Some individuals thought that a "pulse" was "a bad hurt or sickness," "a nerve," or "temperature." An "intern" was thought to be "boy that helps in the hospital," "same as an orderly," "drugstore man," "a man nurse," and "a doctor with no degree." The "abdomen" was misidentified as "sides," "buttocks," "back," "uterus," "heart," "bladder," and the "area below the waist." More recent studies show that patients correctly interpret medical words only about 36 percent of the time (Hadlow & Pitts, 1991). Furthermore, doctors themselves are technically incorrect in their word usage about 30 percent of the time (Hadlow & Pitts, 1991).

What doctors say and what patients think . . .

Doctor:	Patient:
D and C	The Capital of the USA
Sickle cell anemia	Sick-as-hell anemia
Fibroids in the uterus	Fireballs in the Eucharist
Varicose veins	Very close veins
Incubation	In an Incubator
Colic	Something to do with a sheep dog
Internist	An Intern
G. I. series	Medical tests for war veterans
Staph infection	An infection caused by the medical staff
Hypertension	Being tense and "hyper"
For water retention	Take to retain water

FIGURE 3.1 Medical jargon.

Although the average patient is somewhat more medically knowledgeable and sophisticated than was the case thirty years ago, there is still plenty of chance for miscommunication. A study by Thompson and Pledger (1993) attempted to determine whether the medical knowledge of the general public had increased over the thirty years since Samora's study. This time, 224 adults (71% of them with a college education) were administered a list of fifty general medical terms. The college-educated participants defined more words correctly than did less-educated subjects, and there was evidence that word recognition had improved over the past three decades. Only ten participants defined all fifty words correctly, however, and there was not a single word that every participant was able to define correctly. In another set of studies on the communication between physicians-in-training and mothers of their pediatric patients, researchers found that nearly all of the physicians used words that confused and perplexed the mothers (Korsch & Negrete, 1972). These words were fairly rudimentary medical terms such as **incubation period** (which is the period of time from exposure to a disease to development of symptoms). But the words were unfamiliar and caused patients considerable anxiety. The mothers attempted to "puzzle out" the meaning of the words rather than ask for explanation. For example, several reasoned that "incubation period" sounds like "incubator." Therefore, the baby was going to have to go into an incubator and be hospitalized!

The Consequences of Imprecise Communication

Confusion

One recent study linked technical language to less satisfaction, comprehension, and recall on the part of patients (Jackson, 1992). In fact, a patient can become confused or even terrified when he or she misunderstands a medical professional's words. Medical educator Eric Cassell (1985b, p. 181) tells the story of a woman who was extremely upset because of the imprecise words used by her former physician. The physician said, ". . . looks like your diaphragm is immobilized . . . like paralyzed" even though there was no paralysis at all and her condition was not even serious. She had a severe muscle spasm, but knew roughly what paralyzed meant and pictured herself ending up in an iron lung (a device into which the patient's entire body is placed and immobilized to assist breathing). The physician may not have known that the word "paralyzed" would terrify the patient. The physician failed, however, to check the patient's comprehension and understanding so that he could modify certain explanations if that proved to be necessary.

Nonadherence

Imprecise communication exacts a heavy toll in medicine, and perhaps one of the largest effects is seen for patient adherence. Patients are likely to be nonadherent if they do not understand what it is that they are to do, do not agree that their treatment represents the most appropriate form of action, or do not have the resources to carry out instructions. The severity of the patient's problems, the side effects of the treatment, and the length and complexity of the regimen are just some of the factors that influence adherence and are themselves affected by the communication that occurs between doctor and patient. When patients do not adhere to their medical regimens, a variety of negative outcomes are likely, including exacerbation of symptoms, incorrect diagnoses, improper changes to the regimen based on its perceived "ineffectiveness," and additional time and money spent on medical visits. Recent review books on this subject include those by Myers and Midence (1998) and Schumaker and colleagues (1998).

Antibiotic Resistance

One common, and dangerous, result of nonadherence is the emergence of antibiotic-resistant strains of bacteria (Harrison, 1995; Rao, 1998). When an antibiotic is prescribed for an infection, the patient typically starts to feel better within a couple of days. Most prescriptions, however, direct the patient to continue taking the antibiotic drug for seven to ten days. Often, however, when patients begin to feel better they decide that they no longer need the antibiotic. The problem with this choice, of course, is that even though the patient is feeling better, he or she is likely *not* to be completely rid of the bacteria that caused the infection. Remaining bacteria reproduce and many mutations (most of which are inconsequential) occur. Some mutations give the "new and improved" bacteria some advantage over previous versions, making them less susceptible to the antibiotic. A new strain of bacteria emerges and subsequent treatment with the antibiotic may be less effective. Sometimes a strain mutates and evolves successfully into such a hardy strain that none of the available antibiotics can affect it. It is at this point that patients can be in serious danger!

Of course, antibiotic-resistant strains of bacteria can also develop as a result of antibiotic overuse through overprescription by physicians (such as for a viral infection like a cold or the flu, against which antibiotics are not effective), and by the abundant use of antibacterial products. Regarding the first issue, it appears that in an effort to give "something" to their patients during the medical interaction, many physicians prescribe antibiotics even when they are not necessary. We might wonder whether effective communication, careful listening, and evidence of interpersonal caring and connection might serve this purpose better. Regarding the second issue, it is clear that antibacterial soaps, scrubs, wipes, sprays, and even toys upset the bacterial balance in individuals' environments and when antibacterial products are used to kill off innocuous bacteria, the ones that remain can proliferate and even mutate, improving their own chances for survival but causing problems for human beings.

Patient Dissatisfaction

Returning to the issue of imprecise communication, we see that it is not only a problem for patients—it directly affects doctors as well. When patients are not (or do not feel) understood by their physicians, they are less likely to adhere to recommended treatments and are more likely to switch from doctor to doctor, looking for one who meets their needs (Frankel, 1995). These patients are also more likely to sue for malpractice. One interesting study found that primary care doctors who spent more time with their patients, who were clear in telling patients what to expect, who encouraged patients to share their concerns and opinions, and who used humor, were less likely to be sued than their less interactive peers (Levinson et al., 1997). Litigation was more common against primary care doctors who seemed less open to their patients' needs and less willing to be engaged in friendly, interactive discourse.

Listening to Patients

"The doctor didn't listen to anything I tried to say" is a common complaint among patients. Listening is a key factor in assessment and diagnosis, yet the medical practitioner's failure to listen is one of the most common complaints of patients (Probst et al., 1997). Patients typically know, although perhaps not consciously, a great deal of information about their conditions. They alone have the experience of the specific character and timing of their symptoms. They alone know their pain, and by describing it can give clues to the type of problem that might be causing it. To take advantage of the patient's unique perspective, the medical practitioner must allow the patient to provide valuable information and must listen carefully to it. Listening closely to the patient also helps the practitioner to avoid the tendency to settle too quickly on a diagnosis and helps the practitioner to consider all available empirical evidence and avoid trying to fit the information collected later in the interview to a hypothesis formulated early. Listening conveys respect to the patient and emphasizes that the physician is willing to establish a mutual-participation approach to the physician-patient relationship (Stone, 1979).

In practice, listening tends to be rather difficult for physicians to do effectively. At the very least, listening requires not talking, yet major empirical studies have shown that patients don't have much of a chance to talk because physicians talk so much (Bain, 1976; Davis, 1971; Freemon et al., 1971; Stiles et al., 1979). These studies involved tape recordings of physician-patient interactions and tabulations of each person's utterances. In spite of the various settings of the studies and the various backgrounds of the patients, physicians were found to verbalize quite extensively. They spent much more time talking than did their patients. They incorrectly believed, however, that their patients talked more (Waitzkin & Stoeckle, 1976).

Understanding patients' communications fully requires not only listening to the content of what they say, but also taking the context into account. Patients sometimes report their actions and behaviors accurately, but because they usually desire the approval of their physicians, they may (consciously or not) alter their communications in order to receive positive feedback. For instance, researchers have found that patients sometimes exaggerate their role in actions that have potentially harmful health consequences and that patients take more responsibility for these actions than is warranted (du Pre & Beck, 1997). This tends, in turn, to elicit reassurance and compliments from the physician. It is not unlike a person who complains, "I'm just no good at sports—I'm so clumsy," while hoping that others will respond, "You're not clumsy, and you are good at sports!" It is clear from this research that patients want their doctors' approval, and that some of what goes on in physician-patient interactions is focused on helping patients to feel better about themselves.

Educating Patients

Physicians may talk a lot, but what they say often doesn't give patients much information. In several of the studies cited above, the physicians' utterances and verbalizations typically took the form of questions, acknowledgments (e.g., "uh-huh"), reflections (e.g., "So, your foot hurts."), clarifications (e.g., "So, you mean you have felt at least some pain there."), and commands (e.g., "Sit back and let me examine your foot."). Very little of what was said to patients was helpful in raising their knowledge of their illness or of the best ways to care for themselves. These studies, as well as more recent research, have found that physicians actually spend less than 10 percent of their interaction time with patients informing and educating them (Bain, 1976; Davis, 1971; Freemon et al., 1971; Stiles et al., 1979; Waitzkin, 1984, 1985). In their classic study, Waitzkin and Stoeckle (1976) found that during the medical visit, which lasted an average of 20 minutes, physicians spent, on average, less than one minute communicating information to the patient. Those same physicians estimated that they spent between 10 and 15 minutes (that is, 50 to 75% of the interaction time) giving information to their patients. In the Waitzkin (1985) study, out of an average interaction time of 16.5 minutes, physicians spent an average of 1.3 minutes giving information to their patients. When asked to estimate how much time they spent, however, these physicians guessed an average of 8.9 minutes! One study observed physician-patient interactions (Svarstad, 1976) and examined the manner in which physicians gave instructions to their patients regarding the medications they were to take. Of 347 drugs prescribed to patients, 60 were never even discussed during the observed visit. In 90 percent of the incidents in which drugs were prescribed, the physicians gave their patients no specific verbal advice on how to use the medication. Very often, the physicians made changes in patients' medication dosages or scheduling, and after once mentioning the change verbally, neither wrote down the change nor checked to see whether the patient really understood it. As Waitzkin (1985) found by analyzing tape recordings of 336 medical encounters in several outpatient settings, "doctors spent little time informing their patients, overestimated the time they did spend, and underestimated patients' desire for information" (p. 81). One study of patients' satisfaction with the information they received surveyed patients at four different hospitals. It was found that 45 percent of patients were highly dissatisfied with the information their doctors gave them regarding their condition (Phillips, 1996). These patients reported that their doctors often communicated poorly, were insensitive, and even evaded straightforward questions. Clearly, there is much room for improvement in providing patients with important medical information.

Helping Patients to Ask Questions

Patients rarely ask for explanations, conceptual or otherwise. In fact, they ask very few questions. Patients rarely tell their practitioners that they wish to have more information than they are getting and they rarely assert that they do not understand what their practitioner has told them. The studies cited above, which tabulated what actually occurs in physician-patient interactions, provide some insight into this phenomenon.

In these studies, patients spent less than 7 percent of the interaction time asking their physicians any questions at all, including questions about specific problems and treatments. In fact, one study found that patients asked an average of 1.5 questions per medical visit while their physicians asked 27.3 questions (Waitzkin et al., 1996). When misunderstandings are clearly occurring, patients tend not to correct their physicians' apparent misunderstandings of what they have said to them. They do not even politely challenge what their physicians state incorrectly or request precision when physicians are vague. Patients are typically reluctant to betray their ignorance or to appear to distrust the expertise of the physician (c.f., Matthews, 1983).

When a patient asks questions of a practitioner, he or she certainly can acquire some important information that would otherwise not be available. Something else happens as well, however. By asking questions, the patient signals to the practitioner a desire to be an active partner in his or her own medical care and to have an active role in medical decisions. The message is sent that these decisions must be made with the patient's full knowledge, consent, and contribution. When a patient is passive and unassertive, he or she places responsibility for personal well-being into the hands of the practitioner and relinquishes control. This can have harmful consequences because practitioners and patients sometimes have different goals in the medical care process. Patients need to remain vigilant, inquisitive, and assertive in order to maintain their own interests.

Research shows that patients can be taught to communicate more effectively with their practitioners and to ask more questions (McGee & Cegala, 1998). The intervention required to achieve increased communication can be very simple, such as a leaflet that directs patients toward more interactive behaviors and suggests ways to be more actively involved in care (Frederikson & Bull, 1995; McCann & Weinman, 1996). In turn, it has been shown that patients who are assertive, who ask more questions, and who are more expressive of their own feelings during the visit actually

Patients need information in order to care for themselves effectively. Written materials can supplement clear explanations and open discussion.

receive more information from their physicians than do those who are passive and uninvolved (Putnam & Stiles, 1993; Street, 1991, 1992).

Helping Patients to Remember

Another serious problem in communication is that patients usually forget a great deal of what they are told during their visits with medical practitioners. One study found that shortly after their consultation with a medical practitioner, clinic outpatients forgot about one-third of what was told to them during the visit (Ley & Spelman, 1965). They forgot 56 percent of the instructions and 48 percent of the statements about treatment. Subsequent research by Philip Ley (1979) indicated that more information tended to be forgotten when there was a large amount of information presented, when the patient had limited medical knowledge, and when his or her anxiety was high. Interestingly, there do not seem to be age-related differences in recall. In one study of younger (18–44) and older (60–82) adults, the younger adults remembered somewhat more medical information immediately after the session, but at the one-week and one-month follow-ups, both groups remembered the same amount of information (McGuire, 1996).

Research has shown that there are certain consistencies in what and how much patients forget. First, the more a patient is told, the greater the proportion of information she or he forgets. And, although patients forget much of what a doctor tells them, they tend to forget instructions and advice more often than other information, a fact that may help to shed some light on the problem of patient noncompliance with treatment. Patients remember best what they consider most important and what they were told first (Ley, 1979). While there are no significant differences in recall ability by patients of different ages and levels of intelligence, patient anxiety does seem to make a difference. A moderate level of anxiety in a patient results in the best recall, but if anxiety is too high or too low, a patient may forget a great deal. Also, the more medical knowledge a patient has, the more he or she will remember what is said by the practitioner (presumably because there is a context or framework in which to put the information). There is some evidence that when patients know their doctors well, they tend to recall oral instructions better than when they are less well acquainted with their doctors (Heffer et al., 1997). This may be because the doctor and patient have reached an understanding about the patient's knowledge level and so the doctor speaks at this level. Another explanation is that when the patient knows the physician well, there may be less anxiety distracting the patient's attention away from the instructions.

Finally, simply writing things down doesn't seem to help patients a great deal. A patient must first *understand* what needs to be remembered (Cassata, 1978). Once that understanding has been achieved, written notes on what the doctor says might be quite helpful. Putting written communication in clear, simple language and giving explicit instructions instead of general rules is best (Bradshaw et al., 1975). For patients who have limited reading and writing skills, the innovative technique of pairing the verbal messages with pictures can be quite successful. In one study, in which pictures were used, recall of what to do for a fever and a sore mouth increased from just 14 percent up to 85 percent (Houts et al., 1998). Clearly, cooperating with medical treatment can be extremely difficult when patients cannot remember what their health professionals have suggested that they do. While effective practitioner-patient communication is certainly not the only determinant of the patient's ability to follow through with recommendations, it is one of the most important components.

Box 3.2 deals with a very challenging medical regimen that requires exceptional patient understanding, recollection, and motivation—the care of HIV infection. As you read it, think about the principles we've learned.

BOX 3.2

Research Close-up

Better Treatments for AIDS Depend on Patients Taking Their Pills

In the early 1990s, Magic Johnson, a former Los Angeles Lakers basketball player and now co-owner of the team, publicly announced that he had acquired HIV, the virus that causes AIDS. He immediately underwent treatment for the infection with drugs that cause temporary suppression of the virus, and he remains healthy. Not every individual who acquires HIV is as fortunate, however. As of June 2000, 438,795 people in the United States had died because of the disease (CDC, 2000).

In 1996, a new class of antiretroviral drugs was developed and represented a significant advance in the treatment of HIV. These drugs work in combination with previously used medications, such as AZT, and appear to be much more effective than previous therapies. The outlook for many patients is much brighter, although these drugs must be taken precisely as prescribed, even down to the exact time of day. As with any medical treatment, however, adherence to the regimen is essential to its success (as we discuss in both this and the next chapter). Patients with a disease as dangerous and life-threatening as HIV/AIDS are often assumed to be highly vigilant in their adherence and highly motivated to comply perfectly with their prescribed treatments. After all, these new drugs present their opportunity to survive. Research has examined the issue of adherence with anti-retroviral therapies, and has found some surprising results.

In a sample of both African Americans and Caucasians, nearly one-third of AIDS patients missed at least one dose of their medication in the previously reported five days (Catz et al., 2000)! Over the previous three months, nearly one-fifth of these patients reported having missed doses on a weekly basis and half reported missing a dose at least once a month. This degree of nonadherence is very serious given the gravity of the health situation for these patients. In fact, the researchers were able to demonstrate that poor adherence had a direct relationship to greater viral load (a marker for greater disease progression). Those patients who reported having missed no pills in the previous three months had the best treatment health outcomes. Among patients who were perfectly adherent, 62 percent had no detectable viral load.

The act of taking a pill is not necessarily an easy one; many barriers can interfere with an individual's success at following his or her medication regimen. In the sample described above, such barriers included being depressed, experiencing severe side effects, and having poor social support. Helping such patients overcome these barriers is essential to good medical care, however, because the consequences of nonadherence are so high. Adherence could mean the difference between life and death.

In the 1980s and 1990s, we have experienced an era in which, for many areas of the country, there has been a surplus of physicians. Patients no longer need to choose between technical skills and communication skills in their doctors. They can insist on both. This is an adaptive choice. Both clinical and empirical studies have shown that good doctoring involves sound medical practices, effective talking, and good listening. There is therapeutic value to avoiding the uncertainty, panic, and hopelessness that can arise in a patient when communication is poor and the patient does not understand his or her medical condition. It is important to remember that words can be very powerful and very reassuring. But, nonverbal messages are also important.

Nonverbal Communication and Practitioner-Patient Relationships

"So, how are things going, Barry?" asked Dr. Bouchet. Are you able to take your medications twice a day? Or are there some difficulties we need to work out?" Dr. Bouchet had just finished taking Barry's blood pressure. He held Barry's arm firmly as he removed the blood pressure cuff, and then checked Barry's wrist pulse. "Oh. I guess I'm, uh, doing okay . . ." Barry said, looking away.

Dr. Bouchet recognized Barry's discomfort in his halting speech and averted glance. Something was not right. He decided to pursue the issue further.

Dr. Bouchet let go of Barry's wrist. "Are the medications themselves giving you any problems? You know, a few people run into some difficulties with these medications. There are alternatives." Barry began hesitatingly . . . "Uh, well, I don't know if it's the medications or what, but I started having some problems with, you know, with my wife, uh, soon after I started them. . . ." He looked down at the floor tiles. ". . . sexual problems?" Dr Bouchet asked gently. Barry nodded.

"Difficulty getting or maintaining an erection?" asked Dr. Bouchet. "Uh, huh," answered Barry without looking up. "So I, uh, I stopped taking them for a while."

"I can understand that," Dr. Bouchet said supportively. "Sometimes this type of medication can bring erectile dysfunction as a side effect. Let's look into changing your medications and clear up this problem right away, okay?"

In this example, the physician recognized Barry's embarrassment and its relationship to his difficulties in following the treatment regimen. Dr. Bouchet was sensitive to Barry's initial reluctance to discuss things, and he met Barry's disclosures with understanding and support. Of course, the fact that Dr. Bouchet did these things may be obvious, but how he did them needs some analysis. Note, for example, that Dr. Bouchet first established some legitimate physical contact with his patient by checking his wrist pulse and taking his blood pressure. Although the nurse checked Barry's blood pressure just before Dr. Bouchet arrived in the examining room, he chose to do it again himself. Such contact helps to break down barriers that patients may feel between themselves and their doctor. Dr. Bouchet also paid attention when Barry looked away as he answered the first question. Barry was clearly uncomfortable about something. Dr. Bouchet paid attention to the patient's halting speech and his use of "uh" several times in a few sentences. Dr. Bouchet noticed that his patient looked embarrassed. By continuing to be warm and accepting, Dr. Bouchet provided a safe environment in which the patient could disclose his distress.

Metacommunication

Messages of warmth, empathy, understanding, and the essence of "bedside manner" are not always communicated directly through words. In fact, particularly in the medical setting, such messages are conveyed instead through **metacommunication**, which is defined as "communication about communication." Consider the following example. With a smile on her face, looking directly at her patient, the physician says in a kind, jovial voice: "Now, get out of here. I don't want to see you for at least two months!" What conclusion do you draw? Is the physician angry, or rejecting? Despite her words, she probably is not. Rather, she may be joking or, even more likely, encouraging. She may be happily telling the patient that good health is returning and that there is little need for further treatments, at least for a while. Suppose, on the other hand, a physician answers an inquisitive patient with the following response: "Sure, Mrs. Lipton, we'll talk about it." While saying this, however, the physician looks away from Mrs. Lipton, stands up with body oriented away from the patient, and places one hand on the knob of the door leading out of the examining room. Do you have much faith that Mrs. Lipton will get her questions answered? Clearly, metamessages tell a great deal more than do simple words. Suppose that a nurse tells a patient that changing the dressings on a very sore wound may be painful. While explaining what must be done, the nurse places one hand firmly on the patient's shoulder, makes eye contact with the patient, and speaks in a kind and comforting voice. The total message is that the treatment is necessary, that it may be somewhat painful, and that the nurse will provide as much comfort as the patient needs. The nurse clearly is empathizing with the patient's distress.

In human social interaction, a great deal of information can be communicated through nonverbal cues. This is true in medical encounters as well, where health professionals control various aspects of the interaction by speaking longer, pausing more often, and initiating touch more often than their patients do (Street & Buller, 1987). Health professionals may communicate affiliation with metamessages conveyed through eye contact, certain gestures, and body orientations. Patients who experience more of this kind of interchange perceive their doctors to be more affiliative, and these patients are more satisfied with the care they receive.

Metamessages can be simple or they can be quite complex. In the absence of any other cues, a smile will probably convey good will of some sort. But the intensity and the intention of that goodwill may be unclear. A more complex message might combine a smile with five seconds of eye contact. (Try it . . . that's a surprisingly long time!). The communication is becoming more immediate and more intense. Then, pair this message with the verbal statement, "I think you're going to be okay." This complex message gives a lucky patient good reason for optimism and hope. Metamessages are sometimes, but not always, intentional. At the beginning of a consultation, a practitioner may use very specific cues of body orientation and gaze (away from the patient, focused, perhaps, on the chart) to indicate that the patient should not yet begin describing his or her chief complaint (Robinson, 1998). This is an intentional message, and patients typically respond by waiting until their doctors appear ready to listen to their concerns. On the other hand, however, some metamessages are unintentional, although they may be quite informative. Suppose that a patient is being prepared for minor surgery. Lying on the operating table, he exhibits tremendous muscular tension. He fails to respond quickly to several of the physician's verbal commands such as to turn his head. He asks the same question three times because he cannot remember the answer he has been given. The sensitive nurse recognizes these metamessages, although not done purposely, as cues that the patient is quite anxious. He says to the patient, "You're doing very well. This will be all done before you know it," and he asks the patient what would help to make him feel more comfortable. The patient, who initially felt distress, now relaxes and feels that his concerns are understood. He is in good hands.

Not all metamessages are clear and straightforward. A patient may wish to hide the fact that he or she has been inconsistent in taking the prescribed medication. The physician asks whether the patient has followed the medication regimen as prescribed, and the patient answers, "Of course, why wouldn't I?" But, the patient looks away, despite the physician's attempt to maintain eye contact. This metacommunication says that something is amiss, although precisely what may be very unclear. The patient's failure to maintain eye contact with the physician is a comment on the words—a communication about the communication. There is no way to know precisely what the metamessage means, however. It is a comment on the message, but that is all. In the case above, the patient may be unintentionally indicating that his or her words are not true. On the other hand, the patient may be conveying that such an issue is none of the doctor's business. Perhaps the patient is even reacting negatively to the doctor's question because his or her spouse also nags about the medication and the question is tiresome. Metamessages can be of various sorts and can even consist of actions. For example, a patient may say that she is satisfied with her physician's treatment but she refuses to pay, or even work out terms to pay, her bill. One message communicates satisfaction, while another conveys just the opposite. Many metamessages are conveyed through nonverbal cues, but they are not limited to the nonverbal channel of communication.

While the meanings of words can be checked in the dictionary and people can be held to the precise meaning of what they say, there is no exact metacommunication lexicon. Although some people may claim that they know the exact meaning of various nonverbal cues, such claims are not supported by research. There are some consistencies in meaning, as we will see, but these are by no means simple or absolute. Other types of metacommunications—actions for example—can also be complex. Not paying a bill or not returning to a particular physician may indicate anger and disappointment . . . or something completely different. The existence of metacommunication cues admonishes the receiver of the message to explore the precise meaning of the whole picture that is communicated.

The Importance of Nonverbal Communication

Health psychologists working with medical professionals have learned a great deal about the role of one major type of metacommunication in medical settings—nonverbal communication. The recognition of the role of empathy and the importance of the physician's affective (emotional) behavior with the patient has further encouraged the study of nonverbal communication between patients and medical practitioners (Harrigan et al., 1985). Let us take a look at an example of how nonverbal messages can operate in patient care.

> The young intern was ebullient. After only one month on the service, she made a definitive diagnosis that had eluded her colleagues and even her teachers. She burst into the patient's room just in time for the beginning of morning rounds. It was 8 AM. She began describing the case to the residents and the attending physician. "Mr. Anglin is a 45-year-old man who entered the hospital seven days ago with a chief complaint of severe headaches." In her intensity and excitement, she did not acknowledge Mr. Anglin who lay in the bed before her. The intern described several of the findings from the physical examinations and tests and then she summed up. "On the basis of new data from the bronchoscopy and biopsy, I suggest the diagnosis of a right lung primary with brain metastasis." "Brilliant, Doctor," responded the attending physician, a stern old man who rarely gave anyone a compliment. "Excellent work." The intern was beaming; her resident smiled with pride. The young intern had been the one to suggest the workup to rule out lung cancer. But it wasn't ruled out. And it had spread to the patient's brain. A look of happiness and excitement appeared on the faces of the young physicians on the medical team. They were proud to be experiencing firsthand the diagnostic capabilities of modern medicine. They had been intensely frustrated for an entire week, trying to diagnose the patient's headaches. They were puzzled by what looked like tumors on the patient's brain. Mr. Anglin looked up at them, and for a moment, caught their exuberance. He smiled.
>
> And then, Mr. Anglin watched the faces of the physicians metamorphose into a kind of horror. A couple of the faces twitched with tension. A few eyes widened. Some jaws were clenched. And in two seconds the whole display was over. He saw the faces harden one by one into sternness, thought, and purpose. The patient was unable to put into words what he was perceiving. He did not know the meaning of the medical terms the doctors were using, and he did not know what was wrong with him. But some part of his consciousness recognized the truth precisely and without hesitation. His heart began to race; he felt faint. Yet he could not articulate anything. It all seemed remote and unreal. Mr. Anglin's eyes, huge and pleading, met the intern's, but she looked away. Then, the doctors walked out of the room one by one to continue their rounds and the busy routine of diagnosis.

As we see here, patients are extremely sensitive to the metacommunications of the medical professionals who care for them. The verbal messages that patients encounter in medical settings are often confusing, and sometimes providers simply withhold information from their patients. They may not have the time or the inclination to explain things. As we noted earlier, however, patients do not exist comfortably in an information vacuum. They try to find out, for example, how serious their condition really is and its likely prognosis. For many reasons, including their own peace of mind and desire to take control of their own lives, patients search for the answers they need. In fact, as one study has shown, the provision of information to and good communication with cancer patients can result in their greater feelings of control, and in lower levels of depression (Rutter et al., 1996). Illness often forces patients into a dependent state, and many look to the nonverbal cues of their health professionals for important information. Patients who know little about the technical aspects of their medical care may attempt to judge its quality on the basis of their practitioner's interpersonal behavior (DiMatteo & DiNicola, 1982). They may also look for cues that they are liked or favored by those who care for them (Friedman, 1982). They may try to judge whether things are going well in their treatment by looking to their practitioners' nonverbal cues (Friedman, 1982). Because patients often perceive themselves as powerless and with little control, they may be particularly attentive to the nonverbal cues that their practitioners emit.

Potential problems can arise, of course, when patients interpret nonverbal cues in ways that were not intended. For example, a patient may interpret a facial expression brought about by the practitioner's fatigue, confusion, or distress about an entirely different matter as evidence that the practitioner is trying to conceal the patient's grave condition. This, of course, can result in a lot of unnecessary anxiety for the patient. One study demonstrated that patients who received information from a physician who was worried were more anxious and distressed, and recalled the information more poorly, than did those who received information from a physician who was not worried (Shapiro et al., 1992). Thus, even the correct detection of nonverbal cues may lead to faulty inferences if the intentions of the cues are misinterpreted.

Alternatively, nonverbally expressed emotions might be misread entirely. For example, one study found that it can be difficult to distinguish anger from anxiety in a medical interaction (Hall et al., 1981). Imagine a practitioner who enters an examining room to find a patient who seems angry. The doctor might become somewhat defensive or hostile in return, and the interaction could deteriorate rapidly. Perhaps, however, the patient wasn't angry at all, but instead was very anxious about his or her condition. The misinterpretation of the emotion expressed nonverbally could, in a case like this, do a great deal of harm.

By means of their nonverbal cues, medical practitioners signal to their patients the extent to which they are willing and able to really listen to their patients' expressions of pain, frustration, confusion, and sadness. ". . . One might ask how often physicians signal that they cannot endure their patients' pain, putting a stop to sharing even before it gets started" (Bertman & Krant, 1977, p. 643). A recent analysis of the nonverbal exchanges between doctors and patients offers insight into the nonverbal indicators that doctors often use to show their readiness to hear what the patient has to say. For the most part, doctors use gaze and body orientation (turning toward the patient and looking at him or her) to indicate when they are willing to listen to the patient's chief complaints (Robinson, 1998). Patients are sensitive to these cues. They rarely jump in and begin to describe their symptoms, but instead tend to wait for their doctors to indicate receptivity, or even to ask directly about their complaints.

Physicians tend to exert control over the medical interaction by using other nonverbal cues as well. Research shows that they talk for longer stretches than do patients;

they touch patients more than they are touched by patients, even when touch is not required for examination purposes; and they have more frequent pauses during their speech (Harrigan et al., 1985; Street & Buller, 1987). Physicians sometimes choose to overlook patient's questions, and they frequently interrupt patients who are trying to describe their symptoms (West, 1983). Studies also indicate that the types of cues provided by doctors are not always consistent from patient to patient. For instance, physicians sometimes demonstrate more domineering behavior with older adult patients than they do with younger ones, and are often dismissive, parental, inattentive, and critical (Adelman et al., 1992). Several major studies have shown that practitioners who are able to control their nonverbal cues and convey precisely what they want to their patients elicit greater satisfaction and cooperation than do those without such skill (DiMatteo et al., 1986; DiMatteo et al., 1980). Patients care a great deal about the "personal touch" and the quality of interpersonal communication that they experience in their medical interactions. These are the things that patients remember and often comment on.

So far, we have focused almost exclusively on the nonverbal cues provided by the practitioner. As we saw earlier, however, patients experience a wide range of complex emotions during the process of their medical treatment. There may be very few opportunities for patients to express their feelings verbally. Patients are often too intimidated by the treatment situation and by the behavior of their health professionals to say what they feel, and so their emotions tend to be expressed through nonverbal cues (Beisecker & Beisecker, 1990). Most patients, for example, are reluctant to say (and may be actively discouraged from saying) that they are distressed or confused or angry about a prescribed treatment regimen. Instead, they may look uncomfortable and anxious, avert their eyes or turn their heads, or appear confused (Patterson, 1983). Further, when patients are asked in the perfunctory manner typical of modern medical care: "Any questions?" they say "no" with their words. But often they say something else with their bodies and their faces. Patients' metacommunications can convey that "no" is not the complete truth (Cormier et al., 1984). In an attempt to engage their doctors in further communication without directly asking for it, patients have been observed to do a number of things including being silent until the physician looks at them and kicking their legs back and forth while sitting on the examination table to gain the physician's attention (Heath, 1984). Typically, patients have little experience hiding or controlling their expressions of emotion in the medical setting. Patients' nonverbal cues can thus provide a valuable window to their feelings such as noted in Figure 3.2 (Friedman, 1982). The medical practitioner who can recognize a patient's confusion and tension and pick up cues to other emotions is able to gather much needed information to care for the patient. If the practitioner can recognize cues of dissatisfaction, negative affect, and distress, he or she can deal with the problems from which these emotions arise before the patient terminates the therapeutic relationship, calls a halt to the treatment, or retaliates with malpractice litigation. Likewise, the practitioner may recognize signs of patients' enthusiasm and optimism, and harness these positive emotions in support of the patient's recovery.

The nonverbal communication skills of many physicians have been studied in research using various ways of measuring interpersonal communication. These mea-

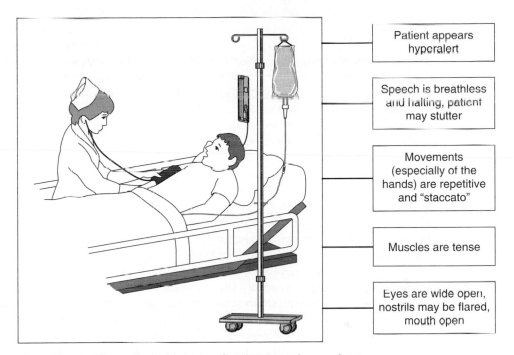

FIGURE 3.2   Nonverbal messages of patient's anxiety and worry.

surement instruments assess both nonverbal **decoding** (that is, the ability to understand what patients are communicating with their nonverbal expressions) and **encoding** (the ability to control emotional expressions via nonverbal cues). In several studies, researchers have assessed the ability of physicians to understand the emotion conveyed in others' facial expressions, body movements, and tone of voice. They have also examined the ability of these physicians to express emotion intentionally through their own nonverbal cues of facial expression, body movement, and voice tone. In several studies, a sample of each physician's patients was interviewed about their satisfaction with the physician's bedside manner. In one study, patients' cooperation in returning for scheduled medical visits in the clinic was also examined. It was found that the physicians who scored high on the tests of nonverbal communication skill received significantly higher evaluations and greater cooperation from their patients than did those who scored low (DiMatteo et al., 1986; DiMatteo et al., 1980).

Dissecting Nonverbal Cues

Considerable research has been conducted on nonverbal communication in medical as well as other settings. Let us address some of the individual components of nonverbal communication and examine the implications that these research findings have for patient care.

Touch

Possibly more than any other aspect of nonverbal communication, **touch** is believed to serve the goal of practitioner-patient rapport. The idea of an association between healing and touch is ancient (Older, 1984). Touch can be extremely soothing to ill patients and can communicate reassurance, comfort, and caring (Blondis & Jackson, 1977; Montagu, 1978). The pressure of touch in the form of massage usually induces relaxation accompanied by a decrease in physiological arousal and stress hormones (Field, 1996). It should be noted, however, that touch can communicate some other not so helpful messages as well. As with all metacommunication, the precise meaning of a touch cannot be known, but depends upon the context (particularly the emotional context) in which the touch takes place. Suppose that a patient is on his way to surgery. His kind, empathic surgeon with whom he has rapport stands next to him as he is about to be wheeled into the operating room. The surgeon puts her hand on the patient's arm, squeezes it firmly, and says: "Are you ready to do this together? I'm ready if you are. . . ." The therapeutic alliance is forged. Another patient, however, meets with her doctor and tries to express concern that she does not understand some things about her intended surgery. That physician interrupts her statements of concern, puts her hand on the patient's arm and squeezes it gently, saying: "My dear, my dear. Why do you ask so many questions? You don't need to bother yourself about these things. I'm the doctor." This latter touch occurs in a very different (verbal) context than the former.

Touch can be a powerful indicator of caring, concern, and solidarity; or it can simply be an indicator of power (Henley, 1977). Health professionals touch patients, but patients typically do not touch health professionals. In fact, were you to reach out and touch your doctor first, before he or she touched you, you might experience an awkward interpersonal moment. The meaning of the touch would not be as clear as if the physician initiated it. People who initiate touching of others (particularly if the touch is not reciprocated) are often viewed as more powerful, dominant, and assertive (Goldberg & Katz, 1990; Major & Heslin, 1982). As we have seen, this is often the situation for doctors and patients. Therefore, the assumption that touching patients is always good is an incorrect one. Like all nonverbal cues, touch depends upon context. One study, for example, analyzed the videotapes of thirty-four first-time visits between patients and their new family physicians (Larsen & Smith, 1981). Only the initial interview portion of the visit was studied. Trained judges recorded, among other things, whether and how much the physician touched the patient. After the visit, each patient filled out a questionnaire regarding his or her satisfaction with the visit. The surprising finding was that, the more patients were touched by their physicians, the less satisfied they were with the visit. The authors suggested that because these were initial interviews, touching may have been interpreted by patients not as supportive but rather as aggressive and as an indication of power. It seems that it was necessary for the physicians to have first established rapport with their patients before touching them. A further finding was that patients who were touched more were found to understand less of what their physicians told them—perhaps because being touched during the initial medical visit was distracting or disconcerting to them.

Eye Contact

Eye contact can be a very powerful nonverbal cue that can intensify the emotion present in a given situation. A pleasant interaction in which the health professional is warm and understanding with a patient is likely to be experienced as even more positive when accompanied by eye contact (La Crosse, 1975). An upsetting or threatening situation, on the other hand, will be experienced as even more negative when accompanied by eye contact (Ellsworth et al., 1978). If a patient is having a hostile interchange with a medical professional, chances are good that things will be worse if the health professional stares him or her straight in the eye than if the health professional fails to make eye contact. Of course, excessive, almost constant staring at a patient can have a very negative interpersonal effect no matter what the context (Friedman, 1982; Larsen & Smith, 1981). In fact, physicians judged to have a high degree of rapport with their patients have been found to engage in only moderate eye contact, less than that exhibited by some physicians rated as having low rapport with their patients (Harrigan et al., 1985). Excessive staring is not usually the problem in medical interactions, however. Typically, health professionals fail to maintain enough eye contact. They look at the chart or at the patient's body more than at the patient's face. They tend to avoid the intimacy and immediacy that eye contact represents (Harrigan et al., 1985). When doctors do monitor their patients through gaze, they are generally better able to identify their patients' level of anxiety and distress (Bensing et al., 1995). This, of course, can provide the doctor with a distinct advantage as she or he attempts to engage the patient in the most effective discourse.

How much eye contact is just right is not precisely clear. Health professionals must gauge the effects of their behavior on patients, in an effort to determine what contributes to, and what detracts from, good bedside manner. The patient's personality characteristics, cultural background, gender, and level of emotional arousal are all factors that can influence receptivity to eye contact (Davidhizar, 1992). One thing is clear, however. Eye contact is a very powerful means of metacommunication. Used wisely, it can significantly enhance the positive emotional impact of the therapeutic relationship and thus aid in promoting the well-being of the patient.

Facial Expression

Facial expressions can tell a great deal about a person, particularly his or her physical and emotional state (Izard, 1977). Fatigue may appear as a long-lasting expression, distrust as a fleeting one. But what makes facial expressions intriguing and sometimes difficult to pin down is that, more than any other nonverbal cue, they can be controlled (Ekman & Friesen, 1974). Research demonstrates that when physicians can control their facial expressions of emotion and convey what they intend, their patients are quite satisfied with the medical care they receive. Further, medical professionals who can understand the meaning of others' facial expressions of emotion have been found in research to be able to elicit greater satisfaction and cooperation with treatment (DiMatteo et al., 1986; DiMatteo et al., 1980).

Tone of Voice

How a physician or a patient says something is perhaps as important as *what* is said. Variations in pitch, loudness, emphasis, and the pacing of speech, as well as stutters and pauses, convey information about emotional states. These are called **extralinguistic cues**—language-related cues that are outside the verbal content of what is said. While we cannot always identify the precise extralinguistic cues we have heard, we rarely miss the emotional impact of these cues when we are spoken to. We know, for example, when we have heard an angry, hostile communication, although we might not identify it as faster and louder than a kind, relaxed communication. We probably would not notice that the hostile message is the one having more vocal emphasis on the verbs.

Although patients may be unable to identify precisely what cues they have heard, the **voice tone** and the specific vocal quality of their medical practitioner does influence them. One study found that the anger perceived in a physician's voice when talking about alcoholics could be used to predict accurately their rate of failure when trying to get alcoholic patients to enter a treatment program (Milmoe et al., 1967). In another study, the degree of hostility judged to be in the voices of both physicians and patients reflected the discomfort and interpersonal difficulties that resulted when patients attempted to ask questions (Hall et al., 1981). Physicians' voice tone has also been linked to patients' ability to recall information (Ray & Ray, 1990). Thus, medical professionals can convey a great deal, good and bad, to their patients through their voice tone. They can also learn a lot about their patients' emotions by listening carefully to what is conveyed in their patients' voices.

Body Language

Body movements and postures (termed **body language**) can convey a considerable amount of information about an individual's emotional state. This is true particularly because body cues are typically the least controlled of all nonverbal messages. People may monitor their facial expressions, but typically do not (or cannot) monitor their body movements very well. Emotional expressions have been found in research to "leak" unintentionally through the body movement channel. Thus, a patient's anxiety, depression, and distress, or conversely his or her energy and positivity, may best be learned by watching how the patient walks, moves about, changes position, and so on. A person's stride may reveal self-confidence and hopefulness about the outcomes of the medical condition. Fidgeting and self-touching (such as pulling on earlobes, or playing with hair) may signify anxiety and the individual's unsureness about what she or he is stating verbally. These behaviors may even signal efforts to deceive (Friedman et al., 1985; Riggio & Friedman, 1983).

Despite the fact that we do not know exactly what every nonverbal cue means, certain body movements and postures do convey certain important messages. Particular gestures of the health professional tend to be perceived positively by patients. For example, while closed arm positions tend to communicate coldness and rejection, open arm positions convey warmth and immediacy (Spiegel & Machotka, 1974). Physicians judged to have a high degree of rapport with their patients were found in one study to

Nonverbal cues of depression include a slumped posture and sad facial expression.

exhibit more open arm and leg positions, greater forward lean, and more orientation of their bodies toward the patient than physicians judged to have a low degree of rapport. High-rapport physicians also sat closer to their patients (Harrigan et al., 1985). Patients have been found to be most satisfied with a physician who orients his or her body in the patient's direction and who leans forward toward the patient instead of backward and away from the patient (Larsen & Smith, 1981). Similarly, in research on psychotherapists, head nods, hand gestures, and a slight forward lean when talking with clients has been found to increase clients' perceptions of the warmth and friendliness of their therapists (La Crosse, 1975).

In the mid-1960s, psychologists began studying what came to be known as "interactional synchrony," which describes the coordinated interplay between the nonverbal behaviors of two or more interactants (Bernieri & Rosenthal, 1991; Condon & Ogston, 1967). This synchrony or coordination seems to be one of the important components of rapport, which we will address in more detail a little later in this chapter (Tickle-Degnen & Rosenthal, 1990). When the interaction between a doctor and patient is "in sync," they respond to each other in a way that might almost resemble a rehearsed script. They pause at appropriate times to allow the other to speak, they nod at one another, their gestures flow smoothly, and their postures mesh. Synchronized interactions feel comfortable and harmonious for the participants; they are not awkward or difficult (Koss & Rosenthal, 1997).

Are some nonverbal cues more important than others in the medical therapeutic setting? One study examined the combined impact of many nonverbal cues by medical professionals in order to determine which were the most important in conveying an overall positive impression in interaction with a patient (Harrigan et al., 1985). In this study, nine family practice residents were videotaped during the interview portion of medical visits with two of their patients. The initial minute of the interview and a minute chosen randomly from the midportion of the interview were selected from each of the two interviews for each doctor. The physicians were evaluated by independent judges (psychiatric nurses) on a global measure of their rapport with the patient. Several nonverbal cues were found to differentially affect judgments of rapport. Cues of bodily alignment (particularly body orientation and arm and leg position) tended to be more important in influencing the ratings than did specific nonverbal actions such as smiles, gestures, and nods, although the latter were still important. Body orientation toward the patient, and open arm and leg positions tended to have a very strong effect on ratings of rapport. These conveyed immediacy and a strong emotional connection particularly when coupled with forward lean and mutual gaze (Mehrabian, 1972).

Table 3.1 summarizes nonverbal cues, and Box 3.3 examines the role of cultural variation in use and interpretation of nonverbal cues in doctor-patient interaction.

TABLE 3.1   Nonverbal Cues

Touch:	A powerful nonverbal cue that can contribute positively to the physician-patient relationship but that can vary in meaning depending upon context.
Eye contact:	Its use can intensify the emotion present in a given situation; typically health professionals fail to maintain enough eye contact with their patients.
Facial expressions:	Their use can reveal a great deal about physical and emotional state; allow physicians to convey what they intend, resulting in patient satisfaction.
Tone of voice:	Variations in pitch, loudness, emphasis, and the pacing of speech, as well as stutters and pauses (which are extralinguistic cues or language-related cues outside the verbal content); provides clues to underlying affect.
Body movements and postures:	Typically the least controlled of all nonverbal messages; can convey a great deal about a person's emotional state.

BOX **3.3**

Across Cultures

We Aren't All Playing by the Same Rules!

Even if a healthcare practitioner and a patient are both doing their best to communicate effectively with one another, cultural differences in nonverbal expressions can sabotage their efforts. One of the broadest cultural categorizations, first described over thirty years ago, is that of "contact" versus "noncontact" (Watson, 1970). People from contact cultures (for example, Latin Americans, Southern Europeans, and Arabs) tend to interact closely, face each other directly, look into one another's eyes, touch each other often, and speak somewhat loudly. Conversely, those from noncontact cultures (such as Asians, Northern Europeans, and North Americans) tend to maintain more personal distance, look into each other's eyes less, rarely touch each other, and speak more softly.

You can imagine how a cultural mismatch of nonverbal styles might cause some problems in a medical encounter. Let's look at an example. George is from a noncontact culture and has been sick with a bad cold for over two weeks. He has been coughing a lot and is now feeling some chest pain when he takes a deep breath; he's worried that he might be developing pneumonia. George's physician, Dr. Zaera, is from a contact culture. When he enters the room he comes right up to George, puts his hand on George's shoulder, and asks how he is feeling. When Dr. Zaera stands close to ask him some questions, George feels uncomfortable and intimidated. George is seated on the examination table so he can't move away; in an effort to relieve the discomfort he feels from too much closeness, George lowers his eyes and does not meet those of his doctor. He answers Dr. Zaera's questions as thoroughly as he can, but he does so quietly. He tells Dr. Zaera that his chest hurts, but the statement seems to fall a little "flat" in comparison with the doctor's more flamboyant conversational style. Dr. Zaera assures George that he does not have pneumonia and writes down the name of a special tea and some over-the-counter expectorant cough syrup to loosen the congestion in George's chest. He encourages George to drink a lot of fluids and to rest, and Dr. Zaera ends the visit with a hearty handshake and another warm touch on the shoulder.

George leaves the office with a nagging suspicion that Dr. Zaera didn't really understand just how badly his chest hurts. He thinks that someday soon he should try to find a doctor who is easier to talk to and who is less "pushy." When he gets home, George decides that tea and cough medicine are not going to do him any good with this kind of pain! He tosses the paper into the wastebasket as he passes.

Clearly, something went wrong here. Dr. Zaera certainly cared about George and wanted to help him feel better. He was friendly and warm and probably thought he was doing all the right things to help George feel comfortable. George demonstrated conscientiousness by coming in to see the doctor and he stated his problem clearly. Nonetheless, he felt overpowered by his physician and didn't feel that the visit helped him to solve his health problem. Dr. Zaera's nonverbal behaviors intimidated George, who was unable to overcome his own nonverbal style in order to be more assertive. Dr. Zaera did not understand the nonverbal cues that indicated George's discomfort.

Situations like these are not uncommon. Healthcare practitioners in the United States may interact with people from many different cultural and ethnic backgrounds every day, and it is difficult enough to read nonverbal cues within one's own culture, let alone be sensitive to the nuances demonstrated by other groups. What makes things even more complex is that within a given culture, there can be subcultural variations. For example, even though Costa Ricans and Panamanians are both part of the Latin American group, Costa Ricans interact much more

(continued)

BOX **3.3**   (Continued)

closely, have more eye contact, and touch more than do Panamanians (Schuter, 1977). Sometimes, too, a cultural or subcultural group may demonstrate a mix of contact and noncontact characteristics (Halberstadt, 1985). For example, in one subculture it may be common to keep a lot of distance between individuals but this may be coupled with frequent instances of reaching out and touching others.

So, how does one know what nonverbal rules to play by? Does a lot of hand gesturing mean that people are angry and upset, or is it just their style? If people gesture very little, does it mean that they are in too much pain to move, or is this simply how they have learned to behave? If people gaze deeply into your eyes, are they suspicious of you and trying to see if you are lying, are they conveying concern and empathy, or might they be falling in love with you?

Certainly, healthcare professionals should be familiar with the norms of the cultural groups that they interact with often (Davidhizar, 1992). Familiarity and awareness do not assure success, however, because of subcultural variations and individual differences such as noted earlier. One effective way to foster good communication with people is to synchronize your responses to their responses, that is, by letting their nonverbal cues guide your own nonverbal displays (Bernieri & Rosenthal, 1991; Koss & Rosenthal, 1997). It is important, however, that this mirroring be as natural as possible. Understandably, people tend to become uncomfortable if they feel that someone is mimicking their behavior, or that they are being purposely manipulated (Manusov, 1993).

Communication of Emotion

As we saw above, nonverbal cues can operate alone to convey an emotion, or they can add subtle information to a verbal message. Nonverbal cues can show how each person feels about what he or she is saying, and these messages may or may not be under the person's conscious control. Physicians sometimes respond, behaviorally, in a more negative way to their sicker patients; and sicker patients also exhibit more negative behaviors than do healthier patients (Hall et al., 1995). Thus, a downward cycle may be started during the interaction that is ultimately harmful to both parties involved.

Nonverbal messages can be extremely powerful. As we noted before, when a physician appears to be worried as he or she relays test results to a patient, the patient is likely to have more anxiety, to recall less of what is said, and to be more alarmed (Shapiro et al., 1992). Entire medical interactions may be regulated by the nonverbal cues of one or more of the interactants. A practitioner may completely determine, with his or her own nonverbal cues, just how much information the patient is able to convey and the number and quality of questions the patient is able to ask. These cues may include the avoidance of eye contact, a frowning facial expression, and the orientation of his or her head away from the patient, focusing totally on the chart. The practitioner might also interrupt the patient and dominate the interaction with the amplitude (strength) of his or her voice. Of course, a practitioner can also convey supportive messages with nonverbal cues, as we noted above. Encouraging patients to voice their concerns and responding to these in an informative and supportive way can significantly decrease the anxiety of the patient (Hamilton et al., 1994).

Understanding patients' nonverbal communications can give a medical practitioner an important advantage in caring for patients. By recognizing cues of dissatisfaction and negative affect in the body language of a patient, a practitioner can become aware of problems that the patient has not articulated. These can then be dealt with and remedied before the patient leaves the relationship, fails to cooperate with treatment, or retaliates with malpractice litigation. There is growing evidence, then, that a practitioner's bedside manner consists partly of his or her ability to understand patients' metamessages and to convey metamessages that are supportive and beneficial to patients.

Bedside Manner

When patients do not feel understood, they are more likely to be dissatisfied with their medical care, to "doctor shop," and to be less adherent to their medical regimens. They are also more likely to bring about malpractice litigation (e.g., Frankel, 1995; Levinson et al., 1997). Understanding requires a certain level of emotional connection on the part of the listener, and it is such empathy that contributes greatly to good **bedside manner**. Bedside manner is a broad and informal term used to refer to a medical practitioner's interpersonal behavior toward patients; it typically refers to the physician's ability to instill trust and to respond to patients' emotional needs. Hippocrates wrote in the fourth century BC of the enormous power of bedside manner: "The patient, though conscious that his condition is perilous, may recover his health simply through his contentment with the goodness of the physician" (Hippocrates, 1923 translation). Bedside manner is viewed by some as a magical "special edge," "certain something," or even "the right chemistry." But while a large part of bedside manner involves being polite, too often in medical interactions politeness is dispensed with (Mayerson, 1976). Many medical professionals fail to exhibit the most rudimentary etiquette, such as introducing themselves, exchanging pleasant words, and looking at the patient as they talk to him or her (DiMatteo & DiNicola, 1982). As we will see, bedside manner is not something a person either has or does not; it requires attention, effort, and learning. Research shows that when medical educators emphasize bedside manner, somehow their students learn it (Seeman & Evans, 1961a, 1961b). On the other hand, when teachers consider bedside manner unimportant, that fact becomes quite clear to everyone around them. Insensitive, callous teachers turn out insensitive, callous apprentices (Klass, 1987a).

Many believe that good "bedside medicine" was once common and that it has largely fallen by the wayside as medicine has become dominated by technology. While this may be the case, the increasing incidence of long-term chronic illnesses is tending to move issues of communication and bedside manner into the forefront of medical practice. The importance of good bedside manner and the flow of nonverbal communication are being recognized as necessary elements of medical training and practice (e.g., Roter & Hall, 1992; Zinn, 1993). In the last ten years, considerable emphasis has been placed on patient-related psychosocial issues in the training of primary care doctors during their residency programs. In addition, during their practice years, more and more physicians are attending continuing education programs and seminars that teach the critical elements of interpersonal patient care through discussion, videotape analysis, and role-play. This interest on the part of the medical profession has provided psychologists with greater opportunities to collaborate with the medical care team in order to provide patients with more comprehensive healthcare (McDaniel, 1995). These issues provide a common ground for physicians and psychologists to till together (Matarazzo, 1994).

Current research in the field of health psychology has been focused on the phenomenon of bedside manner and its relationship to patient care outcomes. Many researchers have worked in conjunction with medical professionals to define precisely what bedside manner consists of and how it can be optimized. They have found that effective physician-patient communication and bedside manner most definitely can be taught (Langewitz et al., 1998; Mason et al., 1988; Smith et al., 1995). Let us examine some of that research now.

As we have seen, one important research method for studying medical practitioner-patient interactions involves the recording (video or audio) of the behaviors that actually occur in the medical interaction, the careful analysis of these behaviors, and the assessment of their effects on patient satisfaction with care. One review of the many studies using this approach examined various aspects of bedside manner and their effects on patient satisfaction and patient compliance with medical regimens (Hall et al., 1988). Patient satisfaction with medical care was found in this review to be higher when physicians provided more social conversation, more positive talk, and less negative talk; among the most important aspects of bedside manner were the specific positive and supportive nonverbal cues of the medical professionals.

Training doctors to be more effective communicators certainly can have an effect on the behaviors of both physicians and their patients. In one study, researchers found that doctors who took a brief training session in communication were better at eliciting active participation from their patients than were those who did not have the training. In this study, the trained physicians were more facilitative of communication with their patients as they asked more open-ended questions. Further, their patients used more positive talk and gave more information when compared to the untrained group of physicians and their patients. Furthermore, trained observers judged the trained physicians to be more interested and friendly and their patients to be more dominant, responsive, and friendly. Not surprisingly, these patients were also more positive and more satisfied with their care (Roter et al., 1998). Another study found that providing intensive training to residents on communicating and understanding patients led their patients to be more confident in them and to have a higher level of satisfaction with their care (Smith et al., 1995).

Of course, at the very basis of the practitioner's bedside manner is his or her recognition of the importance of psychosocial as well as biological issues in treating a patient. The medical practitioner must overcome the purely biomedical view of the patient as a collection of parts needing an adjustment and approach the patient as someone whose feelings are worth understanding. In reality, however, less than half of the average medical visit is spent dealing at all with psychological or psychosocial issues related to illness and patient care (Cape, 1996; Greene & Adelman, 1996).

Empathy

The heart attack patient in room 507 was beginning to annoy the nurses. They complained about his aggressive behavior and his continual disregard of the medical recommendations to avoid strenuous exercise. They found him doing push-ups on the floor of his hospital room the day after his heart attack. They complained that he would pat or pinch them as they passed by him and that he harassed them with sexual innuendoes and invitations. Caitlin Peters, R.N., was not looking forward to meeting him. Yet, when she entered his room, the first thing she saw was the face of a very sad and very frightened man. He tried his usual antics with her at first, but she was not put off. She continued to look into his eyes. While she gave him his medications and checked his vital signs, she maintained a quiet, intense focus on the person in the bed before her.

Finally, he began to talk to her about what he felt. He was devastated by the recognition of his own mortality, fearful of the loss of his sexual potency, and terrified of being an invalid. Caitlin was not afraid of his feelings. She knew that by being there, by understanding him and not pulling away, she could reduce some of the tremendous loneliness he felt. And she would gain something critically important as well. She would have the opportunity to begin facing some of her own fears of death and disability, to connect briefly to another human being, and to feel that she had made a difference in someone's life.

In the past few decades, tremendous advances in medical and surgical techniques have saved countless lives and have vastly improved the quality of living for victims of illness and injury. For example, people who, ten years ago, would have died or been severely disabled by their heart attacks today often survive to lead healthy and productive lives. Many victims of serious accidents can now be restored to high levels of functioning by well-trained trauma specialists using the latest advances in lifesaving technologies. Patients who develop chronic illnesses are now spared many devastating consequences because of newly developed medications and carefully designed medical treatment regimens.

These advances have not, however, eliminated the complications of emotional distress that typically accompany illness and injury. In fact, sophisticated medical technology has created a common ground of concern for health psychologists and other healthcare professionals (Matarazzo, 1994). As we will examine in detail in Chapter 11, serious illness and bodily injury can cause severe emotional responses that patients may be unprepared to handle. Pleasures and life-enhancing activities may be lost. Caught in a web of pain, disappointment, threat, and confusion, most patients feel anger, profound sadness, and a host of other distressing emotions. They may vacillate between feelings of dependency and rebelliousness or between disruptive behavior and withdrawal (Moos & Tsu, 1977). Fears may even surface among some patients who are simply undergoing medical care that is quite routine. Patients typically react to simple medical and surgical problems with at least some degree of emotional upset. Routine care for well-controlled hypertension or a simple yearly physical exam, for example, can unearth a patient's fear that a serious condition will be discovered. The medical setting (uniforms, equipment, the smell of antiseptics) may trigger feelings of threat to one's body image, and emphasize one's sense of physical vulnerability. Fear and anxiety can overwhelm a patient who dreads pain and disfigurement. These feelings may significantly strain his or her emotional controls. Like Dena, whom we met at the beginning of this chapter, a patient may feel confused and disoriented, as if "falling to pieces."

Understanding what patients are feeling is the first step in helping them to cope emotionally with illness. But, to fully understand every aspect of what a patient feels about being ill, a medical professional would have to have experienced precisely what the patient is going through. The medical professional would have to have faced the same physical pain, emotional distress, and uncertainty as the patient. This is impossible, of course, since each patient faces a unique situation with a unique set of personal circumstances. Thus, the medical professional attempts to grasp the full meaning of the patient's experience through the process of empathy.

Empathy is a central concept in the fields of psychology, psychotherapy, and medical communication (Cormier et al., 1984; Goldstein, 1980; Northouse & Northouse, 1985). The pioneering work of the psychologist Carl Rogers best describes its meaning (1951, 1957). Although he conceptualized empathy primarily in terms of the psychotherapeutic relationship, Rogers's definition can apply easily to the medical professional-patient relationship as well. According to Rogers, empathy is a process that involves being sensitive to another individual's changing feelings and "connecting" emotionally to that other person. Empathy involves a process of "living for a time in the other person's life," entering his or her private perceptual world, and seeing events through his or her eyes. Empathy involves avoiding *judgments* about what the other is feeling and instead trying to fully *understand* the feelings from the person's perspective. Health professionals witness countless cues to a patient's emotional experience. These cues are found in what the patient says and how he or she says it, as well as in the patient's actions and expressions. Empathy involves correctly perceiving what a patient is conveying through both verbal and nonverbal cues and responding in a manner that suggests understanding. It also involves behaviors that make patients feel comfortable and valued (Colliver et al., 1998). This task of integrating the patient's life experiences with his or her presenting problems is both rewarding and challenging to physicians (Engel, 1997). A practitioner's accurate reading of the emotion displayed on the patient's face or expressed in the patient's voice, body movements, and other nonverbal cues is central to grasping what the individual is feeling and, hence, to empathizing with the patient (DiMatteo & Taranta, 1979). Thus, empathy is positively related to good doctor-patient communication skills (Feighny et al., 1995).

Empathy is not the same as sympathy. Sympathy is the concern, sorrow, or pity that one person may feel or show for another. But ". . . Empathy is an attempt to feel with another person, to understand the other's feelings from the other's point of view. Empathy is the sharing of another's feelings and not the expression of one's own feelings" (Northouse & Northouse, 1985, p. 31). Thus, in empathy, the focus is on the client with the problem, and not on the listener. "Empathy is not denial, avoidance, false optimism, obfuscation of the issues by clever professional jargon, nor inappropriate cheering. An empathic therapeutic bond, on the contrary, requires contact, an accurate description and sharing of knowledge, . . . and the creation of a safe environment to share inner doubts" (Bertman & Krant, 1977, p. 643). The necessity of focusing solely on the experience of the patient requires subverting the experience and feelings of the health professional. In the therapeutic interaction, only one individual's emotional needs can be dealt with at a given time. The goal of the medical practitioner-patient relationship is for the former to care for the latter, not vice versa. In the most effective of therapeutic interactions, the health professional's feelings can be expressed *only* if doing so is in the best interest of the patient.

Developing Empathy

People vary widely in their skills of understanding and expressing nonverbal cues as well as in their sensitivity to the feelings of other people. Because empathy is so important in the care of patients, medical practitioners whose skills are lacking can (and should) develop their capacity for empathic communication with patients (Feighny et al., 1995). This development requires effort and discipline on three important dimensions (Bertman & Krant, 1977). The **cognitive component of empathy** requires the professional to carefully observe patient behavior and to know the meaning of what is observed. Empathy depends upon knowing (intellectually, at least) what constitutes the physical experience of a particular illness or injury and what its psychological effects might be on the patient. Important facts (such as in Chapter 11) about the psychological realities of illness are available from the field of health psychology. These include the effects of being faced with the crisis of illness on patients' thoughts, emotions, and behaviors. The **affective component of empathy** involves, as described above, being sensitive to the patient's feelings and listening to what the patient is saying about those feelings in words, in gestures, and in actions. The affective component of empathy involves the health professional privately attempting to relate his or her perception of the patient's emotions to his or her own emotional experience and, in doing so, trying to understand what the patient is feeling. Finally, the **communicative component of empathy** focuses on conveying to the patient that he or she is understood, and that the health professional knows the facts about what the patient is experiencing and perceives accurately what the patient is currently feeling. Empathy requires that the health professional somehow communicates back to the patient that his or her emotional experience is taken seriously.

The Outcomes of Empathy

A medical practitioner's empathy for a patient's emotional state can have some important implications for the care and treatment of that patient. First, the accuracy of diagnosis can sometimes be enhanced when the medical practitioner is aware of and understands the emotional, as well as the physical, state of the patient. For example, a patient who experiences rapid pulse and breathing, sweating, and general agitation might be experiencing severe anxiety or panic, may have hyperthyroidism (an overactive thyroid gland), or may have a prolapse of the mitral valve of the heart. The practitioner who is aware of the true (rather than just the externally apparent) emotional state of the patient will be able to distinguish between a physical and an emotional explanation for the presenting problem. At least he or she will know which possibility to pursue first. Taking into account the patient's true feelings will significantly enhance the accuracy of diagnosis.

Second, empathy can enhance the process of medical treatment. Studies show that when medical practitioners are empathic, their patients experience less distress (e.g., Olson & Hanchett, 1997). Consider the patient who has had a heart attack. Panic and feelings of terror can be extremely dangerous for this patient. Research has demonstrated that frightening, upsetting, or negative emotional situations can have a very disturbing effect on cardiac rhythms and the electrical impulses in the hearts of cardiac patients (Lynch et al., 1974). Yet, typical emergency care from home to hospital room attends very little to calming the patient and helping him or her to feel secure and emotionally at ease. Instead, practitioners hurry about and treat the patient impersonally rather than as a thinking, feeling human being. The patient is not in control of what is done to him or her (Cousins, 1983). Obviously, it is always good medicine for practitioners to attend to the patient's emotions as well as to his or her physical condition. Calming the patient with sensitivity and understanding may, in this case, actually save his or her life.

Third, when patients feel understood by their medical practitioners, they are also more likely to follow treatment recommendations (Stewart, 1995). When given the opportunity to express their emotional needs and concerns, patients have more trust that their practitioners will act in their best interests. They feel that their real concerns have been addressed and that they have contributed to the decisions made about their care. In fact, the medical practitioner's ability to empathize with patients and to understand their concerns is a strong determinant of patients' satisfaction with care and their willingness to return to the practitioner in the future (Doyle & Ware, 1977; Sato et al., 1995). On the other hand, studies show that patients who are not satisfied with the interpersonal aspects of the care they receive from their practitioners engage in "doctor-shopping" until they find a doctor they feel cares about them (DiMatteo & DiNicola, 1982; Sato et al., 1995). Of course, an additional incentive to the medical practitioner in these days of oversupply and increasing competition among medical professionals is that greater patient satisfaction often translates into greater popularity among patients, more referrals, and a more successful and lucrative practice.

Finally, when patients are satisfied with the emotional care provided by their medical professionals, they are less likely to bring malpractice suits when they are dissatisfied with the outcome of their treatment. A medical professional who has empathy for a patient is able to explore the patient's feelings of disappointment at a poor outcome and work with the patient to find a solution that is mutually acceptable. Research shows that patients often become angry when treatments fail, even if they knew ahead of time the risks that accompanied them. If their medical professionals are cold and rejecting toward them, patients tend to express their anger through a third party, the malpractice attorney (Vaccarino, 1977). This is not to suggest that **malpractice**, the negligent practice of medicine, does not occur or is only in the mind of an emotionally distressed patient. Things do sometimes go wrong, and medical professionals do make mistakes. But research shows that medical professionals who are sued by their patients tend to be those who are unwilling to communicate openly and to work out a mutually satisfactory solution (Frankel, 1995). Instead, they tend to be emotionally or even physically "unavailable," and yet send their bill as usual (Levinson et al., 1997; Vaccarino, 1977). On the other hand, medical practitioners who have empathy for their patients' feelings are willing and able to work constructively with them to rectify what went wrong and to compensate them for their losses while avoiding litigation.

Empathy and Practitioner-Patient Rapport

Rapport, a term that is used in several places in this chapter and throughout this book, is central to understanding the medical practitioner-patient relationship. The term rapport, depending on how it is used, may be vague or it may be precise (Hall et al., 1995). A vague "sensitizing definition" of rapport is a rather abstract characterization, something along the lines of "a good relationship." A "conceptual definition" (as might be used by a researcher) is more specific and describes a relationship characterized by mutual trust and emotional affinity, or liking (Snipe, 1979). The word "mutual" suggests that both practitioner and patient respect each other and meet on the common ground of their desire to achieve the patient's health. Psychologists Linda Tickle-Degnen and Robert Rosenthal (1990) believe that rapport is made up conceptually of three different components. One of these we have already discussed: coordination. Coordination refers to the synchrony of the interactants' behaviors. The other two components are positivity (feelings and behaviors that are warm and positive) and mutual attentiveness (each interactant paying attention to what the other is saying and doing).

The research on rapport to date reveals that health psychologists sometimes vary in their use of the term when it comes to its "operational definition" (the definition that describes the way in which rapport will be measured in a particular study). In one study, for example, researchers had ten female psychiatric social workers evaluate the interpersonal style of nine family practice residents during videotaped interactions with their patients (Harrigan et al., 1985). They rated the physicians' behavior—those who were rated as most accepting, open, active, and pleasant, and highest on closeness,

Rapport in an interaction has three components: behavioral synchrony, positivity, and mutual attentiveness.

positivity, leniency, calmness, and friendliness were identified as the "high rapport" physicians. Other researchers have identified as high in rapport those physicians who were liked most by their patients, that is, who received high scores on measures of patient satisfaction (DiMatteo & Taranta, 1979). Although these studies varied in their methods, it is clear that rapport consistently emerges as a very important factor in effective practitioner-patient communication (DiMatteo, 1993; Stabler, 1993).

Maintaining Optimism and the Will to Live

Another important aspect of a practitioner's bedside manner involves fostering patients' **optimism** and the will to live (Cousins, 1976). Optimism is defined as the tendency to see things in a positive light and to expect positive outcomes. Although optimism is a rather stable and traitlike characteristic (that is, some people are naturally more optimistic than others), practitioners can say and do things that give patients hope and help them to believe that they can achieve positive outcomes. A positive outcome is usually defined as better health, but if better health is not possible, a positive outcome can involve successfully coping with and adjusting to illness. A heart attack victim, for example, is likely to be strongly influenced by the expectations of medical practitioners for his or her recovery (Cousins, 1983). A woman who has had a mastectomy (surgical removal of the breast because of cancer) may initially be tremendously affected by the response of various health professionals to her appearance after her surgery (Berger & Bostwick, 1984). Patients' feelings of hope or despair can thus be heightened by the behavior of their medical professionals.

Medical professionals can strongly affect patients' expectations partly because patients typically have little experience with the illness conditions they are facing. They may not know the statistics for survival; they may be unaware of different possibilities for recovery. They turn to their medical professionals for clues about what to expect. These clues come in various forms, but almost always have an impact on patients. Practitioners' expectations can operate in the manner of a **self-fulfilling prophecy** (see Rosenthal, 1969). While positive expectations can spur patients on to work toward recovery, poor expectations can bring about poor outcomes. And, patients can be led by pronouncements of doom from their physicians to give up hope for their recovery.

The potential for medical practitioners to influence the psychological, and in turn the physical, state of patients has been demonstrated in research. One study found a significant increase in the sudden deaths of heart attack patients in the hospital during or immediately after ward rounds conducted by the medical staff (Jarvinen, 1955). Ward rounds are formal procedures in which patients are presented as cases before many doctors and other health professionals. The cases are discussed while patients are present, but they are typically unable to participate. Patients are examined while members of the healthcare team look on. Sudden death may have been precipitated in cardiac patients by ward rounds because the emotional distress experienced by patients had a dangerous, negative effect on their cardiac rhythms (Lynch et al., 1974).

As we have noted, many patients, particularly those in busy hospitals, desperately desire information about their medical conditions and treatments but cannot get it. Some try to gather clues even from irrelevant sources. For example, a patient may try to "read" clues about his or her condition from the facial expressions of the medical professionals who stand at the bedside. Or, the patient may conclude that there is some significance in the rate or manner in which the physician writes things down in the chart. Very often, patients misinterpret ambiguous statements or responses. For example, a physician might mention that the patient has malignant hypertension, which is high blood pressure that is progressively getting worse. The patient may assume that this term means he or she has cancer (which it does not) and may experience hopelessness and depression as a result.

Expectations can, on the other hand, contribute positively to a patient's condition. Studies have shown that providing individuals with concrete and objective information actually tends to reduce their anxiety and other negative emotional reactions (e.g., Clark, 1997; see also Rutter et al., 1996). Furthermore, "self-regulation theory" (which we will discuss in Chapter 6) proposes that providing concrete information facilitates coping by reducing the difference between an individual's expectations and his or her actual experience (Clark, 1997). That is, by providing patients with information on what they can expect about a particular experience, they will likely have less anxiety and cope better with the experience.

Perhaps the best known general expectation phenomenon in medicine is the placebo response. The **placebo** response is "a change in the body (or the body-mind unit) that occurs as the result of the symbolic significance which one attributes to an event or object in the healing environment" (Brody, 2000, p. 9). A placebo is something that has symbolic significance. It can be a pill, a touch, a word, and it can have a physiological as well as a psychological effect upon a person (Shapiro & Shapiro, 1997). The medical practitioner's expectations for a good outcome can also serve as a placebo in that these expectations can be transmitted to the patient and can serve to better the patient's physical state. Practitioners who are confident and reassuring and who have rapport with their patients and empathy for patients' feelings can bring about positive therapeutic effects. The practitioner's faith in the treatment and in the patient's response to it may foster more positive health outcomes in the patient.

The strength of positive expectations has been one of the primary forces motivating the success of medicine throughout its entire history. In the early days of medicine, patients were given dangerous substances such as arsenic tonics and they were subjected to treatments such as bloodletting and having holes drilled in their heads (Shapiro, 1960). Despite these barbaric treatments, patients often regained their health—primarily because of the strength of positive expectations and the therapeutic effect of the practitioner-patient relationship (DiMatteo & DiNicola, 1982). Likewise, in today's medicine, with its emphasis on high technology, the therapeutic effect of positive expectations is still of central importance to effective patient care.

Emotional Regression

Illness and injury cause many patients to regress. **Regression** is a term used by psychologists and psychiatrists to indicate that a person has reverted to aspects of a child-like, dependent role that is characteristic of an earlier stage in his or her development (Lederer, 1952; Nemiah, 1961). Patients often remember details of being ill or injured as children and may react as they did then, when they had few emotional resources with which to adjust to being ill. Since many medical care professionals tend to infantilize patients when they are caring for them, it is not surprising that many patients regress, sometimes to states of childishness and helplessness (Lorber, 1975).

Medical professionals see patients' pain, fear, anger, sadness, depression, anxiety, and terror of death. They are with patients when patients' emotions are taxed to the greatest degree. Medical professionals witness patients' failures and triumphs as they struggle to contend physically and emotionally with sometimes overwhelming difficulties. Because of patients' struggles, there is inherent in the medical professional-patient relationship an opportunity for intense closeness and emotional intimacy (Cousins, 1976, 1983).

Who Are the Best Communicators?

Empathy in medical professionals has been found to be related to a number of characteristics. For instance, younger physicians and those with fewer years in medical practice have been found to be more empathic than those who are older and have been practicing longer as physicians (Carmel & Glick, 1996). Whether this is simply a cohort effect or empathy actually does tend to be diminished over time is unclear. There is some evidence in the literature, however, that as medical students go through their training they lose some of their ability to relate to patients and to successfully elicit patients' psychosocial concerns (e.g., Helfer, 1970).

The following is a quote from an exceptional study of 100 routine medical visits (Hall et al., 1994): "Female physicians conducted longer visits, made more positive statements, made more partnership statements, asked more questions, made more back-channel responses, and smiled and nodded more" (p. 384). The researchers analyzed, in detail, the interactions of both male and female physicians with both male and female patients. The researchers were careful to study equal numbers of all four types of dyads. Overall, the best communication was observed in the female-female situations, and the worst occurred in the male-male dyads. Female physicians typically communicated in ways that were optimal for eliciting information from all of their patients; male physicians did this considerably less often. Women doctors, more often than men, actively encouraged their patients' responses, used back-channel communications (things like saying "uh-huh" while another person is talking) to indicate that they were listening and understanding, and made more partnership statements (collaborative statements using terms like "we" rather than "you"). Correspondingly, female patients were more talkative than were their male counterparts. Findings from other research are in agreement. For example, in one study, women physicians typically spent more time interacting with their patients than did men. They talked more, listened more, asked more questions, gave more information, and took more active steps to build a collaborative relationship (Roter et al., 1991). Female physicians have been found to be more empathic than male physicians when dealing with postpartum depression which is often experienced by women following the birth of a child (Lepper et al., 1994). Female medical students have been found to be more empathic than male medical students in several different domains (Kliszcz & Rembowski, 1998). Women physicians are also more likely to consider psychological issues in patient care (Weisman & Teitelbaum, 1985).

In terms of gender congruence in the physician-patient dyad (when physician and patient are of the same sex), some research shows that same sex interactions tend to be characterized by more effective communication and by stronger rapport than are opposite sex dyads (Weisman & Teitelbaum, 1985). Other research shows, however, that female-female medical care interactions exhibit the best communication and male-male interactions the worst (Hall et al., 1994). Gender congruence, of course, may be only one of the important factors in promoting communication, establishing rapport, and facilitating negotiation. While some research has found that patients may have a slightly greater liking for women physicians, overall, patients do not appear to have strong preferences for doctors of a specific gender.

It is important to remember, of course, that while female doctors are better communicators "on average" than males, it is *not* the case that every doctor who happens to be a woman is better in this regard than every doctor who happens to be a man. The communication skills of these two groups comprise what are called "overlapping distributions," which means that although the mean, or average, scores for the two groups are different from one another, there are many individuals in each group that fall well above or below their group mean and therefore could also fit, numerically, into the distribution of the alternative group. So, for example, a woman might score very low on communication skill—so low, in fact, that the measure of her skill is way out in the left tail of the distribution, which would not only put her far below the "average" female doctor, but far below the mean for males as well. Also, perhaps because of the rigors of training, female medical students have shown declines in empathy as they progress through medical school. In one study their empathy levels were found to be similar to those of male students by their last year of medical school (Kliszcz & Rembowski, 1998). Fortunately for patients and practitioners alike, there is a great deal of evidence to suggest that training in better communication does lead to improved interactions and outcomes (e.g., Langewitz et al., 1998). A variety of programs exist to teach practitioners to be better communicators, and these often result in higher levels of satisfaction for patients.

In this chapter, we examined briefly the typical frustrations and difficulties that patients face when they are ill. These are examined in further detail in Chapter 11, while here we focused on issues of communication. We also examined the practitioner-patient relationship, particularly the role of medical communication professionals in helping patients to deal with the emotional aspects of illness. We saw how important such help can be to a patient's emotional well-being. Also in this chapter, we examined how that understanding is conveyed through nonverbal cues and other aspects of meta-communication. And, finally, we discussed what it means to be empathic and the kinds of outcomes that practitioners can elicit with their verbal and their nonverbal communication. In the next chapter we will examine the frustrations and difficulties of being a medical practitioner. We will see how the stresses and pressures of delivering medical care can sometimes lead practitioners to be less than supportive in their treatment of patients. As we will see, medical professionals do not remain unaffected by their closeness to patients' experiences. They often feel personal emotional distress in response to what their patients are feeling. We will see how some health professionals are hurt by their own failed expectations and by a system of training that can be quite unresponsive to their needs as human beings.

Summary

1. Medical practitioners and patients interact in the medical context and affect each other. Physicians and patients agree that there is not enough time available to satisfy them. Because of their different perspectives, patients and physicians differ somewhat in what they consider a satisfactory encounter.

2. Several things can make the medical interview more effective.

   - Patients will be more accurate in their responses if they are helped to remember and if embarrassment is avoided. Interviewers sometimes inadvertently reinforce poor responses from patients in health interviews.
   - Medical jargon makes speech more efficient when it is used by people who understand it, but it impedes effective communication between medical practitioners and patients. Jargon confuses those who do not understand the meaning of the words; it also frustrates them and contributes to their dissatisfaction.
   - When patients do not understand what is wrong with them or what they are supposed to do about it, they are less able to take an active role in their own care.

3. Listening to patients is an important component of effective patient care. Practitioners who listen closely to what patients say are more likely to reach more accurate diagnoses and to make more appropriate treatment recommendations.

4. When physicians talk to patients, they often do not give very much information. Patients typically ask few questions. They generally fail to ask for clarifications and do not speak up to correct inaccuracies in their physicians' statements. Asking questions allows patients to be actively involved in their own medical care.

5. Patients forget a great deal of what they are told during medical visits.

   - Patients are better at remembering what they are told first and what they think is most important.
   - They have better recall when interacting with a doctor that they know well.

6. Metacommunication (communication about communication) can convey a lot of information between practitioners and their patients. Metacommunications come in all forms—from nonverbal cues such as smiling to behaviors such as failure to pay a bill.

   - Metamessages can be simple or complex, intentional or unintentional, and clear or confusing.

7. Patients are very sensitive to the nonverbal cues of their practitioners. Medical professionals who are able to control their nonverbal messages (and thereby

convey the meanings they intend) have patients who are more satisfied. Practitioners who can read the nonverbal cues of their patients are better able to respond to their patient needs.

8. Nonverbal cues include touch, eye contact, facial expression, tone of voice, and body language. Although each is important, body language cues somewhat more heavily influence interpersonal interactions than do other nonverbal cues.

9. Bedside manner involves the way in which a medical practitioner interacts with his or her patients. Good bedside manner combines skills of nonverbal encoding and decoding with empathy (the ability to take the perspective of another person).

   ■ Empathy is not the same as sympathy (pity or feeling sorry for). Because empathy requires the focus to be on the patient, empathic health professionals will express their own feelings only if this is in the patient's best interest.

   ■ People vary in their innate levels of empathy, but to some degree at least, empathy can be learned. Learning to be empathic requires attention to (a) the cognitive component, (b) the affective component, and (c) the communicative component.

   ■ When their practitioners express empathy for them, patients are less distressed, more adherent, more satisfied, and less likely to sue if something goes wrong.

10. The practitioner's ability to foster optimism and the will to live in patients is an important element of effective medical care. Empathy and communication skills among physicians vary with certain characteristics.

   ■ Younger physicians and those with fewer years in medical practice have been found to be more empathic.

   ■ Women (physicians, nurses, and medical students) have been shown to be more empathic, on average, than men. On average, female physicians spend more time with their patients, make more positive statements, ask more questions, smile more, listen more, and make more partnership-building statements.

   ■ Empathy, effective communication (verbal and nonverbal), and good bedside manner can all be increased with training and attention.

THINKING CRITICALLY

1. What kind of intervention would you design to teach patients to interact more effectively with their doctors? Would you vary the intervention for different patient groups (i.e., particular ethnic groups, people of certain ages, etc.)? Would it be very expensive?

2. What are some of the nonverbal cues that you have received from your doctor, dentist, or nurse? How did you interpret them? After reading this chapter, would you reevaluate any of your initial interpretations? Do

you think you have ever mistakenly sent the "wrong" nonverbal message to your healthcare providers?

3. What are some of the legal and ethical issues that healthcare professionals must keep in mind when using touch? How might these issues be different from those of a psychologist? What are some of the benefits of touch and cautions regarding it?

4. What do we know about the association between gender and effective communica-

tion? What can medical schools do to help both men and women become better communicators? What kinds of incentives for

communication might be placed in the health care delivery system itself?

GLOSSARY

Affective component of empathy: Component of empathy involving sensitivity to the patient's feelings and attention to the patient's words, gestures, and actions.

Bedside manner: A medical practitioner's behavior toward patients; typically refers to the ability to instill trust and to respond to patients' emotional needs.

Body language: Nonverbal cues that involve body movements and positions.

Cognitive component of empathy: A health professional's careful observation of patient behavior and knowledge of the meaning of what is observed.

Communicative component of empathy: Communicating back to a person that he or she is understood.

Decoding: Recognition and understanding of patient's nonverbal expressions.

Doctor-talk: High-sounding, formal, and sometimes frightening language used by physicians in their communication with patients.

Empathy: Being sensitive to another individual's changing feelings and "connecting" emotionally to that person; understanding another's private perceptions.

Encoding: The ability to control emotional expressions via nonverbal cues.

Extralinguistic cues: Cues apart from the spoken language, including pauses, stutters, sighs.

Eye contact: A potentially powerful nonverbal cue involving eye to eye gaze.

Facial expressions: Nonverbal cues exhibited on the face and easily controlled.

Incubation period: Time from exposure to disease to development of symptoms.

Malpractice: The negligent practice of medicine.

Medical professionals: Professionals who care for patients, including physicians, nurses, chiroprac-

tors, respiratory therapists, physicians' assistants, pharmacists, x-ray technicians, physical therapists, nurse practitioners, nurse midwives, phlebotomists, medical psychologists, medical social workers, and others.

Medspeak: Another term for medical jargon, or medical terms that patients do not understand.

Metacommunication: Communication about communication.

Negotiation: The action or process of arriving at the settlement of some matter through discussion and compromise.

Optimism: Tendency to see things as positive and to expect good outcomes.

Placebo response: A change in the body that results from the symbolic significance which one attributes to an event or object in the healing environment.

Rapport: Characteristic of a relationship with mutual trust and emotional affinity.

Regression: A term to indicate that a person has reverted to aspects of a childlike, dependent role characteristic of an earlier stage of development.

Self-fulfilling prophecy: Acting in a way that causes fulfillment of one's expectations, even if they are initially incorrect.

Socioemotional aspects of medical care: Components of treatment that deal with patients' emotions and with the social context of their illnesses.

Technical quality of medical care: The technical expertise of the medical practitioner in the realms of diagnosis and treatment.

Touch: A nonverbal cue that is believed to be very important in the practitioner-patient relationship. Touch can convey reassurance, comfort, and caring.

Voice tone: Character and emphasis of the voice in the communication of emotion.

4 Medical Professionals in Training and Practice

It was Rosa Sanchez's fourth year in medical school. On the first day of her new rotation in pulmonary medicine, she entered her patient's room, ready to examine him. But she was not at all prepared for what she saw.

The man propped up against the pillows in front of her could have been her own father-in-law; the resemblance was uncanny. She stopped dead in her tracks, then slowly began to cross the room. Her patient's damp hair rested on a slightly rumpled pillowcase and his eyelids fluttered in sleep. His skin was very swollen in appearance and he looked very uncomfortable. She crossed the room to sit beside him, but even from the doorway his labored breathing was apparent.

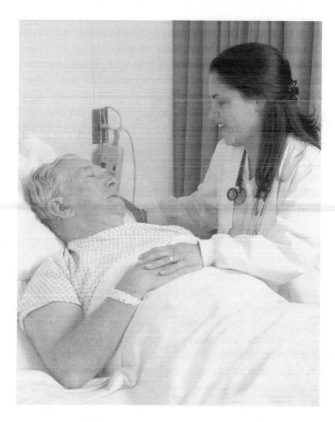

She knew that this man was suffering from both lung cancer and emphysema, and that he would probably not live more than a few more weeks. In a wave, all of the memories she held about her own father-in-law's slow and painful death from cancer came rushing back. She tried to distance herself emotionally as she read the chart and checked on her patient.

So intent was Rosa on Mr. Green that it was some time before she noticed Mrs. Green, huddled in a chair in the corner. She looked exhausted, and seemed numb with emotional pain. As Rosa listened to her patient's breathing with her stethoscope and reviewed the nurse's notes written in the chart, she could feel the eyes of his wife following her. "I need to draw some blood now," Rosa said, not really speaking to either of them. She took a needle and two glass tubes from the plastic case she had brought in with her, but as she reached out to Mr. Green, she heard a faint protest that ended in a sob, "Hasn't he been hurt enough? Can't you people just leave him alone? Please . . . he doesn't want any more of this." It was Mrs. Green, and Rosa immediately felt the competing emotions of nervousness and profound sympathy. She knew that if she did not draw the blood that had been requested, her intern would be upset with her. On the other hand, she knew how this woman must feel as she sat, day after day, watching her husband die an agonizing death. Rosa felt tears burning at the corners of her eyes, and she knew in that moment that she would not draw the blood. If necessary, she would argue with her intern. The patient's wishes, and those of his wife, had to be respected, and plenty of other people on the medical team would back her up. She sat down next to Mrs. Green and put her arm around her. "This is very hard for you, I know," she whispered, and she supported Mrs. Green while the woman sobbed.

In the process of providing patient care, medical professionals experience unusual and sometimes overwhelming pressures. They are expected to have a large body of knowledge and well-developed skills at their disposal and to be able to call upon these under the most extreme circumstances. The work that medical professionals do can have serious consequences. A mistake can be much more than inconvenient. A mistake can kill. And as they deal with some of the most difficult of human experiences, they are expected to maintain the highest levels of emotional control and to comfort and care for their patients.

In this chapter, we will examine both the physical and the psychological pressures inherent in the role of a medical professional. We will look closely at the process of medical and nursing training and consider how such training can affect those who undergo it. We will examine the many (and sometimes serious) consequences of the physical and emotional exhaustion of medical practitioners. These consequences include potential callousness toward their patients, as well as their own physical and emotional impairment. Next, we will probe the process of decision making by medical practitioners and discuss how their decisions can sometimes become biased and inaccurate. Some of most serious difficulties associated with medical decisions are discussed in Box 4.1. Finally, we will examine healthcare systems and the ways in which the systems themselves influence the type and quality of care that patients receive. In preparation for our analysis of the stresses of medical training, Box 4.2 presents a brief overview of the progression of medical school from the early years through residency.

BOX 4.1
Hot Topic

Iatrogenic Illness

Errors of judgment in patient care can be far more serious than errors of judgment in most other fields of endeavor. Drawing the wrong conclusion, making a hasty decision, or making an incorrect assumption about a missing piece of data can kill a patient or seriously jeopardize his or her well-being. Problems that result from errors on the part of medical professionals are called *iatrogenic* illnesses or conditions. Obviously, many of the medical miracles of today come with a certain degree of risk. With a clear idea of what that risk might be, the patient and physician together may decide that the benefits of intervention outweigh potential harm. Iatrogenic episodes present unplanned costs, however. The patient is harmed as the result of an error in diagnosis or treatment.

Up to 98,000 people per year die because of medical error. Many deaths result from problems in the medical system itself (see report at http://lab.nap.edu/catalog/9728.html). "Distressingly, much of the disease one encountered in the high-technology hospital setting was actually caused by previous treatment" (Hellerstein, 1986, p. 8). These problems are the result of (among other things) the erroneous interpretation of test results, inaccurate diagnoses, drug allergies, drug interaction effects, incorrect treatment choices, poor surgical techniques, and **nosocomial infections**. (Nosocomial infections are hospital-acquired infections, transmitted to the patient as a result of infractions in required sterile technique by hospital personnel.) Eugene Robin, M.D., professor of medicine at Stanford University, gives many examples of iatrogenic illness (1984). One case clearly illustrates the "cascade effect," in which one problem leads to another, bigger problem, which leads to another, bigger problem, and so on. A young man was to be operated on for an ingrown toenail. He entered the hospital and was given general anesthesia because he was apprehensive. While the anesthesia was being administered, his heart stopped. The surgeon had to open his chest, with no time for sterile technique, in order to start his heart. The patient survived, but developed a serious infection of the lining of the heart. Also, while being wheeled to his hospital room after surgery, his leg was broken in an elevator accident. The young man then developed a pulmonary embolus (blood clot in his lung) as a result of his leg fracture, the further surgery on his heart to drain the infection, and the high dose of antibiotics he was given intravenously. When the young man was administered an anticlotting drug to dissolve the blood clot, he had massive bleeding from his stomach ulcer. After several months, he was discharged from the hospital, although his ingrown toenail had never been fixed. Why did all these problems occur? The original error in treatment was to give the young man general anesthesia for the trivial surgical procedure required to fix his ingrown toenail.

How can a patient protect him- or herself from iatrogenic illness? Dr. Robin recommends finding a physician whose competence is high. The patient must also remain constantly vigilant and aware of decisions that are made for him or her. The patient must follow the logic of the medical reasoning done on his or her behalf, and must question decisions that do not make sense. The patient must also find out whether decisions about treatment will be affected by the results of diagnostic tests before submitting to those tests. If they will not, the tests should be declined. Before accepting any treatment decision, the patient must know the risks, the potential costs, and the potential benefits of the intervention. And, he or she must hope to be one of the lucky ones who is helped, rather than harmed, by modern medicine.

BOX 4.2

Hot Topic

The Facts about Medical Training

Training to be a physician is a long and arduous process. Almost from the first day of college, the future physician must put virtually all of his or her energies into preparing for medical school. The competition for acceptance is very intense, and although only the most accomplished students apply to medical school in the first place, most applicants are rejected. The student must earn a high grade point average, particularly in science courses, study for and take the demanding Medical College Admissions Test (MCAT), and undergo intensive and stressful application and interview procedures.

Once in medical school, students spend the first two years learning the basic sciences that form the foundation of medical practice. Among these are biochemistry, physiology, and anatomy. They are faced with an overwhelming amount of material to memorize, and sometimes they have difficulty seeing the relevance of it to their clinical work with patients. At this point, they begin to face the first signs of their limitations.

It is during the third and fourth years of medical school, however, that actual contact with patients begins. During these clinical years, the medical student serves as a clinical clerk on services such as surgery, internal medicine, obstetrics, or pediatrics. The medical student occupies the lowest position on the team and is required to carry out a considerable amount of patient care activity under the direction of a supervising (or attending) physician and several residents and interns. At this stage of their training, medical students are referred to as "doctor" in front of patients and must assume the professional role, even if they do not really know what they are doing. Fortunately, this is a time for them to learn, and medical students are supervised closely.

After graduation from medical school comes the internship, which is perhaps the most difficult year of all. An intern may spend as many as every third night in the hospital working all night. The other days may be filled with work, from 7 AM to 7 PM or later. The maintenance of life outside the hospital can be taxing, or impossible. The next several years of training, the residency years, bring somewhat shorter hours but increasing responsibility for the final decisions regarding patient care.

The Structural and Physical Pressures

Medical professionals are required to function effectively in all sorts of physically demanding situations and often under tremendous time pressures. They experience various physical stresses such as sleep deprivation, irregular schedules for meals, poor nutrition, and few opportunities for relaxation and exercise.

Time Pressures

From the first days of medical school and throughout their entire careers, physicians are plagued by severe time pressures. During the first two years of medical school, students are universally concerned that the amount of material they are required to learn is overwhelming and impossible to cover in the time available (Lloyd & Gartrell, 1983;

Murphy et al., 1984). Many students complain that they are "lectured to death," that their curriculum is poorly organized, and that they are given an overwhelming amount of unintegrated technical information (Awbrey, 1985). In the face of difficulties accessing and assimilating the information they need, most medical students feel tremendous pressure to succeed academically (Lloyd & Gartrell, 1983). During the clinical years of medical school and during the internship and residency, a physician in training is likely to spend more than 80 hours per week in patient care. This time is very often characterized by rushing from one patient care or charting activity to another. Interruptions are frequent, making concentrated, focused thought and effort sometimes impossible (Lurie et al., 1989; McCue, 1985). Time pressures and continuous interruptions also characterize the clinical aspects of nursing training (Heron, 1987).

Time pressure is also one of the most distressing aspects of medical practice (Elovainio & Kivimaki, 1998; Richardsen & Burke, 1991, 1993). A dedicated physician in full-time practice tends to work between 50 and 60 hours per week, and much of his or her "off" time at home (including suppertime, weekends, and the middle of the night) is interrupted by work-related telephone calls and pages (Linn et al., 1985; Rout, 1996). Among the medical specialties, neonatologists (who care for sick newborns and premature neonates) report particularly high levels of stress from caring for a (typically) large number of very sick young patients (Clarke et al., 1984). While practicing nurses, nurses in training, and technicians usually work closer to 40 hours per week, their work is strenuous and demanding and time shifts are often out of synchrony with the rest of the working world (say, 3 PM to 11 PM, or 11 PM to 7 AM), adding additional pressures to the course of everyday living.

Sleep Deprivation

It is not unusual for medical professionals, particularly physicians on call, to function with four or fewer hours of sleep in a 24-hour period. The few hours that they are able to sleep are often spent uncomfortably, on a cot in an "on call room." They are interrupted and oftentimes have considerable difficulty sleeping effectively, even when there is an opportunity to do so. Studies of how interns and residents spend their nights on call in the hospital show that even when they can spend a total of nearly five hours in bed trying to sleep, they have difficulty falling asleep and actually spend only about three and a half hours sleeping (Lurie et al., 1989; Richardson et al., 1996). Even this was not continuous sleep because they were often paged to answer questions about patient care. For the most part, length of their uninterrupted sleep tended to range from only 40 to 86 minutes, and no physician got to sleep longer than an hour and 26 minutes at a stretch! Several other studies have also documented the punishing sleep deprivation that occurs during clinical medical training (McCue, 1985; Sheehan et al., 1990; Richardson et al., 1996).

Although research has found that interns and residents (also called "house officers") can function after only a few hours of sleep, such functioning occurs at a relatively rudimentary level. They can walk, talk, access basic rote memory, and perform physical tasks that they know how to do very well. Studies have shown that eye-hand coordination and tasks requiring manual dexterity are not much affected by sleep loss

A poll of U.S. medical school deans suggested that they found the idea of medical student abuse almost ridiculous and that they believed abuse never occurred in their schools (Rosenberg & Silver, 1984). Surveys of present and former medical students paint an entirely different picture, however. In one study, 85 percent of a class of third-year medical students reported being "yelled at or shouted at" at least once in their medical training, and 73 percent being cursed or sworn at (Sheehan et al., 1990). Forty-four percent of these students also reported being placed at unnecessary medical risk by supervising physicians and nurses (for example, risking a needle stick through inexperience while doing a venipuncture on a patient with AIDS). Three-quarters of these students reported that these types of experiences had made them more cynical about medicine than they had ever been, and some said they would have chosen a different profession if they had known how pervasive mistreatment during their medical training would be. In another study, there were similar findings, and two-thirds of the physicians surveyed found the abuse to be of major importance and experienced it as very upsetting (Silver & Glicken, 1990). Another study recently found that 96 percent of medical students were mistreated at least once during their medical training, and the average was thirty-three incidents over the course of their schooling including being treated in a rude or hostile manner and shouted at by residents, interns, or nurses (Wolf, 1997). Studies from countries as diverse as Finland, Israel, and Canada all indicate similar patterns, including sexual harassment and discrimination, verbal abuse, emotional abuse such as humiliation and degrading slurs, and physical mistreatment and threats of bodily harm (Lebenthal et al., 1996; Margittai et al., 1996; Uhari et al., 1994). Mistreatment rates appear to be lower for those studying family medicine, and are highest for surgery and obstetrics-gynecology (Lebenthal et al., 1996; Richardson et al., 1997).

Why are physicians in training expected to endure sleep deprivation, poor nutrition, and other forms of physical and emotional hardship? Do such strains provide good preparation for being a physician, or are they simply part of a "hazing" process? Three basic categories of reasons are suggested to explain the punishing format of medical training (McCue, 1985). First, it is argued that the clinical years of medical school, internship, and residency serve as intensive training for the difficult events that physicians experience at all hours of day or night in practice. The physical punishment of internship and residency, it is believed, provides good preparation for being called upon in the middle of the night to perform a procedure or to make a decision. Unfortunately, studies of how nights on call are spent show that residents carry out little patient care and receive virtually no faculty instruction during the night. They spend most of their time writing in patients' charts and responding to nurses' questions (Lurie et al., 1989). Second, the brutal schedules of medical training represent a sort of hazing in which the young physician "proves" him- or herself. Surviving residency may take on a ritualistic meaning justifying a sense of superiority and separateness from other people (Gapen, 1980). A third explanation is that to learn a great deal about medicine, a resident needs to see and care for as many patients as possible and to see the progression of disease/illness from admission to discharge. Several medical educators argue, however, that the in-depth knowledge and care of fewer patients is more valuable to the learning of the treatment of disease than the superficial care of many patients (Kleinman, 1988; McCue, 1985). Of course, a somewhat more cynical fourth explanation is an economic one, which notes that interns and residents provide a very inexpensive labor force for the hospital. They work over 80 hours per week although they are paid a relatively low salary based on a 40-hour workweek.

The Emotional Challenges of Medicine

The challenges of medical training and practice are heavily emotional. These challenges affect not only physicians but other medical professionals as well. Many of the difficulties are so pervasive that they can damage health professionals' coping mechanisms, affect their attitudes toward patients, and severely limit their social support (McCue, 1982).

Personal and Family Relationships

One of the greatest difficulties of medical training, particularly internship and residency, is the social isolation it brings. By virtue of spending so much time working, those in clinical medical training have little or no free time, particularly quality time in which they are awake and feeling well, to interact with their loved ones and friends (Rout, 1996). They are usually isolated from the people who are closest to them as they spend their days and nights at the hospital. When they are home, they are often exhausted and regularly interrupted with patient-care needs. Medical marriages and family lives do suffer because of this (Rout, 1996). Yet, in order to cope with the emotional demands of medical practice, physicians need social support from family and friends; this support contributes more to their work satisfaction than do job-related factors. Family and friends are among the greatest contributors to overall life satisfaction (Linn et al., 1986). In response to the intellectual, physical, and emotional demands of patient care, however, many health professionals tend to withdraw from loved ones and retreat from family life (Fine, 1981). Emotional separation and withdrawal from the family occurs progressively, and eventually the willingness and ability to share feelings may be lost. This comes about as time spent with family is limited by late work hours, interruptions of family time by telephone calls and pages, and visits to hospitalized patients even on days off. The consequences of such withdrawal can be devastating (Linn et al., 1986; May & Revicki, 1985; Rout, 1996).

Why, then, do physicians allow the erosion of their family lives and peer relationships to occur? Why do they jeopardize the elements of their lives that bring them the greatest satisfaction and opportunity for successful coping? There are several reasons (McCue, 1982). First, there is peer pressure. A hardworking physician who surrenders a happy personal life to the care of his or her patients wins the respect of colleagues. Second, a physician who works all the time cannot be faulted for a poor patient outcome. After all, she or he did everything possible but the misfortune still occurred. Thus, working all the time tends to help a physician deal with the inevitable uncertainties of medical practice. Third, the physician may feel uncomfortable with economic prosperity and feel that only long hours and fatigue can justify it. Finally, a physician may gain greater ego gratification and a sense of self-importance in the process of patient care than in normal day-to-day life. At the hospital, where the pace is fast and exciting, the physician is in charge. At home, the physician is just another spouse or parent.

Dealing with Patients

Medicine is one of the few professions in which one must not only deal every day with people who are sick and not at their best, but also endure work that is physically demanding and entails tremendous responsibility for the lives of other people. Only a few professions come close. For example, air traffic controllers have considerable responsibility for the lives of others. Fire fighters and police officers risk their own lives in addition to having others depend upon them. These jobs, just as medicine, can take a heavy physical toll on those who perform them. Medical professionals face some unique emotional challenges, however. As we saw in the case of Rosa Sanchez, the medical professional's connection to patients is often intense and immediate. In their direct involvement with the details of patients' lives, medical professionals often experience one sad human situation after another. They witness suffering and they are expected to help alleviate it. They are reminded constantly that human life can involve tragedy, and they are reminded of their own mortality and that of their loved ones. For some physicians, these reminders occur daily (Klass, 1987a). In one study of neonatol-

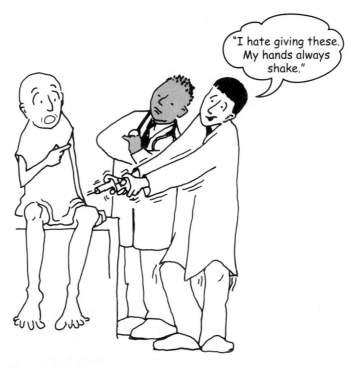

FIGURE 4.1   The challenge of caring for patients.

ogists, the greatest source of stress involved dealing every day with sick or dying patients. This stress was high enough to cause a significant number of these physicians to consider changing specialty (Clarke et al., 1984). Further, uncertainty about many things (e.g., the correctness of diagnoses, the efficacy of treatments) immerses medical practitioners in a day-to-day existence that can be unsettling at best (McCue, 1982, Wood, 1998).

Many students who select medicine as a career expect to be rewarded with satisfying interactions with patients (Krol et al., 1998; McCue, 1982), and such relationships are important sources of satisfaction for those in the medical profession (Linn et al., 1986; Shore & Franks, 1986). Satisfying encounters with patients can happen all too infrequently, however. Medical practitioners regularly encounter sick people who, because of the burdens of their illnesses, are often anxious, uncomfortable, distressed, and at their worst when dealing with their physicians (McCue, 1982). In addition, patients sometimes expect more comfort and understanding from their physicians than the physicians are able to provide (Kleinman, 1988; McCue, 1982). Even when a patient's expectations are unreasonable, a physician who fails to meet them may find him- or herself on the receiving end of the patient's anger. Feelings of inadequacy may follow.

Medical professionals typically have little recourse when they are faced with patients who are unpleasant to work with. Those who are noncompliant, demanding, clinging, and who consistently do not respond to treatment can be a major source of stress for physicians (Krakowski, 1982; McCue, 1982). Furthermore, clinical training typically does not provide medical practitioners with intellectual and emotional tools for dealing with patients' complex psychosocial problems or for dealing with their own complicated feelings toward these patients. Although doctors generally rate their overall medical training as good, they report that particularly in inpatient settings there are more deficiencies in training to meet psychosocial needs than in other areas (Eisenthal & Stoeckle, 1998). They report that their medical training provides them with a good knowledge base regarding the diagnosis and treatment of physical illness, but leaves them relatively unprepared to deal with the emotional and interpersonal aspects of medicine. In addition to being beneficial for patients, such training would likely benefit doctors because they would be better able to address psychosocial issues effectively and thus experience lower levels of personal distress related to the socioemotional aspects of medical care.

Sometimes, medical practitioners face emotional conflicts because the issues they face are highly symbolic for them and these issues represent other salient areas in their lives. When treating older patients, for example, medical professionals may be constantly reminded of the potential for sickness and infirmity in their own parents. Or, they may feel engulfed by the dependency of their patients and fear or feel ashamed of their own feelings of dependency. Some medical professionals may have difficulty setting limits on what patients can demand and thus allow patients' needs to overshadow their own lives (Hellerstein, 1986). If medical professionals have many unresolved emotional issues and symbolic conflicts in their own lives, these are less likely to be resolved in the stressful environment of medical care delivery than they would be in a less stressful environment. Medical training and practice do not provide a protective atmosphere for a vulnerable personality.

Failed Expectations about Medicine

Many medical professionals once dreamed of having power over life and death. Wave the magic wand of medical science and people's miserable lives are transformed. They become happy. That's what happened on the old TV shows like "Ben Casey," "Young Dr. Kildare," and "Marcus Welby, M.D.," and still does, although less often, on newer ones such as "E.R." Most patients have diseases that can be managed but not cured. ". . . [D]uring your training you have to come to terms, all by yourself, with the reality that most of what you do has little to do with curing. Sometimes you make people better. Often they get better by themselves. Sometimes you make them more comfortable while they get sicker. Sometimes you make them more miserable while they get sicker." (Klass, 1987a, p. 205). Unless they are comfortable providing other kinds of help and emotional support to their patients, physicians tend to feel helpless when faced with patients who do not get better (Kleinman, 1988). "There's a lot of hope that the hospital may be able to offer . . . hope for improved quality of life, longer life—but not cure. Get that word right out of your mind" (Klass, 1987a, p. 201). ". . . It's frustrating to want to cure, to carry with you the expectation that somehow you should be able to cure, and then not be able to cure. It can make you dislike particular diseases, and even particular patients" (p. 203).

Medical intervention probably only clearly improves a patient's health status about 10 percent of the time. In another 10 percent of cases, medical intervention actually renders the patient worse off than if he or she never sought care at all (Robin, 1984). In the rest of the cases, medical intervention might help some but not a lot because the condition is self-limiting (and would have gotten better on its own), or because the problem is caused by the patient's own health-damaging behaviors such as smoking, alcohol abuse, or obesity, which likely continue (DiMatteo & DiNicola, 1982). Sometimes the symptoms stem from emotional factors like depression or anxiety that, if recognized, can be treated medically in combination with psychological interventions. Even when medical practitioners can offer patients the means to achieve better health, a large percentage of patients reject the opportunity and are noncompliant with treatment regimens (DiMatteo & DiNicola, 1982).

The Loss of Idealism

Certainly, idealism exists, and service to patients in need is a goal of medical training. As we have seen so far, however, some aspects of this picture also involve physical and emotional brutality inflicted on those in training and a subsequent loss of their idealistic views of medical practice (Sheehan et al., 1990).

In the first two years of medical school, for example, the student's idealistic goals of learning everything there is to know in medicine are put aside in favor of a more realistic approach and a more self-protective one. Students typically discover what the faculty considers important and what will be covered on the tests. During the first year, students develop what sociologists Becker and Geer called "student culture" (1958). They work together and try to help one another with their studies; they support and console one another over the challenges. During the second year of medical school, contact with patients begins. Students are taught techniques of interviewing and how to do physical examinations. During the third and fourth years of medical school, as students become involved in day-to-day patient care, studies show that cynicism tends to overtake idealism and students tend to become less concerned than they once were about their patients as human beings. Emotional abuse by supervising personnel and other aspects of the physical and emotional stress of training cause as many as a third of medical students in the third year to consider dropping out of medicine and as many as three-fourths to state that they have become more cynical about academic life and the medical profession (Sheehan et al., 1990). One-fourth report that if they had known what it would be like they would have chosen a different profession.

Several other factors contribute to the development of cynicism. One way of achieving distance from the anxiety of patient care is the process of **intellectualization**, which involves a total focus of energies on the intellectual and technical aspects of patient care. It involves becoming totally absorbed in the technical aspects of the case and guarding against emotional vulnerability. Such an approach usually maximizes academic success, and, since there is little time to get to know patients as people, it is usually not difficult to view the patient as simply a "case." The values and expectations of doctors vary with work situation and even seem to affect their choice of specialty. One study of physicians over a twenty-five-year period found that individuals who, early on, expressed stronger social values were more likely to later be practicing in a "people-oriented" specialty such as general medicine, family medicine, or pediatrics than were their less socially focused peers who were more likely to have chosen a more "technology-oriented" specialty such as radiology or pathology (Hojat

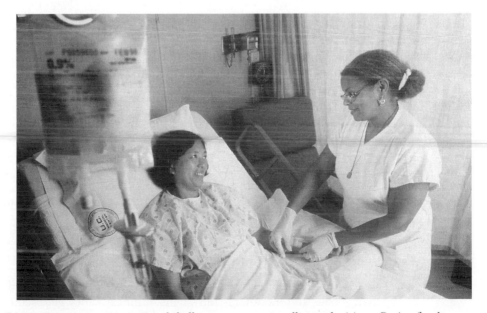

Patient care can present emotional challenges to nurses as well as to physicians. Caring for the psychosocial needs of patients can be particularly difficult in the hospital context.

et al., 1998). Thus, values may influence choice of specialty, and the experiences encountered through the practice of that specialty might in turn foster maintenance of those original guiding values.

Among nurses, expressions of idealism and optimism tend to vary with the work situations that the nurses find themselves in during nursing practice. Young nursing students often expect that they can influence their patients in many ways (for example, to change unhealthy habits or to cope with the distressing circumstances of their illnesses). However, the reality of caring for the psychosocial needs of patients often demonstrates that it is quite difficult to do. For example, despite what they may know about noncompliance, nurses may feel a great deal of frustration or helplessness when they realize that their patients are failing to follow dietary or other special requirements. Studies of nursing students have found that while idealism is usually high among those in the first year, optimism about how much they can help patients and contribute to their lives usually falls by the senior year when they become more disease-oriented and less patient-centered (Aiken, 1983). Nurses do tend to be taken for granted in the process of medical care. Until they are hospitalized, few people recognize what a major role nurses play; nurses regularly observe their hospitalized patients and are responsible for solving problems that arise, often without the consultation of a physician. Nurses dress wounds, administer intravenous medications, and assess patients' vital signs, among other essential patient care tasks. They talk to patients and listen to them, and they are usually instrumental in recognizing the role that patients' emotions play in their illnesses; nurses provide patients with the important information they need but may not get from their doctors (Heron, 1987). (The important role played by nurse-practitioners is examined in detail in Box 4.3.)

Can anything be done to restore some of the idealism that first drew these individuals to the field of medical care? Research suggests that the answer is "yes." While values and ideals are not typically included as part of the formal medical curriculum (Stern, 1998), one program, the Schweitzer Fellows Program, encourages participants to use their skills to complete a community-based project that meets a specific healthcare need. It is named for Albert Schweitzer, who believed strongly in transforming compassionate medical ideals into action. These projects not only benefit communities, but also help health professionals in training to interweave their career development with their ideals (Forrow & Wolf, 1998). Another effective way of helping medical students to nurture idealism and altruistic values is to expose them to the great needs in underdeveloped countries (Taylor, 1994). By serving overseas, students are able to do a tremendous service, and in turn they have the chance to see what compassion and altruism can do. They are often better able to relate to the healthcare needs of others when they return to their own country.

The Need to Control Emotions

Most medical professionals eventually become accustomed to the sight of blood, needles, human tissue, and the sounds and smells of illness. They get used to examining people and sometimes to cutting into people's bodies. They even get used to giving bad news. But not entirely. Many medical professionals are shaken considerably by the discovery that people they are caring for have become seriously or even terminally ill.

Research Close-up

How Does the Care Provided by Nurse Practitioners and Physicians Compare?

There have been times in history when nurses provided most of what medical care existed (Lindeman, 1984). Before the advent of male-dominated, scientific medicine, care consisted of supporting the patient's physical and emotional needs while his or her body healed itself. Nurses fulfilled this role very well. As medicine changed, however, the nursing profession was forced to take a back seat. One example of this shift of responsibility is the long-time attempt by physicians to prevent nurse-midwives from delivering babies both in and out of the hospital. It has been argued that although nurses were once independent, they have been forced into the role of helpers to physicians. This may be due, of course, to the fact that over 90 percent of nurses in the United States are women, and medicine has been, and to some extent still is, a male-dominated profession.

As medical care gets more and more expensive, however, payers of such care have looked for alternatives to traditional care. One such alternative is to have patients cared for by a nurse practitioner (NP) instead of by a medical doctor (MD). An NP is a nurse with more extensive training than basic nursing education. He or she is more autonomous and can diagnose and treat patients and even write prescriptions. NPs and MDs are trained from somewhat different perspectives and traditions, the former being more holistic in nature. They both have the ability to provide some of the same types of care, and so we might ask whether patients achieve the same outcomes following care from each professional. Are patients who are seen by NPs more or less satisfied with their care than patients see by MDs? Do patients achieve better health out-

comes when seen by an NP or by an MD? Who uses more subsequent healthcare, the patient seen by an NP or the patient seen by an MD?

In an experimental trial, with the goal of addressing these questions, patients were randomly assigned to receive follow-up and ongoing care from either a nurse practitioner or a medical doctor (Mundinger et al., 2000). These patients were initially seen in an emergency or urgent care clinic and had no regular source of care. Many of them did not have health insurance. Six months following their initial care, these patients were followed up and interviewed about their satisfaction, health status, and healthcare utilization. At one year following their initial care, their utilization was also assessed.

The care provided by the NPs and the MDs was found to be quite comparable. Results were very much the same in the two groups of patients in terms of their health status and satisfaction at six months and their healthcare utilization at six months and one year after the initial appointment. Only two differences were found. Those hypertensive patients who were seen by an NP achieved lower diastolic blood pressure (a better health outcome) than did those who were seen by an MD. And at the six-month interview, patients who were seen by an MD rated their provider higher on "provider attributes," one of the four measures of satisfaction, than did those seen by an NP. This study suggests that in a large sample of randomly assigned patients, outcomes of care by NPs and MDs were highly comparable. Perhaps the less expensive route to receiving care from a NP is a good alternative for those conditions that NPs are qualified to treat.

Although most health professionals learn to cope with human suffering and tragedy, they do not become immune to these experiences. Suffering can engender strong feelings in medical professionals. They are sometimes profoundly affected by what happens to their patients (McCue, 1982).

Janet Caron, M.D., was in her family practice office on Tuesday morning when the blood test results arrived from the laboratory. She flipped through them quickly, intending to analyze each one in detail later in the day when she reviewed her patients' charts. One finding caught her eye. She bit her lower lip. Ann Smith's HIV test was positive. Dr. Caron's stomach tightened. She began to feel the same dull ache she had experienced over and over during medical training, whenever she knew she had some devastating news to tell a patient. Alone in her office, she sat back in her big swivel chair and tried to brace her body against the tears that were filling her eyes. She looked at the pile of patient charts on her desk, and at the full appointment schedule in front of her. She thought of Ann, a young woman she had treated for several years and had grown to like very much. "Why can't this be just a job?" she asked herself. "Why does this always have to hurt so much?" Then she picked up the phone and left a message on Ann's voice mail, asking her to set up an appointment to come in to the office as soon as possible.

One problem with having these feelings is that medical professionals are expected not to express them. They are expected to hide sadness, anger, and despair from their patients and colleagues; to do so they must often hide these emotions from themselves (Hellerstein, 1986). Medical professionals typically do not allow the expression of emotion even among themselves. In fact, young physicians and nurses sometimes idealize those who have the greatest emotional detachment (Hellerstein, 1986). They often hold up as heroes the physicians who can slice into the chest of a human being and never acknowledge the enormity of such an action. They admire those who can walk away from the bedside of a patient who has just died and coolly manipulate the emotions of the family to get them to agree to an autopsy. They are impressed by people who can watch the autopsy while they eat their lunch. Medical professionals who want to be truly "macho" don't flinch. "Macho can refer to your willingness to get tough with your patients. . . . It can refer to your eagerness to do invasive procedures . . ." (Klass, 1987a, p. 77). ". . . When the disease has essentially won and the patient continues to present the challenge, the macho doctor is left with no appropriate response. He cannot sidestep the challenge by offering comfort rather than combat, because comfort is not in his repertoire. And unable to do battle against the disease to any real effect, he may feel almost ready to battle the patient" (Klass, 1987a, p. 79).

As we noted previously, one way of being tough in the world of medicine is to distance oneself through the process of intellectualization. This focus on the technical aspects of individual cases helps practitioners to keep from becoming emotionally involved in the lives of their patients. Further, they are regularly supported for "disowning" their own emotions, particularly their frustration, anger, and sadness. **Emotional disowning** is a common coping mechanism among medical professionals in which feelings that are held very strongly are presented as foreign to oneself (Branden, 1971). To some extent, medical professionals are chosen for their ability to disown their emotions. Students with a single-minded focus on science, apparently uninterested in emotion are, at many medical schools, the most successful applicants. Despite the greater emphasis on caring in the nursing profession, technical skills and emotional detachment are the qualities that, particularly in critical care (emergency or intensive care), become the most highly valued (Heron, 1987). Most important, perhaps, is the fact that medical professionals hide their emotions from one another. Although they are the very people who best understand the stresses and emotional complexities of patient care, their efforts to appear emotionally controlled with one another deprive them of a potentially valuable system of support.

Callous Humor

"This patient is an LOL with GOK and at present seems to be CTD." Spoken in front of the patient, this sentence might confuse and alienate. But confusion would be better than what she would feel if she heard her doctors say what they really mean: "This patient is a Little Old Lady with God-Only-Knows and at present seems to be Circling the Drain." Circling the Drain is a medical professional's "in-group" term that means the patient is on her way "out." In this case, the patient is probably going to die and nobody knows what's wrong with her. It is common for medical professionals to use humor to reduce the tension of their pressure-filled work. Their jokes, although they might be considered by many to be in poor taste, often serve the purpose of separating health professionals from their patients and reducing the chances of identifying too closely with them. **Medical humor** is a well-established coping mechanism for physicians and nurses, and psychologists and sociologists have studied it at length. Humor serves to enhance the cohesiveness of the group of medical professionals who form a team and it demonstrates their recognition of each other's professional identity and acknowledgment of the stressful nature of their work (Nelson, 1992). Medical professionals' humor may serve to reduce their tension and to enhance solidarity on the medical team. Some have argued, however, that such humor also reflects a certain degree of callousness. Those who hear and appreciate jokes and humorous statements about the tragic conditions of their patients' lives and health are bound to be affected. They may fail to take very seriously the misery that their patients are feeling, or they may learn to view their patients from an unaffected position that makes them immune to the suffering around them. Others have argued that medical professionals are not laughing at patients at all, but at themselves, at their own errors, their fears, and their foibles. A resident in pediatrics, for example, was called upon to treat the severe chest pain of the grandfather of one of her young patients. Although she is a pediatrician and remembers almost nothing from her medical school days about the treatment of potential heart attacks, everyone turned to her because she's the doctor. As she relates this story to her fellow physicians, they laugh, not at the unfortunate grandfather whose life may have been in danger, but at the position in which this doctor found herself, and perhaps at the dilemmas presented by the specialization of medicine today (Klass, 1987b).

The Consequences of the Physical and Emotional Pressures

Not every health professional is vulnerable to distress from the physical and emotional pressures of medical care training. Each health professional's unique history, life experiences, and personality interact with the environmental pressure to affect work performance, emotional reactions, personal and family relationships, relationships with patients, and the adaptiveness of methods chosen for coping (Murphy et al., 1984). Some health professionals do very well, but for the unfortunate few who are vulnerable, the outcomes of these pressures can be serious problems. The costs of a career in medicine can be tremendous.

Anxiety, Depression, and Suicide

During their training, medical professionals (particularly physicians) face intensely stressful experiences and assume responsibility for extremely difficult issues involving death and disability. Very mature behavior is demanded of physicians who, because of their commitments to premedical and medical education, have had to ignore their personal development and may never have had the chance to live independent adult lives. The insulated world of the teaching hospital contributes to delays in emotional maturation (Pfeiffer, 1983; Ziegler et al., 1984). Unfortunately, lack of maturity is not the only consequence of the physical and emotional pressures of training. By the end of their first year of medical training, many students report feeling depressed and anxious (Wolf et al., 1998). At least a third of interns have frequent or severe emotional distress (Valko & Clayton, 1975), and the stresses of medical training, particularly residency, have been found to be a major factor in the precipitation of episodes of depression (Baldwin et al., 1997; May & Revicki, 1985; Reuben, 1985; Samkoff & Jacques, 1991; Weinstein, 1983). In the first year of residency alone, at least 30 percent of residents experience serious depression (Reuben & Noble, 1990). And there is evidence that the emotional impairment of physicians may be increasing (Hardison, 1986; Smith et al., 1986).

Both depression and anxiety seem to be regular accompaniments of a career in medicine. In a survey of academic and clinical faculty of a major medical school, at least mild depression was reported by approximately 13 percent of the physicians. Four percent reported moderate to severe depression. Anxiety levels were considerably higher, with 27 percent reporting beyond-normal anxiety and 13 percent reporting moderate or severe anxiety (Linn et al., 1985). Rates of anxiety among physicians seem to be quite a bit higher than those in the general community, perhaps because of the fast-paced nature of their busy lifestyles and the many responsibilities they face (Linn et al., 1985). Compared with medical students just beginning their training, students toward the end of their first year are quite worried about their capabilities and competence as budding physicians, are questioning their ability to endure the rigors of medicine, and are distressed at their inability to have an extracurricular life (Stewart et al., 1997). Students with more concerns such as these are also more likely to be anxious and depressed than those whose coping styles allow them to minimize these concerns (Stewart et al., 1997).

What is the ultimate outcome of all this emotional distress for physicians and physicians-in-training? The answer of just a few years ago was shocking. Studies in the late 1960s through the early 1980s showed that during internship and residency, at least 25 percent of physicians had serious thoughts of committing suicide (McCue, 1985), and that the leading cause of death of physicians under 40 was suicide (Blachly et al., 1968; Everson & Fraumeni, 1975; McCue, 1985). Every year, an entire medical school class (average size, 130 students) had to be trained to replace the physicians in the United States who killed themselves and, overall, the suicide rate of physicians was two to three times greater than that in the general population (Rose & Rosow, 1973; Ross, 1971). Suicide among male physicians across all age groups was shown to be about 1.5 times the rate of suicide in males in the general population, while that for female physicians was four times that among females in the general population (Pitts et al., 1979; Weinstein, 1983). This trend seems to be changing, however. One comprehensive study of 101 U.S. medical schools found that from August 1989 to May 1994 only fifteen medical students committed suicide (and nine of these students had a history of psychiatric problems) (Hays et al., 1996). The results of this study show lower suicide rates than other studies have previously reported, and this study was more comprehensive than previous studies (with 80% of the 126 medical schools in the United States reporting). This decline in suicides may be due, in part, to training programs that enable earlier identification of those who are experiencing emotional difficulties and struggling to deal with the pressures of their training or professional lives. For example, some medical schools have instituted "student well-being committees," which are geared toward identifying medical students at risk for stress-related mental problems and providing them with timely mental health services (Pasnau & Stoessel, 1994). Another successful program offers special training for new residents as they transition from the role of intern to hospital team-leader. Residents are taught leadership and problem-solving skills, as well as how to recognize depression, burnout, and signs of substance abuse in those they supervise. This program has received high praise by those who have undergone its training (Wipf et al., 1995). Thus, although training and professional practice in medicine is certainly stressful, in many settings mechanisms are now in place to aid physicians and medical students toward effective coping with these stresses.

Physician Impairment

Physician impairment is defined as the inability of the physician to practice medicine adequately because of physical or mental illness, including alcoholism or drug dependence (Reuben & Noble, 1990). You may be surprised to know that physician impairment is not uncommon. On the simplest level, emotional stress affects health professionals' job effectiveness. For example, in medical school and medical practice, stress and fatigue tend to result in poor academic performance (Jacques et al., 1990; Murphy et al., 1984) as well as in compromised patient care (Firth-Cozens, & Greenhalgh, 1997; Linn & Zeppa, 1984; Spiegel et al., 1986). But impairment can go well beyond the inability to do the job effectively because of stress, overwork, or sleep deprivation. Impairment can also involve the inability to function because of alcohol or other drug use.

Alcoholism and drug abuse occur among medical professionals with about the same frequency as in the general population (Baldwin et al., 1991; Croen et al., 1997; Flaherty & Richman, 1993; Hughes et al., 1992; McAuliffe et al., 1991). Rates of alcohol use among medical students are high, but not significantly higher than in the general public and, in fact, alcohol use, cigarette smoking, and marijuana use actually appear to decrease slightly when students enter medical school (Kuzel et al., 1991; Schwartz et al., 1990). Some studies have demonstrated a slightly higher rate of tranquilizer use among medical students and physicians, and a slight increase in tranquilizer use over the course of medical training (Baldwin et al., 1991; Croen et al., 1997; Hughes et al., 1992). A recent study of medical students in the northeast United States showed that although drug use rates varied widely (up to 5.8% for benzodiazepines; 29.4% for marijuana; and 96.9% for alcohol), relatively few (less than 6%) were at risk for substance dependence. The most interesting aspect of this study was that none of the students who were experiencing substance-related problems had come to the attention of the administration, and only half of the students who were aware of their classmates' substance use problems had done anything about it (Croen et al., 1997). Thus, although there seems to be no special substance abuse risk associated with medical training or practice, substance abuse problems within the medical field might be easily overlooked by colleagues and supervisors.

The problem of physician impairment deserves serious attention, whether it results from exhaustion, poor nutrition, emotional overload, or chemical substances. Impairment can interfere with a physician's ability to carry out effective patient care. His or her judgment, memory, and manual dexterity can be severely compromised, and sensitivity to patients' emotional needs may suffer. Medical professionals are usually not inclined to seek assistance for their impairment—a situation that makes detection and treatment quite difficult. Medical training seems to reinforce tendencies toward self-deprivation and avoidance of emotional assistance, and thus problems may not be recognized or addressed until situations are severe. Medical education also provides substantial knowledge about, and access to, prescription drugs, fostering the belief that doses can be managed and control can be maintained. To deal with this problem, several county and state medical and nursing societies have developed programs for identifying and helping impaired medical professionals. In these programs, physicians and nurses work with members of their own profession to help those who are impaired to recognize and confront their problems.

Relationships with Patients

The disowning of emotions can lead medical professionals to numb themselves against the feelings of their patients and to lose their capacity to recognize and respond to emotions in others. They may expect patients to deny their own feelings, and as a result patients may feel misunderstood (Lazarus, 1985). Indeed, the personal warmth and caring necessary for an effective physician-patient relationship is likely to be missing when physicians experience serious personal deprivations. Those who are treated badly may, in turn, treat their patients badly (Kassebaum & Cutler, 1998). Thus, when health professionals attempt to avoid acknowledging their own feelings about patient care, they ignore their patients' emotions and tend to diminish the importance of the human side of treatment (Lazarus, 1985). One psychologist has described this problem as **trivializing patients' distress** (Lazarus, 1985), which involves the health professional's avoiding patients' pain and the severe compromises of illness, and instead encouraging them in the most superficial manner to "put on a happy face." To really empathize with what patients are feeling can be extremely painful for the professional, so instead "professional distance" is created. As we saw in Chapter 3, however, it is only by sharing the patients' perspectives for a time that the health professional can provide understanding and help to reduce patients' feelings of fear, sadness, and helplessness. Because of their own emotional conflicts, medical professionals might fail to even recognize their patients' distress. In one study of the practice of medical internists, more than half of the eighty-seven patients studied were seriously distressed about something (finances, work, sex) and 10 percent had suicidal tendencies. Yet, "except in the most obvious instances, internists repeatedly underestimated patients' distress—even after long experience with them—despite the fact that the patients were not at all reluctant to reveal such feelings when asked" (Lazarus, 1985, pp. 288–289). Practitioners' own distress may also be manifested in pessimism about their patients; thus, when practitioners feel that their patients have poor prospects for improving their lives or their health, they may refrain from presenting much information to them and withhold offers of help.

There is also a tendency for health professionals, particularly those overly burdened emotionally, to see patients' problems as the patients' fault. They may even feel that their patients would not be sick if they had not done something "wrong" such as engage in unhealthy behaviors. The mechanism of "blaming the victim" is put into operation. **Blaming the victim** is a psychological phenomenon in which the victim of an untoward event is blamed for having brought misfortune upon him- or herself (Ryan, 1971). Such a conclusion tends to stem from **belief in a just world** (Lerner, 1980), which involves an individual's conviction that people get what they deserve and deserve what they get. Thus, someone who is the victim of illness is blamed for doing something that brought that illness on. Medical professionals are as prone as other people to the natural tendency to believe that bad things happen, not randomly, but systematically to people who deserve them (Lazarus, 1985). Psychological equilibrium is thus maintained through self-deceit. Further, health professionals may come to believe that certain patients have particular problems because of their flawed personalities (for example, someone has heart problems because they refuse to relax). Such an approach involves not only self-deception but also the inability to support patients emotionally when they need support.

Job Dissatisfaction and Burnout

The stresses associated with delivering medical care can be overwhelming. Occupational stress among doctors has been linked consistently with lower levels of job satisfaction, with negative attitudes toward patients and the practice of medicine, and with burnout (Richardsen & Burke, 1991, 1993). In the past decades, the phenomenon of **burnout** has received interest among psychologists. Burnout is a negative psychological state characterized by physical and emotional exhaustion, an increased cynicism about and dehumanization of patients, a decreased concern and respect for patients, a loss of positive feeling for others, and a tendency to blame others for distress. Common results of burnout include quitting the job that has brought burnout, abusing drugs and alcohol, and an increase in mental illness as well as marital and interpersonal discord. Burnout occurs among individuals whose job it is to care for other people, particularly when the demands are seen as excessive. These individuals include human service workers and medical professionals (Maslach, 1976, 1982). Medical practitioners who care for very ill or dying children and for psychotic patients have been found to be particularly prone to burnout (Clarke et al., 1984), as have those with excessive patient loads and the inability to have much input into their practice (Deckard et al., 1994; Wilters, 1998). Burnout involves the tendency of the professional to disparage the recipients of their care, as well as to care less and focus less effort and emotion on these patients. Individuals with burnout focus on the problems they encounter rather than on the positive, rewarding aspects of their jobs. The chances of developing burnout increase drastically in settings where the probability of successful intervention is low and workers see that their efforts make little difference in the lives of their clients. Burnout increases when staff members have higher expectations for patients than is warranted by the reality of their situation and when they are unable to see a resolution of the problem (usually true in cases of chronic, degenerative illness). Burnout also increases when patients' anger is directed at caregivers.

The term "burnout" has come to be used very loosely and inaccurately. Burnout is not just fatigue. The exhaustion that accompanies burnout is primarily emotional, although it may be manifested in physical fatigue as well. Some researchers have suggested that burnout among medical practitioners results from their attempts to disown the complex and sometimes disquieting emotions they feel in the course of caring for their patients. Others argue that burnout is the natural outcome of practitioners' expectations for patient gratitude, appreciation, and admiration for their selfless care. Still others argue that the primary cause of burnout is the unavoidable result of continual face-to-face involvement with people (Edelwich & Brodsky, 1980; Jones, 1981). Whichever the case, burnout rates are notoriously high in the medical field. Recent studies indicate very low morale for physicians (Sullivan & Buske, 1998; Wilters, 1998), with as many as 58 percent reporting high levels of emotional exhaustion and 35 percent reporting feeling depersonalized from their patients (Deckard et al., 1994). When one considers the important roles that interpersonal warmth and empathy play in effective patient care, these statistics become alarming.

Can burnout be cured? Can a health professional whose emotional well-being is severely threatened by burnout return to his or her previous level of functioning? Research on the prevention and treatment of burnout is beginning to suggest the importance of providing medical professionals with encouragement and the opportunity for emotional expression. In some cases, support groups have been helpful in reducing the stress that medical professionals feel. In other cases, mental health professionals such as psychologists and psychiatrists work with physicians and nurses. They help them to become aware of and to understand their emotions and aid them in determining the best courses of action to follow in caring for their patients. The health professionals are encouraged to attend to their own needs as well as to the needs of others. They are encouraged to engage in actively reducing their stress through physical exercise and relaxation training (Wood, 1998). Medical professionals are also helped to reevaluate the meaning of their work as part of a process. They are encouraged to share their feelings with their families, and they are helped to communicate effectively with other staff members to enhance their ability to deal with the pressures of patient care.

Women in Medicine:
The Struggle and the Ideal

More and more, these days, young women whose interests lie in patient care are choosing to go to medical school. Approximately 42 percent of the medical students in the United States are women (Williams, 1999), a statistic that represents a big change from the 1960s when women comprised only about 6 percent of medical school classes. In the past two decades, a successful medical career has become more and more of a possibility for a woman. Specialties such as surgery and obstetrics-gynecology, once closed to women, are opening their doors (although women are still more likely than men to experience discrimination and discouragement from pursuing certain specialties) (Field & Lennox, 1996). Careers in academic medicine are being pursued successfully by women who combine a medical career with family and children (Brown, 1992; Gross, 1992; Williams, 1999).

Women who entered medicine in the decades of the 1950s, 1960s, and 1970s were trailblazers in medical education. They endured tremendous personal difficulties to become physicians. They received criticism from colleagues that they were not upholding traditional feminine roles, and many of their male colleagues were reluctant to make room for women in medicine. Although today women in medicine refuse to accept such ill treatment, are backed up by laws against sexual harassment, and are able to turn to one another for support, obstacles to female success still exist. Even though direct abuse seems to be no greater toward women than men in medical school, women medical students still experience a significant degree of more "underhanded abuse" in the form of sexual harassment (Moscarello et al., 1994; Sheehan et al., 1990; Silver & Glicken, 1990). They must fight slurs and prejudices and challenge sexist remarks. Even today, women who venture into male-dominated specialties such as surgery can face considerable hostility (Field & Lennox, 1996; Lillemoe et al., 1994; Richman & Flaherty, 1986).

Current research on women's reactions to medical training suggests that, at least in some realms, women may experience somewhat more stress than men. Although women have been found during the early years of medical school to have lower stress levels and higher mental health than men, later clinical training tends to embody more stressors for females than for males (Richman & Flaherty, 1990). These include distress over separation from family, friends, and loved ones during clinical training, and feelings of loneliness, stress, being out of place, and being unable to achieve their goals (Lillemoe et al., 1994; Spiegel et al., 1986). Whether gender differences in occupational stress are found depends, at least to some degree, on the method of data collection used. One recent survey of nearly 1,000 physicians in Scotland found that women generally experienced more satisfaction with their jobs than did men (Swanson et al., 1996). Other research on female physicians indicates that despite feeling overloaded and overwhelmed by the competing demands of their lives, women in medicine are nonetheless well adjusted and are not more anxious or depressed than women who are not physicians, or than their male-physician peers (Brown, 1992; Lewis et al., 1994). A recent review found that when stress inventories were used, gender differences did not emerge, but that open-ended questions were more likely to show male-female differences (Gross, 1998).

Women physicians who also have spouses and children do tend to face limitations in their professional career advancement. Studies show that when women physicians marry, the majority (between 50% and 75%) choose husbands who are also physicians (Uhlenberg & Cooney, 1990). Others marry professionals such as attorneys. In most cases, the husbands are highly career-oriented and do not cut back on their own work to support their wives' careers. Instead, women physicians, particularly those who have children, tend to take salaried hospital positions or work in health maintenance organizations. In these cases, they are able to work fewer hours per week, with some additional time on call (Hojat et al., 1995). As a result, their earnings are typically lower than those of male physicians (Uhlenberg & Cooney, 1990). It is worth pointing out that although male physicians have out-earned female physicians for years, when equating specialty and number of hours worked, this difference seems to be diminishing. Although there are still male-female differences in some specialties (and some of these favor women), on average, young female and male physicians earn comparable wages (Baker, 1996). Another interesting male-female difference is that women physicians are often responsible in their families for virtually all of the housework, shopping, cooking, child care, and money management (Gross, 1992; Rout, 1996; Woodward et al., 1996). And, while their physical juggling of all these responsibilities is difficult enough, the emotional aspects of their role conflicts are even greater. If a woman physician wants to take a few years off to have and care for her children, she may lose the necessary diagnostic and/or surgical skills she has worked so hard to acquire. When she does go back to work and is caring for her patients, she may feel she is neglecting her children. When home with her children, she worries about patients who might need her (Cartwright, 1977, 1978; Warde et al., 1996).

In recent years, there has been a recognition of the important contribution that women physicians make to the profession of medicine. Women have been found, on average, to have a slightly greater tendency than men to express the personal characteristics of sensitivity and empathy for patients that we have seen are so valuable in patient care (Miller, 1994). In their attitudes, they have been found to be (on average) more sensitive than male physicians to the doctor-patient relationship, more accepting of patients' feelings, more empathic, and more open to the social and humanistic aspects of patient care (Hojat et al., 1995; Kliszcz & Rembowski, 1998; McFarland & Rhoades, 1998). In addition to more positive attitudes toward the psychosocial aspects of patient care, women physicians are more likely than men to engage in medical care practices that promote the psychological and social well-being of their patients, such as counseling regarding preventive health care (Bertakis et al., 1995; Frank & Harvey, 1996; Maheux et al., 1990; Woodward et al., 1996). Women are also more likely to choose the primary care specialties than are men (McFarland & Rhoades, 1998).

It might seem obvious that if women are generally somewhat more empathic healthcare providers, people will automatically prefer a female practitioner to a male one. As it happens, this isn't the case. Preference for female family medicine physicians has been documented, but gender preferences for other types of healthcare professionals have been virtually ignored. One interesting recent study examined patient preferences for thirteen health professionals, including surgeons, neurologists, anesthetists, internists, general practitioners, psychiatrists, psychologists, social workers, nurses, home helpers, gynecologists, and midwives (Kerssens et al., 1997). For the more "instrumental" professions (like surgeons) there were no gender preferences, but there were gender preferences when highly personal and/or psychosocial issues were likely to be relevant (such as in the case of a gynecologist). One particularly interesting finding of this study was that even when gender preferences were expressed, these did not necessarily conform to sex stereotypes related to the healthcare provider. Patients who said they preferred a woman physician said that this was because they felt more at ease with a woman and could talk more easily to a woman. Patients who expressed a preference for a male physician said that they felt more comfortable with and could talk more easily to a man!

Another distinction between male and female physicians is that women physicians tend to be more concerned than males about balancing work responsibilities and family life, so that their own emotional needs and social support, as well as the welfare of their families, are not sacrificed (McFarland & Rhoades, 1998). They are more likely than men to spend their leisure time with family and friends and are less willing to work exceptionally many hours (McFarland & Rhoades, 1998). Although women physicians can help to change medicine for the better, simply admitting more women into medicine will not be enough to enhance the psychosocial care of patients and the mental health and adaptiveness of physicians (Eisenberg, 1989). Rather, "the task will be to cultivate the humane qualities in all health professionals by making career paths, and the reward structure that reinforces them, consonant with that goal" (Eisenberg, 1989, p. 1544).

Just as with empathy and communication, cultural awareness and sensitivity are also essential elements in patient care. Box 4.4 examines this issue in an analysis of the important treatment perspectives that are provided by minority physicians.

BOX 4.4
Across Cultures

The Equitable Minority Doctor

Are doctors from ethnic minority groups less likely to have ethnic biases regarding their patients? Or are they at least better at removing these biases from their decision-making processes? Some research suggests that the answer is "yes." In a recent study, a group of 164 medical students was randomly assigned to watch a video of either a white or a black patient, with each presenting the very same symptoms of angina. Even though the "patients" (who were really actors) were using identical scripts, the diagnoses reached by the nonminority medical students differed significantly according to the ethnicity of the patient. Nonminority students

(continued)

BOX 4.4   (Continued)

tended to rate the white patient as healthier than the black patient, and were also more likely when the patient was white to make the correct diagnosis of angina. The minority students, in contrast, accurately judged the two patients as similar; their judgments were not affected by patient ethnicity (Rathore et al., 2000).

This intriguing study of medical students is not the first to show that ethnicity can act as an independent factor influencing the type of diagnosis or treatment recommendation that a patient receives. For example, another similar study, this time of 720 practicing physicians, demonstrated that both female "patients" and black "patients" were less likely to be referred for cardiac catheterization than their white male counterparts (Schulman et al., 1999). These findings are particularly important in light of the rapidly changing demographic makeup of many parts of the United States, such as California.

In recent years the Latino population in California has grown rapidly, and this group now makes up almost one-third of the state's nearly 35 million residents. But, according to recent statistics, fewer than 5 percent of the state's 74,345 physicians are Latino (Hayes-Bautista et al., 2000). And, it doesn't look like things will improve anytime soon, since only 11 percent of incoming medical students at University of California medical schools are from minority groups,

Latino or otherwise. So, must minority patients risk receiving biased care from their doctors because there are so few minority physicians available to them? What can be done?

One solution is to train more minority physicians so that they will be available to provide culturally competent care to patients from minority groups. Steps toward this goal involve both active recruitment and strategies to maximize retention of minority medical students. A recent survey of African American medical students enrolled at the University of Kentucky showed that early exposure to the health professions, early outreach strategies, availability of social networks, and ongoing financial support were all important factors in determining students' enrollment and success in medical school (Wiggs & Elam, 2000). Some schools have instituted their own minority support mechanisms, such as the Ohio University College of Osteopathic Medicine which has six different academic enrichment programs in place to aid underrepresented minority students as they pursue medical training (Thompson & Weiser, 1999). Some medical schools, such as the University of Pennsylvania School of Medicine, focus efforts on recruiting faculty members from minority groups and on training minority students to become medical school faculty themselves (Johnson et al., 1998).

Humanizing Medicine

How might medicine be changed to foster both the personal development of physicians and their psychosocial orientation to patients? Researchers and medical educators have suggested some necessary elements for change. First, medical practitioners themselves should be helped to recognize that there typically exists a conspiracy of silence regarding the difficult feelings engendered by medical practice (McCue, 1985). Early recognition of the complex emotional aspects of patient care and awareness and examination of these feelings are critical (Weinstein, 1983). Opportunities for peer discussion and confidential counseling for impairment should be available so that medical professionals can be supported to deal with the difficulties they encounter in caring for patients (Weinstein, 1983). The mental health and social support needs of medical professionals at all levels of training need to be recognized and assisted (Awbrey, 1985). Second,

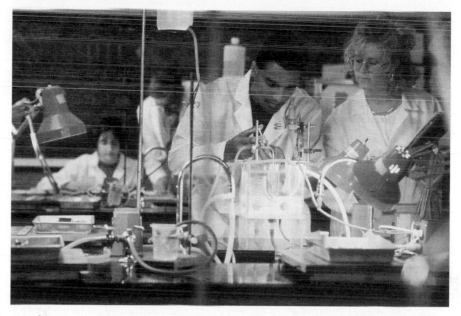

Emotional support and the opportunity for discussion of feelings can be critically important during all levels of medical training, even during the undergraduate premedical years.

it is critically important to attend to reducing or eliminating the more punishing aspects of medical training and practice (Silver & Glicken, 1990). Time for family relationships must be guarded, and a medical professional's efforts to develop and nurture his or her family life should be valued and protected (Eisenberg, 1989). Third, humanistic values should be selected for as well as nurtured in the process of medical education. ". . . Medical school admission is geared to the very bright, achievement-oriented students who have accumulated top grades in scientific subjects. This necessarily selects qualities of intense competitiveness, intellectual narrowness—belonging to young people who often have neglected interpersonal relations and have not permitted the leavening of their own sensibilities and their capacities to 'reach out' " (Lown, 1983, p. 25). In addition to selecting students with compassionate and humanistic values, training programs can be implemented to foster shared learning and communication as well as sensitivity and compassion (Freeth & Nicol, 1998; Pfeiffer et al., 1998). Some have already been described in this chapter in terms of their role in promoting idealism and humanistic values (Forrow & Wolf, 1998; Taylor, 1994). Although these types of programs are relatively new, medical students indicate that they gain useful insights from these programs and that their time in the sessions has been well spent.

Medical Practitioners and the Puzzle of Illness

So far in this book, we have examined the emotional aspects of medical treatment, not only from the point of view of patients but from the perspective of medical practitioners as well. Now we turn to an examination of the difficulties and complexities of making medical decisions that can significantly affect patients' lives and well-being. We will examine the ways in which those decisions can be made most effectively, as well as the ways in which the decision-making process can go awry.

In today's modern world, very high expectations are held both for the scientific field of medicine and for the members of the medical professions. Implicit in these expectations are demands for diagnostic and treatment miracles occurring on a regular basis (McCue, 1982; Mizrahi, 1984). Lay people turn to medical professionals for answers about the state of their bodies and about what they can do to achieve and maintain health. And, as you will see in Chapters 7 and 8, some people express emotional pain through their bodies and expect their medical professionals to provide not only the alleviation of their physical distress, but some measure of happiness and emotional fulfillment as well. In recent decades, developments in medicine have been astounding. Yet, despite all that medicine can do, the field and its practitioners have limitations. Sometimes physicians cannot figure out what is wrong with a patient. Necessary information about diagnosis and treatment may be unavailable because medical knowledge has not developed far enough or because the medical professional's own capacity for processing and integrating the relevant information may be limited. Sometimes, no cure or acceptable management strategy exists. Medical care can even be dangerous, such as when certain diagnostic tests and treatments bring about additional problems that then require treatment. There is even a name for a physician-induced medical problem. It is **"iatrogenic,"** which means that it results from the treatment efforts (*Dorland's Illustrated Medical Dictionary* [DIMD], 1994) (again, see Box 4.1). In the interests of patients' well-being, these limitations must be acknowledged.

Medical Diagnosis

Medical professionals deal with patients under conditions of uncertainty. A medical professional almost never knows for sure the state of a patient's body—only what is probable or likely. Despite the wonders of modern medicine, caring for patients is almost always a matter of dealing with unknowns and probabilities (Allman et al., 1985). Patients present their symptoms to medical professionals and are often surprised to learn that medical diagnosis is not a simple one-to-one matching between the patient's bodily condition and a diagnostic label. Diagnosing illness can be like completing a puzzle.

As an illustration of this process, consider the case of a patient who may have epilepsy with grand mal seizures. He might come to the doctor complaining of "passing out several times during the past month." There are several things that a doctor might check, such as blood sugar levels, blood pressure, and cardiac rhythm. If these are all normal and the patient can think of no environmental cause (such as toxic fumes or hyperventilation) for the losses of consciousness, these fainting spells might be *presumptive* manifestations of some sort of seizure, indicating epilepsy. That is, they make the doctor *suspect* that the patient has epilepsy and suggest a possible diagnosis, but not with a high degree of confidence. Suppose that several weeks later this patient again loses consciousness, but this time it is while standing in line at the grocery store. The paramedics are called and they note that his body is very rigid (grand mal seizures are characterized by "tonus" or rigidity and "clonus" or jerking); this paramedic record accompanies the patient to the hospital. Now there is a *probable* manifestation of epilepsy, an event that reflects a substantial probability of, although does not confirm, the diagnosis of epilepsy with grand mal seizure. Nonetheless, the doctor cannot be sure of the diagnosis without a *positive* manifestation that would confirm the diagnosis beyond doubt and involve the actual demonstration of a grand mal seizure. To reach a final diagnosis, the physician might have the patient come into the lab to see if a seizure can be induced. To gain this kind of positive evidence, the patient has electrodes attached to his scalp to measure the electrical activity of the brain. This is called an **electroencephalogram** (EEG). Next, the patient lies down and is instructed to relax for a while so that a baseline reading of brain activity may be taken. Then, strobe lights are flashed at varying speeds to induce the uncontrolled and escalating neuronal firing that is definitive of an epileptic attack. If the attempt is successful (that is, the patient experiences a seizure), he is given the diagnosis of epilepsy with grand mal seizures. If the attempt is unsuccessful, however, the diagnosis of epilepsy with grand mal seizures is less likely to be accurate and other diagnostic options may be pursued.

The point of this discussion is to illustrate that what goes on inside the human body is often not apparent on the outside and must be deduced by examining signs and symptoms. The health professional collects these data and attempts to integrate the information in an effective manner (Pauker & Kassirer, 1987). Pregnancy is an example of a fairly easy condition to diagnose because noninvasive positive tests, such as ultrasound, are available and, if they were not, the truth would eventually become apparent at delivery! Other medical conditions, however, do not offer such clear-cut answers. For example, the signs and symptoms of an alteration in liver functioning may or may not indicate liver cancer. Gathering information from the patient's history is the least invasive approach, but may provide only presumptive signs of disease. Certain diagnostic tests (such as an x-ray liver scan) may provide probable signs. But tests that provide positive signs of liver cancer tend to be invasive, such as biopsy in which a portion of the presumed tumor is surgically removed and subjected to histological examination. Where to stop on this continuum in attempting to rule out the existence of liver cancer in a patient involves a subjective decision on the part of the physician, ideally in conjunction with the patient. Greater certainty comes at increasing cost to the patient, not only in terms of money but also in terms of pain, distress, and risk (Allman et al., 1985). Because of this, it is extremely important that patients be involved, whenever possible, in decisions regarding all types of medical care, including diagnostic tests. As we discussed in Chapter 2, outcomes for both patients and practitioners are better when there is active collaboration in the decision-making process.

With any condition, finding out what is going on in a person's body involves a process of **clinical reasoning**. The medical practitioner collects information from the patient during the medical visit (in a manner such as described in Chapter 2). He or she may conduct several laboratory tests as well. The process of diagnosis involves interpreting data, developing and revising hypotheses, constructing a diagnostic plan, and then testing and reevaluating that plan. Of course, this process is based upon likelihood and probability. The practitioner sees a set of signs and symptoms that look like a particular syndrome, but each patient's case will be unique. The practitioner must decide whether the signs and symptoms displayed by the patient are indicative of a particular disease and must differentiate the patients' signs and symptoms from others that indicate other possible conditions. The practitioner's job during the clinical reasoning process is to show that the patients' signs and symptoms are more like those that would manifest with a particular disease entity and are differentiated from signs and symptoms that would manifest with another. This process is called **differential diagnosis**.

Decision Making by Medical Professionals

Clinical reasoning skills are fundamental to the practice of medicine. Clinical reasoning requires logical thinking, the incorporation of all the available data, and the avoidance of biases. As shown in Figure 4.2, many factors affect clinical reasoning. Often, disagreements among "experts" regarding both diagnosis and treatment can be the result of differences in their subjective judgments and the clinical reasoning process (Eddy, 1982; Eraker & Politser, 1982).

Many things can influence subjective clinical judgments, which combine assessments of costs, insurance status, legal issues, ethical concerns, and quality of patient care (Burns et al., 1997; Leist & Konen, 1996). A particular practitioner's clinical experience can determine the emphasis that he or she places on certain facts, and a health professional's own values can influence differential emphasis placed on varying types of

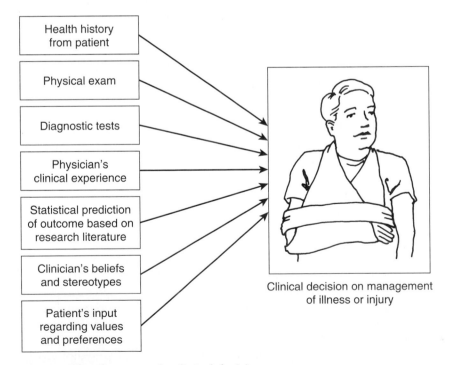

FIGURE 4.2   The elements of a clinical decision.

information. In one study, experience heavily influenced physicians' decisions to discuss resuscitation efforts with their AIDS patients who had *Pneumocistis carinii* pneumonia. Physicians who had more experience taking care of AIDS patients (and who thus had a good understanding of the hopelessness of resuscitation efforts) were more likely than those who had less experience to initiate discussion with their patients about the possibility of foregoing intubation and resuscitation (Wachter et al., 1988).

In other research, estimates of the probabilities of certain clinical outcomes have been found to be affected by physicians' own clinical experience. For example, in cases in which the literature suggested a modest success rate for a particular intervention but most of a physician's patients did well on the treatment, the probability of success with future patients was overestimated (Eraker & Politser, 1982; Tversky & Kahneman, 1974).

Some physicians rely most heavily on **statistical predictions** of outcomes such as prognosis after cancer therapy. They focus on data from large samples of people who have received that particular therapy and how many of them have had various outcomes, such as cure, temporary remission, or death. Other physicians rely more heavily on their **clinical experience**—that is, on what outcomes they themselves have seen occur in their own clinical work (Sawyer, 1966). Which approach is better is not easy to say. Suppose that a cancer patient who is young and generally physically robust asks a physician to quote the statistics on long-term survival with treatment for his or her type of cancer. The average survival rates might be quite low, and the patient might be quite distressed, as well as misled, if he or she were to take them as indications of his or her own chances. These statistics are meaningful in that they are based upon controlled research studies, but they need to be qualified by the fact that the patients in those studies likely were considerably older and less healthy to begin with than this patient. Should the physician instead rely solely on personal experience and judgment in providing a recommendation to the patient? Probably not. Instead, the combination of statistical predictions and clinical experience will likely lead to the best decisions in medicine.

How practitioners process and present medical information can have great implications not only for their own diagnostic conclusions, but for patients' preferences as well. For example, how statistics are presented to patients can significantly affect their choices of various therapies (Tversky & Kahneman, 1981). In one study, people were asked to decide between surgery and radiation therapy for lung cancer. Choices depended a great deal upon how the expected outcomes were presented, specifically in terms of the probability of living or dying. For example, respondents favored surgery more when the outcomes were presented in terms of the probability of surviving than when they were presented in terms of the probability of dying, even though the odds were the same in both cases (McNeil et al., 1982).

In terms of medical decision making, advanced technology has certain distinct advantages and disadvantages. The use of sophisticated equipment and diagnostic procedures can help a practitioner to make an accurate differential diagnosis, which will be of value *if* it affects the choice of treatment. Such technology may also lead, however, to the detection of **"pseudodisease,"** which, although technically disease, has little or no consequence. New technologies may also present treatment dilemmas when the "problems" they detect might be better left alone (Fisher & Welch, 1999). These diagnoses are likely to lead to treatments that are at best unnecessary and at worst dangerous. Take, for example, the case of Travis Townsend, an 80-year-old man who has just discovered, through a blood test his doctor recommended, that he likely has the early stages of prostate cancer. Mr. Townsend also has several other medical conditions (hypertension, cardiovascular disease [CVD], and glaucoma), and, although he does manage to get around, his CVD and hypertension make it very likely that he will die of a heart attack or stroke before he reaches age 90. It is extremely unlikely that if Mr. Townsend does have prostate cancer, it will advance much in the next ten years. In fact, had Mr. Townsend not had the blood test, he would probably never have known that he might have cancer lurking in his body. But now Mr. Townsend worries; the word "cancer" strikes fear in him, as it does in many people, even when the odds suggest that there is no need for alarm. Even though his doctor has told him that surgery would not be necessary if there is a cancer, Mr. Townsend says that he would feel too distressed and frightened to leave a cancer inside of him. Therefore, Mr. Townsend wants further testing and his doctor is willing to support his decision. If a biopsy indicates cancer, Mr. Townsend wants it removed. His age, hypertension, and CVD are quite likely to make surgery dangerous, however, presenting more decisional dilemmas. In Mr. Townsend's case it probably would have been better if he had never had the blood test at all.

Errors in Clinical Decisions

Research suggests that among medical professionals, differences of opinion and even errors can occur because of limitations in the precision of diagnoses, deficiencies in reasoning processes, and biases in subjective judgments (e.g., Wood, 1998). In choosing a diagnosis, many physicians have been found to make an error referred to as **premature closure**. Premature closure tends to occur when a certain amount of information is available, but there is not enough to make a clear diagnosis. Yet, the physician decides upon an initial course of treatment anyway, presuming (or filling in) the answer to the missing pieces of the diagnostic puzzle (Voytovich et al., 1985). This is problematic, of course, because an initial plan that is wrong cannot be remedied by the most carefully determined later steps. In addition, once they have decided upon a diagnosis, no matter how early and prematurely, physicians are more likely than not to establish a cognitive set (a particular way of thinking) and to fit subsequent data to their initial formulations, ignoring what does not fit. Among medical students, one of the most frequent errors is the use of accurate, but nondiscriminating, evidence to support a diagnostic conclusion (Friedman et al., 1998). Students rely unduly on presumptive manifestations of a particular disease or disorder. After a student has decided on the diagnosis (even if the decision is only in his or her own mind and has not been articulated), the student is likely to search for evidence in support of his or her conclusion about the patient's health status. If a diagnosis has been reached, of course, the sought-after evidence is confirmatory rather than explanatory—that is, it focuses on confirming the diagnosis believed to be correct rather than open-mindedly searching for clues that will eventually solve the diagnostic puzzle. Many indicators and symptoms, of course, are common to several (or even many) disease states. Their presence, however, confirms in the mind of the student that a correct diagnosis has been made because, "Yes, you would expect to see this in a person with Disease A." The student might have forgotten that this symptom also occurs in Diseases B through Q!

While it is relatively rare for a physician to simply ignore an important clinical clue such as a serious symptom or an abnormal test result or to draw a conclusion that completely contradicts the data, premature closure in which the diagnosis is maintained even when later data does not support it is quite common. In one study, fifty-eight physicians at several levels of training (medical school, residency, and faculty) were given three hypothetical clinical cases with all the relevant data and were asked to indicate what diagnostic conclusions were warranted (Voytovich et al., 1985). Fifty-three of the fifty-eight physicians made at least one error of premature closure (17 on only one case, 15 on two cases, and 21 on all three cases). Surprisingly, the errors were not related to the physicians' level of experience. Senior residents and faculty made just as many such errors as did medical students. Some research shows that as early as the third year of medical school, certain students can be identified by faculty as having consistent difficulties with clinical reasoning (Coggan et al., 1985). Premature closure in diagnosis can, of course, lead to the wrong treatment as well as to a false sense of confidence that the correct treatment has been chosen. There may be a long delay before it is discovered that the wrong pathway is being pursued. In the meantime, the patient's real problem is not dealt with and he or she receives inappropriate therapy.

Even in situations where the data do support the diagnosis, **primacy effects** influence the decisions made. A primacy effect occurs when greater weight is given to information or input that is received first. In one study, when medical students were presented with data that equally supported two different diagnoses, they were significantly more likely to favor the diagnosis for which they received information first (Cunnington et al., 1997). Although such diagnoses were not themselves necessarily in error, selecting them as more likely was unwarranted based on the data and might subsequently have led to erroneous conclusions. Other research has found that **recency effects** (additional weight given to the last, or most recent, input received) also influence decisions. Doctors in this study read patient vignettes and were asked to estimate the probability that the patient had experienced a transient ischemic attack (TIA, often a predictor of a stroke). When distracting information regarding the patient's cancer history was presented at the end of the vignette, doctors rated the likelihood of TIA as lower than when cancer information was presented earlier (Chapman et al., 1996).

How can such reasoning errors come about? There are several possible explanations. First, most medical decisions tend to be made in a hurry, whether or not they need to be. Although speed is certainly valued in emergency situations, most medical decisions are not emergencies. Physicians tend to make decisions rather quickly because of habit, practice time constraints (e.g., an office full of patients), and other pressures and professional demands, including financial pressures (May & Revicki, 1985). In their haste, some physicians may be prone to infer information they do not have and to draw inferences from incomplete data. Second, physicians vary in their tolerance for uncertainty. Some require "certainty" (or its approximation given the limitations of testing), while others are willing to make a decision on the basis of a small amount of information. These differences have important implications for the extensiveness of testing that physicians may order (Allman et al., 1985). Third, some clinical decisions are complex and not at all routine. Each individual patient has a unique history, laboratory values, and clinical findings, all of which must be integrated in order to arrive at a decision that is right for that individual patient. Such integration may be difficult to do effectively, particularly in a brief time frame. Recently, quantitative methods have been developed for incorporating data about individual patients into clinical decisions. These methods are part of the field of decision analysis (Pauker & Kassirer, 1987) and they function something like an actuarial table. That is, available data (such as the patient's age, what medications he or she is currently taking, the severity of his or her symptoms, etc.) are entered into a weighted statistical program that will quickly evaluate the likelihood of various outcomes. Although this sort of approach may be most efficient in the aggregate (that is, it may minimize the number of "bad decisions" overall), in its present form it is somewhat less promising in any individual case. Some argue that the application of quantitative approaches, such as decision analysis, to medical problems is inappropriate if that is the only approach used. That is, these methods must be supplemented by other, more qualitative approaches (Rizzo, 1993).

In addition, medical professionals have certain biases that affect the accuracy of the presumptions they make, and these biases can strongly affect the ways that they assess clinical problems. When people obtain medical care, they usually think they are being offered all the options available for treatment. What they may be unaware of, however, is the important role played by the specialty orientation of their medical practitioner. The "Law of the Knife" refers to the phenomenon in which the available tools actually define the problem. Consider Ron, a young man who was experiencing some minor oral discomfort. He had an overbite, and every month or so his lower teeth irritated the roof of his mouth. The area became red, swollen, and tender. When this happened, he avoided spicy foods and tried to keep his lower teeth from digging into the roof of his mouth. The problem was somewhat annoying but nothing he really worried about, until one day, while cleaning his teeth, his hygienist noted the inflammation. She called it to the attention of the dentist, who seemed somewhat alarmed. She told Ron that this could be serious and that if he allowed the problem to continue, he might one day lose his front teeth. This would be years in coming, of course, but the prospect startled Ron and he decided to seek appropriate treatment immediately. The dentist referred Ron to an oral surgeon who made detailed molds of Ron's teeth and gums. Ron was rather shocked that the oral surgeon immediately recommended jaw surgery. Specifically, the bone of his lower jaw would be completely cut, then slid forward, and wired into place. He would be unable to open his mouth at all for several weeks. The surgeon also noted that this process would likely make his chin protrude too much, so he proposed doing an additional "simple" surgery, which would nip off the tip of Ron's chin, rendering it more aesthetically pleasing. Ron left the oral surgeon's office in a daze. He didn't like the idea of surgery and wondered if this was really the only alternative. As it turned out, the answer to that question was "no." Ron next scheduled an appointment with an orthodontist, who specialized not in surgery but in moving teeth. The orthodontist told Ron that the problem could be corrected by simply adjusting the placement of some of the teeth in his mouth; he would only need to wear braces for about nine months. Relieved, Ron scheduled an appointment to have his braces put on.

Why did Ron get two very different treatment recommendations? The answer is that the two specialists he saw had training in two very different areas. Each had been taught to view problems in a certain way and to solve them using certain tools and techniques. The oral surgeon was trained to operate. The orthodontist was trained to move teeth with braces. Some people might have preferred to opt for the oral surgery rather than endure nine months of wearing braces. If one did not mind the risks associated with general anesthetic and could handle a few weeks of pain and one's mouth wired shut, this might be a preferable option. Someone opting for braces would have to face months of avoiding certain types of foods, lots of extra tooth-brushing, and altered physical appearance. For Ron, the latter option was preferable.

In many cases, there are several options for medical treatment, and none of the options is necessarily "wrong" or "right" in a technical sense. Each comes with its own set of advantages and disadvantages. The diagnosis and recommended treatment is likely to depend a great deal upon the orientation and experience of the doctor, but this inclination may not be best in terms of meeting the individual patient's needs. This is why it is so vitally important that patients play an active role in medical decision making. Only they can adequately inform the healthcare professional about their preferences, their fears, and those things that they *know* they will be unwilling or unable to do or cope with.

Stereotypes as Barriers to Clinical Decisions

Within the first few minutes of a clinical encounter, a health professional begins to generate hypotheses about what might be wrong with a patient. These hypotheses are typically based upon cues from the patient and preliminary information disclosed by him or her, as well as on the practitioner's observations. In interpreting this early information, a practitioner may be subtly influenced by the nature of his or her relationship with the patient and by the patient's characteristics. In many studies, it has been found that perceptions of a patient's social class, economic background, sex, and physical appearance do indeed affect physicians' clinical decisions. **Stereotypes** (that is, exaggerated beliefs, oversimplifications, and uncritical judgments) held about certain patients can strongly influence physicians' clinical decisions (McKinlay et al., 1996). In one study, the diagnosis of obesity was more than twice as likely to be given to women patients as it was to men patients, although in this study more men than women were actually obese (Franks et al., 1982). In other research, students at a school of osteopathy watched videotapes of five different simulated patients, each presenting with the same physical complaint (Johnson et al., 1986). The students viewed some patients more positively on the basis of irrelevant characteristics such as the patient's attractiveness or being Caucasian. These views had implications for diagnosis, such as when the patient was judged as being open, honest, and reliable as an information source. Of course, the patient's attractiveness and race do not provide an adequate basis for drawing conclusions about the reliability of their reports. Such views could, however, lead a physician to believe information that does not make sense or is clearly inaccurate from a patient who is thought to be reliable, or to doubt information that is accurate and clinically relevant from a patient who is thought to be unreliable.

Stereotyping may be a convenient way to cope with the complexities of dealing with many different kinds of patients, but stereotyping can lead to serious problems in clinical reasoning. A physician's stereotyped views about a patient's psychological makeup can strongly influence the conclusions that he or she draws about the origin of the patient's problem and hence about the treatment prescribed. For example, in this country, twice as many women as men take prescription tranquilizers, and three times as many women as men use antidepressants and sedatives. Research suggests that physicians are more likely to see psychological disturbance at the root of, or associated with, the problems of women patients than those of men patients, and to prescribe medication for this disturbance (Fisher, 1986). Physicians are also strongly influenced by their assessments of their patients' motivation and ability to care for themselves, although their assessments are often made rapidly and on the basis of implicit stereotypes rather than on the basis of patients' real capabilities. Some research suggests that physicians sometimes see only what they expect to see and have been trained to recognize. In a study of 123 residents in five training hospitals, researchers found that despite the unique opportunity that exists for physicians to recognize alcohol problems from reports of patient behavior and from manifested medical complications, physicians frequently remain unaware of alcohol problems in their patients (Warburg et al., 1987). Even when they are aware, they often undertreat or fail to treat these problems. The good news is that when doctors were trained to recognize and deal with alcoholism, their awareness of their patients' alcohol problems was raised and they were more likely to refer alcoholic patients to experts. Physicians' decisions, even those that concern whether a patient is "dead on arrival" (DOA) at the hospital, can also be influenced by their values. In one observational study, car accident victims who had been drunk, destitute, and old were more likely to be classified as DOA by emergency room physicians, who made no efforts at resuscitation. On the other hand, resuscitation was typically attempted on children, even when they appeared to be already dead (Roth, 1972).

Making rational decisions is one of the great challenges of medical practice. Many factors indigenous to the world of medicine can make logical thinking difficult. As we have seen in this chapter, these factors include emotional distress, lack of adequate time, and cognitive deficits resulting from enormous fatigue (Webb, 1982). Pressures to save time can promote stereotyping as well as premature conclusions that are unwarranted by the data available from the patient. Physicians' values cannot help but affect their evaluations of patients and the decisions they make about patient care. And, these are not the only components of the medical equation. The medical system itself exerts a variety of pressures on both patients and their doctors, and these are reflected in the care that is delivered. We turn next to examine the healthcare system, and the elements of it that affect healthcare for patients.

Contemporary U.S. Healthcare Systems

In many countries, including the United States, the healthcare industry is bigger than any other industry. In 1997, healthcare spending in the United States comprised 14 percent of the Gross Domestic Product (GDP), and healthcare expenditures are expected to reach 18 percent of the GDP by 2005 (Anderson & Poullier, 1999; Burner & Waldo, 1995). As we saw in Chapter 1, however, it was not always the case that expenditures were so high. Until rather recently, families and friends cared for one another and doctors were relatively scarce. The few doctors there were had little in the way of medical equipment and medicines with which to care for their patients, and medical treatments were often bartered rather than purchased with money.

Today, in the United States, we have a very complex healthcare system. Medical care is typically delivered either through private physicians' offices, hospitals, or clinics. Hospitals may be public, private, or corporate. Corporate hospital organizations (such as HMOs) function under a single umbrella—that is, the same organization or company owns the hospital and clinics and hires the doctors, nurses, and technicians that work in the buildings. Public hospitals work in much the same way, except that they are governed at the state or federal level rather than being owned and controlled by a corporation. Private hospitals function a bit differently in that physicians are usually not employed by the hospital itself, but rather are paid directly by patients or their insurance companies.

In addition to the different structures that provide healthcare, there are also many different kinds of physician providers. For instance, general practitioners and those in family medicine and general internal medicine have broader training and typically care for patients over a long period of time—both dealing with illnesses as they arise and working with the patient to achieve and maintain health. Specialists are physicians who have chosen to concentrate their expertise in a more specific area. They typically do not see the same patients over and over again, but instead provide specialized care in more discrete time frames. For instance, a family practice doctor would certainly not perform surgery on his or her patients, but instead would refer them to a specialist (for example, to a cardiac surgeon or a vascular surgeon depending on the nature of the required surgery, or to a specialist such as a cardiologist for consultation in managing a heart problem). Because of the rising costs of healthcare, there has been increasing pressure to minimize the role of specialists and to have primary care practitioners provide an increasing proportion of care (McEldowney & Berry, 1995). Primary care practitioners are those who provide point-of-entry care for patients and often see patients over long periods of time, dealing with preventive medicine and chronic health problems, as well as more acute situations. Certainly, specialists play a necessary role in healthcare, but primary care practitioners such as internists, family physicians, pediatricians, nurse practitioners, and physician assistants with their broader perspectives and training can increase the efficiency and lower the costs of healthcare delivery.

Although it may at first seem surprising, the goals of individuals within the healthcare system are not always compatible. For instance, administrators of an HMO may strongly desire to minimize costs (and thus may be reluctant to allow a physician to perform many expensive diagnostic tests). At the same time, the physician's main goal might be to make a positive diagnosis in a puzzling case (a goal that may require a number of expensive diagnostic tests to accomplish). In another case, an x-ray technician may be worried about staying on schedule and not allowing a backup in his or her waiting room, while the radiologist values clear and precise x-rays, no matter how long it takes or how long the lines get. These are some examples of competing agendas, and they can be extremely common, given the complex nature of the delivery of healthcare.

Insurance Reimbursement and the Delivery of Care

Most Americans now receive their healthcare through some kind of managed care organization (often an HMO) (Martin & Bjerknes, 1996; Spragins, 1996). These HMOs function according to a system of **capitation**, which means that members (or their employers) pay a fixed fee, and all of the members' healthcare needs are covered under this payment. Physicians in this system often practice in their own offices. Some HMOs fall under the "staff model" in which physicians are employed by the organization, are paid a salary, and usually work in a designated facility such as a clinic (Wagner, 1989). Sometimes these doctors are given bonuses based on their performance or on the amount of money they are able to earn for the organization (that is, how much of the up-front revenue from patients and employers remains at the end of the covered period of time). Depending on the "bottom line" and philosophy of the company, physicians may experience many restrictions in terms of which diagnostic tests they can order and which treatments they can recommend to their patients.

Other types of HMOs include the following: the *group model* in which the HMO contracts with a group of physicians (therefore, individual physicians are employed by their group, rather than directly by the HMO); the *network model* in which the HMO works with several group practices; the *independent practice association model* in which various small groups of independent physicians are contracted by the HMO; and the *preferred provider organization model*, in which a more loosely organized group of healthcare providers (who remain independent but have agreed to abide by certain rules) contracts with insurance companies or company health plans (Madlem, 1997).

Constraints on Professionals and the Impact on Care

Has the increasing dominance of managed care in healthcare in the United States changed the way the system works? Has managed care influenced the way medical services are delivered? The answer is an unequivocal "yes," although the precise impact of these changes can be very complex. In some ways members of the public have benefited greatly, while in other ways they may have been harmed. Until the emergence of managed care, healthcare costs were increasing exponentially and no relief was in sight. There was little cost-containment within the industry, and many patients were unable to afford health insurance or adequate healthcare. And under the fee-for-service system, many unnecessary procedures were commonly performed (Mechanic, 1997; Reagan, 1992). The combination of the fee-for-service and third-party-payer (insurance) systems created an environment in which abuses could easily occur. Doctors and hospitals were paid for individual procedures and products provided, and in many cases they billed these charges directly to insurance companies. The insurance companies honored claims based on whether or not they were reasonable and typical—but prices were designated by those doing the billing. For example, according to this philosophy, if every hospital charged $1.00 per cotton ball, the insurance companies would be likely to pay it because, in reviewing "typical" charges, they would see that this was indeed the "going rate" for cotton balls. Patients were unlikely to complain or ask their doctors if certain tests or treatments were really necessary because, after all, they weren't paying for it.

The managed care system has done much to remove the incentives for overutilization that existed in the fee-for-service system, thus making the healthcare industry more efficient and opening up more opportunities for people from all walks of life, and at all income levels, to have adequate primary, secondary, and tertiary care. In fact, not only has overutilization been discouraged, but there are now plenty of incentives for prevention in place because patients who stay healthy do not use as many healthcare dollars and thus are more "valuable" under a capitation system. In some ways, managed care represents a positive change for physicians, as well. In a recent study, researchers found that doctors who were employed by an HMO or other hospital group tended, on average, to work fewer hours, see fewer patients, and spend more time with patients than did doctors in private practice (Kikano et al., 1998). Although job satisfaction was equal for both physician groups, employed physicians were able to enjoy more time relaxing with their families. This is an important finding because, as we have seen throughout this chapter, the life of a physician is very stressful. We also saw that relationships with family and friends are extremely important sources of strength for most physicians. It seems that physicians who are not self-employed, and are thus able to work a more limited number of hours, might be more relaxed and have an opportunity to engage in some of the activities that help to balance out the stresses in their lives.

Working within the managed care system also seems to change the way that care is delivered. One recent study asked physicians about the types of treatment they would recommend for patients with various problems. The independent variable was the type of insurance the patient had (capitated vs. fee-for-service). Physicians were more likely to prescribe expensive medications and make referrals to specialists if the patient was portrayed as having standard, fee-for-service insurance (Shen & Wenger, 1998). In this study, capitation predicted less treatment, and physicians perceived more conflict between what they felt was the most appropriate treatment and the costs of that treatment when the described patient had capitated insurance. It must be pointed out, however, that less treatment is not *always* negative. There are certainly cases in which watchful waiting, or a relatively minor and conservative treatment, better serves the patient's interests than a more aggressive approach. Potential costs, as well as potential benefits associated with any treatment must be weighed, and the balance will not always come out on the side of the more aggressive treatment. Thus, we can see that capitation is a two-edged sword. In many ways managed care's influence has been positive, but it may also have some negative effects. Because HMOs and other managed care organizations are *businesses,* they are necessarily concerned with making a profit (and even nonprofit HMOs need to keep their bottom lines "out of the red"). In their pursuit of financial gain, however, they may place excessive restrictions on care, and patients may be denied diagnostic tests or treatments that really are warranted.

All of this puts the physician in a difficult position. On the one hand, he or she is encouraged by the company to be as efficient as possible, to keep people healthy (a good thing), and minimize healthcare utilization (a good thing only if decreased utilization reflects better health and less need for care). On the other hand, the physician must try to meet patient needs, and sometimes these needs are quite costly. When this is the case, the physician may have to make tough decisions about whether a certain treatment option is appropriate, both in terms of the patient's health and well-being and in terms of what the company is willing or able to provide.

It should be clear by now that the process of medical care is very complex. Not only are puzzling questions and symptoms brought to the medical encounter by patients, but medical professionals have a number of physical and emotional pressures of their own that influence the care that they deliver. And, both parties are working within a much bigger system of healthcare delivery that exerts temporal and monetary influence on the practitioner-patient interaction. The fact that the system is complex does not mean that we cannot understand it and manage it. Maximizing the cost-efficiency and effectiveness of medical care is a topic of very real concern and an important area of empirical research. As we gain answers to the questions that have been addressed in Chapters 2, 3, and 4, we will be able to create better hospitals, better doctors, healthier patients, and better health maintenance teams.

Summary

1. In the process of providing patient care, medical professionals experience many unusual and sometimes overwhelming pressures. These include various physical stresses such as sleep deprivation, irregular meal schedules, poor nutrition, and few opportunities for relaxation and exercise. Emotional pressures can disrupt family life and friendships.

   - Medical training oftentimes involves mistreatment, including verbal attacks and public humiliation, threats of bodily harm, physical mistreatment, sexual harassment, and unwanted sexual advances.
   - Medical professionals sometimes lose their idealistic views of medical practice, are dismayed by the limitations of medical science, and hide their emotions from their patients, colleagues, and even from themselves.

2. The pressures of medical training can have serious consequences. Many medical students experience emotional distress and depression. Suicide was once much more prevalent among physicians than in the general population. Physician impairment may result from lack of sleep, overwork, alcoholism, or drug dependence.

3. Currently, approximately 40 percent of U.S. medical students are women, up from 6 percent in the 1960s. In recent years, there has been recognition of the important contribution of women physicians to the profession of medicine. Women tend to more easily express the personal characteristics of sensitivity and empathy for patients.

   - Women physicians tend to be more concerned than males about balancing work responsibilities and family life. In some realms, women physicians experience more stress than do men, but on average are just as well adjusted.

4. Caring for patients is almost always a matter of dealing with unknowns and probabilities.

   ■ Finding out what is going on in a person's body involves a process of clinical reasoning in which the medical practitioner collects information from the history, examination, and diagnostic tests. The goal is to reach a differential diagnosis.
   ■ Clinical decisions are made on the basis of both statistical predictions and clinical experience.
   ■ Many physicians have been found to make reasoning errors of premature closure.
   ■ Stereotypes and perceptions of a patient's social class, economic background, sex, and physical appearance affect physicians' clinical decisions.

5. U.S. healthcare systems have changed a great deal in the last century. Individuals once held primary responsibility for their own health maintenance and the cost of medical services. Now many insurance companies carry out this function.

6. Managed care has emerged as the dominant form of healthcare delivery in the nation and has changed the face of U.S. healthcare. Some of these changes have been positive and some have not.

   ■ Managed care is helping to bring healthcare costs under control by removing incentives for overutilization and providing incentives for preventive care.
   ■ Physicians who are employed, rather than self-employed, tend to spend more time with patients and also enjoy more leisure time with their families.
   ■ Physicians are less likely to prescribe expensive medications or refer a patient to a specialist if that patient is insured under a capitation program.
   ■ The emphasis that managed care companies place on cost-containment can put physicians in the uncomfortable and ethically delicate situation of having to weigh patient outcomes against financial costs.

THINKING CRITICALLY

1. Weigh the costs and benefits of the current medical training model. Do you think that the benefits outweigh the costs? If so, why? If not, why not? What would you do to change the system, if you had the power to do so? How would you measure whether your changes produced the desired effects?

2. How might the family relationships of a pediatric oncologist (who deals with children who have cancer) be affected by his or her job? In instances where job requirements (for physicians, or anyone) might have a strong impact on personal relationships, what role might a health psychologist play in fostering more positive personal interactions?

3. Should there be stricter controls on the access of medical personnel to prescription drugs? If so, how could this be done? If not, how would you justify maintenance of the status quo?

4. Intellectualization serves one useful purpose by allowing medical professionals to distance themselves from traumatic events. Does it serve any other useful purposes? How can it be harmful?

patients to stop smoking (Taira et al., 1997). This study concluded that physicians need to improve their communication with all patients about many health-related issues such as seatbelt use, alcohol use, safer sex, smoking, diet, and exercise. Many different methods can be used to help patients obtain the information they need from their doctors. For instance, as a patient you can prompt yourself to ask questions by writing out a list before going into the doctor's office and then consulting the list during the visit to be sure that everything has been asked. Or, you might meet briefly with a nurse before seeing the doctor so that you can review your questions and practice asking them (Sander et al., 1996).

Health communication involves not only the interactions you have with doctors. Health messages are targeted at you every day. For example, commercials on TV and ads in magazines promote medicines for all kinds of things, including high blood pressure, incontinence, asthma, allergies, headaches, colds, and erectile dysfunction. We are constantly reminded of our need for multivitamins, herbal supplements, and nutritional drinks or bars. If we weigh more than is ideal, there are plenty of diet soft drinks, fat-free foods, meal-replacement shakes, and pills that can help us to lose the extra pounds. And in the realm of exercise, we see attractive people on television and in print ads promising us a lean and beautiful body if only we would join a particular gym or buy a particular product. All of these stimuli affect our views of health and what it means to be healthy. These messages work in concert with the information we receive from our doctors, families, and friends to create our "ideal" vision of a healthy self and our plans for getting there. If we lack information about what the pursuit of health involves, we will probably be less healthy. On the other hand, if we have a good idea of what we want to achieve, we have a better chance of achieving it. The trick is, however, to have accurate information and to use appropriate and effective methods for achieving health goals.

In this chapter, we examine our societal progress toward eradicating or managing a number of diseases as well as preventing many unhealthy conditions. We also examine health-enhancement methods that are supported by much research on health and health behavior, as well as common deterrents to achieving good health behaviors and enhanced health.

Prevention of Disease/Impairments

Imagine life in the year 1900. If you had lived at that time in Boston, Massachusetts, you would have had access to the most sophisticated medical treatment available in the United States, and probably in the world. Yet, the most likely cause of your death would have been a bacterial infection that could today be cured with a ten-day course of antibiotics. In the year 1900, almost 2 percent of the population of the United States died, many from illnesses that we no longer consider to be extremely serious (Thomas, 1979). In 1900, almost 12 percent of deaths were caused by pneumonia and influenza (or the "flu"), which today are common and from which most people recover fully. Over 11 percent of deaths in 1900 were from tuberculosis, and over 8 percent were caused by dysentery (diarrhea), enteritis (bowel inflammation), and intestinal ulcers. These illnesses presented such problems because no antibiotics were available to eradicate bacterial pneumonia, tuberculosis, and intestinal infection, and medicine could provide little in the way of effective supportive therapy for those who had contracted severe viral infections such as influenza. Public health standards were so poor (for example, sewage systems were primitive or nonexistent and cities were dirty) that infectious diseases spread rapidly and epidemics were common (Torrens, 1978).

Obviously, the world has changed tremendously since 1900. The introduction of antibiotics in the 1940s completely changed the face of medicine. There was finally a means to cure bacterial infections that had plagued human beings throughout history (although the improper use of antibiotics has led to an upsurge in the number of antibiotic-resistant strains of bacteria, an issue that was addressed in Chapter 3). Ways of caring for individuals with viral infections have also become available, and immunizations to prevent the more problematic viruses (e.g., smallpox, polio, measles, mumps, rubella, and influenza) have contributed tremendously to the health and well-being of Americans. In the 1990s, influenza and pneumonia caused less than 4 percent of deaths (U.S. Bureau of the Census [USBC], 1998), and these deaths were usually among the elderly and among those already critically ill. These days, Americans suffer from some very different health problems than in the past. Let's examine what they are.

Degenerative Diseases

In the last decade of the twentieth century, people were much healthier than they were in the first decade. They also lived considerably longer. Deaths occurred later and from different, often avoidable, causes. In 1995 almost 75 percent of all deaths in the 25- to 64-year-old range were from chronic diseases (National Center for Health Statistics [NCHS], 1998). In 1996 the leading fatal diseases in the United States were cardiovascular diseases (41% of deaths) and cancer (23% of deaths) (USBC, 1998). Such diseases are now prevalent partly because people live long enough to develop them. In the past, death from communicable disease often came well before cancer or cardiovascular disease had a chance to occur. In 1900, for example, the average person in the United States died before reaching the age at which most people now develop cancer or heart disease or have strokes (Thomas, 1979). These present-day killers, as well as some others such as Type II diabetes and cirrhosis of the liver, are unlike communicable diseases. They are believed to be caused not by a pathogen such as a bacterium or a virus but instead to be multifactorial in nature—that is, they stem from many factors such as heredity and behavior and are referred to as the **chronic degenerative diseases**. These conditions are contributed to by the failure to carry out some important health behaviors (Baum & Posluszny, 1999).

Heart Disease

Heart disease is the primary cause of death in the United States, and it is estimated that in 1995, $79 billion in direct medical costs were due to heart disease (NCHS, 1998). Most heart attacks are attributable to coronary artery disease caused by **atherosclerosis,** a condition in which fatty, fibrous plaques narrow the opening of the coronary arteries, thus reducing the amount of blood that can get to the heart. When these arteries become blocked, the heart muscle can be deprived of blood and hence of oxygen. This condition is called a **myocardial infarction** (or more commonly, a heart attack), and it can cause part of the heart muscle to be damaged or destroyed. Myocardial infarction can cause mild to severe debilitation and can also cause death from heart failure (*Professional Guide to Diseases* [PGD], 1998).

Atherosclerosis has been linked to many factors, only some of which can be changed or controlled: obesity, smoking, hypertension, uncontrolled diabetes mellitus, emotional stress reactions (which we examine in Chapter 9), and high serum cholesterol/HDL ratio. In the past it was rare for premenopausal women to have atherosclerosis, but this is no longer true possibly because more women are now smoking, overweight, working in high stress jobs, and taking oral contraceptives (PGD, 1998). Research has shown that several of the risk factors for heart disease can be reduced or eliminated when people change their behavior. Carefully following treatments for high blood pressure and diabetes (both predisposing factors), maintaining normal weight and a low-fat diet, avoiding smoking, engaging in regular exercise, and modifying stress reactions can help to reduce heart disease risk.

Cancer

Cancer is the second leading cause of death in the United States. (It kills over 550,000 people each year). (See Figure 5.1 for site distributions of the most common cancers.) Cancer is not one disease, but a category of conditions characterized by the transformation of ordinary cells into neoplastic cells (cells that are larger and divide more quickly than do normal cells). Malignant (cancerous) cells proliferate, and a mass of

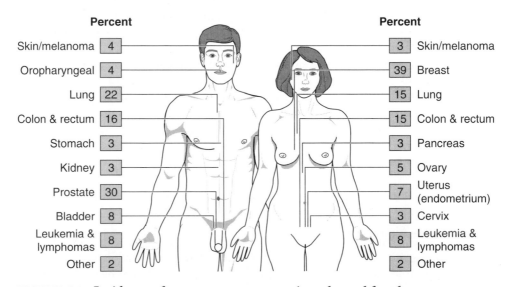

FIGURE 5.1   Incidence of most common cancers in males and females.

them can form a tumor. These cells can also spread throughout the body, sometimes very quickly (PGD, 1998).

A tremendous amount of research has been devoted to discovering the cause of and cure for cancer. However, there are not yet enough answers available. The malignant transformation of cells can result from a complex interaction of viruses, physical and chemical **carcinogens** (cancer-causing agents), genetic predisposition, compromises of the immune system, and diet. Theoretically, the human body develops cancer cells continuously in response, for example, to carcinogens like environmental toxins, cigarettes, certain foods, and food additives. An intact, well-functioning immune system can hunt out and destroy these cells. But, certain factors can inhibit the immune system: aging, toxic drugs, emotional stress (see Chapter 9), radiation, and even cancer itself (PGD, 1998).

Scientists do not yet understand the precise mechanism by which a carcinogen renders a cell malignant or the factors that enhance or depress the immune system's ability to destroy the cancer cell. Thus, the general mechanism by which cancer comes about and the means to prevent cancer are not yet known. A great deal of empirical research has been conducted, however, on individual cancers and their particular risk factors. Many of these risk factors are behavioral, and research has provided us with some important information about cancer prevention.

There are many known cancer-causing agents, such as the chemicals asbestos and benzene in buildings and polluted waters. Obviously, preventing cancer involves avoiding these substances, a goal that may depend a great deal upon knowing what is in one's environment and being able to control it. Some drugs, such as diethylstilbestrol (DES), are clearly carcinogenic. DES has been shown to cause reproductive organ cancers in young people who were exposed to DES prenatally (**in utero**). Certain substances that are encountered in everyday life are also carcinogenic, such as the smoke from one's own or other people's cigarettes. Not all carcinogens can be avoided; people may be exposed unknowingly to asbestos at work or may be taking medications now that will later prove to be carcinogenic. There are circumstances, of course, in which an individual can minimize his or her exposure to harmful environmental factors by avoiding such things as secondhand smoke and the midday sun and by not smoking.

Health psychologists are concerned with the *behavioral risk factors* of cancer—the factors in our everyday activities that contribute to cancer risk. Cigarette smoking is the leading cause of preventable disease and death in this country. It increases considerably a smoker's risk of lung cancer, emphysema, and heart disease. More than 400,000 deaths each year are due to cigarette smoking. That's nearly 1,200 people each day! Smoking costs Americans more than $50 billion each year in direct medical costs (NCHS, 1998). About 80 percent of people with lung cancer are smokers (PGD, 1998), the other 20 percent include people who are exposed to environmental toxins (including sidestream smoke) or whose cancer cause is undetermined. Even sun tanning (exposing the skin to the sun's ultraviolet rays) can cause disfiguring skin cancers as well as a deadly form of cancer called malignant melanoma. Box 5.1 presents some current statistics on skin cancer and describes health psychology research focused on increasing prevention through sun avoidance and sunscreen use.

BOX **5.1**

Research Close-up

Skin Cancer: Information and Prevention

"It's suntan turnover time," cooed the disc jockey after a half-hour of pop-music and acne medication commercials. "And this song is for all you lovely young ladies who are working on your deep, dark tans this weekend . . ." The beach, as usual, was blanket-to-blanket people. Nearly all of them were lying in the hot sunshine hour after hour, hoping to turn their skin golden brown. Many, instead, would burn from overexposure and because they failed to use sunscreen properly. Some did not use sunscreen at all!

Sunbathing is a risky activity, particularly for fair-skinned people, but, amazingly, about one-fourth of Caucasian Americans sunbathe, and a quarter of those don't use sunscreen properly (Koh et al., 1997). Sun exposure vastly increases the chances of developing skin cancer. Three major types of skin cancer are related to ultraviolet radiation exposure from sunlight. These are basal cell carcinoma, squamous cell carcinoma, and malignant melanoma. Basal cell carcinoma is slow-growing and almost never **metastasizes** (spreads to other parts of the body). Squamous cell carcinoma can spread to internal organs or lymph nodes, but together basal and squamous cell cancers have a high cure rate (around 90%). Malignant melanoma, on the other hand, can be deadly. It is the most serious form of skin cancer, and although it accounts for a small number of total malignancies, the death rate from this disease was steadily increasing from the 1950s until just a few years ago. It is now slowly starting to decrease (Lee, 1997). Melanoma is treatable if caught early, but if not treated promptly it can spread throughout the body, with devastating results.

Although many effective treatments do exist, the best medicine is prevention. Prevention involves limiting one's exposure to sunlight as well as correctly using sunscreens. It also requires regular checking of one's entire body

for skin lesions or moles that look suspicious and bringing these to the attention of a doctor. Preventive behavior in the realm of sun exposure and cancer prevention has had relatively little study. Keesling and Friedman (1987) conducted an extensive study to determine the factors that influenced people's sun exposure and use of sunscreens. They interviewed 120 sunbathers on California beaches. Sunbathers with the darkest tans, who spent a good deal of time in the sun, were found to have little knowledge about skin cancer. They were more relaxed, liked to take risks, and were more likely to perform activities related to their appearance. They were also influenced by groups of friends who valued a tan. Those who more regularly and effectively used sunscreen had higher anxiety, were more likely to know people who had skin cancer, had greater knowledge about skin cancer, and were more likely to be women. Interestingly, health beliefs did not predict suntanning or sunscreen use. Another, more recent, study found that Caucasian men who are young and have no history of cancer are the least likely to take precautions against sun overexposure (Hall et al., 1997).

Many people know they are at risk but they sunbathe anyway. By way of intervention, researchers are attempting to increase people's understanding of the severity of skin cancer by showing that it can be very disfiguring, and that malignant melanoma is one of the cancers most likely to be fatal. Health professionals are also trying to educate people about precisely how to use sunscreens for maximum protection, and how to examine their skin for cancerous or pre-cancerous growths. Intervention programs that simply provide information are helpful, but knowledge does not necessarily translate into safer behaviors. Comprehensive prevention programs are significantly better at changing behaviors, attitudes, and beliefs, and these gains are maintained for longer periods of time following the intervention (Rodrigue, 1996). Such programs not only provide information but also address other issues, such as helping people find practical ways to protect themselves and remind themselves to take precautions. Further, these programs provide social support for carrying out preventive behaviors.

In the case of cancer, prevention also involves screening for early detection. Most forms of cancer have higher survival rates the earlier in the disease process the cancer is discovered (Battista & Fletcher, 1988). Breast cancer has a very high survival rate following treatment if it is caught early, when the breast tumor is very small. The overall five-year survival rate for breast cancer is now 95 percent; it was only 72 percent in the 1940s. This change probably results because breast cancer is now often caught in the early stages and there are many effective treatments available. Proper screening for breast cancer includes self-examination, clinical examination, and regular mammograms. The best method for detecting breast cancer is doing a monthly breast self-exam (BSE) and immediately following up on any abnormality (PGD, 1998). Despite the fact that many women do not regularly examine their breasts, most lumps are found by women themselves, not by doctors (George, 2000; Newman, 1997). Thus, regular (once a month) BSE is critically important for a woman to perform in order to enhance her chances of stopping a cancer early in its development. A woman should also have a physician or other trained medical practitioner perform an annual clinical breast exam. And, physicians following guidelines from the American Cancer Society recommend mammograms (x-ray studies of the breast) every one to two years for women 40 to 50 years old and annually after age 50, with a baseline mammogram at age 35.

Despite campaigns by the American Cancer Society and the National Cancer Institute, many women do not check their breasts regularly, and when they do, many do it incorrectly (Stevens et al., 1994). Many older women (approximately 40%) also do not get mammograms because they are embarrassed, it is uncomfortable, or they fear finding cancer (PGD, 1998; USBC, 1998).

Cancer experts recommend that men perform self-examinations for testicular cancer (which mostly affects young to middle-aged men). Monthly testicular self-examination is the most effective means for detecting tumors, and, if caught early, chances of full recovery are very high (Barling & Lehmann, 1999; Katz et al., 1995). Self-screening for cancer also includes measures to detect skin cancers—regularly checking one's skin for changes in the appearance or texture of moles and for new growths or patches of discoloration.

Of course, the individual cannot do all cancer screening at home. Physician palpation for breast or testicular growths is also necessary, and (as noted above) mammograms can help detect breast cancer. Tests also exist to detect cervical cancer (the Pap test, recommended roughly every two years for all women) and cancer of the endometrial lining of the uterus (the endometrial biopsy, recommended for post-menopausal women who are at risk for endometrial cancer). Finally, to detect colorectal (colon and

Combined with breast self-examination and clinical breast exams, mammography is the best method for early detection of breast cancer.

rectal) cancer, the American Cancer Society recommends that everyone over 40 should have an annual digital rectal examination by a physician and everyone over 50 should also have one of the following: an annual fecal occult blood test (FOBT) with flexible sigmoidoscopy every five years, a colonoscopy every ten years, or a double contrast barium enema every five to ten years. People at higher risk (due to family history, etc.) should have more frequent screening tests (American Cancer Society [ACS], 2000). The American Cancer Society recommends that every individual exercise self-responsibility and pay attention to the seven warning signs of cancer, with the acronym CAUTION: Change in bowel or bladder habits; A sore that does not heal; Unusual bleeding or discharge; Thickening or lump in breast or elsewhere; Indigestion or difficulty in swallowing; Obvious change in a wart or mole; Nagging cough or hoarseness.

Although cancer is more common in older individuals than in younger ones, it does occur in young adults, teenagers, and even children. Attending to the warning signs of cancer and conducting the relevant self-examinations regularly may be time consuming or even emotionally threatening to the individual (ACS, 2000). In Chapter 6, we will examine in detail the factors that contribute to an individual's decision to carry out health promoting actions.

Stroke

Stroke (also known as a **cerebrovascular accident** or CVA) is a sudden impairment of circulation to the brain. A stroke usually occurs because a blood vessel has been blocked (for example, by a blood clot or a fat deposit). This blockage deprives a portion of brain tissue of oxygen and damages it permanently. CVA is the third most common cause of death in the United States today (NCHS, 1998), and approximately half of its victims die. Of those who do survive, about half remain permanently disabled and approximately half experience another stroke. The aftermath of a stroke can be devastating, as many individuals are left paralyzed and/or without the ability to speak. Some experience cognitive deficits such as the inability to identify certain objects with words (Krantz & Deckel, 1983).

Prevention of stroke requires lifetime control of its risk factors, since most strokes occur in the aged population. One of the most important factors in preventing stroke is the control of **hypertension** or high blood pressure (PGD, 1998). Those who are obese, have atherosclerosis, and smoke cigarettes are most at risk. In addition, the use of oral contraceptives increases the risk of CVA, primarily among women who smoke cigarettes.

Primary Prevention and Behavioral Outcomes

The diseases and conditions described above cannot, at the present time, be eradicated. They are not amenable to treatment in the relatively simple way that bacterial infections are cured with antibiotics. And, unlike many viruses (such as polio), the conditions of stroke, heart disease, and cancer cannot be prevented with immunizations. Some scientists believe that new discoveries in medicine and technology may someday provide cures or immunizations for preventing such diseases, but at present the only option available is adopting preventive health behaviors.

Above, we have considered a few of the major health risks that can be controlled, if not eliminated, with appropriate health actions. Now, we will examine specific health behaviors in detail. As we do this, however, it is important to keep in mind that not all medical conditions can be prevented by simply changing one's habits. There are likely some contributing factors that are not yet known (for example, an infectious process), or that are known and uncontrollable (for example, one's genetic predisposition). However, because in many cases taking certain preventive actions can reduce some component of health risk, a considerable amount of suffering, disability, and mortality may be prevented with behavior change.

Let us examine **preventive health behaviors,** which are actions taken by an individual to prevent disease from developing or to forestall the negative outcomes of a disease condition. These include diet and exercise, the prevention of alcohol and drug abuse, quitting cigarette smoking, using automobile safety belts, and obtaining vaccinations.

Primary prevention, a term that has gained considerable popularity in recent years, refers to activities that are undertaken by apparently disease-free individuals with the intent of helping them to achieve maximum well-being and avoid disease (Elias & Murphy, 1986). This is done before there is evidence of illness, or even of an increased risk. One example would be a fit and healthy person taking up power-walking as a way of maintaining cardiovascular fitness. Primary prevention includes both health promotion and disease prevention. Many people these days try to attain good health and vigor, and attempt to forestall the ravages of disease and old age. Fortunately, such a goal is within their reach. We will look at some of the more important primary prevention activities, or preventive health behaviors, and examine the effects they can have on life and well-being.

Secondary prevention becomes relevant once a person has developed a condition in which he or she is "at risk" for further health damage. Secondary prevention involves taking preventive health measures in order to forestall potential negative outcomes. Such a condition might be hypertension (high blood pressure), which, if uncontrolled, can lead to stroke. Another might be hypercholesterolemia (high serum cholesterol), which, if uncontrolled, can lead to a heart attack. Both these conditions may need to be managed with medication, special diet, and an exercise program.

Tertiary prevention involves taking measures specifically designed to cure a disease or to control its progress. Examples are the faithful taking of medication by the patient with an acute infection or cooperation with various aspects of treatment such as radiation or surgery by the patient who has cancer. Tertiary prevention measures are designed to prevent further disability and handicap (Alberman, 1986). Below, we examine methods of primary prevention, summarized in Table 5.1.

Safety Restraints

Kaiesha totaled her car. Something went wrong with her steering mechanism, and she hit a pole on the side of the freeway exit ramp going 40 miles per hour. She was wearing her safety belt correctly, and although she was shaken up, she escaped without injury. Everyone who looked at the mutilated car was amazed that Kaiesha was still alive.

TABLE 5.1   A Summary of Basic Preventive Health Practices

Primary prevention: Activities undertaken by apparently disease-free individuals with the intent of helping them to achieve maximum well-being and avoid disease.

They include:

- Safety Restraints/Automobile Safety Belts
- Immunizations
- Safer Sex
- Nutrition and Diet
- Control of Weight and Obesity
- Sleep
- Avoidance of Cigarette Smoking
- Avoidance of Alcoholism and Problem Drinking, and Drug Abuse.

April was doing some errands close to home and didn't think she needed her safety belt. Unfortunately, a too-eager teenage driver ran a red light and slammed into her car in an intersection. Her car was going only 15 miles an hour and his was going 20, but when the impact occurred, she was thrown forward and hit her jaw hard on the steering wheel. The day after the accident, April felt sore and stiff in her neck, shoulders, and back. The accident marked the beginning of back pain and severe headaches for April, because the jolt caused structural damage to her neck, back, and jaw. She had to give up dancing and start physical therapy and was told by her doctor that she might require surgery to repair the damage.

Trauma is the leading cause of death in people under the age of 35 (PGD, 1998), and many of these traumatic injuries are the result of automobile accidents. Statistics about the value of automobile seat belts and shoulder harnesses (together known as safety belts) are very convincing: Safety belts are about 42 percent effective in preventing automobile fatalities, and they can also prevent injuries (Evans, 1996; Viano, 1995). They protect an individual from being thrown from the car or against the windshield, dashboard, or steering wheel. Chest injuries, for example, account for one-fourth of all trauma deaths in the United States, and most blunt chest injuries result from auto accidents in which the driver is thrown against the steering wheel. Belted drivers can better maintain control of their cars. Even in cases in which a driver or passenger must get out of the car in a hurry (such as in a fire, or when the car plummets into water), a safety belt allows him or her to maintain consciousness during the initial impact so that it is then *possible* to leave the car. Safety belts transfer the energy of a sudden stop and impact from the smaller, more vulnerable parts of a person's body (such as the head) and spread it out over stronger parts, such as the pelvis and rib cage.

The addition of airbags prevents an additional 12 percent of fatalities (Viano, 1995), but drivers who depend on their airbags alone and do not use their safety belts dramatically increase their risks of serious injury (Evans, 1990). It is important, however, for drivers and passengers to be at least 12 inches away from the airbag. Small children should never be in a seat that has an airbag because of the potential for injury from it. Safety seats for children placed in the back seat are especially effective in preventing injury and death. Many studies have shown that even at relatively low speeds, sudden braking or impact can send a baby or small child flying out of an adult's arms and into the windshield of a car (e.g., Agran, 1981). Children sitting on an adult's lap and restrained by a seat belt around both passengers risk serious injury from being crushed by the adult's body in an impact. The difference between the ideal and what people are actually doing is vast. One recent study of 5,900 children who should have been in child safety seats found that only about half of them actually were. Most of the remaining children *were* restrained in adult safety belts that were ineffective because of the child's small size. For those that *were* in child safety seats, only about 20 percent of the seats were installed correctly or being used properly (Decina & Knoebel, 1997).

Despite the clear advantages that safety belts provide in a crash, adults have been surprisingly slow to adopt their use. In 1974, for example, when all new automobiles were equipped with safety belts, only 6 percent of people used them. Current estimates of safety belt use range from 48 percent to 95 percent (Hunt et al., 1995; Lange & Voas,

1998). In states with laws that require safety belt use, 25 percent more people do in fact "buckle up" (Nelson et al., 1998). Why do some people fail to use safety belts? Many say that they are uncomfortable, that they forget, or that they are only driving a short distance and therefore don't feel that they need the restraint (Hunt et al., 1995). Physicians who treat adults rarely remind their patients to use safety belts—one recent study found that only about 4 percent counseled their patients about safety belt use (Hunt et al., 1995). This is one area in which safety researchers are calling upon physicians to educate their patients that using safety belts can cut their risk of death or severe injury almost in half (Kizer & Trent, 1991).

Immunizations

During the 1940s and 1950s in the United States, there was an **epidemic** (widely diffused and rapidly spreading occurrence) of a potentially deadly virus called poliomyelitis (often referred to as polio). Polio is an acute communicable disease that causes death in 5 to 10 percent of cases (PGD, 1982). It can also cause partial or complete paralysis. In 1955, a **vaccine** became available, developed by Dr. Jonas Salk, for immunization against polio. This vaccine has been called one of the wonder drugs of medicine. The vaccine stimulates the production of antibodies in the human body, so that encounters with the virus do not result in infection. While the Salk vaccine involves an injection, another form of the vaccine, the Sabin (named for its developer) can be taken orally. The polio vaccine has so effectively eliminated polio in the United States that today it is very difficult for many young people to appreciate how truly feared the disease was. In some ways, that fear is comparable to current fears surrounding HIV and AIDS. Polio, however, is much more easily transmitted than is HIV. The polio virus can be passed through touching, using another's towel or toothbrush, or licking another's ice cream cone. Thus, polio could spread easily among children.

Outbreaks of polio occur even today, although it is easy for anyone to obtain an oral vaccine, without cost, at nearly any county health department in the country. In 1979, for example, there was a minor polio epidemic among the Amish of Pennsylvania who had failed, for the most part, to immunize their children. And, in 1994, there was a large outbreak of measles (another less serious disease for which there is immunization easily available) among Christian Science students in Missouri and Illinois. Why do people fail to use immunizations, which are low cost (and often free) and have been shown to be highly effective? Some of the very earliest research on health behaviors was conducted to try to determine precisely this. It concluded that when people believed that a disease was not serious or could not harm them, or that getting vaccinated was not worth the trouble, they tended to fail to take advantage of the immunizations available to them (Rosenstock, 1974). We examine this research in greater detail in Chapter 6.

Safer Sex

Sexually transmitted diseases are common and are transmitted between individuals who are sexually intimate (whether this is through intercourse or other activities). These diseases include herpes, gonorrhea, syphilis, chlamydia, and hepatitis. Each of these diseases is serious, and hepatitis, in particular, has recently presented an increasing health concern. There are several kinds of hepatitis (A, B, C, D, and E, with B being transmitted through blood, needles, or sexual contact).

Acquired Immune Deficiency Syndrome (AIDS) is the most deadly sexually transmitted disease. It is an illness that impairs its victim's immune system and hence his or her ability to fight infection. The person with AIDS is extremely susceptible to disease and typically dies of an infection, such as a serious lung condition called *Pneumocystis carinii* pneumonia, a form of cancer called Kaposi's sarcoma, or a virus called cytomegalovirus. Although AIDS was originally a disease that claimed mostly gay men and intravenous drug users in this country, it has increasingly afflicted heterosexuals—particularly women. There is not much difference between men and women in terms of the clinical course that AIDS takes, although women are somewhat less likely to develop Kaposi's sarcoma and somewhat more likely to develop bacterial pneumonia (Melnick et al., 1994; Phillips et al., 1994). Another interesting factor is that one of the most common early symptoms of AIDS for women is a gynecological infection. Such infections are common and not often associated with AIDS, and women with this type of manifestation may not be diagnosed until much later, once the disease has progressed farther. The incidence of AIDS diagnosis is increasing for women. In 1985, women accounted for only about 6 percent of the cases, but in 1996 they accounted for 20 percent (USDHHS, 1998a). Minority groups have also been disproportionately affected by the AIDS epidemic, with blacks accounting for nearly half of the HIV infections in 1996 and Latinos comprising about 20 percent (USDHHS, 1998b).

AIDS is caused by the retrovirus HIV (human immunodeficiency virus, type I) which is transmitted from one person to another through the exchange of bodily fluids, including blood, semen, and vaginal secretions. Such exchange can occur during sexual contact or needle-sharing when injecting intravenous drugs. HIV can also be transmitted by means of transfusion with infected blood. Because of this, blood donations are now screened (using ELISA with Western Blot) for antibodies to HIV. If the blood contains the antibodies, it is immediately discarded and the donor is notified. This same test is available from private physicians and clinics for those who are concerned that they may have been exposed to HIV. Those at highest risk for contracting AIDS are homosexual and bisexual men, intravenous drug users, babies of HIV-infected women, those who received blood transfusions before 1985, and heterosexual partners of people in the above groups (PGD, 1998). As of 1988, there were about 70,000 diagnosed cases of AIDS in the United States. In the following years there was a steady increase in AIDS reporting, with over 41,000 new cases in 1990, 43,000 in 1991, and 45,000 in 1992. The peak was in 1993 with over 103,000 new cases of AIDS. Since then there has been a steady decline, with about 78,000 new cases in 1994, 71,000 in 1995, 67,000 in 1996, and 58,000 in 1997 (USBC, 1998). We should point out that in 1992 the Centers for Disease Control broadened the definition of HIV infection and AIDS. This change is partially responsible for the dramatic jump in incidence rates from 1992 to 1993. However, since the AIDS epidemic began in 1981, it is estimated that over 30 million individuals worldwide have been infected, and almost 7 million have died (Holmberg, 1996). AIDS has, thus far, proven to be almost always eventually fatal.

The **incubation period** (time from HIV exposure to AIDS diagnosis) is about eight to ten years, although it can be shorter or longer depending upon many factors (PGD, 1998). During this time, the individual may be symptom free and pass the virus on to others. Within the first several weeks of HIV infection, an individual typically experiences some mild (and common) symptoms, such as headache, fever, or sore throat. These don't last long, however, and soon the person enters the much longer latency (or incubation) period. This incubation period ends with symptoms that often include swollen lymph nodes, night sweats, diarrhea, anorexia, and fevers, and a diagnosis of AIDS. Eventually, the person transitions to the later stage of AIDS, in which the immune system is severely compromised, and the body's T-lymphocyte cell count drops to 200 or fewer per cc of blood. Soon after, the person may die.

There is currently no cure for AIDS, but there are several ways of slowing its progression. Antiretroviral treatments, such as AZT and DDI, have come into widespread usage. In fact, until rather recently, these were the primary forms of treatment. Now, protease inhibitors are proving to be very effective in treating HIV-infected individuals, and highly active antiretroviral therapies (HAARTs) work so well that in many cases the virus is not even detectable in the blood of the infected person (Bonfanti et al., 1999; Shafer & Vuitton, 1999). HAART is a general term that refers to a combination of several antiretroviral drugs, usually including drugs from at least two of the three categories of antiretrovirals (nucleoside analog reverse transcriptase inhibitors, non-nucleoside analog reverse transcriptase inhibitors, and protease inhibitors). These combinations work extremely well for those whose HIV infections have never been treated with other drugs, but they are very expensive and require strict adherence to the complex dosage schedule. This schedule is very demanding and tends to be difficult for many people to achieve. When used properly, however, these drug treatments can dramatically slow the progression of HIV infection. When coupled with the adoption of other health behaviors such as quitting smoking and drinking, lives can be prolonged (Folkman, 1993; Kelly et al., 1998).

What can a person do to protect him- or herself from exposure to this killer? Avoiding all forms of intravenous drug use is an important health measure in general, and is particularly critical for the avoidance of HIV infection. In addition, certain sexual practices have been determined to be quite risky (such as anal intercourse and vaginal intercourse without a condom), since they raise the chances of spreading the infection during sexual contact. The best method for preventing the spread of the disease through homosexual or heterosexual contact is abstinence or monogamous sexual relations with an uninfected person. Beyond that, the use of condoms with spermicidal creme or jelly that contains the chemical Nonoxynol 9 is considered safer than unprotected sexual relations. The birth control pill does not protect against HIV infection or any other sexually transmitted disease.

Research demonstrates that knowledge about HIV and ways to practice safer sex have changed the behaviors of homosexual men, who are at high risk for infection. Research shows that homosexual men in the United States were quick to make radical changes in their behavior in order to prevent the further spread of HIV (e.g., Becker & Joseph, 1988; Ekstrand & Coates, 1990). Although behaviors have changed, however, there is evidence that among young gay men (for whom the panic of the rise of the epidemic is less salient), there are still many who engage in unsafe sex (Penkower et al., 1991). Perceived susceptibility, social support, and self-efficacy (the belief that one can accomplish a goal) have all been shown to be important predictors of whether individuals will adopt safer-sex behaviors (Steers et al., 1996). Although there is still considerable disagreement as to which interventions are most effective, programs that integrate safer-sex messages across a variety of domains (e.g., pregnancy prevention, AIDS prevention, and the prevention of other sexually transmitted diseases such as syphilis and hepatitis) seem to be most effective (Cates & Cates, 1999; DiClemente, 1998).

Box 5.2 examines one public health crisis—the growing HIV epidemic in the former Soviet Union.

Nutrition and Diet

Think about someone you know who is described as a "meat and potatoes man" or as having a "sweet tooth." These labels reveal something important about how deeply ingrained eating habits can be. Anyone who has tried to change his or her own eating habits knows that food choices and diet are difficult to alter! Change may be critical to health and survival, however. Considerable evidence is accumulating that our dietary choices can affect our susceptibility to disease. A diet low in saturated fat may help to reduce the risk of heart disease. The control of dietary sodium can affect levels of blood pressure and ultimately cardiovascular disease. And while high levels of dietary **cholesterol** may lead to atherosclerosis and ultimately to coronary heart disease, certain foods (oat bran, for example) can reduce serum cholesterol.

The reduction of serum cholesterol through dietary interventions has been shown to lower coronary heart disease (CHD) mortality (death) and morbidity (illness). The average U.S. diet contains about 40 percent fat, but experts recommend reducing it to somewhere between 20 and 30 percent, and particularly eliminating saturated fats. Experts encourage eating fish and poultry rather than red meat, and foods that are broiled or baked rather than fried. Ice cream, butter, and other high fat foods should be eaten rarely if at all (American Heart Association [AHA], 1984).

A person's diet is not easily changed, because we eat according to habit and our habits are strongly influenced by our environments, our culture, and our personal likes and dislikes. As you may know from experience, changing your diet is easy for a few hours or days, but it's very difficult to do in the long term. Nonetheless, Americans are slowly improving their diets (at least in some ways). For instance, the average American ate about 105 pounds of fresh fruit in 1980, but by 1996 this number had increased to 129 pounds (USBC, 1998). In the next chapter we will examine in detail the factors that are likely to promote many health behaviors, including dietary change.

Obesity and Weight Control

Obesity and excess weight are common problems in the United States today. Definitions of obesity vary, as do the ways of measuring it. Body weight and mass, appearance, percent body fat, and level of fitness are all factors that are important to think about when trying to determine whether someone is overweight or "obese." For

BOX **5.2**

Across Cultures

The Former Soviet States and HIV

As most people are keenly aware, contact with infected bodily fluids can transmit HIV, the AIDS virus. Infection usually occurs through unprotected sex, injection drug use with infected needles, and transfusion with tainted blood (extremely rare with today's standards). HIV cannot be contracted through casual contact or kissing, from mosquitoes, or from a toilet seat. Throughout the world, various countries have experienced periodic epidemics in the number of persons acquiring HIV, and these epidemics have occurred for a variety of societal reasons. The United States witnessed an HIV epidemic in the male homosexual population in the early 1980s, and then again in the early 1990s among intravenous drug users.

Currently, the countries of the former Soviet Union are witnessing such an epidemic (Atlani et al., 2000). This epidemic is of particular concern because of the political, social, and economic state of affairs in these countries. The situation in the former Soviet Union is fairly unique and does not parallel epidemics in other areas of the world. The political and economic structure of the former Soviet countries is highly stressed, resulting in severely limited health resources. Living standards after the collapse of the communist system have dropped markedly for individuals who are dependent upon public assistance. Failure to adjust to the rapid and severe changes in these countries has caused poverty to become widespread (Atlani et al., 2000). In such conditions of political, social, and economic upheaval, many people turned to drugs and sexual behavior to escape from their pain and suffering. In these countries, injection drug use and a strong drug culture are driving the HIV epidemic (Atlani et al., 2000). For example, in the Ukrainian city of Odessa, the estimated HIV infection rate among IV drug users was 1.4 percent in January 1995, 13.0 percent in August 1995, and 31.0 percent in January 1996. Nykolayev, a second Ukrainian city, shows similar figures among the IV drug-using populace: 0.3 percent in 1994 had acquired HIV, 17 percent in 1995, and 57 percent in January 1996. It is difficult not to be astounded by these figures!

Observers of the IV drug-using population note a very strong group culture and very high rates of sharing of needles and other drug implements (Atlani et al., 2000). Some of these drugs are actually sold prepackaged in (usually nonsterile) ready-to-use syringes. Others are injected at "shooting galleries" or parks where groups of young people congregate. This situation has been referred to as the "Odessa syndrome" among the professionals who are working to reduce the drug use rates and harmful practices.

A growing commercial sex industry and increased mobility among persons living in these regions is causing great concern that HIV will begin to proliferate in non-drug-using populations. Due to the widespread poverty, a surprising number of women in these countries have turned to the sex industry to support their children. They unwittingly "bridge" the populations of high-risk and low-risk individuals. For example, they may engage in high-risk sexual behavior with infected IV drug users, acquire the virus, and then pass it on to men (and in turn to their wives) who have no drug background and who would otherwise be at very low risk for acquiring HIV. Prevention through the use of condoms may not be an option because of their unavailability and expense and refusal of clients to use them.

instance, a very athletic 16 year old might weigh a good deal more than a very thin one, but *not* be considered overweight and might even be in much better physical health than the thinner peer. In general, someone who is more than 20 percent above his or her ideal weight is considered obese, but other factors must also be taken into account. Percentage of body fat is perhaps most important, as is the distribution of the fat. There are very precise ways of measuring the percentage and/or distribution of body fat (such as by immersion in water or by using ultrasound), but most people do not have easy access to these methods, which are costly and complicated. The skinfold technique (where folds of skin are measured with calipers) is popular, but is not terribly accurate (Bray, 1992). Another easy, and relatively accurate, method of assessment is body mass index (**BMI**), which has been adopted by many researchers as a standard indicator. BMI is calculated as weight in kilograms divided by height in meters squared (kg/m^2). It has been suggested that BMIs of greater than 27.7 for men and 27.2 for women can be considered "obese" (Williamson, 1993). It has also been suggested that women should have 20 to 27 percent body fat and men should have 15 to 22 percent, and that those above this are considered obese.

Current estimates indicate that about one-third of the population qualifies as obese (Battle & Brownell, 1996), and Americans are getting fatter. Between 1971 and 1980 the number of overweight adults stayed constant, but then the increase began, and by 1994 nearly 40 percent of Americans were overweight (although not all of these qualified as "obese") (NCHS, 1998). Once an individual becomes obese, the condition tends to be self-perpetuating. His or her internal metabolic mechanisms readjust to maintain the higher weight. Excess girth makes it difficult to move around, and the overweight individual becomes more and more sedentary, further exacerbating the obesity (Stunkard, 1979).

Excess weight contributes to many health problems. The greatest risk is of heart disease, but hypertension and stroke are also potential outcomes. The risk of some forms of cancer is also associated with being overweight, and obesity can cause adult-onset diabetes. Losing weight and keeping it off can be difficult, however, and people who lose weight through dieting usually gain it back rather quickly (Agras et al., 1996). In one study, subjects typical of overweight individuals in general participated in a dieting program (Wilson, 1980). At the five-month point, the average participant had lost 40 percent of his or her target goal for weight loss. By fourteen months, however, the average dieter had gained most of that weight back. Losing and regaining weight can have detrimental metabolic and health effects. Repeated cycles of weight loss and regain have been found to be associated with increased metabolic efficiency (Foster et al., 1996). With such efficiency, weight is maintained with fewer and fewer calories per day. Over time, it becomes more and more difficult for an individual to lose weight. Also, it has been found that when weight that was lost is regained, negative effects on blood pressure and cholesterol level (both risk factors for heart disease) may outweigh the positive effects of losing weight in the first place (Brownell et al., 1986).

Research shows that simple dieting alone usually does not work to get weight off and keep it off (Straw, 1983). An individual needs to consume fewer calories than he or she expends in energy, but because the metabolism has a tendency to become more efficient with dieting, simply eating less and cutting down one's calorie intake is not effective. The best way for an individual to lose weight and keep it off is to develop sound eating habits and to engage in regular physical exercise to raise the metabolic rate (Brownell & Stunkard, 1980). A recent meta-analysis that compared twenty-five years worth of studies on diet, exercise, and combined diet/exercise programs for weight loss showed that although dieting alone was nearly as effective for weight loss in the short term, programs that combined diet and exercise were more successful over the long term (Miller, Koceja, et al., 1997). Low-fat diet and exercise are even more effective than pharmacological (drug) interventions (Epstein & Wing, 1980).

While the answer to weight loss seems to lie in lifestyle change, there are many barriers to such change. For instance, there are many environmental factors that influence what and how we eat. In our society, food is almost constantly available, and we tend to be served (and to eat) large portions. There are many tantalizing and attractive foods that are energy-dense and high in saturated fat. In addition, we are bombarded with TV commercials that portray mouthwatering delicacies. Obtaining calorie-dense foods is also easy in modern times. Driving in our automobiles and not actually expending any physical energy, we can zip down to the supermarket or restaurant to indulge our food cravings. Further, we are coaxed to spend hours sitting at our computers, video games, or in front of our TV sets burning few calories. All of these factors promote obesity and make healthy lifestyle change difficult to achieve (Hill & Peters, 1998).

Various psychological factors also play an important role, as we will examine in more detail in Chapter 6, which deals with changing health behaviors. Whether a person believes that he or she can stick to a healthy diet may influence whether there is even an *attempt* to eat healthfully. Many individuals use food as a method of coping with difficulties or stress in their lives (such as by eating fattening "comfort foods"). The constant cultural pressure to be thin or to have a muscular physique may lead a person who is less than perfect, as most of us are, to simply give up in despair. These barriers, and others like them, make primary prevention a standard that can be exceedingly difficult to achieve.

Box 5.3 examines important new research that sheds light on the age-old question: "Why Are We Hooked on French Fries?"

Exercise

Jack is 55 years old, overweight, and has never exercised a day in his life. He is in middle management and is firmly convinced that exercise is dangerous, as well as being unpleasant. He is quick to point out the sudden death of a famous marathon runner from heart failure. That's the kind of news report he remembers! Sudden, strenuous exercise would obviously be unwise for Jack, or any person his age who is sedentary and overweight. Rather, a medically supervised program of gradual weight loss and light exercise, such as walking, would be about all he could manage right now. Of course, it would be possible for him to build up to a program of more vigorous exercise and weight control that could lengthen his life and enhance his well-being. But Jack is not interested.

BOX 5.3

Research Close-up

Why Are We Hooked on French Fries?

Even though we know that eating fatty foods increases our risks for a variety of negative health outcomes, including obesity, diabetes, hypertension, and some cancers, we still crave them! Why? It's partly because of their **orosensory properties** (the sensations that these foods provide when we have them in our mouths) (Drewnowski, 1995). Other factors, such as convenience, habit, and cognitive/emotional associations also play a role, of course. Recent research, however, indicates that preferences for high fat foods have both learned and biological (genetic) components (Warwick & Schiffman, 1992).

For many years we were taught in textbooks that taste nerves generate only four qualities: sweet, salty, sour, and bitter. Recent research indicates, however, that taste nerves aid in the perception of a number of other qualities, such as fatty, metallic, and chalky tastes (Gilbertson et al., 1997; Schiffman, 1997). Some people (termed "supertasters") are more sensitive than others to bitter tastes. Supertasters can easily be identified in the general population with a simple test. In fact, you may have tried this experiment in a biology or other science class. Two bitter chemicals (called PTC and PROP) are readily available through laboratory supply companies.

These chemicals are embedded in thin strips of paper called "taste papers," which can be placed on the tongue. Most individuals taste nothing when they do this, or perhaps they taste a slight bitterness. But supertasters, on the other hand, have a much stronger reaction. They snatch the papers from their tongues, grimace, and usually run for the nearest drinking fountain while saying something like, "Oh yuck, that is so disgusting!" Interestingly, these individuals are also more sensitive to the orosensory properties of fat and have more taste receptors than average on their tongues (Tepper & Nurse, 1997).

Differential sensitivity to dietary fat might make it more difficult for certain individuals, such as supertasters, to cut down on the fat in their diets. They can easily detect, and often dislike, the low-fat version of their favorite dish. There are now products on the market that either imitate some of the orosensory properties of fat, or that (although technically "fat") are only partially metabolized and thus don't provide as many calories as "regular" fat (one such product is "olestra"). These products are not calorie free, so a person can still gain weight by overeating them. Nonetheless, they may help supertasters to conquer their high-fat cravings and maintain a healthier lifestyle.

Jack's attitude is typical of that held by many people only several decades ago. But these ideas are gradually becoming outmoded as more and more Americans are coming to value exercise. Undertaken regularly over the course of one's life, **aerobic exercise** (defined as exercise that dramatically increases oxygen consumption over an extended period of time) can bring some important benefits to health and well-being (DiLorenzo et al., 1999). Examples of this are brisk walking, running, swimming, or cycling. Exercise helps to lower high blood pressure, contributes tremendously to weight control, and raises high-density lipoprotein cholesterol. Exercise strengthens an individual's cardiovascular system, making the heart and lungs work more effectively and efficiently, and reducing the risk of cardiovascular disease (Paffenbarger et al., 1978). Weight-bearing exercise (including walking, running, and aerobic dancing) prevents **osteoporosis**, a condition to which older women are most prone. In osteoporosis, bones become brittle and weak and fracture easily. Exercise also reduces the aerobic requirements of day-to-day activities and makes muscles more efficient, rendering everyday activities easier in terms of their stress and strain on the body. Exercise helps to delay the onset of debilitation from old age and chronic disease and exercise increases both "active life expectancy" and life expectancy itself. Exercise preserves bodily functioning and prolongs independent living in older persons (Yeater & Ullrich, 1985). Exercise also contributes to a better (subjectively rated) quality of life. Many people report more restful sleep when they have exercised regularly, and exercisers (especially runners) list the psychological benefits of exercise nearly as often as they list the physiological benefits (Harris, 1981). They report feeling lower levels of anxiety and depression and increased self-esteem. Even in prospective research, both self-selected and randomly assigned (experimental group) exercisers had lower depression levels than controls who did not exercise (Brown et al., 1978; McCann & Holmes, 1984). Other studies have shown that exercise can help to reduce situational (short-term) anxiety (Focht & Koltyn, 1999; Harper, 1978; Long, 1984). Regular exercise also seems to be related to enhanced feelings of self-esteem (Sonstroem, 1984). In fact, a review of the literature indicates that aerobic exercise significantly reduces depression, anxiety, distress, and coronary-prone behavior, while it enhances mood, cognitive functioning, and self-concept (Anthony, 1991).

During the 1980s, the commonly held belief was that the minimum amount of activity needed to attain these benefits was twenty minutes, three times a week, in aerobic exercise at a minimum of 70 to 85 percent of maximum heart rate (220 minus the individual's age) (Larson & Bruce, 1987). However, recent evidence indicates that more moderate and less structured physical activity is nearly as effective in promoting health (including cardiovascular fitness) as other, more regimented programs (Andersen et al., 1999; Pate et al., 1995; Pratt, 1999). Psychological benefits, even from a relatively short exercise-promotion intervention, can be long-lasting. A twelve-week program to increase aerobic fitness showed that not only were participants better off physiologically and psychologically at the end of the twelve weeks, but they were better off twelve months later, too (DiLorenzo, et al., 1999)!

The value of regular exercise is acknowledged by many Americans (over 70% in some surveys). But only about 40 percent actually engage in any regular physical exercise (Dunn et al., 1999). And, only about 50 percent of those who have begun an exercise program are still exercising six months later. Despite the immediate and long-term benefits, many people find exercise to be an extremely difficult endeavor. They do not enjoy exercising (or they have not found an exercise they do enjoy). They become bored with the routine or feel they cannot spare the time. Once they lose the physical conditioning they gained, it becomes unpleasant and difficult to regain it. Other statistics bear this out as well. Most adult fitness programs report success rates of only 40 to 65 percent in the first year, with a substantial drop-off after that time. Even when the exercise is for the purpose of rehabilitation from a cardiac problem, 30 to 50 percent of participants drop out during the first twelve months. Forty-five to 80 percent drop out within two years (Ice, 1985). The pressure to exercise for health reasons may be one factor that motivates people to get regular exercise, but it takes more than the knowledge of health risks. It requires dedication and appropriate mechanisms for support or help in doing the activity (Fuchs, 1996).

Despite the fact that only about 10 percent of Americans participate in regular, *vigorous* physical activity (USBC, 1998), we now know that many health benefits may accrue from more moderate exercise. Walking, yard work, climbing stairs, and many other common activities are all quite beneficial and can lead to many of the same health benefits that more vigorous exercise fosters (Pratt, 1999; USDHHS, 1996). Even incorporating these in an informal way (such as taking the stairs instead of riding in the elevator, walking to class instead of driving across campus, or mowing the lawn and washing the windows instead of paying someone to do it) will increase fitness and result in health benefits.

Sleep

Sleep is an extremely important health behavior, and one that is an essential element of primary prevention. Healthy sleep has been established in research to be at least as important, and possibly more important, than diet and exercise in predicting longevity. So says Dr. William Dement, a physician and the world's leading authority on sleep, sleep deprivation, and the diagnosis and treatment of sleep disorders. In his book *The Promise of Sleep* (Dement & Vaughn, 1999), he documents the critical role of sleep in human health. After more than four decades of research, it is very clear that getting enough sleep is essential to longevity and the avoidance of many diseases.

Sleep represents a "perceptual wall" between the conscious mind and the outside world, a regularly occurring "disconnection" between the mind and outside stimuli that (unlike the situation when a person is in a coma) is immediately reversible with external sensory stimuli (such as the sound of an alarm clock). When people sleep less than the ideal number of hours for them, they accumulate a "sleep debt," which must be "paid off" in order for them to function optimally. Getting one hour less sleep than one needs each night Monday through Thursday can result in a four-hour sleep debt by Friday night. The tendency to "sleep in" on weekends is an attempt to pay off that sleep debt. The good news is that the number of hours needed to pay off the sleep debt does not have a perfect one-to-one relationship with the number of hours of sleep lost. Usually, the sleep debt can be paid off in a somewhat shorter time, although the test of successful "payoff" is that the individual no longer feels at all sleepy during the day.

Hardly anyone is a stranger to the feeling of drowsiness. The eyelids feel heavy, and it is difficult to keep them open. Drowsiness is the last step before sleep. When drowsiness occurs during an activity that requires alertness, such as driving a car, it is extremely dangerous. Daytime drowsiness is not "normal," even if it is early afternoon, a person has just eaten lunch, and he or she is sitting in a "boring" class. When people are bored, they tend to fidget, doodle, or daydream. Sleepiness is a sign that one is not getting the sleep one needs. Studies show that most people need somewhere between seven and a half and nine hours of sleep per night, with the average being about eight hours. Very few people need much less or much more sleep than that. Most people in the United States get far less sleep then they need, however. Many college students regularly get only about five or six hours a night and don't completely make up for the sleep loss on weekends.

Sleepiness is one of the greatest causes of traffic accidents in the United States. In fact, it is estimated that as many as 24,000 people die each year in car accidents that are caused directly or indirectly by falling asleep at the wheel (Dement & Vaughn, 1999). Sleep debt was ruled by the National Transportation Safety Board (NTSB) to be the cause of the *Exxon Valdez* oil tanker running aground in Prince William Sound in Alaska in March of 1989. The third mate on the ship had slept only six hours in the previous forty-eight and made some critical errors that caused the worst U.S. oil spill in history. Investigation of the explosion of the Space Shuttle *Challenger* revealed that the severe sleep deprivation of the managers at NASA was a major factor in the incident.

We live in a nation of chronically sleep-deprived people. Many say they do not have time to sleep as many hours as they would like. The electric light bulb, television, computers, and the Internet have provided many opportunities for stimulation well past the onset of darkness. The demands of modern life push us to stay up well past our "biological bedtime." Often, by the time the average adult has fulfilled all of his or her daily tasks of work, studying, hobbies, caring for children, the most inviting thing is to relax by watching a movie or the late night news, by catching up on email, or by browsing the Internet. These can be wonderful conveniences of modern life, of course, and few people want to significantly limit what they accomplish in their lives in order to sleep. But sleeping enough can have some advantages that might be worth considering.

Studies show a direct correlation between the quality of an individual's mental performance and getting enough sleep. People who get adequate sleep are more hopeful, their senses are more acute, and their minds more receptive to ideas and to people. They have a greater sense of well-being than those who are sleep-deprived. In terms of longevity, sleep is more important than most people think. For example, in a study of over a million Americans, those who slept an average of eight hours per night lived the longest. Getting enough sleep promotes more effective immune functioning. The amount and quantity of sleep one has gotten before being exposed to a virus or infection is a significant factor in whether one becomes ill. Sleeping too little tends to promote unpleasant mood, hopelessness, and even depression, as well as mental fogginess and limited creativity. Sleep debt is implicated as a cause of stomach upset and increased sensitivity to pain, and in studies with rats, extreme sleep deprivation caused a complete shutting down of the immune system.

Some things certainly interfere with sleep, and many of these can be controlled. Hyperarousal and stress (in response to problems as well as to favorable and exciting things) can interfere temporarily with sleep. Time zone and schedule changes can hinder sleep, as can difficult sleeping environments (a noisy apartment building, a snoring spouse, a snoring dog (!), or a bedroom that is too hot or too cold). Other common causes of sleep interference include restless legs syndrome, heartburn, or gastro-esophageal reflux disease (treatable with medication and lifestyle change), and fibromyalgia (a condition marked by significant pain in muscles and connective tissue). Insomnia is a problem for some people, and in many cases it can be treated easily; following the good sleep habits listed on the next page can help. Many times insomnia is brought about simply by anxiety about not being able to sleep. The sleep medication zolpidem (trade name Ambien), which is a short-acting hypnotic, is metabolized before the night is over and so there is no morning grogginess. It induces sleep with the fewest side effects. Over-the-counter sleep medications that consist of antihistamines often leave users groggy in the morning and make them vulnerable to rebound insomnia the next night.

For most college students, habitual behaviors are the factors that interfere most with getting enough good quality sleep. Experts suggest the following "sleep hygiene" techniques for effectively carrying out this important health behavior:

(1) Avoid caffeine (in sodas, coffee, tea, chocolate, and other sources) within eight hours of bedtime. Some people can be kept awake by having any at all during the day; some can't sleep if they have any after 10 AM!

(2) Set a regular sleep time that gives you the sleep you need (say 11 PM to 7 AM). Stick to this schedule seven days a week, and make up any sleep loss or a sleep debt will be incurred.

(3) Control external stimuli before sleep time; stay away from things that could be exciting, upsetting, or cause anxiety or anger (e.g., bills, email). Pick another time of the day to worry if you feel you need to.

(4) Do something enjoyable and relaxing but not too exciting before going to sleep. Read something that you find pleasant.

(5) Take advantage of a paradoxical intervention that works. Try *not* to fall asleep! Lie in bed quietly with the lights off and *try* to stay awake and think about a math puzzle like the following: Start with the number 1000, and count backward by 17. You'll be asleep before you know it!

Sleep debt and driving are a dangerous combination. Drowsiness while driving is a warning sign that must be heeded because it signals oncoming sleep that can occur suddenly without the individual's awareness or control. The effects of even small amounts of alcohol, well below the legal limit, can be intensified if an individual is driving with a sleep debt. Alcohol can make a sleepy driver much more likely to fall asleep while driving. Dr. Dement strongly recommends that if you become drowsy while driving, you should let someone else drive if at all possible. If not, he recommends pulling off the road very soon and taking a brief nap. Ingesting some caffeine can help, but it takes about 15 minutes for the caffeine to take effect. A brief nap during that 15 minutes can do wonders to increase alertness. These are emergency measures, however. There is no substitute for being well rested regularly, especially when driving.

Cigarette Smoking

There are few habits as potentially deadly as smoking cigarettes. As noted earlier, more than $50 billion is spent each year on medical costs for diseases caused by smoking, and every day nearly 1,200 people in the United States die sooner than they would be expected to as a direct result of smoking cigarettes (NCHS, 1998). Needless to say, these deaths usually come after protracted, painful, and debilitating illnesses such as heart disease, stroke, emphysema, or cancer. Cigarette smoking during pregnancy may result in lower birth weights and retardation of the fetus's brain growth, as well as increasing the risk of Sudden Infant Death Syndrome (see Chapter 13) and of malignancy in the baby (Harrison, 1986).

Smokers are ill considerably more often than are nonsmokers. The frequency of acute illness among male smokers is 14 percent higher than for male nonsmokers and they lose 33 percent more workdays. For females, the difference is 21 percent higher acute illness and the loss of 45 percent more workdays. Generally, smokers are less healthy than nonsmokers and they have almost twice the chance of dying in any given year (1.7 times) (Tucker, 1985). Roughly 25 percent of the adults in the United States smoke cigarettes (USBC, 1998). This percentage is lower than in 1955, when 53 percent of the population smoked, or even the early 1980s, when about one-third of the population smoked. In 1964, the first Surgeon General's report on smoking (USD-HEW and USPHS, 1964) highlighted the dangers of smoking and an extensive publicity campaign was launched. Yet, while the percentage of male smokers in the United States decreased to 39 percent by 1975, the percentage of female smokers rose (from 25% to 29%). The percentage of male and female adult smokers is now estimated to be about 26 percent and 23 percent respectively. The U. S. Surgeon General's Reports of 1964 and 1974 likely had a significant impact on smoking behavior. From 1920 to 1964, cigarette consumption had increased at a very rapid rate and peaked in 1963. But between 1964 and 1979, it is estimated that 29 million Americans quit smoking. Since the mid-1960s, there has been considerable effort on the part of government agencies, the American Cancer Society, the American Lung Association, the American Heart Association, and other organizations to get the word out that smoking is dangerous.

If smoking is such an unhealthy activity, why haven't more people quit? One reason is that smoking is addicting both physically and psychologically (despite what the tobacco companies may say). The nicotine in cigarettes is primarily responsible for the physical addiction (Schachter, 1980). Nicotine is a stimulant that raises blood pressure and increases heart rate. Some people are so addicted to nicotine that they can't get through a whole night without a cigarette. Some smoke a cigarette as soon as they wake up in the morning and even smoke when they are sick. But the physical addiction is not the only determinant. Psychologically, cigarettes provide a kind of "crutch," by giving the individual something to do in tense, uncomfortable, or boring situations. Furthermore, events, people, and places that have been paired with smoking may serve (in the manner of classical conditioning) to trigger the desire to smoke.

Why do people start smoking in the first place? The first puffs are often accompanied by dizziness and even nausea. Yet, the (usually young) individual who starts to smoke tends to respond to other cues as well. Those who persist in smoking do so typically because the reinforcement value of smoking outweighs these negatives. Peer pressure on young people may be particularly strong, for example (Evans et al., 1984; Presti et al., 1992). There may be immediate positive consequences provided by feeling grown up, sophisticated, and accepted (Dinh et al., 1995). The immediate negative physical feelings of smoking then eventually give way to the rewarding effects of the stimulant drug, nicotine. People probably smoke for various reasons beyond those we have discussed. For some it is simply a deeply ingrained habit, to which they may even be oblivious. Others smoke to reduce distress, anxiety, and other negative feelings. Some may smoke to increase stimulation, to feel relaxed, or to gratify sensorimotor needs. There is no simple explanation, but instead many reasons, for why people smoke (Lichtenstein & Glasgow, 1992).

What works to help people quit? Early research in the mid-1970s found that **aversion therapy** was somewhat successful. The smoker was forced to take a puff every six seconds until satiated and then to continue until smoking became aversive. It was believed that (in an operant conditioning model) the negative feelings that followed taking a puff of the cigarette would serve to reduce the probability of continued smoking. Rapid smoking was, however, found to be dangerous. In some cases, the practice led to cardiovascular stress and heart attack in people who had latent cardiac problems (Hackett & Horan, 1978). Other aversive techniques, such as imagining disgusting things associated with cigarettes or pairing electric shock with smoking (see Figure 5.2), do have initial success rates (quit rates) as high as 60 to 90 percent but relapse occurs if the distressing associations are forgotten over time (Leventhal & Cleary, 1980). In general, quitting seems to be determined by three basic factors: (1) the person's level of motivation, which includes readiness to quit and persistence in the face of obstacles (note that Prochaska's "Transtheoretical Model of Change" addresses readiness to quit and is presented in detail in the Chapter 6); (2) the person's level of addiction; and (3) the combination of supportive factors and barriers to quitting that are present in the environment

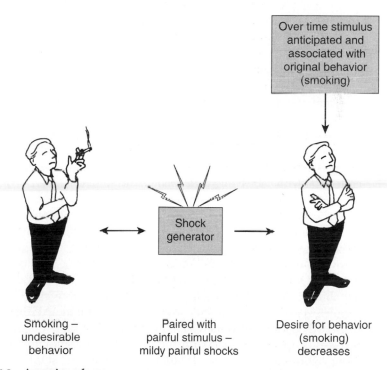

FIGURE 5.2 Aversion therapy.

(Lichtenstein & Glasgow, 1997). A variety of nicotine replacement gums, skin patches, and even fake cigarettes (so that the would-be ex-smoker can pretend to be smoking, and even receive a dosage of nicotine) are now available in stores everywhere. These enable the smoker to begin to unlearn his or her smoking habits, and to deal with the environmental cues to smoking as well as to tackle the physiological withdrawal from nicotine, which can then be reduced gradually over time. Nicotine replacement therapy seems to be quite effective in helping some people who want to stop smoking (Hughes, 1993). Exercise is another promising aid for smoking cessation and has been found both to help people quit and to prevent their return to smoking (Brownell et al., 1986). Other therapies use operant conditioning principles such as external rewards for not smoking, self-observation, self-monitoring, cognitive interventions such as self-talk, and even self-hypnosis. (We will examine behavioral and cognitive therapies in Chapter 6.) Probably every combination of these therapies has been tried with high initial success rates (Leventhal & Cleary, 1980). One study showed that 95 percent of people who quit have done so on their own (Surgeon General, 1979) and another study reported that self-quitting (with no professional help) had a success rate over 60 percent (with quitting maintained for over seven years) (Schachter, 1982). These findings suggest that people who attend smoking cessation clinics may be those who initially failed at their own personal attempts and have sought professional guidance. Thus, they may not represent the average population of smokers. In clinical studies, smoking cessation proves to be decidedly difficult to maintain. The rate of failure of smokers trying to kick the habit is as high or higher than the failure rate of those who try to overcome heroin addiction (Hunt et al., 1971; Lichtenstein, 1982).

Why do would-be quitters have so much trouble staying away from cigarettes? The answer is multifaceted and the subject of much study. **Relapse** is particularly common in addictions (Brownell et al., 1986). Relapse is defined as a recurrence of symptoms of a condition after a period of improvement. (This concept is discussed in more detail in Chapter 6). In the case of smoking, relapse refers to returning to being a smoker after a period of having quit. Environment can play an important part in smoking relapse. This is true particularly because smoking may have become connected to many aspects of the person's social and physical environment. For example, the individual's smoking may have become associated with drinking alcohol and/or coffee and with socializing with friends who smoke. In fact, having friends who smoke is a good predictor of whether someone will relapse (Mermelstein et al., 1986). Some researchers have suggested that environmental associations actually elicit the physiological reactions that once occurred when the individual smoked. Under such circumstances, ex-smokers report feeling an overwhelming urge or craving to smoke (Brownell et al., 1986; Shumaker & Grunberg, 1986). Physiological factors cannot be ignored. Quitting smoking often brings the classic withdrawal symptoms of headache, irritability, and sleeplessness that may last for days or weeks (Clavel et al., 1987). Many people experience weight gain after quitting smoking (McBride et al., 1996). This is true partly because nicotine speeds up the metabolism (Audrain et al., 1995) and partly because people often deal with the difficulties of smoking cessation by consuming more calories (French et al., 1996). For some people, smoking assists in dealing with emotional distress. An individual may turn back to smoking to provide a positive experience in the midst of distressing emotions, or to help eliminate those distressing feelings directly. In one study, 71 percent of relapsed smokers had some kind of negative emotional experience immediately preceding their relapse. Most common were anxiety, anger, frustration, and depression (Shiffman, 1982). Some people go back to smoking when they no longer believe they have the ability to maintain control in avoiding cigarettes and when their motivation to maintain the behavioral change has decreased (Shumaker & Grunberg, 1986). Social factors can be important as well. Support to refrain from smoking can be a powerful determinant of success, whereas pressure from others (for example, a spouse who smokes) to accept a cigarette can derail an attempt to stay away from cigarettes (Lichtenstein, 1982).

Alcoholism and Problem Drinking

The excessive use of alcohol is a hazardous practice that can threaten life and health. It can cause cirrhosis of the liver, fetal alcohol syndrome (physiological and cognitive abnormalities in a fetus), and an increase in the risk for some cancers (Finncy & Moos, 1991). About one-tenth of the U.S. adult population (over 18 million individuals) are either alcoholics or problem drinkers (Dorgan & Editue, 1995), and almost one-fifth of people between the ages of 25 and 49 report heavy alcohol use (having five or more drinks on at least one occasion in the past month). Men are almost three times as likely as women to report heavy drinking (NCHS, 1998). About half of Americans use alcohol at least monthly, which is a decrease from 1979 when about 88 percent of the population drank alcohol at least once per month (USBC, 1998). The 10 percent of the U.S. population that has drinking problems uses about 50 percent of the alcohol that is consumed in the United States (NIAAA, 1981).

An **alcoholic** is someone who is physically and psychologically addicted to alcohol and experiences health and social problems from its consumption (USDHHS, 1981). Alcoholics are physically addicted to alcohol, have high tolerance for it, and have little ability to control their intake. They experience severe physical symptoms of withdrawal when they attempt to stop drinking. **Problem drinkers**, on the other hand, may not evidence withdrawal symptoms but nevertheless experience social, psychological, and health problems as a result of their drinking. Alcoholics and problem drinkers usually need alcohol every day and are unable to limit the time and quantity of their intake. They continue to drink despite cognitive (e.g., memory), health, and social impairments due to drinking. The excessive consumption of alcohol can produce some serious health problems. **Cirrhosis of the liver** is the primary cause of death among alcoholics. Cirrhosis is an accumulation of scar tissue on the liver, causing loss of functioning in this vital organ (Eckhardt et al., 1981). Heavy alcohol use can also affect the constriction of the heart muscle, making it function less efficiently, and can cause nerve damage. Alcohol affects brain chemistry, and long-term heavy drinking can produce severe memory problems, disorientation, and visual disorders (Eckhardt et al., 1981). Heavy alcohol consumption can cause infertility, and alcohol can have a direct negative effect on pregnancy and fetal development. The **fetal alcohol syndrome** affects infants of mothers who drank during pregnancy. Fetal alcohol syndrome includes mental retardation, central nervous system disorders, and growth and

Alcohol consumption is accepted and widespread in our society, but it can be problematic if excessive or combined with driving.

facial abnormalities (Pratt, 1982). Even light to moderate drinking is believed to be dangerous to the fetus, especially during the early months of pregnancy.

Problem drinkers and alcoholics put others in danger when they drive automobiles. Almost 2 percent of all deaths in the United States are due to motor vehicle accidents (USBC, 1998), and about half of these involve drunk drivers. In fact, people who drive while intoxicated are three to fifteen times more likely to have a fatal traffic accident than nondrinking drivers. Of course, drinking even moderate levels of alcohol can increase driving risk. Driving can be adversely affected by as few as three glasses of beer in a 190-pound man, and by as little as one glass of wine in a 120-pound woman (Eckhardt et al., 1981). Alcohol also figures prominently in homicides and suicides, which are leading causes of death in people under age 40.

Does alcohol use bring any benefits? Some research has suggested that less than one or two drinks per day may provide some protection against cardiovascular disease by raising a subfraction of HDL (high-density lipoprotein, the "good" cholesterol that is negatively associated with heart disease) and by lowering LDL (low-density lipoprotein, the "bad" cholesterol that is positively associated with heart disease) (Gordon & Doyle, 1987; Gordon & Kannel, 1984; Weidner et al., 1991).

There are many theories about why people drink to excess. Many believe that it reduces their tension and acts as a sedative and anxiety reducer, particularly in comfortable, pleasant surroundings. While this simple hypothesis has not found much support in research, a modified version of it has. High levels of alcohol consumption tend to decrease the strength of one's physiological responses to distressing stimuli (Seeman et al., 1988; Sher & Levenson, 1982). When people are dealing with a lot of stressors in their lives, they are more likely than at relaxed times to abuse alcohol (Catalano et al., 1993; Greenberg & Grunberg, 1995; Sadava & Pak, 1994). Furthermore, drinking can interfere with self-depreciating cognitions, making thoughts more superficial and decreasing negative ideas about oneself while increasing positive emotions (Cooper et al., 1995; Hull, 1981).

The **disease theory of alcoholism** has given rise to medically oriented treatment programs and decreased the stigma associated with alcoholism. The theory is based partly on the genetic component in alcoholism (Cloninger, 1987; Glenn et al., 1989), and partly on the large body of research on the pharmacological treatment of alcoholism (Anton et al., 1995; Garbutt et al., 1999; Johnson & Ait-Daoud, 2000). Medications, such as opiate antagonists, are now available that target neuroreceptors critical in the addiction process. These drugs can lessen cravings for alcohol, thus making abstinence easier than it would be without the drugs (O'Brien, 1994; O'Malley, 1996; Tinsley et al., 1998). Alcoholism is not an easily treated condition, and it should probably be thought of as a chronic disease that requires long-term management, much the way diabetes does.

Research suggests that many of the effects of alcohol, including loss of control, are as closely tied to expectations, beliefs, and behavioral and cultural factors as they are to biological factors (Ennett & Bauman, 1991; Lesch & Walter, 1996; Marlatt & Rohsenow, 1980; Tinsley et al., 1998; Zucker & Gomberg, 1986). Some studies have shown that the best outcomes are achieved when alcoholics are subtyped according to various dimensions (biological, sociological, psychological), and treatments are tailored to meet the specific needs of that subtype (Johnson & Ait-Daoud, 2000; Lesch & Walter, 1996). Furthermore, studies show that even severely dependent drinkers can often learn to control their alcohol intake (Moos & Finney, 1983). Based on these findings, current treatment programs for alcoholism and problem drinking typically use a multimodal approach. They attend to biological, psychological, social, and environmental factors simultaneously. People learn new behaviors that are not compatible with alcohol abuse, and they learn to modify their activities and environments to eliminate their association with alcohol. Many programs involve a short-term, intensive, inpatient stay (for example, from ten to sixty days) with follow-up sessions. Medical "detoxification" may first be necessary for those with serious addictions to alcohol. Once the severe symptoms of detoxification have passed, therapy can begin.

Because addiction involves both psychosocial and biological components, it is important that treatments address both areas. Drugs are available that interact with dopaminergic and glutamatergic neural systems, and these can be helpful in breaking the biological portion of the addiction cycle (Johnson & Ait-Daoud, 2000; Tsai et al., 1995). To address the behavioral element of the addiction, aversion therapy is used and has proven to be a successful approach. In aversion therapy, drinking alcohol is paired with an aversive event such as nausea and vomiting (caused by a drug). Other aversion therapy programs pair electric shock with alcohol consumption. Successful maintenance of alcohol avoidance tends to require continued aversive conditioning outside of therapy (Mahoney & Thoreson, 1974). Aversive conditioning does work in combination with other forms of therapy (USDHHS, 1981), in particular with approaches that help the individual to recognize and change the factors in his or her life that contributed to the drinking. Some programs, for example, are geared to training individuals to develop the skills necessary to cope with stressful events in their lives and to develop social skills that they can use instead of relying on alcohol (Marlatt, 1982). Family therapy is also valuable in helping to identify and change the family dynamics that might rekindle and support the alcohol problem. Research suggests that the most successful programs are multimodal, and the most successful patients are those who have families to return home to, who have good job situations, and who enjoy their work (Moos & Finney, 1983; Wanberg & Horn, 1983).

The question of whether former alcoholics and problem drinkers can ever drink again is a subject of heated debate among many researchers. Groups such as Alcoholics Anonymous (AA) maintain that a recovered alcoholic can never drink in moderation and must abstain from alcohol for the rest of his or her life. While return to moderate drinking tends to bring about relapse in some individuals, a small group of recovered alcoholics who fit a particular profile may be able to drink in moderation. They are those who are young, employed, who drank for only a short time, and who live in supportive environments (Marlatt et al., 1993).

Secondary and Tertiary Prevention and Behavioral Outcomes

Disease onset, as well as management of disease, are affected by two broad categories of variables: those that are related to the individual, and those that are environmental (Adler & Matthews, 1994; Taylor et al., 1997). If an intervention is to be truly effective, it must address both these domains. Below, we examine some factors that are associated with effective intervention programs. Then, in Chapter 6 we examine in more detail some of the specific things that influence whether patients comply with treatments that are recommended by their physicians.

Components of Interventions That Work

In general, interventions that combine various approaches appear to be more effective than those that focus on only one method of changing behavior. For example, a recent meta-analysis of the literature on patient education and counseling for preventive health behaviors found that using several channels of communication, such as the media and one-on-one discussion, results in better outcomes for things like smoking, control of alcohol use, nutrition, and weight loss (Mullen et al., 1997). Interventions that take place in the social environment itself can also be quite effective. For instance, another recent meta-analysis of school-based interventions to help kids eat more healthfully found that these multifaceted programs are generally quite effective (McArthur, 1998). Additionally, specific characteristics of both the target population and the healthcare system must be taken into consideration when designing an intervention (Sarnoff & Rundall, 1998). A multifaceted intervention that does not address the *particular facets* of importance to a community will not be effective; and, if the healthcare delivery system cannot keep up with the demands created by the intervention, it cannot work. Case studies show that listening with an open mind to people within a community allows for the development of programs that are culturally sensitive and tailored to the needs of the group (Wang & Abbott, 1998).

Let's look at a specific example. First, assume that a physician wants to encourage a patient to become more physically fit, because she or he knows that there are both physical and mental health benefits. Following psychological principles can make the intervention more effective. A fitness assessment should be done, which will let the patient know his or her current status. This should be coupled with discussion to make sure that the patient understands the importance of, and benefits associated with, being physically fit. Next, the physician should help the patient to set *realistic* fitness goals and make sure that the patient understands why a particular plan will help him or her to achieve the goals. In addition, it is a good idea to inform the patient of the absolute minimum activities that will help to improve his or her condition. Next, the physician should work with the patient to create a convenient and enjoyable program of exercise. Finally, she or he should provide adequate supervision over the program and give positive reinforcement when the patient is successful in carrying out the plan (Anthony, 1991). As you can see, this is a fairly lengthy process, with many steps. However, it is only when interventions are thorough and address potential problems ahead of time that they are likely to be successful.

Another type of intervention that is often effective is an incentive program. Incentive programs reward people for accomplishing goals, thus giving them additional motivation to work hard. Increasingly, large organizations such as insurance companies and employers are instituting these types of programs to encourage their employees or clients to strive for good health. A recent meta-analysis of incentive programs to encourage the use of safety belts indicates that several factors of incentive programs are important, including initial baseline rate of the behavior, the population involved, whether the incentive was given based on group or individual behavior, and when the incentives were received (immediately or after a delay) (Hagenzieker et al., 1997). These factors would likely be important considerations for any incentive program.

Controlling Hypertension

Now, let's look at an example of secondary prevention in action. Hypertension, or high blood pressure, is an unusual disorder in that it has no overt symptoms. A person can have a dangerously high blood pressure and never even suspect it, because subjective feelings of blood pressure level are generally not at all accurate (Meyer et al., 1985). Although the name may lead people to believe that blood pressure is elevated only when a person feels "hyper" or "tense," even very relaxed people can have hypertension. About 15 to 20 percent of adults in the United States have hypertension, and it is a major cause of cardiac disease, stroke, and renal failure (PGD, 1998). Fortunately, if it is detected early, and if treatment is followed diligently by the patient, hypertension can be controlled and the potential negative outcomes can be forestalled.

The treatment for hypertension is multifaceted. Diligence in monitoring blood pressure regularly is necessary. The National Institutes of Health recommend that treatment follow a stepwise pattern. The first step involves lifestyle change, such as losing weight, exercising regularly, quitting smoking, and reducing alcohol and sodium intake. In many cases, these changes bring blood pressure back into the normal range. If the patient still has high blood pressure after step 1, the second step involves drug therapy. Beta-blockers or diuretics (which reduce blood volume) are usually used and together with the lifestyle changes are generally effective. For some patients, however, even these measures are not enough, and treatment moves to step 3, which involves increasing the drug dosage, trying a different drug instead of the current one, or adding another drug to the one already being taken (PGD, 1998). Lifelong behavior changes and drug schedules are not easy to maintain, however. In the first year, more than 20 percent of hypertensives completely drop out of treatment. Even among those who remain in treatment, fewer than 50 percent carry out their regimens as prescribed (DiMatteo & DiNicola, 1982).

Controlling Diabetes

Now let's look at another example, this time from the perspective of tertiary prevention. Diabetes is a metabolic disease that is characterized by abnormalities in the body's ability to secrete or to effectively utilize insulin. The failure to metabolize sugar causes an excess of glucose in the blood, a situation that can have significant health-damaging effects. In 1995, the seventh leading cause of death in the United States was diabetes (accounting for almost 3% of all deaths), and mortality from diabetes is increasing. Between 1990 and 1995, death rates from diabetes increased by about 17 percent for men and 12 percent for women (NCHS, 1998). Diabetes is also a risk factor for a variety of other problems, such as heart disease, kidney failure, and blindness. Insulin-dependent diabetes (Type I) develops in children, usually between ages 5 and 6 or between ages 10 and 13. Type I diabetes is managed primarily with daily injections of insulin (American Diabetes Association [ADA], 1976). Type II diabetes, on the other hand, usually develops after age 40, although it can develop in persons much younger. It is not as serious as Type I, and the individual produces some, though not enough, insulin. Most type II diabetics are obese (ADA, 1976). Diabetes can result in coma and death if it remains uncontrolled. Poor control of the disease can result in blindness and loss of extremities (for example, toes can develop gangrene from poor circulation and need to be amputated). For both Type I and Type II diabetes, control is complex and lifelong, requiring many behavioral changes. Diet must be restricted, sometimes severely. Eating must take place on a regular schedule. Blood must be tested several times every day, and (in the case of Type I) daily self-injections of insulin must be taken. Safety measures (such as checking toes for sores) must be done, and exercise routines must be followed every day. Because diabetes cannot be cured, the most any patient can hope for is preventing its terrible consequences. Yet, despite the serious potential outcomes of diabetes, its sufferers typically maintain very poor long-term cooperation with treatment regimens. One study found that 80 percent of diabetics incorrectly administered their insulin; 73 percent did not follow their diet; 50 percent carried out poor foot care; 45 percent incorrectly tested their urine. Only 7 percent of the diabetes patients in the study complied with all the steps for good control (Rosenstock, 1985).

Why do patients fail to carry out their regimens accurately when the consequences can be so serious? A number of factors are related to adherence in general, and these are discussed in more detail in Chapter 6. Particularly in the case of diabetes, however, social pressures to eat (and the tantalizing nature and easy availability of high-fat, high-sugar foods) seem to diminish adherence (Goodall & Halford, 1991). Also, management of diabetes requires a complex regimen, so there are lots of opportunities for people to fail. Since the severe complications of diabetes usually take years to develop, people may not feel that their noncompliance creates a real (or at least an immediate) threat to their health.

Individual Differences and Personal Characteristics

Many individual characteristics are related to the likelihood of carrying out certain health behaviors. Some of these are very specific, while others apply more broadly to a variety of preventive or risk behaviors. Various demographic, psychological and cognitive factors (such as age, education, marital status, ethnicity, personality, self-efficacy, perceived barriers to the behavior, perceptions of severity, social influence, sense of identity, and self-confidence), as well as certain personality characteristics, have been shown to be related to health behaviors (Lantz et al., 1998; Mayer-Oakes et al., 1996; Sands et al., 1998). In Chapter 6 we will outline several theories that incorporate these elements into frameworks for understanding general health behaviors.

One individual characteristic that has been much explored is that of gender. Some studies show that men are more likely to exercise than women (Felton et al., 1997), while women are more likely to relax and do other sorts of health-promoting behaviors. Other studies fail to confirm this, however, such as a recent study that found no gender differences in exercise levels or nutritionally sound diets (Kohlmann et al., 1997). So, although many studies do find gender differences of one sort or another, the overall picture of how the health behaviors of men and women might be different from one another is still somewhat murky. Women's self-efficacy for maintaining a healthy diet and controlling alcohol intake does seem higher than that of men, but men are more effective regarding physical activity. Both men and women cite time constraints, being tired, and not having social support as primary reasons for failing to carry out an exercise program, and social events are listed as the top barriers to smoking cessation and alcohol reduction or abstinence (Milligan et al., 1997). Researchers have found that women practice better automobile-related safety and drug avoidance than do men. Both of these differences were due to the fact that women were less likely to mentally avoid issues that troubled them, and were more likely to think about the issues and face them directly (Kohlmann et al., 1997).

For adolescents, the value placed on health, the perceived negative effects of risky behaviors, and the example set by parents are all important factors in predicting a variety of general health behaviors. Having a positive orientation to school, friends who set a good example, engaging in prosocial activities, and going to church are also predictive of better health habits (Jessor et al., 1998). In the realm of sun-avoidance, female adolescents have been found to be more diligent than males about protecting themselves from the sun's harmful rays (Brayne et al., 1998). Also, in adolescents, the

Awareness of the future consequences of sun damage is essential to taking precautions while in the sun.

personality trait of psychoticism (which involves elements of impulsivity, tough-mindedness, shrewdness, and tendency toward psychopathology) has been found to be related to riskier behavior regarding sun exposure. In another study of adolescents' alcohol use, nutrition, and AIDS-prevention behaviors, it was found that a strong sense of identity, self-confidence, and self-efficacy were important in carrying out sound health practices. Perceived barriers to prevention, perceptions of the severity of the consequences of risk taking, and social influences were also important determinants of behavior (Sands et al., 1998).

A new construct has recently been proposed for explaining one more piece of the puzzle concerning people's health behaviors. It is called "consideration of future consequences (CFC)," and it is a stable individual difference in people's tendency to think about immediate, as opposed to distant, consequences of their behavior (Strathman et al., 1994). This construct has been shown to predict health behaviors more efficiently than some other similar constructs do, and it also seems to influence the degree to which people are swayed by persuasive communications and messages.

Covariation of Health Behaviors

The various activities that we have considered in this chapter (such as maintaining normal weight, exercising, and avoiding smoking) are preventive health behaviors (Kasl & Cobb, 1966). Some people, like Charlie Baxter at the beginning of this chapter, carry out several actions to guard their health. Others do only one or two things (see Figure 5.3). Researchers have found that preventive health behaviors are not necessarily all practiced by a given person. The individual who maintains normal weight and who exercises may also smoke cigarettes and fail to use safety belts (Baumann, 1961). But, some health behaviors, such as good diet, toothbrushing, safety-belt use, and exercise do tend to co-occur (Neumark-Sztainer et al., 1997). Also, among young adults, the use of various "substances" such as cigarettes, alcohol, and recreational drugs tends to occur either simultaneously or serially (Brenner & Collins, 1998; Hays et al., 1984).

Health behaviors may fail to covary precisely because they are not seen to be health behaviors at all. In fact, people tend to perceive many such activities as only distantly related to health (Mechanic, 1979). For example, they may lose weight and exercise for the sake of appearance, and for the same reason refuse to wrinkle their clothing with a safety belt. They may smoke because it feels attractive and sophisticated, and because it helps them relax in social situations. Actions that seem incongruous on the dimension of health may be perfectly consistent on the dimension of appearance.

In order to understand fully the many factors that contribute to a person's decision to engage in a particular health behavior, we must understand a great deal about his or her evaluation of that particular behavior. As we will see in the next chapter, we must be aware of precisely what a person understands, believes, feels, wants, believes

FIGURE 5.3   The covariation of health behaviors.

other people want, intends to do, and is able to do. Only then can we understand and predict what the person is likely to do to promote his or her health!

Summary

1. In the twenty-first century, health experts are primarily focused on combating chronic diseases such as hypertension, heart disease, cancer, and stroke. Infectious diseases are less a threat these days than 100 years ago. Preventing and managing chronic diseases such as these require a life-span approach, which incorporates numerous factors, including healthy diet, regular exercise, healthy sleep patterns, limited use of alcohol, abstinence from smoking, using sun protection, practicing safer sex, wearing a safety belt in the car, and wearing a head protecting helmet while bicycling.

2. Preventive behaviors come in three general forms: primary (undertaken before one is at risk), secondary (undertaken when one has developed specific risk factors for a disease), and tertiary (undertaken to manage or reverse the course of a disease).

3. Healthcare providers are increasingly encouraging prevention at the primary and secondary levels; it is far more cost effective to prevent a disease than to treat one. Despite the fact that most people recognize the health benefits associated with exercising, eating a healthy diet, sleeping enough, and not smoking, many fail to adhere to basic health principles. The reasons are personality, social pressures, cultural norms, habits learned in childhood, values, beliefs, and lack of resources.

4. Interventions that are designed with the needs of a particular person or group in mind will be more effective in changing behavior than general interventions applied to everyone. Physicians are excellent (although certainly not the only) sources of health information and have considerable potential influence in helping their patients to achieve and maintain optimal health.

   - The degree of influence of physicians is very much dependent upon their communication with their patients.
   - In the most effective relationships, physicians determine what precise health behaviors the patient is engaging in.
   - Physicians can help their patients set reasonable goals and help patients understand and agree with the importance of each behavior change.
   - Effective physicians assist their patients in prevention by formulating and supervising detailed plans of action, and giving patients feedback about their progress and positive reinforcement when appropriate.

5. Other important sources of information and aid include the media and the advice/counsel of family members and other social/cultural groups.

THINKING CRITICALLY

1. Most people want to be healthy. Why, then, is it not enough to simply provide people with accurate and thorough information about what they need to do to improve and maintain their health?

2. What are the differences among primary, secondary, and tertiary prevention efforts? How might one combine these in order to maximize positive outcomes (that is, to best help someone who needs primary prevention in one area, and secondary or even tertiary preventive measures in another)?

3. Of the various health behaviors discussed in this chapter (nutrition and diet, exercise, safety belt use, safer sex, avoiding smoking, limiting alcohol consumption, etc.), which is the biggest challenge for those you know? What are some of the difficulties that people face in achieving health?

4. If personality characteristics (which, by definition, are at least somewhat stable) are part of what determines health behavior, is it reasonable to think that we can change health behaviors at all? What are the important factors in determining the success of behavior-change programs and how might they be affected by personality?

GLOSSARY

Acquired Immune Deficiency Syndrome (AIDS): A disease that impairs the immune system of its victims, making them unable to fight off infections.

Aerobic exercise: Exercise that dramatically increases oxygen consumption over an extended period of time (for example, walking, running, swimming, cycling).

Alcoholic: A person who is physically and psychologically addicted to alcohol and who experiences health and social problems from its consumption.

Atherosclerosis: A disease condition in which fatty, fibrous plaques narrow the opening of an artery, threatening blood flow to the heart or brain or other vital organs.

Aversion therapy: A type of behavior modification in which punishment in the form of an aversive stimulus (e.g., electric shock) is used to extinguish a behavior.

BMI: Body mass index, which is one way of estimating obesity; it is calculated as weight in kilograms divided by height in meters squared (kg/m²).

Carcinogen: Cancer-causing agent.

Cerebrovascular accident: (CVA) See stroke.

Cholesterol: A fatlike substance found in the blood and in organs of the body; an important component of stones in the gallbladder and plaque on the coronary arteries.

Chronic degenerative disease: Chronic disease conditions that become progressively worse over time; some are contributed to by poor health behaviors.

Cirrhosis of the liver: A disease caused by an accumulation of scar tissue on the liver, causing loss of functioning of this vital organ; usually the result of alcoholism.

Disease theory of alcoholism: A theory of alcoholism that recognizes the biological components of addiction, as well as the psychological; it has given rise to medically oriented treatment programs and lessened the stigma associated with alcoholism.

Epidemic: Widely diffused and rapidly spreading occurrence of disease.

Fetal Alcohol Syndrome: Mental retardation, central nervous system disorders, and growth and facial abnormalities in babies resulting from maternal alcohol consumption.

Hypertension: High blood pressure.

In utero: While still in the uterus; prenatal.

Incubation period: The time from exposure to infection to the onset of symptoms of the disease.

Metastasis: Spread of cancer from its original site to other parts of the body.

Myocardial infarction (heart attack): A disease condition that can cause part of the heart muscle to be damaged or destroyed because of a lack of blood flow to the heart.

Orosensory properties: Sensations produced by foods in the mouth.

Osteoporosis: A disease in which bones become brittle, weak, and fracture easily.

Preventive health behavior: Actions taken by an individual to prevent disease from developing or to forestall the negative outcomes of a disease condition, including diet, exercise, stopping alcohol and drug abuse, stopping cigarette smoking, using automobile safety restraints, using sun and bike helmet protection, and obtaining vaccinations.

Primary prevention: All the activities undertaken by apparently disease-free individuals to help themselves achieve maximum well-being and avoid disease.

Problem drinkers: Persons who may not evidence withdrawal symptoms but do experience social, psychological, and health problems as a result of drinking alcohol.

Relapse: A recurrence of symptoms after a period of improvement. In the case of smoking, relapse refers to returning to being a smoker after a period of having quit.

Secondary prevention: Term referring to activities that are undertaken by people who are at increased risk of a particular disease in order to forestall its occurrence.

Stroke (cerebrovascular accident, CVA): Sudden impairment of circulation to the brain; usually occurs because a blood vessel has been blocked by a blood clot or a fat deposit or has leaked blood into the brain.

Tertiary prevention: Term referring to activities that are undertaken by people who have a particular disease in order to cure it or to slow its progress.

Vaccine: A substance that stimulates the production of antibodies in the human body, so that encounters with a pathogen (for example, a virus or bacterium) do not result in infection; a vaccine is delivered during an immunization.

CHAPTER

6

Health Recommendations and Behavior Change

Bill Dawson sits at the table, staring out the kitchen window. It is noon and he is trying to remember which of his array of medications should be taken with lunch. "Now, which pills did the doc say I was supposed to cut in half?" he asks himself out loud. "And do I take 'em before or after meals? No . . . these were supposed to be on an empty stomach . . . I think. I shoulda wrote it down. Where'd I put that clinic number?"

Bill, age 65, has hypertension. He also has arthritis, adult onset diabetes, and glaucoma. Although he is not overweight, his doctor has recommended that

he follow a low fat, heart-healthy diet and that he begin a program of daily walking. His doctor has also prescribed several different medications. The diet, exercise, and medication are expected to help reduce his blood pressure, control his diabetes, minimize the effects of his glaucoma, and increase the mobility of his joints, which are swollen and sore from arthritis. There is little question that Bill would feel better and would be healthier if he could stick with a program of light exercise, but he can't seem to get around to it. The diet is a problem because often Bill feels very bored and lonely, and to make himself feel better he eats high fat, high sodium snacks while watching a ball game. And, living alone as he does, he has some real problems remembering when and how to take his medications.

In Chapter 5, we examined primary prevention and considered various degenerative diseases. We looked in depth at the health behaviors necessary to prevent or forestall these conditions, examined the details of individual health behaviors, and considered some of the reasons why people fail to take these steps to promote their own health. In this chapter, we examine preventive behavior in more detail, and look at the psychological factors that contribute to an individual's success or failure in efforts to adopt and maintain the health actions of primary, secondary, and tertiary prevention. As we will see in this chapter, diabetes and hypertension are among the most difficult conditions for physicians to treat. This is because so much of the treatment depends upon the patient's compliance with the medical regimen. Many reasons account for why people fail to regulate their own behavior to care for themselves; not the least of these is that some treatments require almost complete lifestyle change. Deeply ingrained habits must be broken and replaced with new ones. Finding out why they have so much difficulty in doing so can lead the way to helping patients follow through with treatment regimens to maintain their health and prevent further disease.

An Overview of the Determinants of Prevention and Treatment Behaviors

Why might a person adopt a particular health habit such as taking hypertension medication, using sunscreen at the beach, or exercising for cardiovascular fitness? Common sense tells us that several things are important: having information, believing that the health goals are valuable, and having the ability to take the necessary steps. While these three elements are critical, they are not sufficient in themselves, however. Personality characteristics may play an important part in behavior change in that they make altering habits easier for some people than for others. Personality can even influence the environments people choose and the ways in which they structure their lives. As we will see in Chapter 9, personality characteristics can influence physical health outcomes directly through physiological processes, or indirectly by affecting individuals' health behaviors. For example, individuals who are high on sensation-seeking are more likely to take risks than are those who score lower on this dimension (Zuckerman, 1983), and conscientious individuals take fewer risks, smoke less, and drink less alcohol than do less conscientious people (Friedman et al., 1995). Therefore, as we discuss the processes related to behavior change throughout this chapter, it is important to keep in mind that there are other underlying factors such as personality that work along with informational and motivational influences to determine whether people will make positive changes to their health behaviors.

Adherence to Medical Regimens

Researchers have been very actively concerned with primary, secondary, and tertiary prevention. As you will recall from Chapter 5, **primary prevention** refers to preventive health behaviors that one undertakes before there is any indication of illness or even increased risk; **secondary prevention** involves actions that a person may take when "at risk" for a particular health problem; and **tertiary prevention** describes actions that a person who already has a disease may take in order to manage the condition (cure it or slow down its progress).

For decades, researchers in the fields of medicine, psychology, sociology, nursing, pharmacy, and public health have examined a phenomenon known as patient **adherence** to or **compliance** with medical regimens (DiMatteo & DiNicola, 1982; DiMatteo & Lepper, 1998). These terms refer to the degree of success a patient has in carrying out the prevention or medical treatment recommendations given to him or her by a health professional (a nurse or a physician, for example). **Noncompliance** or **nonadherence**, on the other hand, refers to the patient's ignoring, forgetting, or misunderstanding the regimen as directed by the medical professional and thus carrying it out incorrectly or not at all (as was the case with Bill at the beginning of our chapter). Even though medical technology has greatly increased the potential for good health, noncompliance is still a very real threat to successful health maintenance (Trostle, 1997).

The term compliance is an important one in the history of health psychology. Most research on health promotion and disease prevention can be found in the literature under the heading "patient compliance." Although many researchers now prefer to use other terms such as cooperation and patient decision making, the terms compliance and adherence have become traditional. So, most research on this topic involves either the term compliance or adherence, and noncompliance or nonadherence. We will use these words interchangeably. We should keep in mind, however, that the word "compliance" could be seen to imply an attitude that the regimen should be strictly "obeyed." The term might be thought to presume that if there is any disagreement as to what should be done, the health professional's judgment is superior to that of the patient, and the patient should acquiesce. As we will see throughout this and other chapters, however, such a presumption is not necessarily correct. There are many times when patients fail to follow their health professionals' recommendations precisely because they have made a different, but well-thought-out, decision on their own. While the term adherence may be somewhat less value-laden than the term compliance, the terms that are used matter less than the recognition that patients are essentially self-determining.

The phenomenon of nonadherence continues to be a major problem in the delivery of effective medical care and severely threatens the outcomes of such care (Trostle, 1997). The development of drug-resistant pathogens, particularly bacteria and resistant strains of the HIV virus, is a serious outcome that can be traced directly to problems of noncompliance of patients with drug regimens (Graham, 1998; Harrison, 1995; Rao, 1998). Nonadherence is quite common; one very comprehensive review, published in 1979, summarized over 500 studies and found surprisingly high rates (Sackett & Snow, 1979). Patients kept only 50 to 75 percent of their scheduled appointments and failed to take medications as directed anywhere from 23 to 50 percent of the time. Nonadherence rates were highest when the medications had to be taken over a long period of time. In terms of lifestyle recommendations (such as making changes in diet), patients also averaged an adherence rate of only about 50 percent. And, recent studies indicate that things haven't changed much. The nonadherence rate for short-term treatment regimens is approximately 38 percent, and it jumps to 45 percent for long-term interventions (DiMatteo, 1994; Epstein & Clauss, 1982). A good guideline is that patients fail to comply with medical recommendations about half of the time (Dishman & Buckworth, 1997; Haynes et al., 1996).

Why wouldn't patients do everything in their power to achieve optimal health, including follow "doctor's orders"? There is no simple answer. Many patients stop taking medications when they feel that they no longer need them, such as when their symptoms disappear, or when they feel they are "doing better." Some patients who are prescribed an antibiotic take it for a few days, feel better, and decide to save the rest of the prescription for the next time they feel sick. As you will recall from Chapter 3, this type of behavior can pose serious health risks, not just for the individual, but even for society as a whole by fostering drug-resistant strains of bacteria. People also fail to comply when they perceive that the illness they have, or to which they might fall prey, is not very severe. Medical regimens that are long-term and/or are very complex are also less likely to be carried out correctly, partly because they are more inconvenient and are more difficult to remember. These and other factors were discussed in detail in Chapter 3. What is perhaps most important to remember in this chapter is that actions toward the goal of health promotion (especially at the primary and secondary prevention levels) may be especially difficult because individuals are not yet ill. When people feel fine, they may be considerably less motivated to change than if they were trying to eradicate a disease and its troublesome symptoms. If Bill, whom we met at the beginning of this chapter, had been in pain he might easily remember to take medications designed to relieve it. Or, if he had experienced frightening heart palpitations when he got his dosages wrong, he would probably take the proper number of pills at the prescribed times. When symptoms and the effects of the treatments are more subtle, patient motivation for adherence drops off.

Overview of a Model of Compliance

What specific factors cause people to engage in the activities necessary to promote their good health, prevent illness before it occurs, and treat disease before its consequences are devastating? Throughout this chapter, we will see that the following simple message comes through loud and clear: A person will not carry out a health behavior if significant barriers stand in the way or if the steps necessary to carry out the behavior actually interfere with favorite or essential activities. Impediments such as excessive cost or impracticality must somehow be overcome. Certain sources of support (such as family enthusiasm and encouraging self-talk) can help a person carry out the new behavior, but his or her commitment is absolutely essential. Commitment that is true and internally motivated comes only when a person believes that the health behavior will bring valued outcomes (for example, avoiding skin cancer, or achieving fitness and living longer). Real commitment comes after careful consideration of all the pros and cons of the action from many perspectives, including consideration of the wishes of family, friends, and social or cultural group. Of course, people are influenced by the clarity and the content of the health message, such as why and how to use sunscreen or engage in exercise that enhances cardiovascular fitness, as well as by how they feel about the source of the recommendation, such as the health professional or the media (Wilson & Sherrell, 1993).

These are the important adherence-determining factors in a very large nutshell. When commitment results from careful consideration of these factors, the individual can be helped to overcome the various difficulties inherent in attempting health behavior change. Let us now examine each of these issues systematically.

Sources of Health Information

Health information is the first necessary component and a key ingredient in any attempt to bring about health behavior. People usually will not stop engaging in unhealthy behaviors unless they know that these behaviors are dangerous; they will not initiate new health behaviors unless they learn somehow that these are important for preserving health. Until the early 1960s, for example, cigarette smoking was generally believed to be safe. Then reports in the scientific literature made their way into the popular press and other media; the word was out that smoking was very dangerous (Surgeon General, 1964).

These days, we are learning more and more about the dangers of overexposure to the sun and the increased risks of skin cancer. We are also finding out that certain diets, high in saturated fat and low in fiber, may increase our risk of heart disease and certain cancers. We are learning that safer sex practices, such as the use of condoms, can help prevent the spread of HIV and AIDS. Of course, this does not mean that health messages affect everyone equally. In one Harris survey (cited in Fisher & Rost, 1986), health professionals ranked "not smoking" as the number one health protective action a person can take, while the public ranked it tenth!

The ideal health message is one that changes a person's health behavior for the better. For example, a message about the importance of a monthly breast self-exam would present the facts to a woman about the importance of conducting the examination and would teach her precisely how to do it properly. Then she would carry out the examination monthly, without fail. Health messages that are individualized (in the person's own vocabulary, targeting their individual values, etc.) are most effective (Simons-Morton et al., 1997), but even with a well-designed message, there's still a big step to a regularly executed health behavior. This step is made considerably more difficult when an individual faces an overwhelming number of health messages—particularly if some of these messages contradict one another.

Most people know that smoking can cause disease and death. The effects of tobacco on other aspects of life are only now being widely recognized.

The Media

Health messages surround us on television and radio, in newspapers and magazines, and on billboards. No sooner are the studies published in scientific journals than we hear reports on the evening news, see articles in our favorite fashion magazines, and witness the advertising pitches of the manufacturers who make health-promoting products. For the most part, these messages are getting through to us. Recent studies show that television is the most frequent source of health-related information in the United States (Krishnan, 1996). With so many messages about health around us, it can be difficult to sort out what is worth believing and doing something about, and what is not. We are bombarded with messages about "dangers" or risks to health, ranging from eating meat that is not well cooked to eating meat that has been charred, from not drinking enough water to drinking too much caffeine. When faced with an overwhelming number of precautions and pieces of advice, one might be tempted to simply give up and not worry about all the risks (see Fisher & Rost, 1986). But, some risks are definitely greater than others and, after years of research, some behaviors (such as cigarette smoking) continue to be confirmed serious threats to health.

Another problem with health messages is that public information campaigns often bypass the very people who are at the greatest health risk and are most in need of information (Klapper, 1960). Those with the greatest health knowledge are the most likely to attend to health messages in the first place. The relatively poor and uneducated, on the other hand, are less likely to be reached (DiMatteo & DiNicola, 1982; Friedman & Martin, 1999). In general, mass media campaigns to change health behavior show fairly limited, although somewhat positive, results (Grilli et al., 1998). Information campaigns to encourage seat belt use, prevent unwanted pregnancies, stop smoking, increase skin cancer awareness, and increase physical activity show, at best, transitory, short-lived change and, at worst, no change at all (Cavill, 1998; Del Mar et al., 1997; Lau et al., 1980). Many intended recipients tune out messages they do not want to hear, and are particularly oblivious to general information that focuses on abstract issues (such as "eating healthy or "avoiding sun exposure") and that fails to suggest specific actions that individuals should take. Mass media appeals are typically helpful only in alerting people to change health habits they may not know are dangerous (Lau et al., 1980). Examples of these are the alerts early in the 1960s regarding the health risks of smoking and warnings during the later 1980s regarding the need for condoms to prevent infection from HIV.

The media also sends "inadvertent" health messages, that are not framed as health messages, but that nevertheless help to shape beliefs about health. The television and movie industry is particularly important here, as many movies and TV programs depict people living their lives and provide examples of habits and behaviors. Sometimes these messages are positive, such as when characters forego sexual activity with people they just met, or choose a designated driver who does not drink any alcohol. Many of these messages are negative, however, such as when dramatic and commercial actors smoke cigarettes, practice unsafe sex, drink alcohol excessively, binge eat junk food, and fail to use automobile safety belts. These negative behaviors are often portrayed as "hip" and glamorous. If seen often enough, these messages begin to influence the behavior of viewers, especially adolescents. People who spend more time watching TV have been found to develop more inaccurate ideas about health than those who watch less TV (Signorielli, 1998).

Medical Interaction

One potentially important source of health information is an individual's physician. The opportunity exists in the physician-patient interaction for the communication of specific information that is directly relevant to an individual's health. In this interaction, the physician can suggest specific behavioral steps that are needed to achieve the intended health goal. Physicians, however, often fail to teach their patients how to maintain their health and they devote surprisingly little time to giving information about illness prevention. One survey of smokers, for example, found that only 44 percent reported that they had ever been told to quit smoking by a physician (Anda et al., 1987), and a survey of patients with AIDS showed that only 38 percent had ever been told by their physician how they could prevent transmitting the virus to others (Valdisseri et al., 1988). Not only do approximately half of patients fail to get adequate information from their medical professionals, but almost half of health professionals fail to stay current in obtaining that information themselves, in continuing education classes (O'Brien, 1997). Of course, these statistics may reflect the ineffectiveness of many physicians at communicating recommendations to their patients, an issue that was examined in detail in Chapter 3. Thus, although research demonstrates that patient compliance is enhanced when physicians give patients information and answer their questions, this aspect of the physician's role is surprisingly often neglected (Hall et al., 1988).

The picture is further complicated by the fact that when it comes to prevention, patients have certain expectations for what their physicians will tell them and may ignore communications they don't want to hear (Ashenden et al., 1997). For example, smokers generally expect to be told to quit by their doctors, and they may use various cognitive strategies to lessen the blow. If doctors are too persistent in advising such patients to quit, they may annoy or alienate the patient with guilt, further diminishing the patient's chances for successful cessation (Butler et al., 1998). They might be unconvincing or unenthusiastic (see Figure 6.1). Former smokers often report that they quit because they made their own evaluation and decided to do it on their own, not because of the advice of their doctors (Butler et al., 1998; Pederson et

FIGURE 6.1   Medical visits sometimes lack essential health information.

al., 1996). One participant in a study on patients' perceptions of advice to quit smoking said, "Everyone knows the dangers of smoking now. It's not like it's a top secret. If that smoker don't want to stop smoking, the doctor could be three hours talking to him and he'll walk out of the surgery and have a [cigarette] and thank God for that. I think everyone has heard of the consequences of what smoking does to you . . . so I can't see there is any good in going into great detail about it . . ." (Butler et al., 1998).

Support Networks

Family members and friends are also important sources of health information. Older family members may recommend traditional remedies for illness, such as teas or poultices. Brothers and sisters may share information that they have learned in school about the most effective ways of losing weight or increasing muscle mass. Friends may share their personal experiences and give advice about something that they themselves have gone through. In our search for the "right answers," we evaluate the messages received from friends and family and combine this information with that received from other sources, such as the media and our healthcare providers. Sometimes individuals rely primarily on their support networks for medical information and advice (Berg & Lipson, 1999). Because we care what the people in our support networks think of us, their input can be quite powerful in affecting our decisions. See Figure 6.2, which summarizes the many sources of health information regarding pregnancy care.

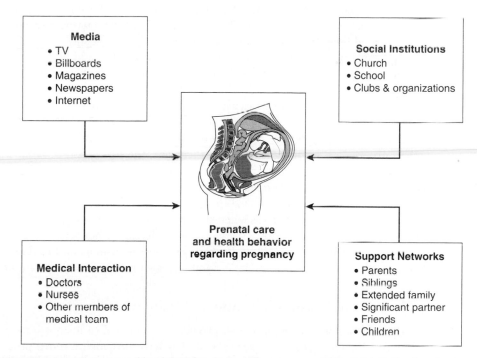

FIGURE 6.2   Sources of health information about care and healthy behavior during pregnancy.

Historical Perspectives

In the last century, we have witnessed (and many have experienced) the tremendous advances in medicine. Because of high-tech equipment and sophisticated drugs, we now live longer and, as a society, deal with fewer acute diseases than we did 100 years ago. We are not disease-free, however, and depending on how health is defined, some might argue that we are no healthier than we used to be; our problems are just different than in the past. Chronic diseases have become more problematic, and some of the most serious and life-threatening diseases we face are tied directly to our own poor health behaviors: high-fat diet, lack of exercise, smoking, sexual behavior, sun exposure, and alcohol or drug use. In many ways, we are "in the driver's seat" with respect to our own health. This is both good and bad news, however. Being able to affect our own health is encouraging, but establishing and maintaining good health behaviors isn't always easy. Many factors influence an individual's decision to engage in valuable health behaviors; not the least of these are beliefs, attitudes, and intentions.

Health Belief Model

The **Health Belief Model** (HBM) was developed specifically to help understand preventive health behaviors (Rosenstock, 1974). The HBM proposes that whether a person performs a particular health behavior is influenced by two major factors: (1) the degree to which the disease (negative outcome) is perceived by the person as *threatening*, and (2) the degree to which the health behavior is believed to be *effective* in reducing the risk of a negative health outcome. The first factor, perceived threat, is determined by whether someone believes he or she is susceptible to (that is, likely to get) the disease, and how severe that person believes it would be if it developed. The second factor, perceived effectiveness of the preventive behavior, takes into account not only whether the person thinks the behavior is useful, but how costly (in terms of money, time, effort) it is to carry out the preventive behavior. Hypotheses generated by the HBM have been generally supported by research. When health messages demonstrate to people that there is a real threat to their health and also convince them that a particular behavior can reduce their risk, the likelihood of behavior change is greatly increased (e.g., Klohn & Rogers, 1991; Ronis, 1992). When the health behavior of concern is very complex, however, this model tends to be less successful than when the behavior is simple. For instance, teens with diabetes were found to adhere best to their medical regimens when they believed that these regimens were important and useful. They also adhered best when they felt less (rather than more) threatened by their disease (Bond et al., 1992). Perhaps greater threat in a complex behavioral situation is simply too overwhelming and interferes with successful behavior change.

Theories of Reasoned Action and Planned Behavior

Although the Health Belief Model provides a good deal of insight into some precursors of behavior change, subsequent models have provided a more process-oriented approach. According to the **Theory of Reasoned Action** (**TRA**; Ajzen & Fishbein,

1980), a behavior results from an intention to carry out the behavior. A **behavioral intention** is an individual's commitment (to self or others) to carry out a behavior. An intention is brought about by two things: (1) the individual's *attitude* toward the action and (2) his or her **subjective norms** regarding it. As we will examine in more detail below, a subjective norm involves the individual's beliefs about what others (whose opinions are valued) want him or her to do.

According to the theory, attitudes and beliefs are related to each other in the following way. Attitudes are a function of the individual's beliefs regarding the likely outcomes of a health action and the individual's evaluation of that outcome. Thus, Karen's attitude toward quitting smoking will depend upon the extent to which she believes that quitting will lead to health and upon how much she values health. Furthermore, Karen's subjective norms regarding quitting (that is, what she thinks other people who matter to her want her to do) will combine with her attitude toward quitting to determine her intention to quit. Her intention is expected to be a strong determinant of whether she will actually quit.

In 1985, the original model was revised to include the element of perceived behavioral control. Perceived behavioral control is simply the degree to which a person believes that he or she has control over a particular behavior of his or her own. It is an additional component that influences the intention to perform the behavior. Because the model applies only to planned or purposeful behavior, the model was renamed the **Theory of Planned Behavior (TPB**; Ajzen, 1985).

A recent analysis has been done of all published research on the ability of TRA and TPB to predict exercise behavior (using the statistical technique called meta-analysis, which combines results from independent studies). This analysis has shown that both are successful in accounting for exercise, but that TPB does a somewhat better job. The analysis also found that expectations are better predictors of exercise behavior than are intentions (Hausenblas et al., 1997). Both TRA and TPB have considerable support from empirical research, however, and do nicely predict many types of health behaviors, including contraceptive use, mammography screening, AIDS risk-related behaviors, weight loss, smoking cessation, exercise, and drug and alcohol use (Doll & Orth, 1993; Fishbein, 1980; Fisher et al., 1995; Godin & Kok, 1996; Hillhouse et al., 1996; Montano & Taplin, 1991; van Ryn et al., 1996; Wallston & Wallston, 1983).

Specific Beliefs about Health

Our analysis of the path from health information to health behavior is built on the assumption that people act rationally on the basis of realistic and logical conclusions. This approach assumes that health behavior is not driven by hidden unconscious motivations such as the desire to be self-destructive (though other approaches might include such a component). Rather, this rational model of health action presupposes that if a person is convinced that a particular action will bring him or her closer to things that are valued, or if that action is seen to be in his or her best interest, the individual will make a rational decision to pursue it (Ajzen & Fishbein, 1977, 1980). Furthermore, if a person appears, at first glance, to exhibit irrational and self-destructive actions, we must look deeper at the underlying thought processes. What appears to be an irrational choice may, in fact, have been arrived at using facts to which only the individual has access or using a reasoning process that only the individual understands. To fully understand health decisions, we must analyze the process by which people evaluate health information.

First, let us define very carefully some terms that are central to understanding and predicting health-related behaviors (Stang & Wrightsman, 1981). These are terms that most of us use every day. However, each has a specific meaning in psychology in general and in the context of models of health behavior in particular. A **belief** is a hypothetical construct that involves an assertion, often of the relationship between some object, action, or idea (for example, "smoking") and some attribute (for example, "is expensive" or "causes cancer"). While some beliefs may derive from direct experience, others may result from secondhand experience or knowledge conveyed from another person. An **attitude** is a hypothetical construct that is used to explain consistencies within people in their affective reactions to (that is, their feelings about) an object or phenomenon (for example, their dislike of brussel sprouts or final examinations) (c.f., Stang & Wrightsman, 1981). Most psychological investigators agree that an attitude represents a person's emotional evaluation of an entity and that an attitude follows from a belief (Ajzen & Fishbein, 1980). (How attitudes and beliefs affect health behavior was outlined in Theories of Reasoned Action and Planned Behavior.)

Evaluations of Health Outcomes and the Value of Health

The belief that certain actions will lead to a certain outcome matters only if that outcome (in this case, health) is valued. If you believe that exercise will help to make you physically strong and you value being physically strong, your attitude toward exercise will be positive. But, if physical strength means nothing to you, or if you equate it with pain, you might avoid exercise altogether. Research has shown that even when people believe that certain actions will lead to health, they will carry out those actions only if they value health in the first place (Lau et al., 1986). In fact, the value placed on health is an excellent predictor of both intentions and health behaviors (Eiser & Gentle, 1988; Weiss et al., 1996). We might expect that everyone would value health very highly, but this is not the case. Other values, such as excitement and freedom, may take precedence. A person who enjoys riding a bicycle without a helmet, feeling the wind and feeling carefree, might value this dangerous practice above health. (The bumper sticker that says [in Figure 5.3] "I drive way too fast to worry about cholesterol" might be endorsed by someone with such priorities!) Research in the general population has shown that although, on average, health is the highest ranked of eighteen values, between 20 and 40 percent of respondents do not rank health among their five highest values (Ware & Young, 1979).

The current status of one's own health can affect the value placed on health in general. When people are healthy and feeling well, they tend to place a lower value on health than they do when they are facing serious illness. The value of health also varies with culture and social class. One study found that persons of lower social class were more likely to attach high value to being clean, owning a home, having insurance, and living in a good neighborhood than to good health (Larson & Sutker, 1966). Middle-

and upper-class persons most valued being in good health, having a good education, being respected by people, having children, and having friends. Lower social class persons were necessarily more concerned with having their basic survival needs met than were those in the middle and upper classes, who may have taken these things for granted. Researchers have developed a way to measure the variability in the value placed on health by using the Value of Health Scale (Lau et al., 1986). Respondents are asked, for example, to indicate their degree of agreement with statements such as: "If you don't have your health, you don't have anything" and, conversely, "There are many things I care about more than my health." The researchers found that adults tend to place a higher value on health than do children. Adults appear to no longer take good health for granted, perhaps because they already have experienced health problems and limitations.

Can beliefs and attitudes be modified? The answer can be found in the social psychological research on belief and attitude change.

Persuasion: Changing Beliefs and Attitudes

In this first decade of the twenty-first century in the United States, there is probably a greater emphasis on health promotion and disease prevention than in any previous time in our history. As a result, we are exposed to myriad health messages intended to persuade us to engage in good health practices and avoid dangerous ones. The American Cancer Society and the American Heart Association, for example, regularly warn us of the dangers of smoking cigarettes. We see television advertisements for products to increase our dietary fiber and reduce our risk of cancer. Billboard messages, at least in some of our major cities, persuade us to practice safer sex. Our friends and loved ones argue that we should lose weight, exercise more, and reduce our intake of saturated fats.

As we saw earlier in this chapter, health beliefs do not arise out of nowhere. Every day, information comes our way from many sources. We accept some health messages and ignore others. What determines this difference? Generally, people come to believe in something if they are convinced it is true. This "convincing" is carried out by the process of **persuasion**. Persuasion is defined as a form of social influence in which one person uses a verbal appeal to change the beliefs and attitudes of another person (Stang & Wrightsman, 1981). Persuasion can alter beliefs and attitudes and thereby affect an individual's intentions to behave in a particular way. In the field of social psychology, there has been a great deal of research delineating the specific factors that influence beliefs and attitudes and cause them to change. Most relevant here are the findings of the early Yale University research program on attitude change (Hovland, 1959; Hovland et al., 1953; Rosenberg & Hovland, 1960). This research has determined several important characteristics of messages that persuade successfully.

If we wish to persuade you with our message, we must convey more than just the facts. Our message must put together information in ways you might never have considered and present new ideas you might never have thought of before. Our message must have four characteristics: First, it must grab your attention. It must be something out of the ordinary, distinguished from the rest of the environment around you.

Second, it must be something you can understand. It must make sense to you in the context of what you already know. Third, it must be something you can accept and a message worth considering, not rejecting. And fourth, it must be retained or remembered. Often, because of time pressures, those who deliver persuasive messages present only one side of an issue. But research shows that it is better for an individual to hear both sides of an argument (for example, the advantages and the disadvantages of exercising). The person can then decide for him- or herself which to believe. If the person becomes convinced by only one set of arguments, but then encounters arguments or experiences consequences from the other point of view, those initial beliefs may falter. When health professionals, such as patient educators, work one-on-one with a patient, their most effective strategy is to help the patient to actively examine arguments for and against the target health behavior.

Fear Induction

You may remember seeing the "Red Asphalt" videos during driver's education class in high school. These videos showed very graphic images of people injured or killed in grisly automobile crashes in an effort to scare students into driving carefully. Or perhaps you have seen the television ad in which a raspy-voiced woman describes her struggle (and failure) to quit smoking—and then takes a deep drag of her cigarette through a permanent hole (called a stoma) in her neck! Such graphic displays of the horrible consequences of unhealthy behavior might grab your attention for a moment, but focusing too much attention on these kinds of images is disturbing, so you might distract yourself or change the channel. You might even remember them as being in poor taste.

Do scare tactics work? By themselves, they usually do not. Messages that arouse tremendous fear, such as pictures that show very decayed teeth, or diseased lungs, or unsightly cancerous facial growths, usually do make people upset. However, they actually may reduce the chances that a person will change his or her beliefs and behavior (Beck & Frankel, 1981). Threatening or fear-arousing messages alone tend to be unsuccessful because they increase an individual's anxiety to such a level that he or she may deny that anything is wrong and instead simply "tune out" the message. The individual might also view the case as extreme and think, "That's really an exceptional case. Nothing like that could possibly happen to me." When people are confronted with ideas or facts about their health behaviors that are very disturbing to them, they may actively work to change their views of the behavior in order to relieve their stress or even to justify continuing the behavior (Gerrard et al., 1996).

A threatening health message can work to change health behavior in some situations, however. In order to do so, the message must enhance the individual's feeling that something can be done to change the potential outcome, and that she or he is not entirely powerless. Threatening or fear-arousing health warnings can produce change only when the warnings actually convince people first that their health is in danger *and*, second, that they can reduce this danger by taking the recommended steps. Furthermore, people must believe that they are capable of carrying out the recommended action (Beck & Frankel, 1981). In order to achieve change, an individual must be convinced that he or she can do what is necessary to avoid the terrible outcomes presented.

Therefore, a fear-arousing message should also carry specific behavioral recommendations. In order to be effective, pictures of faces ravaged by skin cancer must be combined with information about the use of sunscreen and the precise steps necessary to avoid sun exposure. A recent study of fear tactics used in AIDS public-service announcements (PSAs) has shown that when the PSAs ended with a statement about the use of condoms to reduce the risk of HIV infection, male participants took significantly more condoms offered to them than did those who heard only a fear-arousing message (Struckman-Johnson & Struckman-Johnson, 1996).

Exposure to Persuasive Messages

Early research on persuasive messages showed that the more often a person hears a generally pleasing message, the more likely he or she is to remember it and be persuaded by it (Zajonc, 1968). It is important that the message not be boring and that it be initially acceptable to the recipient. If a person is "put off" by a message, hearing or seeing it over and over will probably antagonize him or her and increase any initial level of skepticism associated with the concept. An important related phenomenon in research on persuasion is what psychologists call the **sleeper effect**. The sleeper effect occurs when, a long time after exposure to a persuasive message, the recipient changes his or her belief but does not remember what influenced this change (Cook & Flay, 1978; McGuire, 1969). Although we generally prefer that behavior change be initiated right away, the sleeper effect can be utilized in situations where the risky situation has not yet been encountered. For instance, preadolescents may view sex as a "cool" and a "grown-up" thing to do, but not yet be engaging in sexual activity. Persuasive messages about protecting against

The most effective persuader is enthusiastic, interested, dynamic, and confident.

disease and unwanted pregnancy might be presented that have no immediate effect on their beliefs about sex, but later, when they are faced with real, sex-related decisions, their beliefs may be influenced by the previously encountered messages. In order for a belief to withstand external pressures, such as challenge by others, it must be stabilized (Johnson & Matross, 1975). First, the person's new belief (say, that smoking is dangerous) must be thoroughly integrated with his or her other beliefs. For example, if a person comes to believe that health can be enhanced by one's own actions, any previous belief that his or her health is beyond personal control will be called into question. Somehow these beliefs need to be resolved, such as by changing the latter. Second, an individual must review why he or she has a particular belief. The reasoning process that supports the belief must be reiterated. Third, an individual must inoculate him- or herself against conflicting arguments; that is, arguments against the belief must not be ignored, but rather examined and logically counteracted. For example, arguments that smoking is fine because "you gotta go sometime" must be refuted with evidence that smoking leads to premature death and disability. Finally, the belief change must come from personal free choice, not from coercion by others (Johnson & Matross, 1975).

The techniques of persuasion examined above really do work as evidenced by a great deal of research. They can be used by health professionals, by organizations, and by concerned friends in an effort to promote healthy beliefs, attitudes, and behaviors. These techniques increase the salience of important health information and make it more accessible to those who might potentially benefit from it.

The Persuasive Person

The persuasiveness of a message is determined partly by the characteristics of the communicator. Simply put, a message is more persuasive when it comes from a communicator who is liked than from one who is not. The most effective persuader is one who is enthusiastic, interested, dynamic, and confident (Rosenberg & Hovland, 1960). The effective persuader believes the message he or she transmits and is perceived to be trustworthy, dependable, predictable, honest, and to have motives that are in the receiver's best interest (Zimbardo et al., 1977). This can be a tall order for a health professional to fill.

The factors in effective persuasion are summarized in Table 6.1.

Social Cognitive Theory

Social cognitive theory grew out of social learning theory, which was proposed as an alternative to purely behaviorist approaches to understanding what people do and why (Bandura, 1977, 1986). A purely behaviorist approach focuses on the importance of classical conditioning of responses and reinforcement of behaviors (operant conditioning) to the exclusion of cognitive (thought) processes. Clearly, we can learn many behaviors without any classical conditioning or operant reinforcement. This can be done through a process called **vicarious learning** (learning by observation). We learn this way when someone behaves in a given manner and we observe the consequences of what they do. In order for behavior change to occur through vicarious learning,

---

TABLE 6.1 The Factors in Effective Persuasion

The Message Must:
- Grab attention
- Be understandable
- Be something acceptable and worth considering
- Be retained and remembered
- Present both sides of an issue
- Show precise steps to take to avoid dire consequences if the message is fear arousing

The Person Being Persuaded Must:
- Thoroughly integrate the new message with other beliefs (stabilize the belief)
- Review why he or she has certain beliefs
- Be inoculated against conflicting arguments

The Persuasive Person Must:
- Be a communicator who is liked
- Be enthusiastic, interested, dynamic, and confident
- Believe what he or she is saying
- Be perceived as trustworthy, dependable, predictable, honest, and as having the receiver's best interests at heart

---

however, we must believe that engaging in that particular behavior will produce a specific (and desired) outcome for us. This is called an **outcome expectation**. In addition, we must believe that we have the ability to perform the behavior—that is, that we have **self-efficacy**. Let's look at an example. Benicio wants to lose weight and have more energy by exercising regularly. He must first believe that this exercise will really help him to drop pounds by burning more calories and perhaps by helping to curb his appetite. He can arrive at this belief after having seen one of his friends lose weight by taking up jogging. Then, he must also believe that he can stick to an exercise schedule long enough to achieve his desired outcome. Some people may be incorrect in this belief, of course. Instead of sticking to a long-range, moderate plan, they instead establish a grand and grueling workout scheme that lasts only a few days. While it is important to have this sense of self-efficacy (without it the behavior change would never even be attempted), one needs to be careful to insure that it is sustainable. Also, it is important to recognize that self-efficacy is not a constant factor, but instead tends to vary according to situation and mood. Benicio may have a very high level of general self-efficacy immediately after practicing music with his band. The music energizes him, and he feels good about himself. He also may have a high level of self-efficacy regarding exercise on Mondays when he works out with his friend Tomás. His exercise self-efficacy may be low, however, on Wednesdays and Fridays, when Tomás is not available. Because of the importance of self-efficacy, it is worthwhile to structure any proposed behavior change so that it coincides, whenever possible, with high self-efficacy. For example, Benicio might try to schedule band practice in the late afternoons on Wednesdays and Fridays so that his workouts can follow. In this way, his

BOX 6.1
Hot Topic

Self-Efficacy and Health Behavior

What kinds of people work at staying healthy? Are they people of cast-iron will who decide to commit themselves to exercise and really stick to it? Are they people with unusual self-control who modify their unhealthy dietary practices and rarely fall back into bad patterns? Who are the people who give up smoking forever because they made a decision that once and for all it's time to quit? Are they different from those who fail or don't even try? Well, it turns out that there is nothing very unusual about them at all. Mostly, they are people who *believe* they can make a difference in their lives and in their own health.

People who believe that what they do matters are high in the characteristic that psychologists term **self-efficacy**. Self-efficacy refers to an individual's personal judgment of his or her own ability. This ability can be specific (to carry out a particular behavior) or more general (to accomplish things and be successful). People whose self-concept involves efficacy in one arena of health action often feel effective in other areas as

well. Self-efficacy is a very useful concept for understanding why some people stick to their diets or stay off cigarettes for good.

Several studies have found that people who believe in themselves when it comes to health behavior (for example, who believe they can quit smoking) are more likely to succeed than people who have low self-efficacy. In one study, smokers' confidence in their own ability to quit was the single most important predictor of whether they even tried to do so (Eiser & van der Plight, 1986). In another, people with high self-efficacy were less likely to relapse after quitting smoking than were those with low self-efficacy (Yates & Thain, 1985). Self-efficacy is also positively associated with maintaining an exercise program; having the belief that one can be physically active helps to achieve that goal (Calfras et al., 1997; Clark & Dodge, 1999). A high level of self-efficacy has also been related to better disease management, such as using medicines as prescribed, managing stress, and following a recommended diet (Clark & Dodge, 1999).

---

heightened level of general self-efficacy can be channeled into an effective workout motivator. This sort of environmental manipulation is addressed in more detail in the section that deals with transforming commitment into behavior.

Box 6.1 further examines self-efficacy as a factor in health behavior change.

Self-Regulative Theories

Self-regulative theories also include the element of cognition. These theories combine the ideas of self-knowledge with planned and directed action toward changing behaviors. The **transtheoretical model** is one of these self-regulative theories, and it defines six stages of change and outlines the process that occurs at each stage (Prochaska & DiClemente, 1984). The first stage is called *precontemplation*, and it occurs when the person is not even thinking about changing his or her behavior. At this stage, people depend on input from others because they do not see (or they are denying) that their health behavior is a problem. The second stage is *contemplation*, during which the person recognizes that a problem exists and starts to think about making a change. Strategies that work well for people at this stage include information gathering and emotional arousal (perhaps by reading a story about someone who experienced health difficulties because of failure to make a change). *Preparation* is the third stage. In it, a person is almost ready to instigate change and spends time thinking about how to implement the new behavior, ideally focusing on the expected positive outcomes. Someone at this stage needs to create a very specific plan of action and make that plan public so that others can help maintain motivation. The fourth stage is *action*, during which the person finally begins the actual behavior change. Such behavior change is most likely to be successful if the person is committed and allows him- or herself rewards as motivators. Placing oneself in environments that are "friendly" to the new behavior and discourage the old behavior also can be helpful. The fifth stage is called *maintenance*. In it, the person tries to avoid temptations to revert to old habits and learns to negotiate various pitfalls that might sabotage the new behavior. The strategies for this stage are the same as for the action stage; rewards need to be maintained long-term. The last stage is referred to as *termination*, and in this stage the behavior has become completely integrated into the person's lifestyle and there is no longer any danger of slip-ups. It is possible that no one ever truly reaches this stage, but instead, efforts at maintenance just become less intense. When interventions to change health behaviors are individualized and match the stage that the person is in, the results are much better than when general strategies are applied to everyone regardless of what stage they are in (Prochaska & Velicer, 1997). People at different stages in the transtheoretical model's framework are also affected differently by the factors of perceived severity, vulnerability, and efficacy. Those in the precontemplation stage are most affected by messages that highlight their vulnerability, whereas those in the contemplation stage are most affected by messages regarding severity. Those in the action stage are most motivated by efficacy messages (Block & Keller, 1998).

Subjective Social Norms: What Other People Think

Beliefs and attitudes were once thought to have a very simple relationship to behavior. Psychologists once proposed that behavior followed directly from attitudes (Allport, 1935). In fact, an attitude was defined as a state of readiness to exhibit a behavioral response. But the assumption of a direct link between attitudes and behavior was based partly on the premise that the wishes, approval, or disapproval of others do not influence people. In fact, many people are highly influenced by the approval or disapproval (real or imagined) of close friends and loved ones, as well as by the social and cultural groups to which they belong. Such influence can provide support for health actions, making healthy behavior easier to attain. Of course, the influence of others can be destructive as well, interfering with and jeopardizing the attainment of healthy action. The term *subjective social norms* is used to refer to the expectations of others (real or imagined) for one's actions. These norms serve an important function by giving cues about what are appropriate and inappropriate actions. For example, norms for style of dress in a business presentation may be quite valuable for a person to know, so that attention is given not to his or her attire but instead to what he or she is communicating about the issues of concern. Some norms contribute to the smooth collective functioning of a large group of people. Without certain expectations for behavior, there may be chaos (Rokeach, 1973).

In matters of health, certain norms become salient to an individual very early in life. These norms, usually communicated from the family of origin, may involve personal hygiene and are often concerned with such specific activities as brushing one's teeth, keeping clean, and avoiding using other people's towels and silverware. Other norms may arise out of the expectations of one's cultural group and involve such issues as the best foods to eat, the value of exercise, and the causes of and treatment of disease (Hampson et al., 1990; Pratt, 1976). People typically are not even aware of the norms that govern their behavior until they have violated these norms and they witness the reactions of others to their deviance (Hewitt, 1979). Of course, people vary considerably in the extent to which their intended actions are influenced by social expectations (Fishbein & Ajzen, 1975; Triandis, 1977). Some may act independently with respect to relevant norms for their health behavior. Some may gather facts from other people but evaluate those facts independently of the opinions of others. Some may rely on other people to evaluate various courses of action for them and then simply tell them what to do. The Theory of Reasoned Action takes account of differences in the salience of social norms.

It is important to keep in mind, of course, that not everyone is influenced by the same norms. Jelisa might be strongly motivated to fulfill the expectations of her friends, while Daniel is affected only by what he thinks his family wants him to do. In the spirit of rebellion, Anna might even decide to do precisely the opposite of what she perceives to be the wishes of those around her. And Nirav might be influenced strongly by what he thinks are appropriate behaviors for a member of his cultural group, particularly if he has a strong sense of cultural identity (Mechanic, 1978).

The Theory of Reasoned Action presents a scheme for systematically analyzing the influence of other people on an individual's commitment to a particular behavior (Ajzen & Fishbein, 1980). Let us examine how the influence of various members of an individual's social network, specific people as well as actual or imagined groups of people, can be analyzed. First, these individuals or groups must be listed: for example, parents, spouse or significant other, close friends, the people at work, heroes, and members of the cultural group. Different normative sources are likely to encourage different behaviors, and so in order to analyze the net effect of the influence of others, one must delineate precisely what each individual or group wants and one's motivation to comply with these desires. Let's consider this example. Janet is trying to make a decision about whether to commit herself to an exercise program that involves weight training. She is influenced by the wishes of several people in her family, by her boyfriend, and by what she thinks are the values of her peers:

Goal: Weight training three times a week to develop physical strength.

Person or group	Value orientation	Janet's motivation to comply
Father	positive	high
Sister	very negative	low
Boyfriend	very positive	very high
Peers	negative	very high

Note that Janet's father and boyfriend are quite positive about her proposed program. She is motivated to comply with their desires and tends to be influenced by their appraisal of her potential actions. On the other hand, Janet's sister is very much against the whole idea of weight training. However, Janet is not eager to follow her sister's wishes anyway. The chances for the behavioral program are good, so far. One possible snag, however, is Janet's perception of what her peers think of a young woman who lifts weights. She is particularly uncomfortable with the idea that other young women may tell her that she looks "unfeminine" with well-developed muscles. The net effect of the influence on Janet of her social norms is likely to be positive. However, the influence of norms would be more strongly positive if she perceived other young women to be in favor of weight training or if her motivation to comply with the current value orientation of her peers were quite low. Box 6.2 examines another type of social norm that sometimes directly affects health behavior, that of religious beliefs.

BOX 6.2

Across Cultures

Religious Subcultures in the United States: Their Influence on Health Behaviors

Ethnic traditions are not the only cultural elements that affect health behaviors; religious beliefs often play very important roles as well. Let us examine four major religious subcultures found in the United States and the ways in which their doctrines influence health behaviors. The groups we will focus on are Latter Day Saints (Mormons), Seventh-day Adventists, Jehovah's Witnesses, and Christian Scientists.

In terms of their general health messages, these four groups have many similarities. All advocate healthful living, exercise, and an integration of spirituality into one's life in order to achieve optimal mental and physical health. Each of the four groups teaches abstinence from tobacco and recreational drugs, and all but Jehovah's Witnesses also recommend abstention from alcohol. Family values and a high moral code are important, and these groups encourage their members to practice sexual abstinence before marriage and fidelity after marriage. Both Seventh-day Adventists and Mormons follow dietary guidelines that limit meat eating and encourage consumption of fruits, vegetables, and grains. Because these behaviors are strongly encouraged by the church, there is strong incentive for members to follow good-health guidelines. Social supports for doing so are firmly in place. As a result, practicing members of these groups are often healthier than their nonmember peers (for example, they have better cardiovascular health and experience fewer sexually transmitted diseases).

Religious health doctrines are not unilaterally positive, however. For example, Jehovah's Witnesses believe that they should not receive

(continued)

BOX 6.2   (Continued)

blood transfusions from another person. Thus, they do not accept blood even in cases of emergency, even if their lives are in grave danger. Although this has kept their rates of certain bloodborne diseases (such as AIDS and hepatitis) low, it poses great risk in situations where a person has lost a good deal of blood, such as in an automobile accident. Because the Bible does not make specific references to a person's own blood, patients anticipating surgery may choose to donate their own blood for use during the surgery. Also, because the Bible does not comment on blood fractions, vaccines that contain minor blood fractions may be received if the patient desires. For Jehovah's Witnesses these are "gray areas," thus the decisions are a matter of personal choice.

Christian Scientists do not believe in seeking medical treatment of any sort. They believe that faith and prayer are the best methods of healing and that to couple these with traditional medical treatments is counterproductive. If Christian Scientists do choose to seek medical treatment, however, they are not condemned or dropped from church membership. There is variability among Christian Scientists in terms of whether and when to seek medical help. Many Christian Scientists say that they have had bones set and mended solely through prayer while others may have a doctor set the break, but then rely on prayer for healing. Although they will not break legal mandates by refusing vaccinations, they do not believe that these are effective and they do not obtain vaccinations that are not required by law.

Why is all of this meaningful to a health psychologist or other healthcare provider? These examples highlight the importance of understanding the individual patient's world during the medical decision-making process. For example, suppose that a young woman is brought to the emergency room after a hiking accident. She has lost a lot of blood and needs to have a transfusion. As she is propped up on the stretcher, she refuses to give her consent and says that she does not want to have a transfusion. There may be a few possible explanations for her refusal. First, she may simply be afraid, fearing the transmission of AIDS. She may feel that her condition isn't serious enough to warrant a transfusion, given the risks that she believes are associated. If this is the case, a careful explanation of why she really *does* need the transfusion, along with information about the screening processes for blood (against AIDS and other bloodborne diseases), will probably convince her that her health will be best served by receiving the transfusion. If, on the other hand, she is refusing the transfusion for religious reasons, these reassurances and explanations are unlikely to have any effect. Instead, the health practitioner might try to work within the "gray area" and find out if the patient would be willing to receive a transfusion from a family member or if there is some other religiously acceptable alternative for her.

Intentions and Commitment

In considering beliefs, attitudes, and social norms, we have been working toward an understanding of the formation of behavioral intentions (i.e., stated or acknowledged commitments to carry out action). As we noted above, a positive attitude and supportive social norms do not *necessarily* change health behavior but they do contribute to establishing the intention to act. When there are no barriers standing in the way, intentions are good predictors of overt action (Ajzen & Fishbein, 1980; Triandis, 1977). The most successful intentions are those that are accompanied by a clear understanding of the problem, an organized plan of attack, and a high level of self-efficacy (Strecher et al., 1995). A stated intention (stated to oneself or to others) involves a commitment, a pledging, or a binding to a particular course of action (Kiesler & Saka-mura, 1966); many studies have shown that if a person makes a commitment to a par-ticular health behavior, there is a greater chance than if no commitment has been made that the behavior will be carried out (see, for example, Kulik & Carlino, 1987). Certain troublesome factors, such as lack of money or time, might stand in the way. But the belief that the behavior will achieve valued health goals, combined with the support of social norms and a stated commitment, can work together to help the indi-vidual follow through with the behavior. Commitment involves a promise to take steps to carry out the behavior and must follow from the individual's perception that he or she is free to act otherwise. Commitment can come in several forms: a promise to one-self, a commitment to a family member, and even a written contract with a health pro-fessional. For some people, the independent decision and a resulting promise to the self are most effective. For others, the expectations of family members or friends might be more salient and thus a more powerful motivating force.

Turning Commitment into Behavior

Commitment is not the final step in behavior change, however. Even when people have made a promise to themselves or to others, they can still fail. The actions they intend may be too much trouble or other priorities may capture their attention. Peo-ple cannot always do what they intend because of a lack of resources, knowledge, and useful tactics. Health messages may convince, and intentions may be serious, but the typically low success rate of New Year's resolutions suggests that behavior change is difficult, even for the most well-intentioned. Commitment does not provide an indi-vidual with the skills needed to make behavioral changes. People who want to be healthy, and practitioners who want to help them, need techniques to enhance the development and maintenance of health behaviors. Here are some of those techniques.

Behavior Modification

Despite the power of their good intentions, many people find that their behaviors (good and bad) are regulated by habit. The environment and day-to-day events often seem to control an individual's health behavior. The force of habit must be tamed if an intention is to be translated into a consistent health behavior. Indeed, once an inten-tion has been established, continued practice of the desired behavior is perhaps the greatest single factor that determines whether it will be acquired. The desired health behavior itself must become a powerful habit (Becker & Maiman, 1980).

Let's examine some strategies for bridging the gap between intentions and actual behavior change. These strategies are based on the fact that much of health behavior is learned and that destructive behavior patterns can be replaced with newer, healthier ones (Kasl, 1975). The behavioral approach is among the most fruitful for establishing healthy behaviors once an intention has been stated. In fact, an entire field known as "Behavioral Medicine" applies the experimental analysis of behavioral techniques to the prevention or management of illness problems (Katz & Zlutnick, 1975).

The **behavioral approach** to health holds that with appropriate learning, a person can change his or her destructive behaviors and take action toward the achievement of health. Once a person has made a commitment to the behavior change, success can be a matter of finding the right behavioral program to meet his or her needs. Using a behavioral approach, problems are defined in terms of specific behaviors and involve exactly what the person does, where he or she does it, when, and with whom. Explanations that focus on an individual's personal characteristics are avoided. Consider Carolyn, who has a problem with binge eating. Too often now, Carolyn comes home from work and heads straight for the refrigerator. She has developed a habit of eating large quantities of processed, high-fat, high-calorie foods. They include ice cream, cookies, potato chips, and cola and are clearly not nutritious for an active young woman in her 20s. Carolyn's problem, in behavioral terms, is not that she's "uncontrolled" or a "binge eater." Such labels are derogatory and unproductive. Rather, her problem behavior is that she allows herself to become exceedingly hungry by skipping lunch. She drinks coffee all afternoon, a habit that makes her feel anxious and causes her blood sugar level to fall quite low at the end of the afternoon. In addition, she has developed a habit of eating immediately after arriving at home. She uses food to reduce the tension she experiences from her work.

One solution to Carolyn's binge eating problem would be to develop different habits. For example, she could eat balanced meals throughout the day and after work she could take a warm bath to relax. She might also practice yoga or take an exercise class. She could then prepare a nutritious dinner for herself. She might be careful to

Yoga is an excellent approach to achieving relaxation, strength, and emotional balance.

keep only nutritious foods in the house and avoid stocking up on dessert items when she shops. By focusing on specific behaviors, Carolyn could lose weight and be healthier as well as find more effective ways to deal with her work stresses. By doing so, she would avoid self-deprecating labels that might be damaging to her self-concept.

As we noted in Chapter 5, a basic principle of the behavioral approach is that reinforcement of a particular behavior will increase the frequency of that behavior. Basically, reinforcement is anything that increases the probability of the occurrence of a particular behavior; rewards of various sorts, for example, can serve as reinforcements. Any behavior can be removed from the control of environmental reinforcements and brought under control of self-imposed reinforcements (Goldstein & Kanfer, 1979).

Behavioral Self-Control

The ultimate goal of the behavioral approach, as we examine it here, is for an individual to translate his or her intentions into behaviors and to maintain the performance of those behaviors. A common term for such activity is **self-control**. Although other people such as health professionals or family members can certainly assist an individual in carrying out health behaviors, no one else can consistently monitor an individual's behavior and dispense rewards or punishments accordingly. Rather, the patient's own behavioral regimen must be based upon self-control and self-management. The capacity for self-control involves not something that one "is" but rather something that one "does" (Thoreson & Mahoney, 1974). Self-control is a skill that one can acquire (Goldstein & Kanfer, 1979). Let's review, in somewhat more detail, a few of the basic behavioral principles that were referred to briefly in Chapter 5. Some excellent references in this field are books by Bandura (1969); Rimm and Masters (1974); Stuart and Davis (1972); and Mahoney and Thoreson (1974).

Classical or respondent conditioning is a process by which a behavior comes to be evoked by a once-neutral stimulus because that stimulus was paired with one that automatically evoked the behavior. As an example, imagine that you "munch" (popcorn, peanuts, M&Ms, and other delicious, enticing goodies) nearly every time you study. Pretty soon, the stimulus of opening your book will evoke your desire to munch. Some smokers report that smoking is sometimes so automatically triggered by external stimuli (such as a cup of coffee or the sight of their desk at home) that they find themselves halfway through a cigarette with no recollection of having lit up! Classical conditioning of unhealthy behaviors can occur readily and inadvertently. An individual who wishes to be in control of his or her behavior must be constantly aware of stimuli in the environment and his or her responses to them. Suppose that Brent wants to control the stimuli in his house that cue him to snack when he is bored. In order to do so, he must limit his eating to one and only one place in the house (the kitchen table). He must allow himself to eat only when sitting down, with a place setting, and with a limited portion of food. These restrictions prevent him from eating when he is not hungry, just because eating may feel like a fairly pleasurable way to keep busy. By making eating a less convenient activity, Brent will be able to limit the amount of time he spends eating and perhaps find other diversions for himself. In this same manner, a student can limit snacking to study "break time" and have something healthy to eat far away from the books. This will limit the cues that trigger the desire to eat "junk food" unintentionally. Of course, classical conditioning principles can be used not only to eliminate unhealthy behaviors but to enhance healthy behaviors as well. For example, by taking vitamins with every breakfast, John can increase the likelihood that breakfast will serve as a cue or reminder for him to take his vitamins.

Operant conditioning is based on the principle that behavior is shaped by the consequences that follow it. Psychologist B. F. Skinner (1938) persuasively demonstrated the powerful force of operant conditioning, and considerable research has been done since his time on this aspect of behavior modification (Bandura, 1969; Karoly, 1980). Operant behavior that is rewarded or reinforced (by the individual or by the environment) is more likely to be repeated. Reinforcement, of course, can be positive or negative. **Positive reinforcement** increases the probability that a behavior will be enacted by providing the individual with something that he or she values after enacting the target behavior. **Negative reinforcement** occurs when an individual is removed from a negatively valued state (for example, one that is uncomfortable) as a result of enacting the behavior. Thus, alcohol abuse may be negatively reinforced (and thus increase in probability of occurrence) if the result is a reduction in anxiety or physical discomfort. Of course, operant behavior that is punished will diminish in frequency of occurrence.

Graduated treatment implementation, or **shaping**, involves the application of reinforcement for successive approximations of the desired behavior. Shaping involves initially rewarding anything that vaguely resembles the target action, such as putting on the running shoes and walking lazily around outside. Over time, only progressively closer approximations to the desired behavior are reinforced. Eventually, the individual must walk briskly or run the entire target distance in order to receive reinforcement. Thus, the individual moves in a stepwise fashion to build a behavioral repertoire (Matthews & Hingson, 1977).

Self-imposed operant conditioning occurs through the process of **self-regulation**. Self-regulation has three stages. The first, **self-monitoring** or **self-observation**, involves deliberately and carefully attending to the precise details of one's own behavior. For example, it may include keeping records of exactly what one eats. Complete details of behavior might be recorded in a diary, such as the exact foods eaten and their quantities, as well as the location, times, antecedent and consequent events, and feelings. The individual can then analyze his or her own behavioral patterns, to find out what moods trigger overeating. A great deal can be revealed that will help in behavior change. The second stage in self-regulation is **self-evaluation**. The behaviors assessed through self-monitoring are compared against a specific criterion or ideal. For example, a person might compare the percentage of his or her daily calories obtained from saturated fat with the ideal, which experts believe should be kept below 10 percent (Trevisan et al., 1990). Sometimes, so much is revealed to a person by self-monitoring and self-evaluation that behavior is modified without further intervention. More often, however, behavior must be changed with some form of reinforcement. The third stage of self-regulation is called **self-reinforcement**. The individual rewards or reinforces him- or herself for behavior that matches or approximates the behavioral goal. For example, an hour of exercise might be regularly rewarded with ten minutes in the health club's steam room. Poor choices for rewards, of course, are those that actually sabotage the goal, such as having several hot fudge sundaes after a week of successfully cutting out desserts!

People may fail to translate their intentions into health behaviors because they lack awareness of their own current behavior and ways to modify it. Their performance criteria may be vague (e.g., they want to "get in shape" but really don't know how to exercise with maximum effectiveness). People may even have incorrect notions about the timing of rewards. Some may think it's fine to take the reward before performing the target behavior! This, of course, is an approach that is likely to fail miserably. Thus, patient education can contribute a great deal by assisting a person in self-regulation toward the goal of developing healthier habits.

Other Behavioral Strategies

What initially triggers the health behavior that is to be reinforced? Usually the behavior is triggered by some kind of **prompt** or **reminder**. A person might tack a note on the refrigerator door to remember to choose fruit for a snack. Another person might place a pill bottle next to the toothbrush to remember to take medication in the morning and at night. Toothbrushing before bed and after breakfast then serves as the stimulus, or reminder, for taking the medication. Some people use special pill packages and calendar packs such as those that come with oral contraceptive medication (birth control pills). These can help an individual to keep track of daily pill intake. Other behavioral prompts might include setting a wristwatch alarm for the time of each pill dosage or arranging to be paged at pill time. Remember Bill from the beginning of the chapter? He might find it useful to make a chart and post it on his refrigerator. The chart could list what he is required to take each day and provide a small space in which he could record what has already been done. Reminders from family members can be extremely helpful, as can reminder post cards and calls from health professionals to prompt behaviors ranging from pill taking to follow-up medical and dental visits (Haynes, 1979). Indeed, compliance with long-term regimens, such as medication and lifestyle changes for the treatment of hypertension, require an intensive, long-term program of initiating behaviors with consistent prompts and reminders, and then reinforcing those behaviors. Fortunately, the longer a person has engaged successfully in a behavior, the more environmental stimuli there are to serve as prompts and reminders to carry out the behavior. After one has acquired the habit of exercising regularly, for example, many things in the environment serve as prompts to exercise (such as the shoes one uses for running or the hand weights one uses for muscle conditioning). Prompts and reminders can be used to one's advantage. Purposely keeping exercise gear nearby (in the car, for example) or interacting with people who exercise regularly can provide the necessary prompts to maintain the desired behavior.

Cognitive Modification.   Research suggests that the most effective methods for modifying health behaviors involve a combination of cognitive and behavioral modification techniques (Brownell & Cohen, 1995). A behavioral strategy for change can be enhanced with cognitive modification; even after a person has established a strong behavioral intention to act, cognitive factors might continue to affect change. Thoughts play an important role in behavioral control; assessments of and expectations for their own abilities can decisively affect people's maintenance of behavior change (Conn, 1998; Hausenblas et al., 1997). The best behavioral regimen can be ruined by a person's use of negative self-statements. Suppose that one evening you give in to your over-whelming craving for a double hot fudge sundae (with French vanilla and double-chocolate fudge ice cream). You've "broken" your diet and failed at your behavioral regimen. You might then torture yourself with such thoughts as "See, I really have no control. I am doomed. I may as well forget the idea of ever getting into shape." Such negative self-talk can lead you to abandon your behavioral regimen altogether and give up your goals. This is often the outcome of one lapse by a dieter, a person who has quit smoking, or ex-drinker who takes a drink. One mistake can begin a round of self-deprecation that ends in feelings of hopelessness and in disaster for the good intentions.

A better approach for the relapsing would-be self-controller is to focus on thoughts of the intended behavior while saying encouraging rather than discouraging self-statements. In order to really succeed at long-term maintenance and control, an individual must become aware of his or her own potentially damaging negative self-statements and learn to use self-instructions that are compatible with success (Brownell et al., 1986). Behavioral approaches work well when internal dialogues support, rather than interfere with, the process of behavioral self-control. When internal dialogues are negative, there is significant risk that self-regulation will be undermined. An individual can, however, learn to replace negative, self-deprecating thoughts with positive, encouraging ones by applying the three self-regulation principles just described (self-monitoring, self-evaluation, and self-reinforcement) to thoughts. The individual must first become aware of the damaging self-statements by making them conscious and analyzing them. This might be accomplished by saying all thoughts about oneself, as they occur, out loud into a tape recorder or by writing them down in a journal at regular intervals during the day. Then, the individual needs to evaluate these statements and determine the extent to which they are encouraging or not. The discouraging, negative self-statements need to be replaced with positive ones (see Table 6.2). Finally, the person must then practice the positive statements and reinforce them (Atkins, 1981).

Practical Supports and Barriers to Behavior Change.   Certain practical aspects of people's lives can either enhance their ability to carry out intended health actions or make these actions relatively impossible to accomplish. Obviously, an individual's access to health services of various types (for example, immunizations) can affect whether he or she will actually use them. The longer a person is required to wait to follow through on a target health practice, such as seeing a physician or nurse to check blood pressure, the less likely he or she is to do it. Many other factors in people's lives can hinder their receiving medical care at all, such as the inability to get a baby sitter and the lack of transportation (DiMatteo & DiNicola, 1982). The cost of medical care, and of certain preventive measures, is often cited as the explanation for an individual's failure to carry out intended health behaviors. Certainly, a lack of financial and other resources can constitute an impediment to the best of intentions. Many patients, for example, cite financial need as the explanation for their noncompliance with both therapeutic and preventive regimens. Even when treatment is free, however, many

TABLE 6.2   Replacing Negative Self-Statements with Positive Ones

1. Negative:	"Exercising is uncomfortable. I wish it were over and done with."
Positive:	"This doesn't feel too bad. When it's over, I'll feel invigorated and glad I exercised."
2. Negative:	"I feel stupid walking around this neighborhood. Everyone thinks I'm crazy for doing this."
Positive:	"Probably nobody is watching me. If they are, they probably admire my dedication to my health."
3. Negative:	"I've only run one mile and I'm already tired. How will I ever cover another mile?"
Positive:	"I've run one mile already. I'm halfway there. I'm into the home stretch."
4. Negative:	"I can't imagine taking this medication every day from now on. That's too overwhelming."
Positive:	"I can do this one day at a time."

people still don't avail themselves of it (Cody & Robinson, 1977). And, some health behaviors actually save people money (e.g., quitting smoking, eating less). Reducing prohibitive costs tends to work only when a person has already stated an intention to carry out the action. Once the intention has been stated, reducing the financial burden on the patient can make the target behavior as easy as possible to carry out (DiMatteo & DiNicola, 1982).

Not surprisingly, a complex treatment regimen is more difficult to follow than is a simple one. Taking one or two pills a day, for example, can be relatively easy. The action of taking a pill can be paired with a regularly occurring activity such as getting up in the morning, brushing one's teeth, or retiring to bed at night. Taking three pills a day is challenging, however, and taking four pills is more challenging still. Lunch and dinner may occur irregularly, if at all. The pill bottle may be forgotten at home as often as it is brought along to work. Furthermore, because some pills may need to be taken on an empty stomach, while others must be taken with food or milk, scheduling can be inconvenient at best! Even if these details are worked out, the pattern of regularly scheduled prompts and reminders (such as daily events or visits from friends) that are relied upon to trigger behavior may occur inconsistently, causing pills to be missed. Special pill packages, such as those used for oral contraceptives, can help patients to remember to take their pills and to keep track of how many they have taken (Smith, 1989). Research suggests, however, that each time the number of pills per day is increased (from two to three, or from three to four) and another pill is added with its own unique schedule, failure to comply with the prescribed dosage increases dramatically (Graveley & Oseasohn, 1991).

In general, it is better for an individual to tackle one behavior at a time and then link the successful health behaviors together. Taking on too many health resolutions at one time or making more than one change in daily lifestyle can be overwhelming and can make one so frustrated that it is tempting to "just forget it." Suppose that you are a health psychologist and have a client named Iris who wants to change several of her health behaviors. You can increase her chances of success by approaching them in sequence. You might first help her to develop a behavioral regimen of self-regulation for one of her health goals, say, riding her stationary exercise bicycle four times a week. Only after this regular exercise has become a habit, reinforced perhaps with a relaxing hot shower afterward, would you advise her to begin to add on. The next step, for example, might be to improve her diet. Together you and Iris would develop a self-regulation regimen to reduce the fat content of her diet (first to 30% and then to 20%) and cut in half her intake of simple sugars. Her rewards might include purchasing some attractive, fashionable clothing and getting a massage once a month to reduce the tension that once inspired that terrible diet. She might even make a point to pay for these with money she put aside every time she wanted to purchase a hot fudge sundae but resisted the urge. Now, the good physical feelings that accompany exercise, a hot shower, and a massage, as well as the psychological boost that comes from looking better and wearing new clothes, can become the reinforcers for her healthier diet.

Social Support.   Family and friends play a crucial role in providing encouragement for achieving health goals; they provide the all-important ingredient called **social support**. Social support has been defined as any input that furthers the goals of the receiver of the support (Caplan, 1979). There are two major kinds of social support: **tangible support,** including physical resources that benefit the individual in some way, and **psychological support** that provides the individual with help to develop affective or emotional states that engender well-being. Tangible social support helps the person out; psychological support helps him or her to feel better. Social support from family and close friends can play an important role in assisting a person to translate intentions into health behaviors. Lack of social support, on the other hand, can be quite devastating to the health goal. Consider the example of smoking. One review found that the ". . . best predictors of relapse following cessation among adults are the smoking habits of family and friends . . . It is commonplace for relapsed smokers to report obtaining the cigarette with which they relapsed from a friend who may even have offered it. Those attempting to stay off cigarettes report high and troublesome levels of friends smoking in their presence" (Fisher & Rost, 1986, p. 555). On the other hand, time spent with nonsmokers, as well as sustained participation in smoking cessation programs with others who have the same goal, helps maintain quitting (Fisher & Rost, 1986). In general, the positive presence of people who are either verbally encouraging or who themselves enact the target behavior can do much to facilitate the translation of intentions into behaviors.

Mental Control Strategies.   Throughout this chapter we have described a number of mental control strategies that might be coupled with more overt behavioral control strategies in order to maximize behavior change. Anything that serves to keep one focused and motivated toward behavior change can be considered a mental control strategy, including goal-setting, relaxation and stress management, self-monitoring, cognitive restructuring, imagery, and mental rehearsal. These strategies, as a group, do aid behavior change. For example, a recent review of the literature showed that when people are trying to increase their performance in a particular sport, setting goals, managing their levels of arousal, and using cognitive self-regulation and imagery all lead to better performance (Murphy, 1995). Some "mental control strategies" do not work, however. If you are often tempted to overeat, you might resolve to simply stop thinking about food. You reason that if you don't think about it, you won't be tempted. This may be true, but it's very difficult, if not impossible, to simply stop thinking about something. In fact, you probably know from experience that deciding not to think about something often moves the topic to the forefront of your mind and makes it more difficult to forget! Researchers have found that even when people are asked to "not think about white bears," something they probably wouldn't think of ordinarily, they become more likely to think of that very thing (Wegner, 1990; Wegner et al., 1991). The counterproductive effects of trying not to think about something are even stronger when what one is trying to avoid is a real issue instead of something contrived, like a white bear (Becker et al., 1998). Clearly, when exercising mental control, it pays to know what works and what does not. For instance, it's not likely that just *trying* to stop thinking about all those delicious snacks will work, but distracting oneself with an interesting activity may enable one to forget about snacking for hours.

Preventing Relapse.   Perhaps the biggest problem facing the individual who strives to adopt healthy practices and eliminate unhealthy ones is **relapse**. As we noted in Chapter 5, relapse is defined as the recurrence of symptoms (or behaviors) after a period of improvement. The ex-smoker, who has abstained from cigarettes for months, begins to smoke regularly; the patient who has been treated successfully for obesity begins to steadily gain weight; the diabetic, whose blood sugar levels have remained steady, loses dietary control and stops taking insulin regularly.

Not all **backsliding** (returning briefly to the past behavior) leads to relapse. Less serious is the **lapse**, described as a mistake, an error, or a slip-up that involves a reemergence of the previous habit but may or may not lead to a state of relapse. In fact, how a person looks at such a slip-up or lapse can influence whether he or she remains in control or turns a lapse into a full relapse. Research has demonstrated that the attribution a person makes for his or her lapse may determine whether a relapse occurs. Those who relapsed were found to have more internal, character-based explanations for the slip than did those who did not relapse. Those who relapsed blamed themselves and their own personal characteristics more than they did the setting (Brownell et al., 1986). "The chief obstacles to maintenance of any new behavior are high-risk situations for which the individual lacks coping skills" (Rosenstock, 1985, p. 614). These situations vary from person to person, but usually include negative emotional states such as anger and frustration, interpersonal conflicts such as arguments with a spouse or disagreements with people at work, and social pressures such as temptations at gatherings in which other people are engaging in the behavior that the individual is trying to avoid (Brownell et al., 1986). When circumstances constitute a high-risk situation, the chances of slip-up in one's established health behaviors can easily occur.

Avoidance of high-risk situations is certainly a wise approach, provided doing so does not deprive the individual of experiencing other aspects of life that are highly valued. Sometimes avoidance is not possible, such as when the boss is having a cocktail party and failure to attend might put one's job in jeopardy. In fact, a high-pressure situation that cannot be avoided (such as the party) may trigger enough anxiety and negative emo-

At some social events, the temptations of high-calorie, high-fat foods can lead to behavioral lapses among those attempting to eat a healthy diet.

tion that the individual uses the forbidden behavior (smoking, drinking alcohol, overeating) as a crutch to deal with the distress. In such a case, it is still possible for an individual to stop the lapse or slip-up from turning into a full relapse. He or she must recognize that the unique environmental circumstances, not his or her shortcomings, are responsible for the initial failure. And the individual may need to develop specific methods for coping with such circumstances in the future (e.g., doing focused relaxation and eating a healthy snack before the party; ordering a soft drink at the party; avoiding smokers).

In sum, relapse can be caused by a combination of the following factors: negative emotional states, inadequate initial motivation, lack of skills to cope with the pressures to relapse, physiological factors (such as craving), lack of social support for continuing the health behavior, and environmental stimuli and contingencies that favor the unhealthy behavior (Brownell et al., 1986). Research suggests that there are three stages in the prevention of relapse (Brownell et al., 1986): (1) enhancing one's motivation to continue the health behavior by providing oneself with regular rewards and/or by focusing on the rewarding natural consequences of the behavior; (2) acquiring and practicing skills to prevent and to deal with lapses, which probably will occur; (3) maintaining the health behavior by continued careful monitoring, general lifestyle change, and seeking out social support. With effort, positive health behaviors and the avoidance of negative ones can be maintained indefinitely. With knowledge, skill and support, people really can change their lives and improve their health.

Box 6.3 examines yet another reason that the achievement of adherence is so important to health. Regardless of what people are trying to do, their health seems to get better when they are successful at adhering.

BOX **6.3**

Research Close-up

Compliance Alone Can Improve Health

Most people under a doctor's care are able to achieve and maintain control over their diseases if they carefully follow the treatment recommendations their doctors have given them. For example, patients who cooperate with their antihypertensive regimens are more likely to have lowered blood pressure than are those who fail to comply with prescribed medications and health behaviors (Shapiro & Goldstein, 1982). Heart disease patients who take their prescribed medications are less likely to die (of all causes, not just heart attack) than are those who do not (Gallagher et al., 1993; Horowitz et al., 1990). The apparent success of a treatment when the patient actually does follow it is considered evidence for the effectiveness of the drug or the health action prescribed. If a prescribed treatment is the correct one, then it is not surprising that patients benefit from following it. What may be rather astounding, however, is research showing that people benefit from adhering even to treatment recommendations that have no direct physiological effect—that is, to placebo medications.

As we learned in Chapter 3, a **placebo** is something that has symbolic significance and can effect a change in the body. A placebo can improve the patient's health or eliminate symptoms. One example of a placebo is an inert substance such as a "sugar pill" that is administered, unbeknownst to the patient, by a health professional who conveys his or her expectation that it will work. Ideally, the health professional also thinks that the inert substance is a certain medication. Thus, in a **double blind situation** (which usually, and ideally, occurs in research), neither the patient nor the physician knows which "medication" administered is the one being tested and which is the sugar pill. What is important is that the health professional conveys to the patient his or her positive expectations. The physician him- or herself may even act as a

sort of placebo, by adopting a reassuring manner which serves to instill hope and belief in the patient (Brody, 1997, 2000).

Nearly two decades ago, a health psychology researcher conducted an extensive review of the literature on adherence to medications (Epstein, 1984). He collected only studies in which the outcome was a measured variable (for example, number of pounds lost) and in which the researchers tested both the outcome of the placebo versus the real medication and the outcome from compliance versus noncompliance, as well as the interaction of these two variables. He found five studies that met the criteria, and in all five studies, there was a significant effect of compliance on outcome. Subjects who were more adherent did better on the outcome measures, regardless of whether they were taking the real drug or a placebo. In one study, women who received regular injections lost more weight than those who did not get their injections regularly, regardless of whether what was injected was a weight-loss-hormone or an inert placebo. Other outcomes that were aided by adherence were alcohol abstinence, prevention of relapse in schizophrenics, reduction in fever or infection in cancer patients, and prevention of mortality in coronary patients. A recent study assessed the treatment of over 1,100 patients who had a myocardial infarction and evaluated their adherence over two years to the drug Amiodarone or to a placebo. The results showed that poor adherence was associated with a greater risk of mortality, whether adherence was to the real medication or to the placebo (Irvine et al., 1999).

What could account for the beneficial effects of adherence alone in predicting health outcomes? It may be that over the course of treatment, people who make the effort to comply come to expect better health outcomes than those who do not, and positive expectations serve

(continued)

BOX **6.3** (Continued)

a self-fulfilling prophecy. A recent systematic review of the literature on expectancies and placebo effects suggests that this may be the case (Crow et al., 1999). These researchers found that enhancing patients' positive expectations in a variety of areas (including their expectations for the process of medical procedures, their ability to manage their illnesses, and the likely effects of their medical interventions) led to more positive patient outcomes. A second explanation is that the act of complying may generate new habits and cognitive patterns that bring about improvement. Complying may engender feelings of well-being and confidence so that related health behaviors are affected as well. People who are doing something about one aspect of their health may begin to do something in other areas as well and thereby improve their health outcomes.

Since there are several ways in which patient adherence is clearly fundamental to health outcomes, how can adherence be improved? As we saw in our analysis of health behaviors, simply educating patients about the benefits of adhering and the potentially negative effects of failing to adhere is not sufficient to bring about change. Strategies that focus on behavior change are more successful than purely informational methods, but what seem to work best are approaches that combine both. A recent meta-analysis of the effectiveness of various interventions aimed at improving adherence found that although most programs are at least somewhat effective, the more comprehensive programs (which combine affective, behavioral, cognitive, and educational interventions) result in the highest levels of adherence (Roter et al., 1998).

A Personal Note

Psychologists tell us that adopting a new health behavior is easier than dropping an old habit but that both can be quite difficult. As we write this book, we are trying to modify some of our own health behaviors. We want to add some good ones and take some bad ones away! One of us (R.D.) is actively working on improving her diet, a goal she has been trying to achieve for more years than she cares to admit! This involves cutting down on fat intake and eating more complex carbohydrates, including whole grains, fruits, and vegetables. And she is still trying to learn to relax! We are both trying to get into regular routines of taking vitamins and of doing aerobic exercise three to four times each week. We have very strong beliefs that these behavioral goals are valuable and that they represent the path to good health. We are surrounded by supportive social norms and lots of tangible help and emotional support. Prompts and reminders greet us everywhere we turn. We have developed valuable behavioral and cognitive strategies. And they work like a charm. Most of the time. Sometimes, however, we suspend rationality and we just get tired of being good. It's been a long day, and it's more enticing to lie around and watch TV than to put on the running shoes and go for a jog. That ice cream is begging to be eaten and that's all there is to it. So we give in. A week or so later, when extra pounds are becoming obvious and energy levels feel low, we reform again and hope that the period of bad behavior has not done too much to undermine good health.

At this writing, we are basically healthy. The diseases we might prevent by improving our diets would likely befall us seemingly far in the future, if they do at all. And, when we fail to eat a proper diet, we remember that we have stuck to our exercise plans, or that we've taken those vitamins regularly, or that we don't smoke. It is a little like bargaining with some imaginary Calculator in the Sky: one dish of ice cream for a half-hour on the treadmill at the gym. We wonder, though, how things might be different if diabetes were part of the picture, and a slightly uncontrolled diet could result in a coma or death. What would happen if alcohol, instead of ice cream, was the big temptation? We find that we are not at all surprised at the noncompliance figures in the research literature. No wonder so much attempted health behavior results in failure. Changing can be very difficult. We also realize, however, that if a person tries, he or she will probably make some progress. Cutting down on fat, even if there are some slip-ups, is much better than ignoring nutrition and subsisting on chocolate and french fries. Walking from the dorm to classes may not be quite as good as taking aerobics four times a week, but, compared to taking the campus shuttle everywhere, it is a big step toward overcoming the negative effects of a sedentary lifestyle. The psychological constructs that we have examined in this chapter (such as health beliefs, attitudes, commitment, and the techniques of self-monitoring, self-reinforcement, shaping, and cognitive modification), whether they happen naturally or are instigated by a clinician or health psychologist, do move people along the road to better health. Most of us probably have quite a long way to go to perfect health. But, health psychology can help us make a good start.

Summary

1. There are many factors that affect health behaviors at the primary, secondary, and tertiary prevention levels.
2. Compliance with (or adherence to) treatment regimens is important to health-care outcomes, and health information influences the creation and maintenance of health behaviors. There are several important sources of information about health and health-related behaviors: the media, medical interactions, family members, and friends.
3. Processes related to behavioral change may be explained using several different models that incorporate not just the level of information that a person has, but also his or her beliefs, attitudes, and intentions.

   - The Health Belief Model proposes that health behavior is influenced by (a) the degree to which the disease is seen as threatening and (b) the degree to which the health behavior is thought to reduce the threat.
   - The Theory of Reasoned Action (TRA) posits that behavior results from an intention and the intention reflects a person's commitment to self (or others) to take action. This intention is influenced by the individual's attitude toward the action and his or her subjective norms regarding it.
   - The Theory of Planned Behavior grew out of the TRA and added the element of perceived control.

- Attitudes and beliefs relate to health outcomes. Behavior will be changed only if the expected result is a desired one (e.g., good health is valued).

4. One may become convinced that a particular behavior is valuable and worth carrying out through the process of persuasion (social influence to change the beliefs and attitudes of another person).

   - Persuasive messages are attention-grabbing, understandable, acceptable, and remembered and are most compelling if both sides of the argument are presented. Fear tactics persuade only if they are not overly graphic and are paired with specific information about how to avoid the fearful outcome.
   - Persuasive messages are more effective with repetition as long as they are not annoying or unpleasant; a "sleeper effect" involves exposure to a message with resultant delay in belief or attitude change.
   - A persuasive person is one who is liked, enthusiastic, interested, dynamic, confident, believes the message, and is perceived as trustworthy, dependable, predictable, and honest.

5. Social-cognitive and self-regulative theories seek to understand the adoption of health behaviors; cognitions are important in determining whether people attempt behavior change and persevere at it.

   - The transtheoretical model is a self-regulative theory that defines six separate stages of change: precontemplation, contemplation, preparation, action, maintenance, and termination.

6. Commitment and intention are essential but also require skill.

   - Behavior modification translates intentions into actual behavior change.
   - Behavioral self-control uses principles of behavioral theory (classical and operant conditioning) to regulate one's own behavior. Self-regulation involves (a) self-monitoring (or self-observation), (b) self-evaluation, and (c) self-reinforcement.
   - Other behavioral strategies include shaping and using prompts or reminders.
   - Cognitive modification involves replacing negative self-statements with positive ones, particularly to deal with failure to maintain the behavior.

7. Supports for intended health behavior change can include family and other social support. Barriers include lack of access to health services, lack of child care, inadequate monetary resources, lack of transportation, and complexity of the regimen.

8. Mental control strategies serve to keep one focused and motivated toward behavior change. Effective strategies include relaxation, distraction, cognitive restructuring, imagery, and mental rehearsal. Avoidance of thinking does not work well.

9. Relapse is the recurrence of symptoms or behaviors after a period of improvement; it can be made less likely by avoiding high risk situations or finding effective coping strategies for them.

THINKING CRITICALLY

1. What do you think would be the most effective combination of interventions to instill good eating habits in third-grade children? Why is a multipronged approach more likely to work than a single intervention? What elements of the behavioral modification equation might be out of your control?

2. Think of one of your own health behaviors (or health misbehaviors!). Apply the Health Belief Model to your situation. How well does this model explain what you do or don't do? Does the Theory of Reasoned Action provide a better explanation? How about the Theory of Planned Behavior?

3. Imagine that you were hired by the health department to direct a 30-second television PSA (public service announcement) aimed at getting motorists to wear safety belts all the time. What elements would your persuasive commercial include? Why?

4. If you were working with recent immigrants to the United States, trying to aid their adoption of good health behaviors, what factors would you need to pay particular attention to?

GLOSSARY

Adherence: An alternative term for compliance.

Attitude: A hypothetical construct used to explain consistencies within people in their affective reactions to (or feelings about) an object or phenomenon. An attitude represents an emotional evaluation of an entity; the attitude follows from a belief. Attitude has been defined as a state of readiness to exhibit a behavioral response.

Backsliding: Returning briefly to past behavior, leading to relapse.

Behavioral approach: An approach to the achievement of health behaviors that holds that with appropriate learning, behavior can be changed.

Behavioral intention: A stated or acknowledged commitment (to oneself or to others) to carry out a particular course of action.

Belief: A hypothetical construct that involves an assertion, often of the relationship between some attitude object (e.g., smoking) and some attribute (e.g., causes cancer).

Classical or respondent conditioning: A process by which a behavior (or response) comes to be evoked by a once-neutral stimulus because that stimulus was paired with one that automatically evoked the behavior.

Compliance: The degree of success a patient has in carrying out the prevention or medical treatment recommendations given to him or her by a health professional.

Double blind situation: Situation in which neither patient nor physician knows whether a medication is real or a placebo.

Health Belief Model (HBM): A model of the relationship between health beliefs and health behaviors.

Lapse: A less serious mistake than relapse; involves reemergence of a previous habit; may lead to a state of relapse, depending upon interpretation and regaining control.

Negative reinforcement: Consequences of removal from a negatively valued state as a result of enacting the behavior; increases behavior.

Nonadherence: See noncompliance.

Noncompliance: The patient's ignoring, forgetting, or misunderstanding the regimen as directed and carrying it out incorrectly or not at all.

Operant conditioning: Technique for modifying behavior based on the principle that behavior is shaped by the consequences that follow it.

Outcome expectation: A person's belief that a specific and desired outcome will follow a particular behavior.

Persuasion: A form of social influence in which one person uses a verbal appeal to change the beliefs and attitudes of another person.

Placebo: Something that has symbolic significance and can effect a change in the body. A placebo can improve the patient's health or eliminate symptoms.

Positive reinforcement: Consequences that increase the probability that a behavior will be enacted; provides individual with something valued after enacting the behavior.

Primary prevention: Actions taken to preserve health before any disease has developed and when there is no special "risk" present.

Prompts and reminders: The initial triggers for health behavior.

Psychological support: Help for the individual in developing and maintaining affective or emotional states that engender well-being.

Relapse: The recurrence of symptoms (or undesired behaviors) after a period of improvement.

Secondary prevention: Actions taken once a person has developed a condition in which he or she is "at risk" for further health damage; involves taking preventive health measures in order to forestall potential negative outcomes.

Self-control: The ultimate goal of the behavioral approach; an individual translates his or her intentions into behaviors and maintains the performance of those behaviors.

Self-efficacy: An individual's personal judgment of his or her own ability (e.g., specifically to carry out a particular behavior, or generally to be successful).

Self-evaluation: The second stage in self-regulation; the individual assesses what was learned through self-monitoring and compares present behavior with a criterion.

Self-monitoring or self-observation: The first stage of self-regulation, which involves the individual deliberately and carefully attending to his or her own behavior.

Self-regulation: Self-imposed operant conditioning that involves three stages (self-monitoring, self-evaluation, and self-reinforcement).

Self-regulative theories: Theories that combine ideas of self-knowledge with planned, directed action toward changing behaviors.

Self-reinforcement: The third stage in self-regulation; the individual rewards or reinforces him- or herself for behavior that matches or approximates the goal.

Shaping (also called graduated treatment implementation): The application of reinforcement for successive approximations to the desired behavior.

Sleeper effect: A phenomenon in which a long time after exposure to a persuasive message a person may change his or her belief and not remember why.

Social cognitive theory: A theory that proposes that thoughts (or cognitions) are important in social learning and that these enable learning to take place in the absence of classical conditioning and reinforcement (e.g., vicariously).

Social support: Any input from other people that furthers the goals of the receiver of the support; includes tangible support and psychological support.

Subjective (social) norm: The individual's beliefs about what others (with whom the individual is motivated to cooperate) want him or her to do.

Tangible support: Social support in the form of physical resources.

Tertiary prevention: The taking of measures specifically designed to cure a disease or to control its progress and prevent further disability and handicap.

Theory of Planned Behavior: A modification of the Theory of Reasoned Action that includes the element of perceived behavioral control; involves purposeful behaviors.

Theory of Reasoned Action: A social-psychological theory that health behavior results partly from behavioral intention, which is made up of two components: attitudes toward an action and subjective norms regarding the action.

Transtheoretical model: Based on self-regulative theory; a model that proposes six stages of change: precontemplation, contemplation, preparation, action, maintenance, and termination.

Vicarious learning: Learning by observation.

CHAPTER 7

The Process of Illness

As Li Ming leaned forward in the cool leather chair of the doctor's waiting room chair, she thought for the first time that something might be seriously wrong with her. The idea crossed her mind that a brain tumor could be causing her problems, and the concept was pretty terrifying. Li Ming had been experiencing increasingly severe headaches for the past six months, and although she'd been to see her doctor twice about them, the pain had only gotten worse. Even more disturbing was the fact that her doctor, someone she knew and trusted a great deal, couldn't find any explanation for her pain. Now she was to see a specialist—a neurologist—and to Li Ming this meant the possibility that there really was a serious problem. She felt conflicting emotions. On the one hand, she was anxious to hear what this new doctor would have to say. Perhaps she would even be able to offer a simple solution. On the other hand, she dreaded what the neurologist

might find and worried that the diagnosis might be much worse than the pain itself. She thought that if it was a brain tumor, she might even die!

She was jolted out of her reverie by the receptionist's summons: "Li Ming Zhang . . . Dr. Renard is ready for you." Once inside the examining room, Li Ming was greeted warmly by Dr. Renard. For about five minutes the two of them talked, with Dr. Renard jotting a note in Li Ming's chart from time to time. Dr. Renard had clearly done her homework, and she already knew many of the details of Li Ming's past six months, but there were a few things yet to cover. When they were finished, Dr. Renard faced Li Ming squarely and looked into her eyes. "I don't want to alarm you, but it is possible that this is serious. I would like to schedule you for an MRI (magnetic resonance imaging) scan as soon as possible. The first opening they have is this Wednesday afternoon at 2. I'd like you to do this as soon as possible, okay?"

At that point, Li Ming wasn't really surprised, just sort of tired and resigned. Of course she would go on Wednesday. She would have to miss her chemistry lab, but what did that matter, when she might have a brain tumor? What good would an education do her if she weren't even alive? Li Ming thanked Dr. Renard and, in a daze, waited for the receptionist to make her appointment for the MRI. Then she drove home and lay on the couch, gazing at the ceiling.

A week later Li Ming once again found herself in a comfortable leather chair in Dr. Renard's waiting room. But she did not feel comfortable. Li Ming had found out the day before that her MRI had been completely normal. She wished she could be happy about that, but her headaches hadn't stopped. In fact, she'd had the most excruciatingly painful headache of all just the night before. Today she was here to discuss possible treatments with Dr. Renard. Certainly she felt relieved, but to Li Ming's mind not knowing what was wrong was almost as bad as having a terrible diagnosis. How could she be treated if the problem couldn't even be identified?

Dr. Renard seemed as warm and kind as she did in their first visit. She suggested that what Li Ming had was a particularly severe form of tension headaches that also had some characteristics of severe migraine headaches. Dr. Renard prescribed some medication and told Li Ming she had to do something to manage her tension. She mentioned the word "psychosomatic," which Li Ming took to mean that the pain was somehow not real, or that she had imagined it. Dr. Renard suggested that Li Ming consider seeking psychological counseling and perhaps relaxation therapy to deal with her stress.

Li Ming felt frustrated and didn't really know what to do next. She didn't feel like talking to any of her friends about the issue because they all seemed so tired of hearing about her headaches. She didn't believe that her pain could be caused by emotions and stress, although she wondered if she might be wrong. Could something psychological really cause such severe physical pain?

In Chapters 5 and 6, we examined the prevention of disease and the measures that people can take to try to remain healthy. Despite their health-related efforts, however, human beings do sometimes fall prey to external threats such as viruses, bacteria, toxins, and injuries. Not all diseases and degenerative conditions can be prevented or even forestalled. But even when a real external threat is involved, becoming ill is not a clear-cut event like throwing a switch or blowing a fuse. There is often no simple distinction between healthy and ill states, and there are many gradations of each. For example, one can be healthy in all respects but still suffer from osteoarthritis of the knee or allergic sinusitis. The seriousness of various conditions can be graded from mild (e.g., a simple cold) to severe (e.g., cancer of the lung). And, the label of "healthy" or "ill" that is placed on a person depends upon the integration of a multitude of factors including test results, clinical findings, physical functioning, objective capabilities, self-definitions, interference with usual activities, and the nuances of diagnostic decisions.

In this chapter, we examine the phenomenon of illness from the perspectives of both patient and health professional. We consider some important questions such as these: How do individuals make the decision that they are ill? How do health professionals diagnose diseases? What prompts a person to conclude that his or her symptoms are serious and that it is time to seek treatment? Why would a person ignore the symptoms of a heart attack or the clear signs of cancer? What does a person do when there is no clear definition of the problem and when there is no name for what he or she is feeling? Under what circumstances might a person use illness as an excuse to take a break from the difficulties of life? What special privileges does illness bring? What would make a person accept those privileges or pass them up? How does emotional stress influence this process? And, how can a person overcome the limitations of illness and accomplish great things against the odds?

Health, Illness, and Disease

In order to answer the questions we have posed, we need to understand the sometimes frustrating and always complex concept of **illness**. Most of us have used this word throughout our lives, believing that we know what it means. But if you dissect the concept, you will find more about human behavior and psychological processes than you might have imagined. Consider this simple definition: Illness is "a condition marked by the pronounced deviation from the normal healthy state" (*Dorland's Illustrated Medical Dictionary*, 1965, p. 725). When ill, an individual is unable to carry out normal day-to-day activities. Further, his or her body does not have the expected level of stamina, and there may be pain, nausea, fatigue, or perhaps just a sense of feeling unwell and unhealthy. As you can see from this definition, illness is a subjective phenomenon. It depends upon an individual's evaluation of his or her own internal state and ability to function. The definition leaves room for the effects of both physical and emotional factors. The subjectivity of illness does not make it whimsical or unreal, but it does complicate the phenomenon by making it difficult to define objectively. And, because people usually wait until they *feel* sick to go to the doctor, the subjective definition of a person's bodily state is what typically brings him or her to seek help from a health professional.

When caring for a patient, a health professional usually looks for something called **disease**. Disease is a more narrow concept than illness. Disease is "an interruption, cessation, or disorder of body function, systems, or organs . . . a morbid entity characterized usually by at least two of these criteria: recognized etiologic agent(s), identifiable group of signs and symptoms, or consistent anatomical alterations . . . the opposite of ease, when something is wrong with a bodily function" (*Stedman's Medical Dictionary*, 1995, p. 492). It is possible for a person to have disease but (for a time, at least) to have no outward signs, no marked deviation in functioning, and no subjective feelings of limitation or disability. In other words, until disease is discovered, it is possible for a person to be considered well and even to consider him- or herself quite healthy. A disease process can be highly progressed before an individual has signs or acknowledges feeling ill. For instance, an individual may live normally and feel perfectly healthy for months despite the rapid growth of a brain tumor. It is only when the tumor is large enough to affect the nervous system that the individual begins to feel ill (and the disease becomes apparent). This was the fear that Li Ming, whom we met at the beginning of the chapter, entertained.

Health is not simply the absence of disease. A person might have no identifiable pathology and yet not be healthy. Certainly, any deviation from a person's normal, self-defined healthy state of feeling and functioning suggests that he or she is not healthy. But, as more and more is learned about the critical role of specific preventive behaviors, as well as physical (and even psychological) fitness, the concept of health is broadened even further. The World Health Organization adopted a comprehensive view of health back in 1946, stating that "[h]ealth is the state of complete physical, mental, and social well-being, and is not merely the absence of disease or infirmity" (World Health Organization, adopted 1946). These definitions of health, illness, and disease are somewhat vague because their definitions rely on complex issues that are themselves imprecise. These definitions do, however, present guidelines to help us understand what we encounter when we consider real cases. For example, imagine a man who is ". . . . fully recovered from a myocardial infarction [heart attack, in which there is some damage to the heart muscle]. He takes no medication, observes manageable restrictions in his diet and daily activities, appears perfectly healthy in every respect—yet he does have heart disease. Do you interrupt this man in the middle of a red-hot tennis game to tell him he's sick?" (*Professional Guide to Diseases* [PGD], 1982, p. xxii). This man has heart disease, yet he does not define himself as ill. One problem with the subjectivity of illness is that we only know a person is ill if he or she says so or demonstrates obvious illness behaviors (such as moving slowly, with bent posture, and holding a hand to the lower back). A person may complain that he or she does not have a normal level of energy or cannot function in the usual way. The label of illness must be based upon the person's notion of what is right and what is not right for him or her individually (Mechanic, 1968). The term illness would apply to a marathoner who suddenly could not run more than five miles without collapsing in exhaustion or to a student who usually takes six courses each quarter and now has barely enough energy for three. If a person cannot perform usual activities, a self-definition of "illness" is likely to be applied. This subjectivity of illness, and the fact that it is different from disease, makes the following paradox possible.

The Paradox of Health and Illness

Jerdall had felt exhausted for months. He had a great deal of trouble getting up in the morning, and he seemed to drag himself through the day. He was continuously looking for opportunities to take a nap, and every evening after work he fell into bed, exhausted. He regularly passed up the chance to go out with friends because he was not feeling well. The woman he was dating stopped returning his calls because she was tired of his constant excuses for not going out and of his promises of fun excursions when he "got caught up on things." The fatigue that Jerdall felt was so powerful that nothing else mattered to him as much as being able to go to sleep. He felt his life was coming apart. All the things that once had mattered a great deal to him no longer made him feel the least bit of enthusiasm. He was beginning to doubt his own motivations and capabilities, and his self-esteem was suffering considerably.

Hoping that his problem could be diagnosed and cured, Jerdall finally went to see his doctor. He had a single complaint—fatigue—and it was a common one among the patients who were seen at this office. The doctor followed up with all the requisite blood tests, but the results were completely normal. Jerdall did not have infectious mononucleosis, he was not anemic, and he had no hidden infection. So what was wrong?

His doctor suggested that he might have **Chronic Fatigue Syndrome** (CFS), and, although Jerdall wasn't exactly sure what this was, he felt relieved to finally have an explanation (if not a cure) for his tiredness and lethargy. He now had at least some explanation to tell his friends who were disappointed in his lack of social availability and his boss who was dissatisfied with his work. Jerdall's diagnosis is not an unusual one—in fact, it has become increasingly common over the past two decades. But what does it mean?

The concept of chronic, overwhelming fatigue is not new. A hundred years ago in Europe this illness would likely have been called neurasthenia, but the symptoms would have looked quite the same. In the mid-1980s **Epstein-Barr Virus** (EBV; a virus that causes infectious mononucleosis) began to be associated with chronic fatigue because there was some evidence that high levels of EBV antibodies were present in those who experienced chronic fatigue. Upon closer investigation, however, the U.S. Centers for Disease Control (CDC) found that most people with CFS had levels of EBV antibodies that fell within the normal range and that there did not seem to be a clear link between the level of the antibody and the level of fatigue (Payer, 1992). Nonetheless, there was now a label to apply to chronic fatigue—Chronic EBV Syndrome (or CEBV).

The CEBV label was loosely defined, however, and there was a great degree of variability in how this new syndrome was diagnosed. Also, there was increasing pressure to change the name of the syndrome since there was really no clear-cut evidence to link it to the Epstein-Barr Virus. In 1986 the CDC officially named the disorder Chronic Fatigue Syndrome (CFS) and formalized the definition to include these requirements for diagnosis: (a) The person's fatigue must be severe enough to reduce his or her daily activities by half; (b) the person must have at least eight of fourteen additional symptoms such as sore throat, muscle weakness, and fever; and (c) all other causes for the person's fatigue (including psychiatric) must be ruled out.

Having a formal name and definition for CFS does not mean, however, that it is understood very well. Its diagnosis is still very subjective. For instance, how do we know whether our activity level has really been cut in half, or whether we are remembering ourselves as having been more active and productive than we really were? How do we define "muscle weakness"? At what point does a physician decide that *all* competing causes for the fatigue have been ruled out? Also, even though there is a name for the experience of CFS, and it can be defined, there is still no clear answer about what causes it. Hypotheses include various immunologic abnormalities, hypotension, and autonomic nervous system malfunction, but the evidence for each of these is equivocal (Pagani & Lucini, 1999; Rowe & Calkins, 1998; Whiteside & Friberg, 1998). Chronic Fatigue Syndrome is not the only illness that is defined subjectively. As we will see later in this chapter, most illnesses have at least some subjective component, and some are almost completely subjective in their diagnosis.

The term **"functional somatic syndrome"** refers to a group of related syndromes that are characterized by functional disability and self-reported symptoms rather than clearly demonstrable organic problems (Barsky & Borus, 1999; Wessely et al., 1999). These include things like irritable bowel syndrome, chronic fatigue syndrome, multiple chemical sensitivity, and repetitive stress injuries. With all of these illnesses, people are disabled to one degree or another, and yet it is difficult for medical practitioners to find something specific that is physically wrong with them. Thus, it is difficult to treat or "cure" them. Why, with all of the medical technology available, are healthcare practitioners unable to find the causes of these illnesses? Why are nonconventional techniques sometimes helpful when modern technology has failed? And why are these illnesses becoming more common?

By *objective* standards, the health of U.S. citizens is quite good and has been getting better over the years. Average life expectancy has been rising steadily over the past decades. In 1900, life expectancy was only 47.3 years, and in 1996 it was 76.1 years (K. D. Peters et al., 1998). Preliminary 1997 vital statistics reports indicate that life expectancy increased another 0.4 percent from 1996–1997, resulting in an all-time high of 76.5 years (Ventura et al., 1998). Mortality has declined for people of all ages, even those over 85 years old, and infant mortality rates have been declining steadily for the past forty years. They now stand at only 7.1 per 1,000 live births (K. D. Peters et al., 1998; Ventura et al., 1998). In 1928, there were effective treatments available for only about 5 to 10 percent of the 360 most serious diseases. Now the figure is well over 50 percent (Barsky, 1988). However, "during the past 20 to 30 years, people's subjective sense of healthiness has not kept pace with improvements in health status; indeed, it appears to have declined. According to nationwide polls and community surveys, the proportion of Americans who are satisfied with their health and physical condition has fallen from 61% in the 1970s to 55% in the mid-1980s . . . People report more frequent and longer-lasting episodes of serious, acute illness now than they did 60 years ago, despite the introduction of antibiotics during the intervening period" (Barsky, 1988, p. 415).

In the 1920s, large-scale community surveys found that the average respondent reported fewer than one (0.82) episode per year of a serious acute disabling illness. The average length of the illness was 16 days. In the early 1980s, on the other hand, the average respondent reported 2.12 episodes of acute disabling illness, each lasting an average of 19 days. Another aspect of the trend toward a greater incidence of illness can be found in large nationwide surveys of somatic symptoms. In these surveys, respondents were asked about common somatic (bodily) complaints like dyspnea (difficult or labored breathing), heart palpitations, and pain. According to Barsky, people reported significantly more symptoms in 1976 than in 1957, and from 1976 onward there has been a steady decline in the proportion of respondents who reported having no symptoms at all.

Certainly there are many possible explanations for the paradox that while objectively Americans are healthier than ever before, they say they feel worse. One explanation is that the threshold and tolerance for mild discomfort is now lower than it was in the past. People more readily seek medical help for isolated symptoms, and they are more likely than in the past to acknowledge to others that they feel ill. The standards for health have been raised so high that people are now aware of, and disturbed by, impairments and symptoms that they would have once ignored (Barsky & Borus, 1995). Medicine can offer more treatments than ever before for all sorts of ailments, from the life threatening to the simply inconvenient. Chronic illnesses such as diabetes, rheumatoid arthritis, and heart disease cannot be cured outright, but they can be controlled. Thus, one explanation for the paradox of "doing better but feeling worse" is

Door-to-door household surveys over the past several decades have shown a steady increase in reported somatic symptoms.

that today people live long enough to experience chronic illnesses that leave them with various nagging symptoms, impairments, and disabilities that medical professionals can possibly help control but not cure. In addition, people seem to have raised their standards of what is healthy to a much higher level than ever before. Compared to the past, people today are willing to tolerate less impairment as a normal part of daily living. People have a heightened awareness of health, with many Americans now focusing some of their energies on attaining "a healthy lifestyle." The search for healthy diets and the physical fitness boom probably serve to focus people's attention on their internal bodily feelings and encourage them to expect that they can feel good most of the time (Barsky, 1988).

When examining the functional somatic syndromes, there are some other interesting things to note. Patients with these syndromes generally have very elaborate self-diagnoses, their symptoms can often be ameliorated by explanation and reassurance, and they tend to experience high co-occurrence rates with other similar syndromes. There is also a high prevalence of co-occurring psychiatric symptoms (Barsky & Borus, 1999). For some of these patients, a physical cause for their problem will eventually be diagnosed but, until then, the suffering experienced by these patients is exacerbated by the psychosocial factors that encourage and reinforce their beliefs that they have a serious disease (see Figure 7.1). A social climate that encourages these beliefs (such as a media that sensationalizes issues like multiple chemical sensitivity, or the prolitigation attitudes of some consumers) perpetuates the distress of these patients and likely prolongs and worsens their disability (Barsky & Borus, 1999).

FIGURE 7.1   Seeking help for medical symptoms.

The Physician's Dilemma

The paradox of doing better-but-feeling-worse and the subjective character of illness itself can be sources of frustration for physicians. About half of all primary care visits are due to a small number of common physical-health symptoms, and only 10 to 15 percent of these result in the definitive diagnosis of an organic disease (Katon & Walker, 1998). Thus, a patient may arrive with vehement complaints of discomfort, but discussion with the physician and a careful review of systems may reveal no consistent pattern of symptoms. The physical examination and diagnostic tests may demonstrate no clear pathology. Understandably, the physician is perplexed.

Consider this real case history:

This 49-year-old woman [HF], widowed eight years previously, lived alone and did not work. She had one daughter aged 27. HF and her husband having been fairly prosperous, her investments gave her an adequate income. With a teacher's diploma, she taught for a while before she got married, but had not since. HF had had a hysterectomy at the age for 45 for **menorrhagia** [abnormal premenopausal bleeding]. Twelve years previously she had had a **laparotomy** [exploratory surgery of the abdomen] because of persistent abdominal pain. She had had mixed tension [muscle contraction] and vascular [migraine] headaches since her teens. The patient now complained of various pains in the chest, abdomen, and lower back, headache, pressure in her chest, and dizziness. These symptoms lasted throughout most of the day. There were odd days when she felt better, but never entirely free of symptoms. Abdominal pain had started about thirteen years previously, at a time when she had serious marital difficulties. She appeared to improve for a while, but her symptoms became more severe about one year after her husband died. She had been convinced for about five years that she had a physical disease that none of the doctors had discovered; they had told her different diagnoses and she believed one day the true cause would be found . . . (Kellner, 1986, pp. 300–301).

This patient presents a challenge to the physician—both to find out what's wrong with her and to try to help improve her health and functioning. It is quite possible, of course, to accomplish the latter without accomplishing the former. To do this, however, it is necessary to avoid the assumption that there is a one-to-one correspondence between physical tissue damage (or disease) and patients' subjective feelings of pain or discomfort (illness). A dilemma arises only when illness is looked at in the limited traditional way—as a purely biomedical rather than as a biopsychosocial phenomenon.

The Biomedical versus
the Biopsychosocial Model

As we examined in Chapter 1, the dominant model of disease today is biomedical. The **biomedical model** assumes that illness can be *fully* accounted for by a patient's deviations from the norm on measurable biological variables. The model holds that even the most complex illness phenomena can be reduced to certain measurable physical abnormalities. Although the means to measure all of these variables may not yet be available, such measurement is at least theoretically possible (Engel, 1997).

The biomedical model is certainly an improvement over the approach in previous centuries that emphasized demons as the cause of disease. However, the biomedical model is limited in its ability to account for much health-related phenomena. For example, the presence of a biological deviation does not always result in an individual's expression of illness through his or her behavior (Bakal, 1999). The person with a definable abnormality may feel fine and look and act perfectly normal. In addition, a particular physical abnormality can affect different people in vastly different ways (Robinson, 1971). Finally, it is clear that illness can be manifested in behavior even when there are no corresponding physical parameters that point to disease. In other words, the biomedical model leads to yet another paradox. Some people with objective physical findings (such as abnormal laboratory test results) are told they are in need of treatment, when they are, in fact, feeling quite well. Others may feel astoundingly ill but are assured that they have no disease. Unfortunately, the biomedical model does not adequately describe the *reality of illness* in human experience (Bakal, 1999; Kleinman, 1988).

Let's consider an example of how the biomedical model fails to account for the vast differences in human behavior that result from the same physical phenomena. As we saw above, Jerdall, who was introduced at the beginning of this chapter, was diagnosed with chronic fatigue syndrome (CFS). Another CFS sufferer is Michelle Akers, who at age 33 held the distinction of being the oldest member of the 1999 U.S. World Cup soccer team. She also had the best goals-to-games ratio in U.S. soccer history (with 100 goals in 128 international matches). She played these matches with both CFS and damaged knees. Despite her apparent disadvantages, Michelle played an outstanding game in front of a packed Rose Bowl stadium. She had to leave the game early, but not before she spearheaded the attack, and ultimate World Cup victory, against the team from China. How could Michelle and Jerdall, with the same diagnosis of CFS, function so differently? Clearly, illness is a considerably more complex phenomenon than the biomedical model allows. A much broader approach is needed.

The **biopsychosocial model** requires that psychological and social factors must be included along with the biological in any attempts to understand a person's response (positive or negative) to physical symptoms and the experience of illness (Bakal, 1999; Engel, 1997). Such an approach incorporates various important psychological phenomena along with biological parameters. These include (1) the meaning a person attaches to his or her condition (whether it is something that will prevent the achievement of goals or something to be overcome); (2) what the individual consciously or unconsciously wants (for example, to fail or to succeed; to be taken care of or to maintain independence); and (3) the individual's own response style (such as whether he or she enhances or tries to minimize personal disabilities and discomforts). The biopsychosocial model also incorporates the individual's social expectations about illness, particularly patterns learned from family and culture, for the appropriate ways to respond to symptoms. The biopsychosocial model takes into account the person's psychological state, such as the extent to which she or he is anxious or depressed. And, it takes into account the present social context of the illness (that is, how the illness affects the individual's relationships with other people).

As we will see in detail below, there is a great deal of evidence that psychological and social factors such as these are every bit as important as tissue damage in determining people's experience of illness. "A phenomenon often approached with fascination by practitioners, lay persons, and social scientists alike is the tremendous variation among people in their responses to what appear to be similar medical conditions. While one individual may hardly acknowledge a symptom, another (with perhaps an even milder form of the same condition) will withdraw from his or her particular daily responsibilities, refrain from going to work, exhibit emotional distress, and display significant social and psychological disability" (DiMatteo & DiNicola, 1982, p. 112). In the next section, we will employ the biopsychosocial model as we examine how people respond to and interpret their physical symptoms. Before that, however, in Box 7.1 we

---

BOX 7.1

Research Close-up

Physical Symptoms and HIV

Beth has been feeling very poorly lately. She has been losing weight, experiencing extreme fatigue, catching numerous colds, and feeling achy and feverish and sick to her stomach. She went to see her doctor, who could not find evidence of a sinus or a "strep" infection, or of infectious mononucleosis.

Beth has not been totally honest with herself or with her doctor about her sexual history, however. Over the years, Beth has had unprotected sex numerous times, even with men she did not know very well. She has not shared this information with anyone, including her current boyfriend. She doesn't want to face the possibility that something might be seriously wrong with her. It may be time to do so, however, and to admit the possibility that she may have acquired a sexually transmitted disease such as chlamydia, cytomegalovirus, viral hepatitis, gonorrhea, or syphilis. There is even a chance that she may have contracted HIV, the AIDS virus.

The curious phenomenon of HIV infection is that infected individuals typically do not know about their infection unless they are either tested for the virus or develop the symptoms of AIDS. Generally, HIV itself does not cause symptoms until considerable damage has been done to the immune system. Even the symptoms of AIDS can be confusing to patients and health professionals alike, because they are so similar to many other illnesses. One of the primary ways that healthcare professionals come to even consider the possibility of HIV infection is through the information provided by the patient about his or her high risk behaviors (primarily intra-

venous drugs use and unprotected sex). If that information is not forthcoming, such as in Beth's case (or if the health professional fears angering the patient by suggesting it), diagnosis may take a long time and waste a valuable opportunity for early treatment. When HIV symptoms are attributed to some other illness, or even to stress, the patient does not seek HIV testing (Siegel et al., 1999). Such delay can be quite detrimental to the individual's health, because treatment for the illness is more successful when it is started early. Even before symptoms of AIDS emerge, some treatment and watchful waiting are essential.

The misattribution of symptoms is not the only barrier to seeking testing or treatment for HIV, of course. One of the biggest barriers is emotional. Delay in seeking testing and care is often associated with significant psychological distress about the results (Raveis et al., 1998). In fact, among women, greater psychological upset about HIV was a good predictor of avoiding testing and early care (Raveis et al., 1998). It is easy to understand why a person in emotional distress might wait months or even years before seeking the answer to the terrifying question of whether he or she has contracted HIV.

Currently, a great deal of research and clinical practice is being focused on helping high-risk individuals to initiate HIV testing and, if necessary, early treatment. This work is hindered, however, by misattributions about symptoms and by the enormous emotional barriers that individuals use to protect themselves against frightening possibilities regarding their health status.

examine the often ambiguous symptoms of HIV infection, and the psychological barriers to testing and early treatment.

Recognizing and Attending to Physical Symptoms

Some people pay a great deal of attention to the state of their bodies. They connect what they ate for lunch to the amount of energy they have in the afternoon. At any given moment they can tell you exactly how their bodies feel and where they have discomfort, twinges, muscle spasms, and feelings of heaviness or bloating. They are aware of varying degrees of fatigue, slight fluctuations in physical coordination, varying gradations of blush or pallor in their skin, and any and all limitations in their movement. Other people barely acknowledge their physical state on a conscious level. They actually seem to ignore it. Even when they feel very much out-of-sorts, they don't try to determine the origin of their misery. Their irritability, grumpiness, and lethargy may be the only clues that something is wrong with them. When others point out that they appear "not themselves," they require considerable time to recognize that bad feelings in their bodies are the source of their less-than-congenial behavior. They don't even seem to have the words to describe physical distress.

Several factors have been found to influence people's reactions to their physical symptoms: First, people vary in the extent to which they focus their attention on threatening events such as symptoms. Some people minimize the implications of these events and behave as though the occurrences are minor. Others become vigilant, seek information, and actively confront the threat (Goldstein, 1973; Miller & Mangan, 1983). One psychological factor that has often been related to reporting of physical symptoms is the personality trait neuroticism (Brown & Moskowitz, 1997; Costa & McCrae, 1987; Katon & Walker, 1998; Neitzert et al., 1997). People who are high in neuroticism tend to be anxious and somewhat "high-strung." This may be reflected in their tendency to exaggerate small symptoms and to complain a lot. In fact, when more objective outcomes, such as mortality, are used, individuals high in neuroticism do not seem to be any worse off than those low in neuroticism, pointing to the likelihood that it is their perceptions and interpretations (rather than their objective health status) that are different (Costa & McCrae, 1987). There is some evidence that neuroticism might be important in influencing symptom reporting mostly for individuals who are already sick; the relationship between neuroticism and symptom reporting has been found to be less strong in completely healthy populations (Brown & Moskowitz, 1997). Depression has also been linked consistently to higher rates of symptom reporting, with more depressed people being more likely to complain about their physical symptoms (Katon & Walker, 1998; Neitzert et al., 1997). Anxiety (which is one element of neuroticism and a psychological state and consistent pattern of emotional experience in itself) has also been linked to symptom reporting in its own right (Barsky et al., 1998a, 1998b).

Second, attention to bodily symptoms often depends upon their salience. People tend to focus most on bodily symptoms when issues of their health and body-integrity occupy their attention. When a close relative or friend is ill or has died of a particular condition, for example, there is a tendency for many people to focus their attention on the vulnerability of their own bodies. Many focus specifically on the organ affected in the friend or loved one (Mechanic, 1972). This phenomenon is magnified in medical students who have a high prevalence (approximately 70%) of experiencing symptoms that they attribute to a pathological process (Mechanic, 1972; Niemi & Vainiomacki, 1999).

Third, some individuals chronically scrutinize their bodily states. They may have a greater than usual body awareness, vigilance, and self-consciousness (Bakal, 1999; Barsky, 1988), sometimes called "private body consciousness" or "somatic focus." Some studies even show that this bodily attention may be a better predictor of symptom reporting than is anxiety (Arntz & de Jong, 1993; Arntz et al., 1991). Their increased scrutiny tends to amplify their discomfort (Barsky et al., 1996; Ferguson & Ahles, 1998; Martin et al., 1991). It has even been suggested that some people, particularly those who depend upon modern medical "hype" (e.g., the latest diet, the latest cure-all scheme, the latest commercial product) may have lost faith and confidence in their own bodies. Rather than view their bodies as strong and capable, they feel weak and vulnerable, prey to the rhinoviruses on bathroom basins and to the sudden stoppage of their hearts for no apparent reason. In general, in U.S. culture, there is more of a focus on health than ever before. This can be seen in the number of self-help health books and health-enhancement products available, as well as the increasing availability of healthy food alternatives, such as fat-free potato chips and soy burgers. While these products may be valuable in achieving certain goals such as weight management, the increased focus on health and on expectations of vitality may serve to accentuate, for an individual who is predisposed to pay attention to the issue, those areas in his or her health that are less than optimal.

Fourth, as we will see in more detail in Chapter 8, research has found that people differ in their thresholds and tolerance levels for symptoms, particularly pain. The "pain threshold" is the level of intensity of a stimulus at which pain is identified. The corresponding "tolerance level" is the point of intensity of the stimulus at which the individual can no longer tolerate or stand the pain and (in research at least) asks that it be stopped (Hirsch & Liebert, 1998; Weisenberg, 1977).

Fifth, our childhood experiences contribute to our patterns of dealing with symptoms. The manner in which others have behaved toward us when ill, as well as particular behaviors of ours that were encouraged or discouraged, tend to affect whether we ignore our bad feelings or express them to others (Hotopf et al., 1999).

> *Consider Grandma:*   Grandma moans and holds her hand toward you. "Look," she encourages. "See what my arthritis is doing?" Her joints do look swollen. She holds her hand stiffly. "Oh, these fingers." Then, clutching her hand over her heart she exclaims, "Ah . . . this arthritis is gonna kill me . . . Dear God what a curse." She rolls her eyes heavenward. You are 5 years old. You assume this is how everyone behaves when something hurts him or her.

Sixth, our cultural background tends to affect our responses to symptoms. In a New York City hospital, one classic research study examined the reactions of patients from varied ethnic backgrounds (Zborowski, 1952). People of Jewish and Italian ancestry responded to pain in a very emotional fashion. They talked about their pain, describing it verbally and expressing it with gestures. People of "Old American" ancestry, on the other hand, were stoical and talked objectively about their pain, as if it were an entity separate from themselves. The Irish denied feelings of pain even when they presented to the clinic with objective symptoms. Cultural norms are important in helping to determine many aspects of illness ranging from which symptoms are important and how to respond to them to determining the most appropriate ways of dealing with those that are sick (Payer, 1988).

Seventh, the circumstances of an individual's life at a given time can influence the degree of attention that he or she pays to physical symptoms. It is quite possible to be too busy to notice one's pain or discomfort and much too focused on outside activities to pay attention to the nuances of one's bodily functioning. On the other hand, a person who is in a boring situation or who lives alone without the company of other people can tend to focus much more attention on his or her internal state than does someone who is involved in many activities (Pennebaker, 1983).

Eighth, a person's gender is a potentially important factor as well. Studies consistently show that women generally perceive and report more physical symptoms than do men (Goldberg et al., 1998; Neitzert et al., 1997). There are many potential explanations for this. For example, women may pay more attention than men to sensations in their bodies; they may define the causes for these sensations differently; or they may have different sorts of information about what the sensations indicate (van Wijk & Kolk, 1997).

Finally, cognitive factors may strongly affect an individual's attention and reaction to symptoms. The meaning of the symptom, for example, can be quite important (as we will see in more detail when we examine pain in Chapter 8). Surgical patients who sustained tissue damage similar to that experienced by men wounded in war were found to react much more negatively, to express the fact that they were in pain, and to request more pain killers than did the wounded soldiers (Beecher, 1959). The men wounded in battle seemed to tolerate their wounds with equanimity. The tissue damage was actually interpreted as positive by the men in war because it meant that they had escaped death and would go home as heroes. Surgical patients, however, viewed their tissue damage as quite negative, as a loss of capacity, as a deviation from normal, and as an interference in their daily lives. Other cognitive factors are also important. If one's symptoms are recognizable from the past and are believed to be unimportant or explainable, such as muscle aches after an athletic competition, they probably will be ignored. However, if the symptoms represent a new feeling that is strange and terrifying, they will likely be attended to (Safer et al., 1979). Symptoms gain a person's attention if they attack a salient part of the body such as the face or eyes, or the one that is particularly important to the individual (such as the heart for a person whose father died of heart disease) (Safer et al., 1979).

So far, we have examined the factors that prompt an individual to attend to certain symptoms that arise in his or her body (summarized in Table 7.1). Now let us turn to an examination of the actions that people take when they experience certain symptoms, particularly why and how they seek medical treatment.

TABLE 7.1 Factors That Influence Reactions to Physical Symptoms

1. Degree to which people focus attention on threatening events, like symptoms. This tendency is related to the personality characteristic of neuroticism.
2. Salience of bodily symptoms.
3. General tendency to scrutinize one's own bodily states (also called private body consciousness or somatic focus).
4. Threshold of and tolerance for symptoms, especially pain.
5. Childhood experiences regarding symptoms.
6. Cultural background.
7. Life circumstances at the time the physical symptoms are experienced.
8. Gender (which may play its role through a variety of pathways, including socialization to gender norms, differences in attention, or different types of available information).
9. Cognitive factors such as the meaning attributed to the symptoms.

Seeking Medical Help for Symptoms

Research in the general population shows that at any given time, 75 to 90 percent of people experience symptoms that *could* be considered clinically relevant (Kellner, 1986). However, only about 20 to 30 percent of them seek medical help (Bruijnzeels et al., 1998; Kellner, 1986). In one study, university students and hospital staff (who at the time were taking no medications and undergoing no medical treatments) filled out a questionnaire indicating which symptoms they had experienced in the last 72 hours. The list included things like loss of appetite, nausea, weakness, heart palpitations, dizziness on first standing up, and pain in joints and muscles. Over 80 percent of the respondents had experienced at least one of the symptoms. The median number of symptoms was two, and almost 5 percent of the respondents experienced six or more symptoms (Reidenberg & Lowenthal, 1968). In another study, on a 12-item symptom rating scale, over 800 of the 1,000 students surveyed at two universities (80%) reported at least one somatic symptom (Pennebaker et al., 1977). Yet another study found that 75 percent of 1,000 surveyed adults reported having an episode of illness in a given month, but only 25 percent consulted a physician about it (White et al., 1961). Thus, many people who appear to be "healthy" and functioning well in day-to-day life may be simply compensating for or ignoring their clinically important symptoms. Although some conditions are self-limiting (a backache or the cough of a cold), others may persist or grow worse. Usually, at some point, the person stops tolerating the symptoms and attempts to identify the condition and find treatment for it. How and when the decision is made to tell others about the symptoms depends at least as heavily on an individual's psychology as it does on the objective seriousness of his or her symptoms.

Psychological Triggers for Seeking Help

What are the psychological factors that bring an individual to seek medical help for the symptoms he or she is experiencing? Some of the models introduced in Chapter 6 to explain preventive and health-maintenance behaviors are also applicable here. You will recall that we first examined the Health Belief Model, which posits that health behavior is predicted by (1) the perceived susceptibility to and severity of the disease (threat) and (2) the perceived benefits associated with the health-enhancing behavior, as well as the barriers that impede that behavior. In terms of our current question, then, we might say that whether a person seeks medical help is determined by his or her perceptions of how serious the symptoms are, his or her beliefs about medicine's ability to alleviate the symptoms, and the perceived barriers to getting help. We also discussed the Theory of Reasoned Action and Theory of Planned Behavior, both of which point to behavior as governed by intentions, which are in turn influenced by attitudes and beliefs. The Theory of Planned Behavior also takes into account the degree to which an individual feels that he or she has control over personal behaviors. According to these models, whether a person seeks help for medical symptoms will be determined by whether the individual intends to do so. Intention, in turn, will be determined by attitudes and beliefs about help seeking and about the symptoms being experienced.

Research studies have tested many of the hypotheses that one might formulate based on these general models. Let us examine some of them. As highlighted by the Health Belief Model, susceptibility to disease and the severity of symptoms are important factors. And, as we see in the Theories of Reasoned Action and Planned Behavior, attitudes and beliefs are also important. We have just finished describing the personality characteristic of neuroticism that influence individuals' ideas about severity and susceptibility. Someone who is quite low on this neuroticism dimension is not likely to notice a lot of symptoms in the first place and is not particularly likely to decide that an uncomfortable bodily sensation deserves to be called a "symptom." But someone high on this dimension is likely to view many bodily sensations as potentially serious medical matters and is therefore likely to rate his or her susceptibility to illness as quite high.

Symptoms that are highly visible are, of course, more difficult to ignore or discount, so a person is more likely to seek medical care if a symptom is very obvious (Mechanic, 1978). A symptom that interferes with one's vocational or physical activity (for instance, a severe back pain that makes sitting in class unbearable or blurred vision that makes it impossible for one to focus on the computer screen) is difficult to ignore and thus is likely to be attended to (Pennebaker & Watson, 1991; Wells, 1991).

The perceived threat associated with a symptom is affected by past experience. A person usually will attend to a symptom if he or she recalls that in the past this same symptom was a serious one (Goff et al., 1998; Scherck, 1997; Zola, 1973). The labels that people apply to their symptoms (because of past experience and their level of knowledge about their symptoms) are important in determining whether people seek help (Benyamini et al., 1997; Leventhal & Diefenbach, 1991). For instance, two people might be experiencing frequent headaches, but the person who associates these with a serious condition, such as a possible brain tumor, is more likely to make a doctor's appointment. The one who believes that the headaches are due to temporary stress and will soon subside may wait some time to find out if things get better on their own. Further, when the nature and quality of the symptoms are new for that person and differ significantly from what is familiar, he or she is likely to seek expert help.

People often decide to seek medical care for ambiguous symptoms after they have experienced an interpersonal crisis or a great deal of stress (Cameron et al., 1995). A crisis in an individual's relationships with other people might include marital difficulties or a major argument with a boss or co-worker. An interpersonal crisis can raise a person's level of anxiety, making some symptoms (or uncertainty about them) intolerable. Or, it might trigger attention to illness symptoms, and the self-definition of illness might bring enough sympathy and extra attention to resolve the interpersonal crisis or at least minimize its importance. A person might even seek to establish a warm, supportive relationship with a medical practitioner to take the place of the relationship that has been lost or threatened by the interpersonal crisis. Just as interpersonal problems can precipitate help seeking, when a symptom threatens a person's ability to relate to others, it is likely to prompt the individual to seek help (Zola, 1973). Symptoms that limit social interactions, such as unsightly rashes, apparent contagiousness, and overwhelming fatigue are often attended to, and medical help is sought. People don't want to be left lonely by illness.

Finally, the decision to seek medical care is usually made when other people are supportive of it. For example, when friends suggest that you see a doctor, you can stop being concerned that you are overreacting to your symptoms. Approval from another person is an important trigger to seeking care (Zola, 1973). Table 7.2 summarizes factors that bring people to seek medical help for symptoms.

TABLE 7.2   Factors That Bring People to Seek Medical Help for Symptoms

1. Susceptibility to disease is viewed as high.

2. Symptoms are perceived to be severe.

3. Symptoms are highly visible, difficult to ignore or discount.

4. Symptoms interfere with important daily activities.

5. Symptoms are new and different or are familiar and serious.

6. Anxiety or stress is high, particularly as regards interpersonal crisis, and symptoms are ambiguous.

7. Symptoms are limiting social interactions or threatening personal relationships.

8. Other people are supportive of the individual's help-seeking efforts.

The Lay Referral Network

Very often the process of diagnosis begins before an individual even reaches the doctor's office. The **lay referral network** consists of friends and family members who help the individual to attach a meaning to his or her symptoms (Freidson, 1970). Family members, friends, and co-workers typically offer advice about whether the person should seek care from a physician or instead treat the condition with a home remedy (or simply ignore it and wait for it to go away) (Stoller, 1984). Home remedies that are prescribed by lay referral networks may incorporate cultural traditions that might be considered odd or superstitious by those who don't share the cultural beliefs (Landrine & Klonoff, 1994), and lay referral networks may direct people to alternative practitioners as well as to traditional physicians (Astin, 1998; Eisenberg et al., 1993).

It has been suggested that there developed in the 1980s and 1990s a societal tendency to approve of and encourage the seeking of medical care. In fact, some say that there now exists a kind of "medicalization of daily life." People visit their doctors for everything from difficulty sleeping, to fatigue, to a bad complexion, to erectile dysfunction. Although they may be living lives that are very hectic and include very little sleep (e.g., work all day and cruise the Internet for a lot of the night) or very much out of balance (all work and no play), people expect medicine to provide solutions (Barsky, 1988).

Additional Determinants of Medical Care Utilization

It is important for us to note that psychological factors are not the only determinants of the use of health services. Let us briefly examine the few consistent findings available from studies of **medical care utilization** in order to get a clearer picture.

At various points in the life span, people are more likely than at other times to need and to utilize health services. Children and elderly people receive medical care more often than do adolescents and young adults (Garland & Ziegler, 1994). During adolescence and young adulthood, most people are quite healthy, although they usually visit their pediatricians regularly not only to treat their childhood illnesses but also to receive their immunizations and to determine whether they are developing normally. As people age, the onset of chronic disease often forces them to utilize more health services than they did when they were younger (Leventhal & Diefenbach, 1991).

Women use health services significantly more than do men, even for conditions that are unrelated to menstruation, pregnancy, and childbirth (Fuller et al., 1993; Nathanson, 1977). It has been suggested that women are more sensitive than men to bodily dysfunctions, especially minor ones, and so are more likely to seek medical treatment (Goldberg et al., 1998; Neitzert et al., 1997). Of course, women may simply be more willing than are men to express pain and discomfort and to seek help, perhaps in part because female gender roles allow more help seeking than do male roles that emphasize being independent and strong (Klonoff & Landrine, 1992; Waldron, 1997).

Compared with people of higher socioeconomic status, those with lower incomes are less likely to use medical care services even though they report lower levels of health. Medical care is costly, and those with limited resources often have limited access to it (Herman, 1972). Even with the availability of free public clinics and programs like Medicare for the elderly and Medicaid (or MediCal in California) for the poor, those in the most economically disadvantaged social classes are less likely to have a regular physician and instead typically are able to obtain care only when a health emergency arises (Rundell & Wheeler, 1979).

Delay in Seeking Treatment

A myocardial infarction (MI), or heart attack, can come on suddenly and without warning. The symptoms can include tightness, pressure, squeezing or pain in the chest (sometimes radiating to the shoulders, neck, jaw, and arms), shortness of breath, nausea, and/or profuse sweating. Medical studies show that if immediate action is taken, the prognosis for recovery from a heart attack is quite good. Unfortunately, almost half of the deaths due to heart attack occur within an hour of the time the symptoms start and before the person ever gets to the hospital (PGD, 1998).

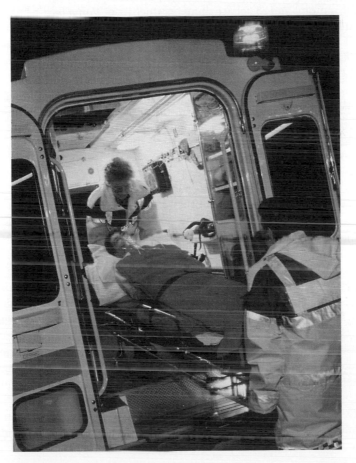

Life-saving treatment for a heart attack can be provided by paramedics within moments of dialing 911, but many people delay receiving medical assistance.

Nearly everywhere in the country it is possible to receive life-saving treatment from a paramedic unit within moments of dialing 911. Although it is usually possible to receive the necessary help to prevent death from a heart attack, many people fail to get it. Why? Research suggests that heart attack victims fail to receive timely medical assistance for two reasons: (1) They attribute their symptoms incorrectly to conditions other than a heart attack, and (2) they delay unnecessarily even after they have decided to seek medical care. Once symptoms start, it takes some people a considerable amount of time to decide that something is wrong. Deciding to seek help can take between 30 minutes and 12 hours, and actually seeking help (calling 911 or going to a hospital) takes on average from $1\frac{1}{2}$ hours to slightly over 20 hours (Hedges et al., 1998)! Many patients initially attribute heart attack symptoms to conditions such as indigestion, ulcers, gallbladder disease, or the flu (Scherck, 1997). Even after someone decides that medical attention should be sought, valuable time is lost when people do unnecessary things such as calling the family physician (only to be told to go right to the emergency room) or changing into nicer clothes (Hedges et al., 1998). Thus, even after they have correctly attributed the symptoms to a serious condition such as a heart attack, people often waste considerable time before taking the necessary action to receive treatment.

Psychological factors seem to be most responsible for leading a heart attack victim to ignore symptoms and to delay calling paramedics or going to the hospital. Many victims of a myocardial infarction fail to seek medical help because they are afraid of looking silly if they have misinterpreted their symptoms and their problem turns out to be trivial. Many do not want to bother others with their problems, or they are afraid of what might happen if they do seek treatment (Dracup & Moser, 1997). Another person (a spouse or a friend) usually insists on bringing the patient to the hospital emergency room. When alone, however, many heart attack victims miss the opportunity to save their own lives.

Delay in seeking medical care for all types of problems, not just emergency ones, has been an interesting and important area for research. In general, delay in seeking medical care is composed of three parts. **Appraisal time** is the time it takes the patient to appraise his or her symptoms as illness and to decide that the sensations mean that something important is wrong. **Illness delay** is the time from the patient's decision that he or she is ill to the decision to seek care; this delay might be caused by the patient's belief that the condition cannot be ameliorated with medical intervention. **Utilization delay** is the time from the decision to seek care to the actual obtaining of medical services. This time involves the individual's choosing medical care that he or she feels is worth the costs, and then overcoming any barriers to utilization such as finding a doctor and getting the money to pay for the medical visit. **Total delay** is the total length of time it takes for a person to move from recognition of the symptom to arrival at the clinic or emergency room (Safer et al., 1979). When people are going through the process, from first recognizing symptoms to ultimately seeking care, a number of stages are traversed (Rushton et al., 1998; Scherck, 1997). People first must notice and attend to their symptoms. Next, they evaluate these symptoms and compare them with their general knowledge about health issues and their previous experience. This is usually followed by some sort of action, and if the action is preliminary, there will be a reevaluation and then a final action (Rushton et al., 1998).

It is during the evaluation stage that patients' levels of knowledge are most critical. If the person interprets those first symptoms as being related to a heart attack, he or she is more likely to seek immediate help. Most people who have had heart attacks say that the experience was much different than they had ever imagined before actually going through it (Rushton et al., 1998). In one study, most people (nearly 90%) associated chest pain with a heart attack, but numbness and arm pain were seen as important symptoms by only 67 percent of people, shortness-of-breath by only 50 percent, and sweating by only 21 percent. Seven other common heart attack symptoms were recognized by fewer than 21 percent of people. In fact, the median number of correctly identified heart attack symptoms was only three (out of a possible 11) (Goff et al., 1998). These symptoms are admittedly difficult to interpret and differentiate from others. One study surveyed ten world-renowned cardiologists who had heart attacks. On average, they delayed seeking help for 48 hours, presumably because they misinterpreted the symptoms they were feeling (Julian, 1996).

When people's actual symptoms more closely match their own prototype for what a heart attack is like, they are much more likely to take their symptoms seriously and seek help (Scherck, 1997). Previous experience with heart attack is also an important factor. People who have had a previous heart attack and those who identify themselves as "at risk" do not delay as long in seeking medical care (Goff et al., 1998; Rushton et al., 1998). People who are older and who have lower socioeconomic status are more likely to delay in seeking care (Dracup & Moser, 1997). It is interesting to note that strongly sensing one is quite ill, or being afraid of what the doctor might say, can sometimes cause longer delay rather than making action more immediate (Safer et al., 1979; Temoshok et al., 1984). This is particularly true when people feel afraid of treatment and have strong negative images of it. Under such circumstances, people tend to remain passive and to simply think about their symptoms rather than do something about them.

For a disease like cancer, too, delay can be life threatening. The number of people whose lives are actually saved by cancer treatment is significantly lower than the number who hypothetically could survive. The reason is that, in practice, many people delay receiving treatment for so long that their disease has progressed much too far for them to be helped by modern treatments such as surgery, chemotherapy, and radiation. Many cancers can be completely cured if detected early. Patients take longer to detect symptoms that are vague or difficult to discern (such as small lesions or lesions in awkward-to-see places) (Temoshok et al., 1984), and once a symptom, such as a skin lesion, mole, or breast lump, is detected, many patients do not immediately seek treatment. As many as 68 percent of individuals who note signs of melanoma do not go to see a doctor right away (Hennrikus et al., 1991). Many of these patients think that the symptoms are not serious and that they will go away on their own. One study showed that the average delay between noticing a melanoma and getting appropriate help was over eleven months, with almost ten of these being due to the patients' own delay in seeking help (Krige et al., 1991).

Another common cancer, breast cancer, is most often noticed first by the woman herself. About a third of women who become aware of a breast abnormality or lump, however, wait three months or more before seeking medical care. A recent study of women with breast cancer showed that younger women and those from lower socioeconomic status were less likely to seek help for symptoms, as were women who had fatalistic ideas about breast cancer. Women were more likely to seek help quickly if they feared that they may have cancer, thought delaying would make it worse, and were accustomed to using medical services (Facione et al., 1997). Fear of cancer does not always prompt people to seek care, however. Sometimes people avoid going to the doctor because they don't want to hear any potential bad news and prefer to ignore the problem (Temoshok et al., 1984). Because of fear of the disease and its treatment, many people allow their cancer to grow to the point where more debilitating interventions are required and cure is much less likely.

Many people, even those who seem least likely to do so, may delay treatment for suspicious symptoms. One surgeon who, at age 37, was diagnosed as having a malignant, non-Hodgkins lymphoma (cancer of the lymph nodes) delayed defining his symptoms as a possible serious illness (cancer) even though he was trained to identify the importance of such symptoms in his patients. ". . . I noticed a small lump at the angle of my jaw while shaving one morning. It was with more curiosity than dread. What could happen to me? I was full of myself and invincible . . . My denial systems were activated and I ignored it. Time went by . . . When it slowly enlarged I showed it to physician friends in a casual way. They said not to worry. Maybe they didn't and I didn't hear them. . . . Finally one night at a dinner party a psychiatrist's wife with no medical training said, . . . 'What is that thing under your jaw?' Still believing all was well, I saw a surgeon who scheduled a biopsy" (Shlain, 1979, p. 176). Dr. Shlain eventually underwent surgery and five months of radiation treatment, and fortunately he survived.

The Sick Role

Why do social and psychological factors have the power to trigger people's decisions to seek medical care? Why is it that these factors can cause a person to ignore the symptoms of disease and delay treatment? As we noted earlier, illness depends upon self-definition. If you say you are ill, it would be unusual indeed for other people to doubt your word. Your subjective account of your pain is proof enough of its existence (Kosa & Robertson, 1975). In a society such as ours that values independence, competition, and achievement, illness is considered such a negative state that no one would voluntarily adopt it for no good reason . . . at least in theory (Parsons, 1975).

Being ill involves adopting a social role known as the sick role. The sick role brings privileges as well as responsibilities (see Figure 7.2). You may enter the sick role by declaring yourself ill (and simply that). However, once you enter the sick role, you are expected to behave in the correct manner. You must view the sick role as negative (you do not, for example, run around yelling, "Yippee, I'm sick, now I get to stay home from work," or exhibiting other expressions of satisfaction). If you fail to view illness as negative, your motives might be somewhat suspect. In addition, you are expected to seek competent medical help (a health professional, and not a tarot card reader, for example). You cannot maintain the self-definition of illness indefinitely without hav-

FIGURE 7.2 The sick role.

ing a doctor legitimize your claim (Parsons, 1975). Physicians are, in effect, the "gate-keepers" of the sick role. So, while you can complain all you want to about your illness, you are expected to back up your claim with a visit to the doctor. And you are expected to cooperate with the doctor's recommendations. Note that to maintain the sick role, a clear diagnosis is not required. Self-definition, combined with the fulfillment of these obligations, is all it takes to acquire the sick role and to maintain it. One can remain in the sick role even while a diagnosis eludes physicians, as long as one is trying to get better.

Occupying the sick role can have its advantages. The sick role is guarded by the above social sanctions and comes with certain responsibilities precisely *because* it brings special privileges. These privileges are referred to as **secondary gains** and are the positive outcomes that balance some of the more negative aspects of being ill. A person who enters the sick role can be exempt from working, from caring for others, and from caring for him- or herself. Pain and illness bring increased attention from others, a chance to rest, and an opportunity to be taken care of. Pain and illness can put a stop to criticism from others and sometimes allow the individual to relinquish any blame for his or her condition or behaviors, such as with alcoholism. Of course, this is not always the case. Alcoholics still tend to be viewed by many as at least partially to blame for their illness, and personal responsibility is often assigned for other illnesses such as AIDS. Illness can sometimes enhance family harmony, at least temporarily. On a deeper level, the secondary gains of illness might include an excuse for why one does not succeed in life. Illness may provide a break from a job or even a style of life with which one is dissatisfied. It may provide a sense of purpose for an individual who feels that life is devoid of meaning. Illness can provide a focus for one's chronic anxiety and a place to channel emotional distress. Finally, the secondary gains of illness can even be tangible, such as money in the form of insurance payments or workers' compensation.

Of course, there can also be many negatives associated with illness and the sick role. Health practitioners, friends, and family members may scrutinize an ill individual's behavior and may be quick to view any noncooperation or hesitancy in seeking care as evidence of an illegitimate attempt to gain unfair advantage by being ill. For most people, despite any possible secondary gains, the negative aspects of illness, including uncertainty, discomfort, limitations, and emotional distress, far outweigh the positives.

Illness as an Expression of Emotional Needs

The fact that secondary gains can sometimes make illness attractive suggests that the expression of physical distress sometimes fulfills certain psychological needs. As we noted earlier in this chapter, particular aspects of one's cultural background, upbringing, daily life circumstances, and personality can make illness a natural outlet for the expression of emotional distress. Ideally, a person would find the direct expression of his or her emotions perfectly acceptable. A person who is in touch with his or her own emotional life might readily admit to feeling angry, anxious, or depressed with no smokescreen and no conscious or unconscious need to disguise those feelings. For another, however, it may be safer to complain about the purely physical manifestations of distress. Instead of stating, "I feel very anxious," the individual describes a pounding heart, lightheadedness, and difficulty breathing. Instead of expressing feelings of depression, he or she describes fatigue, lack of energy, and problems sleeping. Some people might actually be unable to express or describe in words the emotions they feel and cannot even identify those emotions. Instead, they may describe only their physical symptoms. Psychiatrists refer to this condition as **alexithymia** (Sifneos, 1996).

People with a **generalized anxiety disorder** (unrealistic or excessive anxiety) often experience a variety of physical symptoms. These can include feelings of shakiness, muscle tension, muscle aches, dizziness, nausea, irritability, and insomnia. Anxious feelings that involve panic can result in shortness of breath, heart palpitations, and chest pain as they trigger the biological *suffocation alarm system* (Klein, 1993). These latter symptoms can lead physician and patient to significant concern about the possibility of a dangerous cardiac condition.

As we noted earlier in this chapter, it is not the case that illness is a purely physical *or* a purely emotional phenomenon. A person who feels anxious typically does have tense muscles, a rapid heartbeat, and cold clammy hands. A person who is emotionally depressed, perhaps in reaction to the death of a loved one or loss of a relationship, is slowed down and feels fatigued. What matters in determining whether the individual will adopt a psychological or a somatic interpretation is where the individual focuses attention, the interpretation of what is being felt, and how distress is explained.

Most people exhibit something between the extremes of the purely physical and the purely psychological expression of distress. They may have a sense of emotional distress, but are unable to find the right words to describe their psychological state. They may have been taught to repress and deny psychological interpretations of their experiences and to hide their feelings from others (as in "boys don't cry"). If the very things that they need, such as attention, emotional support, or practical help, become available when they complain of physical illness, the scales will likely be tipped toward physical rather than psychological interpretations of experience.

Usually, the decision to express physical instead of emotional distress is not made consciously. When a depressed patient comes to the physician complaining of fatigue, he or she is likely to be unaware of the emotional explanation for the fatigue. Instead, a long period of time may elapse before the true source of the problem is found. If the patient is particularly good at hiding (both from self and others) evidence of psychological distress, the physician may continue to search at length, and sometimes in vain, for the physical abnormality that explains the patient's subjective feelings of illness. Sometimes in the process such patients receive unnecessary medications, treatments, and surgeries. For example, in one study, women in a hospital neurological service who had expressed their distress in physical terms were more likely to have received a hysterectomy at some point in their lives than were women in a psychiatric service, who had expressed their distress in primarily psychological terms (52% vs. 21%) (Bart, 1968).

Research suggests that expressing distress with somatic (bodily) vocabulary is not at all uncommon. In a substantial proportion of people who seek medical treatment for somatic complaints, no organic problem can be found no matter how much testing is done (Barsky & Borus, 1995). Most studies estimate that in the care of between 10 and 30 percent of patients, no organic basis for illness can be found (Kellner, 1986). In these cases, patients are also more likely to be experiencing psychological problems, including anxiety and depression (Katon & Walker, 1998; Kisely et al., 1997). This does not mean that their symptoms are not real, but it does suggest that anxiety or depression may be interacting with their physical symptoms, exacerbating them or being strengthened by them.

It is possible, of course, that there are limitations in medicine that make it impossible to find the organic basis for some illnesses that truly do have an organic origin. Further, it is possible that the inability to find an explanation for their physical distress can lead a patient to become anxious or depressed. Traditional medicine does not have a diagnosis for every ailment. Some syndromes such as "chronic fatigue syndrome" are in the process of being identified, their signs and symptoms mapped out, and their etiology, incidence, and prognosis identified empirically. Other ailments are not so well described, such as chest muscle tightness and spasm due to emotional tension. In fact, there are so many conditions that patients report that have no apparent cause that the medical term **idiopathic**, which means "arising spontaneously or from an obscure or unknown cause," is used quite commonly.

Somatization and Conversion

In some cases, the puzzle of symptoms cannot be solved at all using a purely medical approach because the symptoms don't make sense physiologically. Consider **glove anesthesia**. Glove anesthesia is the term for a condition in which only the hand, but no part of the arm, loses all sensation and is unable to function. The disorder cannot be caused by an organic impairment because the neural pathways that conduct sensation to the hand also serve the rest of the arm. If any nerve damage had occurred, either part of the hand and one side of the arm would be affected, or all of the hand and the entire arm would be devoid of sensation. Sigmund Freud treated several such cases, and with his colleague Pierre Janet (1929), identified a number of **conversion responses**, including loss of sight, speech, or hearing, and various forms of muscular paralysis. Conversion responses are believed to be primitive responses to emotional conflict (cognitively primitive in the sense that they arise from very early childhood conflicts and emotional patterns). Conversion symptoms make sense in that they tend to solve the emotional conflict facing the person who suffers from them. A man who unconsciously wishes to attack his brother may find himself unable to move his arm; a married woman who is overwhelmed with guilt because of her sexual attraction to another man may find herself unable to see. These are extreme examples, of course, although they occurred with surprising frequency in Freud's time. Such disorders are not often presented to physicians these days. Now, less extreme examples are more common. They involve **somatization**, which is defined as a general tendency to experience and communicate emotional distress through somatic complaints (Piccinelli & Simon, 1997). Examples include the experience of stomach upset when one is highly anxious and of headache when one is under tremendous pressure. In Box 7.2, the ways in which two individuals describe their symptoms are compared as they vary in their degree of somatization.

In Chapter 9, we will deal in more detail with somatization responses that result from the experience of stress. Here we consider the role of the medical professional in attempting to understand the patient's illness experience. Unfortunately, using a biomedical model, many medical professionals ascribe to psychological causes any symptoms for which they can find no organic explanation. They often do this by default—that is, when they can find no other explanation for what ails the patient (DiMatteo, 1979). Certainly it is possible that any given patient is expressing emotional distress through physical channels, as described above. But in a biopsychosocial model, diagnoses of somatization and conversion require evidence beyond the mere fact that nothing organic can be found to explain the symptoms. They require an understanding of the patient's psychological and social circumstances as well as his or her biomedical status.

Understandably, few patients react positively when told that their pain is "just nerves" or "in their head." In fact, many feel bewildered and upset. They feel rejected by the physician and sometimes quite hopeless because they believe nothing can be done to help them. Sometimes they get angry and transfer their care to another doctor (Baur, 1988).

BOX **7.2**

Hot Topic

The Telling of the Story

Consider these two responses to the question, "Tell me about your symptoms; what have you experienced over the past two weeks?"

Chris: "I've had a lot of pain. The pain feels like it starts almost exactly in middle of my head, and then sometimes goes down into my neck a little bit. The pain can vary, also. Sometimes it's a dull pain and I can deal with it by just ignoring it or taking aspirin. But sometimes, when it starts to go into my neck, it gets really intense and even taking several aspirin doesn't help. When it does this, it feels more like a really tight squeezing than anything else. I feel like my head's going to explode! Since my neck hurts, I try not to turn my head too much, plus any jarring motion also makes it hurt worse. I usually just try to lie down and hope it goes away."

Tony: "I've had a lot of pain. I noticed it about a month ago when I started waking up in the morning with a slight headache. It would usually go away within an hour or two, and I thought maybe it had something to do with drinking too much coffee. Then, about two weeks ago it started getting worse and sometimes would last past lunch. I also noticed that sometimes it would get very intense and feel like it was starting in the middle of my head and extending down into my neck a little bit. Whenever it does this, it feels like something is squeezing very tightly and the pain is intense! I feel like my head's going to explode! It's gotten to the point this week where this is happening every day or two,

and all I can do is lie down and wait for it to go away. Aspirin doesn't help at all when it's bad like that, and I usually have to lie down and relax, trying not to move my neck or jolt my head, for at least an hour or so before it starts to ease up."

Although both of these individuals are describing almost identical symptoms, there is something important that distinguishes their stories—chronological development. Chris focuses on the experience of the pain and provides a description of the symptoms thematically. Tony tells the story chronologically, organizing the events according to the time frame in which they were experienced.

Researchers have recently discovered that the failure to develop the story of symptoms chronologically and to place them in a temporal framework is characteristic of "somatizers" (individuals who experience symptoms for which a specific organic cause cannot be identified) (Elderkin-Thompson et al., 1998). In this study, 116 patients were videotaped as they interacted with their primary care physicians. These interactions were then transcribed and examined qualitatively. The narratives of somatizing and nonsomatizing patients were very similar in that they described symptoms with the same degree of emotion and they use similar words to explain what they felt. But somatizers focused on theme rather than chronology and did not provide a clear time frame for their symptoms. This difference was significant and warrants additional research into the topic. This difference may prove to be a useful tool in attempting to assess somatization!

A Patient with Psychosomatic Illness

Let's look at an example. A patient's chest pain is appropriately attributed to anxiety because the pattern of chest pain is consistent with tension-related muscle spasms. Specific treatment for these spasms (muscle relaxants, physical therapy, massage, stretching) can be prescribed to alleviate them. But when "tension" is given as the explanation and the patient is left with no hope of specific treatment, the patient is likely to be noticeably distressed. In this example, we see an excellent illustration of the phenomenon of **psychosomatic illness**, an illness condition that results from, or is exacerbated by, psychological factors. Chest pain is an excellent example of a condition that can develop as a consequence of anxiety and psychological stress (an issue that we will examine in greater detail in Chapter 9), although it can certainly signal a serious heart problem as well. While it is essential for the physician to rule out a cardiac problem, once that it done, the physician needs to help the patient recognize that anxiety can be affecting his or her body in this particular way. A patient who is chronically tense and anxious is likely to brace his or her back, neck, and chest muscles constantly, causing a reduction in blood flow to the muscles and a buildup of lactic acid in them. The result

FIGURE 7.3   Somatization and hypochondriasis.

is pain (Feldenkreis, 1981). There is a clear connection between the psychological phenomenon and the physical findings. An astute physician will recognize this pattern in the patient and help him or her to find specific ways to counteract it. Certainly the method illustrated in Figure 7.3, though humorous, could not be expected to be an effective one.

The following example of a physician talking with a patient who has this exact problem was *adapted* from a real conversation that was reported verbatim and analyzed by Eric Cassell (1985b, pp. 158-159). The dialogue demonstrates an effective and supportive method for communicating a diagnostic conclusion of psychosomatic illness.

> **DOCTOR:** Well, I do think it's emotional in origin, the result of a lot of stress and tension and anxiety. But that's not a sufficient answer. We'll work on it until we get one. Now, what you've told me is that lately you've had a lot of extra problems and lots more work because your new boss won't let up. Did I hear that correctly?
>
> **PATIENT:** Yeah.
>
> **DOCTOR:** Well, I think that might cause you to brace yourself; your back, neck, and chest. It causes pain, but fortunately no lasting damage. So we have to treat the symptoms of the pain, and get at the root of what's causing your muscles to tense so much. . . . what's going on in your emotions. But fortunately we don't have to deal with any damage to your body so far . . . are you with me?
>
> **PATIENT:** Yeah, I am . . .
>
> **DOCTOR::** Well, to see if my explanation is the right one, which I really think it is, and to try to help you with this discomfort, we need to make a dent in the process. We need to try and relax those tight muscles and see whether that changes how you feel. . . . I think it will. Of course, we also need to try to get at some of the underlying feelings that are causing you problems.
>
> **PATIENT:** Yeah. I hold in my feelings a lot.
>
> **DOCTOR:** I know that. Now it's not in my expertise to help you make lots of changes in how you feel about things and the ways in which you react emotionally. But we can find you someone who can help. What I can do is start you off by changing the discomfort. I'm going to give you some diazepam to take at night, to get those muscles in your back, chest, and neck to relax a little. I want you to get yourself into a steam room or hot-tub at the gym, and get a couple of real good massages to relax those muscles. Work on that body, okay?

The physician above is extremely reassuring and is focused on solving the problem. This doctor makes sure that the patient knows that there is no long-term damage to worry about, tells the patient that there are several things that will start the healing process, and explains how the problem likely came about in the first place. He gives the patient hope that an active orientation to the pain and its underlying causes can result in pain reduction. The patient can look forward to feeling better. As Epstein and colleagues (1999) would recommend, this physician avoids the common mistake of trying to separate a patient's experience of illness from its organic cause, and instead listens to what is happening in the patient's life. This physician helps the patient to gain a sense of control over the illness experience and to focus on returning to full functioning.

The solicitousness of others may perpetuate a heightened concern about bodily symptoms.

Many problems have been avoided, which could arise if the patient's illness experience and the doctor's diagnostic criteria do not match up (Epstein et al., 1999).

Psychological factors can play a significant role in physical complaints, and emotions can have a truly serious effect on the body. As noted above, emotional distress can manifest itself, among other ways, in tight muscles that can cause pain. Chronic emotional arousal can also raise blood pressure and severely tax the cardiovascular and immune systems. In Chapter 9, we will discuss in detail the role of psychological factors in causing actual physical damage to the human body.

Hypochondria

The phenomenon of **hypochondria** or **hypochondriasis** is well known, even in the popular culture. People informally refer to others that they feel are overly concerned with their own health as "hypochondriacs." Although the lay public may be less discriminating than are health professionals in placing such a label on an individual, the same term is typically used. Hypochondriasis is a phenomenon in which an individual displays more than just an overattention to bodily symptoms. True hypochondriacs convert personal emotional distress into physical distress. They report symptoms that are diffuse and may change from one occasion to another. Their complaints tend to be of symptoms that occur very commonly in a large number of people and that are typically associated with stress. Yet, hypochondriacs are convinced that, for them, these symptoms indicate serious disease. "Hypochondriasis is an exaggerated and obsessive concern about the body and health, with delusion of disease or bodily dysfunction. It is often associated with a multitude of symptoms and complaints that reflect real suffering despite the absence of organic pathology" (PGD, 1982, p. 83).

Because it is possible to use the sick role to one's advantage, hypochondria might sometimes appear to be a form of **malingering,** which is a conscious, purposeful use of somatic complaints to achieve exemption from one's obligations. Most experts agree, however, that hypochondria involves no conscious manipulation at all, but rather the misinterpretation of vague symptoms as disease. "Hypochondria is not malingering, in which a person intentionally pretends to be sick, and it is not psychosomatic illness in which psychological stress triggers, exacerbates, or maintains a physical problem . . ." (Baur, 1988, p. 4).

A related condition is that of **factitious disorder**, in which an individual intentionally creates symptoms in order to receive a diagnosis and medical treatment. The compulsion to do this does not seem to be under the person's control, but because the planning and production of the symptoms requires thought and attention to detail, the behavior is said to be "voluntary."

One form of hypochondria is quite common among medical students. As we noted earlier in this chapter, the "medical student syndrome" (or *morbid medicans*) has a high prevalence. About 70 percent of physicians experience it for some period of time during their medical training. The factors contributing to this temporary "hypochondriasis" or "nosophobia" include stress (from internal or external sources), feelings of anxiety (usually about tests or other methods of performance evaluation), and physical symptoms (common ones, such as forgetfulness, fatigue, and rapid heart rate) (Niemi & Vainiomaeki, 1999). The medical student attaches an inordinate importance to his or her symptoms because of an incomplete knowledge of the diseases studied. The student knows enough to be worried, but not enough to be reassured. The disease that the medical student is concerned about having is often something that is modeled after a recently encountered anecdote, medical case, or patient condition. Several components are necessary to promote this form of hypochondriasis in the medical student: limited information, identification with another person, definable symptoms, and anxiety or feelings of stress. Most young physicians recover quite nicely from their maladies, usually after they have received reassurance from a faculty member who knows more than they do, or they have gained sufficient knowledge and sharpened their own medical judgment (Hunter et al., 1964; Mechanic, 1968).

Patients with true, chronic hypochondriasis are typically not reassured, no matter what they are told. They have a significant amount of anxiety about illness that persists throughout their lives. The resolution of one situation gives way to a new concern because hypochondria is a stable characteristic (Barsky et al., 1998a). This is not to say that hypochondriacs never have disease. Certainly they do, but objective measures usually do not support their subjective complaints, which may be considerably more extensive than, or even independent of, what is measurably wrong with them.

Hypochondriacs do feel real distress, much of which is emotional. Study after study has shown that patients who present physical symptoms for which no organic basis can be found are significantly more depressed and anxious than are patients for whom a diagnosis can be reached (Katon & Walker, 1998; Neitzert et al., 1997). These

Across Cultures

Somatic Symptoms across the World

In 1992, the World Health Organization completed a study of fourteen countries across five continents. Over 5,000 primary care patients underwent a structured assessment to determine their levels of depression and somatic complaints (see Kisley et al., 1997, and Simon et al., 1999). Of particular interest were symptoms such as headache, constipation, weakness, and back pain. For some of these patients, their somatic complaints had a medical reason, whereas for others no medical reason could be found. Of the 21 percent who were classified as being clinically depressed, a large proportion (69%) reported *only* somatic symptoms to their physician and did not even mention any psychological symptoms at all. Of these depressed patients, 11 percent explicitly denied their depression when asked, and more than 50 percent reported somatic symptoms that remained medically unexplained.

In this large international study, it was found that respondents with five or more reported symptoms had higher rates of psychiatric morbidity and poorer social functioning than did patients who had fewer somatic complaints. Interestingly, few cultural differences were found between the two groups; that is, the relationship between somatic complaints and psychiatric and social problems appeared to hold across all fourteen nations. Another important finding was that somatic complaints were higher among individuals who did not have a steady primary care provider. Regardless of nation, those who did have an ongoing relationship with a single primary care physician had fewer somatic complaints.

patients are not simply depressed because nobody can diagnose their problems; their depression has been found typically to precede, rather than to follow, their symptoms (Kellner, 1986).

Box 7.3 examines the connection between depression and the reporting of somatic symptoms in a large international study.

Psychological Factors and the Delivery of Health Services

It would be a gross oversimplification to conclude that emotional distress generally causes the seeking of healthcare. Instead, there exists a complex relationship between emotional distress and patterns of illness-related behavior. A combination of the individual's general propensity to choose medical treatment as a solution to symptoms and feelings of stress that exacerbate those symptoms appears to be necessary to bring a person to seek the care of a physician (Bakal, 1999; Mechanic & Volkart, 1961).

A number of researchers have found that individuals with higher levels of emotional distress are more likely to utilize a variety of health services than are those who have better emotional adjustment (Compton & Purviance, 1992; Connelly et al., 1991; Follette & Cummings, 1967; Piccinelli & Simon, 1997). Further, it has been demonstrated that patterns of medical care utilization can be changed by dealing directly with patients' psychological concerns. In one study, researchers divided patients who were described as emotionally distressed into three groups and matched them on relevant variables. One experimental group was given one free visit for psychotherapy. The other experimental group was given two to eight free psychotherapy sessions. The control group received no psychotherapeutic intervention. Patients who received one session only, with no repeat psychological visits, reduced their medical utilization by 60 percent over the next five years, with the most rapid decline in medical utilization occurring during the second year. Utilization was reduced by 75 percent in those who received brief psychotherapy (2–8 sessions). There was no change in utilization rates for the control group. And, although patients appeared to benefit from the psychotherapy sessions, there was no resultant increase in demand for psychotherapy services so patients did not overtax that facet of the system (Follette & Cummings, 1967). Another study provided twelve psychotherapy sessions for a group of patients with a wide range of serious medical problems. None of these patients was terminally ill or in continuous pain. During their therapy sessions, time was spent validating their feelings, helping them to problem solve, and giving them interpersonal support and understanding. All of the patients who participated in this study reported that their sense of well-being increased, and there was a moderate reduction in clinic healthcare utilization during the course of the treatment (Compton & Purviance, 1992). Both of these studies highlight the value of including psychosocial and emotional support for patients. The therapy sessions provided in each case were relatively inexpensive and were able to reduce the patients' use of medical services. The patients were able to voice their concerns and to receive understanding. Patients who were helped to discover and deal with their deep-seated concerns may have even been spared the problems of some unnecessary surgeries and drug therapies, as well as the risks of multiple diagnostic tests. In all, psychotherapeutic interventions appear to be a cost-effective way of increasing the success of medical interventions.

In the next chapter, we turn to pain as a traditional medical problem that can be best understood and treated using a biopsychosocial approach.

Summary

1. Illness is subjective and depends upon objective physical symptoms, subjective evaluation of internal state and ability to function, and reactions of others. A person can be "ill" without the presence of disease, or have a disease but not self-define as ill.
2. "Functional somatic syndrome" is a group of related conditions characterized by functional disability and self-reported symptoms, rather than clearly demonstrable organic problems; symptoms can often be ameliorated by explanation and reassurance; this syndrome often involves co-occurrence with psychiatric symptoms.
3. Biomedical models of illness assume that illness can be fully accounted for by a patient's deviations from the norm on measurable biological variables; biopsychosocial models include psychological and social factors as components of the illness process.
4. Individuals vary in their responses to similar medical conditions and focus of attention on symptoms. Factors affecting this variation are focus of attention on threatening events, personality characteristics (such as neuroticism), attention to

bodily experience, salience of symptoms, levels of body awareness and self-consciousness, thresholds and tolerance levels for pain, childhood experiences, cultural background, current life circumstances, gender, and cognitions (meaning of the symptoms).

5. Help seeking once symptoms are noticed and acknowledged is also variable. Factors that influence help seeking are perceptions of the seriousness of the symptoms, beliefs about medicine's ability to alleviate them, perceived barriers to getting help, attitudes toward being ill, visibility of the symptoms and degree to which they interfere with everyday life, current level of stress, level of external support (emotional, informational, and monetary) from the lay referral network for help seeking.

6. Unnecessary delays in seeking medical treatment can be dangerous. Incorrect interpretation of symptoms can result from fear of serious diagnosis and fear of embarrassment if symptoms are not serious. Delay involves three components:

   ■ Appraisal time (time it takes to decide that symptoms are meaningful).
   ■ Illness delay (time from deciding symptoms are important to deciding to seek medical care for them).
   ■ Utilization delay (time from deciding to seek medical care to actually doing it).

7. The sick role has privileges and responsibilities; entrance to it initially requires self-definition as well as seeking help and following medical advice.

   ■ Doctors or other medical professionals are needed in order to legitimize the sick role, particularly if the person maintains it extensively.
   ■ Secondary gains associated with the sick role include being cared for, receiving attention, having a way to channel dissatisfactions, and even monetary gains such as insurance payments or worker's compensation.
   ■ Individuals with no diagnosed organic disease may occupy the sick role; their condition may have psychological "overlay" such as anxiety or depression; they may also have alexithymia, hypochondriasis, conversion disorder, or factitious disorder.

THINKING CRITICALLY

1. How would you go about determining whether someone actually has a disease, or whether they are simply malingering or suffering from factitious disorder?

2. Why is it that some diseases and syndromes keep changing—their names change, the list of symptoms changes, and the preferred treatments change? Can you give some examples?

3. What are the social factors that might contribute to the fact that women report more symptoms than do men? That they seek treatment more often than do men?

4. Think about your own social groups—what examples are there in your family, or among your friends, of a "lay referral network"? Would you say that this network is an adaptive one, or does it cause unnecessary delays or other problems?

5. What does it mean to say that illness is not completely biological, nor is it completely psychological?

GLOSSARY

Alexithymia: The inability to express or describe emotions.

Appraisal time: The time it takes a patient to appraise his or her symptoms as illness and to decide that the sensations mean that something important is wrong.

Biomedical model: A model that assumes that illness can be fully accounted for by a person's deviations from the norm on measurable biological variables.

Biopsychosocial model: An approach that requires that psychological and social factors must also be included along with the biological in any attempts to understand a person's response to symptoms and the experience of illness.

Chronic Fatigue Syndrome (CFS): A syndrome characterized by long-term fatigue and the general absence of any clearly discernible organic cause.

Conversion responses: Symptoms such as loss of sight or speech or hearing and various forms of muscular paralysis. Conversion responses are believed to be primitive responses to emotional conflict and make sense in that they tend to solve the conflict.

Disease: A much more narrow concept than illness; disease is a morbid process having characteristic symptoms and may affect the whole body or any of its parts; its etiology, pathology, and prognosis may be known or unknown.

Epstein-Barr Virus: A virus that causes infectious mononucleosis.

Factitious disorder: A disorder in which an individual intentionally creates symptoms in order to receive a diagnosis and medical treatment.

Functional somatic syndrome: Syndrome characterized by functional disability and self-reported symptoms rather than clearly demonstrable organic problems.

Generalized anxiety disorder: Disorder in which a person experiences unrealistic or excessive anxiety or worry.

Glove anesthesia: The term for a condition in which only the hand, but no other parts of the arm, loses sensation and is unable to function.

Health: One definition is a state of complete physical, mental, and social well-being, not merely the absence of disease or infirmity.

Hypochondria/Hypochondriasis: Propensity to pay more attention than most people to bodily symptoms and to be convinced that they signal disease; involves conversion of personal emotional distress into physical distress and reporting of diffuse, changeable symptoms.

Idiopathic: Medical term meaning "arising spontaneously or from an obscure or unknown cause."

Illness: Condition of pronounced deviation from the normal healthy state.

Illness delay: The time from the patient's decision that he or she is ill until the decision to seek care.

Laparotomy: Exploratory surgery of the abdomen.

Lay referral network: Network of friends and family who help attach meaning to symptoms and offer home remedies or advice to seek medical care.

Magnetic Resonance Imaging (MRI): Procedure for imaging internal structures in the body using protons in a magnetic field.

Malingering: A conscious, purposeful using of somatic complaints to achieve exemption from one's obligations.

Medical care utilization: The use of healthcare services.

Menorrhagia: Abnormal premenopausal bleeding.

Morbid medicans: Form of hypochondriasis in which medical students believe that they have the symptoms of the diseases they are studying.

Psychosomatic illness: Illness that results from, or is exacerbated by, psychological factors.

Secondary gains: Positive outcomes that balance negative aspects of being ill.

Sick role: A social role adopted by an individual who presents symptoms of illness. The sick role brings privileges as well as responsibilities.

Somatization: A general tendency to experience and communicate emotional distress through somatic (bodily) complaints.

Total delay: Total length of time for a person to move from recognition of the symptoms to arrival at the clinic, emergency room, or doctor's office.

Utilization delay: The time from the decision to seek care to actually obtaining medical services.

CHAPTER

8

Pain

Sharonda was disappointed when her exam by the endodontist was completely normal. She had hoped that this dentist, who specializes in caring for the tooth pulp, would find that some kind of damage to her tooth's nerve would explain her pain, and that he would quickly alleviate it. Instead, her endodontist told her that her damaged tooth could not account for her pain. For Sharonda, this was very frustrating—there was no explanation for what she was experiencing!

About a year earlier Sharonda had been in a car accident in which she lost her front four teeth. Even though it was a relatively minor accident, Sharonda's face hit the steering wheel because she was not wearing her safety belt. She was

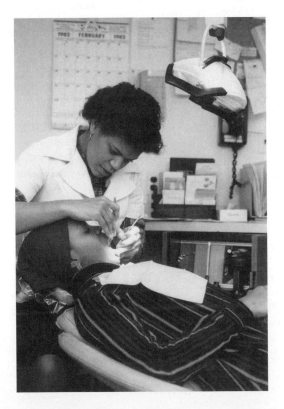

lucky that the injury wasn't worse and that the roots of her teeth were intact. She did, however, have to undergo several painful root canals, as the trauma to her mouth slowly killed the roots of her teeth and they became infected. Despite the root canal on her right front tooth (the right central incisor), she still felt enormous pain that kept her awake at night and prevented her from eating anything hot or cold. Her pain was taking a toll on her family life; she was constantly irritable and edgy because she wasn't sleeping. Sharonda no longer enjoyed family dinnertime conversations, concentrating instead on preventing hot or cold foods or drinks from touching her tooth as she ate. Her regular dentist had not been much help, as he assured her that "nothing was wrong." The tooth that hurt had no nerve and therefore could not transmit pain, according to her dentist. Sharonda was angry that he thought the pain was "all in her head." The pain was very real in Sharonda's view, and it was ruining her life.

Sharonda was insistent that she had hurt badly, although her endodontist said it was impossible for a tooth with no nerve to cause pain. To prove it, he applied a piece of hot rubber to the tooth, and she closed her eyes in anticipation of horrible pain. But Sharonda was dumbstruck when she felt nothing! When her dentist touched the nearby teeth that had not received root canal, however, Sharonda felt sharp pain in her right central incisor, one tooth away! The puzzle was solved: Sharonda was experiencing **referred pain** that originated in one tooth but was subjectively felt in another tooth. So that day she had yet another root canal and eventually her pain disappeared.

The struggle to understand pain—what it is, what causes it, and how to control it—is an extremely important endeavor for health psychologists. In the past three decades, however, psychological and medical research have prompted great strides in solving the problems of pain that until recently remained very poorly understood. New developments have benefited the lives of those who have been touched, and sometimes devastated, by pain.

As we will see in this chapter, the mind plays an important role in the perception and interpretation of pain. We will examine what pain is, how the experience of pain can be affected by individual differences, and the toll that pain can take on both cognitive functioning and the immune system. We will explore the many treatments available for the management of pain, and we will see how patients in pain can be helped to live happy and productive lives.

The Significance of Pain

Pain is an extremely salient phenomenon in human life and is typically the symptom that brings a person to seek medical care (Safer et al., 1979). People will often tolerate the most annoying and sometimes the most apparently serious symptoms (such as lumps and abnormal bleeding) as long as they feel no pain. For many, the presence of pain is what suggests danger. When in pain, they fear for their well-being or simply want the pain stopped (Zborowski, 1952).

There is often little relationship, however, between the severity of pain and the danger that its associated condition can pose. A cancerous lump may be life threatening but bring no pain at all; a serious heart attack may simply involve a feeling of indigestion. Unfortunately, the lack of pain may diminish the person's incentive to seek medical treatment. Among those who have heart attacks, there is typically a long delay in going to the hospital or calling 911 if the pain is not severe (e.g., Meischke et al., 1995). This can be very dangerous, since every minute counts!

Most people fear ever having to experience terrible pain. Fear of pain causes some people to avoid preventive medical examinations, necessary dental care, and even recommended medical treatments such as surgery (Drewry & Chu, 1995; Lin & Ball, 1997). Most people are aware that pain may have the potential to overwhelm their ability to cope with it. When people are in pain, they can feel quite overcome by it, and alleviation of pain can become even more important than satisfying basic needs such as hunger and thirst (Sternbach, 1968). In some cases an individual's pain can become so bad that he or she cannot imagine life beyond it. Families can be destroyed by pain, and severe pain can even prompt some people to consider suicide (Seale & Addington-Hall, 1994). The possibility of suffering **intractable pain** (pain that cannot be relieved) is one of the things people fear most about serious illnesses such as cancer, and many people fear uncontrolled pain more than they fear death (Melzack, 1973). These days, of course, pain control techniques and medications, used properly, should be able to keep patients comfortable.

Sometimes the pain experience can extend beyond the illness or disability itself and involve a variety of elements such as eligibility for disability and release from unpleasant tasks and responsibilities; often, the entire family or social system of the individual is affected. As we will see in this chapter, it is particularly important that pain be treated from a biopsychosocial point of view—one that addresses the physical, emotional, and social elements of the pain experience.

Pain and the Costs of Healthcare Utilization

The phenomenon of pain has tremendous economic consequences. The U.S. workforce experiences approximately 13.2 million nonfatal injuries and 862,200 illnesses each year. These are estimated to cost over $170 billion annually, and it is recognized that this figure is likely a significant underestimate because some illnesses and injuries are not reported and because costs associated with pain and suffering are difficult to tally (Leigh et al., 1997). About 31 million Americans experience back pain, which is the primary cause of limited activity for young adults. Back pain alone results in about $28 billion in lost work productivity annually (Rizzo et al., 1998). In one group of patients who had spine injury and associated pain, total costs of care averaged $41,727 per case (Earman et al., 1996).

Although the use of healthcare services is affected by numerous factors, pain plays a significant role in utilization, particularly in the elderly (Cronan et al., 1995). Among back pain patients, most of the costs of care are generated by a relatively small number of patients (Engel et al., 1996). One study of community-dwelling elders who were suffering from chronic pain found that they depended as much on themselves as they did on formal services for pain relief (Cook & Thomas, 1994). Most took over-the-counter analgesics and accepted pain as a part of their everyday lives. Annual costs of over-the-counter pain treatments in this country are estimated at over $100 billion a year (Bonica, 1992; Dworkin, 1994).

Psychological factors affect perceptions of pain, and the more pain an individual experiences, the more likely he or she is to utilize healthcare services. When patients have a heightened sense of bodily awareness, are more verbal about reporting their bodily sensations, and misunderstand those sensations, they are much more likely to seek medical care. Somatization (which, as we will see in detail later, is an expression of emotional distress through bodily or somatic symptoms) can lead further to increased healthcare utilization for several reasons, one of which is the experience of pain. In fact, pain is one of the most frequently reported complaints associated with somatization. A recent review of patterns in medical care use demonstrates that many individuals who are having mental health difficulties instead seek care by presenting physical symptoms to a physician (Ford, 1995). In addition, medical patients with more mental health problems and more reported pain have longer hospital stays (about 40%), higher healthcare costs (about 35%), and more procedures done while in the hospital than those who do not (Levenson et al., 1990). It is important to recognize, however, that the direction of causality in these associations is not fully understood.

What Is Pain?

Pain is generally described as emotional and sensory discomfort that is usually (although not always) related to tissue damage. More globally, pain is defined as "a state of physical, emotional or mental lack of well-being or . . . uneasiness that ranges from mild discomfort or dull distress to acute often unbearable agony, may be generalized or localized, and is the consequence of being injured or hurt physically or mentally . . . and that usually produces a reaction of wanting to avoid, escape, or destroy the causative factor and its effects" (Merriam Webster's Medical Desk Dictionary [MWMDD], 1996). Pain involves the "total experience of some noxious stimulus which is influenced by current context of the pain, previous experiences, learning history, and cognitive processes" (Feuerstein et al., 1987, p. 243). Pain has also been defined as a psychological experience that includes "(1) a personal, private sensation of hurt; (2) a harmful stimulus which signals current or impending tissue damage; and (3) a pattern of responses which operate to protect the organism from harm" (Sternbach, 1968, p. 12). "In some respects [pain] is a sensation, and in other respects it is an emotional-motivational phenomenon that leads to escape and avoidance behavior" (Weisenberg, 1977, p. 1009).

These definitions suggest that defining pain as a construct can be difficult and confusing (although to the person who is suffering, the experience of pain is quite unmistakable). One important distinction is that between nociception and pain. **Nociception** is ". . . mechanical, thermal, or chemical energy impinging on specialized nerve endings that in turn activate A-delta and C fibers, thus initiating a signal to the central nervous system that aversive events are occurring" (Fordyce, 1988, p. 278).

Nociception can be observed because activity in certain nerve fibers and their synaptic connections can be measured. Pain may be perceived as a result of the stimulation of these nerve fibers, but it is also possible for pain to be perceived in the absence of nociception and for nociception to occur without any pain being perceived at all.

How Is Pain Perceived?

When a person's body is injured, signals of tissue damage flow from afferent neurons of the peripheral nervous system to the dorsal horn of the spinal cord and then to various areas of the brain, including the thalamus, hypothalamus, and cerebral cortex. The afferent nerve endings that respond to pain stimuli are called **nociceptors** (Chapman, 1984). When activated, these nerve endings generate impulses that travel to the central nervous system. The afferent peripheral fibers that transmit pain impulses are A-delta fibers and C fibers. A-delta fibers transmit impulses very quickly, sending their messages through the thalamus on their way to the brain's cerebral cortex. These messages are associated with sharp, distinct pain and thus command immediate attention. C fibers transmit impulses more slowly and send their messages to the brainstem and lower portions of the forebrain; they are involved when pain is diffuse, dull, or aching and are believed to affect mood, general emotional state, and motivation (Bonica, 1990; Melzack & Wall, 1982).

Perceiving pain is not always straightforward, of course. *Referred pain* involves pain that originates in tissue in one part of the body but is perceived as coming from another part. For example, pain inside the ear may be caused by irritation to the temporomandibular joint of the jaw (Melzack & Wall, 1982), or, as in Sharonda's case, pain in one tooth may be the result of sensitivity in adjoining teeth. When different sensory impulses use the same pathways to the spinal cord, the person perceiving the pain sometimes mislabels the origin of the pain message.

Sometimes pain is experienced in the absence of apparent tissue damage or a noxious stimulus. **Neuralgia**, defined as ". . . pain radiating along the course of one or more nerves usually without demonstrable changes in the nerve structure" (MWMDD, 1996) is one such extremely painful condition. Neuralgia episodes can occur quite suddenly and pain can be provoked by minimal stimulation such as a light wind. **Causalgia** involves severe burning pain and sometimes results after a wound has healed and damaged nerves have regenerated. Like neuralgia, causalgia can be triggered by minor stimulation. Neuralgia and causalgia are believed to be sometimes caused by infections (viral or bacterial) that result in nonobvious neural damage (Hare & Milano, 1985).

Phantom-limb pain occurs when a patient who has had an amputation, or one who has damage to the peripheral nervous system, still feels pain in the missing or damaged part of the body; amputees almost universally report sensations and/or pain in the amputated limb (Melzack, 1995). These sensations were once attributed to spinal processes that are still active or to other peripheral nervous system factors, but a new theory proposes that innate neural networks can actually function in the absence of input from the body (Melzack, 1995, 1999). Conditioned initially by sensory inputs, these networks can continue to create sensation without external provocation. This idea is addressed further when we consider the Neuromatrix Theory of Pain.

Theories of Pain

Let's examine the history of theories of pain in an effort to more fully understand what pain is and how it can be controlled.

Specificity Theory

In the late nineteenth century, with the **Specificity Theory of Pain,** medical professionals proposed a specific bodily system responsible for pain perception. Pain was believed to be an independent sensation like heat, cold, or touch (e.g., Mountcastle, 1974). It was held that specialized skin receptors responded to particular stimuli and that specific routes of transmission in the central nervous system and special centers in the brain were responsible for registering and interpreting (only) pain (Melzack, 1983). Evidence soon contradicted this theory because pain is not an experience separate from other sensory experiences; it can result from excessive heat, cold, or pressure.

Pattern Theory

The classic **Pattern Theory** holds that pain results from the patterning, intensity, and quality of stimulation from peripheral nerve endings (Goldschneider, 1886, cited in Melzack, 1973; Melzack, 1983, 1993). In a particular area of the body, for example, mild stimulation might cause the sensation of touch but intense stimulation may cause the sensation of pain. This theory also holds that sensations can summate and that nerve impulses conducted to the spinal column reach the brain only after achieving a certain threshold. This summation might account for the short delay between the onset of tissue damage in a cut or burn and the recognition of pain.

Neither theory above can adequately explain the pain experience, yet each provides a partial explanation for what we know of the physiology of pain. As Specificity Theory suggests, specific nerve fibers do conduct pain, although others can also give rise to pain when they are stimulated beyond a certain threshold. As Pattern Theory predicts, receptors do respond to patterned information. There is, however, no direct connection between the pain receptors in the peripheral nervous system and the brain center where pain would be perceived (Melzack, 1993).

Affect Theory

Affect Theory was the only early theory of pain to allow for emotions to color the perceptions of all sensory events. According to Affect Theory, pain has a negative quality that drives the individual into action focused on stopping the stimulus that is causing the pain. All physiological effects of a stimulus are believed to be accompanied by motivational and affective factors and to result in the "unique, distinctly unpleasant affective quality that differentiates (pain) from other sensory experiences such as sight, hearing, and touch" (Melzack, 1983, p. 3). This theory, however, does not add information regarding how the physiological system perceives and the brain reacts to painful stimuli.

Gate Control Theory

The **Gate Control Theory** more adequately deals with the physiological findings of pain research than do the Pattern and Specificity theories (Melzack, 1993; Melzack & Wall, 1965, 1982). The Gate Control Theory acknowledges specificity in pain transmission as well as the importance of patterning and the summation of impulses, but also allows for the role of psychological processes in pain experience and control, and is thus valuable in clinical application.

The Gate Control Theory holds that pain impulses do not go directly from nerve endings to the brain but instead that nerve messages of nociception flow from the peripheral nervous system to the central nervous system through the dorsal horns of the spinal cord, where they are modulated by a neural "gating" mechanism. Melzack and Wall (1965) originally proposed that certain transmission cells in the substantia gelitinosa of the spinal cord, if activated, would facilitate the sensation of pain. The activity of these transmission cells is partly dependent on the ratio of A-beta, A-delta, and C fiber activity. The degree of pain that is felt is linked to the level of transmission cell activation (that is, higher levels of activity open the "gate"). As we noted earlier, pain perception involves a complex interplay of different facets of the brain and central nervous system. The Gate Control Theory proposes that as nerve fibers throughout the body conduct pain sensations and project them onto various parts of the brain (including the hypothalamus, thalamus, and cerebral cortex), the brain provides feedback to the spinal cord, which inhibits some pain messages and facilitates others. This mechanism is referred to as the central control mechanism, and it is this involvement of the cerebral cortex that is believed to make cognitive judgments about the *meaning* of pain. If the higher centers of the brain interpret an event as painful, the gating mechanism will be open, and the sensation of pain will be transmitted to the brain (Melzack & Wall, 1982).

When no painful stimuli are involved, peripheral nerves directly transmit sensations to the spinal column and up to the brain, and the hypothesized spinal gating mechanism is closed. But when the stimulation of appropriate nerve endings is strong enough, and the upper centers of the brain interpret the event as painful (for example, by recognizing that the body has sustained some damage), the gate opens to allow painful sensations to enter. On the other hand, the large A-beta fibers, when stimulated, decrease the level of transmission cell activity and thereby close the pain gate to nociception stimuli. The gate can be opened, and pain experienced, when the ratio of A-delta and C fibers to A-beta activation is high (when there is a lot of nociception stimulation), but A-beta fibers can be stimulated directly in an effort to reduce pain. Acupuncture and electrical stimulation are both used in this way to interfere with the transmission of pain messages to the brain. A person's psychological or mental status may also influence the activation of A-beta fibers, thereby influencing susceptibility to pain impulses.

Gate Control Theory thus proposes that three factors are involved in determining how much pain is felt. Activity in the small pain fibers (A-delta and C; determined partly by the strength of the noxious stimuli) influences the strength of the pain message transmitted. The amount of activity in large diameter fibers (A-beta) closes the gate and inhibits the pain perception. And messages that descend from the brain close the gate and inhibit the transmission of pain signals. The Gate Control Theory of Pain is illustrated in Figure 8.1.

A few clinical implications for the control of pain are suggested. First, stimulation of A-beta fibers (that close the pain gate) limits the perception of pain and these can be affected *chemically* (such as with medications) or stimulated *electrically* (such as with mild transcutaneous [through the skin] electrical nerve stimulation) or *physically* (such as with counterstimulation like heat and massage). Second, the pain experience can be affected by factors such as thoughts or emotional reactions. Pain messages can be modified or inhibited if they are not interpreted as such by higher centers of cognition. Positive emotions, intense concentration, relaxation, and involvement in pleasurable activities can close the pain gate and negative emotions, anxiety, worry, tension, depression, focus on the pain, boredom, and lack of involvement in life activities can open it (Chapman et al., 1985; Turk et al., 1983).

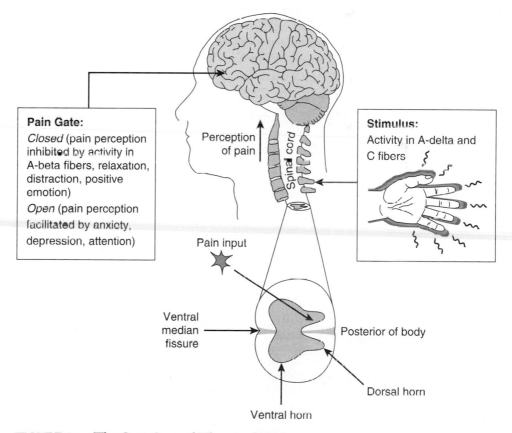

FIGURE 8.1   The Gate Control Theory of Pain.

Although Melzack and Wall's original conceptualization of the Gate Control Theory provided an excellent model for understanding nociception modulation at the level of the spinal cord, the neurophysiology and neuroanatomy associated with this process has proven to be even more complex than indicated in early models (Coderre et al., 1993; Humphries et al., 1996). Despite this, there is substantial evidence in basic support of the Gate Control Theory. One recent prediction, based on the Gate Control Theory, was that when a painful stimulus that activated both large-diameter and small-diameter nerves was suddenly stopped, there would be a pulse of increased pain. This pulse was predicted to occur when the stimulus was removed because the A-beta activity would cease almost immediately due to relatively rapid simultaneous conduction along the large-diameter fibers. The A-delta and C fiber activity would diminish more slowly due to their relatively small diameter and correspondingly slower transmission. Thus, for a short period, the level of nociceptive neural input to the dorsal horns of the spinal cord would remain unchanged, while the inhibitory action of the A-beta fibers would be gone, resulting in an increased "net" pain message. This hypothesis was supported. (Humphries et al., 1996).

Neuromatrix Theory

The most recent theory of pain is the **Neuromatrix Theory of Pain** (Melzack, 1989, 1995, 1999). This theory is based on four basic tenets: (1) The areas of the brain that correspond to particular body parts exist and are active, whether or not they are receiving inputs from the body; (2) neural patterns that underlie "experience" originate in neural networks in the brain; (3) the experience of "self" as distinct from the environment is due to central neural processes, not peripheral nervous system (PNS) or spinal cord inputs; and (4) these neural processes, although modified by experience, are innate. Neuromatrix theory suggests that every individual has an innate, genetically prescribed neural network (called the "neuromatrix") that consists of feedback loops between the thalamus and cortex and between the cortex and limbic system. Furthermore, these loops are modified through experiences with pain. When sensory inputs are received, they cycle through this matrix and are synthesized, creating a unique pattern (called a "neurosignature"). Thus, all sensory inputs become imprinted on the neuromatrix, and these neurosignatures are projected to specific brain areas known as the "sentient neural hub" where they are converted to consciousness. It is at this point that the neurosignature may also activate an "action neuromatrix" to produce bodily movement (Melzack, 1995, 1999).

Although this is a relatively new theory, there is evidence to support it. First, we already know that removing specific somatosensory areas of the thalamus or cortex does not relieve phantom-limb pain (pain "felt" in a limb that no longer exists) (White & Sweet, 1969). This is one piece of evidence in support of the theory because the neuromatrix is distributed selectively throughout the whole brain and it would be impossible to destroy it (Melzack, 1995). In addition, several studies with rats have indicated that injecting an anesthetic into particular brain areas important for neuromatrix functioning (e.g., lateral hypothalamus, cingulum bundle, and other reticular and limbic areas) does in fact reduce the pain of the formalin test (a test that is believed to mimic the pain humans feel in response to injury), while leaving spinally mediated pain reflexes unaffected (Tasker et al., 1987; Vaccarino & Melzack, 1992).

Neurochemical Basis of Pain and Pain Inhibition

Evidence in support of the Gate Control Theory of Pain demonstrates that the brain can indeed control the amount of pain an individual experiences by transmitting messages down the spinal cord to block the transmission of pain signals (Melzack, 1993; Melzack & Wall, 1965, 1982). Studies showing that electrical stimulation of the brain can block the perception of pain impulses led to the discovery of a neurochemical basis of pain and the identification of **endogenous opioids**. Endogenous opioids are opiate-like substances that regulate pain and are produced within the body. They appear to behave in the same way as exogenous opioids, such as the drugs heroin and morphine, in that they produce pain analgesia and feelings of well-being (Snyder, 1977; Winters, 1985). Researchers have identified three main groups of these endogenous opioids: beta-endorphins, proenkephalin, and prodynorphins (Akil et al., 1984).

The system of endogenous opioids and their function in the body is very complex. These substances appear to be released in response to stressful circumstances and can produce natural pain suppression. Some evidence shows, for example, that intense physical exercise can trigger the release of beta-endorphin, which results in natural, short-term pain suppression and a subjective feeling of physical well-being (Akil et al., 1984; Fournier et al., 1997; Harte et al., 1995; Heitkamp et al., 1996; Heitkamp et al., 1998). Not all studies have found such an effect, however (Kraemer et al., 1990; Williams & Getty, 1986). There is empirical evidence that *various* types of activities, some not strenuous at all, can produce better moods and similar feelings of well-being. For instance, a recent study compared the mood-altering effects of two very different activities (running and meditation) and showed that both groups experienced elevated moods after engaging in their activity (Harte et al., 1995). Only the runners had increased beta-endorphin levels, but corticotropin releasing hormone (CRH), which is associated with circulating beta-endorphin, increased for both groups.

Just as endogenous systems can inhibit pain, they can also facilitate the experience of pain (Meagher, in press). This phenomenon has been much less studied than the analgesic properties of endogenous systems, and the neural systems that underlie this phenomenon are not well understood. Environmentally induced hyperalgesia (experiencing significant pain in response to stimulation) does appear to be due to both fear reactions and the sensitization of pain circuits within the individual. It is clear that the same stimulus can either enhance or diminish the pain experience, depending upon its severity (Meagher et al., in review). Mildly to moderately intense stimuli seem to facilitate pain, while more severe stimuli actually engage inhibitory processes. The emotional states that are linked to hyperalgesia include anxiety about pain, high levels of attention to pain, and expectations of pain (Meagher, in press).

Pain and the Immune System

The study of the immune system and psychological processes (an area known as psy-choneuroimmunology) has made enormous advancements during the past twenty years. (Chapter 9 provides further detail about this exciting field.) The effect of phys-ical pain on immune functioning has been studied recently (e.g., Page & Ben-Eliyahu, 1997), and it is clear that this research has numerous implications for the health of patients as well as for the costs of uncontrolled pain. Researchers have stated that "pain not only results in suffering but is a pathogen itself, capable of facilitating the pro-gression of metastatic disease. Adequate pain relief decreases these risks" (Page & Ben-Eliyahu, 1997). These researchers found that experimental animals that had tumors and who underwent pain-inducing surgery had fewer subsequent metastases if they received morphine for their pain. The experience of uncontrollable, severe pain appeared to exacerbate the proliferation of malignancy (Page & Ben-Eliyahu, 1997). In another example, patients with sciatic pain were found to have elevated morning lev-els of interleukin-6 and cortisol in comparison to healthy controls; both of these are indicators of a suppressed immune system (Geiss et al., 1997). Of course, these findings are intriguing, but much more empirical work is required in order to understand fully the impact of pain on immune system functioning.

Cognitive Outcomes of Pain

Have you ever been in pain and unable to focus on anything else but finding a way to relieve it? Consider how you would perform on a test just a day or two after breaking your leg. How do you think you would perform during a business meeting while suf-fering from a migraine headache or chronic back pain? The negative impact of pain on the performance of individuals is very real. Performance, particularly that requiring mental attention, is most reduced in individuals who report high levels of pain inten-sity and somatic awareness (Eccleston et al., 1997). In other words, it becomes increas-ingly difficult to concentrate and pay attention to tasks when levels of pain and body awareness are high. Painful episodes appear to actually reduce the available cognitive resources needed for the performance of some tasks. When one is focusing on pain, one is less able to think clearly. During an experimentally induced painful episode (in which an ischemic upper-arm tourniquet was applied), volunteers responded less accu-rately and more slowly to questions than did volunteers who were not undergoing painful stimulation (Lorenz & Bromm, 1997). The ability to perform a distraction task has also been shown to be affected by experimentally induced pain (a cold pressor pain stimulus test; Johnson & Petrie, 1997).

Everyone must perform various tasks in daily life and their capacity to do so can be seriously disrupted by pain. What, then, are the implications for those who suffer from pain? It has been shown that when pain is underpredicted and worse than antic-ipated, there is a greater disruption in cognitive functioning than when pain is correctly predicted, even when the two levels of pain are perceived to be at the same intensity (Arntz & Hopmans, 1998). One experiment demonstrated that task performance is reduced significantly just after the onset of a painful episode, but that this effect disappears after the pain has been present for a while and also when the pain ceases (Crombez et al., 1996). This research suggests that cognitive performance may be reduced primarily when pain is new to the individual and unexpected. After a time of adjustment, however, pain has less effect on performance.

Different Types of Pain

Pain cannot be measured objectively because it is a wholly subjective experience; only the person who has the pain can feel it. While the tissue damage that causes the pain might be identified and examined in detail, the pain itself cannot be perceived or described by anyone other than the person who is in pain.

The Quality of Pain

Various highly descriptive words help to depict various types of pain experience. For example, pain may be "dull" versus "sharp," or "constant" versus "throbbing," "shooting" versus "still," "diffused" versus "focused," "stabbing" versus "pinching." The type of pain experienced will sometimes, though not always, depend upon the type of irritation or damage to the body and the part of the body that has been affected. As with other bodily experiences, there is probably a limit to what can be communicated with words (Schiffman, 1976). In one study, patients with low back pain, rheumatoid arthritis, and chronic headaches and healthy volunteers were asked to make similarity judgments for a set of twelve descriptions of pain (Morley & Pallin, 1995). Overall the descriptions were sorted into three groups labeled "tolerability," "focus of attention," and "minor emotional reaction." This study reaffirmed the idea that the pain experience is verbalized in a multidimensional fashion, and that there is some consistency in pain descriptors even across diverse types of pain. In general, people agree on how to describe various types of pain.

The Intensity of Pain

Pain can be experienced at different levels of intensity. As is true of the quality of pain, the communication of pain intensity may also be very difficult. A ten-point scale may begin to impose some objectivity on the intensity of pain, but people vary in their choice of a number depending upon other factors besides their pain. One person's four, for example, may be another person's seven. Measuring the intensity of an individual's pain is difficult, but it is critical to understanding and assessing the effects of clinical interventions on pain perceptions. One may wish to know whether a particular treatment makes a patient feel better and have less pain.

Pain Threshold and Tolerance

Two concepts are central to understanding pain intensity: **threshold** and **tolerance**. Pain threshold is the point at which a person first perceives a stimulus as painful. A light touch of one's wrist with a fingernail may bring the sensation of mild pressure while a sensation of pain may eventually be identified if the fingernail scratches the wrist; the stimulus has crossed the pain threshold. Tolerance refers to the point at which the individual is not willing to accept stimulation of a higher magnitude; if the stimulation increases beyond this point, it is perceived as unbearable. Threshold appears to be determined mainly by physiological variables, whereas tolerance appears to be influenced by psychological variables such as attitudes and motivations (Hirsch & Liebert, 1998).

Tolerance and threshold may be factors that are based upon prior as well as present experience. Veterans who had serious past war injuries were found to have higher thresholds and tolerance levels, but women who currently suffered with fibromyalgia reported greater pain qualitatively and quantitatively than healthy women exposed to the same stimuli (Bendtsen et al., 1997). Box 8.1 examines genetic versus behavioral factors as determinants of pain in an important study of twins.

BOX **8.1**

Research Close-up

Explaining Joint Pain: Genetics or Health Behaviors?

As you know, there are two types of twins, fraternal and identical. Fraternal twins are no more similar genetically than are regular siblings, whereas identical twins are perfectly matched genetically. Much psychological and biological research has used twin studies to examine the heritability of certain traits. These twin studies examine identical twins reared together and identical twins reared apart (where the twins were adopted into different families) to determine the relative influence of genetic and environmental factors. One issue of interest is that of chronic joint pain, which does appear to run in families. Certainly, family members share a common genetic link (such as a gene that affects the collagen in cartilage), but they also typically share an environment and similar health behaviors (such as poor exercise habits and obesity). The relative contributions of genetic predisposition and environmental risk to joint pain are important to assess, and this question is answerable with twin research.

A study of Swedish twins sought to explore the factors contributing to self-reported joint pain (Charles et al., 1999). The psychologists conducting the study examined several health behaviors that are known risk factors for joint pain, including previous exercise, work-related physical activity, and obesity. They also explored the contributions of neuroticism, gender, and of course, genetics. Of the 335 twin pairs that were examined, 190 were female and 145 were male, and they had an average age of 62 years. The measure of joint pain was subjective: Individuals reported whether they had any knee or hip joint pain for at least three months or if they were currently taking medication for joint problems or arthritis. Some information was gathered as early as the 1970s to predict joint pain outcomes in 1993; the time between initial assessment of personality and health behaviors and the outcome of self-reported joint pain was twenty-three years. The results suggested that behavior had a much greater influence on future joint pain than did genetics, which explained only 12 percent of the variance. Behavioral factors included obesity, exercise, not caring for injured joints, engaging in overly strenuous activities, and having specific joint injuries. Although men and women did not differ in terms of their location of joint pain (hip versus knee), men who had the highest risk for joint pain were those who had poor exercise habits and who had performed more strenuous work for a living. Obesity was the only risk factor for women.

Acute versus Chronic Pain

Acute pain is temporary and lasts less than six months (Turk et al., 1983). A toothache, the discomforts of childbirth, and even the pain of postoperative recovery are relatively short-lived. Acute pain can cause considerable anxiety and distress, but these typically subside when the condition resolves (Fordyce & Steger, 1979). Pain sometimes lingers on, however, and once it has lasted longer than six months, it is considered to be chronic. **Chronic pain** can be intermittent or constant, mild or severe, and pain that starts out as "acute" may persist and after a time become "chronic." **Chronic recurrent pain** (e.g., neuralgia) is not life threatening but produces intense episodes of pain followed by periods of relief (Turk et al., 1983). **Chronic intractable benign pain** (e.g., low back pain) is always present but unrelated to a progressive condition. **Chronic progressive pain** (e.g., metastatic cancer, advancing arthritis) involves continuous discomfort that becomes progressively more intense as the condition worsens.

When faced with acute pain, a patient can obtain information about the likely course of the condition and expect the pain eventually to dissipate, such as when a broken limb heals. When pain endures for months or even years despite measures to relieve it, the person in chronic pain can become very discouraged. Someone in chronic pain might restrict activities to control pain, and in doing so have to give up favorite hobbies, time spent with family and friends, and even their job (Jackson et al., 1996; Karoly & Ruehlman, 1996; Linton & Buer, 1995). People in chronic pain can become preoccupied with **somatic** (bodily) concerns, feel a heightened sense of dependency, and even experience a heightened incidence of depression and hopelessness (Melzack & Wall, 1982; Ogden-Niemeyer & Jacobs, 1989).

What Does Pain Look Like?

Pain behavior is a general term that reflects the actions people carry out or signals they emit when they are in pain. These include facial and vocal expressions of distress like moaning or grimacing, distorted movements and guarded postures, expressions of negative affect, and avoidance of activity (Turk et al., 1985). These behaviors may arise in response to nociception or for other reasons. A person may groan or grimace in response to being ignored, while another with stabbing pain might not flinch. A person might verbally report pain but demonstrate no pain behaviors. Thus, nociception may be thought of as the input, pain as the perceptual experience, and pain behavior as the output. This input-output system necessarily involves the brain, and "prior experience, expectancies, and perceived or anticipated consequences all play a role" (Fordyce, 1988, p. 278).

Two researchers have recently proposed a model of pain expression (in particular, facial expressions of pain) that involves the pain experience as well as the encoding (emitted by the pain patient) and decoding (what another person sees) of pain expressions (Prkachin & Craig, 1995). The model states that as a person experiences a painful episode, the face expresses information about the experience, which is then observed by the person who is interacting with the patient (the "interactant"). This person then interprets the expression and chooses to react in some way to this facial expression.

Numerous factors influence the timing of the first encoding (expression) of the pain and the manner in which the interactant interprets and responds to the expression. The expression of pain on a face does seem to be consistent across individuals (Craig, 1992; Craig et al., 1992) and to involve ". . . tightening of the orbital muscles surrounding the eye, leading to a narrowing of the eye aperture and raising of the cheeks . . . muscle groups lower the eyebrows and wrinkle the bridge of the nose . . . raise the upper lip and may produce wrinkles at the side of the nose . . . the eyelids may close altogether" (Prkachin & Craig, 1995, p. 195). Studies have found this expression in preterm infants, in full-term infants, and in adults, suggesting that this expression is not learned, but is instead an innate mechanism for expressing pain (Craig et al., 1994; Grunau et al., 1990; Johnston et al., 1993). Of course, this expression can also come under voluntary control.

Pain and the Medical Encounter

Pain control is not an area of great strength in medical training and practice, either in the United States or in other countries. Bonica (1992) noted, in his review of the seventeen top medicine, surgery, and oncology textbooks in the United States that only about one-half of one percent of the textbook pages were devoted to the issue of pain management. Healthcare providers tend to have only marginal knowledge about pain (Lebovits et al., 1997) and their attitudes, demographics, and patients' pain behaviors all influence the pain management they provide (Levin et al., 1998; Turk & Okifuji, 1997). It has also been shown that medical specialty affects the type and extent of pain management. Oncologists were found to have knowledge and attitudes toward pain closer to "ideal" than primary care physicians (due to greater experience), although their actions in managing their patients' pain were less than ideal (Levin et al., 1998).

Sometimes the responsibility for achieving effective pain relief must fall on the patient. As noted in Chapter 4, practitioner-patient communication is an essential component of the therapeutic relationship and is central to patient satisfaction, adherence, and even the outcomes of treatment. Pain can introduce significant misunderstanding between medical practitioners and their patients. To a physician, pain is only one of the signs and symptoms relevant to diagnosis. Most medical practitioners are committed to minimizing or eliminating their patients' pain whenever they believe it is possible and safe to do so. But medical practitioners often see people in pain all day long, and it may become easy to remain unaware of patients' pain experiences. The timing of pain relief may also cause misunderstanding between physicians and patients. Sometimes pain-relieving medications must be withheld until the source of the pain is found, such as in the diagnosis of appendicitis. Some patients continue to have pain despite the fact that medical professionals can find no organic cause. When patients complain about pain and the physical evidence of nociception is not forthcoming, medical professionals sometimes become frustrated and may even believe that their patients are malingering or seeking secondary gains (as described in Chapter 7).

Pain can be affected and modified by psychological mechanisms, but this by no means implies that pain is "all in a person's head" or that people can consciously con-

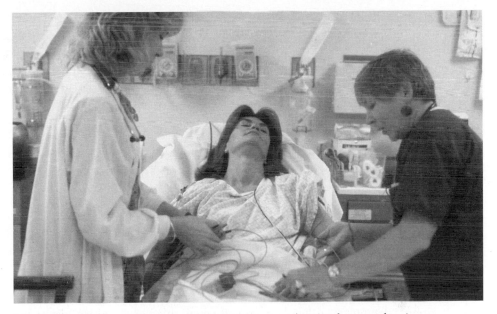

Misunderstandings regarding pain management can occur between doctors and patients.

trol the psychological processes that regulate pain. People do not have pain because they want to, and they should not be expected to simply "wish" their pain away. Psychological factors may contribute to pain experience, but do not completely control it, a fact that may be forgotten by some medical practitioners. Researchers have found that some medical practitioners gave placebo medications only to patients they disliked. Instead of an adjunct to therapy, the placebo was used as evidence that patients' pain had no physiological basis (Goodwin et al., 1979).

Psychological Factors and Pain

Emotional distress often acts as a magnifier of pain experiences (Fisher & Johnston, 1998). Depression has a profound impact on the ability of a patient to cope with many aspect of life, and in the face of physical pain depressed patients give higher pain ratings and are more emotionally affected by pain than nondepressed patients (Burckhardt et al., 1997; Sist et al., 1998). Pain is strongly influenced by other psychological factors such as thoughts, emotions, attention, and expectations. **Distraction**, for example, can sometimes lessen our perceptions of pain; in the midst of a competition, for example, an athlete may not even notice his or her injury because attention is fully focused on something else. When outside stimulation is minimized, such as when someone with lower back pain stays home in bed, pain sensations can be more unpleasant (Turk et al., 1983). The meaning attached to pain partly determines how it is perceived and experienced. Actual tissue damage can be less important in determining pain reaction than setting and meaning. Men wounded in battle during World War II rarely needed medication to control their pain; only 25 percent wanted narcotic relief, whereas over 80 percent of surgery patients with similar wounds wanted such relief (Beecher, 1956). For soldiers, being wounded meant leaving the front lines and perhaps even going home as heroes. Surgical patients, on the other hand, were missing out on the pleasurable aspects of their lives. The meaning of pain also affected the perceived disability and functioning in cancer patients compared with those of noncancer pain patients, although their levels of perceived pain severity were rated as equivalent (Turk et al., 1998). Despite similar levels of reported pain experience, cancer patients had greater disability and lower activity when compared with noncancer patients. Beliefs about the severity of cancer (e.g., that it is a "killer") may have contributed to lower levels of functioning despite equivalent pain.

Expectations

Expectations can significantly influence pain perceptions (e.g., Cipher & Fernandez, 1997). Practitioners can communicate positive or negative expectations to their patients and actually affect (positively or negatively) their patients' individual perceptions of pain (Melzack & Wall, 1982). For centuries, physicians have known the important effect that suggestibility has on perceptions of symptoms, and clinical evidence consistently demonstrates that the power of a medication often lies in the patient's belief in its effectiveness. Throughout the history of medicine, instant pain relief could be brought about with colored water that the doctor pretended was a potent medicine. As we saw in Chapters 3 and 6, the term that is usually used for such an inert substance is placebo, from the Latin meaning "I will please" (Shapiro, 1960). Practitioners' expectations for the good (or the bad) sequelae of a treatment have been found to be transmitted quite effectively to patients and to produce, on average, a 35 percent more positive (or negative) outcome than when no expectations are present (Shapiro, 1960). Today's research to test new drug therapies requires, in addition to an experimental treatment group, two control groups—a **placebo control group** (that receives the placebo medication) and a **zero control group** (that receive no treatment at all). Researchers can tell whether, and how well, the actual drug outperforms the expectations held for it.

While it is commonly thought that patients must "believe" in the placebo in order for it to have its effect, placebos are valuable tools and deception is not a necessary component to their effective use (Brody, 1982). When positive meaning is created within the illness experience, the opportunity is fashioned for organic change and positive patient outcomes generally result (Brody, 1997, 2000). Meaning includes having a comprehensible explanation of the illness, feeling cared for, and believing that there is a possibility to control or eliminate the symptoms. Even without trying to do so, practitioners can communicate their own expectations to their patients and can actually affect patients' individual perceptions of pain (Melzack & Wall, 1982).

Anxiety

Anxiety tends to be a magnifier of pain. Anxiety interferes with the relaxation needed to cope with pain and serves to worsen anticipation about pain (known as **anticipatory anxiety)**. Being anxious has been found to increase the fear of pain and the likelihood that one will attempt to avoid it (Asmundson et al., 1997; Asmundson & Taylor, 1996). This is important in medical settings because anxious patients may avoid necessary medical procedures or be combative toward their health professionals.

Perceived Control

A **sense of control**, particularly a belief in one's ability to control pain, affects its perception (Weisenberg, 1987). The ability to control aspects of a painful episode, such as its timing, is an effective coping aid. One experiment demonstrated that giving volunteers advance warning prior to receiving cold-pressor pain (either 0, 30, or 180 seconds), actually decreased the level of pain they reported (Weisenberg et al., 1996). Having a higher level of self-efficacy provides a buffer in raising pain thresholds and tolerance for pain. Arthritis patients were assessed for their level of arthritis self-efficacy and then subjected to thermal pain. Those with the highest ratings on efficacy had the highest pain thresholds and tolerances and rated the pain episode as the least unpleasant (Keefe et al., 1997).

Individual Differences in Reactions to Pain

Reactions to pain vary widely from one person to another. Faced with a painful back spasm, one person will continue to go to work and fulfill his or her family obligations while another will go to bed, take "painkillers," and do little but watch television and sleep. One person might tolerate pain for weeks or months before seeking medical help while another goes to see a doctor at the first twinge of discomfort. Research demonstrates that individuals' reactions to pain vary significantly depending upon several different factors, including personality, age, sex, and social and cultural backgrounds. Let us examine these factors in further detail.

Personality Differences

The personality factor most related to pain perceptions is neuroticism, which involves a propensity to experience anxiety, emotional liability, insecurity, and reactivity. Being high in neuroticism is associated not only with perceptions of pain, but also with more pain behaviors (Lauver & Johnson, 1997). Another trait associated with pain perceptions is private body consciousness (PBC) (or attentional self-focus), which refers to the tendency to pay close attention to physical sensations. College students higher in PBC and anxiety tend to report more severe aches and pains (Ahles et al., 1987), and patients undergoing a diagnostic procedure (MRI) reported more symptoms during the procedure if they were high in PBC and anxiety (Martin et al., 1991). Among patients suffering from chronic pain, individuals higher in PBC reported more pain (Ferguson & Ahles, 1998).

One important personality variable relating individual reactions to painful stimuli is the one that classifies people as **augmenters** or **reducers**. Those who are most tolerant of pain tend to be perceptual reducers; they see stimuli around them as part of the larger "field" in which the stimuli are embedded. Reducers tend to have a body image with definite boundaries; they are extroverted, have low levels of anxiety, and minimize stimulation (Sternbach, 1968). Augmenters characteristically perceive stimulation as greater than average. Also termed "sensitizers," they respond to external stimuli directly by trying to do something to deal with it. Reducers (or avoiders), on the other hand, play down external stimulation and deny it (Goldstein, 1973). Not all research verifies perceptual reactance in pain perceptions, however.

In general, "readiness to use pain as a symptom" occurs most often among people who are older, more neurotic and self-punishing, and have had more pain experiences in their lives (Weisenberg, 1977, p. 1019). Pain as a symptom appears with the highest incidence in people who have high anxiety. For certain groups of patients, pain expression can be greater than might be expected based on the extent of tissue damage experienced. These are (a) patients who show high levels of hypochondriasis (see Chapter 7); (b) people who have reactive depression; (c) people who tend to have somatic (bodily) reactions to their psychological states; and (d) people who use their pain to manipulate others (Sternbach, 1974).

Age Differences

Until recently, most research on age differences and pain has shown that the threshold for pain increases steadily with age (Kenshalo, 1986; Lautenbacher & Strain, 1991; Sternbach, 1968; Tucker et al., 1989). This might be due to diminishing sensitivity that occurs with aging or an increasing reluctance among older persons to label noxious stimuli as painful (Harkins & Chapman, 1976). In more recent studies, it has become apparent that the effect of age on pain thresholds and sensitivity is not as well understood as previously thought. Some researchers have failed to find an age effect at all (Harkins et al., 1986), and some recent findings actually indicate that there may be a slight *decrease* in pain thresholds as people get older (Heft et al., 1996). One promising research avenue lies in a recent study of the differential effects of aging for different types of pain transmission. Scientists in Australia are investigating the differences between A-delta and C fiber transmission of pain (Chakour et al., 1996). They have found that older adults rely more heavily on input from C fibers when reporting pain, while younger adults use a more even balance of C fiber and A-delta fiber input. Although older adults did have a higher pain threshold overall, this effect was eliminated when younger adults had A-delta fiber input blocked.

Understanding the changes in pain threshold across the life span may be particularly important in pediatric medical and dental care, since children often present behavioral problems in response to pain (e.g., screaming, pulling away). Such behavioral difficulties probably reflect their somewhat greater sensitivity to pain relative to the adults who treat them; it may be incorrect to conclude that a child's report of pain is exaggerated. It is quite possible that a child feels more pain (such as from a needle insertion) than does an adult. Some studies have shown (e.g., Lander & Fowler-Kerry, 1991) that younger children report more pain when having blood drawn than do older children; not all research supports such an age-related difference, however (e.g., Hogeweg et al., 1996). It is important to keep in mind that many psychosocial factors affect children's reactions to pain, such as their parents' own pain behaviors and the reinforcements that parents provide for their children's pain behaviors (Bush, 1987; Naber et al., 1995; Schechter et al., 1991).

Infants and Young Children

A long-held belief by many in the medical community has been that infants do not experience pain. Pain is essentially a subjective and psychological phenomenon, and an infant cannot articulate his or her experience. An unfortunate outcome of this belief has been the common practice of circumcising young infant boys without any local anesthetic; this practice is finally changing, however. Because pain in infants is difficult to assess, it is often treated ineffectively or neglected altogether (Prkachin & Craig, 1995; Stevens & Johnston, 1993). As we saw earlier, however, infants exhibit the same facial expressions in response to painful stimuli that adults do. The inability of infants and young children to use words to report pain requires particular attention to their pain *behaviors* (Anand & Craig, 1996).

In the care of toddlers and young children, a common practice is the attempt by parents to avoid "reacting" when their child gets hurt. The parent may not want to reinforce the child's pain behaviors and may fear "spoiling" the child by responding to every bump and bruise. Boys and girls are often socialized differently, of course, and even though there is evidence that boys and girls do not differ substantially in their ability to sense pain (Hogeweg et al., 1996), their pain experiences and their interactions related to pain have been found to be very different. Fearon and colleagues (1996) found that among children ages 2 to 6, girls were more distressed and received more physical comfort from adults in response to painful events than did boys. The girls were more verbal in their responses to pain and more often solicited the help of nearby adults. Help seeking was less frequent among the older children than the younger ones. Children who experienced the most bumps and bruises were also the most reactive, suggesting a heightened pain sensitization, rather than desensitization.

Gender Differences

Men and women, boys and girls, tend to differ somewhat in their experiences of and reactions to pain. Many studies have examined sex differences in threshold and tolerance for pain, and although several have failed to find any sex differences at all (e.g., Alon et al., 1999), some have identified them. It is only when one attempts to integrate the findings from these numerous studies that the complexity of this issue becomes apparent. Studies in which sex differences in pain have been documented appear primarily to be those that used very specific, experimentally manipulated somatic stimuli (such as electrical and pressure stimuli as opposed to thermal stimuli). In a recent review, Berkley (1997) points out that in these specific experimental situations, women are generally found to have slightly lower pain thresholds, lower pain tolerance, and greater ability to make fine discriminations among painful stimuli. She also notes, however, that these differences are small, that they apply only to certain kinds of stimulation, and that they are influenced by a multitude of situational variables. She concludes that with so complex a phenomenon, and with so many important variables interacting, ". . . the most striking feature of sex differences in reported pain experience is the apparent overall lack of them." Males and females do seem to have somewhat different attitudes toward pain (e.g., Liddell & Locker, 1997), which perhaps arise from the differences in their early experiences (e.g., Fearon et al., 1996). In general, women tend to report more pain than men, different manners of coping with the pain, and different responses to treatment. For example, a recent study by Walker and Carmody (1998) found that ibuprofen (a widely used nonsteroidal anti-inflammatory drug, or NSAID) did not reduce experimental pain for women, although it did reduce pain for men. The authors point out that this finding has important implications. Many painful diseases for which NSAIDS are typically prescribed (e.g., rheumatoid arthritis) are more common in women.

Why might differences in experimental pain perception, endogenous pain experience, attitudes toward pain, and treatment responses exist? One partial explanation may be hormonal. Although men and women both have estrogen, progesterone, and testosterone, the levels of each hormone differ between them, and while they tend to remain relatively stable for men, they fluctuate monthly for women. In addition, researchers are finding evidence of structural and neuronal organization differences in the brains of males and females, which may play some role. Subtle variations may also be partially explained by social and cultural factors.

Social/Cultural Differences

Substantial cultural and social group differences exist in reactions to pain. These are very significant, for they can affect clinical diagnosis and even the choice of treatment. Researchers have studied Italians, Irish, Jews, New Englanders, Eskimos and American Indians, and an assortment of racial and ethnic categories around the world and have found intriguing diversity (Weisenberg, 1977).

First, variations in reactions to pain may be related to tolerance (which is highly affected by psychological factors) rather than to threshold (which tends to be the result of physiological factors) (Weisenberg, 1977). Cultural and social differences in pain tolerance appear to be caused by anxiety stemming from certain pain-related attitudes that involve two approaches: (1) the willingness to deny or to avoid dealing with pain and (2) the desire to avoid or eliminate pain at all (if necessary, even before finding out its cause). These cultural attitudes affect psychological functioning and pain experience, pain behaviors, and ways of coping with pain are all influenced by the socialization process (Tursky & Sternbach, 1967). Protestants of British descent, for example, have been found to have a matter-of-fact orientation to pain and tend to adapt faster than any other cultural group to research-induced electric shock. Irish subjects directly inhibit their expressions of suffering and do not show what they are feeling, but instead remain very stoic. Italians, on the other hand, are expressive about pain, complain loudly, and in the laboratory display the highest heart rate in reaction to pain (probably reflecting their anxiety). In clinical situations, Jewish subjects tend to have the lowest heart rate in reaction to pain and are very future oriented, insisting on finding out the significance of their pain for their health (Zborowski, 1969). Researchers have also interviewed chronic pain patients and compared those of Anglo, Latino, and Polish descent living in New

England, and those from Puerto Rico (Bates et al., 1997). In the New England sample, patients tended to hold to a purely biomedical view of the separation of mind and body, leading to higher levels of stress and feelings of alienation as compared with the Puerto Rican sample. The latter held the view that chronic pain is biopsychosocial in nature, and this belief helped patients to experience less stress related to their treatment.

How do cultural factors come to influence such a private, albeit ambiguous, experience as pain? Social learning and social comparison are probably responsible (Weisenberg, 1977). Comparison with other people helps an individual to determine what reactions and expressions are most appropriate. Is it permissible to cry, for example, or to ask for help? Should pain be masked with analgesic medications? An individual's earliest models for appropriate behavior regarding pain are likely to have been members of the family, who provide a particularly potent source of cultural group norms. Parental anxiety, for example, has been found to correlate with (and possibly to cause) children's difficulties in facing painful medical treatments (Bush et al., 1986; Zastowny et al., 1986). The social environment can also influence the meaning of pain to an individual, and reactions to pain can become reinforced independent of the original physiological sensation and tissue damage. In some social and cultural groups, others may attend to a person's wincing. (They ask, "Fred . . . are you in pain? Sit down. What can we do for you?") In other groups, expressions of pain may be completely ignored and ultimately extinguished because they are not reinforced. In some environments, people learn that certain sensations are to be ignored, whereas in others the same sensations demand expressions of great distress. Knowledge of the role of family, cultural, and social influences on pain is critical to effective pain control and therapy.

Culture may also play a role in the utilization of health services for somatization disorders (pain disorders being one of these) (Ford, 1995). In one study of over 13,000 elderly cancer patients living in U.S. nursing homes across the country, ethnicity was a significant predictor of recorded pain levels by staff as well as of patients' own self-reported pain levels (Bernabei et al., 1998). White patients had significantly more episodes of pain expression recorded in their medical charts as compared with nonwhite patients, independent of language difficulties in the reporting; nonwhite patients self-reported higher levels of overall pain. Table 8.1 summarizes the numerous factors

TABLE 8.1 Factors That Affect the Perception and Expression of Pain

Emotional distress including:
  Depression
  Anxiety
	Personality including:
	  Neuroticism
	  Private body consciousness/attentional self-focus
	  Augmenter/reducer
	  Readiness to use pain as a symptom

Perception of control of pain	
Muscular tension and difficulty relaxing	Age
Attention	Sex
Meaning of the pain	Social and cultural background
Expectations	Childhood experiences
Sense of control	

that affect pain perceptions and responses to pain, and Box 8.2 further examines cultural issues and the meaning of pain in a group of international subjects.

BOX 8.2

Across Cultures

Variations in the Meaning of Pain within a Culture

The measurement of pain would be considerably easier if there existed such a device as a "pain-meter," or if one could see a reading of the associated pain along with a picture of tissue damage on a CAT scan. Pain is a subjective, personal, and private experience, however, and nobody can know another's precise feeling of pain. A mother can listen to her child's cries, and a physician can hear a verbal description of pain. But we cannot know that another is in pain unless they communicate it to us or exhibit pain behaviors.

People also attach various meanings to their pain. A person with a sedentary job might consider knee pain just a nuisance, while an aspiring World Cup soccer player might consider it the end of a dream. One woman may get through childbirth with relative ease while another begs for pain medication. One toddler may scream uncontrollably in response to an immunization injection while another barely takes his eyes off his toy. As we have seen in this chapter, the meanings that we attach and the reactions we have to our pain vary considerably by our cultural background.

Some research done in Sweden supports the idea that although pain perceptions and meaning vary across cultures, these phenomena vary within cultures as well. In Sweden, which is a culturally homogeneous country, an individual must have a medical diagnosis in order to be compensated for disability (or what is termed "sick-listed"). One study there interviewed women about the meaning of their pain experience as they suffered from chronic, "undefined" (i.e., undiagnosed) pain (Johansson et al., 1999). Each of these women was of lower-middle class; half were employed full-time, the other half part-time, and all but one had children. Through

analysis of open-ended interviews, the researchers noted four different underlying themes of the women's descriptions of their pain: (1) as a *bodily presentation*; (2) using an *explanatory model*; (3) stating the pain's *consequences for life*; or (4) stating the pain's *consequences for self-perception*.

The *bodily presentation* of pain often signaled a loss of control, and a threat of something wrong internally. One 60-year-old woman stated ". . . I really thought I had some sort of serious neurological disease. I thought I had better pay close attention before I became paralyzed and lost my sense of touch, so that I could commit suicide before I turned into a vegetable" (p. 1795). Such catastrophic thinking portrayed pain as unpredictable, and a kind of invisible enemy.

Women who provided an *explanatory model* for pain tried to explain the root cause of their pain. Explanatory models were generally quite simple and specific, such that pain was described as being work-related, a form of punishment, or as having an origin in the environment or in tensions and worries. One 49-year-old woman stated, "I kind of believe in fate. In a way you want to think that everything has a meaning. And I had these thoughts that I was punished for doing this abortion. I don't think so any longer though; that it was God's punishment that forced me to stop knitting, and weaving, and that my world collapsed" (pp. 1795–1796).

Some women expressed distress at pain's *consequences for life*. They often felt they had let others down, and were unable to attend to their normal chores and raise their children as they had envisioned. One woman felt pain made her irritable and she feared being viewed by her family as complaining and nagging. A 60-year-old grandmother stated, "The pain makes it hard to handle small children. I feel stung, because I know there are people saying that grandchildren are the most wonderful experience on earth. I don't have that feeling. Is that horrible? I don't live up to the ideal grandma." (p. 1796).

Finally, some women described their pain as having *consequences for self-perception*. Many felt their own reputations had been diminished in the eyes of others because they had not received an "official" diagnosis for their pain, and that others viewed them with mistrust because they worked less and needed more assistance in caring

for their families. One woman was denied the opportunity to adopt a child because of her health condition. Several of the women indicated that the pain affected their sexual relationships with their husbands. A 40-year-old wife stated, ". . . It consumes a whole lot of the desire" (p. 1797). Several women openly discussed the effect of having an undiagnosed medical problem on their relationships with their physicians. One 34-year-old woman stated, "I was stressed, but I didn't talk about that with the doctor, he might have considered me a psycho" (p. 1798).

Ways to Measure Pain

Because of the subjective nature of the pain experience, pain can be challenging to measure. Clinicians and researchers have developed many techniques to assess pain, each with its certain advantages and limitations. Measures of pain can be classified into three basic types: (1) psychophysiological measures such as blood pressure, heart rate, and respiration rate; (2) behavioral measures such as observations of pain behaviors (grimacing, moaning, and complaining), and (3) verbal self-report measures such as the patient's written or spoken description of the character and intensity of the pain. The latter are usually relied upon most heavily by clinicians.

Psychophysiological measures assess pain as it is reflected in changes produced in an individual's physiological activity (Lykken, 1987). One measure is the **electromyograph** or EMG that records electrical activity in muscles, assessing their level of tension. Headache patients, for example, demonstrate different EMG patterns when they are having headaches than when they are not (Blanchard & Andrasik, 1985). **Autonomic activity** such as heart rate, respiration rate, blood pressure, and skin conductance are used to assess generalized arousal (which may be the result of reactions to the pain or to other stimuli). Measures of autonomic activity are believed to be most useful in assessing the emotional components of pain (Chapman et al., 1985). The **electroencephalograph** (EEG) measures electrical changes in the brain; pain stimuli produce **evoked potentials** that correlate with subjective reports of pain. EEG responses increase with the intense stimulation of pain and decrease when subjects take analgesic (pain-reducing) medication (Chapman et al., 1985).

Behavioral measures of pain involve observation of a patient in both daily activities and structured clinical situations as they express pain behaviors. These involve, as we have seen, nonverbal expressions (including facial and vocal cues), distortions in movement and posture, irritability, and restrictions of activity. Measurement of pain might involve recording the amount of time spent in bed due to pain, the number of complaints the person expresses, or the extent to which the person is cautious and hesitant while bending. Individuals who live with pain patients, particularly spouses, are often the best people to make these assessments (Fordyce, 1976). A spouse might, for example, keep a pain diary for the patient and record episodes of pain expression. Such a diary might facilitate discussion of the thoughts and feelings of the patient and spouse, as well as an assessment of the effectiveness of treatments to control the pain.

Self-report measures of pain are relied upon most by clinicians and the lay public. Verbal reports depend upon the individual's verbal (or written) description of the character and intensity of the pain he or she experiences (see Figure 8.2). Self-report measures can take the form of interviews (in which pain is described verbally), rating scales (which ask the patient to quantify his or her pain level), and questionnaires (which ask about many aspects of pain including its emotional components). Interviews about pain with a patient and his or her family can be very informative and can tell a clinician a great deal about the patient's pain behaviors and how they affect the other members of the household. Rating scales provide very direct measures of pain intensity, and involve having the individual rate his or her discomfort on a numerical scale. The person might choose a number from one (meaning "nonexistent" pain) to ten (meaning "excruciating" pain). Or, a person might choose a label for his or her pain ranging in increasing intensity from "mild" to "distressing" to "intense," to "excruciating." Rating scales are useful for pain sufferers to record their pain levels at various

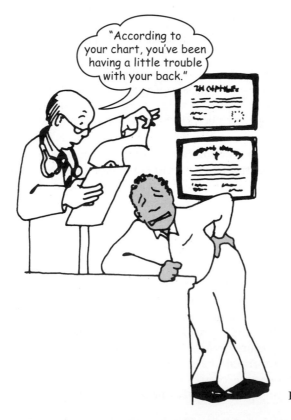

FIGURE 8.2   **Pain behavior.**

times of the day and to examine fluctuations in pain intensity as they relate to various activities and states of mind. Repeated ratings can also point out to the pain patient and his or her family that pain is not constant, but may vary a great deal depending upon circumstances (Turk et al., 1983).

The experience of pain depends, of course, not only on intensity but also on its character, quality, and how it affects a person emotionally. In an effort to characterize pain completely, Melzack and Torgerson (1971) divided 102 "pain-describing terms" into three classes: (1) sensory quality descriptors (for example, "spreading," "crushing," "burning"); (2) affective quality descriptors (such as "exhausting," "awful," "nauseating"); and (3) evaluative descriptors of the intensity of the experience (such as "agonizing," "excruciating," and "miserable"). The sensory and affective components of pain are not merely summated, but rather are combined in a unique weighting (Fernandez & Milburn, 1994). The McGill Pain Questionnaire provides a method for assessing, through self-report, a patient's subjective experience of the sensory, affective, and evaluative quality of pain (Melzack, 1983). This measure asks the individual to select the words that best describe the pain he or she feels from 20 subclasses. Each word in each class has an assigned value based on the degree of pain it reflects. The sum of points across the 20 subclasses is called the pain rating index, and several dimensions of pain can be assessed at once. The questionnaire requires fine distinctions among words in English, however, and may be very difficult for people from other cultural groups and those who have limited vocabulary. Another common self-report measure of physical pain is the West Haven-Yale Multiphasic Pain Inventory (WHYMPI; Kerns et al., 1985), which includes assessments of the impact of pain on the patient's life, the ways that others respond to the patient's pain, and the degree to which the patient can carry out everyday activities. There are other self-report measures of the pain experience, including the Multidimensional Pain Inventory (MPI) and the Pain Behavior Check List (PBCL). Each of these self-report measures provides a slightly different "picture" of pain, and no single measure provides a complete record of an individual's pain experience.

The Significance of Pain Assessment

Lacking words to describe the character of pain, an individual may be able to say only that something hurts. But, *how* something hurts can give important clues to what may be causing the pain in the first place. Consider, for example, a headache. Not all headaches are alike. Two that are quite different from one another are the **muscle contraction (or tension-type) headache** and the **migraine (or vascular) headache** (Blanchard & Andrasik, 1985). Tension-type headaches usually produce dull, persistent aches; spots that are sore and tender on the head, neck, and jaw; and feelings of tightness around the head. Sometimes the patient describes the pain as being like "a stake or a knife in my head." The patient often describes the pain as severe, constant, and unrelenting. Headache of a vascular nature is caused by dilation of the cranial blood vessels. Migraine pain is described as unilateral or bilateral "aching" or "throbbing" pain. The migraine headache often brings prodromal symptoms that include nausea, vomiting, sensitivity to light and noise, and sensory disturbances. It is possible for migraine headache and tension-type headache to co-occur. In the rare cases in which head pain is caused by a tumor, the patient may find the pain to be most severe when he or she awakens. And if bleeding inside the cranium causes headache, such as in cerebral hemorrhage, there may be accompanying neurological deficits such as muscle weakness and perceptual disturbances.

A detailed description of headache pain is essential to its medical diagnosis, which in turn will determine the treatment—pharmacological and even psychological methods such as biofeedback for constricting dilated cranial blood vessels in migraine headaches, and pharmacological, psychological, and physical means to relax the muscles involved in tension headaches. Of course, recognition from the patient's description of a possible tumor or cerebral hemorrhage can be essential. Detailed description of headache includes the duration and location of the headache as well as its nature and characteristics, concurrent symptoms, and precipitating factors. Technological measurements of the patient's physiological status may be valuable, but diagnosis of many medical conditions, including headache, requires a clear picture of the character of the patient's subjective pain experience.

Despite the existence of detailed assessment instruments, such as the McGill Pain Questionnaire, clinicians often report that one of the best ways to assess and diagnose a patient's pain experience is to make the simple request: "Tell me about your pain" (Cassell, 1985a). A patient's hypothesis about his or her pain can also be very illuminating. Many years ago, the famous medical educator, Sir William Osler (1899), told medical students that they must listen to the patient because he or she will reveal the diagnosis. Many modern physicians, who have all the most recent technological innovations at their disposal, believe that the patient has the best perspective on his or her illness and that the diagnosis can be revealed in the story that the patient tells about pain (Cassell, 1985a). "I asked a woman with left upper quadrant abdominal pain what she thought the trouble was. (That is a useful question, because patients are frequently correct, and if not, it is a very direct way of finding out what worries them.) She said, 'Well, of course, I know it's heart disease, because my whole family has heart disease. But sometimes, when I think to myself that maybe it isn't heart disease, then I think, well maybe my kidney has a big cyst and it's bumping against my ribs.' Bull's-eye! That was precisely correct" (Cassell, 1985b, p. 31).

How Is Pain Treated?

When Harold got the bad news from the orthopedist, his pain grew even worse. The discomfort in his lower back and the burning sensations down his legs could now be explained. He had a "slipped" or herniated disc in the lumbar region of his spine. The soft, mucoid material in the fibrous disk between two vertebrae had been forced through the disk's torn outer rim and was impinging on spinal nerve routes. The physician believed that this caused his severe back pain.

Harold's back had been hurting badly ever since he tried to pick up a heavy box at work, and as a result he called in sick several times a week and finally stopped going to work altogether. He lay in bed a good portion of each day, watching old movies and reading his favorite science fiction novels. The more he lay there, the weaker he became. Harold filed for workers' compensation, which required certification by a doctor of his disability. Harold visited his family doctor and was referred to an orthopedic surgeon for tests, including a CT scan. The surgeon recommended surgery and Harold didn't argue. He wanted the pain taken away.

But after Harold had his surgery, the pain remained. The doctors were not sure why, but the pain was so bad that Harold could not bear it without narcotic painkillers combined with a good deal of alcohol. He was fully disabled and could not work at all, collecting full compensation from his employer. Harold rarely saw his friends and depended almost solely upon his wife for companionship. Unfortunately, her life was becoming unbearably limited.

Someone suggested that they go to the pain center at the local university hospital. Desperate, Harold and his wife contacted the staff, and they started him on a program of rehabilitation. Within weeks, he was off pain medications and alcohol, and he was moving around despite his discomfort. His pain had not been taken away, but he was learning to manage it using relaxation techniques, biofeedback, exercise, and correct body postures. Harold also began training for a new career that he could manage with his physical limitations.

With Harold's knowledge and consent, his wife was taught to reward him with attention for ignoring his pain, instead of for describing how badly he felt. She interacted with him only when he turned his own attention outward and did not dwell on his discomfort. Consequently, he became more and more involved in outside activities and stopped focusing on his pain. Harold and his wife received support and guidance as they worked hard to achieve their goals. They accomplished the difficult task of relearning on many levels because they were both devoted to each other and to improving their lives. The pain clinic helped Harold and his wife achieve a happier relationship, and Harold again became a productive individual who was able to live a satisfying life.

During the past few decades, various physical and psychological interventions have been developed for treating both chronic and acute pain problems. Successful pain control involves two elements: (1) the elimination of pain or its reduction and (2) increased functioning (in which the individual learns to tolerate his or her pain and, if necessary, to live with it and still have a satisfying and productive life).

Surgical Treatment of Pain

The Western medical model relies almost exclusively on surgery and medication to treat pain. Surgical treatments involve intervention in the transmission of pain impulses to the brain by removing or disconnecting portions of the peripheral nervous system from the spinal cord. Surgical methods are drastic and the least holistic of all approaches. Surgery can produce numbness and sometimes paralysis in the area affected by the nerves; its use is much less common in recent years because effectiveness is relatively low and other problematic consequences are high. If it works, surgical treatment of pain usually has only short-term effectiveness because the transmission of pain impulses is not as specific as was once believed. Blocked nerve pathways are eventually circumvented and new pathways form, bringing pain messages to the brain by new routes (Melzack & Wall, 1982). Despite its ineffectiveness, surgery has even recently been the most expensive approach to the treatment of pain, accounting for up to 20 percent of all treatment costs for pain (Earman et al., 1996).

Drug Treatments

Today, the most common medical treatment for pain involves pain relieving medications, called analgesics, of which there are several types. **Local anesthetics** are quite familiar to anyone who has ever had a tooth repaired. Novocaine and lidocaine, for example, can be applied topically or injected into the site of the pain's origin (for example, skin that is being cut or stitched). Affected nerve cells are prevented from generating pain impulses (Hare & Milano, 1985; Winters, 1985). Local anesthetics work well to block impulses in pain fibers, but they block impulses in motor neurons as well. A dental patient typically has little or no control over areas of the mouth, tongue, lips, and cheeks for several hours after a dental procedure during which he or she received an injection of novocaine.

Sedatives (e.g., barbiturates) and **tranquilizers** (e.g., diazepam) help to depress pain responses by decreasing the transmission of nerve impulses throughout the central nervous system. In doing so, they depress the individual's entire repertoire of responses and bodily functions (Aronoff et al., 1986). These drugs likely do not directly affect pain, but rather reduce patient anxiety and help the patient to sleep, thereby escaping the pain for a while and, with rest, better tolerating the pain when awake. Related medications that tend to help patients who are in pain are **antidepressants** (e.g., tricyclic antidepressants), which work directly by affecting pain-related neurotransmitters and also by reducing the depression that may accompany pain. **Peripherally acting analgesics** are probably the best known of all pain medications. These include aspirin and other over-the-counter nonsteroidal anti-inflammatory (NSAID) medications such as ibuprofen (e.g., Advil, Motrin IB) and naproxin sodium (e.g., Aleve), as well as acetaminophen (e.g., Tylenol). Prescription anti-inflammatory drugs also fall into this category. These drugs work by reducing inflammation at the site of tissue damage and inhibiting the synthesis, in the peripheral nervous system, of neurochemicals that facilitate the transmission of pain impulses (Winters, 1985).

Centrally acting analgesics, also called **narcotics,** are pain-killing medications that work by binding to opiate receptors in the central nervous system (Aronoff et al., 1986). Examples are codeine, morphine, heroin, and methadone. Narcotics are very effective in reducing severe pain and can be taken orally or injected (which results in more potent action) (Winters, 1985). These drugs have tremendous potential to produce tolerance so that a person needs higher and higher doses to achieve the same effect, and they can be addicting (Aronoff et al., 1986).

One drawback of some of the pain medications available (particularly sedatives and centrally acting analgesics) is that they usually dull the person's sensory perceptions, impairing his or her ability to walk, talk, drive a car, and make decisions. The use of pharmacologic agents for hospitalized patients or among those at home during bed rest can be quite successful, at least in the short term, but taking these pain medications can impair everyday functioning.

It has been argued that analgesic medications work mostly by affecting the individual's predisposition to complain about pain (Beecher, 1972). Morphine, for example, is believed to reduce not so much the sensation of pain as the desire to express distress. The patient may feel the pain but remain unconcerned about it. In experimental studies in which laboratory pain is induced in subjects, pain is typically unaffected by morphine and there is no difference between reactions to morphine and to a saline solution. On the other hand, morphine can be very effective for clinical pain (caused by a clinical problem). The explanation for this phenomenon probably has to do with the combined effects of pain and anxiety about pain, limitation, disfigurement, and death. In the laboratory, such anxiety is typically missing because the subject in the pain experiment knows precisely what is causing the pain and when it will end. Reducing pain reactions in the clinical setting requires the reduction of the individual's anxiety, which both morphine and placebos do very well (Beecher, 1972). As we will see later in this chapter, there are other, nonpharmacologic methods for reducing anxiety (e.g., hypnosis, biofeedback) that work very well to treat clinical pain.

There is some controversy about the impact of opioid use on a person's intellectual capacities. In one study, morphine significantly reduced normal intellectual functioning and recall in a small group of hospice cancer patients (Wood et al., 1998). In another study, however, opioid use did not deleteriously affect cognitive functioning and even increased psychomotor speed and sustained attention (perhaps by alleviating the pain) (Haythornthwaite et al., 1998). The first study was done with terminal cancer patients while the second involved noncancer pain patients, a variation that may have also contributed to the vastly different results.

Use of Pain Medications

Under certain circumstances, pharmaceutical interventions can be quite effective in controlling pain. Narcotics are typically administered for a period of time after surgery to reduce or eliminate acute pain, and when the severe acute pain is past and tissue has begun to heal, narcotics may no longer be necessary. For patients with progressive, debilitating, painful diseases such as terminal cancer, narcotic analgesics are valuable and well-accepted approaches to controlling pain and maintaining comfort (Jamison et al., 1994). Issues of addiction may be less relevant for patients suffering from terminal illnesses (Bressler et al., 1991; Paice et al., 1998). Many medical professionals long held the belief that they must withhold high dosages of pain medications such as morphine because of the dangers of addiction (Buck & Paice, 1994; Schug et al., 1991; Tucker, 1990). But research shows that such a fear is largely unfounded. Patients are generally successful in withdrawing from their pain medications when their acute pain subsides, and they do not become addicted to medications that are used to combat severe, acute pain (Citron et al., 1986; Schug et al., 1991).

Narcotics have not typically been viewed as appropriate for the treatment of chronic, noncancer pain because clinicians have been concerned about effectiveness, side effects, tolerance, and addiction. Even pharmacists have apprehensions about stocking and dispensing these drugs; many have concerns about robberies and government regulations (Greenwald & Narcessian, 1999). Some even feel that the use of opioids for the treatment of nonmalignant pain is morally unacceptable. Despite this dim view of opioid therapy for nonmalignant chronic pain, recent studies show that in some cases such therapy may be quite effective. Among patients with various types of chronic pain (including neuropathies and back pain), opioids (morphine and others) have been shown to work well (Jamison et al., 1994; Valentino et al., 1998; Zenz et al., 1992). Patients not only experience less pain, but they are also able to resume some of their daily activities previously curtailed by the pain. In one study, there was little evidence of the development of tolerance over a one-year period (Valentino et al., 1998), and side effects were minimal (and comparable to those that are seen with cancer patients). Thus, even for patients who are not terminally ill, opioid therapy might be a useful addition to the pain control arsenal.

Nonsteroidal anti-inflammatory drugs (NSAIDs) are the most common choices for chronic pain management (Kanner, 1986; Schnitzer, 1998). Of course, NSAIDs have their own negative side effects, such as gastrointestinal and renal toxicities. Recent studies have also shown that for the management of mild to moderate pain from osteroarthritis, NSAIDs don't work well for some patients (particularly females; Walker & Carmody, 1998). Acetaminophen has been found to be just as effective as NSAIDs for many people (Schnitzer, 1998). Another analgesic, tramadol hydrochloride (which has both opioid and nonopioid actions) appeared on the market in 1994 and is useful for patients whose pain is not relieved by acetaminophen and who cannot take NSAIDs for various reasons (Schnitzer, 1998). Some recent studies have suggested that NMDA (N-methyl-D-aspartate) receptor antagonists (e.g., Dextromethorphan) might be effective for alleviating chronic pain by decreasing the rate of firing of neurons in the dorsal horns of the spinal cord, although this approach is not well understood (Mercadante et al., 1998). In general, the use of nonnarcotic medications for relatively severe chronic pain (such as back pain) can be effective if combined with psychological interventions such as those described below.

Oftentimes, patients find the medical encounter regarding the issue of pain to be frustrating and unsatisfying. Many physicians and nurses have particular attitudes and beliefs regarding pain management, and often these are based on incomplete or misinformation. Many are influenced strongly by patient behavior and do not recognize the tremendous variations that exist in patients' expressions of their pain experience. In one study, 191 chronic noncancer pain patients were referred to a multidisciplinary pain clinic (Turk & Okifuji, 1997). The care provided by the physicians, such as prescribing opioid medication, was not influenced by the patient's pain severity, objective physical pathology, or demographics. Rather, the prescribing patterns of physicians were most influenced by how patients expressed their pain. Those who showed the most behavioral manifestations of pain, who were the most distressed, who portrayed the most suffering (through pain behaviors), and who reported the lowest levels of physical functioning received the most pain medication. Upon further statistical analysis, Turk and Okifuji found that the only factor that determined opioid prescription was observed pain behavior of the patient. Regardless of the actual levels of pain that patients claimed to be experiencing, it was the most behaviorally expressive patients who received the most medication. This is a worrisome finding, of course, because some individuals may simply be less expressive than others due to personality factors,

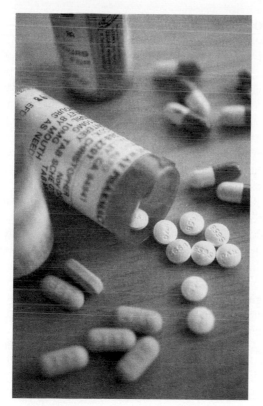

The use of nonnarcotic medication can be effective in controlling chronic pain when combined with psychological interventions.

social upbringing, and cultural factors, and as a result their pain may be treated inadequately or not at all.

Patient-controlled analgesia (PCA) is an effective pain management tool, which, like most pain control issues, is not without controversy. PCA is a method by which a patient has control over the administration of (usually narcotic) medication in accord with his or her own needs, through the use of a pump or other mechanical mechanism. The administration of PCA can be intravenous, subcutaneous, intramuscular, epidural, or oral, and the mechanical "feeder" usually incorporates a lockout period so that the drug can be administered only once within a specified time period (e.g., every 30 minutes) to prevent overdosing. PCA allows the patient to receive medication immediately when the previous dose wears off and enables the patient to titrate his or her dosage according to experienced levels of pain and desire for cognitive clarity. For these reasons, it is associated with both greater safety and greater satisfaction for patients (Schug et al., 1991), as well as faster recovery times (Roseveare et al., 1998). "The most effective pharmacological treatment of acute pain requires the active participation of the patient" (Owen & Plummer, 1997, p. 203). Not every patient, however, wants to play such an active role in his or her pain management (Taylor et al., 1996). Further, some very sick patients may be quite debilitated and unable to remember what to do when they are in pain.

Cognitive Methods of Pain Control

Faulty logic and the emotional distress that can result from it often distorts the reality of the pain that an individual experiences, leading to some serious negative psychological consequences and interference with the individuals' ability to deal effectively with pain. Alteration of damaging cognitions, on the other hand, can facilitate an individual's ability to cope with pain and actually diminish its intensity and distress. Recall that the pain experience is comprised of threshold, perceived intensity, and tolerance. Cognitive strategies to control pain or to react calmly to it may produce differing results depending on whether a patient is trying to raise his or her threshold, reduce perceived intensity, or increase tolerance. One study found a positive effect of "nondirective suggestions" on pain tolerance but there was little or no effect on pain threshold or maximum perceived intensity (Neumann et al., 1997). In this research, simply giving a group of volunteers information about general pain theory and suggestions for coping with pain helped them to better tolerate the experimentally induced pain compared with volunteers who did not receive such information. A meta-analysis (a research technique that combines the effects of several studies) examined 47 studies on the effects of cognitive strategies to control pain. This analysis found that cognitive strategies are indeed effective tools to use. Fernandez and Turk (1989, p. 131) stated that ". . . 85% of investigations showed cognitive strategies to have a positive effect in enhancing pain tolerance/threshold or attenuating pain ratings as compared to no treatment."

Various cognitive errors can interfere with an individual's ability to deal effectively with pain and may contribute to depression (Ciccone & Grzesiak, 1984; Ogden-Niemeyer & Jacobs, 1989). These include (1) *catastrophizing* (overestimating the adverse consequences of the injury), (2) *overgeneralizing* (believing that suffering will endure forever), (3) *low frustration tolerance* (avoiding present discomfort at the expense of long-range objectives), (4) *external locus of control* (believing that one is being operated on by forces beyond one's control), (5) *mislabeling somatic sensations* (interpreting all bodily feelings as pain), (6) *feelings of worthlessness* (feeling diminished role status because of pain), (7) *feelings of having experienced injustice* (feeling unfairly treated by fate), (8) *cognitive rehearsal* (thinking about pain over and over and experiencing it along with a high degree of anxiety). What an individual thinks about his or her chronic pain problem can significantly affect the perception and consequences of that pain. Cognitive appraisal that emphasizes the situation as long term, hopeless, out of the patient's control, and unable to be contended with (as in, "I can't stand it. It is too awful to bear.") can lead to significant distress in the form of anxiety and depression (Ciccone & Grzesiak, 1984). Interference with these negative cognitions and substitution of positive and hopeful thoughts (redefinition) can do much to help a pain patient contend successfully with pain and minimize its intrusiveness in his or her life (Turk et al., 1983). Both anxiety and a lack of control over pain can heighten the severity and intensity of pain; thus, intervention techniques that work with patients to reduce their anxiety and increase their sense of personal control over the pain can be very effective in helping them to cope. When volunteers were provided with information about ways to cope with pain, they actually had higher levels of pain tolerance and less severe physiological responses to pain (Weisenberg et al., 1996).

Diversion of attention (or distraction) from the pain or the source of pain onto a different stimulus also reduces pain experience when pain is mild to moderate, although not as well when it is severe (Eccleston, 1995; Fernandez, 1986). If a person is receiving an injection or a dental treatment, for example, he or she might deal best with the pain by attending to nonthreatening stimuli in the environment (perhaps music playing on headphones) or thinking about a different issue (such as solving a math problem or remembering the words to a popular song). Even for chronic pain patients, engrossing activities such as a movie or interesting reading can provide some pain relief, although more severe pain and higher levels of somatic awareness make the diversion of attention less effective (Eccleston et al., 1997). Simply doing a word distraction task can help low back pain patients to increase their time in and repetitions of exercise without increasing their pain levels (Johnson & Petrie, 1997). Among children, the distracting effect of a toy during a routine venipuncture helped them cope better with the procedure (Vessey et al., 1994). In this research, the children who received a kaleidoscope to play with during the procedure coped better than did those who received attention and physical touch.

A more complex strategy than diversion of attention is the use of nonpain imagery. Discomfort is alleviated by conjuring up a mental scene that is incompatible with the pain (Fernandez, 1986). A person might imagine a scene that is extremely pleasant, such as a beautiful valley in a mountain forest. The individual's task is to imagine visually the sight of the valley, to "smell" the evergreen trees, to "hear" the sounds of birds chirping and leaves rustling in the wind, and to "feel" the freshness of the air. While focusing so much attention on the scene, the individual is less able to attend to the details of the pain experience. Imagery works best for mild to moderate pain and requires considerable involvement and concentration on the part of the patient (Turk et al., 1983).

The use of positive, present-oriented coping self-statements is also an effective method of pain control. Such statements might include "I'm okay," "The pain is manageable," and "I am coping well with this." In one study of low back pain patients who experienced pain produced by physical activity, such statements were highly effective in increasing their range of motion (McCracken et al., 1998). Hoping or catastrophizing, on the other hand, led to greater anticipatory anxiety, greater anxiety during the activity, greater pain, reduced range of motion, and reduced ability to perform activities. Generally, cognitive interventions designed to reduce pain or to increase a person's ability to cope with it can be useful in both inpatient and outpatient situations. Compliance with them tends to be higher and more effective in the former setting, however, suggesting that the expense of an inpatient program may be worthwhile as a long-term cost-cutting tool (Williams et al., 1996).

Box 8.3 describes the way in which other cognitive factors, those related to motivation, can affect pain perceptions such as when pain is "compensated" financially.

BOX **8.3**

Hot Topic

Back Pain and Compensation

Can monetary compensation for pain cause it to persist longer than it otherwise might? Does the fact that a person can stay home from work and still receive income actually interfere with efforts to overcome pain and return to work? Research suggests that the answer is yes.

As we have seen in this chapter, psychological and behavioral factors can influence the maintenance of pain and the limitations that pain places on an individual. A work injury that might otherwise have caused short-term restriction can sometimes become a deeply ingrained, long-term problem when monetary compensation is available. Research shows that people who are eligible for wage replacement funding take significantly more time off from work than do people who are not eligible (Fordyce, 1985). Unfortunately, patients who receive compensation (from private insurance, workers' compensation, or Social Security Disability Insurance [SSDI]) may not be aware that their incentive to get well is being compromised. They may no longer be willing to expend the effort necessary to overcome the debilitating effects of their pain and to return to a productive life.

Back pain is a common example. Back problems account for 27 percent of lost workdays in the United States. The average cost of workers' compensation claims related to back pain caused by injury at work (e.g., from a fall, lifting of a heavy object, or repetitive strain such as at a keyboard) is more than twice the average cost for all other compensable claims (Rizzo et al., 1998). To gain compensation from Social Security Disability Insurance, an individual must be declared by a physician to be totally disabled. These benefits are not intended to go on indefinitely. Once declared disabled, however, most people maintain the label and never get better unless they have a targeted intervention to help them (Fordyce, 1985).

Although insurance claims for low back pain have been decreasing over the past few years (Murphy & Volinn, 1999), a disproportionate amount of money spent on back injuries goes to a small number of individuals who are incapacitated for a long period of time (Hashemi et al., 1998; Williams et al., 1998). Back pain remains a major problem in the United States, with almost 2 percent of workers filing claims annually (Murphy & Volinn, 1999).

Low back pain—in fact, pain itself—does not fit well into a biomedical approach because pain is a biopsychosocial phenomenon. Pain can persist without any evidence of underlying tissue, nerve, or bone damage. A person's experience of pain is identified solely on the basis of self-reports and pain behaviors such as grimacing and stiff or limited movement. Thus, physicians often find themselves in an awkward situation when their patients with low back pain seek certification of injury in order to receive compensation. Even when a physician cannot find anything organically wrong with the patient (which is quite common), he or she often feels compelled to help the individual who displays obvious signs of suffering. Although initially helping the suffering person, however, monetary compensation that is not linked to active participation in rehabilitation might actually interfere with functional recovery (Fordyce, 1985, 1988).

Cognitive-Behavioral Methods of Pain Control

As we examined earlier in this chapter, an individual's thoughts about pain can significantly influence pain perceptions and the impact of pain on his or her life. Negative thoughts about pain can focus attention on unpleasant issues and make the pain feel worse, often by increasing muscle tension (Turk & Rudy, 1986; Turk et al., 1983). Cognitive strategies such as the following can help tremendously: redefinition (or reframing) of the situation, change in the individual's focus of attention, change in the mental images that surround pain, and change in the ways in which thoughts are translated into bodily experience (Fernandez, 1986).

Progressive Relaxation

Relaxation is proving to be an extremely useful intervention for controlling both acute and chronic pain. Researchers have found that muscle tension causes lactic acid buildup in muscles and decreases their blood flow, significantly increasing the experience of pain. Psychologists have developed various techniques of progressive muscle relaxation that work either on one muscle group or on several and can place an individual into an overall state of low arousal (Blanchard et al., 1986). Relaxation can be accomplished by various methods, the simplest of which is to consciously tense and then relax certain muscles, imagining that they are extremely heavy. Simultaneously, the person might empty the mind of all thoughts and focus on one calming image. An important part of the relaxation is deep breathing, as the individual brings his or her body and mind into a state of peace. Progressive relaxation has been used successfully to treat many different types of pain including arthritis, headache (both migraine and tension), and low back pain (Blanchard & Andrasik, 1985). Relaxation is one component (and in fact may be the most important component) in bringing about the analgesic effects of hypnosis (considered below). Relaxation training alone has been found to significantly reduce the pain of chronic tension headaches in many patients (although about 50% of tension headaches do not yield fully to simple relaxation [Blanchard & Andrasik, 1985]). Regardless of the source of pain (e.g., back strain, childbirth, surgery), relaxation does contribute considerably to pain reduction and is even effective in helping children who suffer from migraine headaches. Progressive relaxation and stress management have been found to be more effective than the drug metoprolol in controlling the pain from a migraine headache, and this effect lasted over the eight-month period of the study (Sartory et al., 1998).

Meditation

Meditation is similar to relaxation but incorporates additional elements of focus, particularly on current sensory experience. The technique of mindfulness meditation has been used successfully to alleviate both pain and negative emotional symptoms and involves deep breathing and relaxation. It requires the individual to actually focus on the pain, but with "detached observation," an approach that reduces the emotional distress associated with pain. Reappraisal of the pain and association of it with relaxation have been shown to reduce its impact and to decrease negative feelings and symptoms related to the pain (Kabat-Zinn et al., 1985; Roth & Creaser, 1997). Mindfulness meditation works with many types of pain, and seems to be useful not only in reducing negative effects, but also in fostering positive effects such as heightened activity levels and greater self-esteem (Kabat-Zinn et al., 1985; Roth & Creaser, 1997). In addition, these improvements are long lasting, with continuing levels of pain reduction and positive psychological and physical experiences reported as long as fifteen months later (Kabat-Zinn et al., 1985).

Biofeedback

Biofeedback involves a mechanical system whereby an individual is signaled by means of a light or a buzzer to bring about some particular behavior (usually quite subtle) in his or her body. For example, tension in the frontalis muscle in the forehead, the amount of blood flow to the extremities, or the temperature of the skin might be measured with electrodes attached to those parts of the body. Biofeedback that measures muscle tension is called **EMG biofeedback.** EMG stands for electromyogram, a measure of the electrical charge of the muscles. **Thermal biofeedback**, on the other hand, measures temperature and blood flow. Biofeedback works on the principles of classical conditioning and teaches people to be aware of their bodily processes and to alter these consciously. It is a very effective treatment with some kinds of pain. For example, using thermal biofeedback, migraine headache sufferers can learn to bring blood to their hands ("hand warming"), thus reducing cranial blood flow (blood flow to the head) and the pain that is caused by dilated cranial blood vessels. Biofeedback relaxation therapy works as well as medication to reduce migraine headache (Holroyd & Penzien, 1990). Patients whose tension headache pain is caused by chronically tensed muscles in the head and neck and jaw can be taught to reduce this tension using EMG biofeedback (Blanchard & Epstein, 1977). Although biofeedback may be used in a very specific way to deal with a specific pain problem, the power of biofeedback can be quite general as well. Using biofeedback, people have been taught to activate their parasympathetic nervous system (which produces relaxation in response to the activation of the sympathetic nervous system during periods of stress, fear, or anxiety).

How well does biofeedback work? Is it more effective than other, less complicated and less expensive techniques? Some research suggests that simple relaxation techniques may work just as well as EMG biofeedback in achieving muscle relaxation (Blanchard et al., 1982; Bush et al., 1985). This issue is still debated, however. Some people who use biofeedback report decreased headache pain regardless of whether they receive feedback for raising, lowering, or producing no change in their forehead muscle tension. This suggests that just the fact of using the biofeedback technique and focusing on muscle tension and relaxation may contribute to improvement. Furthermore, at the end of their biofeedback training, people usually need to be "weaned off" the electronic biofeedback equipment and learn to associate the desired states with other cues. Relaxation techniques are much less expensive than biofeedback; they can be used anywhere and are available to anyone who will practice them.

Hypnosis

Hypnosis is a very old technique that was used as early as the nineteenth century for pain control during surgery (Hilgard & Hilgard, 1975). It has received substantial research interest in the past twenty years (Margolis, 1997; Tan & Leucht, 1997), although clinical interest in hypnosis within the medical profession waxes and wanes

(Chaves & Dworkin, 1997). Hypnosis is an altered state of consciousness which involves several components: (1) relaxation; (2) distraction (the diversion of attention from the pain—also referred to as "narrowing of attention"), and (3) suggestion (that the pain has diminished and is replaced by a more pleasant sensation such as warmth). Hypnosis can also include the attachment of a meaning, other than threat, to the pain (Barber, 1986). Hypnosis can be very helpful in pain relief, although researchers have been unsure of whether hypnosis actually blocks pain or simply interferes with the reporting of it. In hypnosis for pain control, a suggestion of analgesia to the patient (that he or she does not feel any pain) has been shown to be a critically important ingredient. Without it, hypnotized people have reported as much pain as did those who were not hypnotized (Hilgard, 1978). Under hypnosis with a hypnotic suggestion of analgesia people have still shown the classic physiological reactions to painful stimuli such as changes in respiration and increased heart rate and blood pressure (Orne, 1989). They have tended to show no behavioral signs of pain (such as grimacing and tensing their muscles), however, and they have verbally reported feeling no discomfort (Hilgard & Hilgard, 1975). Although they may continue to recognize that they are in pain (say, by writing down their evaluation of the pain), individuals under hypnosis often indicate that the pain is not affecting them and does not matter to them at all.

One recent study attempted to separate the affective and sensory components of pain in an effort to understand how the process of hypnosis might differentially affect these components (Rainville et al., 1999). These researchers hypnotized their subjects and then induced pain experimentally. In some cases the focus was on hypnotically manipulating the affective component of pain (unpleasantness), while in other cases the focus was on altering the actual sensation of pain (intensity). It was found that hypnosis could be used effectively to lessen both aspects of pain. When the focus was on making the pain experience less unpleasant, hypnosis helped to accomplish this, and the decrease in unpleasantness was independent of variations in intensity. When hypnosis was focused on decreasing the intensity of the pain, that goal was accomplished and a decrease in unpleasantness generally followed. Hypnosis can be used to control both the affective and the physiological components of pain, depending on the type of instructions that the hypnotized individual receives (Rainville et al., 1999).

Contrary to popular fears, people under hypnosis will not carry out actions they would not normally do (such as things to which they are morally opposed). They often can do things they would like to do, however, including things they did not realize were possible for them, such as remaining completely calm during a medical procedure. Researchers such as Barber (1982) suggest that hypnosis may not be due to a trance state at all, but rather to very powerful suggestions for comfort, anxiety reduction, and well-being.

In summary, strong evidence, some of it from laboratory and case studies and some from clinical experimentation, suggests that hypnosis can be used very successfully in the control of pain (Barber, 1982; Sellick & Zaza, 1998). Precisely which people and what kinds of pain problems benefit most from hypnosis has yet to be determined, although there is promising evidence that a variety of painful medical situations, such as invasive procedures (Lang et al., 2000) and long-term cancer pain (Sellick & Zaza, 1998) can be reduced with hypnosis. Hypnosis does not work for everyone, however. In fact, there are significant individual differences in susceptibility to hypnosis and a complete understanding of the hypnotic state has not yet been achieved.

Behavior Modification in Chronic Pain

As we have seen, patients in pain may signal their experience in a variety of ways. They might verbally describe the location, quality, and intensity of the pain; they might sigh, moan, limp, grimace, or massage the painful area. Their behavior serves as a signal to the social environment that they are in pain, and this signal typically elicits some response from others. Pain behavior serves many purposes. "Behavior may elicit medication from the physician, indicate to the spouse that sex is out of the question, or communicate to the boss that the person cannot perform the job effectively." (Pinkerton et al., 1982, p. 264). When an individual's pain is long-term and chronic, pain behaviors can come to manipulate the environment in such a way as to become a disadvantage to the patient. Chronic pain is not an event, but rather a state of existence, and the suffering patient may be limited to bearing the pain and trying to live as normal a life as possible. In the presence of consistent pain behaviors, however, other people may pity the patient, make excuses for him or her, or expect little. Some may even become suspicious that the patient is malingering. With vastly limited behavioral options, an individual may become hopeless and despairing, and the patient's self-concept may eventually become distorted (Ogden-Niemeyer & Jacobs, 1989). The patient may underestimate his or her abilities and overestimate limitations. For example, the patient may state that it is impossible to sit for more than twenty minutes without pain medication, but he or she might go without pain medication for hours if involved in something that is very interesting.

Some researchers and clinicians approach the control of chronic pain as a problem requiring operant conditioning (Sanders, 1996). Remember from Chapter 6 that operant methods involve rewarding behaviors that one wishes to enhance and ignoring or punishing behaviors that one wants to eliminate or extinguish. The **operant method of pain control** approaches the problem of chronic pain by emphasizing the role of environmental factors and by rewarding behaviors one wishes to enhance (such as moving) and ignoring behaviors one wishes to extinguish (such as grimacing). Pain behaviors, although initially "respondents" (behaviors in response) to sensations of discomfort, can quickly become operant behaviors that trigger direct positive reinforcement (such as affection), or negative reinforcement (such as "time out" from aversive activities). Pain behaviors can come to have very high reward value, bringing attention, sympathy, and relief from social and work obligations. When this occurs, there may be little or no reinforcement for "well behaviors" and the individual's entire behavioral repertoire becomes one of pain expression (Roberts, 1986).

The value of behavioral methods is well illustrated by the case of a woman who had experienced constant low back pain for twenty years. She had four different surgical operations; medical evaluation revealed no neurological damage, but normal day-to-day activities were becoming increasingly difficult for her. A treatment was designed that involved taking pain-relieving medication on a timed schedule rather than when she experienced or complained of pain. In addition, with her consent her family was taught to give her attention and praise for increasing her activities, and for well (non-pain) behaviors such as walking. The family (and hospital staff where she was treated on an inpatient basis) ignored such behaviors as moaning and grimacing. The patient was provided with programmed rest periods as rewards for greater involvement in physical and occupational therapy. After three weeks of inpatient and twenty-two weeks of outpatient treatment, she could remain physically active for up to two hours at a time without needing rest or complaining of pain and without pain medications. After having been almost totally disabled, this patient was walking further and faster than she had ever been able to before, and in many areas of her life she was functioning well (Pinkerton et al., 1982).

Physical Therapies for Pain

The principle of **counterirritation** is an important basis for the several physical therapies currently available for the treatment of pain. One form of discomfort can minimize or cancel out another (Melzack & Wall, 1982). For example, one might vigorously rub the site of an injection in an effort to override the pain caused by the needle. Counterirritation can relieve pain by diverting the individual's attention away from it. Furthermore, signals of counterirritation carried by the peripheral fibers can "close the pain gate" and inhibit the transmission of the primary pain signals to the brain.

The Gate Control Theory of pain explains the effectiveness of a pain control technique called **transcutaneous electrical nerve stimulation** or TENS, which is very effective in reducing pain in many patients (Chabal et al., 1998). TENS involves the placing of electrodes on the skin near where the patient feels pain and sending a mild electrical current supplied by a portable device that looks like a small tape recorder; the electrical stimulation of the peripheral nerves interferes with the transmission of pain signals to the brain. The long-term impact of TENS has been found to be highly effective and cost efficient, with up to a 55 percent decrease in medication use a 69 percent reduction in physical therapy use (Chabal et al., 1998).

Acupuncture is an ancient Chinese pain control technique. Fine metal needles are inserted under the skin and twirled or electrically charged to create stimulation to the peripheral nerves believed to be associated with distally located parts of the body (Melzack & Wall, 1982). For example, points on the foot might be associated with internal organs such as the kidneys. Acupuncture can work to provide such high levels of analgesia that in some cases people have undergone major surgery with only acupuncture for pain control (Melzack, 1973), and many studies show that acupuncture is effective in controlling pain while having few, if any, side effects (Berman et al., 1999; Ceniceros & Brown, 1998; Leng, 1999). Not all studies find acupuncture to be superior to a placebo, however (Ernst & White, 1998; Shlay et al., 1998; Volmink et al., 1996; White & Ernst, 1999). It is possible that the acupuncture procedure may interact in important ways with various personal characteristics or illness/pain characteristics to make it effective for some people in some domains of pain. More empirical research is needed in this area before a conclusion can be drawn.

What are the possible mechanisms through which acupuncture might affect pain? First, it is possible that needle insertion and movement might stimulate peripheral nerve fibers and thereby close the pain gate. Perhaps when patients believe acupuncture will work, it functions as an effective placebo. Acupuncture may also reduce pain by distracting the individual, or it may trigger the release of endorphins that in turn reduce the experience of pain.

Physical therapy involves a variety of approaches to help patients who suffer from both acute and chronic pain. One example of this approach is water exercise to help an arthritis patient maintain joint flexibility (Wickersham, 1984). Exercise is extremely helpful for back pain patients who need to maintain flexibility and develop strength in key muscles to provide support for their spines and joints. As part of an exercise program, patients are typically taught body mechanics and proper posture to prevent further injuries. Deep muscle massage and the application of heat and cold are also used quite effectively to treat chronic pain conditions such as back pain and tension headaches (Hare & Milano, 1985).

Which approach to **pain control** works best? The answer depends upon what the outcome of interest happens to be. In a study comparing the effectiveness of cognitive-behavioral treatments and physical therapy for pain control among patients with back pain, researchers found that their subjects in chronic pain benefited from both approaches (Heinrich et al., 1985). Improvements were greatest in physical functioning among the patients who received physical therapy. Psychosocial adjustment was better among patients who received the cognitive-behavioral intervention. Of course, in practice the application of several modalities of treatment may serve patients very well, helping to reduce their pain and improve their lives.

Formal fitness programs are also promising treatments for chronic pain. One study compared a group of back pain patients who attended a formal exercise fitness program to a group of patients who practiced exercise at home. Formal exercise reduced pain and disability by about 8 percent, whereas home exercise had a reduction of only 3 percent (Frost et al., 1998). These positive effects of formal exercise on chronic low back pain were evident up to two years after the initial intervention.

A combination of cognitive, behavioral, and physical therapies seems to be the most beneficial for many pain patients. Helping a patient to think about his or her pain differently, changing typical pain behaviors, and increasing physical movement may help to diminish a patient's feelings of "pain helplessness" and increase his or her physical endurance (Burns et al., 1998).

Preoperative Treatments for Postoperative Pain

Another important issue in the control of pain involves what occurs following a surgical procedure. Postoperative pain of various intensities, durations, and qualities can be expected to occur, and being able to control this pain is very important to the recovery of the patient. A patient who has undergone knee surgery, for instance, needs to be active within a few days to maintain muscle tone and to recover from the trauma. Too

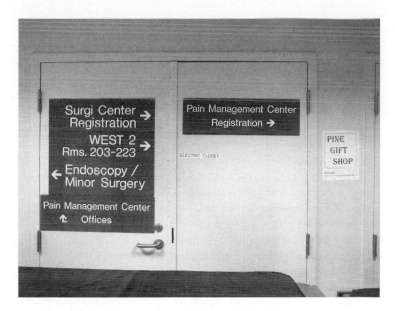

The best pain management centers provide therapies that combine behavioral, cognitive, physical, and analgesic approaches to pain control.

much pain will likely lead the patient to limit his or her activity. New research suggests that treating pain preoperatively, with relaxation training prior to surgery and helping the patient to prepare mentally for the upcoming pain, reduces both long-term levels of analgesic use and reports of pain by patients (Manyande & Salmon, 1998). Related to this is the general issue of patient control in the delivery of pain medication. A recent study showed that when colonoscopy patients were allowed to control their own pain and sedation during the procedure, they sedated themselves less, tolerated higher levels of pain, had smaller decreases in systolic blood pressure, and recovered four times faster than patients who were treated in the conventional manner in which pain medication was controlled by the health professional (Roseveare et al., 1998). Giving patients adequate preparation and more control leads to better post-surgical outcomes.

Pain Clinics: Multidimensional Treatment Programs

The most effective current pain treatments involve a combination of behavioral, cognitive, physical, and analgesic approaches to pain (Coughlin et al., 2000; Ogden-Niemeyer & Jacobs, 1989). Particularly in the realm of pain control, operant learning, such as described in the behavioral treatments above, needs to be combined with cognitive awareness for long-term change to take place. On a practical level, exercise is incorporated in an effort to increase physical mobility and flexibility and to assist in the release of endogenous endorphins for the effective masking of pain. The judicious use of analgesics is also a part of a multifaceted approach to pain. The goals of interdisciplinary pain programs involve not only reducing the patients' experiences of pain but also decreasing their use of medications, improving daily functioning, and improving psychological and social well-being.

Pain clinics can be quite effective in achieving these stated goals. While they do vary in quality, multidisciplinary programs that incorporate the various approaches considered above tend to have the highest rates of success (Newman & Seres, 1986). Various pain clinics around the country report that as many as 75 to 90 percent of their chronic low back pain patients experience significant improvement in activity levels and reduction in use of pain medication after participating in a multifaceted treatment program. Many go through vocational retraining programs and significantly improve their lives (Ogden-Niemeyer & Jacobs, 1989). Careful screening of candidates is essential, however. Individuals who repress their emotions and those who are highly anxious tend to fare relatively poorly in such programs (Burns, 2000). Those who deny negative affect tend to resist treatment, and those who are highly anxious tend to become more anxious still in response to the pace of exercise and other activities. Program modification may be necessary for such patients.

The field of pain is a dynamic, fast moving area of research. Health professionals must keep up with ever-changing treatment recommendations in order to provide their patients with the newest options for care. With the latest treatments, people who once would have been totally debilitated by pain have the chance to live enjoyable, productive, and fulfilling lives.

Summary

1. Pain is defined as (1) an unpleasant sensory and emotional experience associated with actual or potential tissue damage; (2) a total experience of some noxious stimulus; or (3) a psychological experience that includes a personal, private sensation of hurt. Nociception is mechanical, thermal, or chemical energy impinging on specialized nerve endings that activate nerve fibers and initiate a signal to the central nervous system. Pain can result from nociception or occur in its absence. Nociception can occur without any resulting pain.

2. Pain is an extremely salient phenomenon in human life and has important economic consequences. It is the symptom most likely to bring a person to seek medical care. People fear the possibility of suffering intractable pain.

3. Several theories of pain exist.

   - Specificity Theory posits specific receptors in the skin that respond to a particular kind of stimulus, specific routes of transmission in the central nervous system, and special centers in the brain that register and interpret (only) pain.
   - Pattern Theory holds that pain results from the patterning and quality of stimulation from peripheral nerve endings.
   - Affect Theory posits that emotions color perceptions of pain and sensory events.
   - Gate Control Theory acknowledges specificity in pain transmission as well as patterning and summation of impulses. It also allows for the role of psychological processes in the pain experience and its control.
   - Neuromatrix Theory posits that everyone has an innate, genetically prescribed neural network uniquely modified through pain experiences. The unique patterns that come to be associated with particular sensory inputs are

called "neurosignatures" and each has associated cognitive and emotional meaning. The pain neuromatrix can be activated through means other than nociception.

4. Pain can be experienced in different ways and with differing intensities. Pain is a subjective experience, felt only by the person in pain.

   - Threshold refers to the point at which a person first perceives stimulation as painful; it appears to be determined mainly by physiological factors.
   - Tolerance refers to the point at which the individual is not willing to accept stimulation of a higher magnitude; it is influenced by psychological variables.
   - Measures of pain can be classified into three basic types: (a) psychophysiological measures such as blood pressure and heart rate; (b) behavioral measures that involve observations of pain behaviors such as grimacing, moaning, and complaining; and (c) verbal self-report measures, which involve the patient's written or spoken descriptions of the character and intensity of the pain.
   - A detailed description of pain can be essential to its medical diagnosis, and necessarily includes the duration and location of the pain as well as its nature and characteristics, concurrent symptoms, and precipitating factors.
   - Medical professionals make an important distinction between acute and chronic pain. Acute pain is temporary and lasts less than six months; chronic pain lasts more than six months and can be intermittent or constant, mild or severe.

5. Psychological factors affect pain. The meaning attached to pain partly determines how it is perceived and experienced, as well as how it is reacted to. Pain is also affected by the setting in which tissue damage occurs and what the person thinks about it. Expectations can also significantly influence pain.

   - Pain perceptions depend upon age, sex, social and cultural background, and personality type of the individual. Pain tolerance appears to vary with the individual's attitudes about pain and his or her anxiety about pain.

6. There are many methods for treating pain.

   - Surgical methods represent a drastic approach. Nerve resection or removal may not be successful because recent evidence suggests that blocked nerve pathways are eventually circumvented to carry pain messages to the brain.
   - Today, the most common medical treatment for pain involves pain relieving medications, of which there are several types: local anesthetics, peripherally acting analgesics, centrally acting analgesics, and sedatives or tranquilizers.
   - Narcotics are typically not appropriate for the treatment of chronic pain because they have high addiction potential. They are appropriate for the treatment of short-term severe acute pain and the pain of terminal illness.
   - Cognitive methods for the treatment of pain have been found to be very successful: (a) Altering interpretations of pain can significantly affect the perception and consequences of that pain; (b) the diversion of one's attention from the pain or the source of pain onto a different stimulus can help reduce the perception of pain; (c) the use of nonpain imagery can help reduce pain.

- Progressive relaxation is an extremely useful intervention for controlling both acute and chronic pain. Biofeedback involves a mechanical system whereby an individual is signaled by means of a light or a buzzer to bring about relaxation in a particular set of muscles.
- Hypnosis is an important psychological technique that aids in the control of (particularly acute) pain.
- Behavior modification/operant conditioning to change pain behaviors is another successful approach.
- Physical therapies for pain are based upon the principle of counterirritation. These methods include transcutaneous electrical nerve stimulation, deep muscle massage, acupuncture, and traditional physical therapy, as well as the application of heat and cold.
- The most effective current pain treatments involve a combination of behavioral, cognitive, physical, and analgesic approaches to pain.

THINKING CRITICALLY

1. If you were a health psychologist and a physician referred a patient in need of help for pain with no apparent organic cause, what would you do? What are some of the psychosocial mechanisms that might be at work in this patient's situation? How could you begin to help this patient?

2. Of the pain theories discussed in this chapter, which do you find the most reasonable given your own pain experience or that of people you know? What are the strengths and weaknesses of this approach?

3. Pain threshold and pain tolerance are not the same thing. Would it be possible for someone to have a very low threshold but high tolerance? Vice versa? What underlying mechanisms might make this happen? How might personality characteristics play a role? Social and cultural norms? Previous experiences?

GLOSSARY

Acupuncture: An ancient Chinese pain control technique in which fine metal needles are inserted under the skin to create stimulation to the peripheral nerves.

Acute pain: Pain that lasts less than six months and eventually ends.

Affect Theory of Pain: States that pain has a negative quality that drives action, and the physiological effects of a stimulus are accompanied by motivation and affect.

Anticipatory anxiety: Anxiety produced from the anticipation of an event.

Antidepressants: Medications used in pain control that also reduce the depression that can accompany pain.

Anxiety: Inability to relax; feeling worried, tense, or anxious.

Augmenters: Individuals who characteristically perceive greater environmental stimulation than average (also called sensitizers).

Autonomic activity: A measure of general physiological arousal (such as heart rate, blood pressure, and respiration rate).

Behavioral measures of pain: Measures that involve observations of pain behaviors (such as grimacing, moaning), verbal self-reports, and complaining about pain.

Biofeedback: A system involving signals with a light or buzzer to bring about alteration of bodily state; works on the principles of classical conditioning.

Causalgia: Severe burning pain that sometimes results after a wound has healed and damaged nerves have regenerated.

Centrally acting analgesics: Narcotics such as codeine and morphine that bind to opiate receptors in the central nervous system. Narcotics are effective in reducing pain but they impair sensory and motor functioning and have high addiction potential.

Chronic intractable benign pain: Pain that is present all the time but is not related to any progressive condition.

Chronic pain: Pain that lasts longer than six months.

Chronic progressive pain: Pain that becomes progressively more intense as the condition associated with it worsens.

Chronic recurrent pain: Pain characterized by intense episodes of discomfort followed by relief.

Counterirritation: Basis for several physical therapies for pain; involves a form of discomfort to "close the pain gate" to transmission of the original pain signal, or to divert attention.

Distraction: Turning attention away from pain by focusing on something else.

Electroencephalograph (EEG): Tool to assess electrical changes in the brain.

Electromyograph (EMG): Instrument that measures the electrical activity in muscles.

EMG biofeedback: Biofeedback that measures muscle tension, such as tension in the frontalis muscle in the head that can cause headache.

Endogenous opioids: Opiate like substances produced within the body and released in stressful circumstances; they regulate pain and operate like exogenous opioids such as the drugs heroin and morphine by producing pain analgesia and feelings of well-being. The three main types are beta-endorphin, proenkephalin, and prodynorphin.

Evoked potentials: The electrical brain activity caused by painful stimuli.

Gate Control Theory of Pain: Acknowledges specificity in pain transmission as well as patterning and the summation of impulses; allows for psychological processes in pain experience and control; a valuable theory in terms of its clinical applications.

Hypnosis: An important, and very old, psychological technique that aids in the control of (particularly acute) pain; involves relaxation, distraction, and suggestion.

Intractable pain: Pain that cannot be relieved.

Local anesthetics: Chemicals (e.g., novocaine, lidocaine) that, when applied topically or injected under the skin, prevent nerve cells from generating pain impulses.

Migraine headache: Headache that results from dilation of cranial blood vessels; described as unilateral or bilateral aching or throbbing pain; prodromal symptoms include nausea, vomiting, sensitivity to light and noise, and sensory disturbances.

Muscle contraction headache: Headache that manifests in dull, persistent aching, sore and tender spots on the head and neck and jaw, and a feeling of tightness around the head; patient may describe the pain as being like "a stake or a knife in my head," and the pain as severe, constant, and unrelenting.

Narcotics: *See* centrally acting analgesics.

Neuralgia: A painful condition that is characterized by the absence of apparent tissue damage but in which pain can be provoked by minimal stimulation.

Neuromatrix Theory of Pain: Describes a unique, innate, genetically prescribed neural network (called the "neuromatrix") that is modified through experiences with pain; the "neuromatrix" imparts a unique pattern ("neurosignature") on all sensory inputs to the body, giving experience an affective and cognitive meaning.

Nociception: Mechanical, thermal, or chemical energy impinging on specialized nerve endings that in turn activate A delta and C fibers, initiating a signal to the central nervous system that aversive events are occurring. Nociception can be assessed as activity in certain nerve fibers and their synaptic connections.

Nociceptors: The afferent nerve endings that respond to pain stimuli.

Operant method of pain control: Method that involves rewarding behaviors to enhance, and ignoring or punishing behaviors to eliminate or extinguish. An operant approach to the problem of chronic pain emphasizes the role of environmental factors.

Pain: An unpleasant sensory and emotional experience associated with actual or potential tissue damage; involves the total experience of a noxious stimulus influenced by current context, previous experiences, learning history, and cognitive processes.

Pain behavior: Actions or signals that people emit when they are in pain.

Pain control: Efforts to eliminate pain or reduce it; the goal is to bring an individual to tolerate pain, or to live with it and still have a satisfying and productive life.

Patient-controlled analgesia (PCA): A method that allows patient control over the administration of pain medication using electronic monitoring systems.

Pattern Theory of Pain: Holds that pain results from the patterning and quality of stimulation from peripheral nerve endings; holds that sensations can summate.

Peripherally acting analgesics: Pain control medications taken internally that work by reducing inflammation at the site of tissue damage and inhibiting the synthesis of neurochemicals that facilitate peripheral transmission of pain impulses.

Phantom limb pain: Pain felt "in" an amputated limb.

Physical therapy: A variety of measures to help the pain patient maintain flexibility and develop strength in key muscles and learn proper body posture and movement.

Placebo: An inert substance (such as a sugar pill) used as a control in randomized clinical trials to compare with an active substance in evaluating therapeutic effect.

Placebo control group: In research, the incorporation of a special control group (in addition to the experimental group) to test the success of a new drug or therapy beyond that which would be expected from a placebo.

Psychophysiological measures of pain: Assessments of physical processes such as blood pressure and heart rate that typically increase in response to pain.

Reducers: Individuals who tend to reduce or minimize environmental stimulation and deny or avoid it.

Referred pain: Pain that originates in tissue in one part of the body but is perceived as coming from another part.

Relaxation: Techniques that place an individual into an overall state of low arousal; usually extremely useful for controlling both acute and chronic pain.

Sedatives: Medications that control pain by depressing the individual's responses, reducing anxiety, and helping the patient to sleep.

Self-report measures of pain: Pencil-paper questionnaires or verbal reports, made by a patient, that rely upon a description of the character and intensity of pain.

Sense of control: A feeling that one is able to effect change or exert control. .

Somatic: A term meaning "bodily."

Specificity Theory of Pain: Theory that a specific bodily system is responsible for pain perception independent of perceptions of heat, cold, or touch; specific routes of transmission in the central nervous system and centers in the brain are proposed.

Thermal biofeedback: Biofeedback measuring blood flow to parts of the body.

Threshold: The point at which a person first perceives a stimulus as painful.

Tolerance: The point at which the individual is not willing to accept stimulation of a higher magnitude.

Tranquilizers: *See* sedatives.

Transcutaneous electrical nerve stimulation (TENS): A physical therapy for pain that involves placing electrodes near where the patient feels pain and sending a mild electrical current that interferes with transmission of pain signals to the brain.

Vascular headache: *See* migraine headache.

Zero control group: In a randomized controlled trial, a control group that receives no treatment and no placebo.

CHAPTER

9 Psychological Processes, Stress, and Illness

Atul was having a difficult time. No matter how hard he tried, he just could not seem to get his life in order and running smoothly. He was in his last semester of college, and there seemed to be only a remote possibility of finding a job in the field of study he chose. His three-year relationship with his girlfriend was troubled, and they were growing further apart and considering breaking up. Atul was failing two of his final courses because he couldn't concentrate on his work, and he was sleeping very poorly at night. He tried to cure his insomnia by drinking beer, channel surfing, and watching infomercials. This added to his problems, of course, because alcohol and the stimulation of TV interfere with sleep. Furthermore, Atul charged over $700 of infomercial merchandise on his credit card and he didn't have the money to pay the bill. Stress and fatigue made him more prone to cold sores, and these breakouts added to his embarrassment and insecurity. All of these problems seemed minor, however, when Atul received a phone call from his father telling him that his younger sister was killed in a car accident.

A week later, while at home with his family, Atul woke up from a nap and his legs had become completely numb. He had been experiencing a headache and his back had been hurting a bit for a few days, but he had attributed these to having slept on the floor. His legs were numb to the touch, but fortunately he could walk.

Atul's parents took him to the emergency room. Luckily he was cared for by a young resident who was thinking of zebras and not horses! (This analogy refers to the tendency of inexperienced doctors to expect and look for the exotic diseases and problems that they have learned about in their textbooks—the zebras, rather than the more mundane problems that are typically present, the horses.) He was diagnosed with transverse myelitis, a condition that is believed to be caused by a rare viral infection related to the Herpes Simplex-1 virus that causes cold sores. There is no instant cure for transverse myelitis, although some treatments with corticosteroids seem to be at least partially effective. Atul simply had to wait a few weeks to recover.

Atul is not the first patient to experience frightening physical symptoms after experiencing emotionally distressing events. One described in the early psychological literature was a young woman named Anna O. She was a patient of Joseph Breuer and later of Sigmund Freud and is credited with having inspired the "discovery" of psychoanalysis (Erdelyi, 1985). Anna O. became Breuer's patient in 1880 at the age of 21 when she developed serious symptoms under the pressure of caring for her dying father: intermittent, incapacitating paralysis of her limbs, listlessness, loss of appetite, painful coughing fits, and a blinding squint (Erdelyi, 1985). Breuer treated her successfully with hypnosis, but when her father died, she relapsed. Breuer then treated her using a technique that resembled the talking cure of "psychotherapy" later developed by Freud. Many of Anna's symptoms were relieved by the analysis of their origin in her *unconscious* mind. Her cough, which was often triggered by music, was finally cured when she remembered how it started. One night, while caring for her father in the dark by his bedside, she heard music emanating from a party next door. She found herself wishing that she could go dancing at the lively party instead of attending to her father. She began coughing violently in response to the guilt she felt for such a thought. When Anna recalled the event, with all its painful emotions, her coughing ceased. In fact, the **cathartic technique** developed by Breuer involved reviving inhibited or otherwise inaccessible memories for the purpose of discharging the pathogenic (disease-causing) emotions attached to them. The patient had to recollect the distressing events and relive them in all their intensity in order for the procedure to work. When an intense positive rapport developed between physician and patient, however, Breuer tried to end the therapy abruptly. The patient's distress at this abandonment brought an avalanche of physical symptoms, and Sigmund Freud was called in to treat Anna with psychoanalysis. Anna O. was actually a young woman named Bertha Pappenheimer, who went on to become a feminist and the founder of social work in Germany. Her case demonstrates that as early as the nineteenth century and even earlier (as some have written: c.f., White, 1960), physicians recognized the role of emotions in the development of physical illness.

Psychophysiological Disorders

Atul and his predecessor Anna O. each suffered from a **psychophysiological disorder** in which physical symptoms and/or dysfunctions are intimately linked with psychological factors. A close interplay between psychological and physiological processes can produce such a disorder, making separation and analysis of each component quite difficult. In Chapter 7, we examined in detail how psychological factors such as thoughts, beliefs, and feelings can affect a person's perceptions of his or her bodily state. We saw that an individual's distress from loss or anxiety can lead a person to give more than usual attention to symptoms. In Chapter 8, we examined the manner in which emotional factors can focus attention on pain and exaggerate its effects on the individual. In this chapter, we turn to a more general analysis of psychophysiological disorders and examine how psychological experience, particularly emotion, can predispose an individual to disease and can exacerbate a physical problem.

Let us conceptualize a continuum reflecting the role of psychological factors in disease states. On one side of the continuum, there are conditions identified or brought about because of purely psychological factors—for example, serious illness (or death) caused by the self-starvation of *anorexia nervosa*: "a serious eating disorder . . . that is characterized especially by a pathological fear of weight gain leading to faulty eating patterns, malnutrition, and usually excessive weight loss" (Merriam Webster's Medical Desk Dictionary [MWMDD], 1996, p. 41). On the other end of the continuum lie the few disease conditions believed to be unaffected by psychological states, such as acute appendicitis. In between is a vast array of diseases that are influenced in various ways and to varying degrees, by the interaction between emotions and organic disease processes. Let us look at the two examples we considered earlier.

Anna O.'s physical symptoms were conceptualized as the outward manifestations of her emotional distress. Freud and Breuer proposed a kind of "hydraulic model" of the mind in which pressure builds up in the psyche and metaphorically "leaks" into another the realm of the body. Freud and Breuer explained Anna O.'s symptoms as the expression of emotions through the body. Anna's limb paralysis, for example, reflected her anger at her father for restricting her life with his needs for care. With paralyzed limbs, she was helpless to express her anger and could guarantee that she could not strike out at her father or run away. Her physical condition was so clearly the result of buried emotional conflict that when she was treated using the cathartic method and became aware of her emotional conflicts, her physical problems disappeared.

Following from the work of Freud and Breuer, various clinicians and theoreticians have affirmed (unfortunately without any definitive research) that certain emotional states can actually lead to specific medical conditions (Alexander, 1950). Based upon observations of people in psychoanalytic treatment, Alexander proposed the **Nuclear Conflict Theory**. This theory holds that each physiological disorder is associated with certain specific unconscious emotional conflicts. It is based upon the belief that an individual's repressed psychic energy can be discharged directly (as in the hydraulic model noted above) to affect his or her autonomic nervous system, leading to the impairment of bodily functioning. Despite its lack of evidence, it is an

Let's examine an instance of unique, subjective stress experienced as a dynamic process. Jude goes to visit his invalid grandmother for about an hour every Sunday afternoon. Although he knows that she enjoys seeing him, and he likes bringing some happiness to her life, the visits are stressful for him because he can't bear to see her confined to bed. In this example, the stressful event (visiting his grandmother) takes up only one hour in his week, but as early as Friday morning Jude begins to anticipate the visit and until Sunday afternoon his experience of stress increases. After he leaves his grandmother, Jude feels some degree of relief but he also feels sad about her situation. He usually feels better by Monday morning, but it all starts again on Friday. Thus, although the actual stressor occupies only an hour in his week, the psychological stress is distributed over a much wider time frame. The stress has also become chronic because the event occurs week after week. Chronic stress is one of the three types that researchers have studied, the other two being day-to-day hassles, and major life changes.

Chronic Stress

Debbie works a full-time waitressing job and takes a full course load at her college. Her days are spent driving through traffic congestion to her eight-hour job and then driving to her college campus through a crime-ridden neighborhood where shootings are a regular occurrence. She is constantly aware of the passage of time, never wasting a moment that could be spent studying. Debbie must be extremely organized and juggle her schedule to accommodate the requirements of her day. She does not make enough money at her job to cover all of her bills, and she works extra hard to get good tips from her customers just so that she can survive financially. Her rent and tuition payments are her first priorities, and she has little money available even for necessities such as food and clothing. Because she can afford only a very inexpensive apartment, Debbie lives in a less-than-desirable neighborhood. She is often afraid to go home at night after her classes because of the potential dangers after dark. Although things are likely to change for her in a few years when she gets her degree and a professional job, right now Debbie experiences a life filled with chronic stress.

Chronic stress can result from a life situation that requires significant and persistent adaptation in an environment that is inherently stressful (Gottlieb, 1997; Wheaton, 1994). Stress associated with inadequate resources can result in long-standing, persistent, and debilitating stress responses (Fried, 1982; Lazarus, 1999). One enormous source of chronic stress in today's world is the workplace. Occupational stress has been studied extensively and its importance is particularly recognized because people spend such a large proportion of their lives at work. Occupational stress can affect workers' productivity and health, and such stress can result in more sick days, higher levels of job turnover, and more on-the-job accidents. Excessive workloads, long hours, lack of control, and poor relations with supervisors can all contribute to an increased rate of job-related accidents, emotional distress, and physical health problems (Bromet et al., 1992; Dryson et al., 1996; Shankar & Famuyiwa, 1991; Wilkins & Beaudet, 1998). Certain illnesses have also been found more likely to occur in those who have responsibility for other people. For example, studies of air traffic controllers show that they have very high levels of perceived stress. The hypertension rate among air traffic controllers has been found to be four times greater than that among individuals who have similar jobs but do not have responsibility for people's lives. Air traffic controllers have also been shown to be twice as likely to have diabetes and peptic ulcers (Cobb, 1976).

Workers who have little control over what they do experience considerable stress and are at increased risk for serious illness (Cottington & House, 1987; Linder, 1995). Relatedly, people experience significant job stress when they are given no clear idea what they must do to get ahead and when there are few guidelines or standards for work. Feeling a lack of control can result in chronically elevated blood pressure rates and even in higher rates of cardiovascular disease. Further, people rely heavily on their work for social contacts and for relationships with people who share common interests. Those who have little opportunity to interact with others at work are less satisfied with their jobs and tend to experience more job stress than do those who have greater opportunities for social interaction (House, 1981).

Hassles of Everyday Life

Getting a traffic ticket, misplacing one's keys, or breaking a glass full of milk on the kitchen floor are relatively minor events in the scheme of all the potential problems of human life. **Daily hassles** are minor annoying events for which we have no automatic, adaptive responses; they take us by surprise and always require some degree of adjustment. Daily hassles have been shown over the long term to have negative cumulative effects on health (Arango & Cano, 1998; De Longis et al., 1982; Fernandez & Sheffield, 1996; Kanner et al., 1981; Norman & Malla, 1994; Wu & Lam, 1993). These effects result directly from the stress itself (that is, physiologically) as well as from poorer health behaviors, such as drinking alcohol or snacking on sweets or skipping exercise, that often accompany hassle-filled days (Steptoe et al., 1998). Although the term "hassles" might suggest that these inconveniences are no big deal, they are actually crucially important. In fact, several researchers have examined the relative impact of major stressors versus minor hassles and the latter were even more important influences on physical health than the former (Kanner et al., 1981; Lazarus, 1984; Ruffin, 1993).

In order to study hassles, researchers use an instrument called the Hassles Scale, which lists 117 disruptive day-to-day events. Many are only mildly unpleasant (such as misplacing or losing things or having to deal with other people who are inconsiderate), but some of them are serious (such as having concerns about owing money). All are things that might occur on a daily basis, often stemming from more major life changes (Kanner et al., 1981; Lazarus, 1984, 1999). For instance, when going through the trauma of a divorce, one must deal not only with the psychological aspects of the breakup itself but perhaps also with things like having less money, finding and moving to a new place to live, answering questions from family and friends, having to do more yard work or household chores, and eventually dating. All of these can add up!

The effects on an individual of day-to-day hassles depend to a great extent upon how those hassles are interpreted (for example, "that's life" versus "the world is against me"). One cognitive factor that may be important is optimism. **Optimism** is a psychological term used to describe how an individual perceives the world; an optimist

Daily hassles require some degree of adaptation and can have a serious effect on health.

views the future positively and expects things to work out well. One study found that individuals highest in optimism reported the fewest daily hassles, not because they actually had fewer but rather because they simply saw these events not as stressful but rather as just a part of life (Nelson et al., 1995),

Researchers have found that other aspects of life (more pleasant experiences called **uplifts**) can help to combat the bad feelings that arise from the experience of hassles. Uplifts are believed to "buffer," or prevent the full impact of, the stress of hassles on an individual's physical and mental condition. Uplifts serve to reduce the effects of annoying, frustrating problems or difficulties and serve as sources of peace, satisfaction, and even joy (Kanner et al., 1981). Some examples of uplifts are "saving money," "finding something presumed lost," and "liking fellow workers."

What is the relative contribution of chronic stress and daily hassles to ill health? Some researchers suggest that chronic stress might actually make a person somewhat less vulnerable to small daily hassles because he or she is presumably less affected by small problems in the face of larger ones (Caspi et al., 1987). Others suggest that hassles are inherently more difficult to deal with for people who are already experiencing chronic stress and therefore more physically "vulnerable" to the stress of small daily hassles (Lazarus, 1984). It is likely, of course, that daily hassles and serious chronic stress co-occur; an individual whose life is filled with many daily hassles may have a negative life situation that likely produces ill health.

Major Life Events

To date, most of the research on stress and illness has been conducted on the role of specific stressful life events in predicting ill health. This research tradition is a significant part of the history of the field of health psychology. The conceptualization of stress as resulting from a single event or a collection of life change events represents the first research tradition on this topic and the most extensively studied. **Life change events** are defined as those that bring changes in how the individual lives, and they require considerable adaptation. Examples are marriage, divorce, the death of one's spouse, and moving to a new part of the country. The first large-scale attempt to understand stress was undertaken in the late 1960s (Holmes & Rahe, 1967). Researchers began with the hypothesis that the degree of stress an individual experiences can be understood in terms of the number of life changes he or she has recently undergone. These researchers first had hundreds of people rate the degree of adjustment they thought would be required by each of 43 positive and negative events. Each event was assigned a numerical value from zero to 100 to represent its perceived stressfulness, thus producing the **Social Readjustment Rating Scale** (SRRS). Some of the entries and their readjustment ratings are death of a spouse (100), divorce (73), marriage (50), being fired at work (47), change in residence (20), and vacation (13). The SRRS has since been updated to contain 51 major life events. For this update, 3,122 individuals rated each event in terms of its stressfulness on a scale of 1 to 100, just as described above for the original SRRS (Hobson et al., 1998). These researchers found that people agreed amazingly well about which events were most stressful, and that the most stressful events fell generally into five broad categories: death and dying, health and illness, crime, finances, and family problems.

Research on life change events has been criticized as problematic both conceptually and methodologically, and it is important to understand what those critiques are. First, the earliest studies were retrospective in nature. That is, subjects were asked to remember both the life events and the illness episodes they had experienced in the previous two years. A correlation between stress and illness could have been the result of the expectations of the respondents, including their own belief that personal stress can lead to illness. In answer to this criticism, prospective studies have been conducted and have shown that life change scores do indeed predict with some success the experience of illness. For example, in one study the life events scores were tallied for sailors who were about to embark on a six-month cruise tour of duty. The researchers were able to predict rather accurately which sailors would get sick during the tour and which would not (Rahe et al., 1970). Although a measure such as the SRRS may aid in predicting the *likelihood* of illness, it does not adequately take into account the many factors that ultimately determine health or illness. For example, someone with a very strong immune system might be exposed to an infectious agent and yet not become ill, while someone with a weakened immune system might easily get sick from the same exposure. What people do when they feel sick (that is, how well they take care of themselves) is also important, as is the manifestation, reporting, and reaction to the symptoms themselves. One person with a headache might leave work early and go home to lie down while another might push on with daily activities. Overall, research indicates that life events that are sudden, negative, unexpected, and uncontrollable (as we saw previously, the most "stressful") are more likely to predict illness than are events that are positive, expected, under personal control, or that develop gradually with the opportunity for adjustment.

Mechanisms for the Effects of Stress on Health

How do stress and the need for adaptation affect bodily processes? How might stressful life events lead to illness? Several routes are possible. First, the experience of (particularly high levels of) stress can prompt an individual to engage in behavior that is compromising to his or her health. Chronic daily stress and/or stressful life events can divert an individual's attention away from caring for him- or herself and leave little or no time for exercise, proper diet, and plenty of restful sleep. Even worse, the individual might attempt to cope with the stress by engaging in short-term pleasant, but nevertheless unhealthy, behaviors such as drinking alcohol excessively or eating foods that are high in sugar and fat. Indeed, studies of health behavior suggest that people who are under high stress consume more alcohol, cigarettes, coffee, and "fast food" and exercise less than do people who experience lower levels of stress (Melamed et al., 1997; Ogden & Mitandabari, 1997; Steptoe et al., 1998). An individual under stress might be so distracted that he or she forgets to wear a safety belt while driving or drives so distractedly as to increase the chances of an accident. Under high levels of stress, people are more likely to be injured on the job, in sports activities, while driving a car, and even in accidents at home (Johnson, 1986; Quick & Quick, 1984). Second, as we examined in detail in Chapter 8, some people react to stressful conditions in their lives by adopting the "sick role" and seeking healthcare services (Mechanic, 1972). The embracing of "illness" as the explanation for personal distress allows the individual a reason for not functioning effectively. In doing so, the individual is able to preserve his or her self-concept because illness is a socially acceptable excuse for failing to meet one's obligations. Illness brings secondary gains that allow the individual legitimately to avoid dealing with the events that cause so much stress in the first place. A third explanation, which we will pursue in the remainder of this chapter, involves a direct and detrimental effect of stress on bodily processes. As we will see, stress can produce physiological changes that are conducive to the development of disease. Furthermore, physical vulnerability in the form of a preexisting condition can be exacerbated by stress, and certain diseases can become considerably worse in the presence of stress.

Cross-cutting these three possible explanations is a broad mechanism for the effect of stress on physical health and symptoms. It is personality (see van Heck, 1997 for review). According to van Heck (1997), personality may be the link between the stressful environment and the beginning of the disease process. In fact, one study found that the personality trait of repression has been linked to compromised immune functioning and impaired disease control by the immune system among individuals infected with the Epstein-Barr virus and the herpes virus (Esterling et al., 1990; Esterling et al., 1994). Having a pessimistic outlook has been related to poorer cell-mediated immunity (Kamen-Siegel et al., 1991). We will deal with certain personality characteristics later in this chapter, as well as when we consider personality as it relates to coping in Chapter 10. It is useful to keep in mind, however, the potential role that habitual thought patterns and behaviors (i.e., the individual's personality) might play in affecting the individual's reactions to stress and subsequent health and health behavior.

Physiological Reactions to Stress

As early as the 1850s, the term stress was applied to humans to mean an outside force acting on the body or on mental powers (Mason, 1975). In the early 1900s, Walter Cannon described stress not as a stimulus but rather as the response to a stimulus, particularly to an emergency requiring a person to cope with danger. Cannon named the individual's response to a stressor (stimulus) the *critical stress,* and he identified the now famous **fight-or-flight response** in which the human organism is readied for fighting or taking flight when in danger (Cannon, 1932). Physiologically, this response is quite dramatic. As illustrated in Figure 9.1, the blood pressure rises, heart and respiration

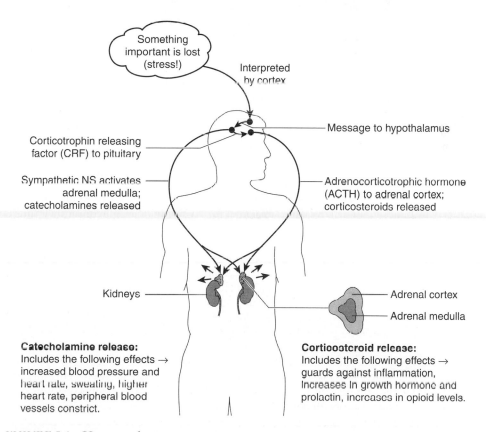

FIGURE 9.1   Hormonal response to stress.

rates increase, and blood sugar levels rise. The palms sweat and the muscles tense (Cannon, 1932). Cannon suggested that the frequent experience of the stress could break down an individual's physiological homeostasis and increase his or her physical vulnerability to illness. Although the fight-or-flight response can be quite adaptive (for example, it could help a person to run from danger or fight to save her own life), continual physiological arousal can be hazardous to the individual because it involves significant physical disruption. Box 9.1 examines one of the first things people tend to do when they feel threatened; they hold their breath! This box examines how breathing is viewed in Western and Eastern medicine and culture and how simple awareness of one's breathing can help with stress responses.

BOX 9.1

Across Cultures

Breathing, East and West

The experience of stress can affect the body in some very obvious ways. One of them is breathing. For many people facing stress, breathing tends to become very "shallow" (little air taken in or breathed out), and the mobility of the diaphragm is reduced (Timmons, 1994). When they experience threat, some people even unconsciously hold their breath. It is also common for people to do what is called "collarbone breathing" (stomach in, shoulders back, chest muscles and rib cage tightened) (Reich, 1942). These patterns can actually communicate to the brain the somatic experience of suffocation and thereby increase the experience of anxiety and stress.

In Eastern cultures, breathing is central to the practice of a number of religious activities and is believed to facilitate the linking of spiritual and physical health. In China, *qi* (pronounced chi) means vital energy or vital breath. In several disciplines, the goal of breathing is concentration of the breath into the abdomen (the *tan tien*, a spot about two inches below the navel). *Qi gong* is a form of exercise that combines graceful movement with deep breathing. *Tai chi* combines breathing with exercise, meditation, and martial arts.

Yoga, which in Sanskrit means "yoking" (the spirit with the body), involves not only physical postures but also breath control (*pranayama*

in hatha yoga). The goal is to establish stable breathing patterns and relax the body.

Western approaches typically lack religious associations, but some practices use breathing retraining for relaxation and focus attention on breathing as a mechanism for coping with stress, as well as for generally improving health. One meditative method for training breathing is the "Relaxation Response," which is discussed in detail in Chapter 11 (Benson et al., 1974). Breathing is also central to gestalt therapy techniques (Bakal, 1999). In bioenergetic therapy (Reich, 1942), it is believed that breathing disturbances are central to blocked physical and psychic energy because they interfere with the internal rhythms of the body.

Can people change the way they breathe? Not easily, according to experts, because breathing is typically not a conscious activity (Bakal, 1999). One of the best recommendations is simply to breathe effortlessly, to relax and expand the diaphragm, and breathe "into" the abdomen. For stress management, one can try to allow breathing to take on a natural relaxed pattern and then to connect relaxed breathing and feelings of somatic well-being and relaxation with thoughts and feelings that cause stress.

The General Adaptation Syndrome

Followers of Cannon's theory, particularly Hans Selye (1956), further examined what happens to the human body in response to stressors (which he defined as "demands to which there are no readily available or automatic adaptive responses" [Antonovsky, 1979, p. 72]). Selye developed the theory of the **General Adaptation Syndrome (GAS)**, which involves three stages: (1) the **Alarm Stage** in which the body is mobilized to respond to stress and there is an increase in adrenal activity as well as cardiovascular and respiratory functioning; (2) the **Resistance Stage** in which the individual makes efforts to take action to overcome the stress, or learns to adjust to it, and continual resistance to stress results in decreased resistance to other stimuli; (3) the **Exhaustion Stage** in which the individual experiences a depletion of physical resources in the process of trying to overcome or adjust to threat. In the GAS, a stressor taxes the body through its initial response, subsequent adjustment, and final depletion of physical resources. According to Selye, these phases combine to produce considerable vulnerability to illness.

Selye's biological model emphasizes the effect of stress on an individual's physiological state (Selye, 1976). Any noxious or aversive event is believed to bring about changes in the adrenal and thymus glands and in the lining of the stomach. In rats, for example, stress reactions resulted in an enlarged adrenal cortex and in an atrophied thymus gland and lymphatic structures (important centers of immune functioning). Stress reactions even resulted in an increased number of stomach ulcers. In fact, in Selye's research nearly everything he did to create stress in an animal elicited the same physiological pattern (Selye, 1976). Selye argued that a stressor can be physical (such as pain), psychological (such as fear), or both, and that regardless of the cause of a threat, the initial response is the same. For the General Adaptation Syndrome to be activated, an organism does not have to be chased by lions and tigers and bears. The daily environment, complete with its traffic jams, midterms, and unreasonable bosses, will do quite nicely. If, for whatever reason, the stress reaction is repeated for a prolonged period of time, according to Selye, the eventual result will be exhaustion, depletion of physical resources, and irreversible physiological damage, including changes in the adrenal glands (particularly the adrenal cortex), as well as respiratory and cardiovascular failure and a reduction in the functioning of the immune system.

Historically, the General Adaptation Syndrome is an important model because it depicts the mechanisms by which stress can lead to physiological damage; early support for it came from independent research on the physical effects of stress. For example, aggression-provoking stimuli were shown to lead to increased adrenal activity (Levi, 1965). Work overload and feelings of a lack of control, as well as major life changes, were found to increase catecholamine levels (Theorell, 1974). Early researchers also found that somewhat different patterns of physiological reactions occurred in response to stressors that elicited feelings of uncertainty, anger, and fear (Mason, 1975). Epinephrine and norepinephrine were found to be secreted in response to purely psychological stimuli (Frankenhaeuser, 1975) and changes in adrenal-pituitary responses followed episodes of distress (Mason, 1975). Early findings led to three lines of research inquiry regarding the role of stress in the development of disease. The first is the exciting new field of psychoneuroimmunology. The second is a major field of research on stress and cardiovascular disease. And the third deals with psychophysiological disorders. We will discuss each of these in turn.

Psychoneuroimmunology

Have you ever noticed that you, your roommate, and your friends seem to catch a cold right about the time finals come around? Well, you are not alone, and it's not your imagination! Even Atul, the young man introduced at the beginning of the chapter, developed an unusual disorder following an acute episode of stress. "Psychological stress seems able to alter susceptibility to infectious agents, influencing the onset, course and outcome of certain infectious pathologies" (Biondi & Zannino, 1997, p. 3). "When demands imposed by events exceed individuals' abilities to cope, a psychological stress response composed of negative cognitive and emotional states is elicited. It is these responses that are thought to influence immune function through their effects on behavioral coping and neuroendocrine response" (Cohen & Herbert, 1996, p. 119). These two statements exemplify what research in psychoneuroimmunology has demonstrated. **Psychoneuroimmunology** (PNI) is a field of study that examines the interrelationships among psychosocial processes and nervous, endocrine, and immune system functioning (Ader, 1981; Ader et al., 1991; Ader & Cohen, 1985; Cohen & Herbert, 1996). Since the early 1980s, phenomenal advances have been made in our understanding of the role that psychology plays in the stability of the human immune system. Much PNI research has focused on the impact that physical stress or emotions have on immune functioning. (Before continuing, please review Box 9.2 and Figure 9.2 for a brief reminder of how the

---

BOX **9.2**

Hot Topic

Stress and Immune Functioning: A Crash Course in Lymphocytes

The immune system is the body's means of guarding against foreign invaders such as bacteria, viruses, and carcinogenic substances. Immune system protection is of two types: (1) *nonspecific immunity* and (2) *specific immunity*. The first involves several mechanisms: actual barriers (such as the skin, which can keep out invaders), phagocytosis (the process whereby special white blood cells engulf and destroy pathogens), inflammation (swelling and increased blood flow that facilitates the movement and function of white blood cells), and the secretion of toxic chemicals (to kill microorganisms such as bacteria and viruses). The

second type, specific immunity, involves the body's ability to protect itself from specific invaders. An example would be the immune response to an encounter with the measles virus after antibodies have been developed from immunizaton.

There are two kinds of specific immunological reactions: *humoral immunity* and *cell-mediated immunity*. Humoral immunity occurs when an antigen (a threatening agent) stimulates B lymphocytes to differentiate into cells that secrete antibodies to fight a foreign invader. Cell-mediated immunity, on the other hand, involves T-lymphocytes from the thymus gland

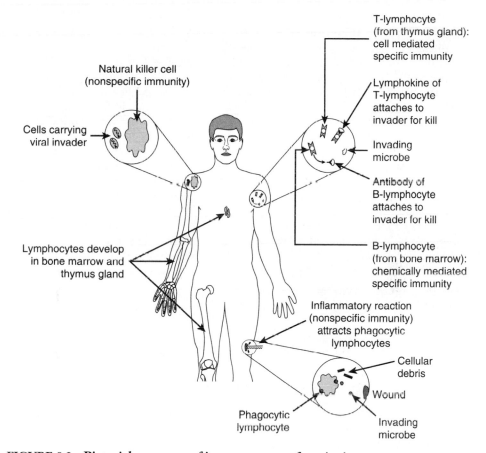

FIGURE 9.2 Pictorial summary of immune system functioning.

and is slower acting. (A T-cell is a type of infection fighting white blood cell. T-cell levels and lymphocyte activity are key elements in immune system functioning.) Instead of releasing antibodies into the blood, cell-mediated immunity occurs in the following way. When stimulated by an antigen, T-cells secrete chemicals that aid in a process by which attacking microorganisms are ingested and destroyed (the "pac man" effect). This process is called *phagocytosis*. Some T-cells (called helper T-cells) appear to aid in humoral immunity, whereas suppressor T-cells may suppress humoral reactions. Many other cells and components of the blood are also involved in immune responses: mast cells, monocytes, macrophages, natural killer (NK) cells, and several others.

The activity of natural killer (NK) cells in response to stress illustrates the complexity of immune system responses. First, the effects of acute stress on NK cell activity have been shown to be both positive and negative, depending upon certain factors (Delahanty et al., 2000). One determinant is the time at which NK activity is measured following an acute stressor. NK activity tends to be increased during or immediately after a stressful activity, whereas NK activity tends to decrease later (such as 48 or 72 hours following the stressor) (see Delahanty et al., 2000). The age of the individuals under study also matters. In younger women (ages 21-41), NK activity was increased following a 12-minute stressful arithmetic task, but no such increased activity was seen for older women (Naliboff et

(continued)

BOX **9.2** (Continued)

al., 1991). Also, the relationship between acute stress and NK activity is affected by time of day (Delahanty et al., 2000). NK cells are most active when participants are exposed to a stressful activity in the late afternoon; they increase in number the most when the stressful activity occurs at noon. Thus, the time of day at which studies are conducted can have an effect on the observations made on the immune system; as noted above, the age of study participants also needs to be taken into account.

Since a great deal of research on stress and immunity is done on undergraduate psychology students under highly controlled situations, the generalizability of findings from some of this research is always a concern. One study with considerable ecological validity examined the immune responses of first-time tandem parachutists before and after their first jump (typically an acutely stressful event) (Schedlowski et al., 1993). Compared with before the jump, these individuals showed increased NK activity immediately following the jump. One hour following the jump, however, the NK activity level was even lower than before the jump! That is, the NK activity was at baseline, then peaked, and then dropped below the baseline level, all within about 90 minutes. This research demonstrates that the immune system is very complex and that fluctuations in immune functioning are affected by many factors.

---

immune system works, and, if necessary, also review the section on immunity in Appendix A so that the findings of PNI research will be better understood.)

Stress, Mood, and Immune Functioning

Let's go back to our original question about the frequency of colds around finals week. Research evidence supports the idea that physical symptoms are related to mental states—in this case, stress. PNI research has found that individuals under severe, chronic stress are more likely to develop symptoms from exposure to the rhinovirus (the common cold) than are individuals under no or only acute stress (Cohen, 1996; Cohen et al., 1998). Individuals reporting greater levels of positive mood over a two-day period have higher levels of natural killer cell activity (a measure of immune functioning) than do those reporting negative moods over the same two days (Valdimarsdottir & Bovbjerg, 1997). Antibody levels have been found among men to be higher on days in which they reported a positive mood (Stone et al., 1994). Furthermore, individuals exposed to a humorous film showed higher levels of salivary immunoglobulin-A (IgA; a measure of immune functioning) than did those exposed to a nonhumorous comparison film (McClelland & Cheriff, 1997). Another study found that while medical students were undergoing the stress of exams, their levels of salivary IgA were suppressed for more than six days following the examination period! Those with suppressed immune functioning did not necessarily acquire an upper respiratory tract infection, however (Deinzer & Schueller, 1998). Perhaps it was the youth and general good health of these students that allowed them to avoid catching a cold despite their suppressed immune systems, or perhaps they were lucky enough to have not been exposed to the cold virus. In another study, a small group of patients who suffered from recurrent oral herpes ("cold sores") was followed over three months and provided ratings of their stress and daily mood fluctuations (Logan et al., 1998). Findings showed that cold-sore outbreaks did vary with stress and mood fluctuations, indicating that the immune system was suppressed enough during stress to allow for the manifestation of a lesion. In fact, the week before the outbreak there was a significant reduction in subjects' levels of natural killer cells in their blood. Another interesting and innovative study examined the speed with which the body *heals* itself under varying levels of stress. Dental students were given two small wounds in their hard palates, one during summer vacation and one right before exams. Wounds healed 40 percent slower just prior to exams, which can reasonably be assumed to be a time of higher stress (Marucha et al., 1998).

PNI research supports the fact that as stress increases, the nervous system responds by increasing cortisol levels, blood pressure, and epinephrine. In turn, these act to suppress immune functioning. Stress also works directly on IgA, another indicator of immune functioning. What must also be remembered, however, is that interactions of the immune system with other systems (physical and mental) are extremely complex. This fact is highlighted in Box 9-2.

Social Support and Immune Functioning

Numerous studies have found significant beneficial effects of social support on the functioning of the cardiovascular, endocrine, and immune systems (see Uchino et al., 1996, for a review). Research on the immune system has demonstrated that poor marital relations and lower levels of social support can have a deleterious effect on one's health (see Cohen & Herbert, 1996). In one study, newlyweds (average age 25)

Having the support of a friend can be essential to effective immune functioning and overall health.

were studied in a hospital research unit over a 24-hour period. Hostile or negative interactions between a husband and wife were associated with increased levels of norepinephrine, epinephrine, growth hormone, and ACTH, and all showed a suppression of the immune system during the 24 hours following the negative interaction (Kiecolt-Glaser et al., 1998). This research also demonstrated, by replicating the study in a group of older married couples, that it is not simply being newly married, but the hostility of any existing conflict, that produces the observable immune changes. Individuals who feel that they have someone to confide in and to share their thoughts and feelings with have better immune functioning than those who do not (Thomas et al., 1985). In Chapter 10, we will further examine the effects of social support on health.

Emotional Health and Immune Functioning

Daily moods, emotions, and clinical psychopathologies can also affect the immune system (Cohen & Herbert, 1996; Valdimarsdottir & Bovbjerg, 1997). Clinical depression has been linked to both suppressed T-cell levels and general suppression of **lymphocyte** activity (Kronfol et al., 1983; Leserman et al., 1997). Depression also alters levels of cytokines, which are chemicals that some white blood cells release to aid in the proliferation of more white blood cells and in the attack on the invading microorganism (Miller, 1998). A **meta-analysis** of the relationship between clinical depression and immune functioning did indeed find that clinically depressed individuals have lower numbers of natural killer cells, higher numbers of circulating white blood cells (indicating that the body is trying hard to ward off a threat), and lower numbers of T-cells, helper T-cells, suppressor T-cells, and B cells (Herbert & Cohen, 1993). While these effects are also present among those who are simply experiencing a depressed mood or overall malaise, the findings are considerably more pronounced in those who are clinically depressed. Anxiety, anger, and hostility have also been found to bring about elevated levels of corticosteroids (such as cortisol) and catecholamines (such as epinephrine), causing immunosuppression and even metabolic disorders (Krantz et al., 1983). Anxiety, in particular, is related to lower natural killer cell activity (Locke et al., 1984).

Research on animals demonstrates that experimentally induced stressors can alter immune regulation and cause immune suppression. Studies of humans show that during times of emotional excitement there is decreased phagocyte activity (that is, phagocytes do not engulf and destroy invaders as quickly as they otherwise might) (Borysenko & Borysenko, 1982). Research has demonstrated that the immune system does not operate independently of the central nervous system. Rather, the brain houses centers that are critical to the regulation of hormones and neurotransmitters that affect immune responses. Until recently, however, there has been little information available as to why or how emotional factors affect resistance to or progression of disease. When psychoneuroimmunologists have studied the biochemical interactions between mood and immunity, they have found that certain emotions can indeed cause suppression of the immune system (Jemmot & Locke, 1984). In this research, depression has been linked to both susceptibility to contracting a disease and to the slower (or limited) recovery from disease (Imboden et al., 1961; Levy, 1985a, 1985b). Others have demonstrated an association between positive mood and improved immune functioning

(Stone et al., 1994). The nervous, cardiovascular, and immune systems are affected by the stress associated with uncontrollable events (Peters, Godaert, et al., 1998). Subjects given an uncontrollable task had higher cortisol levels (an immune response), higher blood pressure (a cardiovascular response), and higher norepinephrine levels (a nervous response) than did subjects given a controllable task.

Precisely how does stress affect immunocompetence? No complete answer is yet available, but it is believed that stress causes the adrenal glands to produce epinephrine and cortisol and that these in turn affect immune cells. Catecholamines (epinephrine and norepinephrine) appear to have a variety of immunosuppressive effects. Epinephrine increases suppressor T-cells and decreases helper T-cells (Antoni, 1987; Borysenko, 1984). Corticosteroids, secreted as anti-inflammatory agents, have an immunosuppressive effect as well, and cortisol inhibits the functioning of phagocytes and lymphocytes (Antoni, 1987; Borysenko, 1984). The connection between stress and suppressed immune functioning may also occur because of stress-stimulated changes in endorphin responses. Kiecolt-Glaser and colleagues have attempted to explain the effects of stress on the immune system and the physiological mechanisms by which these effects appear to come about (Kiecolt-Glaser et al., 1984; Kiecolt-Glaser & Glaser, 1986). In one study (Kiecolt-Glaser et al., 1984), blood samples were taken from first-year medical students during low- and high-stress times associated with their examinations. The blood samples were analyzed for killer T-cell activity and for concentrations of antibodies. Although antibody levels were not found to vary with stress levels, killer T-cell *activity* was lower during high-stress times than during lower-stress times. Higher killer T-cell activity was also associated with feeling less lonely.

Table 9.1 summarizes the common effects of stress.

Stress, HIV, and the Immune System

How does stress affect an already compromised immune system? Due largely to the incidence of HIV around the world, this is a question that has become very pressing. Unfortunately, the link is still unclear because many of the findings are somewhat contradictory and the research results are confusing. Several studies on HIV-infected

---

TABLE 9.1   Common Effects of Stress

Immunological and Cardiovascular	Effect
Events in Response to Stress	
1. Cortisol levels increase ⟶	Phagocytes and lymphocytes inhibited
2. Blood pressure increases ⟶	Pressure and friction on artery walls increase
3. Epinephrine levels increase ⟶	Helper T-cell levels decrease; suppressor T-cell levels increase
4. Salivary IgA levels decrease ⟶	Indicates decreased immune functioning

individuals suggest that both stress and depression levels have a deleterious effect on immune functioning (Leserman et al., 1997; Littrell, 1996; Miller, Kemeny, et al., 1997). Social relationships also affect progression of the disease, and being sensitive to rejection by others had been found to accelerate declines in health status among those with HIV (Cole et al., 1997). While it is unclear whether depression actually accelerates the onset of AIDS, one study found that among initially asymptomatic HIV positive gay men, over a five-year period depression levels were significantly associated with lower helper T-cell numbers, reflecting poorer immune functioning (Burack et al., 1993). Another study of 395 HIV infected men (Page-Shafer et al., 1996) found that men with symptoms of depression had a higher risk of progression of AIDS diagnosis than men who were not depressed. Still another study found depression was associated with increased clinical symptoms in 160 HIV patients (Revicki et al., 1995). Although this evidence is mounting, other studies (e.g., Lyketsos et al., 1993) failed to find an effect, and a recent review (Patterson et al., 1995) notes that the data are mixed regarding the association between depression and HIV/AIDS disease progression. There may soon be enough studies on this topic to allow a more definitive answer with meta-analysis.

An interesting counterintuitive finding in this realm is worthy of note. Among HIV infected gay men, lower levels of loneliness (that is, *not* feeling particularly lonely) have been found to predict faster declines in the immune system than higher levels of loneliness (Miller, Kemeny, et al., 1997). The authors speculated that although an individual may not be lonely, he may be at risk for greater declines in immune function because the nature of his social network is problematic. For example, this network may be filled with people who are intrusive, controlling, or even demean the individual. Thus, this study suggests that in some instances being lonely may be preferable (at least from a health standpoint) to being involved with people who demand much in return for social connection.

Stress, Tuberculosis, and the Immune System

Tuberculosis (TB), like HIV, is an infectious disease. TB is caused by a bacterium that is passed from person to person in airborne droplets, and it is particularly communicable among people in close proximity through sneezing or coughing. For most people, the immune system alone or with the aid of antibiotics is able to resolve the infection. This resolution does leave a scarring in the lungs (which can be seen on an x-ray), however. (Ask your grandparents if they have ever been exposed to TB. In all likelihood, as children, many of them were.) In about 5 to 10 percent of individuals who acquire TB, the infection persists because the immune system cannot fully rid the body of it. In these individuals, the infection may lay dormant for many years, or the bacteria may even find their way into the bloodstream through the lymph nodes and spread to other parts of the body (a condition called miliary TB that can be fatal). At one time, TB was a common cause of death, but with the advent of antibiotics its presence as a major, worldwide killer was greatly diminished. In recent years, however, some strains of the bacterium that causes TB have become resistant to antibiotics so that once again it is a major player in cases of infectious diseases. (Also, recall our discussion of nonadherence and antibiotic-resistant strains of pathogens from Chapter 3.) In fact, at present TB is one of the leading causes of death from infectious diseases globally. Many years ago physicians argued that certain individual factors may actually play a role in the course of TB—that is, whether TB is fought off by the body, or instead lies dormant or even spreads throughout the body (Wittkower, 1953). As early as 1919, one study found that a stressful school environment exacerbated the incidence of TB among schoolchildren and instructors (Ishigami, 1919). By reducing the effectiveness of the immune system, stress can influence the course of TB. In addition, other personal factors appear to play a role as well, particularly in nonadherence to treatment (Sumartojo, 1993).

Stress and Cardiovascular Disorders

The second major line of research on the role of stress in the development of disease involves work on **cardiovascular disorders**. Cardiovascular disorders are disorders of the heart, blood vessels, and blood circulation and are the number one cause of death in the United States today. Stress has been implicated in their direct cause. For example, two studies have found that one form of job stress (expending a lot of effort with little reward) leads to higher rates of the risk factors for cardiovascular disease (Peter et al., 1998; Peter & Siegrist, 1997). In the 1998 study, among the men who had high levels of job effort with little reward, there were higher rates of hypertension, higher total cholesterol, and higher ratios of total cholesterol to high density lipoprotein (HDL) cholesterol. In combining the effects of several different studies of women exposed to stressful laboratory tasks, Benschop and colleagues (1998) found that there were significant and sizable changes in systolic and diastolic blood pressure, heart rate, and natural killer cell activity during stressful tasks.

Hypertension

Hypertension involves having consistently high blood pressure (over 140 systolic and 90 diastolic, usually over several weeks or months). About 30 percent of Americans have hypertension, which is a major risk factor for CHD as well as for other diseases such as stroke and kidney disease (Shapiro & Goldstein, 1982). Hypertension (over 85% of cases) seems to be determined by several risk factors, some of which were examined in detail in Chapter 5. These include obesity, sedentary lifestyle, diet, and alcohol use as well as family history and various psychosocial factors. While hypertension is unlikely to be caused solely by emotional factors, there is evidence that stress, anger, and hostility may play an important role in the development and maintenance of hypertension. Individuals with hypertension have been found to be more likely to experience chronic feelings of hostility than are individuals with normal blood pressure (Diamond, 1982). In both men and women, greater hostility is associated with higher reactive blood pressure levels in response to a situation evoking suspiciousness and mistrust (Weidner et al., 1989). During social interactions, hostile men have been found to have higher systolic blood pressure than men who were not hostile (Guyll &

Contrada, 1998). People in high-stress jobs who suppress their anger have been found to have higher blood pressure than do those who have lower-stress jobs or who express their anger (Cottington et al., 1986). Blood pressure levels among air traffic controllers, for example, have been found to be positively correlated with both their age and the job stress they experience (Cobb & Rose, 1973). Both heart rate and blood pressure have been found to increase under conditions of physical overcrowding (Fleming et al., 1987) and are correlated with living in high stress urban areas, particularly among African Americans (Barnes et al., 1997; Harburg et al., 1973). Blood pressure also seems to be higher among those whose heart rate is affected by emotional factors (Rose & Chesney, 1986).

Coronary Heart Disease (CHD)

Coronary heart disease is a category of diseases that result from the narrowing or blocking of coronary (heart) arteries that supply oxygen-rich blood to the heart muscle. CHD includes angina, arteriosclerosis, atherosclerosis, and myocardial infarction. **Arteriosclerosis** is a condition in which the walls of the coronary (or other) arteries thicken and lose their elasticity; a special case of arteriosclerosis is **atherosclerosis**, in which arterial walls narrow and harden because of the formation of fatty patches or "plaques." These plaques are composed of cholesterol (the fatty substance in the blood both manufactured by the body and introduced with saturated fat foods). Plaques can occur throughout the body. When the plaques forming in the coronary arteries obstruct blood flow, insufficient oxygen is supplied to the muscle of the heart, which can result in **angina pectoris** (chest pain) and myocardial infarction (heart attack). Angina pectoris (also called angina) is a form of heart disease in which the sufferer feels pain and tightness in his or her chest because of brief or incomplete blockages of oxygenated blood to the heart. **Myocardial infarction (MI)**, also known as a "heart attack," involves a severe or prolonged blockage of blood to the heart, which results in the muscle tissue (myocardium) being destroyed. In cardiovascular disease, which is the leading cause of death in Western Europe and the United States, the majority of deaths are due to MI and about half occur within an hour of the onset of symptoms (PGD, 1998).

As we noted in detail in Chapter 5, CHD has many risk factors such as cigarette smoking, obesity, sedentary lifestyle, uncontrolled diabetes, hypertension, high serum cholesterol, and family history. Included in the list is psychological stress, particularly the individual's pattern of responses to stress. In general, researchers have found that in the realm of occupational stress, workers with unsatisfying yet demanding jobs requiring a great deal of responsibility have a higher incidence of CHD than do those whose jobs are less demanding (Quick & Quick, 1984). A buildup in stressful life changes also appears to be associated with a first and repeat myocardial infarction (Garrity & Marx, 1979; Theorell & Rahe, 1975). The critical factor in determining the effect of stress on CHD may be how the individual reacts to stressful situations. Let us turn to an examination of the Type A behavior pattern in an effort to understand reactions to stress as they affect cardiovascular disease.

Type A Behavior and Heart Disease

One major area of research that has linked psychological factors with disease is that of the **Type A Behavior Pattern** (TABP). TABP is more than just a way of behaving. It involves predispositions to think, feel, and act in particular ways in response to environmental demands and conditions. These predispositions are believed to remain fairly consistent over time, and researchers hold that there are definable differences between people who exhibit the TABP and those who do not. This purely dispositional (i.e., personality, and thus psychological) construct has come to be accepted by the medical community as a significant risk factor for heart disease, the leading killer of Americans today. While the construct is complex, and the research evidence sometimes conflicting, TABP has evolved to be a rather well-recognized link between the mind and the body.

In the 1950s, cardiologists Meyer Friedman and Ray Rosenman first described the TABP. They noted a particular way of behaving that seemed to be common among many of their patients with heart disease: persistently agitated, ill-at-ease behavior and a tendency to sit at the edge of their chairs as if ready to bolt away. In fact, Friedman and Rosenman reported that this way of sitting was so common among patients that when the chairs in the office waiting room were reupholstered, the man doing the work commented on the unusual pattern of wear on the front edges of the chairs (Friedman & Rosenman, 1974). In the late 1950s, Rosenman and Friedman applied to the federal government for a grant to study the unusual behavior pattern of their cardiac patients. They were turned down twice for a grant to study "emotional stress" because reviewers doubted that two cardiologists could successfully study emotional matters. Eventually, they changed the label to the innocuous "Type A behavior pattern" (with its opposite called **Type B**) and on its third submission the grant application was funded (Friedman & Ulmer, 1984).

The major elements of TABP involve an individual's aggressive and incessant struggle to achieve more and more in less and less time (Friedman & Rosenman, 1974). The person who is Type A is competitive and achievement striving and has a sense of time urgency, impatience, and aggressiveness toward others. The Type A person easily becomes hostile toward other people and is "overly mobilized" in response to both physical and psychological tasks. Psychologically, this mobilization takes the form of time urgency as well as anger at those who waste (particularly the person's own) time. The Type A person is chronically aroused and may remain keyed up all day, every day, having a great deal of trouble relaxing (Chesney et al., 1985). Earlier research found that this collection of cognitive, emotional, and behavioral predispositions was significantly correlated with CHD (Booth-Kewley & Friedman, 1987). A more recent review, however, suggests that the general construct of TABP, at least as it has been conceptualized and measured in more current research, has a limited relationship to CHD (Myrtek, 1995). Many important questions in this area are still being investigated.

Recent research on the Type A construct has attempted to sort out more precisely which aspects of the TABP might be the most dangerous in their contribution to CHD. For example, people who are energetic, expressive, and animated appear not to have any increased risk for CHD. Rather, those in greater danger of heart disease seem to be the individuals who experience the emotions of chronic hostility, anger, and aggression (Barefoot et al., 1983; Chesney & Rosenman, 1985), particularly those who have a basic distrust of others (Barefoot et al., 1987; Weidner et al., 1987). Thus, it is important to distinguish between behavior patterns that are healthy, animated, expressive, and charismatic, and those that reflect unhealthy, aggressive hostility (Friedman et al., 1984). Being hostile, suspicious, and mistrusting of other people seems to be consistently related to CHD and deaths due to it (Barefoot et al., 1983; Barefoot et al., 1987; Shekelle et al., 1983; Weidner et al., 1987). And although stereotypes suggest that suppressed emotion can play a role in CHD, for the most part the research consensus is that coronary-prone people exhibit exactly the opposite tendency. They do not to suffer in silence, but rather they explode with frequent, open displays of hostility (Cady et al., 1961; Dunbar, 1943).

In an important prospective study of hostility as a risk factor for CHD, 255 medical students filled out a measure of hostility. Almost thirty years later, the health status of these physicians was assessed (Barefoot et al., 1983). There was a nearly fivefold increase in CHD incidence among those physicians with the higher hostility scores: The number of deaths was over six times greater among those with the most hostility as compared to those with the least hostility. We might imagine that dislike and distrust of other people may prevent a person from achieving the level of connection with and social support from others that is necessary to help reduce some of the effects of stressful life experience (a concept that is explored in further detail in Chapter 10). The TABP hostility finding holds true for women as well (Fichera & Andreassi, 1998). Specifically, one study found that women who were both Type A and hostile had higher blood pressure and arterial pressure during the stressful laboratory tasks than women who were Type B and less hostile. In Box 9.3, we examine some of the most

Chronic hostility, anger, aggression, and distrustfulness form a pattern that increases the risk of coronary heart disease.

BOX **9.3**

Research Close-up

Blood Pressure and Expressing Anger Constructively

As we have seen in this chapter, negative emotions and health outcomes appear to be strongly linked. There has been considerable research on the role of anger in cardiovascular disease, but studies have generated conflicting findings. Expressing anger is related to poor health outcomes like high blood pressure and adverse cardiovascular events, both directly and through health damaging behaviors such as smoking and drinking. The suppression of anger is also associated with poor health outcomes such as hypertension, increased reports of symptoms, and heart disease (Davidson et al., 2000).

Should a person express anger, or hide it? Which approach is better for health? The answer has eluded researchers partly because of the problem in conceptualizing responses to anger. *Explosive* anger expression is indeed correlated with poor health outcomes and even untoward cardiovascular events. Another option for expressing anger, however, is doing so constructively and discussing angry feelings (Davidson et al., 2000). Constructive anger expression is a goal-oriented problem-solving method of anger communication that seeks to resolve the situation by understanding the role and point of view of the other person. The researchers taking this approach hypothesized that when someone is angry and expresses his or her anger verbally and constructively, a faster resolution of the stressful anger provoking condition can be reached and blood pressure can be returned to normal even if it was initially reactive to the anger-provoking situation. Such recovery is important because delayed blood pressure recovery places a significant load on the cardiovascular system.

This project involved a general population study in Nova Scotia of 1,862 people, with equal representation of women and men (Davidson et al., 2000). Public health nurses contacted the participants at home and interviewed them about various aspects of their physical health and psychological functioning. Many measures of blood pressure were taken at home and at the clinic session, where subjects were videotaped in a 12-minute interpersonally stressful interview. The stressful interview was a standard instrument called the ESI (Expanded Structured Interview), and it was designed to elicit anger and hostility by asking participants about their characteristic responses to a variety of situations, including anger expression, anger verbalization, and defensiveness. The videotape was later scored for hostility and aggression toward the interviewer, as well as for constructive expression of anger. Among the measures collected were depression, trait anxiety, hostility, and social support.

The results showed that those who expressed anger constructively were less likely to be hostile, anxious, or depressed. (The ESI was unrelated to social support.) While most research has shown that the explosive expression of anger is destructive, this research demonstrated that discussing anger calmly and constructively with a motivation to solve the problem was positively associated with better cardiovascular health and lower blood pressure. These findings held even when analyses were restricted to those who had never been told they had hypertension (in an attempt to eliminate the effects that might occur if people purposely tried to change their anger behavior because of high blood pressure). Thus, a resolution-oriented verbal expression of anger that involves empathy with the other person's point of view appears to result in healthy management of blood pressure and in better cardiovascular health.

recent research findings regarding the effects on blood pressure of anger and its constructive expression.

The (Controversial) Cancer Personality

As the concepts of Type A and Type B personalities gained popularity, the notion that there is a "cancer personality" also found supporters. The history of **"Type C"** illustrates what can go wrong when weaknesses in research methodology actually lead to inaccurate, though popular, conclusions. In 1956, two clinical psychologists published a review of research and theoretical literature (LeShan & Worthington, 1956). In it, they suggested that personality can play a part in the formation and development of cancer. The researchers presented what they considered to be three major threads that ran through all the studies they reviewed: People who had cancer were more likely than those without cancer (1) to be unable successfully to express hostile emotions, (2) to have more unresolved tension concerning a parental figure, and (3) to have more sexual disturbance. As one psychiatrist wrote, the person with cancer is ". . . driven into himself" (Evans, 1926). Type C was the name given to a constellation of characteristics, including the tendency to deny and suppress emotions, to avoid conflict, and to be overly agreeable. Unfortunately, many people jumped to the conclusion that the inability to express hostile feelings as well as the repression of negative emotions and unresolved tensions can cause cancer. Even the popular press picked up the idea, saying that a person with a "cancer personality" is likely to develop malignant neoplasms. This idea worried and distressed many people.

The conclusion was not justified, however. Research up to that point had never addressed the development of cancer. In all the studies that had been reviewed, people who already had cancer were interviewed or subjected to a psychiatric examination. Many patients had recently received their diagnoses. They were asked about their current emotional state, their style of expressing anger, and about areas of conflict in their lives. They were interviewed by psychiatrists and psychologists who already believed in the cancer personality and who knew they had cancer. Cancer patients were compared with those who did not have cancer. As you may already have guessed, the fact that cancer patients had negative and even hostile feelings is not terribly surprising! These patients were suffering a great deal. They were in pain and they felt very uncertain about their future survival. They may have thought: "Why me?" Yet, no matter what they felt, they had to hold back their negative feelings lest they antagonize and alienate their health professionals and others around them. The psychological differences between people with cancer and those without can be easily explained by their state of mind at the time the research was done, as well as by the expectations of those who carried out the research. Studies that avoided the serious methodological flaws of earlier work generally failed to find any relationship between personality style and susceptibility to cancer (Levy, 1985a).

Prospective studies are now being done, and the results are unclear. Generally, direct links have not been demonstrated (Baltrusch et al., 1991; Levenson & Bemis, 1991; Temoshok, 1987). What seems more clear than a "cancer-prone" personality is evidence for the role that personality factors may play once a diagnosis is made. Those who refuse to give up and who demonstrate a fighting spirit generally tend to survive longer than do those who are more passive and accepting of their terminal disease (Baltrusch et al., 1991).

Psychophysiological Disorders and Stress

Now we turn to the third realm of research in which psychological stress has been linked to disease. At the beginning of this chapter, we defined a *psychophysiological disorder* as one that is characterized by physical symptoms and/or dysfunctions that are intimately aligned with psychological factors. Psychological and physiological processes interconnect so closely in psychophysiological disorders that it is impossible to separate them. Throughout this chapter, we have been examining the role that psychological factors can play in the development of cardiovascular diseases and in impairment of the immune system. This set of disorders appears to have a connection to psychological factors, although the precise character of the connection and mechanisms of effect is not known. Many of the diseases in this next category were once referred to as psychosomatic disorders, that is, diseases believed to have psychological factors as their causative agents. (Recall that this issue was introduced in both Chapters 1 and 7.) The implication was that these diseases, or at least their symptoms, were *specifically caused* by psychological factors. Now, of course, we recognize the complex interplay of psychological and physical processes and have evidence that straightforward causal explanations may be too simplistic and inaccurate.

Reviews of the psychological, psychiatric, and medical literature from the past several decades suggest that there is a link between psychological factors (specifically, the experience of chronic negative emotions like anger, hostility, depression, anxiety, and aggression) to the once classically identified psychosomatic diseases including ulcers, arthritis, asthma, and headaches (Friedman & Booth-Kewley, 1987). Each of these diseases is widespread and chronic, and their precise causes are not well understood. Yet each can be identified both as having objective physical findings upon examination and as influenced by psychological factors (such as asthma by anxiety and headaches by unresolved anger). The difficulty inherent in ascertaining the relationship between emotion and a disease process can be demonstrated with the case of ulcers (Levenstein, 1998; Levenstein et al., 1999). Ulcers are circumscribed lesions in the digestive tract (usually the esophagus, stomach, and duodenum). Until recently, they were believed to be due to stress, too much stomach acid (a possible result of stress), or too much spicy food or other irritants such as medications. Then, a medical discovery shook the foundations of this belief—it was found that many people with ulcers also had the bacteria *Heliobacter pylori* (*H. pylori*) in their stomachs. When treated with antibiotics, patients experienced dramatic recoveries from their ulcers. Suddenly stress was "out" as an explanatory mechanism for ulcers, and *H. pylori* was "in"!

As is usually the case in health psychology, however, the story is really more complicated than it might at first appear. Despite the overwhelming evidence that bacterial infections can cause ulcers, it is also the case that psychosocially stressful events (such as wars and earthquakes) are associated with increases in the incidence of ulcers.

The same is true for animals that experience stressful situations and infants who are separated from their mothers. Further, we know that stress can trigger sleep loss, high alcohol consumption, and increased stomach acid secretion, all of which are linked to ulcers. So, what is the "real" cause of ulcers? That is not entirely clear, and it depends upon many factors including how we think about causality. Certainly, if the level of *H. pylori* infection is extensive enough, an ulcer is likely to develop, regardless of the individual's psychological state. More commonly, however, causality is multifaceted. Usually infection is moderate, and stress factors may facilitate the action of the bacteria in doing damage to the stomach. Furthermore, stress may impair the ability of the body to fight off the bacteria in the first place or to heal the ulcer.

Post-Traumatic Stress Disorder

Sometimes people who have undergone very harrowing and extremely stressful events experience serious effects even months or years after the event occurs. These effects can include flattened affect (emotion), sleep disturbances, exaggerated startle responses, extreme guilt, intense watchfulness, and even "reliving" of some of their traumatic experiences (Orr et al., 1995). These individuals are said to be suffering from **post-traumatic stress disorder** (PTSD). PTSD occurs most often following extreme war experiences, but can also be a response to other traumatic events such as rape or natural disasters (Ironson et al., 1997; King et al., 1995). As with other experiences of stress, PTSD has been linked to changes in immune functioning (Ironson et al., 1997). It has also been associated with a variety of hormonal fluctuations such as those we discussed above in our consideration of general stress (Mason et al., 1990).

The Difficulties of Assuming Causation

Despite the temptation to do so, we cannot conclude that chronic negative emotions actually *cause* illness. The research reviewed in this chapter has examined associations, not causal relationships. In fact, emotions could just as easily have been caused by illness as have caused it. Finding an association between asthma and anxiety, for example, means that while anxiety may have contributed to the development and exacerbation of asthma, asthma might just as likely have contributed to the development and exacerbation of anxiety. Gasping for air in the throes of an asthma attack, for example, would probably make anyone consistently anxious. Of course, researchers note that a biological third variable could be the cause of both emotion and disease and could account for the relationship between the two. For example, a hyperresponsive nervous system could be the cause of chronic anxiety and of asthma. Chronic anxiety could thus be the "marker" for asthma but it would fail to play a role in its development. Negative emotion may be related to disease but not cause it (Buck, 1984).

For the moment, let's return to Atul, whom we met at the beginning of this chapter. Atul did indeed have an infection of the Herpes virus, and his overwhelmingly stressful life situation at the time very likely produced an exacerbation of the infection, leading to the manifestation of myelitis. Without his money and job search troubles, and almost certainly without the death of his sister, the underlying infection he had might have remained muted and never noticed.

Much has yet to be learned about the physiological mechanisms that connect emotions with various disease processes. This realm of research is an exciting element of the fast-growing field of health psychology. Stay tuned. . . .

In the next chapter, we will examine the many ways in which individuals under stress try to deal effectively with it. We will consider the consequences of their attempts to prevent stress from adversely affecting their physical and their mental health, and we will examine the most and least effective methods of combating stress, as well as the theories and research that support current thinking about the concept of coping.

Summary

1. Disorders can range from those brought about because of purely psychological factors (e.g., anorexia nervosa) to those that probably have no psychological overlay at all (e.g., appendicitis).

   - Nuclear Conflict Theory holds that each physiological disorder is associated with certain specific unconscious emotional conflicts.

2. Stress is a complicated concept and may refer to physical strain (e.g., taxing an organism beyond its strength) or to psychological strain (e.g., the experience of negative emotions in response to conflict in a relationship).

3. Stress may be viewed as a stimulus, as a physical and psychological response to a stimulus, or as an interaction between the two.

   - Stress is dependent upon primary and secondary cognitive appraisal.
   - Chronic stress can result from a life situation that requires significant and persistent adaptation.
   - Daily hassles are stressful events (usually minor) for which there are no automatic, adaptive responses. They can be balanced by uplifts.
   - Life change events require considerable adjustment in how the individual lives.

4. Stress can significantly affect physical health.

   - The fight-or-flight response is a reaction to the perception of danger.
   - The General Adaptation Syndrome involves three stages in the stress response: mobilization (alarm), resistance, and exhaustion.

5. Psychoneuroimmunology is a field of study that examines the relationship between psychosocial processes and nervous, endocrine, and immune system functioning. Stress can compromise an organism's ability to defend itself against microbial invaders.

6. Stress has also been implicated in the development of cardiovascular disorders, particularly hypertension and coronary heart disease (CHD).

- Type A behavior pattern involves a predisposition to think, feel, and act a certain way in response to environmental demands. Personality characteristics that best predict CHD are hostility, competitiveness, hard-driving aggressiveness, and mistrust of others.

7. Research on psychosomatic disease tends to demonstrate that negative emotions (depression, anger, hostility, and anxiety) are correlated with the incidence of ulcers, arthritis, headaches, and asthma. Causal explanations are difficult, however.

THINKING CRITICALLY

1. What are some of the problems that psychologists encounter when they try to define "stress" as a stimulus or a life event? How do other conceptualizations of stress remedy this difficulty? How do you conceptualize stress? With which theoretical framework does your view best fit?

2. Using what you know about the General Adaptation Syndrome and the different ways in which people view life events, explain why a person who has just recently retired and is

now ready to enjoy "the golden years" suddenly finds him- or herself becoming ill frequently, although he or she has always been very healthy.

3. Does it still make sense to think of TABP as a predictor of cardiovascular disease (CVD)? Now that we have identified the components of TABP that are most predictive of CVD, should we just focus on those both in research and clinically? Why?

GLOSSARY

Alarm Stage: The first stage in the General Adaptation Syndrome during which the body is made ready to respond to threat and there is an increase in adrenal, cardiovascular, and respiratory activity.

Angina pectoris (also called angina): A form of heart disease in which the sufferer feels pain and tightness in his or her chest because of brief or incomplete blockages of oxygenated blood to the heart.

Arteriosclerosis: Condition in which the walls of arteries thicken and lose their elasticity.

Atherosclerosis: A form of arteriosclerosis that involves the formation of fatty plaques in the arteries throughout the body. In the coronary arteries, these plaques obstruct blood flow and oxygen to the heart muscle, which can result in angina pectoris (chest pain), cardiac insufficiency, and myocardial infarction (heart attack).

Cardiovascular disorders: Disorders of the heart, blood vessels, and blood circulation.

Cathartic technique: A technique of psychological treatment which involves reviving inhibited or otherwise inaccessible memories for the purpose

of discharging the pathogenic emotions attached to them.

Chronicity of stress: The chronic character of stress.

Cognitive appraisal: Cognitive interpretations that affect the degree to which an individual experiences physiological stress reactions.

Coronary heart disease: A category of disease that includes myocardial infarction (heart attack), angina (chest pain caused by restriction of oxygen to the heart muscle as a result of occluded coronary arteries), sudden cardiac death, cardiac insufficiency (inability of the heart to perform its function properly), and electrocardiogram abnormalities.

Daily hassles: Daily events for which an individual may have no automatic, adaptive responses and that require adjustment; hassles can pose a threat to health.

Dynamic process of stress: Stress as ongoing and pervasive throughout life.

Exhaustion Stage: The third stage in the General Adaptation Syndrome, in which the organism experiences a depletion of physiological resources for dealing with a threat.

Fight-or-flight response: Response in which the human organism is readied for fighting or taking flight when in danger. In this response, blood pressure, heart rate, respiration rate, and blood sugar rise, there is palmar sweating, and the muscles tense.

General Adaptation Syndrome: Selye's theory of stress involving three stages: alarm, resistance, and exhaustion.

Hypertension: Elevated blood pressure defined as resting blood pressure greater than 140 mm HG (systolic)/90 mm HG (diastolic).

Idiopathic: Of unknown cause.

Life change events: Life events that require considerable adaptation.

Lymphocyte: White blood corpuscles that arise in the reticular tissue of the lymph glands and play a key role in immune system functioning.

Meta-analysis: A methodological tool for combining results from independent studies using quantitative techniques to determine overall effects and significance.

Myocardial infarction ("heart attack"): Involves a severe or prolonged blockage of blood to the heart that results in the muscle tissue (myocardium) being destroyed.

Nuclear Conflict Theory: Proposed by Alexander, this theory holds that each physiological disorder is associated with specific unconscious emotional conflicts.

Optimism: A cognitive style characterized by positive, hopeful views about the future and outcomes in life.

Post-traumatic stress disorder (PTSD): Response (sometimes delayed by months or years) to extremely stressful events, including affect and sleep disturbances, extreme vigilance, and even "reliving" of the traumatic event.

Primary appraisal of stress: A person's determination of whether the event has any potential negative implications for him or her.

Process stress: Stress that changes and develops over time.

Psychoneuroimmunology: A field of study that examines the direct effects of psychological factors and the nervous system on the immune system.

Psychophysiological disorder: Characterized by physical symptoms and/or dysfunctions that are intimately linked with psychological factors.

Resistance Stage: The second stage in the General Adaptation Syndrome during which an organism attempts to take action to overcome a stressor or learns to adjust to it.

Secondary appraisal of stress: The individual's determination of his or her own abilities to overcome the threat of potential harm from a stressful event.

Social Readjustment Rating Scale (SRRS): A measure of life events in terms of their judged salience and impact; death of a spouse receives the highest score of 100.

Stress: Physical strain (such as taxing an organism beyond its strength) or psychological strain (such as emotional distress in a relationship).

Stressor: A stimulus or event that produces stress within the individual.

Threat: The subjective appraisal of potential negative effects of a stressor; dependent upon appraisal of the event as threatening. Threat mobilizes action.

Type A behavior pattern (TABP): A predisposition to think, feel, and act in a particular way in response to stress. The major elements are aggressiveness, competitive striving, sense of time urgency, impatience, and hostility.

Type B behavior pattern: The opposite of Type A behavior pattern—calm, relaxed, and easygoing.

Type C behavior pattern: A constellation of characteristics once believed to predispose people to cancer; characteristics include wanting to make others happy, suppressing emotions and their expression, and being very compliant and overly pleasant.

Uplifts: Positive daily events that can be used to combat negative feelings and cope successfully. Uplifts can "buffer" (prevent the full impact of) the effects of stress on an individual's physical and mental condition and serve as a source of peace and joy.

CHAPTER

10

Coping with Stress: The Role of Psychological Processes in Staying Healthy

Francisco felt a flood of adrenaline pour into his bloodstream as he looked into the cage and realized that the snake had disappeared. He quickly looked beneath the small hiding log and the pygmy bush that made up the animal's habitat, but the snake really was not in the cage. He looked around frantically, thinking that surely this couldn't actually be happening!

This was Francisco's second day at his new job as "head animal care technician." He had been put in charge of caring for more than 100 animals at the university's laboratory facility, and he was proud of his position. He had two assistants that worked under him, and he had responsibility for purchasing food and bedding, for keeping the animals fed and their cages clean, and for identifying any ill animals and reporting them to the university's veterinarian. But now he felt his position was in jeopardy because somehow he had allowed a very rare and expensive, although thankfully not dangerous, snake to escape from its cage.

Francisco's eyes scanned the room frantically. He saw that one of the three outside exit doors was partially open, which meant that the snake might not even be in the room anymore. If the snake had managed to make it outdoors, the chances of ever finding it were slim indeed. His heart was racing and he felt a small trickle of sweat making its way down his backbone; he didn't know what to do or where to look first, so he remained frozen for a few moments.

Then Francisco realized that he had several choices. He could panic and maybe call his supervisor for advice. Or, he could blame the mistake on one of the student workers. He would still be in trouble, although not as much, but that option didn't feel right to him. More adaptively, he could devise a logical plan for searching and worry later about what to do if the snake could not be found. He decided to go with this last option.

Francisco took two slow deep breaths and told himself that his chances of finding the animal were good if he could focus his mind on a search for it. Breathing deeply helped to calm him, and his heart rate began to slow down. He walked to the door, stepped outside, and closed it behind him. He reasoned that the snake had not been out of its cage very long, so if it had gotten outside it probably had not gone far. He also knew that this snake was nocturnal, and it would seek shade and darkness in the middle of the day. So, he quickly looked under each object that was close to the doorway. The snake was not there and so now he felt reasonably sure that the snake had not actually gotten out of the vivarium. So, he returned to the room and began a systematic search. After 15 minutes he felt somewhat discouraged, but kept reminding himself that he needed to be methodical. Five minutes later he was rewarded! The snake had wedged itself between the bottom drawer of the filing cabinet and the floor. If Francisco's search had been less thorough, he would certainly have missed this hiding place. He placed the snake back into its cage and double-checked the latches to make sure that it could not escape again. He then jogged up the stairs and down the hallway to the water fountain. He felt thirsty, and wanted to burn off some of that "fight or flight" energy!

As we saw in Chapter 9, stress can affect the immune system in some important ways, and the experience of stress can compromise an organism's ability to successfully defend itself against microbial invaders (Biondi & Zannino, 1997; Cohen & Herbert, 1996). Death of a spouse, for example, has been found to reduce severely the production of lymphocytes, which are necessary for fighting infections (Irwin et al., 1987). The stresses of college life, including examinations, can also lead to immunosuppression, resulting in increased rates of acute respiratory and other infectious diseases (Deinzer & Schueller, 1998).

Various factors influence whether, and how severely, stress will impair immune functioning. Uncontrollable stressors, for example, appear to produce more adverse effects than do controllable ones. And immune responses depend partly upon an individual's ability to cope with a stressor. In one study of married, separated, and divorced women, certain psychosocial factors predicted their blood test measures of immune functioning. Among the married women, there was a positive correlation between marital satisfaction and immune functioning; as you might guess, those who were less satisfied showed poorer immune system performance. Among the separated and divorced women, those with poorer adjustment to their marital troubles had poorer immune functioning than did those who accepted the fact of the separation or divorce and did not spend much time thinking about their husbands (Kiecolt-Glaser et al., 1987).

One of the most intriguing aspects of the phenomenon of stress is the fact that different people who are exposed to precisely the same stressful life event can experience it in vastly different ways. One person may be overwhelmed physically and emotionally, while another barely notices the event and proceeds relatively unconcerned. One person might instantly tackle the source of the stress while another does little but worry about it for days. One person may be able to relax and put the problem out of mind while another is so distressed that restful sleep is out of the question. The precise character of an event or situation is not a reliable indicator of the degree of stress an individual will feel or of how that stress will affect the individual's physical and psychological health. Many factors can alter or even completely filter out the negative effects of stress, averting the potentially debilitating effects of stress on health.

A difference exists between the concepts of "workload" and "stress," and it is important to make a distinction between the two. Have you ever found yourself really busy with school and work and friends, and at the same time focused, energetic, and having fun? You can accomplish a great deal in a short amount of time despite having an extensive workload. This is a "trying harder" mentality that is a healthy and adaptive way to cope with growing demands (e.g., Gaillard, 1993). Yet at other times, perhaps, you may have felt utterly swamped by a similar, or even smaller, workload. What was the difference? Perhaps it was the way in which you organized your time and prioritized your activities, the manner in which you thought about the work and the things you had to do, the amount and quality of your sleep and nutrition, and perhaps also whether you exercised. Numerous cognitive and behavioral factors can influence the ways in which people attempt to adapt at different points in time, and the effectiveness of those attempts.

In this chapter, we consider the various ways that individuals try to accomplish two goals: (1) to reduce feelings of stress in the face of potentially stressful situations and (2) to manage and reduce stress once it has been experienced. These goals are interrelated, of course. Having ways to manage stress may make it more difficult for stressful events to wreak havoc in the first place. Reducing the potential for stress obviates, to some degree, the need to manage it.

Psychologists have long recognized that what people think, and the meaning they attach to the events they experience, can influence their reactions and subsequently their adjustment (Lazarus & Launier, 1978). As we noted in Chapter 9, cognitive evaluations of an event or stressor are extremely important in determining how an individual will react to them. Stress depends upon the perception of threat of harm as well as upon the discrepancy that the individual perceives between the demands of the situation and his or her ability to meet them. One person who is given a job transfer across the country may view the change as very stressful and may encounter many emotional difficulties attempting to adjust to it. These difficulties may, in turn, compromise his or her health. Another person might view the job change and the cross-country move as an exciting adventure and an opportunity for learning. As we will see, the way a challenging situation is approached and dealt with can make a great deal of difference in how it affects the individual's life.

In this chapter, we will also examine several psychological factors that have been found to mediate the connection between stress (stressful life events, hassles, or chronic stressors) and physical illness. We will consider cognitive factors that affect people's interpretations of what is happening to them, and we will examine the sense of control that people have over what they are experiencing. We will look at long-standing patterns of cognitive and emotional responses to stress, as well as methods for altering thought patterns about stressful events. We will also evaluate training in cognitive coping methods (such as stress inoculation) and will consider problem-solving approaches to stress reduction (such as cognitive behavior modification). We will look at methods aimed at minimizing the physiological arousal that accompanies stress reactions and examine the effectiveness of specific behaviors (such as exercise) that can help to bring about adjustment. Finally, we will discuss the role of more technical psychological interventions (such as progressive muscle relaxation and biofeedback techniques) as well as socioemotional factors (such as social support) in aiding successful coping.

If this chapter has a primary message, it is that stress can be dealt with successfully. A human being's health is not at the mercy of life's events. Stress jeopardizes health only when the stress is not dealt with effectively. This chapter presents the many options that are available to help us to meet the challenges of stress and to remain healthy, both physically and emotionally, despite the vexations and vicissitudes of life.

Coping Processes

Coping is a term that has made its way into popular culture. People talk about trying to cope with their problems. Some say that they need to learn to cope better with balancing work, school, family, and financial pressures, others may note that some of their unhealthy behaviors, such as overeating or failing to exercise, are attempts to cope with stress. Although the psychological definition of coping is not far removed from the popular usage of the term, a precise definition is essential for our examination of coping. "Coping consists of efforts, both action-oriented and intrapsychic, to manage (i.e., master, tolerate, reduce, or minimize) environmental and internal demands and conflicts among them" (Lazarus & Launier, 1978, p. 311).

When people attempt to cope, they try to deal with the differences they perceive between the demands of a stressful situation and their ability to meet those demands. Ideally, people focus their efforts on trying to correct the problems they face. But in trying to deal with differences between situational demands and their own abilities, sometimes people try to escape from or to avoid the things they find threatening (such as by getting drunk). They may also try to simply accept situations they find unmanageable.

While technically the definition of coping can include all attempts (however self-destructive the attempt may be) to deal with stressful situations, here we focus on active coping efforts that can be expected to leave the individual better off physically and psychologically after employing them.

What is meant by "better off"? Efforts to cope are typically successful if they accomplish five general goals (Cohen & Lazarus, 1979). The first and primary task involves contending realistically with the problem. When faced with a stressful experience, an individual who is coping successfully engages in all possible efforts to reduce the harmful environmental conditions that he or she faces and to enhance prospects for survival and recovery. The individual's efforts are oriented toward this critically important task of contending with the realistic demands of the stressful situation. The second, third, and fourth tasks focus on the individual's emotions and thoughts. The individual attempts to tolerate or to adjust emotionally to the negative events or realities; he or she tries to maintain a positive self-image; and the individual tries to preserve his or her emotional equilibrium. The fifth and final task is concerned with the social environment. The individual tries to continue satisfying relationships with other people (Cohen & Lazarus, 1979).

As we saw in the previous chapter, stress can have a profound effect on physical health. Coping is a tool by which an individual deals with stress and tries to solve the problem that he or she faces, or live with its effects. Coping may in fact buffer the effects of stress on the body, as some studies suggest. In one study of adults, for example, the effect of life events and daily hassle stress on the incidence of upper respiratory tract (URT) infections was examined (Cobb & Steptoe, 1996). Despite not differing in their sleep, exercise, or smoking habits, the individuals who experienced greater life events stress before and during the study suffered more URT infections. This effect was buffered by subjects' coping styles, however. The way that the individuals coped with their stress influenced their susceptibility to illness.

Coping is a dynamic process. An individual may attempt several coping strategies, and feedback about the success of one type of effort typically spurs the person on to try it again. Failure, on the other hand, encourages one to try another approach or perhaps give up altogether. The individual continually appraises and reappraises the environment and his or her efforts at coping with it (Lazarus & Folkman, 1984). How do we know when an individual has coped successfully with a stressor? A precise answer to this question has not yet been found, although we can use what we know about stress to suggest one. The most adequate measures of successful coping are likely to be multifaceted. When coping well, an individual should report a reduction in his or her feelings of psychological distress (including anxiety and depression). He or she should also be able to return to the behaviors that were typical for him or her prior to encountering the stress. Successful coping should also show up physiologically in the form of reduced heart rate, breathing rate, skin conductivity, and muscle tension. In addition, blood or urine levels of catecholamines (epinephrine and norepinephrine, which may affect the heart through chronic arousal) and cortocosteroids (which are related to stress and may impair immune functioning) should drop. Complex, multifaceted measures are necessary to give an accurate picture of the quality and effectiveness of coping.

Problem Solving and Emotional Regulation

Coping efforts fall into two major functional categories: problem-solving efforts and emotion-focused coping efforts (Lazarus & Folkman, 1984). **Problem-solving efforts** (also known as **problem-focused coping** efforts) involve taking direct action to change a stressful situation or to prevent or reduce its effects. The goal of problem-focused coping is to reduce the demands of the situation or enhance one's resources to deal with it. Applying for a loan to pay overdue bills is a good example. A person may even seek information in order to cope with a problem (such as learning basic automobile repairs in order to fix a car that breaks down often). Problem-focused coping can even begin before the problem does. This approach is called **proactive coping** (Aspinwall & Taylor, 1997). In this case the individual anticipates potential causes of stress and does things to plan ahead for the situation. Using proactive coping doesn't mean that one will never encounter a stressor, but it can enable a person to be better prepared to handle it. People tend to use problem-focused coping when they believe that there is something that they can do about the stressful situation they face (Lazarus & Folkman, 1984).

Emotion-focused coping involves attempts to regulate or reduce the emotional (and relatedly social) consequences of the stressful event. The individual attempts to regulate his or her emotions. When faced with the breakup of a romantic relationship, for example, people may try to cope with their feelings of distress by distracting their attention with day-to-day activities. In response to stressful events, the emotion-focused coping response may also involve cognitively reevaluating the situation ("The relationship was not very good from the start, so breaking up is the best thing"), seeking emotional support and reassurance from other people, trying to accept the problem if one can do nothing about it, and discharging emotion (by crying or joking).

While both problem-focused and emotion-focused coping are necessary when facing stressful situations, research suggests that people generally tend to use the former more often than the latter. Emotion-focused coping is more likely to be used after stressful events are over, when the situation cannot be changed, and women tend to use more emotion-focused coping strategies than do men (Billings & Moos, 1981). In most cases, however, both problem-solving and emotion-focused approaches are necessary for effective long-term coping. Although coping with the emotional aspects of a stressful event can be extremely important, emotion-focused coping efforts do not deal with the reality of a problem and bring about a long-term solution. Likewise, continuous efforts to solve a problem without concern for its psychological impact on the individual may place him or her in jeopardy. A long-term realistic solution may come at the expense of the individual's psychological health, and long-term problem-solving efforts may fail without the short-term relief of emotion-focused coping.

Consider the earlier example of Francisco and his temporary misplacement of the snake that was his responsibility. Francisco engaged in both problem-focused coping and emotion-focused coping, but it was the former that allowed him to ultimately solve his problem and reduce his stress. Had he maintained his initial emotion-focused reaction, that of blaming a student worker, he might never have focused his attention

TABLE 10.1   Coping Strategies

The coping strategies that an individual chooses depend a great deal upon the situation and the unique interaction of person and situation. Cohen and Lazarus (1979) suggest five major types of strategies.

1. *Seeking information*: Considering what behavioral choices are open and the probable outcome of each, as well as learning precisely how one would follow any particular course of action.
2. *Taking direct action*: Enacting specific behaviors meant to deal directly with the stressor. When direct action is possible (which is not always the case), this coping strategy is more adaptive emotionally and physically than taking no action. Direct action promotes a sense of mastery and control and allows for the discharge of physiological arousal in the fight-or-flight response (Gal & Lazarus, 1975).
3. *Inhibiting action:* Suppressing the desire to take action. Under some circumstances, this approach may be the best course of action (for example, being quiet instead of screaming at one's boss, which could threaten one's long-term interests).
4. *Engaging intrapsychic efforts:* Such actions as suppressing or ignoring upsetting thoughts or reframing them into more positive ideas.
5. *Calling on others:* Asking other people for both physical and emotional support.

on finding the snake and he may have ultimately felt worse and put his job in jeopardy. Instead, Francisco remained calm and took a logical course of action, refusing to allow the stress to overwhelm him.

Table 10.1 presents the five general strategies that individuals can use to cope with stress (Lazarus & Cohen, 1979). When faced with a situation that demands action or adjustment, individuals can choose to seek information, take direct action, do nothing, engage in emotion regulation, or call on others for assistance or support.

Cognitions and Coping

Cognitions refer to one's thoughts about, and interpretations of, events and one's relation to those events. Cognitions can have an important effect on how an individual views a stressful situation because they typically reflect in some way the individual's view of his or her own life and its meaning. For example, the stress of losing a job is likely to be much higher if an individual views job loss as a personal failure than if he or she does not. An individual is likely to experience higher levels of stress if the future is viewed with pessimism than if the job change is seen as a new opportunity. Not surprisingly then, the individual's efforts to manage the distressing thoughts and feelings that arise in response to a problem can reduce the experience of stress.

Cognitive Coping Styles

An individual's **coping style** refers to the *manner* in which and the *degree* to which he or she thinks about stressful life events. Coping styles fall into two general categories: **proactive coping** and **avoidant coping**. Some individuals may minimize or even completely avoid the implications of a threatening event (avoidant coping). Other individuals may confront the trouble directly by gathering information and even by taking straightforward preventive action (proactive coping) (Aspinwall & Taylor, 1997; Goldstein, 1973). Which coping style is the better approach depends a great deal upon the situation. For example, a student behaving in an avoidant manner might ignore recommendations to preregister for courses and instead merely show up on the first day of school and take whatever courses are still open for enrollment. The student who is coping proactively, on the other hand, confronts the situation directly and prepares for preregistration by consulting the course catalogue and list of course requirements. As early as the sophomore year, this student might even plan out the courses needed for graduation, being careful to take all the necessary prerequisites. Nothing is left to chance and situations over which there is some possibility of control usually work out well. Of course, proactive coping may extract a certain price in the form of anxiety at having to deal directly with the issue of concern. Avoiding it might initially bring about greater relaxation, but sometimes the lack of direct action can make the achievement of goals difficult or impossible (i.e., the courses needed for graduation may have reached maximum enrollment). Proactive coping is likely to be the better practical alternative.

Proactive coping involves five stages (Aspinwall & Taylor, 1997). How well a person performs at each of these five stages will depend on a number of factors, such as skills, personality, and internal and external resources:

1. *Resource accumulation* refers to the person's actions to garner help for him- or herself. For instance, getting a good education is one way of accumulating resources, as is gradually building a savings account.
2. *Recognition of potential stressors* occurs when a person tries to anticipate things that might happen or go wrong. For instance, when leaving for an appointment, it is best to realize that traffic might be heavy and cause delay.
3. *Initial appraisal* is defined as one's first assessment of the stressful situation, when it occurs. After finding out that an important check has "bounced," the individual might first assess his or her checking account balance to determine whether there were indeed insufficient funds or instead an error was made by the bank.
4. *Preliminary coping efforts* are those first attempts at dealing with the stressful situation. They may not be completely effective and will likely be altered after feedback is received. They do, however, represent quick action to address the problem after its initial appraisal. Trying to reach a friend who has a computer printer after one's own printer has broken down may be an adaptive first strategy on the night before an important paper is due. If that friend is nowhere to be found, alternative plans must be made.
5. *Elicitation and use of feedback* concerning initial efforts involves the person's attempt to find out how well preliminary coping strategies are working so that

appropriate modifications can be made. Rechecking one's degree plan with the student affairs counselor and making modifications if necessary is a useful, flexible technique for proactive coping.

Reactions to stressful events are influenced not only by the individual's basic coping style but also by his or her need for, and tolerance of, stimulating experiences. For some people, new experiences and a varied routine are absolutely necessary for happiness, whereas other people experience distress whenever their familiar routine is even mildly interrupted. Research demonstrates that individuals with a high need for stimulation tend to adjust better to stressful life events than do those who have a low need for stimulation (Johnson et al., 1979). Of course, it is possible that such a preference makes "stressful events" seem not particularly stressful at all or may even bring about immediate coping measures such as the recognition of **self-efficacy.** Self-efficacy, as we saw in Chapter 6, is the belief that one can indeed accomplish a particular goal (Bandura, 1977; Wheaton, 1983). Thus, the individual who thrives on activity and unpredictability might be the kind of person who feels very capable of dealing with whatever comes along.

Causal Attributions

Causal attributions are reasons that individuals give for why a particular situation has occurred. People usually have some idea about the causes of the events they experience. Such attributions can include: "It is God's will," "Things sometimes happen for no reason," "It happened because I am a bad person," "I am supposed to learn something from this," or "I deserve this." Attributions for a very negative event, such as contracting HIV, can include "poetic justice" or my "personal destiny" (Rudolph & Steins, 1998).

Explanatory Styles

How an individual understands and explains life events (particularly the unfortunate ones) can influence his or her degree of perceived helplessness in the face of those events. An individual's typical way of explaining such events is referred to as his or her **explanatory style**. Explanatory style is comprised of three **attributions** (causes assigned to events):

1. Attributions are either *internal* ("I really messed that up") or *external* ("That task was very difficult").
2. Attributions are either *stable* ("I can never solve problems like this") or *unstable* ("I failed to solve this particular problem").
3. Attributions are either *global* ("This is going to mess up my whole life") or *specific* ("This one area of my life has problems").

The tendency to make internal, stable, and global attributions for negative events is referred to as a **pessimistic** explanatory style. An **optimistic** style, on the other hand, involves the tendency to attribute external, unstable, and specific causes for bad things that happen (Peterson & Seligman, 1987; Peterson et al., 1988). Research shows that if people perceive stressful events in their lives to have internal, global, and stable explanations (that is, if they have a pessimistic explanatory style), they experience greater threats to their motivational, cognitive, and emotional control than if they have an optimistic explanatory style (Peterson & Seligman 1987). This means that when people look at the negative events in their lives and believe (1) that they are personally to blame for these events, (2) that these negative events are likely to be long term, and (3) that the negative events have pervasive effects on many areas of their lives, they are less able to cope effectively with the associated stress. Individuals who make these sorts of attributions feel more helpless than those who do not and feel less able to deal with their problems. Their pessimism in turn influences their behavior. They often *do* deal less effectively with their problems.

In examining explanatory style and attempting to understand how people explain disappointments, misfortunes, and tragedies, researchers have been drawn to the questions of why causal attributions are so important to coping and what effects explanatory style might have on people's health. Research suggests that attributions do indeed affect emotional health, physical health, and even the immune system as illustrated in Figure 10.1 (Segerstrom et al., 1996). For instance, causal attributions regarding why one is sick have been associated with making necessary lifestyle changes to try to become healthy (De Valle & Norman, 1992). They have also been shown to correlate with physician visits among older patients and with getting recommended mammograms among middle-aged women (Rothman et al., 1993; Stoller & Forster, 1994). In addition, attributions are correlated with the management of end-stage renal disease (ESRD), as measured by adherence to fluid intake restrictions among dialysis patients (Friend et al., 1997). In these studies, people who had an optimistic explanatory style took better care of themselves.

In other research with adults, global attributions for bad events significantly predicted poorer subjective health ratings (Dua, 1994). People who were more likely to use global attributions to explain negative events in their lives perceived themselves to be in poorer health. This study also found that the attributions people made for negative events were better predictors of health than their attributions for positive events. When faced with a crisis, it is possible that the assessment of its cause may affect an individual's approach to combating it: giving up in despair or pressing on. Yet another study has demonstrated that among HIV-positive gay men, negative (as opposed to positive) attributions about the self, the future, and control predicted faster helper T-cell decline (an indication of diminishing immune functioning) over an eighteen-month period (Segerstrom et al., 1996). In this study, attributions were not simply related to health-care behaviors, but were actually linked to immune system functioning.

Two important longitudinal studies have looked at early explanatory style and its relationship to health many decades later. One interesting finding comes from research that began in 1946 and followed 99 young men for over forty years. They were roughly 25 years old when the study began and had just graduated from Harvard University.

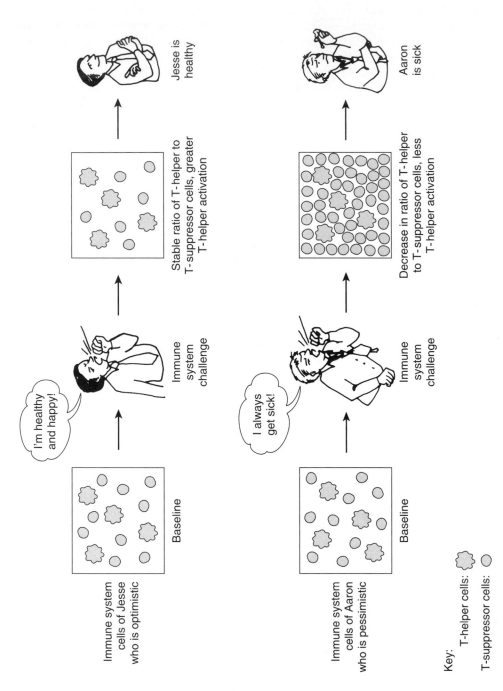

FIGURE 10.1 Pessimism and cell-mediated immunity.

Those who, early in their adulthood, had explained bad events pessimistically (using internal, stable, and global attributions) developed poorer health by age 45 than did those who had explained events in an optimistic (external, unstable, specific) way. Their attributions showed a significant association with their physical health even up to age 60 (Peterson et al., 1988). Another prospective, longitudinal study of over 1,000 men and women has demonstrated that those with a more pessimistic explanatory style were at an increased risk for early death over the next fifty years, compared with their less pessimistic peers (Peterson et al., 1998). More pessimistic individuals were at greater risk for all causes of death, not just suicides. In this study, the most harmful aspect of the pessimistic style was globality, or what these researchers called "catastrophizing." That is, the individuals who were less able to put their concerns into a broader perspective were worse off than were those who could maintain a more balanced point of view.

Additional research supports these findings. For example, in one study, optimism was assessed in surgical candidates for coronary bypass (installation of arterial grafts in the heart to bypass coronary arteries that are blocked by atherosclerotic plaques) (Scheier & Carver, 1987). The assessment was made on the day before this major open-heart surgery. Although they did not know who was who, the hospital staff judged the optimists to be recovering faster than the nonoptimists, and the optimists were ambulatory sooner than the nonoptimists. Another study, this time of older adults, found that those who were more optimistic about their health were less likely to die within the following three years than those who were pessimistic. This occurred despite the fact that the two groups did not actually differ in terms of their physical health status (Borawski et al., 1996).

Why might explanatory style and health be associated? Several interpretations are possible. First, disease may contribute to one's adoption of a particular explanatory style; pessimistic people might be pessimistic because they feel in poor health. The cognitive and emotional manifestations of disease may become apparent long before the physical manifestations do, and so pessimism appears first and physical illness is seen later. It is possible, too, that people who offer stable, global, and internal explanations become passive in the face of illness in its earlier stages, and they are less likely than optimists to take actions to enhance their health. One study, for example, showed that college students with a pessimistic style who developed colds or flu did not take even the simplest of precautions (such as resting) to help themselves (Peterson & Seligman, 1987). In general, pessimistic explanatory style may result in failing to seek medical advice or in not following such advice once it is obtained (Peterson & Seligman, 1987). Relatedly, depression is strongly correlated with patient noncompliance to medical treatment recommendations, perhaps because depression leads to hopelessness, and/or because it interferes with social support and constructive thinking (DiMatteo et al., 2000).

Of course, regularly explaining events pessimistically might cause an individual to experience chronically negative emotions, which, as we saw in Chapter 9, may precipitate or exacerbate certain chronic diseases. For example, it has been suggested that the stress associated with negative explanatory tendencies may increase the risk of heart disease (Dykema et al., 1995). Research also suggests that people who generate pessimistic explanations for bad events show increased immunosuppression and less effective immune system functioning than do those whose explanations are optimistic (Jemmott & Locke, 1984; Peterson et al., 1988). One study even found that the immune system does not generally function as well in pessimistic individuals as it does in optimistic individuals (Kamen-Siegel et al., 1991). In this study, immune function was measured using the ratio of T-helper cells to T-suppressor cells and the level of T-lymphocyte response to an immune system challenge. Individuals with a more pessimistic explanatory style had poorer helper cell ratios and lymphocyte responses than did individuals with a more optimistic outlook (controlling for current health, depression, medication, recent weight change, sleep, and alcohol use). The authors suggested that an increase in T-suppressor cells may underlie the observed immunosuppression.

It is important to recognize that optimism does not refer to superficial positiveness or to carelessness because "everything always works out great." In fact, research shows that when a person's attitude is so positive that it keeps him or her from taking necessary health precautions, very high optimism can actually become a risk factor for ill health and disease (Davidson & Prkachin, 1997; Tennen & Affleck, 1987). One study even found that very cheerful and optimistic children were at increased risk for premature death over their lifetimes compared with those who were less cheerful and optimistic (Friedman et al., 1993). It is important to point out, regarding this last study, that cheerfulness and optimism are not the *same* construct. Optimism involves expectations for the future and attributions for the present, whereas cheerfulness involves an emotional state such as happiness. Additional examination of these individuals indicated that those who were more cheerful and optimistic were also likely to take more risks with their health (smoking, drinking, risky hobbies) (Martin et al., in press).

There is such a thing as "healthy optimism." Healthy optimists are those who, because they expect positive outcomes, are less avoidant and more problem-focused in their coping strategies (Scheier & Carver, 1992). They are people who generally expect positive outcomes, are hopeful, and tend to see problems as manageable rather than catastrophic. Because of this view, they take positive action to promote their own health.

Box 10.1 examines the role of women's explanatory styles in their ability to cope successfully with a diagnosis of breast cancer.

Sense of Control

Cognitions determine how events are interpreted, whether they are seen as threatening, and how much adaptation they require. If an individual regards change as exciting and feels capable of handling it, his or her reaction is likely to be more positive and the stress level lower than if change is viewed as frightening and the individual feels incapable. More specifically, psychologists have found that human beings have a fundamental need for control. Since human survival depends to a great extent upon control of the environment and the expression of one's reasoning processes in action, it may not be surprising to find that when people are put into situations in which their control is jeopardized, they try very hard to regain and maintain it. If all their efforts fail, they become anxious or eventually helpless and depressed.

BOX **10.1**

Hot Topic

Explanatory Styles and Breast Cancer

This chapter has focused substantial attention on individual differences in explanatory style in the process of coping with stress. People vary considerably in how they explain things that happen to them. Some people focus on bad luck, karma, or God's will; others explain events in terms of a lesson to be learned. Some people explain troubles as punishment, and still others view difficult situations as new challenges to be overcome. Generally, people seek explanations for troublesome events partly to feel a greater sense of control in their lives. Although this control may be illusory, it can assist in the belief that the world is orderly and predictable.

One area in which this sense of control is important is the explanation of illness or injury. The diagnosis of cancer is particularly demanding of explanation, and a great deal of research has focused on explanatory style in women with the diagnosis of breast cancer (Taylor et al., 1984). This work is based on a theory of cognitive adaptation. The cause of breast cancer is still unknown, of course, and although many factors have been implicated in its development (e.g., high fat diet, too little exercise, poor stress management, not breastfeeding if one has given birth, family genetics, or emotional repression), none completely accounts for its occurrence. Many women with the diagnosis, however, blame themselves for developing breast cancer and take on responsibility for the disease. Self-blame for illness can generally have both positive and negative implications for adaptation (see Glinder & Campos, 1999, for a review). While some individuals blame themselves and become depressed, others use self-blame to spark their motivation to take positive action. How does self-blame affect adjustment to breast cancer?

A recent study has examined the relationship between self-blame, depression, and anxiety in a group of newly diagnosed breast cancer patients (Glinder & Campos, 1999). In this research, at the time of diagnosis, those who blamed themselves had higher levels of emotional distress in the form of depression and anxiety; self-blame predicted distress levels at six months and one year after diagnosis. Thus, in this sample of breast cancer patients, self-blame did not serve as a motivator to take positive action but instead compounded the distress felt by these women. This line of research suggests the importance of healthcare professionals' awareness of their patients' explanations for disease and the need for attention to, and care for, those who make self-blaming statements.

Another type of explanatory style examined in this chapter is optimism. Combined with mental control strategies and the avoidance of intrusive thoughts, optimism is a positive coping style that can benefit patients in many ways. For women with breast cancer who are trying to cope with the devastating event of diagnosis, such positive coping strategies can be essential. Psychologists have examined coping style in relation to breast cancer and the process of adaptation to it within the first six months of diagnosis and found that optimism is related to less emotional distress at the time of diagnosis as well as six months after (Epping-Jordan et al., 1999). Women who were more pessimistic used more self-blaming and tended to withdraw socially, which appeared to heighten their distress at six months post-diagnosis. Further, intrusive thoughts predicted emotional distress at the time of diagnosis and at three months post-diagnosis, but not at six months. Although these women reported that they did not want to think about their cancer, thoughts of it seemed to, as one woman put it, ". . . jump into my mind." Of course, the relationship between coping style and adjustment to breast cancer is complicated and likely to be affected by many factors including issues of family and social network support, and even public views of breast cancer. In general, assisting women to come to terms with their diagnosis and giving them the support they need requires a full understanding of the power of these cognitive factors in coping and explaining illness.

Coping with a stressful event can be greatly enhanced by a sense of control (Thompson, 1981). Such control can take several forms, including the way the individual thinks about the stressful event. Thoughts of control are referred to generally as **cognitive control** and focus on whether the individual believes that he or she guides, or is guided by, the events in life. One form of cognitive control, **cognitive distraction**, involves the person's consciously attending to something other than the phenomenon that is distressing. A second type of cognitive control strategy involves selectively attending to or focusing on some aspects of a situation, but not on others (that is, **cognitively restructuring** the event). As we will see later in this chapter, in the section on interventions, cognitive control is complex and there are several methods for gaining and maintaining control.

One realm in which cognitive control can significantly help reduce stress is in the medical situation. For example, the patient who must undergo frequent painful examinations might try to think about being somewhere else (such as lying on the sand at the ocean). Thinking about a peaceful environment will serve to focus attention away from the pain and discomfort being experienced. A patient receiving chemotherapy, for example, might try to avoid focusing on the nausea, pain, chills, and fever that result from the powerful drugs and instead focus on positive images of healing. These two aspects of cognitive control can significantly improve an individual's adjustment to aversive events.

Relatedly, **informational control** can be extremely valuable in helping a person to cope with a stressful event. Particularly in the medical realm, gaining information about procedures and what sensations will be experienced can help to promote effective coping as well as later adjustment and recovery (Anderson & Masur, 1983; Thompson, 1981).

Although not a cognitive coping mechanism, another form of control is valuable in helping an individual to cope with stress. The specific behaviors that the individual enacts to control his or her environment determine the level of **behavior control**. In the medical realm, behavioral control allows the patient to lessen the aversiveness of the medical event or to influence it in some way. Here's an example: When DiMatteo's daughter had her first throat culture at the age of 3, she sought to lessen her distress by exerting behavioral control. The nurse had asked her to sit on the examining table and instructed her to open her mouth wide. This assertive, good-natured little girl had her own ideas, however. "Wait," she responded. Then, she proceeded to lie down on the examining table. When comfortable, she said, "Okay . . . now," and opened her mouth wide, as she had been instructed to do, for the throat culture. Adult patients who are similarly given the opportunity to control some aspect, however small, of their experience, are generally better able to tolerate unpleasant medical procedures. Examples of such control include allowing a patient to vary the volume of music to provide a distraction from discomfort in the dentist's chair or teaching a patient to reduce discomfort by relaxing muscles and swallowing when undergoing endoscopy (a procedure in which a tube is passed through the throat into the stomach to allow its examination). Behavioral control helps people tolerate the stress of uncomfortable and/or frightening medical procedures, probably because it enables them to reduce their anxiety in anticipation of and during these noxious events (Thompson, 1981). Of course, control can have a down side as illustrated in Figure 10.2.

"Really, I mean it Mr. Turnbull . . . your son is only six years old. You can't control everything he does on the soccer field."

FIGURE 10.2 Effective coping requires dealing constructively with events that cannot be controlled.

Learned Helplessness

As we saw in Chapter 9, uncontrollable events are perceived as more stressful than are controllable ones. The belief in one's ability to modify or to put an end to an aversive event reduces the degree to which it imposes stress on the individual (Thompson, 1981). Lack of control, on the other hand, can raise stress and increase levels of epinephrine and norepinephrine (Frankenhaeuser, 1986). When an individual is unable to exert even the smallest amount of behavioral control and is unable to change how he or she thinks about stressful events, the individual experiences "helplessness."

Research on the phenomenon of helplessness has shed considerable light on the experience of stress. First of all, helplessness is something that may be learned, possibly even inadvertently. Some of the earliest studies on "learned helplessness" involved animals, such as dogs, and demonstrated that if the animal was kept from helping itself it would eventually stop trying. For instance, in some studies animals stood on a grating that delivered painful electric shocks and there was no means of escape. Later, when they were given a means of escape, and thus of helping themselves, they did not take it. They had learned to be helpless. **Learned helplessness** occurs when our efforts at control continually come to no avail and we are unable to change an intolerable situation. After repeated failures to exert some kind of control, we become helpless in three specific realms (Maier & Seligman, 1976): (1) *motivational* (we stop making efforts to change the outcome), (2) *cognitive* (we fail to learn new responses that could help us to avoid aversive outcomes in the future), and (3) *emotional* (we become depressed). One study of children found that those who were able to establish a feeling of powerfulness versus helplessness during a routine blood draw procedure experienced less fearful anticipation (Carpenter, 1992). Even in addiction, learned helplessness may be important for behavior. Cocaine addicts who scored high on helplessness were less likely to remain in treatment and had poorer outcomes than did addicts who scored low on helplessness (Sterling et al., 1996).

Hardiness

Research in the area of existential personality theory has sought to explain why some people, despite highly stressful conditions, are able to enjoy their lives and maintain or even improve their health. Focusing on the individual's perspective and the meaning he or she attributes to life events, psychologists Salvatore Maddi and Suzanne Kobasa developed the concept of **hardiness**. Hardiness is a psychological construct that refers to an individual's stable, characteristic way of responding to life events. Individuals who exhibit hardiness have generally been found to be less susceptible to experiencing illness in response to stressful conditions in their lives (Funk, 1992; Horner, 1998; Kobasa, 1979, 1982; Kobasa et al., 1994). Psychologically hardy individuals also have less severe illnesses (Maddi et al., 1998). The findings are correlational, however, and effects of hardiness on the experience of physical health or illness have not always been found (Clark & Hartman, 1996). Despite this, it is a valuable concept that helps to guide our understanding of coping with stress.

Hardiness involves three intertwined components: commitment, control, and challenge. Individuals exhibiting hardiness approach life change events from these perspectives. People high in *commitment* become intensely involved in what they are doing and believe in the importance and value of their work. They tend to involve themselves deeply in many aspects of their lives, from work to family interactions to social relationships. They believe that there is an overall purpose to the actions of their day-to-day lives. People high in *control* believe (and act as if) they indeed can influence the events that they encounter rather than remain powerless in the face of outside forces. They place considerable emphasis on their own responsibility for their lives and feel that they are capable of acting on their own, without direction from other people. It is not necessary that they have a great deal of control, just that they believe they can control the important aspects of their lives. Finally, people who have a sense of *challenge* regard life changes to be the norm and are not threatened by them. They anticipate and welcome life change as an opportunity for personal growth. They are open and flexible in their ways of thinking, and they are able to tolerate ambiguous situations.

Having a sense of humor about stressful events is a topic of research that has also received attention. One study found that humor was associated with lower stress levels among female college students (Kuiper et al., 1993). Those who had a better sense of humor were more likely to view a college exam as a positive "challenge," thereby lowering their perceived stress levels. Another study linked a good sense of humor to better immune functioning (McClelland & Cheriff, 1997). Thus, a sense of humor may help individuals cope with stress and may facilitate their good health.

World View and a Sense of Coherence

Another theory of coping, the theory of a **Sense of Coherence** (SOC), arose out of studies of concentration camp survivors who managed, despite terrible life experiences, to remain healthy both physically and psychologically (Antonovsky, 1998). This theory helps to explain how people can cope with very stressful and chaotic circumstances, even when objectively they have no control over the events in their lives.

According to the Sense of Coherence theory, life stressors can be conceptualized broadly, ranging from microbiological to sociocultural. One's family situation and one's job can be significant sources of life stress and so, too, can the social and cultural environment in which one lives. Existing in poverty, living in an unsafe neighborhood, and functioning in an oppressive cultural environment can all be extremely stressful. In the nature of human existence, stressors are inevitable and omnipresent. This theory attempts to understand, despite extreme stress, how some people manage to survive and even to flourish.

According to Antonovsky, it is incorrect to assume that stressful life experiences are inherently bad. Stressors do cause a state of tension in an individual, but the physical outcome of that tension is dependent upon the adequacy of the individual's tension management. Inadequately managed tension may result in a long-term perception of stress and subsequently in the individual's ill health. But ill health is not the necessary or inevitable outcome of life events that require adaptation. In fact, despite terrible circumstances in their lives, many people remain physically healthy. Antonovsky argues that if we really want to understand the interplay of mind and body, of stress and physical illness, we must learn to understand precisely how some people are able to avoid illness and remain quite healthy despite significant stress (Antonovsky, 1998).

Antonovsky has contended that research on stress and illness focuses, to its detriment, on a **pathogenic model**. A pathogenic model of research targets a direct effect of some psychological or physical variable on disease. Current examples of this approach are the effect of Type A behavior on coronary disease and the effect of learned helplessness on immunity. A **salutogenic orientation**, on the other hand, allows us to examine the factors that promote movement toward health rather than toward illness. It is as important to study what causes health as it is to study what causes threats to health.

The salutogenic approach leads the way to the formulation and development of a new type of coping theory. Using a salutogenic approach, we ask how it is that some people do well and feel good despite life problems, impediments to their goals, and even tragedies. An individual's SOC is a major determinant of his or her ability to maintain health and avoid illness. Why?

According to Antonovsky, **General Resistance Resources** (GRRs) are resources (such as money, ego strength, social support, and cultural stability) that help to protect a person against the ill effects of stress. Money is a physical GRR because it can alleviate or minimize the effects of a stressful event by allowing one to pay off a bill, purchase a product, or pay for a service. If one has enough money to solve a practical problem that causes stress, the problem can be eliminated and the stress reduced. Of course, money is a GRR only with regard to the financial effects of a problem. Money can purchase a new car to replace the one that was "totaled" in an accident, but money cannot bring back the loved one who was killed. Alternatively, emotional support from others can make one feel much better but may not directly help in acquiring a means of transportation to work.

An individual's Sense of Coherence is also a GRR. This "global orientation" or world view can "buffer" the effects of stressful events so that they are not felt so intensely. Thus, SOC is an "enduring though dynamic, feeling of confidence that: (1) the stimuli deriving from one's internal and external environments in the course of living are structured, predictable, and explicable; (2) the resources are available to one to meet the demands posed by these stimuli; and (3) these demands are challenges worthy of investment and engagement" (Antonovsky, 1987, p. 19). This was how Antonovsky characterized the people he interviewed who had experienced major trauma but who nevertheless coped exceedingly well. They were people who remained physically healthy despite significant psychological stress. Antonovsky asked these individuals how they viewed their lives, and these three characteristics emerged.

First, they saw the world as comprehensible and as making sense to them. These people expected that the stimuli they would encounter (for example, other people or natural phenomena) would be ordered and explicable. Although certain events were not at all desirable to them, such as career failure, the death of a loved one, or war, they felt they could make sense of them. They explained accidents in terms of certain physical forces or job failure in terms of a lack of key knowledge or a personality clash with the boss. They explained war as the result of a variety of political forces. Such explicability stood in contrast to the more magical beliefs of those without a SOC (such as that a loved one was zapped away by a malevolent universe or that jobs were lost for no understandable reason).

Second, those with a SOC saw the world as manageable and had a solid belief that things would work out as well as can be reasonably expected. This emphasis is a cognitive one that involves a solid capacity to judge reality. Those with a high SOC saw events in life as experiences that could be coped with. They recognized that unfortunate things do happen in life but that such experiences can indeed be survived.

Third, those with a SOC also believed that events in life have meaning. They valued life on a deep emotional level and felt that, for the most part, the problems and demands posed by life were worth the investment of their energy. Although people with a SOC certainly did not welcome troubles, they faced life's burdens as challenges and sought to find meaning in them.

Social Resources and Social Support

One of the most potent factors in helping an individual to deal with stressful life conditions and events is **social support**. Social support is support or help from other individuals such as friends, family, neighbors, co-workers, professionals, and acquaintances. Social support is believed to help reduce stress in three important ways (Coyne et al., 1981; House, 1981; Wills, 1984). First, family members, friends, and acquaintances can provide direct **tangible support** in the form of physical resources (e.g., lending money, doing the grocery shopping, taking care of children). Second, members of one's social network can provide **informational support** by suggesting alternative actions that may help to solve the stress-producing problem. These suggestions may help the person to look at his or her problem in a new way and thus help to solve it or to minimize its impact. Third, those in the social network can provide **emotional support** by reassuring the individual that he or she is a cared for, valued, and esteemed person. These supportive individuals can provide nurturance, acceptance, and love. These types of support have been found to be important in helping an individual to cope with the demands of serious illness (Wortman & Dunkel-Schetter, 1987).

Evidence suggests that people who receive support enjoy better health than do those who do not receive social support. Individuals with more extensive social contacts and community ties have been found to live longer than do those who have few such ties to others (House et al., 1982). Receiving social support has been found to be associated with lower rates of heart attack, with reduced incidence of tuberculosis, with fewer complications during pregnancy, and with lower rates of psychological distress (Billings & Moos, 1982; Williams et al., 1981). Social support seems to modify the magnitude of the effect of stress on immune functioning (Kang et al., 1998). And, failing to take advantage of one's social support system has even been found to be related to the onset of glucose tolerance abnormalities (Fukunishi et al., 1998)!

How and under what circumstances social support helps an individual is not entirely clear and must be explored in more detail through research. It may be the case that social support "buffers" the effects of stress by making situations less likely to be appraised as threatening (Cohen & Wills, 1985) or by rendering stress less likely to trigger deleterious physical responses (such as poor health habits or chronic, exhausting physiological arousal) (Kaplan et al., 1977). It is also possible that social support actually makes potentially stressful events more benign by diffusing or minimizing their initial impact. For example, having a loving and supportive romantic partner may make it much less likely that one will interpret a course grade that is lower than one expected as evidence of personal failure. The person who enjoys a high level of social support may even approach each examination in a course with much less anxiety and distress than he or she might otherwise. Researchers still do not know, however, precisely how social support operates to help an individual cope with stressful situations. Some suggest that social support has a direct effect on health regardless of the amount of stress an individual experiences. Social support may give an individual a more positive outlook on life as well as a greater sense of self-esteem. These positive psychological outcomes may manifest themselves in the individual's greater resistance to disease and engagement in more positive preventive health habits (Cohen & Wills, 1985; Wortman & Dunkel-Schetter, 1987).

Not all kinds of social support can help under all circumstances, however. In fact, the role of social support in helping to maintain and promote health is emerging as rather specific. Under certain circumstances, for example, only one kind of support will be helpful to an individual. In research on younger, widowed people, it was found that the stress of their loss was best buffered by social support from their parents, particularly emotional support. Among working women with newborn babies, however, the only significant source of social support was their spouse (Lieberman, 1982). Obviously, the form of social support received can matter a great deal as well. If one really needs tangible support but receives only encouragement, one may begin to feel frustration and further stress (Cohen & McKay, 1983).

Of course, receiving social support may have some risks as well. Such help may carry with it the implicit requirement to reciprocate, and it is possible that those who try to help will instead become intrusive. For example, receiving suggestions from others may be quite helpful, but having another's solutions vehemently thrust upon one (with accompanying distress and upset if they are not followed) may itself become a burden and a source of further stress. Overly intrusive members of the social network might actually make things worse (Lieberman, 1982). Further, some members of the social network may even encourage the individual to be noncompliant with treatment regimens, and to engage in health-compromising, instead of health-enhancing, behaviors (Suls, 1982).

Emotional Disclosure

Although negative emotions usually accompany traumatic experiences, researchers now know that it is better to express these feelings than to keep them inside. Many studies have demonstrated that when people try to deceive others, their bodies respond physiologically, their heart rates increase, they sweat, and their blood pressure increases (see Waid et al., 1981; Zuckerman et al., 1981 for reviews). James Pennebaker and his colleagues propose that keeping the details and emotions associated with a traumatic event "secret" might lead to the same kinds of effects, and that these, over time, might prove harmful to one's physical health in accordance with the principles of Selye's General Adaptation Syndrome (Pennebaker & Susman, 1988).

Throughout our lives, each of us is faced with numerous experiences we may consider traumatic. For example, we may experience a sizable earthquake, a powerful hurricane, or an unexpected tornado; be injured in an auto accident; see someone hurt or killed; suffer from neglect or abuse; be raped or robbed; get lost in the woods; have the car break down in a blizzard; be painfully betrayed by someone we love. Each of these events can be very traumatic, and each can cause extreme stress that takes a toll on our emotional and physical health. It is likely that you have experienced at least one event in your life that you consider traumatic. Do you remember feeling a need to talk about the event after it happened?

Emotional disclosure is the act of opening up or revealing emotional experiences to other people. This disclosure can take the form of talking or writing. Oftentimes disclosure through talking occurs immediately following the event, when others are usually willing to listen. After a period of time, however, the individual is often pressured by others to stop talking about it. They say, or imply through their behavior, "Enough already!" Perhaps you have wanted to say that to a friend who would not stop talking about a personal traumatic experience. The problem is that people often need a period for disclosure that lasts longer than the period in which others are happy to listen. Research suggests that "bottling up" experiences may be detrimental to our health.

To study the effects of emotional disclosure, psychologist James Pennebaker has conducted numerous studies in which people were either given the opportunity to talk about emotional events or were told to keep their thoughts and feelings to themselves.

He found that people who are given the opportunity to talk or write about their experience are better able to overcome the event, let it go, and move on. This is true whether the event is minor, such as having one's feelings hurt, or major, such as suffering the death of a loved one or being raped. People who talk about the negative events in their lives have lower blood pressure and lower levels of skin conductance, report fewer illness symptoms, and visit their doctors less often than do those who keep things to themselves (Berry & Pennebaker, 1993; Pennebaker, 1997). Keeping a trauma buried or "under wraps" for long periods of time affects the immune system and puts the individual at risk for various health problems (e.g., Berry & Pennebaker, 1993).

Disclosure seems to be important for several reasons. First, traumatic events cause both emotional and physiological reactions. Even thinking about a traumatic event can make one's heart rate and blood pressure climb. Over long periods of time, as we have seen, this can cause damage to the body. Research shows that simply trying not to think about something is usually not effective. In fact, telling yourself, "I'm not going to think about it any more," might even make you think about it more frequently! So, disclosing the event allows for a release of some of the stress and may make it more likely that the event can be forgotten, not merely suppressed.

Second, when people talk about an event, they often have the opportunity for social comparison because the person with whom they are talking may indicate ways in which he or she has had a similar experience. This may provide the discloser with a

Writing in a journal helps to organize one's thoughts, events, and experiences and can help to improve health.

degree of emotional social support. Third, the discloser might receive some sort of aid in response to his or her disclosure. For example, the listener might provide useful advice. Finally, the telling of the story allows the discloser to mentally organize and structure the event. In order to tell (or write to) someone about an event, one must first organize it in one's mind. We don't usually skip from occurrence to occurrence or from thought to thought in random order when we talk or write about events. Instead, we tell a story, starting with precipitating factors. We describe events along the way and conclude with the last events and perhaps our "take" on the situation or our plans for the future. Organizing events in this way makes it easier to find meaning in those events, to bring to them a sense of rationality and coherence. This, in turn, makes coping easier.

It is interesting to note that even when individuals do nothing other than "disclose" their emotions in a journal or diary, they reap health benefits. Clearly, a diary entry cannot provide social comparison, social support, or advice, but writing in a journal does require a certain amount of cognitive organization and the telling of a coherent story. It appears that the act of organizing and telling is important, independent of interpersonal factors. Disclosing traumas that happened long ago, either by talking about them to someone sympathetic or by writing them down in journal form, has been found to significantly improve one's physical health, to reduce short-term work absenteeism rates, to reduce the number of medical visits made for problems, and to increase functioning of the immune system (Berry & Pennebaker, 1993; Cameron & Nicholls, 1998; Francis & Pennebaker, 1992). In addition, individuals are at greater risk for clinical depression when they continually try to keep unwanted thoughts from surfacing (Nolen-Hoeksema, 1990).

Let's look at one specific empirical example. A group of medical students (who had never been exposed to Hepatitis B either through direct exposure or through a vaccine) were randomly assigned to two groups. In one group, the students were asked to write about a neutral event; in the other, they wrote about a past event in their lives that they considered to have been traumatic for them (Petrie et al., 1995). The following day all of the students were inoculated with the Hepatitis B vaccine (something that is a recommended preventive health behavior for their age group and profession). Their participation in the study lasted for six months, during which time they received the necessary Hepatitis B vaccine boosters one and four months after the first shot. The medical students who were asked to write about a traumatic experience showed higher levels of antibody response to the vaccine than did the students who simply wrote about a neutral event. Furthermore, immediately following the writing sessions, the students who were able to disclose a personal event had blood levels showing better immune functioning than did the students who simply wrote about everyday events. This is indeed a powerful example of the health benefits of disclosing emotions.

Helping People Cope: Interventions That Work

One of the primary jobs of a clinical health psychologist is to design ways to enable individuals to live healthier and more productive lives. One way in which this can be done is to create interventions that help reduce the natural stress and anxiety of everyday life. They also create interventions to help those in need of immediate attention (such as those who have just suffered a catastrophe) Many individuals need tools that will help them cope with both acute and chronic stress. These tools come in various forms and have various degrees of support from research. Numerous interventions have been designed to serve specific functions, such as bolstering the immune system, calming the nervous system, eliciting more positive cognitive coping strategies, or giving instrumental and emotional support to the individual under stress. Examples of such interventions include aerobic exercise, biofeedback, relaxation, hypnosis, systematic desensitization, psychotherapy, and cognitive retraining (see Baum et al., 1995, for a review of interventions). Here we will focus on interventions that research has shown to be effective at reducing stress and increasing coping as it relates specifically to physical health outcomes.

Coping strategies and interventions can be classified as behavioral, cognitive, or some combination of the two. Behavioral interventions focus on altering in some way the individual's activities (such as aerobic exercise). Cognitive interventions focus on altering the thought processes or cognitions of the individual to make these more adaptive (such as cognitive retraining). Biofeedback and relaxation combine both cognitive and behavioral aspects to form a sort of intervention "hybrid."

Mental Control

The term mental control conjures up all sorts of images, such as a hypnotist controlling a subject's mind and making him or her behave in bizarre ways, a voodoo master casting a spell, or a religious cult leader controlling the thoughts of followers. These images are far from what psychologists presently think of as mental control. **Mental control** ". . . occurs when people suppress a thought, concentrate on a sensation, inhibit an emotion, maintain a mood, stir up a desire, squelch a craving, or otherwise exert influence on their own mental states" (Wegner & Pennebaker, 1993, p. 1). As you can see from this definition, mental control is the act of controlling one's *own* mental states and not those of others. (You will recall that we also discussed the concept of mental control in Chapter 6 as it relates to changing health behaviors such as smoking and diet.) The concept of mental control came into focus in the literature in the late 1980s, when new research methods and new theories were developed and allowed for its formulation.

Mental control can serve various functions, such as a psychological defense against unwanted emotional states, a strategy for self-regulation of emotion (such as trying to remain happy), a self-control process (such as having strong willpower), a strategy to affect social interactions (such as trying to make a good impression), or a coping technique (Wegner & Pennebaker, 1993).

Coping with stress in general, and coping with the stress that accompanies adverse events in particular, is a major challenge to individual functioning. One of the best times to use mental control strategies is right at a time when coping is needed, simply to get by. You have likely had times when you did not want to think about something (an upcoming exam, a painful breakup, an embarrassing moment). If you were successful in blocking those thoughts from your mind, you used a mental control strategy. You altered your mental state. "Mental control can be understood, then, as a response to stress, a standard reaction to the psychological effects that accrue from exposure to catastrophic life events or the cumulative stresses of living" (Wegner & Pennebaker, 1993, p. 6). Mental control, in terms of coping, is an active response to stress.

What forms do mental control strategies take? When engaging in mental control, an individual will generally make a self-statement about wanting, in some way, to alter his or her present mental state. This might be accomplished through: (1) *thought stopping* (telling a thought to "stop" when it comes into awareness), (2) *cognitive distraction* (thinking about something else), and (3) *thought avoidance* (simply trying not to think about something). Each of these cognitive strategies can be employed to help an individual cope with stress. Their effectiveness likely will vary according to characteristics of the individual and to the levels of stress experienced. Employing these strategies takes work, however, and because thought stopping, avoidance, and distraction involve *not* dealing with and eliminating the problem at hand, these strategies may need to be maintained over time. Further, it is not always possible to maintain mental control over a lengthy period, even with hard work; eventually one will probably have to address the problem in a more direct way.

Box 10.2 examines the role of cognitive-behavioral stress management in reducing distress and enhancing health of HIV seropositive men.

Cognitive Retraining

As we noted in Chapter 9, stress arises from one's cognitive interpretations of events. If an experience is evaluated as threatening to one's well-being *and* one does not believe that he or she has the appropriate resources to cope, a stress response (complete with its physiological and psychological threats to homeostasis) is likely to ensue. Earlier in this chapter, we examined how people's patterns of cognitive interpretation can affect their experience of stress. For example, we saw that the "hardy" individual interprets life changes as challenges instead of problems, experiences himself or herself as "in control" of life, and views the pressures encountered as part of his or her commitment to a meaningful job, family, and community. Likewise, we saw that people who view the world as a coherent, understandable place are usually able to weather very stressful experiences without becoming ill.

While some people have developed health-enhancing cognitions at a young age, there is considerable evidence that most people can change how they think about themselves and the events in their lives and can even eliminate ways of thinking that are destructive to their physical and emotional well-being. Cognitive therapy for stress management is based upon the view that the cognitive representation of the environment, rather than the environment itself, determines stress responses. If thoughts are changed, stress responses can be reduced. Let us examine several approaches in the field of cognitive therapy that are particularly relevant to the management of stress.

Cognitive restructuring is a widely used technique for changing stress-provoking thoughts or beliefs so that they promote, rather than detract from, the individual's well-being. If a student believes that one particular test will make or break his or her entire future, it is likely that the experience of stress while preparing for that test will be extremely high. It is also probable that this belief is irrational and is not based on a

BOX **10.2**
Research Close-up

Cognitive-Behavioral Stress Management in the Care of Men with HIV

When HIV infection progresses to AIDS, one of the symptoms can be the "AIDS wasting syndrome" in which the individual loses a great deal of body mass and becomes quite frail. Studies of male HIV-positive patients have shown that testosterone levels drop as HIV progresses to AIDS and fall even lower when patients develop the wasting syndrome (Cruess et al., 2000). When men with wasting syndrome are given testosterone replacement therapy, they show good improvement in their overall body mass and physical health (Cofrancesco et al., 1997). Interestingly, psychologists have found that testosterone levels tend to go down with low mood and depression (J.L. Mason et al., 1988), prompting the suggestion that the enhancement of mood might actually increase testosterone levels (Cruess et al., 2000).

A recent study examined the effects of a 10-week, group-based cognitive-behavioral stress management (CBSM) intervention on the testosterone levels and emotional distress of a group of HIV-positive gay and bisexual men between the ages of 21 and 49 (Cruess et al., 2000). The purpose of the CBSM intervention in this group of male HIV patients was to determine the extent to which managing stress with cognitive restructuring and relaxation techniques could improve both the emotional health and the testosterone levels of these men. Subjects were randomly assigned to either the CBSM or the control group. Those in the CBSM group attended ten 2½-hour group meetings and were asked to practice their relaxation exercises twice a day between the weekly meetings.

The group meetings involved discussions of personal experiences, role-playing, and review of assigned tasks, as well as identification of cognitive distortions, help in improving coping skills and assertiveness, assistance with utilizing social supports, and help to manage feelings of anger. Both groups of men were followed up one week after the 10-week study and were assessed on their emotional distress and their testosterone levels.

The CBSM intervention was indeed effective at significantly increasing the men's testosterone levels. A quite surprising finding was that the men in the control group showed significant decreases in testosterone levels, presumably due to their deteriorating health status. The men in the CBSM group showed significant emotional and mood improvement, whereas the men in the control group showed no change. This intervention provides support for the notion that testosterone levels appear to be related to emotional health and that both aspects of health can be improved dramatically through a simple psychological intervention.

---

reasonable analysis of the facts. Any single test is only one of several, and futures are not destroyed on the basis of one course grade. Yet, unless the student's irrational beliefs are changed, he or she may be extremely "stressed out" over the test.

An important technique for restructuring irrational thoughts was developed many years ago by the psychologist Albert Ellis (1962, 1977). Ellis's approach to cognitive restructuring is called rational emotive therapy or RET. According to RET, stress appraisal processes, such as we examined early in Chapter 9, tend to go awry when people engage in irrational thinking. Such illogical beliefs may include **catastrophizing**, which involves believing that a disappointing event is not just inconvenient but is truly a disaster from which one may never recover. Irrational beliefs may also include the individual's vast underestimation of his or her ability to accept the consequences of the inconvenient event (e.g., "I won't be able to stand it if I get a B on this test"). The individual might also judge his or her own personal worth on the basis of something like school performance (e.g., " I am a worthless person if I do not get an A"). Such irrational thoughts can be replaced with rational thoughts (for example, "If I do poorly on this test, I will simply have to try harder next time" or "My grade on this test does not reflect my worth as a person"). The success of the cognitive approach to the clinical treatment of stress-related problems has been encouraging (Hamberger & Lohr, 1984).

Compared with the methods we have examined so far, **stress inoculation training** is a somewhat different cognitive approach to the management of stress (Meichenbaum, 1985; Meichenbaum & Cameron, 1983). Stress inoculation training is based upon the theory that the stress experience can be reduced if a person is cognitively *prepared*, much like disease may be thwarted if a person has had appropriate immunizations. Stress inoculation occurs in three steps. During *conceptualization*, client and therapist work together to understand the problems facing the client and to analyze the details of his or her stress experience. During the stage of *skill acquisition and rehearsal*, the individual may learn relaxation and desensitization techniques (such as will be described on page 384) as well as ways to redefine his or her situation in cognitive terms. The client may also incorporate into the program practical aids to overcoming stress-producing problems, such as social skills training for the individual who experiences interactions with other people as stressful. Finally, in the phase of *application and follow-through*, behavioral and cognitive techniques are used to bring about behavior change. For example, client and therapist might use "role playing" to simulate a stress-producing situation so that the client can practice the skills that have been acquired. Or, client and therapist may practice upcoming situations that are expected to be stressful so that the client can apply his or her new abilities.

Exercise

Has anything like this ever happened to you? You felt upset, although you were not clear about why. Maybe something your professor or a friend said to you left you feeling unsure of yourself. In response, your heart was beating faster than usual and your body felt strangely exhausted. But you decided to push yourself to do your workout. You had faith that while your problems would still be there after exercise, your ability to deal with them would be greatly improved; your body would feel relaxed and strong, and you would be able to think more clearly. That is exactly what happened! After a few minutes of exercise, your body felt warm as blood rushed to your muscles and you began to feel stronger. By the time you finished your workout, you felt hopeful; you believed in yourself again.

Research suggests that exercise is an effective coping method (see Baum et al., 1995; Rostad & Long, 1996, for reviews). Exercise helps to decrease the physical strain that can result from stressful events and can help to reduce emotional strain that has already manifested itself in an individual's life. People who exercise regularly and are generally physically fit experience significantly lower levels of anxiety than do people who do not exercise (Blumenthal & McCubbin, 1987). Lower levels of anxiety are likely to reduce the initial impact of a potentially stressful event and may minimize the perception of environmental threat.

Exercise appears to reduce blood pressure and heart rate and particularly to decrease cardiovascular reactivity (Dimsdale et al., 1986; Jennings et al., 1986). Studies suggest that exercise can provide an active outlet for the physiological arousal experienced in response to stress. Regular physical exercise can help to protect health in the face of stressful life events and chronic daily stressors. In general, exercise has been found to enhance the efficiency of the heart, slow it down and regulate its rhythm, and decrease an individual's likelihood of having a heart attack (Epstein et al., 1976; Paffenberger & Hale, 1975). Research links exercise with fewer premature deaths from not only cardiovascular disease but from all causes (Blair et at., 1989). One study even found that exercise can reduce test-taking anxiety in college students (Doan et al., 1995)!

In research on executives under stress, exercise was associated with lower overall illness reports, and this buffering effect was found to be distinct from the personality characteristic of hardiness (Kobasa et al., 1982). Whereas hardiness was found to help limit the stressfulness of events, thereby decreasing their ability to produce sympathetic arousal or physical strain, exercise had a general buffering effect that directly relieved the physical strain on these executives. In subsequent studies of male executives who faced highly stressful conditions, researchers found that exercise worked in conjunction with other resources to help these men increase their resistance to illness (Kobasa et al., 1994). Taken together, hardiness, social support, and exercise substantially decreased their likelihood of becoming ill.

Exercise, particularly with social support, can be an effective coping mechanism and can reduce cardiovascular reactivity and improve health.

Relaxation Techniques

In the realm of stress management, relaxation has been found to reduce effectively not only muscle tension but also heart rate and blood pressure (English & Baker, 1983; Lavey & Taylor, 1985). Two forms of relaxation work particularly well in dealing with stress. **Progressive muscle relaxation** is a technique in which the individual focuses his or her attention on specific muscle groups and alternately tenses and relaxes the muscles. The individual might begin with the feet and leg muscles and work up through the torso to the head, shoulders, and arms. With each muscle group, the individual tenses the muscles for about ten seconds and then relaxes them for about the same amount of time. During the relaxation phase, the individual might be asked to think a pleasant thought, such as how good the relaxation feels. The alternation of tensing and relaxing allows the individual to become aware of the experience of tension in each muscle group and to contrast it with the experience of relaxation. After some training in this technique, an individual is usually able to achieve relaxation by remembering the feelings and thoughts that he or she had during the training.

Meditation involves several techniques that attempt to focus an individual's attention on a single thought or image in an effort to remain undistracted by other thoughts. Although meditation has been associated over the years with various religious frameworks, particularly those from the Far East and India, meditation can involve purely psychological techniques for being aware of one's thoughts as they come and go. The practice of meditation has been found effective in reducing stress and anxiety, as well as in reducing hypertension and even eliminating certain phobias (Shapiro, 1985).

Cardiologist Herbert Benson (Benson, 1974; Benson et al., 1974) developed a meditation-like method of relaxation for stress management. The Relaxation Response is a technique that has been particularly popular with executives because it is fairly easy to accomplish and can be worked into a normal business day routine. The technique combines muscle relaxation with a comfortable position, a passive attitude, a quiet environment, and a repetitive sound, just as does meditation. The individual sits with his or her eyes closed for about 20 minutes and silently repeats the word "one" (or whatever word he or she has chosen). Repeating this single word prevents the intrusion of distracting thoughts that might interfere with the relaxation. In fact, the individual's goal is to let go of any distracting thoughts that enter his or her awareness during the relaxation experience. Relaxation has been a very successful technique in helping people under stress to cope with their experience and to prevent or control stress-related disorders (Lavey & Taylor, 1985).

Systematic Desensitization

In the realm of stress management, relaxation techniques are often used as part of a program of **systematic desensitization**. Systematic desensitization is a way of reducing stress (particularly stress that is generated from fear or anxiety about something specific). The method is based upon the stimulus-response associations of classical conditioning. Systematic desensitization involves a process of "undoing" the associations that have been established in the past between some environmental event and the stress response. For example, a first-year medical resident may begin to experience a frighteningly powerful stress (fight-or-flight) response when asked a question posed by the chief resident. The counterconditioning of systematic desensitization could help this individual to replace the stress response with calmness and relaxation. Here is how it might be done.

A psychologist working with this new resident would use a method that involves a stimulus hierarchy. The situation that elicits the stress response, specifically answering a question posed by the chief resident, would be elicited in the resident's imagination while she engaged in progressive relaxation as described on page 384. For example, she might first sit in the psychologist's office and learn to associate a relaxed state with thoughts of various types of questions, such as one that the chief resident might pose. The next step might involve the resident associating a relaxed state with images of working with patients while the chief was nearby. The next step may involve associating a relaxed physical and mental state with thoughts of asking the chief a question. The resident might then imagine hearing another resident answer the chief's questions. Finally, she would visualize actually answering a direct question posed by the chief. Each of these scenes would be pictured while feeling comfortable and calm. As the resident mentally climbs the hierarchy and more closely approaches the stress-producing activity, discomfort and the stress response may build. When this happens, the psychologist would likely stop and work intensively on the association of that particular step with relaxation until it has been accomplished successfully. Then, the next step on the hierarchy would be approached.

Depending upon how strong the individual's fear is and how intense the stress reaction, the entire process of systematic desensitization may take several sessions with a psychologist, as well as the individual's own personal follow-up on the relaxation and imagery. In addition, basing the systematic desensitization on *images* of the stressful situation may not be enough to quiet the distressing response when it happens in the real world. Some therapists use symbolic contacts with the feared object or event (such as tangible representations or pictures), and some even use **in vivo** contacts (which involve experience of the actual stress-provoking situation). Thus, the therapist might accompany the resident to the hospital where she normally interacts with the chief resident and help her to achieve a relaxed state while there. Systematic desensitization works very well to reduce stress responses to such things as traveling in an airplane, going to the dentist, public speaking, being in high places, and taking tests (Gelfand, 1978).

Biofeedback

In Chapter 8, we examined biofeedback in detail as an effective technique for pain control. Biofeedback, as we noted, can be a very useful method for helping people to relax specific muscles or muscle groups as well as for generally decreasing their state of emotional arousal. **Biofeedback** involves an electromechanical device that emits a signal (a light or a buzzer or a sound of varying frequency) to "feed back" to the individual some information about the state of his or her body. Typically, the information fed back is the degree of tension in specific muscles or the general state of arousal of the individual's sympathetic or parasympathetic nervous system. When the individual

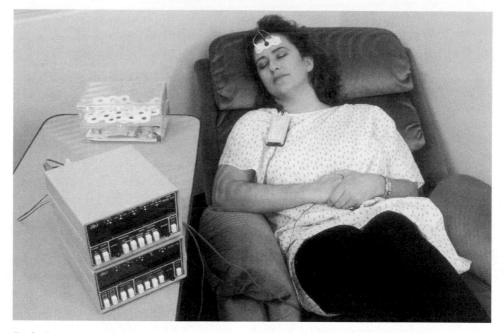

Biofeedback can be helpful in treating stress-related disorders, although self-induced relaxation can be achieved with less expensive methods.

achieves the desired physical state (relaxed muscles or a slower heart rate, for example), the device emits a signal and through the process of operant conditioning, reinforces the individual's efforts.

Biofeedback has been useful, as we noted in Chapter 8, in treating certain stress-related pain disorders, and it appears to have the same level of effectiveness as progressive muscle relaxation for treating headaches (Blanchard & Andrasik, 1985). In general, although biofeedback can be helpful in treating stress and stress-related disorders in some people, the gains over simpler methods such as self-induced relaxation are not considerable, and because of the equipment required, biofeedback can be expensive.

Learning to Cope: Effective Stress Management

The stresses of modern life, the intensity of daily work commitments, pressures to succeed financially, and the loosening of family and community bonds make successful coping difficult to achieve. For many people, "stress management" consists of hitting the bars after work or using drugs for relaxation and coping (Greenberg & Grunberg, 1995). In fact, more than two gallons of alcohol is consumed each year per person over age 14 in the United States (National Center for Health Statistics [NCHS], 1997). Substance use, however, is a poor method of stress management. Alcohol and drugs, and even more benign measures such as hypersomnia (sleeping too much), binge eating, and chronic television addiction, may serve as short-term remedies for stress, but in the long run cause more problems than they solve. The ability to function effectively over time can become jeopardized by the choice of a "quick fix" for problems.

Research on stress management demonstrates that people can learn to cope effectively with, and manage, their stress to prevent the development of both psychological and physical difficulties. Some learn stress management from individual therapists, others from participation in workshops. Others receive training at school or the workplace. Currently, many corporations assist their workers to develop effective means to cope with stress. Such efforts are beneficial to the corporations themselves, since stress-related illnesses may cause employees to miss work, perform poorly, and even suffer work-related injuries and poorer health (Adler & Matthews, 1994; Repetti, 1993). Since the monetary cost of work stress in the United States is high due to things such as absenteeism, inefficiency, and occupational injuries, stress management assistance is indeed cost effective. One study found that individuals who attended a stress management clinic (including relaxation, social skills training, problem-solving training, and lifestyle alteration) were less distressed, less anxious, and had fewer daily hassles than did those who did not attend (Timmerman et al., 1998). Again, these findings reiterate that learning to manage stress can actually relieve some of the hassles of daily living!

Several points are worth noting about stress management programs. First, a successful, multidimensional approach to stress management must involve recognizing the sources of stress in one's life and examining the factors that contribute to feelings of stress. As we noted in this chapter, stress may arise from (among other things) irrational cognitions (e.g., "If I don't succeed at this job, I will never succeed at anything"), from a perceived difference between one's abilities and resources and the demands of the situation, and from ways of thinking about life that leave one feeling vulnerable instead of in control. Adjustments in the source of the stress experience may be necessary, as we have seen throughout this chapter. Second, learning to cope with stress requires learning to modify the physiological effects of the stress reaction. This modification might best be achieved by a combination of exercise and other physical interventions such as deep breathing, deep muscle relaxation, certain forms of meditation, yoga, or hypnosis, which have been found to reduce heart rate, skin conductance measures of stress, muscle tension, blood pressure, and subjects' self reports of feeling tense (English & Baker, 1983). Third, successful stress management programs teach people to figure out which components of a stressful situation are causing their stress reactions and, if possible, to alter those components. It can be very valuable for an individual to learn to distinguish among potentially stressful experiences and to determine which can be avoided, which must be tolerated, and which can be appropriately modified to reduce the experience of stress. And finally, stress management techniques must be incorporated into an individual's daily life and practiced regularly in order to maintain their effectiveness.

In this chapter, we have discussed how people can and do cope with stress. We have examined factors that affect the evaluation of stressful stimuli and that modify the experience of stress. We have also considered approaches to changing the psychological and physiological reactions to events once they have been perceived as stressful. In essence, we have examined the ways in which the tie between stress and illness can be modified and even broken. Much is yet to be learned about stress and its management, but it is one of the most promising and potentially applicable realms of research in the exciting field of health psychology.

Box 10.3 examines some fascinating individuals from the tiny republic of Georgia, and from the United States, who have lived to be over 100. The coping styles and "outlook on life" of these centenarians is of considerable interest to health psychologists.

In the next chapter, we look in detail at a specific kind of stress, the experience of serious illness, and we examine the unique ways in which patients attempt to cope with what are sometimes the greatest crises of their lives.

BOX 10.3
Across Cultures

The Long-Living People

Abkhazia is a tiny republic of Georgia (population 516,600), located on the edge of the Black Sea with the Caucasus Mountains to the north. What makes this place so interesting, though, is its "long-living people." In this country, there is no word such as "old" or "elderly" that can be used to describe people. Instead, those who live to be more than 100 years old are called "long-living people." And, although people tend to be very long-lived in Abkhazia, the region is not filled with doddering, frail folks! They stand tall, very few need glasses or false teeth, and most of them do more physical labor than we do at any age in the United States!

There are many ways in which the Abkhazian culture differs from that of the United States. First, there is no such thing as "retirement" in Abkhazia. People keep working for their entire lives, although at a slower pace when they are older. The long-living people work in the fields, do household chores, and tend to livestock. In Abkhazia, gluttony is considered a serious health risk, and overweight people are viewed as ill. In general, the Abkhazian diet is very healthy (lots of vegetables and fruits, very little meat) and people consume many fewer calories per day than the average American. The low level of stress in this culture is another likely contributor to the longevity of its residents. Competition is frowned upon, and moderation in everything is highly valued. It is not surprising that many people in Abkhazia are "long-living." As we have learned throughout this book, good health habits and the management of stress are critical for maintaining good physical health. It makes sense, then, that a culture that places emphasis on these elements would experience better health, and consequently increased longevity.

Of course, Abkhazia is not the only place where centenarians (people at least 100 years old) can be found! Centenarians are also the fastest growing group of Americans! Here are glimpses of some of them from a fascinating website: http://www.hcoa.org/centenarians/centenarians.htm

Audrey Stubbart was born in 1895 and remembers encounters with Sioux Indians on the plains of Nebraska not long after the historic Battle of Wounded Knee. She was married at age 15 and lived her early married life on the rugged Wyoming prairie. She still has a 40-hour-a-week job as a columnist and proofreader for *The Examiner* in Independence, Missouri.

York Garrett is 101 and he still works as a pharmacist in Durham, NC, as he has for 74 years. He went to Howard University's pharmacy school in 1916. Having suffered racism and discrimination throughout his life as an African American, he says that he is happy to be where he is now, and he hopes that his great-grandchildren and great-great-grandchildren get treated according to what they deserve.

Tom Lane was born in Omaha, Nebraska, in 1894. He is the holder of every national age-group record in master's swim meets, although as Tom says, "I'm the only swimmer in my age group!" He started swimming competitively at age 82. His daily exercise regimen consists of 30 sit-ups and 15 minutes of calisthenics followed by two or three sets of 50 repetitions on pull weights, and then lots of swimming. He also writes poetry. Tom was a World War I pilot and a earned a law degree from the University of Michigan.

What's the secret to living to be 100? To these centenarians, it's simple . . . you just keep going! As health psychologists, we know that many factors interact to produce such positive outcomes. Diet and exercise and safety behaviors (such as wearing a safety belt in the car) are very important. So is social support and optimism. Setting goals and always being willing to try something new keeps life interesting and worth living.

Is life still fun when you are a "long-living person"? It certainly can be! We hope you visit the website that contains fascinating stories of the lives of Tom Lane, York Garrett, Audrey Stubbart, and other centenarians across the country. This website also has links to current research on healthy aging and even lets you view some of the beautiful artwork that has been created by those over the age of 100!

Summary

1. Coping consists of efforts, both problem-focused and emotion-focused, to manage stressful events. It is a dynamic process and efforts to cope are typically centered on accomplishing five main tasks:

   - Contending realistically with the problem
   - Tolerating or adjusting emotionally to the negative events or realities
   - Attempting to maintain a positive self-image
   - Attempting to maintain emotional equilibrium
   - Attempting to continue satisfying relationships with other people

2. Human beings have a fundamental need for control. If all their efforts at control fail, people tend to become anxious or eventually helpless and depressed. Helplessness occurs in three specific realms:

   - Motivationally, by failing to make any efforts to change the outcome
   - Cognitively, by failing to learn new responses that could help avoid aversive outcomes in the future
   - Emotionally, by becoming depressed

3. Coping style refers to an individual's manner of thinking about and dealing with stressful life events.

   - Optimism is defined as a cognitive style, and optimists are problem solvers. Pessimists are convinced that things will turn out badly for them so they tend to give up and stop trying.

■ Hardiness involves three intertwined components: commitment, control, and challenge. Hardy people are more likely to remain healthy in the face of stressful events.

4. Antonovsky has proposed the Sense of Coherence model to explain successful coping with stress and the maintenance of health. Those with a Sense of Coherence believe that events in life have meaning and life "makes sense" to them.

5. The resources available to individuals to deal with stress can significantly affect their successes.

■ Those in the lowest socioeconomic positions in society have been found to suffer the highest rates of illness and mortality.

■ Social support can be very important in helping an individual deal with stressful life conditions and events. Social support may be of three types: tangible, informational, and emotional.

6. Research on stress management demonstrates that people can learn to cope effectively with and manage their stress to prevent the development of both psychological and physical difficulties.

■ Exercise can provide an active outlet for the physiological arousal experienced in response to stress.

■ Cognitive therapy is based on the view that the cognitive representation of the environment, rather than the environment itself, determines stress responses.

■ Relaxation works particularly well to help an individual deal with stress. It may involve meditation, systematic desensitization, progressive muscle relaxation, or biofeedback.

7. A successful, multidimensional approach to stress management involves recognizing the sources of stress as well as the factors that contribute to feelings of stress, learning to modify the physiological effects of stress reactions, and learning to remedy the factors that contribute to stress.

THINKING CRITICALLY

1. If you encountered a person who had been on so many unsuccessful diets that "learned helplessness" had taken over, how might you help him or her to regain a sense of control over his or her eating?

2. Based on Pennebaker's work on emotional disclosure, would you suggest that it would be a good idea for someone to keep a diary? How can the principles learned from Pennebaker's empirical studies be applied to everyday life situations, rather than just to coping with traumatic events?

3. Social support can be a two-edged sword. You are already very familiar with the ways in which social support is good for health. In what ways might social contacts be harmful to it?

4. Think about the last time something bad happened to you. What kinds of attributions did you make? Internal or external? Stable or unstable? Global or specific? Were these attributions typical of you? If so, what does this tell you about your explanatory style? How might this relate to your health?

GLOSSARY

Attribution: The causal association of an event.

Avoidant coping: A coping strategy in which one attempts to minimize the experience by not thinking about it or addressing it.

Behavior control: The specific behaviors that the individual enacts to control his or her environment in order to cope with stress.

Biofeedback: A technique involving an electromechanical device that emits a signal to "feed back" to the individual some information about the state of his or her body, such as muscle tension or arousal of the sympathetic nervous system.

Catastrophizing: Believing that an event that has not gone according to plan is not simply inconvenient but is truly a catastrophe from which one may never recover.

Cognitions: One's thoughts about and interpretations of events or about oneself in relation to those events, including a view of life and its meaning.

Cognitive control: Control over thoughts and other psychological activities.

Cognitive distraction: A mental control strategy whereby an individual tries to forget about an unwanted thought by actively thinking about something else.

Cognitive restructuring: A widely used technique for changing stress-provoking thoughts or beliefs so that they promote the individual's well-being.

Coping: Dynamic efforts by an individual, both action-oriented and intrapsychic, to manage environmental and internal demands and conflicts among them.

Coping style: The manner in which and the amount that an individual thinks about stressful life events.

Emotion-focused coping: Attempts to regulate or reduce the emotional consequences of a stressful event.

Emotional disclosure: The process of talking about (or writing about) an emotionally painful event to resolve the emotional aspects of the problem or occurrence.

Emotional support: Help from members of the social network to reassure the individual that he or she is a cared for, valued, and esteemed person.

Explanatory style: An individual's typical way of explaining events, particularly negative events; includes internal vs. external, stable vs. unstable, and global vs. specific.

General Resistance Resources (GRR): Resources (such as money, ego strength, social support, cultural stability) that help to protect a person against ill effects of stress.

Hardiness: A psychological construct that refers to an individual's stable, characteristic way of responding to life events. Hardiness involves commitment, control, and a sense of challenge.

Informational control: A valuable element in coping, informational control occurs when an individual has knowledge about ways in which to deal with the stressful event.

Informational support: Help from members of the social network in which they suggest alternative actions that may help to solve the stress-producing problem.

In vivo: Contacts that involve experience of the actual stress-provoking stimulus in the real-life situation.

Learned helplessness: Occurs when efforts at control continually come to no avail; helplessness occurs in three realms: motivational, cognitive, and emotional.

Meditation: Techniques that attempt to focus an individual's attention on a single thought or image in an effort to not be distracted by other thoughts, particularly ones of an evaluative or analytic nature; effective in reducing stress and anxiety.

Mental control: The effort an individual exerts to control his or her own thoughts.

Optimistic explanations: Explanations for events that invoke external, temporary, and specific explanations for negative things that happen.

Pathogenic model: A model that posits a direct effect of some psychological or physical variable on disease. Current examples are the effect of Type A behavior on coronary disease and the effect of learned helplessness on immunity.

Pessimistic explanations: Those that invoke internal, stable, and global explanations for negative events.

Proactive coping: Coping efforts that attempt to anticipate and prepare for stressful events before they actually occur.

Problem-focused coping: See problem-solving efforts.

Problem solving efforts: The actions taken to change a stressful situation or to prevent or reduce its effects.

Progressive muscle relaxation: A technique in which the individual focuses his or her attention on specific muscle groups and alternately tenses and relaxes the muscles.

Salutogenic orientation: An approach to research that allows examination of the factors that promote movement toward health rather than toward illness.

Self-efficacy: The belief that one can indeed accomplish a particular goal; self-efficacy may promote positive coping.

Sense of Coherence: A theory of stress that addresses how people who experience very stressful and chaotic existences can still remain healthy.

Social support: Help from other human beings such as friends, family, neighbors, co-workers, and acquaintances. Social support can come in the form of physical assistance and can also involve reminders that one is an esteemed and valued person.

Stress inoculation training: Cognitive preparation for stressful experiences; occurs in three steps: conceptualization, skill acquisition and rehearsal, and application.

Systematic desensitization: A method for reducing stress (particularly that generated from fear of or anxiety about something specific). The method is based upon the stimulus-response associations of classical conditioning.

Tangible support: Help in the form of physical resources (e.g., lending money, doing the grocery shopping, taking care of the children).

Thought avoidance: A mental control strategy whereby the individual tries not to think about an unwanted thought.

Thought stopping: A mental control strategy whereby an individual eliminates a thought by telling it to "stop" when it comes into awareness.

CHAPTER

11

Serious Illness:
The Patient's Perspective

In her dream, Lety struggled to reach the surface of the water, but she seemed to be moving much too slowly, almost in slow motion. She realized with increasing panic that she was stuck under the surface of the water, unable to move. She was sure she was going to die. She tried to scream, but the water burned her throat and lungs as she gasped for air. The dream was terrifying, the most terrifying she had ever had.

Lety awoke and felt someone stroking her forehead. She struggled to open her eyes and take in a deep breath. The pain in her neck and back at first was dull and throbbing, but as she became more fully awake it began to be excruciating. As she lay there in her hospital bed, concentrating on breathing, her mother tried to tell her what happened. She emerged from her dream of drowning and began to remember some of the details of her accident.

A week earlier, Lety had put on her new bathing suit and hurried to the back-yard of her home where her 21st birthday party was already in progress. It was her day. She'd spent the morning shopping with her two sisters, and they had stopped at the caterer's on the way home to pick up food for the party. As her sisters pre-pared the backyard for the party, Lety was ordered not to look until everything was ready! So, she gave herself a manicure and listened to her favorite CD. She put on her new bathing suit and admired herself in the mirror. It was a perfect afternoon.

When the party began and Lety emerged from the house, the backyard erupted with cheers! Everyone joined in singing "Happy Birthday." The DJ played her favorite music. There was dancing and plenty of delicious food, and all of her family and best friends were there. As dusk approached, her father turned on the lights in the pool, and guests began to swim. Now that she was 21, Lety had three celebratory glasses of wine over the course of the party; she felt brave and somewhat heady. Her judgment was quite impaired, however, and thinking she was in the deep end of the pool, she did a beautiful swan dive. Her takeoff was perfect, but to the horror of her friends and family, she dove into the shallow end headfirst. Her head hit the bottom of the pool with a terrible, crushing impact. Her thoughts at that moment were surprisingly clear. She knew something very serious had happened and suddenly she couldn't feel her body, or move it. She was rapidly running out of air, and wondered why no one had come to get her. Were they actually going to let her lie there on the bottom of the pool and drown? She felt panic stricken, but no matter how hard she tried, she couldn't move to struggle to the surface. After what seemed like forever, she felt herself rising to the surface, and then she was lifted from the pool and laid on the grass. She was terrified. She couldn't move, and when she tried to answer her parents' questions, she didn't seem to be able to make the words come out the way she wanted them to. As she waited for the paramedics to arrive, her neck and back began to ache horribly. She closed her eyes and waited.

At the hospital, Lety underwent countless procedures to determine just how much damage her body had sustained. Holes were drilled into her skull so her head could be attached to a metal frame to immobilize her neck and spine. Much of her time was spent in a kind of "limbo," somewhere between waking and sleep-ing. Lety preferred it there. Her sleep was haunted by terrifying dreams of suffo-cating, and when she was awake she couldn't stop thinking about all she may have lost and her uncertain future. Sometimes she felt like she no longer wanted to live. She might never walk again, might never be able to care for herself or do many of the things she had always enjoyed. She knew her life was changed forever.

Josh felt he had everything going for him. He was married to a wonderful woman. He and his wife had a new baby who had just turned 6 months of age and was learning to sit up on her own. He was 30 years old, with a degree in criminology. After a few years of working for the probation department, Josh had decided to follow his dream of working for the FBI. He had just found out he was accepted into their training academy, and he and his wife were excited about looking for a new home in Virginia.

Josh had a nagging ache in his shoulder for a few months, but he didn't think much of it. He had played college baseball and knew lots of other players with the same aches and pains. But Josh's world came tumbling down when he received a call from the physician who had done his FBI physical. Josh had told the doctor about his painful shoulder, and the doctor ordered an x-ray. Now, he was calling with some bad news. Although Josh was generally strong and apparently healthy, the shoulder x-ray showed an uncommon form of bone cancer. The doctor wanted him to see an oncologist immediately to confirm the diagnosis and to determine whether and how far the cancer had spread. Josh simply could not believe what he was hearing!

Josh met with the oncologist who immediately scheduled surgery to remove the bone tumor in his shoulder and recommended that he have chemotherapy. Luckily, tests showed that the cancer had not metastasized to other parts of Josh's body. His prognosis looked good. Josh was optimistic after the surgery, but his optimism was tempered after his first chemotherapy appointment. Josh was severely ill for days and could not get out of bed. He developed a 103-degree fever and violent chills, vomited almost constantly, and was so severely weakened that he could not even talk with his wife or play with his baby daughter. Every week, Josh had to return for chemotherapy treatments. After a month, Josh's hair started to fall out and he had lost 20 pounds. He wondered how he would get through three more months of treatment, then wait six more to find out if the chemotherapy had worked and the cancer was contained.

Josh was not only physically affected by the treatments, but he suffered emotionally as well. He felt very lonely and scared during and after the treatments, when he was unable to get out of bed for days on end. Josh found himself thinking over and over that 30-year-old men with wives, young children, and big hopes for the future do not get cancer! Cancer is for old people! Cancer is for sick people! Cancer is for people who are about to die! He started to withdraw emotionally from his family and did not want to see any of his friends. He simply could not envision anything positive in the future. He was overwhelmingly depressed.

Accidents and serious illness have the potential to transform an individual's life instantly and completely. Illness and injury happen not only to a body, but also to a mind—a consciousness. It is a thinking, feeling human being who suffers. Lety and Josh both faced physical traumas, and their conditions threatened their emotional balance as well as their survival.

In this chapter, we will examine in detail what it is like to be seriously ill or injured. We will explore patients' thoughts, concerns, and feelings. We will examine what patients feel about themselves and about their own lives and prospects for the future. We will examine the difficulties faced in making decisions about diagnosis and treatment, and in fighting for control of one's own life. We will see how patients cope with feelings of helplessness and alienation. We will also examine how patients learn to cope with the tragic circumstances of illness and injury. We will explore some of the conditions under which patients find hope for a future, however different that future might be from what they once expected. We will see the value in patients setting limited, concrete goals and taking small but regular steps toward achieving independence and rebuilding their lives in new ways. Finally, we will continue this examination in Chapter 12, where we address the chronic phase of illness in which patients and their families must learn to adjust to permanent limitations and find ways to lead meaningful lives.

Stages of Illness

Different demands are made on an individual at different stages of illness or physical injury. During the first phase, the **acute phase**, the primary concern of both patient and medical personnel is survival. Moment-to-moment, or day-to-day, the individual's chances of survival depend upon the immediate measures taken to deal with the physical trauma or disease. For the heart attack patient, intervention is initially provided within moments of arrival at the hospital and the effectiveness of that intervention can determine both immediate and long-term survival (Vincent, 1996). For many illnesses, short-term survival (months, or a few years) may be relatively certain. Beyond the short term, however, the length and quality of the individual's life will depend upon appropriate and timely treatment. A person with a newly discovered cancerous tumor might receive swift surgical intervention to remove the tumor and timely chemotherapy to prevent **metastasis** (spread to other organs) by eliminating malignant cells (Stockhorst et al., 1998a). The choices that are made in the acute stages of illness or injury can have a lasting impact on the individual's long-term survival and on the quality of his or her future life. Therefore, the imperative exists for professionals to make the correct diagnosis and to work with the patient to make the best treatment decisions for the patient as an individual.

The acute phase of care is also likely to be accompanied by pain, confusion, and fear on the part of the patient. These emotions can influence the patient's decisions regarding treatment. Josh, whom we encountered at the beginning of this chapter, felt many of these emotions as he underwent surgery and chemotherapy in the acute phase of his cancer treatment. These emotions sometimes competed with his decision to undergo the initial physical and emotional suffering of cancer treatments in an effort to eradicate the cancer from his body and thereby to increase significantly his chances for survival (see Mullan, 1983).

During the next phase, **rehabilitation**, a person who has been bedridden or has been passively cared for by medical professionals must work toward achieving as high a level of health and independent functioning as his or her condition will allow. Tremendous efforts may be required for the patient to walk unassisted, for example, or to talk coherently, or to get dressed and eat. A rehabilitation patient must learn to adjust to these limitations and to come to terms with an altered self-image, and specialists in medical rehabilitation can help the patient to maximize his or her remaining potential. As described in Box 11.1, rehabilitation can take many different forms, depending on the nature of the disability.

When an individual has accomplished as much as possible toward rehabilitation, he or she often must accept the remaining disabilities and limitations as chronic and go on with life. **Chronic conditions** (considered in detail in Chapter 12) are those from which patients are not expected to recover. Facial disfigurement, a limp, or life in a wheelchair may be inescapable realities, and patients must adapt by accepting their impairment, making appropriate behavioral and goal adjustments, and dealing with their new limitations (Charmaz, 1995).

In some cases, an illness progresses to the point where a cure is impossible and the condition is **terminal**. Cancer may metastasize, for example, as neoplastic cells escape from the initial tumor site and travel to other parts of the body such as the

BOX 11.1
Hot Topic

Rehabilitation

The cost of illness and disability can be staggering. Not only is treatment a huge expense, but human potential for productive labor is lost. The process of rehabilitation can reduce these costs significantly by helping a person to attain his or her maximum potential in physical, psychological, social, and vocational realms.

Rehabilitation has a fairly recent history. In ancient times, there was little tolerance for physical infirmity. The Greeks, for example, were so enamored of physical perfection that they killed defective children by throwing them from a precipice or abandoning them on the side of a mountain. Any enlightenment that occurred after that was halted in the Middle Ages when the emphasis on spirits and demons as the cause of illness stood in the way of the humane treatment of those afflicted (Goldenson, 1978a, 1978b). During the 1800s, several institutes for the care of those ill and crippled were opened in Europe and in the United States. It was not until after World War I, however, that the rehabilitation movement took hold and began to develop. Emphasis was on the physical restoration and rehabilitation of those injured in war. The greatest strides in the clinical care of the chronically ill and disabled have come since World War II.

Today, rehabilitation is a *dynamic* process that is geared to the needs of the whole person

(Belgrave, 1998; Bryan, 1999; Falvo, 1999; Fraser & Clemmons, 2000; Gandy et al., 1999; Sife, 1998). It is not limited to restoration of the individual's physical capacities alone but is targeted at several realms. Physical treatments such as medication and surgery are instituted to reduce, as much as possible, the impact of the illness or injury on the individual's physical functioning. Rehabilitation may also involve acquisition and training in the use of a prosthetic device (or prosthesis, which is an artificial substitute for a missing body part). The use of a prosthesis can often bring a person to near normal functioning, such as when an amputee learns to walk with a prosthetic leg.

Current rehabilitation methods also include (a) vocational rehabilitation, which involves counseling, testing, and training toward the goal of job placement or independent self-employment; (b) psychological rehabilitation, which consists of personal counseling and psychotherapy, and supportive measures toward the goal of increased self-acceptance and self-esteem; and (c) social rehabilitation, which includes help in developing and maintaining social relationships and recreational pastimes. Sexual counseling is also provided, so that with some relearning a disabled individual can enjoy a fulfilling sex life.

---

bones, lungs, brain, or liver. A heart attack, or a series of them, may cause irreparable damage to the patient's heart, making it impossible to sustain life. In Chapter 13, we examine in detail the wide range of emotional reactions that patients experience in attempting to come to terms with their terminal conditions and the prospect of death. What is clear is that each individual comes to understand his or her illness in relation to "life themes" made up of past life experiences, current goals, and personal values. These life themes, which vary greatly from person to person, help patients to find meaning in illness and influence the coping strategies that they employ in dealing with it (e.g., Zlatin, 1995). As patients move through the stages from acute to rehabilitation to chronic or terminal, their life themes provide unique frameworks for dealing with the illness experience.

Importance of Focusing on Psychosocial Issues

In this chapter, we will see that serious illness and injury threaten virtually every aspect of an individual's life. Thoughts and feelings inevitably arise from serious threats to the person's well-being (e.g., Penninx et al., 1998; Vilhjalmsson, 1998) and change with the current stage of the person's condition. It is important for medical and psychological professionals, as well as for patients and their families, to understand the psychological outcomes of serious illness and injury in order to help patients to cope with the difficulties they encounter. Furthermore, the character of these thoughts and feelings may not only be affected by, but also affect, the patient's physical condition. For example, the patient's anxiety and fear may deplete the energy he or she needs for healing. Depression and hopelessness may translate into an unwillingness or inability to take the necessary steps toward health and well-being. Knowledge and understanding of these psychological factors can be critical to the patient's achievement of long term-goals (Holzemer et al., 1999).

Serious Illness: The Losses

Dr. Shlain, the young surgeon stricken with cancer, writes of its tremendous emotional impact. "I submit to you that, in the entire dictionary, in any language, you will not find a single word that carries with it such emotional impact as cancer" (Shlain, 1979). He describes his diagnosis as having characteristics of a nightmare in which something horrible is happening, and one can have no control over it. Many today would argue that AIDS fits this profile as well. Life with cancer, AIDS, or any other serious illness or injury can be unpredictable, make little sense, and be filled with threats to self-image. The losses may be profound: losses of self-esteem, of freedom, of day-to-day activities, of feelings of physical comfort, and of the many possibilities for the future.

Threats to Self-Image

The debilitating treatments of cancer, the weakness and limitations of heart disease, and the physical disfigurements of burns and amputations can drastically change an individual's self image. The exhaustion and forced dependency of sickness and disability may seriously threaten an individual's sense of strength and competence. A person's feelings of attractiveness may be drastically altered by facial disfigurement, alopecia (hair loss) resulting from chemotherapy, severe burns, or the loss of a breast to cancer (Fukunishi, 1999; Moyer, 1997; Munstedt et al., 1997; Taylor et al., 1985).

> . . . Mastectomy is so shattering to a woman's self-image that she may feel she is only "passing" for normal. Attention from a man, particularly a man she did not know "before," will overwhelm her with feelings of fraudulence; she knows what he doesn't— that beneath her sweater are scars and a missing breast. (Dackman, 1987, p. 420)

In general, diseases such as cancer of the reproductive organs or disabilities that interfere with sexual activity have the potential to seriously threaten an individual's self-image as a sexual being. The individual may doubt his or her ability to be a loved and desired partner (Dunham, 1978); this is particularly true for younger patients (Spencer et al., 1999). In fact, as we will see in Chapter 12, younger patients who are chronically ill often deal with a number of difficult psychosocial issues that are less salient for older patients.

Overall, one's self image as a whole and independent person may be seriously challenged by the forced dependency of illness and injury (Fukunishi, 1999; Voll & Poustka, 1994). This may be especially true when survival depends upon artificial devices, such as ventilator equipment or cardiac pacemakers, since these devices are constant reminders that the person is no longer completely independent and is living a very different sort of life than prior to the injury (Bertolotti & Carone, 1994). Even before physical changes related to a disease are obvious, a person's self-image may begin to change according to the beliefs that he or she holds about the illness and the fears associated with anticipated disability and loss of independence.

> Upon hearing his diagnosis of cancer, 37-year-old Dr. Shlain reported, "At that moment . . . I was consumed by fear. . . . It was the thought of suffering, of dying slowly, and in the end dying, not as I was in life but rather as a shriveled ghost of myself . . . I feared I would be the object of pity and that people would be afraid of me and withdraw." (Shlain, 1979, p. 177)

Loss of Body Integrity

The physical alteration of one's body can be disorienting and terrifying. Watching one's own blood pour from a serious wound, or recognizing that a body part has been amputated and is permanently gone may at first bring **dissociation**, the experience that "This body isn't me." **Integration** of an altered body image (the process of adjusting one's body image to include physical changes) may take some time and have to be repeated as new losses occur (Charmaz, 1995). For example, the loss of fingers in an industrial accident can be just the first in a series of associated losses, such as skin graft surgeries, further surgical amputations, and knuckle replacement surgery. Reattachment of the fingers is not always successful, so the patient may live for a time with the nonfunctional fingers attached, and then suffer another loss if the reattachment fails months later.

Even when a bodily change is for the better, as in the case of cosmetic or reconstructive surgery, adjustment may be very slow. When a permanent change in physical reality is for the worse, however, as is usually the case in serious injuries, reality is not faced easily, and often not right away (Handron, 1993).

Some diseases or injuries, such as Lety's spinal cord damage, drastically change a person's ability to perform self-care and participate in much-enjoyed activities (see Figure 11.1 for a detailed description of the outcomes of spinal cord injury). One of the most painful disruptions to such a person's life may be the loss of pleasurable hobbies (Kinney & Coyle, 1992; Kleiber et al., 1995). People tend to experience this loss in two domains: They may mourn their inability to physically perform the activity and may also miss the social interaction and camaraderie that was associated with the hobby (Kleiber et al., 1995).

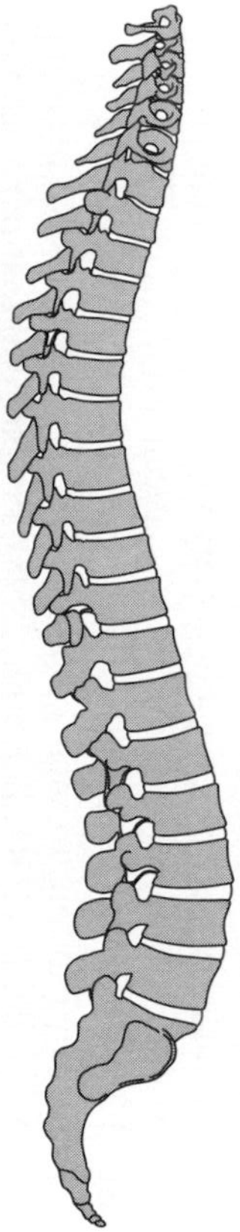

Spinal cord injury at:	Spinal area affected	Motor loss	Sensory loss	Possible psychosocial consequences
1 2 3 4	Cervical nerve routes C1 to C4	– diaphragm – intercostal – skeletal muscles below neck	– neck and below	– threatened self image – loss of body integrity – interruption of work – loss of independence – cognitive deficits – threatened future – strain on interpersonal relationships – strain on family members – complex, conflicting emotions – the stresses of modern medicine – medical treatments – communication with medical professionals – hospitalization – pain, suffering, and possible death
5 6 7	Cervical nerve routes C5 to C7	– intercostal – below shoulders and upper arms	– arms, hands, chest, abdomen, lower extremities	
1 2 3 4 5 6	Thoracic nerve routes T1 to T6	– below midchest	– below midchest	
7 8 9 10 11 12	Thoracic nerve routes T7 to T12	– below waist	– below waist	
1 2 3	Lumbar nerve routes L1 to L3	– leg muscles, pelvis	– lower abdomen and legs	
4 5	Lumbar nerve routes L4 to L5	– lower legs, ankles, feet	– parts of lower legs, feet	
1 2 3 4 5	Sacral nerve routes S1 to S5	– bladder, rectum, feet, ankles	– inner thigh – outside of foot – perineum	

FIGURE 11.1 The biopsychosocial consequences of spinal cord injury.

Appearance is also an important component of body integrity. The patient who has lost a breast to cancer, for example, may delay for a long time looking at the results of her surgery. Women who are very invested in their physical appearance are most traumatized by breast cancer surgeries (Carver et al., 1998). Many women report that the initial viewing was a tremendous shock and that the incorporation of the reality of the amputation into their body image took considerable time. For some, it is never done completely, and the only solution is breast reconstruction (Berger & Bostwick, 1984).

Like breast cancer survivors, burn patients may deny the existence of a severe facial disfigurement by avoiding mirrors. Some patients with facial burns delay looking at themselves for a very long time. The patient's altered appearance is almost always a considerable shock that challenges his or her entire sense of identity (Fukunishi, 1999). Those who are facially disfigured tend to have the most difficulty adjusting, probably because of their inability to hide the disfigurement, the reactions of other people to them, and the role that the face plays in social interaction and the establishment of their self-concept (Macgregor, 1990). One way that burn patients may cope adaptively with this stress is by minimizing the importance of physical appearance to their sense of self. **Denial** is a psychological defense mechanism in which one refuses to acknowledge what has taken place. Denial can be a very effective short term defense mechanism. It allows the individual slowly to come to terms emotionally with the full meaning of his or her altered body image, rather than attempting to deal with the multitude of losses all at once. Most people who must deal with major adjustments in their lives tend, initially at least, to defend their feelings against the full meaning of their deformities. Denial is a common response of patients to such conditions as heart attack, strokes, cancer, and burns (Handron, 1993; Levine et al., 1994). Denial, although sometimes self-deceptive, can serve to help maintain the individual's identity and self-esteem, particularly in the face of negative reactions from other people (Goldbeck, 1997; Hamburg et al., 1953; Handron, 1993; Lazarus, 1983).

Denial can occur when changes are swift and dramatic, such as with traumatic accidents, as well as when they take place more slowly, such as when long-term illness depletes capacities or appearance. These physical changes have a significant emotional effect in both types of situations. Fitzhugh Mullan, M.D., found a cancerous tumor when looking at his own chest x-ray. He was young (32 years old), with a wife and a small daughter, and, although he was able to battle the cancer successfully, it took years of his life and changed him forever. He wrote candidly about his real-life encounter with serious illness in a book entitled *Vital Signs* (Mullan, 1983). In many ways, his experience was like that of Josh, whose life-changing encounter with bone cancer was described earlier in this chapter. After months of cancer treatment, Dr. Mullan found his body altered in a way that made salient the profound physical losses he had experienced because of his cancer.

> There were no mirrors in my hospital room, and while I knew I was losing weight, I had had no opportunity to see my body. Daily, to be sure, I showered and ran my hands over the increasingly bony prominences of myself, but somehow that didn't add up to what had really happened until I came home and saw myself in a full-length mirror. I was staggered. . . . I had felt sick. Now I saw what it was like to look sick. (Mullan, 1983, p. 60)

When an individual's body is altered due to accident or a disease such as cancer, he or she may fear that relationships with others, particularly with loved ones, will be changed drastically because of the new physical appearance (Lichtman, 1982; Moyer, 1997). They fear that they will be rejected or become an object of revulsion or pity. Thus, the reactions that these loved ones actually have can profoundly influence the individual's self-definition. A woman who had had a mastectomy allowed her lover to see the results of her surgery. " 'It's not that bad,' Tom . . . said. He lied. I know because he squeezed me tightly and whispered, 'Oh, you poor darling.' I heard his words of sympathy, and then I heard myself wail as I had wailed only once before— when I thought my life might shortly end" (Dackman, 1987, p. 436). It is not uncommon for people with disabilities to receive conflicting messages—supportive words coupled with nonverbal indications of revulsion, or rejection, or pity (Wortman & Dunkel-Schetter, 1979).

Interruption of Work

When people are seriously ill, their schoolwork and careers must be put on hold. Opportunities for advancement may vanish, the likelihood of returning to school or career may remain unclear for a long time, and resumption of former activities may become impossible. New self-definitions may be slow in coming, as new opportunities for productivity must be discovered or learned.

Many people derive a strong sense of identity from the work that they do—for example, from their role as student, or their devotion to a career. Work is often the outlet for creative ideas, and it provides a view of oneself as a productive person. The ability to support oneself and not be dependent upon others can figure prominently in an individual's self-esteem (Reynolds, 1997). In heart transplant recipients and those with other physical disabilities, employment has been shown to relate to a variety of psychosocial variables, including self-esteem, identity stability, sense of control, independence, depression, body image, quality of life, and life satisfaction (Duitsman & Cychosz, 1994; Kinney & Coyle, 1992). People who are employed experience better psychosocial outcomes. They have higher self-esteem, feel more independent, are less depressed, and express higher levels of satisfaction with their lives than those who are not employed. These individuals derive a sense of competence and control over their lives from their jobs, and for many people a job is an important indicator of their identity and what they think is important. It is often difficult to deal with the changes that serious illness brings, and when the work-related portion of one's life is taken away by the illness, losses may be felt quite strongly.

Various adjustments in the workplace can make it possible for people with illnesses or injuries to return to work (Roessler et al., 1998). Sometimes actually changing the workspace may be necessary. Some employees may need special equipment to restore their previous level of productivity, or they may require a modified work schedule. In some instances, it may be impossible for the individual to return to the exact same duties for which he or she was formerly responsible. In this case, another work assignment might be substituted. These kinds of accommodations require effort—

both on the part of the ill or disabled individual and on the part of the employer. Given the multitude of psychological benefits to the person and the financial rewards of avoiding total disability, however, this is effort well invested. Beyond the issue of a paycheck, the financial costs of serious illness can be tremendous. Family resources may be taxed beyond their capacity. Even with medical insurance coverage, which may eventually vanish if the patient loses his or her job, the costs (such as deductibles and copayments) are often considerable. Without insurance, these costs can be astronomical.

Loss of Independence

> . . . My greatest fear was loss of control over my own destiny. I would have to hand it over to faceless x-ray technicians and people I did not know." (Shlain, 1979, p. 177)

Helplessness and forced dependency are the realities of many serious medical conditions. Because of the limitations that result from illness and injury, a patient must rely on other people such as family members, medical professionals, and attendants, sometimes for his or her most basic needs. Walking, eating, using the bathroom, and other simple tasks may be impossible to face alone and may depend entirely on the assistance of others. Illness and injury can bring to the person who is trapped in a damaged body various limitations and restrictions that may be frustrating and overwhelming. Loss of independence and the inability to do things for oneself can often result in depression (e.g., Koenig & George, 1998; Williamson, 1998). Even when the severity of the illness, age, financial security, social support, and personality variables are taken into account, restricted physical abilities still predict depression (Williamson, 1998). Depression is important not only for the obvious reason that it affects the individual's quality of life, but also because it tends to increase medical costs and the risk of death (Fried et al., 1998; Panzarino, 1998). Depression also threatens physical, cognitive, and social functioning (Evans & Whitney, 1998).

Paradoxically, the best adjustment to the enforced passivity of illness may involve fighting it (Mullan, 1983). A patient who relinquishes independence and control too readily may find that dependence and passivity become habits. Even the things that he or she can do alone may come to require assistance. For example, a recent study found that two of the factors that predicted nursing home placement for older adults who had been hospitalized for a medical problem were their levels of independence prior to hospitalization and how much independence they lost during their hospital stay (Rudberg et al., 1996). Another study (this time of adolescents who had experienced severe illness or injury) showed that when the adolescents were given autonomy and independence by their families, they were more successful in adjusting to their new physical realities (Voll & Poustka, 1994). An additional benefit of maintaining independence is that the patient who (within the confines of medical recommendations) tests his or her capacities continuously is more likely to maintain an accurate assessment of what can and cannot be accomplished alone. In this way, the limits of independence are defined and redefined. Goals for accomplishment can be adjusted and readjusted.

They had an elevator to transport stretchers and wheelchairs to the treatment level. I refused to use it, determined to walk the eight steps downward." (Mullan, 1983, p. 32)

Having to depend constantly on others can be a severe blow to one's sense of self (Van Lankveld et al., 1993). On the other hand, maintaining some independent action, however minimal, is valuable in preventing the depression that can result from helplessness (Seligman, 1975).

Problems can arise if a patient fights passivity at a significant cost to his or her own well-being. For example, the male heart attack patient—for whom rest is essential initially—may do calisthenics in his hospital room in order to prove that he is still robust and strong. While it can be valuable for a patient to do as many things as possible, actions must be carried out within medically recommended guidelines. The best approach may be for the patient to question some of his or her routinely applied restrictions and spend some time negotiating them with the physician so that they reflect his or her own individual capabilities as a patient.

Threats to Cognitive Functioning

Certain medical conditions can interfere directly with cognitive functioning. For example, partly because of the peculiar nature of the Intensive or Coronary Care Units (ICU or CCU) and partly because of the direct effects of certain physical treatments and medications, patients may become completely disoriented for significant periods of time. After open-heart surgery, for example, a patient's delerium may last for several days. This is a well-known condition that has been termed **cardiac delirium** or **cardiac psychosis** (Kimball, 1977). Some cardiac surgery patients experience only transient intellectual deficits while others have gross impairment of their cognitive functioning. Some experience hallucinations and even **paranoid ideations** (mental representations and thoughts of being the target of persecution). To the patient with cardiac psychosis, all environmental stimuli seem equally important and threatening. Stimuli that are normally tuned out remain quite salient. Cardiac psychosis is believed to be caused by small cerebral emboli (blood clots that go to the brain) following surgery. Cardiac psychosis is an example of a specific psychobiological reaction to the assault of illness and surgical treatment. Obviously, it is important for family members and those who care for the patient to know that such reactions are common and temporary.

In less extreme cases, such as for elderly individuals living with chronic conditions, the association between disease and cognitive functioning is less clear. It is these, less severe, deficits that psychologists more commonly encounter. Because of their less obvious nature, understanding them and designing interventions to deal with them is complex and difficult. Strokes are clearly associated with varying levels of cognitive deficits but other problems, such as asthma, bronchitis, high blood pressure, diabetes, and self-reports of general poor health have been found in some studies to be related to decreases in cognitive functioning (although some studies find no such effects) (Jelicic & Kempen, 1997; Zelinski et al., 1998). Of course, there are other diseases, such as Alzheimer's disease, that are primarily diseases *of* cognitive impairment. These types of chronic and degenerative illnesses are addressed further in Chapter 12.

A Threatened Future

The phenomena of illness and injury underscore the fact that life is unpredictable. A hoped-for future and distant goal can suddenly vanish from the realm of possibility when serious illness and injury occur. Plans to have children may be threatened by the discovery of cancer of the reproductive organs (cervical or testicular cancer, for example). Even short-range goals, such as finishing college, running in a marathon, or writing a book may be thwarted temporarily (or forever) by serious medical problems. Despite the uncertainties inherent in anticipating and planning for a future, present actions are usually undertaken in anticipation of their long-term goals. Planning assumes that there is a future to work toward, and that what is envisioned might be achieved. In the context of serious illness, of course, such assumptions may be incorrect.

Would people spend their time differently if they knew that a serious illness or injury would befall them and change their lives forever? People whose lives *have* been changed by serious illness or disabling injury do, in fact, focus on precisely this issue. In attempting to find meaning in their lives, they look back: How have I spent my time? Were my choices wise, given what I know now? What are the things that were and are really important to me? If I had another chance at a healthy life, how would I live it? Dr. Mullan, the physician and cancer patient we learned about earlier, looked back on the time just before his diagnosis and the terrible events that followed:

> It was about five o'clock on a Sunday afternoon. The sun was brilliant gold, illuminating Santa Fe and the Rio Grande Valley stretching to the west. . . . It was a moment of exquisite happiness. . . . In the time that followed that early March afternoon I thought frequently of that moment. I clung to its memory as proof that happiness exists. . . . I clung to the memory of that golden twilight in the belief that bodies were made for something better than what I felt. (Mullan, 1983, p. 26)
>
> In no way do I mean to recommend or endorse serious sickness, but living through it has, I think, left me with a fuller sense of life. (Mullan, 1983, p. 203).

Strain on Relationships with Loved Ones

Hospitalization and the invasive, debilitating treatments of illness and injury can bring both physical separation and emotional alienation from other people. Hospitalized patients, as well as those disabled at home, are very often terribly lonely. Visiting hours may be restricted, and busy schedules of work, school, and household duties may make it difficult for family and friends to spend time with the patient.

Even when loved ones do see the patient regularly and often, the circumstances of hospitalization can prevent normal interactions. Hospital roommates, nurses, and other medical personnel, for example, can severely limit privacy. When such a situation exists for a long period of time, marital and family relationships may become quite strained. Among adolescents suffering from cancer, for example, research has found that conflicts with their mothers seem most psychologically disrupting and stressful (Manne & Miller, 1998). This family dynamic is a particularly important target for family interventions.

Many obligations fall on the loved ones of a person who is ill. Family members typically must carry out many of the tasks that were once the patient's responsibility. The patient may begin to feel like an outsider in his or her own family. During his years fighting cancer, for example, Dr. Mullan watched the relationship between his wife and daughter grow very strong and, at times, appear to exclude him. He knew that the exclusion was not intentional and that it came about as a result of his long absences in the hospital. He also recognized that if he were to die, the closeness that his wife and daughter developed would be extremely important to them both. Yet, he still felt sadly left out (Mullan, 1983).

The severe stress that illness places on a family can challenge its cohesiveness. It has been suggested that the stresses of a serious illness such as cancer typically make a solid, strong marriage much better, and a weak, troubled one considerably worse (Shlain, 1979). While the crisis of illness brings many opportunities for intense emotional intimacy and for the expression of concern and devotion (e.g., Waltz, 1986), illness also presents a tremendous challenge to maintaining trust and open communication (Collins et al., 1990; Taylor, 1989).

Finally, an individual's role in his or her family may change, temporarily or permanently, as a result of illness or disability (Hallett et al., 1994; Johnson et al., 1995). When someone is absent from his or her family while severely ill and hospitalized, other family members must carry on in whatever way they can. For example, a woman who was once dependent upon her husband is forced to become self-sufficient when he is ill. Unless their communication is open and intimate, he may come to feel unneeded. In an effort to forestall such a loss, one woman whose husband was seriously ill with **amyotrophic lateral sclerosis** (or Lou Gehrig's disease, which is an incurable, degenerative disease of the nervous system) made it a point to send the children to their father whenever he was well enough to help them with their problems. This action underscored his continued role as a parent and codecision maker of the household (Safran, 1977). In some cases, role changes may be for the better. The disruption of dysfunctional patterns may give rise to new and better ways for family members to relate to one another.

Facing the Emotional Challenges of Serious Illness

A patient who is seriously ill or injured faces many challenging tasks. Among the greatest of these is to remain an emotionally healthy person in the face of the demands of a serious medical condition.

As we have seen so far in this chapter, there are many aspects of serious illness and injury that can be psychologically extremely stressful to patients. Perhaps the most daunting emotional obstacle a seriously ill person faces is depression. Depressed people view their illnesses more negatively than those who are not depressed and see themselves as less able to control their illnesses (Murphy et al., 1999). Although common sense might dictate that perceptions of greater illness severity should be related to more depression, this has not been found to be universally true. For example, patients with rheumatoid arthritis who believed their condition was curable were more depressed than those who believed it was incurable. Perhaps the latter patients had accepted the disease, while the former patients were disappointed that they had not yet been cured (Schiaffino et al., 1998). This research also found that patients who viewed their symptoms as unpredictable and who held themselves responsible for their illness were more depressed. Depression is an important factor of focus because it predicts a variety of crucial outcomes such as medical costs, functioning, and even death (Evans & Whitney, 1998; Fried et al., 1998; Panzarino, 1998).

Another common emotional reaction to serious illness or injury is anxiety. The ill or injured individual is now forced to live a life, and function in a world, that may be significantly different from what he or she was accustomed to. These changes create obstacles that must be overcome, and anxiety over one's ability to meet these challenges often ensues. Also, the prognosis associated with the illness or injury is often uncertain. Although the individual may hope for (and even believe in) the best possible outcomes, the nagging possibility of more negative outcomes is always present, precipitating anxiety and dread (Jacobson et al., 1995). Furthermore, the uncertainties associated with disease progression often do not go away, and anxiety about the future may actually increase over time, although the focus is on immediate problems (Christman et al., 1988).

Maintaining Identity through Social Support

Serious illness and injury have the capacity to change people significantly, and one of the greatest challenges facing the patient is to maintain his or her own identity. In the face of the physical and emotional demands of illness, even happy, optimistic people can become severely depressed. Intelligent, energetic people can lose their willingness and ability to direct their lives. Mature, reasonable people can become petulant and childish. How extensively a person is changed depends, of course, upon the conditions of the illness, the precise experiences of treatment, the individual's emotional resiliency, and a host of other factors including the social support available to them (Moos & Tsu, 1977). In general, though, illness and injury often bring challenges and losses to the very things that make each person unique, such as his or her appearance and bodily functioning, physical and mental capabilities, plans and future possibilities, and personal philosophy. When many of his or her own unique characteristics are changed or can no longer find expression, the individual must work to develop new aspects of his or her identity.

One way in which the seriously ill or injured can help maintain their own identity is through positive social relations with others (Fife, 1995). Identity maintenance under these trying circumstances requires flexibility in the perception of one's own identity. The individual must make adjustments that maintain his or her self-esteem and optimize functioning despite the impairment. Social support can play a pivotal role by providing an environment that is encouraging of this change.

In the course of illness and injury, having a life partner and other close relationships tends to be linked to lower levels of depression. Emotional support seems to provide a buffering effect against the inevitable onslaught of negative feelings resulting from illness or serious injury (Penninx et al., 1998). Both marital support and support from friends can aid emotional adjustment (Brecht et al., 1994; Hoskins, 1995; Li & Moore, 1998; Reifman, 1995). Such effects last over time. A recent review of longitudinal studies of social relationships and recovery from heart disease and breast cancer found that, over the long term, patients with good social support networks had better outcomes (including survival) than did those with weaker social supports. This was particularly true for those with heart disease (Reifman, 1995).

Maintaining a strong support network in the face of a serious illness can be difficult. Those close to the individual, who are being relied upon for support, may feel the strain associated with both the illness and the patient's reaction to it (Manne & Zautra, 1990; Stein et al., 1992). All family members who are coping with the challenge will likely have special needs surrounding the experience.

Box 11.2 further examines social support, and some of its complexities and cultural variations, in the context of serious illness.

BOX **11.2**

Across Cultures

Social Support, Culture, and Illness

Adjustment to illness and disability can be strongly influenced by the social and emotional resources available to an individual and to a family. **Social support** is particularly important, and may include four components: (1) emotional/informational support (e.g., listening and providing advice), (2) tangible support (e.g., grocery shopping and driving the children to school), (3) affectionate support (e.g., hugs and hand holding), and (4) positive social interaction (e.g., engaging in fun activities) (Sherbourne & Stewart, 1991). Generally, researchers have found that people who receive social support from friends and extended family tend to cope better with illness than do those who receive no such support.

Cultural groups vary in their comfort with such support, however, and with their expectations for who should provide it. Chinese families, particularly those less acculturated to the United States, have been found to be generally uncomfortable allowing distressing information (such as about illness) to be communicated outside the family and even to certain members within the family, such as the children (Ow & Katz, 1999). While such restriction may contribute to what is

seen as "face-saving" and the maintenance of hierarchical roles, "secrets" can limit social support and increase strain between family members. Among low-income Hispanic women with arthritis, coping has been found to depend upon having family members (particularly daughters) rather than friends provide support. Dependence on family is a highly valued cultural norm (Abraido-Lanza et al., 1996). In African American families, religion and spirituality tend to be important components in the utilization of social support networks in the face of illness (Belgrave, 1998; Stroman, 2000). There are important implications of cultural variation for practice in the healthcare setting. Awareness of social support norms is necessary in order to facilitate assistance when patients become ill. Support for caregivers and emotional disclosure within the family and social support network may be necessary.

While it is important to know about individual cultures and their practices, research has shown that it is the degree of group cohesion, rather than culture itself, that predicts psychological well-being (Liu, 1986). In all cultural groups, health professionals need to be aware of the dynamics and the cohesiveness of the support network, as well as of the burdens that are placed on caregivers. Providing physical and emotional care to someone who is ill can be exhausting and leave the caregiver with limited opportunity to focus on his or her own needs. Further, a caregiver's negative emotional state might actually be detrimental to the emotional life of the patient. Therefore, it is especially important that caregivers themselves receive social support. Parents of hospitalized children, for example, have stated that when their needs for support were met, they cared for their children better and coped with the sudden illness/injury more effectively (Ramritu & Croft, 1999). They identified their needs as: (1) services that optimized their child's recovery, (2) services that supported their coping, and (3) services that assisted in the maintenance of family functioning

and stability. Healthcare providers can help to arrange such support.

Even beyond cultural variation, social support is a potentially complicated issue. It is not unusual for those providing support to an ill or disabled loved one to be confronted with their own emotional adjustments. Family alliances may shift and once-stable bonds may be threatened. People stricken by illness or injury often perceive that social support is forthcoming only as long as they are optimistic, and they fear abandonment if they become depressed or uncommunicative. In addition, while tangible social support tends to be fairly straightforward, psychological support can be quite complex. What feels like concern to one person may feel like overprotection and control to another. Family counseling may be imperative in assisting all who are affected to make needed role adjustments in the context of disability and illness.

Emotional Development

Another challenge of illness or injury is for the patient to continue developing psychologically and emotionally. Amidst the impediments and limitations of a serious threat to physical well-being, an individual may find him- or herself struggling to continue to grow psychologically. For the young cancer patient with a wife and children, for example, such development involves continuing to pursue trust and intimacy with a spouse and learning to be consistently supportive and emotionally open and available to children (Mullan, 1983).

The demands of a medical crisis can make it relatively easy for medical practitioners, loved ones, and the patient him- or herself to lose sight of the need to maintain and support the patient's identity and development. During the initial phase of an acute illness or injury, all attention may need to be focused on actions that will insure the patient's survival and minimize his or her long-term disabilities. If the patient does survive, eventually the crisis mode is over and the normal challenges of living must be faced. Even in the midst of physical limitations, emotional development must continue (Moos & Tsu, 1977).

Explaining Illness and Injury

The beliefs that people have about the causes of illnesses can have a profound effect on every stage of clinical management, from the decision by the individual to seek specialist help, to adherence with recommended management and adjustment to prognosis. (Sensky, 1997, p. 565)

Patients who develop life-threatening illnesses such as cancer often try to understand just how their disease came about; they seek an explanation. Several researchers have examined how patients, both adult and pediatric, organize their thoughts and beliefs about illness (Burgess & Haaga, 1998; Mullins et al., 1997; Sensky, 1997). Typically, people form cognitions about the identity, the cause, the duration, and the consequences of their condition (Nerenz & Leventhal, 1983). Of these beliefs, what people think about the causes and the consequences of their illness may be the most important in determining how well they adjust (Meyerowitz, 1983).

People's beliefs (which may or may not be accurate) about the causes of their illness affect every aspect of their reaction to it, from treatment seeking to adherence (Sensky, 1997). For some cultural or religious groups, metaphysical attributions (such as to God, fate, or karma) are made (Kohli & Dalal, 1998). Self-blame is common. In clinical studies, several researchers have found that one-third to one-half of cancer patients blame *themselves*, particularly their own past "sins," for their cancer (Houldin et al., 1996; Moses & Cividali, 1966). Spinal cord injury patients have been found to blame themselves to a greater degree than others hold them responsible (Davis et al., 1996). Some patients blame others and believe that their cancer was caught through contagion or developed because of something another person did to them. Such explanations are typically held implicitly and without awareness, and so may affect the patient's feelings about him- or herself. These explanations may also be rather destructive to the individual's emotional well-being. Some research suggests that self-blame can lead to guilt and self-recrimination, and that patients may feel they should have been able to prevent their illness or accident (Krantz & Deckel, 1983). Their self-blame may also impair willingness and ability to do things necessary to adjust (Houldin et al., 1996).

Research suggests that under some conditions, taking responsibility for one's illness or injury might actually be adaptive. One study found that patients who took responsibility for their spinal cord injuries adjusted better than did those who would not do so (Bulman & Wortman, 1977). Presumably, those who felt responsible were also better able to understand the situation, feel in control of their lives, and come to terms with their tragedy. Research uniformly shows that blaming another person for one's disorder is maladaptive (Bulman & Wortman, 1977; Taylor et al., 1984). Blaming others may reflect either a general tendency to avoid taking responsibility for one's life or an unresolved anger and hostility that may drain energy needed for adjustment.

Interestingly, older people seem to be more likely than younger people to blame both themselves and others for their chronic illnesses (Benedict, 1995). Why might this be the case? This may be evidence of a cohort effect (which is a similarity seen in people who were born during the same time period). It is possible, for instance, that older individuals were taught a great deal of personal responsibility as they were growing up and were encouraged to believe that people get what they deserve in life. This might make them more likely to feel that they somehow "deserve" an illness that befalls them. Younger people may have learned, from their parents and society in general, that sometimes bad things "just happen." Younger people may have more general scientific knowledge about illnesses and may be better able to identify instances in which no person is "to blame" for the illness. Whatever the answer, this is clearly an area that needs further exploration before the observed difference can be explained with any certainty.

Facing Emotional Conflicts

Consider this example: A breast cancer patient is convinced that she is unaffected emotionally by the loss of her breast. She tells everyone, "It's not a big deal." She never allows herself to feel sadness, anxiety, or anger about the change in her image. She acts almost as if nothing had happened. Yet, the loss affects her in other ways. She suddenly becomes very dissatisfied with other aspects of her life. She has terrible fights with her husband. She begins to despise a job that once gave her a great deal of satisfaction. She remains unaware that her emotional amnesia surrounding the loss of her breast is adversely affecting the rest of her life.

Consider another patient who develops fearful associations when he encounters the site or circumstances of an earlier accident. He has intense **phobic reactions,** negative emotional responses that cause him to avoid the accident situation, or anything resembling it, whenever possible. A victim of an automobile crash, for example, may avoid ever riding in an automobile. The successful maintenance of emotional balance in the face of illness and injury would certainly involve overcoming such a phobia and working through the emotional impact of the devastating event. Although the **repression of emotion** (forcing it out of conscious awareness) might protect the individual from immediate distress in the short term, repression is not a long-term solution, and the emotional distress must be faced and dealt with.

These examples illustrate how important it is for an individual to face the impact of illness and injury and to fully understand the effect it can have on his or her thoughts and emotions.

Facing Stressful Medical Treatments

Despite their promise of another chance at life and health, medical treatments for serious illness and injury can present a major source of stress to a patient. Cancer treatment is a good example. Many cancer patients are treated with surgery as well as with radiation and chemotherapy. The surgical excision (removal) of a tumor, if it is successful, removes most or nearly all of the neoplastic (malignant) cells from the patient's body. Cure necessitates the removal of all cancerous cells because these cells can cause recurrence of the disease. Therefore, radiation treatment and/or chemotherapy may be needed to destroy any remaining malignant cells in the patient's body. The physical effects of these treatments are often very unpleasant and sometimes almost intolerable. Radiation treatments can bring nausea, vomiting, and severe weakness. Chemotherapy can bring the same, along with chills and high fever.

While the physical effects of cancer treatment can be debilitating, the psychological effects can be disquieting as well. Radiation treatments, for example, require a huge commitment of time and energy. They usually must be taken every day for several weeks and are administered by a huge, faceless, cobalt machine. Positioned on the table, the patient is left in total isolation, separated from everyone else by heavy lead doors. The cobalt machine might display a light sound a discordant buzzer, or emit no signal at all. The patient is told not to move while the machine directs its radiation to designated parts of the patient's body. The patient knows that the machine is emitting x-rays that destroy both healthy and malignant tissue. Even medically sophisticated patients can be frightened and awed by a machine that dispenses a potentially lethal, yet imperceptible, substance (Shlain, 1979). One way of successfully adapting to the necessary treatments is to acknowledge fear of the machine, accede its power, and recognize that this power is being harnessed in the patient's own best interest.

In addition to discomfort and pain, treatments for some serious illnesses and injuries can call forth a host of dysphoric emotions such as fear, anger, and confusion. Being around other patients, particularly those who are gravely ill, can be depressing. Seeing a fellow patient resuscitated in an emergency because his or her heart or breathing have stopped can cause feelings of terror. Recognizing one's own dependency can even call forth embarrassment (Mullan, 1983).

Much research shows that addressing psychological and cognitive aspects of aggressive treatments for patients can make it easier for them to adjust. Having information about what to expect can help the patient cope with the procedure (e.g., Clark, 1997; Michie et al., 1996). For example, women at a breast clinic who were provided with information regarding their procedures prior to receiving them were less anxious, both about the exam and about what their doctor might find. They also saw their problem as less serious, and felt they had more control over their condition, than did those who had not received information (Michie et al., 1996). Despite the well-established value of psychological interventions to decrease the anxiety and discomfort associated with threatening medical procedures, many patients still don't receive sufficient preparation (Wilson-Barnett, 1998). Perhaps one of the biggest reasons is that medical schools have not traditionally trained physicians to be sensitive and competent in this area. Although this situation is slowly changing and medical schools now address psychosocial issues in their curricula more thoroughly than ever before, there is still relatively little focus on these very important facets of care. Even when they are addressed, these issues are often viewed as "soft science" and a waste of time. Because they do not involve the latest drug or specialized equipment, they may not be viewed as important components of patient care. Finally, attending to the psychosocial and cognitive needs of patients requires time—something that medical care providers are frequently lacking. But, from the long-term perspective, taking a little bit of extra time is often more efficient than rushing through the encounter because with time patients are more satisfied, understand better, and have less anxiety.

Facing the Stresses of Hospitalization

Lety felt some relief as the ambulance pulled into the parking lot of the emergency room. She was at the hospital, about to be cared for by the best doctors. Surely they would be able to fix her up, she thought. Interestingly, Lety found herself relieved that she had survived the ambulance ride. The blaring sirens and wild maneuvers through traffic made her wonder whether they would make it to the hospital at all.

In the emergency room, Lety was surrounded by machines that beeped and whirred. She was aware of several doctors and nurses measuring her vital signs with an intimidating array of equipment and speaking rapidly to one another in words that she did not understand. Nobody talked *to* her, except to ask her if she could feel this or that (and her answer was usually "no"). Then she was given an IV, through which they began administering medication. She was wheeled on a gurney to what seemed like an endless MRI. Her last stop was a large cold room in which the sounds seemed to echo. Lety remembered breathing through a plastic mask and drifting off. She awoke in her bed in the intensive care unit (ICU), unable to move her body and unable to turn her head, which was now held in place by a metal frame bolted to her skull.

The ICU was a strange and disturbing place. It was a large room that held several beds, each with a massive collection of high-tech machines to which the patient in the bed was connected. There was a central station for nurses and doctors and no privacy. The lights remained on all day and night, and the machines made such ominous sounds that Lety couldn't rest. Her condition required almost constant surveillance, but the stress of the ICU was unnerving. She felt like a "case" being managed by the machinery that surrounded her, and while her body was being cared for, everyone but her family seemed to forget that she was a terrified human being. Furthermore, she could sense that her emotional distress was beginning to take its toll on her body.

The experience of being in the hospital has changed a great deal over the past few decades (Weitz, 1996). Acute hospital care is now limited to cases in which advanced technologies are needed, and increasing controls on medical costs by managed care result in less frequent hospitalization for far shorter periods of time than in the past. When patients do have to stay in the hospital, they are likely to be very seriously ill. High-level mechanization and reliance on specialized equipment can limit the personal nature of treatment and make hospitalization generally quite stressful (Weitz, 1996). This is particularly true in the Intensive Care and Cardiac Care Units, where the environments are even more novel and threatening than in the other units. Patients who experience distress in the hospital might be calmed by receiving information that makes their environment and situation more understandable and predictable to them. For instance, studies show that patients who are given information about upcoming procedures and their likely outcomes are less anxious and more satisfied, and report less pain associated with the procedure, than are those who do not receive information (Martin, 1996; McGaughey & Harrisson, 1994).

Hospitalization is also stressful for the family of the patient. Families with a relative in the CCU typically do four things in response to their uncertainty and distress (Jamerson et al., 1996). They *hover* around the patient and medical personnel, they actively *seek information* regarding the patient's status, they *track* the patient's progress by watching and evaluating the process of care and their perceptions of adequacy regarding it, and they *garner resources* (do whatever they feel is necessary to get what they or their relative needs). If these needs are anticipated by hospital staff, they can be promptly and efficiently addressed, thus minimizing the stress felt by the family.

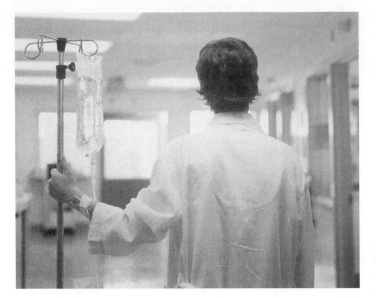

Hospitalization can be very stressful for many patients and can involve alienation from their psychosocial needs.

Maintaining one's individuality in the midst of hospital routine can be a very difficult undertaking. To most staff members, one's identity can become that of "the patient in room 306." Additional identifying characteristics such as "surgical patient," "critically ill patient," or "demanding patient" may be applied. Few people are happy with the role of being a patient, and there are good reasons for their lack of enthusiasm. Hospital routine typically takes over virtually every aspect of an individual's day-to-day life. A normally late sleeper may be awakened each morning at 6 AM by the cleaning crew and again at 7 AM for breakfast. During a hospital day, the patient remains dependent upon everyone else's schedule. Hospital personnel enter at will, giving medication and checking dressings. Doctors, nurses, and laboratory technicians come and go seemingly as they please, and the patient spends each day waiting and adapting. The patient has no schedule of his or her own choosing (see Figure 11.2).

Such routine is obviously necessary for the smooth functioning of such a complex institution as a hospital. Most patients recognize and accept that necessity and try to accommodate it. But acceptance can have its drawbacks. The process of adapting, particularly if one is hospitalized for a long period of time, can result in alienation from one's own needs and wants. The hospital routine becomes the patient's routine, and he or she begins to forget that there is a world outside where one schedules one's own time and controls one's own destiny. To the well-adapted, *good patient*, freedom begins to look terribly frightening (Taylor, 1982). Doing what one is told, not asking questions, and not making trouble become priority behaviors for the good patient. In addition, the good patient suppresses his or her emotions and, as a result, may feel numb, emotionally alienated, and even seriously depressed.

Of course, the oppressive routines and restrictions of freedom can cause some patients to react in the opposite manner and to become cantankerous and troublesome. The *bad patient* may try to hold onto his or her individuality by demanding attention

FIGURE 11.2   Facing the stresses of hospitalization.

and special changes in routine. Such a patient may refuse treatment, not because he or she has carefully thought about options, but for the sake of asserting control. This patient may be very anxious and angry and use a considerable amount of energy rebelling for the sake of rebelling. This patient may fight a system that, although sometimes oppressive and uncomfortable, may actually be working in his or her own best interest.

Taylor (1982) has suggested that patients caught in the maze of hospitalization must act rather than react. It is in a patient's best interest to make his or her wishes known to the medical professionals who provide care. He or she must assert the need for information, not only about diagnosis and treatment but also about the events to be experienced (what tests will be done, when, what they will be like, etc.). As we learned in Chapter 2, the most effective relationships between patients and their physicians are those that are collaborative in nature. When patients do not speak up about their symptoms, questions, and worries, they are unlikely to have all of their needs met. Patients should be active participants in planning the treatments and procedures that affect their lives. They may decide to pursue treatments that differ from the standard protocol, or specifically request that their doctors write orders to deviate from hospital routine (for example, for the patient to receive no medication at night so that he or she can sleep undisturbed).

By being assertive, a patient will be able to work towards his or her own interests of preserving identity and individuality. Such assertiveness may be critically important to the patient's emotional well-being in the face of serious illness (Cousins, 1979). Of course, the passivity of patienthood is underscored when one is in a position that makes taking such control difficult or impossible. The patient on a respirator cannot talk; one who is being given pain medication or who is stricken with panic may be unable to think clearly. Lety, whom we met at the beginning of this chapter, awoke in the ICU with a metal frame bolted to her skull, unable to move her body or turn her head. In such cases, the advocacy of a friend or family member who is comfortable being assertive in a medical setting can be invaluable.

Communicating with Medical Professionals

As we saw in Chapter 3, many medical professionals have a habit of telling patients as little as possible. If information is given at all, it is often too simplistic or too jargon-laden to be helpful. Probably not intentionally, but nonetheless often, they keep patients in the dark. As we also saw in Chapter 3, the communication of information and understanding between medical professionals and their patients can be quite difficult to achieve. The inability to obtain complete information about their conditions and the plans for treatment can be a source of great stress for many patients, however, and can leave them angry, discouraged, frustrated, and fearful that they are losing control over their lives. Such fears are not unfounded, of course. Only with the necessary information can patients make weighty treatment decisions in light of their own values, needs, and life plans.

It is possible, of course, that on a deep emotional level patients who wish to remain in control of their situation also harbor a desire to be cared for when they are ill.

> . . . when you take people who have a strong sense of themselves and put them in a hospital bed with a life-threatening illness, they find themselves in a relationship with their doctor much like a child and his parents. During serious illness patients must give up control over their lives. . . . Most people react to this kind of helplessness and authority just like they did as a child, with a great deal of ambivalence. They put their faith in the attending physician, hoping that he will make them well, but they also harbor a great feeling of anger for being put in their dependent position in the first place. (Shlain, 1979, p. 179)

Facing Pain

A physician assigned to take care of patients with severe burns underscores their suffering:

> It is a semiprivate room set up for burn care . . . The two men here are naked, scraped raw. Their pain stops me, fogs my glasses, raises up sweat between my shoulder blades, under my mask and gown, its presence as strong as the dead-flesh smell that permeates the Burn Unit. (Hellerstein, 1986, p. 185)

As we saw in Chapter 8, pain is one of the most terrifying aspects of serious illness and injury. Even when they are comfortable, many patients worry about the possibility that they will be in pain in the future. Cancer patients, for example, typically express tremendous fear that their pain will become overwhelming, debilitating, and uncontrolled. They anticipate helplessness. Their fears are not unfounded. The pain of severe burns is a good example. Such pain can be excruciating for the patient and continue unabated for weeks, or even months.

Emotions can influence the perception of pain as described in detail in Chapter 8. Negative emotions tend to intensify pain while positive emotions tend to minimize it, even among burn pain patients (Ulmer, 1997). Thus, health psychologists are recognizing that even serious, acute pain can be modified by one's thoughts and feelings about it. Norman Cousins, the former editor of the *Saturday Review*, was considered by his doctors to be terminally ill with a severe collagen disease. As he described it, the pain in his spine and joints was overwhelming and debilitating. As a patient active in his own care, Cousins did a considerable amount of reading about his condition and determined that some of the medications that were being given to him to ease his pain were actually detrimental to his chances of recovering. So he chose to stop taking them. But his pain was very intense, and he had to do something. Cousins reasoned that the perception of pain was partly a function of attitudes and that he could stand his pain if he felt that he was making progress in meeting his body's needs. He established a setup whereby he could view humorous movies and have humorous books read to him. "I made the joyous discovery that 10 minutes of genuine belly laughter has an anesthetic effect and would give me at least two hours of pain-free sleep" (Cousins, 1976, p. 1261).

Psychological factors can figure prominently in treatment difficulties as well as in treatment successes. Chemotherapy, used in the management of cancer, can often bring serious and discomforting side effects such as nausea and vomiting (Stockhorst et al., 1998a). These can be very debilitating and last for hours or even days after treatment. Psychological and emotional factors can influence the severity of these side effects as well (Montgomery et al., 1998; Tyc et al., 1997). For example, after a few courses of chemotherapy, a patient may begin to anticipate the upcoming discomfort. His or her expectations can influence the onset of nausea and vomiting. In one study, 33 percent of chemotherapy patients reported having anticipatory nausea and 11 percent reported having anticipatory vomiting (Van Komen & Redd, 1985). Like a conditioned response (Pavlov, 1927), the reaction comes on even before the drugs are administered, such as when the patient is traveling to the hospital or entering the hospital building (Montgomery et al., 1998). These distressing anticipatory reactions have been found to occur more often among patients who are anxious, despairing, socially isolated, and depressed.

Some researchers have found that anticipatory nausea and vomiting can be reduced and even eliminated by using certain well-established conditioning principles such as systematic relaxation and desensitization (Rimm & Masters, 1979), hypnosis (Jacknow et al., 1994), and cognitive overshadowing (Stockhorst et al., 1998b). Through the process of pairing relaxation with thoughts of the upcoming distressing event (chemotherapy), the patient learns to associate a relaxed and comfortable state with the instigation of the treatment. Typically, the patient starts with imagining scenes that provoke low anxiety and builds to associating his or her relaxed state with scenes that provoke high anxiety. This procedure results in an enhanced ability to tolerate the rigors of chemotherapy.

Facing Death

As we examined earlier, the possibility of death hangs over every seriously ill person. Any illness that carries more than a negligible chance of mortality brings a terrifying confrontation with the possibility that life may be cut short. When the future is threatened by serious illness, the individual may find it difficult or impossible to maintain hope. About half of cancer patients, on average, now live at least five years from the time of their diagnosis. During this time, however, they must deal not only with things like the side effects of their treatments, disabilities, social stigmas, and disappointments related to failed interventions or to relapses, but also with thoughts of their own mortality (Muzzin et al., 1994). This is a very trying time for patients and their families, and it can be virtually impossible to maintain any semblance of "normal" life. In Chapter 13, we discuss the specific reactions that people have when they face death or at least a foreshortened life span, and we examine the psychological aspects of coming to grips with terminal illness.

The Role of Emotions in Healing

As we have seen so far in this chapter, the emotions that attend serious illness can be complicated and terrifying. Many patients feel that they are losing control, and they experience self-blame, a sense of failure, anxiety, apprehension, and confusion.

One of the most important tasks facing a patient is maintaining emotional equilibrium. Several studies have emphasized the central role of maintaining emotional balance in coping successfully with illness and injury (Cohen & Lazarus, 1979). Depression is believed to contribute to more lengthy recovery from serious illness, and low psychological morale is thought directly to affect physiological processes in deleterious ways (Cohen & Lazarus, 1979).

This is not to say that patients must "put on a happy face" in order to recover. As we consider in the Research Close-up Box 11.3, such expectations for a patient can be detrimental to his or her well-being. While a patient should be helped to deal with negative emotions and to avoid becoming overwhelmed and incapacitated by them, some concern and worry on the part of the patient may actually be valuable. Worry that is not paralyzing or debilitating can serve to motivate the patient to follow necessary treatments, ask questions, and make sure that he or she is getting the best care available. The **work of worrying**—mentally rehearsing potentially unpleasant events and gaining information about what to expect—can be very helpful (Janis, 1958).

The expression of feelings, whatever they are, may be best for a patient. Suppressing emotional thoughts as a way of coping has a negative impact on the immune system and is associated with a variety of health problems (Berry & Pennebaker, 1993; Petrie et al., 1998). "Bottling up" feelings has also been associated with shorter survival, while expressing emotions is associated with longer survival (Lazarus, 1999). Research has found that patients survive longer who more frequently express their emotions, including their negative ones. Those who ask for what they want, including emotional support from others, and who express what they are feeling tend to fare bet-

BOX **11.3**
Research Close-up

Can Positive Emotions Facilitate Recovery?

Important in any attempt to cope with serious illness or injury is the maintenance of composure, self-esteem, and happiness. "Positive thinking" involves efforts to avoid or divert thoughts from the negative (such as what has been lost and what can go wrong) to the positive (such as what one still has and hopeful expectations for the future). Positive thinking certainly might make an ill person's life more pleasant, at least in the short run. The power of positive thinking, however, is such an intuitively appealing notion that it is tempting to conclude that it can make people not only happier but physically healthier as well. Is there evidence in the health psychology literature for a happiness-health connection?

The research evidence is strong that *dispositional optimism*, a relatively stable trait or characteristic, is related to more positive outcomes from crisis situations, including serious illness. In one study, optimists not only adjusted better to coronary artery bypass (CABG) surgery, they also recovered faster than did those who were not optimists (Scheier et al., 1989). Optimism has also been related to adjustment to breast cancer and decreased rehospitalization following CABG (Carver et al., 1994; Scheier et al., 1999). An unwillingness to give up and the presence of a "fighting spirit" have been found to relate to longer survival (Spiegel & Kato, 1996). It is important to point out that optimism, as it is measured and conceptualized in these studies, is dispositional and thus is a long-standing feature of the individual's personality. It is unlikely that someone can just decide to become an optimist and succeed (although with a lot of work, certainly behavior and attitudes can be changed).

While not positive thinking, per se, methods of psychological support have been developed to help cancer patients feel greater control over their lives and increase their sense of well-being (e.g., Jacobsen & Hann, 1998). One important study assigned women with breast cancer to one of two groups: traditional medical treatment or traditional treatment plus emotional support. Those in the support group met with fellow patients once each week for an hour and a half. During this time they discussed their experiences with one another and were able to voice their fears. The women who participated in the support groups lived, on average, a year and a half longer than did those who received only the traditional cancer treatment (Spiegel et al., 1989). Not all studies have shown increases in survival with psychological support, however. The most successful interventions have been those that have provided both information and strong psychosocial support for patients (Classen et al., 1998).

There are some important caveats regarding the issue of "positive thinking" in the face of serious illness. It is possible that thinking positive thoughts may be generally beneficial and, by reducing stress, may have some positive effects on health. Expectations that serious illness can be cured by positive thinking can be destructive, however. Those who are ill may admonish themselves when they feel understandably distressed and sad, and other people might even suggest that their recovery depends upon their attitude. In some unfortunate cases, people with serious illnesses may even be blamed for thinking negatively and accused of bringing on their disease or preventing recovery. (This would reflect the psychological phenomenon called **blaming the victim** that we examined in Chapter 4.) In an effort to deal with their outrage and sense of powerlessness when someone they love is very ill, some people may develop an unconscious belief in the victim's own power to get well again or to have avoided the illness in the first place. Those who fail to respond to treatment may be accused of lacking a will to live. The patient may feel subtly blamed for his or her misfortune, and a patient who is very sad because of all the losses

(continued)

B O X **11.3**   (Continued)

experienced in the face of serious illness may be forced to hide his or her true feelings and act happy. Those close to the patient (or even the patient him- or herself) may believe so strongly in a simplistic mind-body connection that the patient who is depressed may be blamed (and feel guilty) for not getting better. The individual might even avoid attempting new treatments because of a fear that failure to recover may bring more blame. Opportunities to help the patient overcome depression with medication and psychotherapy may be missed.

---

ter than do patients who keep their wishes hidden. Recall from Chapter 10 that emotional disclosure helps to bolster the immune system and is related to better health outcomes.

Treatment of Ill Patients

The relationship between a patient and the medical staff can have important implications for his or her survival, as can participation in things like support groups (Spiegel et al., 1989). These interactions and relationships generally have a positive impact on patient health, but sometimes their effects are negative. Although these relationships might, in some ways, be thought of as forms of social support, they are distinct from family and friendship networks. Rather they are a more formal part of the treatment protocol for some patients. These peer support groups might affect patient health by aiding coping, encouraging adherence, or by reducing stress.

Interestingly, it has been found that the relationships formed with hospital roommates influence the very important patient variable of anxiety. Preoperative patients who had postoperative roommates (or roommates who were not having surgery at all) were less anxious than those whose roommates were also preoperative (Kulik et al., 1993). Although selection of roommates has not traditionally been a part of treatment protocol, the authors suggest that these findings be used to inform and direct the roommate selection process in an effort to make the hospital stay more pleasant and psychologically supportive for patients.

Patient-staff interactions may be related to patient outcomes in an even more direct way. It has been suggested that hospital staff might (unconsciously) alter the quality of care that they provide based on their liking or disliking of particular patients (Hall et al., 1993; Segal et al., 1995). For instance, likable patients have been found to receive more "specialized, technically correct evaluations" as compared to unlikable patients (Segal et al., 1995). In fact, physicians appear to like better those patients who are in better health and those patients who are more satisfied with their medical care (Hall et al., 1993). When examining the impact of the relations between providers and patients, the bias toward more likable patients must not be overlooked.

In short, appropriate treatment of seriously ill patients should endeavor to incorporate the elements discussed in this chapter. The effective healthcare provider needs to have an understanding of the myriad challenges that the patient is facing and

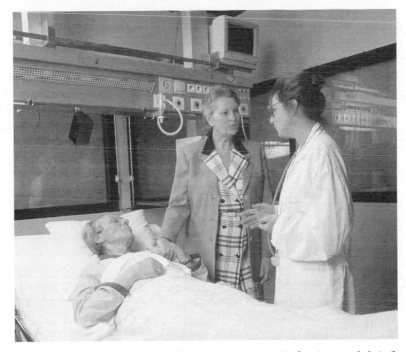

Effective healthcare involves recognizing and attending to the needs of patients and their families for information, comfort, and emotional support.

attempt to meet the patient's needs in as many areas as possible. The effective health-care provider will (1) give the patient information about his or her illness, treatment, and likely outcomes; (2) try to make the patient as comfortable as possible by administering appropriate pain medications and making other pain control modalities available; (3) encourage rehabilitation and help the patient to use adaptive equipment if necessary; and (4) understand that the patient is likely to go through a number of emotional shifts, and thus will need a good deal of patience and support.

Medical Communication and Treatment Outcomes

Communication between doctors and patients is always important. As we learned in Chapter 3, there are many factors that influence the effectiveness of the relationship between physicians and their patients. Their communication, in turn, influences many important outcomes. Due largely to the fear and heightened emotional arousal that the patient and family are experiencing, medical communication may be especially difficult in serious illness. In a recent study of interactions between patients with breast cancer and their medical care teams, 84 percent of the patients said that they had difficulty communicating with their healthcare providers (Lerman et al., 1993). Patients who were less optimistic and less assertive had more problems than their more assertive and optimistic peers. Communication problems were, in turn, associated with more depression, confusion, anger, and anxiety even three months after treatment. An intervention that facilitates better communication might improve a patient's adjustment to illness. Finding ways of increasing optimism and relaxation might enable more effective communication to occur.

When a third person (usually a family member) accompanies an ill person in the medical care encounter, the effect can be quite positive. This individual can provide support and can aid the patient in asking questions and receiving information. The addition of a facilitator or helper does change the dynamics of the doctor-patient relationship, however. Researchers have compared the interactions of dyads (physician and older adult) and triads (physician, older adult, and third person) and found that, although the physician's interactional style was not affected by having the third person present, the patients themselves tended to ask fewer questions and provide less information if a third person was there. Patients were less assertive and less expressive, they participated less in decisions, and they even laughed less. Sometimes, conversations were carried on between the third person and the physician, completely leaving the patient out (Greene et al., 1994). Thus, although having a "helper" may sometimes be necessary, this person must be careful not to undermine the autonomy of the patient and get in the way of direct communication with the physician.

Summary

1. Different demands are made on an individual at different stages of illness or physical injury.

   ■ During the acute phase, the primary concern of both patient and medical personnel is the patient's survival.
   ■ During the rehabilitation phase, the patient must work toward achieving the highest level of health and independent functioning possible.
   ■ When as much as possible has been accomplished toward rehabilitation, the person may need to accept the remaining disabilities and limitations.
   ■ In some cases, an illness progresses to the point at which it cannot be cured or further treated, and the condition is terminal.

2. Serious illness and injury threaten virtually every aspect of an individual's life. Anxiety and fear may deplete the energy needed for healing. Depression and hopelessness may introduce an unwillingness to take the necessary steps toward health and well-being.

   ■ Life with a serious illness or injury is unpredictable; it often makes little sense and can be filled with threats to self-image, freedom, physical comfort, and the future.
   ■ The physical alteration of one's body can be disorienting and terrifying. Integration of an altered body image takes time.
   ■ Denial can be a very effective short-term defense mechanism. It allows the individual slowly to come to terms with his or her altered body and abilities.
   ■ A seriously ill or injured person may fear that relationships with others, particularly loved ones, will be changed drastically. Many obligations fall on the

family of a person who is ill. The severe stress that illness places on a family can challenge its cohesiveness.

- Self-esteem may be threatened by the need to rely on others for financial, physical, and emotional support.
- Certain medical conditions can interfere directly with cognitive functioning.

3. Several important physical and emotional challenges must be met when adjusting to serious illness or injury.

- When personal, unique characteristics are changed or can no longer find expression, the individual must develop new aspects of his or her identity.
- Another challenge is for the individual to continue developing psychologically and emotionally despite the interference of illness.
- Self-blame is common and research suggests that, in moderation, it may be adaptive for certain patients, particularly those with injuries acquired as a result of their own behavior.
- In addition to discomfort and pain, treatments for some serious illnesses and injuries can bring dysphoric emotions such as fear, anger, and confusion. Being around other seriously ill patients can be depressing.
- Communicating with medical professionals can be very difficult. Patients may try to be "good" by not asking too many questions; they must learn to be assertive to assure that their own needs are met.
- Facing pain is a tremendous challenge (see Chapter 8).
- Serious illness and injury may require the patient to face the possibility of death (see Chapter 13). When the future is threatened by serious illness, the individual may find it difficult to maintain hope.
- The expression of feelings, whatever they are, may be best for a patient. "Bottling up" feelings has been associated with shorter survival, and expressing emotions with longer survival.

THINKING CRITICALLY

1. What are the important things a health psychologist would need to take into account when designing interventions for people who are at different stages in the illness process?

2. How might denial of a serious illness or injury be adaptive? At what point would denial become maladaptive? How would a physician or health psychologist identify the point at which a person has crossed the line from using denial effectively to using it in a harmful fashion?

3. Most people love to have a break from work and everyday responsibilities. Why is it, then, that the disruption to one's work is such a harmful aspect of serious illness and injury? If it is truly impossible for someone to return to the work they once did, how can the needs fulfilled by work be met in other ways?

4. Although blaming oneself for illness or accidents is generally thought of as counterproductive, research shows that in some cases a moderate amount of self-blame is actually good. Why might this be so? In what kinds of situations can self-blame be beneficial?

GLOSSARY

Acute phase: The period of illness (or the period following injury) in which the primary concern of patient and medical personnel is the patient's survival.

Amyotrophic lateral sclerosis (or Lou Gehrig's disease): An incurable, degenerative disease of the nervous system.

Blaming the victim: A psychological phenomenon in which the victim of an unfortunate event is held to blame for his or her experience.

Cardiac delirium or cardiac psychosis: A condition in which some cardiac surgery patients experience transient intellectual deficits; others have gross impairment of their cognitive functioning and even hallucinations.

Chronic conditions: Conditions from which patients are not expected to recover.

Denial: A psychological defense mechanism in which one refuses to admit what has occurred; it can serve to help maintain the individual's identity and self-esteem, particularly in the face of negative reactions from other people.

Dissociation: Feeling outside or separate from one's body.

Integration: The process of adjusting to physical alterations and adjusting to the new body image.

Metastasis: Spread (usually of cancer) to organs other than that of the primary site. Neoplastic cells escape from the initial tumor site and travel to other parts of the body such as the bones, lungs, brain, or liver.

Paranoid ideations: Mental presentations and thoughts of being the target of persecution.

Phobic reactions: Negative emotional responses that can cause an individual to avoid certain stimuli.

Rehabilitation: The phase of illness during which the patient must learn to adjust to the limitations of illness and work and try to achieve as high a level of health and independent functioning as his or her condition makes possible.

Repression of emotion: The forcing of emotion out of conscious awareness in an attempt to avoid immediate, short-term emotional distress.

Social support: Aid that one receives from others in coping; may be tangible or psychological in nature.

Terminal: An illness from which a patient will not recover and that will result in the patient's death.

Work of worrying: The mental rehearsal of potentially unpleasant events together with the consideration of what to expect in the future.

12

A Life-Span Perspective on Chronic Illness, Disability, and Aging

After her diving accident, Lety faced a whole new life. Despite the early possibility of complete immobility, she was fortunate because eventually Lety regained the use of her arms. Her rehabilitation process took several years and a lot of hard work, and she had to accept the reality of never walking or being completely independent again. Lety's family was very supportive and encouraged her to do as much for herself as possible.

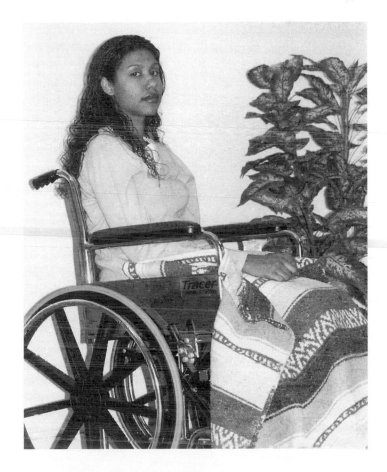

After two years of rehabilitation and therapy, Lety returned to college and finished her degree in computer science. With the help of the placement office at her college, Lety was able to land a well-paying job as a high-level programmer. Most of her work could be done from home and she had to go to the office only once a week. Her social life presented a bigger problem, however. During the first few months after her injury, her friends were wonderfully supportive. They visited and called on the phone often, and she felt very much a part of their lives. As time went on, however, her contacts with friends became less frequent; they all seemed to be so busy. In conversations, her own contributions were limited because most of her experiences were related to her injury and her therapy. She and her friends mutually withdrew from one another, and because it was so hard for Lety to get out, she didn't make any new friends. Her family provided most of her social interaction. Understandably, she was very lonely as she struggled to deal with both her physical challenges and her social limitations.

Josh was very sick for several years, battling his bone cancer and dealing with the physical problems that accompanied his treatment. His body was permanently altered, both in appearance and in functioning. He tired easily. Although his treatment was considered successful, Josh lived every day with the possibility of recurrence. Every simple ache or pain caused him to panic at the possibilities they might represent, and he struggled daily with the idea that he might not see his young daughter grow up.

Serious illness and injury often do not result in the full recovery of health and a return to life as it once was. Like those who are born with or develop chronic disorders, many victims of serious illness and accidents face a lifetime of limitations such as physical impairment, demanding routines of care, and even social isolation. For the chronically ill patient who never really gets better, the threat of a medical crisis always exists. Fears of further constraints and the possibility that the condition may jeopardize his or her life remain constant. Despite precautions, medical crises can become regular events and can absorb tremendous amounts of time, money, and energy. Further, the day-to-day reminders of physical illness and impairment force many victims of illness and injury to live lives that are radically different from the ones they had once planned and hoped for.

Chronic Illness and Disability

Lety and Josh each suffer what is referred to as a **chronic condition.** Lety has a disability, and Josh has a disease in remission. Chronic illness or disability involves one or more impairments or deviations from normal structure and functioning that, whether extensive or not, remain semipermanent or permanent. Chronic conditions are often caused by pathological alterations that are irreversible, or at least very difficult to change. They are usually accompanied by some sort of residual disability. Contending with a chronic condition typically requires treatment, supervision, and special training.

Unlike the acutely ill or injured person who remains hospitalized to receive treatment, the chronically ill or disabled patient must eventually try to incorporate his or her limitations into a relatively normal life. Whether living alone or with others, the individual must attempt to maintain some degree of independence and achieve as high a quality of life as possible within the constraints of the medical condition.

Chronic illness is surprisingly common. In 1995, approximately 22.5 million people in the United States between the ages of 18 and 64 experienced limitations in their activities due to a chronic health problem (National Center for Health Statistics [NCHS], 1998). Some of these conditions represent the aftermath of a serious acute illness or accident and others are gradually degenerative, such as rheumatoid arthritis. Chronic illnesses include such conditions as heart disease, arthritis, back or spine impairments, ulcerative colitis, diabetes, leg or hip impairments, visual impairments, and even psychiatric conditions. The most common chronic conditions of people under 45 are paralysis and limitations of the lower extremities (usually the result of accidents). For people over 45, the most common chronic conditions are rheumatoid arthritis, osteoarthritis, and heart disease. For nonelderly adults (18–64) as a group, the problems accounting for most activity limitation are back, spine, and lower extremity injuries, heart disease, arthritis, and eye problems (NCHS, 1998). The older a person is, the more likely he or she is to have one or more chronic conditions that limit major activities such as work, housework, school, or recreation. Chronic conditions are not limited to older persons, for as we shall see, chronic illness and disability strike the young with surprising frequency. About three-quarters of the healthcare spending in the United States goes toward the management of chronic conditions (Hoffman et al., 1996), and most Americans will have at least one chronic condition by the time they die.

Many patients in acute care hospitals today are being treated either for conditions that likely will eventually become chronic or for medical crises that arise from ongoing chronic illnesses. Examples of the former conditions are heart attacks, cancer, and accidental injuries that result in paralysis. Examples of the latter are repeat heart attacks, diabetic coma, and complications that arise from the treatment of kidney failure with hemodialysis. Of course, some chronic conditions typically require no hospitalization but rather are diagnosed and treated on an outpatient basis. These may be insidious illnesses, like arthritis, that slowly rob the individual of health and vitality and bring gradual deterioration over the course of many years.

Our discussion of chronic illness applies to the many and varied conditions noted so far, including physical disability. Although these conditions vary widely, they have one very important characteristic in common. Chronic conditions, by definition, have no cure. This one fact has many important implications for the psychological and social adjustment of the person stricken with a chronic condition. As you read this chapter, you might think about these issues from several perspectives. You may remember friends or family members who have had to face such conditions. Perhaps you have a chronic illness or disability. You might consider the issues from a clinical perspective and analyze how a healthcare provider can better care for chronically ill patients, both physically and psychologically. Finally, you might think about the research questions that remain unanswered and consider how a health psychologist would address them.

Dealing with Chronic Illness

The stresses of chronic illness and handicap can severely tax the emotional resources of the most tolerant and optimistic person. Chronic illness and handicap must be dealt with day after day, year after year, without the possibility of cure. While chronic conditions do vary in their severity and in the extent to which they interfere with "normal" life, each chronic condition brings with it at least some of the following problems and challenges. Typically, the more disabling the condition, the more problems there are to face.

Managing Medical Crises

When things are going well, a chronically ill person's physical functioning may be quite good. Certain limitations may be imposed, but with effort these may be incorporated into day-to-day routines and often concealed from the scrutiny of others. When things go badly for the chronically ill person, however, he or she can be quite ill and even in significant danger. A person with emphysema, for example, can become so short of breath that she or he collapses in the street. A diabetic can self-administer the wrong dosage of insulin and fall into a coma. The chronically ill individual (and those who are close to him or her, such as the parents of a diabetic child) often must remain vigilant to recognize the signs of an approaching medical crisis. Many chronically ill people must wear identification bracelets so that their conditions can be interpreted correctly if, during a medical crisis, they are unable to communicate. Some must carry with them, at all times, the necessary treatments to deal with a medical crisis. For example, a heart disease patient may need to carry nitroglycerine pills to take for chest pain. Other patients may need to avoid certain situations and environments altogether, lest these precipitate a medical crisis. A cardiac patient, for example, may need to make certain that, when alone, he or she can get to a phone to reach medical personnel. The emphysema patient might completely avoid social interaction in order to reduce the chances of becoming emotionally upset and experiencing impaired breathing. Such vigilance can, in itself, be quite taxing for the chronically ill person and require him or her to learn a considerable amount about self-care in an effort to lead a relatively independent life.

Controlling the Symptoms

Nearly every chronic illness presents some distressing symptoms with which its victims must cope. These symptoms may be as mild as midday fatigue or as debilitating as daily, intractable diarrhea that causes physical exhaustion and social isolation. Certainly, the more debilitating an individual's symptoms, the greater adjustment that may be necessary in order to adapt to chronic illness. Debilitation, of course, is not the only characteristic that determines the undesirability of symptoms. The social acceptability of the symptoms also influences the measures that people must take to control them and how well people are able to adjust. Symptoms that limit the ability to speak coherently, or that make salient bodily processes that are normally private (such as elimination) are likely to be quite difficult to adjust to (Dudley-Brown, 1996; Lenderking et al., 1996; Ludman & Spitz, 1996).

Let's consider the adjustments that have been made by one chronically ill person.

Pete Jackson is 32 years old and has epilepsy. **Epilepsy** is a disease that affects the nervous system, causing seizures that can range from almost unnoticeable tics or short periods of "zoning out" to violent convulsive attacks. Although it cannot be cured, epilepsy can often be controlled through medication, and Pete is lucky because his epilepsy is mild. The disease has a significant impact on his life, nonetheless. Pete's epileptic attacks are usually in the form of blackouts lasting just a few seconds and sometimes accompanied by muscular rigidity. He loses consciousness during these blackouts, which occur several times each week. Because his blackouts do not last long, he is often able to continue whatever activity he was doing, with only a brief pause. It is rare for him to actually fall down during an attack. He does lose consciousness, however, and so Pete is not able to have a driver's license. He lives downtown in a metropolitan area, so he is able to use public transportation to get around to nearly everything, such as to his office for work, to the grocery store, and to see his friends.

Several times, when Pete's seizures have been more dramatic than usual, he has been embarrassed by the reactions of those around him. For instance, one time he slid off his seat on the bus and lay on the floor for nearly 30 seconds before he was able to get up. He drooled a little bit, and several of the other passengers seemed frightened and disgusted by his behavior. They thought he was a drunk or a drug addict. To avoid embarrassment and danger when experiencing a seizure, Pete takes as many precautions as he can. He always tries to get a window seat on the bus. This way, he will have the wall of the bus to support him if he loses control of his body for a moment. He pays careful attention to his surroundings, staying away from curbs and other obstacles as much as possible, so that if a brief attack causes him to lose his balance, he is less likely to stumble and fall. When he goes shopping, he uses a cart to carry his goods, so that his packages will not fall if he has a blackout. He wears an identification bracelet with emergency contacts and medical information so that if he should lose consciousness for a longer period of time or have a severe seizure, people will know what to do to help him. He also must take a complicated regimen of medication, and do so faithfully.

Despite all of these precautions, however, Pete still worries about his epilepsy and it causes him a great deal of distress. He lives an apparently normal life, but only with considerable effort. His constant vigilance is necessary not only to protect his physical health, but also to keep others from seeing him as "different." He tries to work things out so that activities with friends do not require driving. His friends are happy to do the driving, but sometimes he feels badly that he cannot reciprocate. When he meets new people, he always dreads telling them about his disease. He takes care to establish a relationship with them first, so that they will see him as a "normal" person first, and an epileptic second.

Pete Jackson's experience is not unusual. Many people with chronic conditions spend a great deal of their time and energy trying to "**pass**," or function, as normal or unimpaired (Goffman, 1963). Their ability to avoid public notice of their affliction has been shown to influence their success in coping with the disability (Lenderking et al., 1996). These individuals are continually challenged to find ways to hide their symptoms

FIGURE 12.1   The importance of privacy.

and limitations and to live relatively independent lives (a challenge faced by the patient in Figure 12.1). Understandably, some chronically ill persons fear that other people will reject them because of their disabilities (Fried et al., 1995). Indeed, research shows that negative stereotypes about the chronically ill are common (Rounds & Zevon, 1993; Schwarzer & Weiner, 1991). Many people with obvious physical alterations and limitations meet with expressions of pity and disdain from others (Kleck, 1968). Therefore, they work to conceal or minimize the intrusiveness of deformities in their bodies and limitations in their abilities. When symptoms of chronic illnesses are under control, victims can live more enjoyable, productive lives.

Carrying Out Treatment Regimens

As we saw earlier in Chapter 6, despite the importance of symptom control and the established effectiveness of treatments for many chronic illnesses, adherence to medical regimens is surprisingly poor. Nonadherence is a particular problem for patients with chronic illnesses because their treatment regimens are often difficult, complex, and intrusive, and interfere with enjoyable activities. Further, they must be carried out for the rest of the individual's life. These factors have been shown to predict low levels of adherence (Turk & Meichenbaum, 1991).

Consider, for example, the patient who has chosen at-home **peritoneal dialysis** instead of hospital-based hemodialysis. (Dialysis involves the process of cleansing the blood of impurities, a task carried out by the kidneys unless they have been damaged in some way.) Peritoneal dialysis involves the overnight installation of a solution into the abdominal cavity while the patient is connected to a machine via tubes that have been surgically implanted in his or her abdomen. In this way, peritoneal dialysis can take place while the patient sleeps. This process requires connection to the dialysis machine by means of an elaborate sterile technique that can take more than an hour to carry out. This techniques requires considerable care and concentration to avoid mistakes. Errors in the sterile procedure can introduce bacteria into the abdominal cavity, resulting in a serious, life-threatening infection called peritonitis. Many of us have trouble washing our faces and brushing our teeth before bed when we are tired or deeply engrossed in a novel or a television program. Imagine incorporating the elaborate preparations for peritoneal dialysis into each evening's routine!

The complex arrangements that many chronic illnesses demand may be lifelong. As we saw in Chapter 6, patients who fail to carry out treatment regimens for chronic conditions are often trying to manage their daily lives within the confines of many practical, social, and financial constraints. Some treatment regimens may cause the patient a certain amount of emotional distress as well. Examples are the self-administration of injections for the control of diabetes, inhalation medication for asthma, or the application of bad-smelling cremes and ointments for the control of a dermatological condition. Some regimens cause distressing side effects, such as pain or nausea. Others lead to social isolation or tremendous financial stress. In a recent study of patients with Type II diabetes, all were actively trying to control their diabetes, but not one was completely successful in following all of the medical recommendations (Hunt et al., 1998). Nonadherence was associated with limited monetary resources and with the desire to feel and act "normal." Obviously, the more a treatment regimen interferes with daily activities and personal identity and the less it improves physical functioning, the more likely it is that the individual will fail to follow the regimen or will follow it inconsistently or incorrectly (DiMatteo & DiNicola, 1982; DiMatteo & Lepper, 1998).

Increasingly, modern technology tends to make patients passive rather than active participants in their own medical care (Stabler, 1993). Yet, research shows that patients who take an active part in their medical care typically achieve better control of their chronic illnesses than do those who are passive (Anderson et al., 1995; Greenfield et al., 1988; Maly et al., 1999). A recent review of the literature has demonstrated the importance of patient participation in decision making to improving adherence to diabetic self-care regimens (Golin et al., 1996). Patient participation is believed to affect adherence in three different ways. First, patient participation might directly affect adherence such that those who are active in the process of receiving medical care are also active in carrying out their treatment regimens. Second, patient participation might influence the way a patient understands his or her illness or the manner in which self-care can be integrated into his or her lifestyle. Or third, patient participation might lead to a greater sense of satisfaction with the medical care that is received, and this satisfaction may lead the patient to want to adhere more to the regimen, thus gaining approval from the well-liked and respected provider.

The best adjustment to chronic illness is usually achieved by patients who learn what they must do to care for themselves and design their day-to-day lifestyles and environments to meet the requirements of the treatment regimen. These patients also incorporate their personal needs and values into achieving a satisfying life despite the illness. In a recent meta-analysis study of diabetic patients, "balance" was defined as "the determinant metaphor of the experience of diabetes" as people experimented with various strategies for combining illness-management with a lifestyle that was as normal as possible (Paterson et al., 1998).

Self-help groups, consisting of patients with the same disease who get together for regular meetings, can be an important source of information and support for many chronically ill people (Gilden et al., 1992; Spirig, 1998). Often, these groups provide more information and better suggestions for disease control than do physicians who may lack the time, communication skills, and experience required to train patients to carry out complex treatments. These groups can provide practical help and information such as where to buy or rent special equipment or appliances required for home care. They may provide ideas for management of symptoms and for "passing" as well as assistance in dealing with financial matters such as health insurance. Box 12.1 contains a partial list of national self-help organizations.

Coping with an Uncertain Prognosis

> Katrina was stunned by the neurologist's words. "Well, what's going to happen next?" she asked. She was tremendously impatient after all the tests she had been through and all the distressing symptoms she had dealt with. "Well, actually, we don't really know," he answered her. "Multiple sclerosis is such a variable disease that we cannot predict what the precise course will be in your case. Most likely, it won't be fatal. But we are not even totally certain of that. You will probably be limited in some ways by your disease." "Will I be able to walk again?" she asked. "Will my vision improve? Will I ever stop feeling so weak?" "Probably you'll have ups and downs, some relatively healthy times, as well as some bad times. But I can't predict when, or to what degree."

Approximately 350,000 Americans currently suffer from **multiple sclerosis** (MS). MS is a major cause of chronic disability in young adults. In this disease, cellular changes in the brain and spinal cord disrupt proper nerve transmission. Scarlike areas form, destroying the fatty sheaths of **myelin** that cover the nerve-cell extensions called axons. Myelin is essential to the synaptic transmission of nerve impulses, and its destruction causes symptoms that are in some cases transient, in others chronic, and in others severely degenerative (Professional Guide to Diseases [PGD], 1998). The transient symptoms of MS may last for hours or for weeks, coming and going with no particular pattern, and varying from day to day. The symptoms are often bizarre and difficult to understand. They include some or all of the following: muscle dysfunction, weakness, paralysis, spasticity, tremors, ocular dysfunction (including double vision and blurred vision), urinary disturbances (including incontinence), and emotional lability (including mood swings, irritability, euphoria, and depression). There may also be slurred speech and numbness or tingling sensations in various parts of the body.

BOX 12.1
Hot Topic

National Organizations: Sources of Information and Help

Alzheimer's

www.alz.org

919 North Michigan Ave., Suite 1000,
Chicago, IL 60611-1676

Arthritis

www.arthritis.org

Arthritis Foundation, 1330 Peachtree Street,
Atlanta, GA 30309

Burns

www.burns-phoenix-society.org

Phoenix Society, 33 Main Street, Suite 403,
Nashua, NH 03060

Cancer

www.cancer.org

American Cancer Society, 777 3rd Ave.,
New York, NY 10017

www.nci.nih.gov

National Cancer Institute,
Public Inquiries Office, Bldg. 31, Rm. 10A03,
31 Center Drive, Bethesda, MD 20892-2580

Crohn's/Colitis

www.ccfa.org

Crohn's and Colitis Foundation of America,
386 Park Avenue South, 17th Floor,
New York, NY, 10016

Diabetes

www.diabetes.org

American Diabetes Association,
600 5th Ave., New York, NY 10020
Juvenile Diabetes Foundation,
23 E. 26th St. New York, NY 10010

Diet

www.eatright.org

American Dietetic Association,
216 W. Jackson Blvd.,
Chicago, IL 60606-6995

Epilepsy

www.efa.org

Epilepsy Foundation of America,
4351 Garden City Drive,
Landover, MD 20785

Heart Disease

www.amhrt.org

Lung Disease

www.lungusa.org

American Lung Association,
1-800-LUNG-USA

Multiple Sclerosis

www.nmss.org

National Multiple Sclerosis Society,
733 3rd Ave.,
New York, NY 10017

Spinal Injuries

www.apacure.org

American Paralysis Association,
500 Morris Ave.,
Springfield, NJ 07081

The onset of MS occurs most typically in young adulthood, it strikes more women than men, and it tends to run in families. MS is usually not fatal. After more than 100 years of study, the cause of MS is still unknown; theories suggest a slow-acting viral infection, an autoimmune response of the nervous system, or a strong genetic susceptibility component (e.g., Meinl, 1999; Noseworthy, 1999). There is currently no cure for MS, although corticosteroids and the drug ACTH have been found to relieve symptoms and to hasten remission from an attack of serious symptoms. Some antiviral therapies also seem promising. These regimens do not prevent future attacks, however. MS patients must learn to adjust to the disease, although adjustment can be a tremendously difficult task considering the monumental problems that the disease presents. During a period of remission, the MS patient might be able to live a normal life. During exacerbations of the illness, however, he or she might be totally paralyzed, incontinent, and unable to see. Further, in order to live a productive, satisfying life, the person with MS is required to take certain steps to prevent progressive debilitation and to manage the symptoms of the disease. For example, in order to maintain muscle tone, special exercises must be done every day. The patient must be consistently vigilant to avoid infections and must always get adequate rest because fatigue and stress can exacerbate symptoms. Depending on the nature of the symptoms, independence may depend upon developing new ways to perform daily activities. Since flare-ups of the disease are unpredictable, the patient usually has to make many physical and emotional adjustments in his or her lifestyle.

While most chronic conditions are not nearly as unpredictable as MS, many do tend to vary over time in their effects on the patient's life. Someone with rheumatoid arthritis, for example, might be quite energetic and mobile for several days and then experience yet another round of pain and limitation. One of the major difficulties experienced by many victims of chronic illness is their inability to plan many aspects of their lives; they often cannot predict what kind of physical state they will be in at any point in the future. Box 12.2 examines the ways in which diagnoses and related prognoses can vary by the cultural context in which disease is evaluated and defined.

Avoiding or Adjusting to Social Isolation

Chronic illness often brings serious social consequences. The practical limitations of a debilitating physical condition can make it all but impossible to maintain social ties. Contact with friends may diminish considerably, to the point where the patient rarely has contact with anyone outside his or her immediate family (Brodland & Andreasen, 1974). The person who is in treatment for cancer, for instance, may have too little energy to attend social functions or to organize get-togethers with friends. The complex scheduling of renal dialysis for the patient with kidney failure may leave little free time during which to socialize. Medical limitations and specifications may require control over the situations in which time is spent with others. The cardiac patient may need to avoid coffee breaks with co-workers because these situations intensify the desire to smoke cigarettes. The severe diabetic might avoid parties or dinner with friends in order to avoid temptations to deviate from the strict diet necessitated by the

BOX **12.2**
Across Cultures

Medicine and Culture: Varieties of Treatment for
Chronic Disease in Various Countries

Not only do patients' interpretations of and reactions to their symptoms vary with their cultural backgrounds, so do their diagnoses. While medicine views itself as a scientific discipline, evidence is strong that physicians' thinking is often tightly bound to their culture. For example, a group of British patients was assessed as to whether their hypertension was controlled according to the criteria of several different countries and the World Health Organization. The different criteria produced vastly different conclusions. According to U.S. guidelines, only 17.5 percent of the patients had their high blood pressure under control. According to Canadian guidelines, 84.6 percent of those same patients had their hypertension under control.

In another example, North American, Continental European, and English psychiatrists use different criteria to diagnose dememtia. When a group of physicians used the three different criteria on the same Canadian patients, they determined that with the North American system 13.7 percent had dementia, while over four times that number were diagnosed with dementia when using the Continental European criteria. While a total of 449 people fell into the category of having dementia by at least one of the four criteria, only 20 met the criteria under all four systems.

Anthropology researchers have found, in analyzing clinical trials of the anti-ulcer drugs cimetidine and ranitidine, that the drugs themselves were more effective in some countries than in others. In this research, 59 percent of patients in Germany felt better on a placebo; only 7 percent of Brazilian patients did so. Since only 36 percent of Brazilian patients healed on the active drug, it was less effective in Brazil than the placebo was in Germany! Now antibiotics are used to treat the *H. pylori* microorganism that is known to play a role in causing ulcers. The reason for the differences among countries in responses to cimetidine and ranitidine remains unknown, but researchers think that the placebos may have stimulated an immune response to eliminate *H. pylori*.

These studies are reviewed in an interesting publication called *Medicine and Culture Update*. It is edited by Lynn Payer, who is the author of three books, including *Medicine and Culture* (Henry Holt), which was first published in English in 1988 and has since been translated into French, German, Italian, and Japanese (Payer, 1988). Other cultural variations in illness definitions considered in *Medicine and Culture Update* include the following:

1. Low blood pressure is a sign of health in the United States but a sign of sickness in Germany.
2. Older heart patients are treated much more aggressively in the U.S. than in Canada, without any measurable benefit.
3. The Dutch have the lowest rates of antibiotic prescribing in the world; Dutch doctors don't even prescribe antibiotics for acute otitis media infections. They report that they have no more complications from bacterial disease than do other countries, and antibiotic resistance is less of a problem in the Netherlands than in other countries.

Visit the *Medicine and Culture Update* Website at: www.globalppo.com/medculture.htm. To request a sample copy of *Medicine & Culture Update*, send an e-mail with full name and address to payerlj@interport.net, or fax to 1-212-928-3278.

The limitations of physically debilitating conditions may be many and can require tremendous effort to develop and maintain independence.

illness (Benoliel, 1975). Unfortunately, however, this social isolation often acts against the individual's ability to cope. One study of diabetic adults found that one of the most important factors related to their quality of life and psychosocial functioning was diabetes-related social support (Aalto et al., 1997).

Victims of chronic illness must work to normalize their conditions as much as possible. **Normalizing** involves hiding symptoms such as limbs twisted by arthritis or polio and offensive smells from a colostomy. Normalizing also involves adjusting the routines of care so that they will remain unnoticed by others and integrating necessary treatment behaviors into a framework that both appears natural and allows independent, healthy functioning (Goffman, 1963; Robinson, 1993). Sometimes these arrangements must be ingenious and elaborate. Normalizing may be necessary in order to avoid the problem of **identity spread** (Strauss, 1975). When others are unfamiliar with the capabilities of the chronically ill or handicapped person, they tend to overgeneralize from the actual limitations. A blind person is addressed loudly and slowly as if he or she were not only unable to see, but were also deaf and intellectually slow. A handicapped person may be given little chance to show what he or she can really do, while emphasis is placed on what cannot be done. Chronically ill and disabled people sometimes must avoid social contact to maintain their self-image. They may be embarrassed by their required therapeutic nostrums (Lenderking et al., 1996). For example, an individual who suffers from incontinence might prefer to stay at home and watch television rather than risk the public embarrassment of urinary leakage. The products available for dealing with incontinence might feel bulky and "obvious" even though they are quite discreet. An individual might also fear the rejecting responses of others. Even close friends, who eventually make the necessary adjustments to altered appearances and abilities, might initially be taken aback and distressed by how the patient looks and behaves. The reactions of friends can have a very strong impact on the patient (Moos & Tsu, 1977).

Patients who are very distressed and likely in the most need of support may, by their own actions and behaviors, actually reject the people in their support network (Matt & Dean, 1993). Because their level of distress is high, these patients might be demanding and irritable and may even withdraw from social contacts. Providing long-term social support and care can be taxing for the care provider, depleting his or her physical and psychological resources (Kiecolt-Glaser et al., 1995; Mintzer et al., 1992; Schulz et al., 1995). Caregiving (especially for those who have little choice or who feel a great deal of pressure related to their responsibilities) can influence a variety of health behaviors including sleep patterns, exercise, smoking, and alcohol use (Gallant & Connell, 1998; Schulz et al., 1997). Those who *must* provide care, and who have no choice, seem to experience more stress and depression than those who feel they have a choice (Robinson-Whelen & Kiecolt-Glaser, 1997). Further, the perceived "stress-load" is a very important factor. Only about half of caregivers for the chronically ill report actually feeling strained by their duties, but negative psychological and physical health outcomes are more prevalent for these individuals (Schulz et al., 1997). Some researchers have suggested that rather than measuring the objective amount of caregiver burden, researchers should focus on the caregiver's *perceived* stress (Chwalisz & Kisler, 1995).

Many victims of chronic illness and disability eventually do adjust socially. They develop ways to continue relationships with their perceptive and sympathetic friends under conditions that they and the disease can tolerate. Many find that, as a result of the necessary adjustments, they and their friends are able to form deeper and more meaningful attachments (Mages & Mendelsohn, 1979). The stresses of illness and the experience of crises together may lead patients and their loved ones to a strengthening and deepening of their relationships and a keener appreciation of what is important in their lives (Mullan, 1983).

Setting Concrete Goals and Making Plans for the Future

Regardless of their health status, human beings have a need to conceive of their own futures and orient themselves toward goals that they value. Chronic illness can rob people of their future orientation, however. Because chronic illness can render the future so uncertain, the ability to plan and strive for future goals may be severely compromised. Paradoxically, those who cope most successfully with chronic illness tend to be those who do plan and who set and work toward goals that are of value to them (Moos & Tsu, 1977). Granted, the goals may need to remain short-term and limited, such as being able to walk in the academic procession at graduation. These goals often center around family or other members of the individual's support network (Pomeroy et al., 1997). The goals that are chosen must be simple enough to produce initial success, after which the tasks can be gradually increased in difficulty. Those with disfigurements, for example, might first try to appear in public among close friends, and then later try to interact with acquaintances. Only after considerable time might they be ready to meet new people.

In strategizing for the future, the chronically ill person often must consider and even prepare for a range of possible outcomes. For example, as graduation approaches, the person with a mobility limitation may arrange to have a walker or a wheelchair available at the commencement ceremonies in case the goal of walking unassisted cannot be achieved. An even more complex set of alternative plans may need to be made by a patient who faces the possible recurrence of cancer or by one who anticipates the possible rejection of a donor kidney (Adler, 1972). The individual may need to consider possible ways in which an independent lifestyle can be maintained if movements become restricted and/or the environment becomes inaccessible. Many chronic conditions necessitate the continual formulation and revision of alternative short- and long-range plans in order to cope with the changing aspects of the disease and its limitations.

There are many ways in which individuals might cope with their chronic conditions. One useful analysis involves the categorization of **assimilative** versus **accommodative** coping styles (Schmitz et al., 1996). Assimilative coping style is problematic in that it involves the persistent pursuit of unrealistic goals that cannot realistically be attained. The individual continues to strive for goals that he or she has failed in the past to achieve. Accommodative coping style, on the other hand, involves flexibility in goal setting such that the individual focuses on objectives that are attainable. The outcomes of the two strategies were examined, and it was shown that patients who set goals that were somewhat flexible and could be modified according to the person's present capabilities experienced more positive outcomes than did those who set goals and then doggedly pursued them even in the face of failure. Those whose goals were more flexible were able to avoid the negative emotions associated with failure and, instead, enjoyed more successes and feelings of accomplishment.

In addition to having flexible objectives, it is adaptive to have several possible plans worked out cognitively for various situations. The process of rehearsing a variety of alternative strategies and courses of action has been referred to by psychologists as the **work of worrying** (Janis, 1958). The work of worrying is the process of reviewing various potential approaches to a problem and considering how a variety of uncontrollable factors might affect one's life. More recently, psychologists have expanded and modified this concept to better fit the concerns associated with medical decision making. For example, in their book on clinical decisions, Nezu and Nezu (1989) provide guidelines for clinicians who have the task of guiding their patients through an array of possible treatment strategies. The book uses a problem-solving approach and notes that patients can be expected to vary in their orientations to problem solving as well as in their particular problem-solving skills (D'Zurilla & Nezu, 1990). Understanding these individual styles and strengths will enable better treatment decisions. Similar approaches are proposed by others, such as using a decision tree (Speedling & Rose, 1985) or a guiding acronym such as PREPARED™ (DiMatteo et al., 1994; Gambone & Reiter, 1991). (See Chapter 2 for a more detailed discussion of these.) A person who has gone through the process of thinking about outcomes and making careful decisions is unlikely to be caught off guard by life's inevitable "curve-balls." He or she will have various back-up plans, and will be able to transition more smoothly to an alternate, well-considered course of action.

Chronic illness permanently changes an individual's life and forces him or her to face and adjust to restricted life choices. Limitations in certain areas may, however, unexpectedly open up other possibilities. For example, unable to pursue physical endeavors, the chronically disabled individual might choose to pursue an intellectual life and go back to school to begin a new career. Or, the individual might discover hidden artistic talents that might never have been recognized and developed had the disability not occurred. Thus, some of the changes that take place in an individual's life and self-image as a result of chronic illness might actually be for the better.

Chronic Illness in Children and Adolescents

About 6.5 percent of children in the United States have some kind of chronic condition that brings serious concerns about their future as well as limitations in their current activities. It is estimated that these childhood disabilities result in 24 million days of absence from school and 26 million physician contacts each year (Newacheck & Halfon, 1998). Many of these disorders require special treatment, such as a restricted diet or regular medication. In addition, increasing numbers of children with long-term illnesses are able to remain at home with their families, instead of staying in the hospital. Thus, considerable interest is developing among health professionals and parents in the impact and management of the chronic conditions of childhood.

Diseases that were once fatal among children, such as diabetes and severe bronchial asthma, are now survivable and manageable because of advances in medicine and related sciences. While children with chronic diseases are never actually cured, they are able to live relatively normal lives as long as they maintain a regimen of care for their chronic, life-threatening conditions. In addition, in current times children who once would have died from leukemia and various forms of childhood cancer now survive longer than ever before and a great many are eventually cured. Their process of recovery, however, can be extremely long and emotionally draining for the family. Typically, the physical, emotional, social, and financial demands of caring for an ill or disabled child can affect all members of the family in some very profound and complex ways (Silver et al., 1995).

> Jeffrey is a normal, happy 8-year-old—as normal as can be expected, of course, since he has bronchial asthma. Jeffrey's asthma is severe enough to sometimes endanger his life. In the midst of an asthma attack, for example, he is literally suffocating. Because of swollen bronchial passages that are also in spasm, he cannot expel the carbon dioxide in his lungs quickly enough to be able to breathe again and take in needed oxygen. At least once each month, Jeffrey's parents must rush him to the local emergency room to receive treatment. Although extensive testing has been done to identify triggers for Jeffrey's asthma, his parents can't always predict when an attack will occur. Therefore, they must keep extra close watch on him at all times. Even Jeffrey's 10-year-old sister feels she must constantly know his whereabouts when they are out playing or at school, in case he has difficulty breathing.

Jeffrey's environment and activities are quite restricted by his asthma. For example, he must avoid allergens such as pollen, animal dander, dust, and molds. This means that his parents must keep their home absolutely spotless at all times. They cannot have carpeting in their house and instead have installed linoleum flooring that can be mopped every day. They have minimal furniture, so that dusting every day will be easier. They cannot have a pet, much to the disappointment of Jeffrey and his sister. Jeffrey is not allowed to visit the homes of his friends, because the necessary precautions have not been taken there. And, because dampness and humidity are so detrimental to Jeffrey's condition, his parents are planning to move the family from the East Coast to Arizona, where the air is very dry.

Jeffrey typically misses a day or two of school after a serious asthma attack. Unlike the other children, he cannot participate in physical education classes because the exertion of exercise can bring on an attack. Jeffrey is learning to control or avoid emotional states that can trigger an attack, such as fear, anxiety, anger, and even excitement. This makes his life even more restricted, and places a tremendous burden on his family to control the emotional stimuli to which he is exposed. Also, Jeffrey must take preventive medication daily, including a systemic bronchodilator in slow-release tablet form and an aerosolized medication that he has to inhale. These medications help to keep his airways open on a daily basis, and so far he has experienced only mild side effects from them. The medicine doesn't completely control the problem, however, and so he also carries a "rescue inhaler" for emergencies. He initially experienced some problems using the rescue inhaler because by the time he got to it, he was already feeling panicked and unable to breathe. He now has a spacer device that allows the correct amount to be dispensed and keeps him from overdosing. He and his family must learn to anticipate his asthma attacks and to be competent at dealing with them by administering medication, providing physical support for coughing, and helping him to rest and use the relaxation techniques he has learned. Sometimes, even with all of these efforts, Jeffrey must be taken to the hospital.

Jeffrey cannot always be with his parents or his sister, of course. In order to gain the independence that is normal for a developing 8-year-old, Jeffrey must learn to take more and more responsibility for his own care. Such responsibility takes considerable time to develop and tends to be quite stressful for him. Jeffrey's parents worry that if he makes a mistake, he could die. So, they tend to be somewhat controlling with him. They also have a tendency to place some of the responsibility for Jeffrey's life on his 10-year-old sister, and her anxiety level is quite high as a result. Family dynamics are very much influenced by Jeffrey's illness, sometimes in a negative manner. This summer Jeffrey will be attending a summer camp specifically for children with asthma. At this camp, he will not only learn and practice asthma-control techniques, but he will also have an opportunity to interact with many children like himself and have a safe outdoor camping experience.

Insulin dependent diabetes mellitus (IDDM) is one of the four most prevalent chronic illnesses of childhood and, like asthma, requires substantial changes in lifestyle if it is to be successfully managed. It is an incurable metabolic disorder that affects about 150,000 children and their families. Juvenile diabetes must be controlled through careful adherence to a complex regimen of care that includes strict control of food intake and physical activity and the routine, balanced use of insulin replacement. Careful attention must be paid to the management of time, and the diabetic child's behavior must be monitored to control aspects of life (such as food intake) that most people take for granted. For example, the diabetic child cannot spontaneously eat cookies, candy, and other sweets because his or her insulin level will be significantly affected. A great deal of responsibility for treatment regimen adherence falls on the child and his or her family (Gallo & Knafl, 1998; Johnson et al., 1992; Wertlieb et al., 1986).

Parents of a diabetic child carry a heavy responsibility for their child's welfare (Drotar, 1981). Just as they try to maintain the child's adherence to rules of social conduct, they attempt to bring about adherence to the management demands of insulin injections, blood or urine monitoring, dietary regimens, and exercise (Gallo & Knafl, 1998; Wertlieb et al., 1986). All the activities must be done according to schedule and carried out correctly. Organization is a paramount concern. Rebelliousness and failure to follow rules can be annoying and frustrating for parents of a healthy child. But parents of a diabetic child know that their child's refusal or inability to follow the required course of treatment could jeopardize his or her life.

Diabetes presents a significant challenge not only to a child's physical health but also to development and emotional adaptation. As the young diabetic assumes increasing independence and responsibility, parents must help him or her to take over self-care duties. Studies have shown that a supportive family environment is associated with favorable treatment adherence and metabolic control (Jay et al., 1984; La Greca et al., 1995; Martin et al., 1998). In families in which there is avoidance of conflict or lack of conflict resolution, the diabetic child may express rebellion by poorly caring for the disease. Treatment lapses may be used to control parents. Further, research has shown that diabetic adolescents who are independent and can express their feelings are able to maintain better metabolic control than are those who have high levels of conflict in their families. Greater behavioral symptoms and more problems in disease control have been found in diabetic children whose parents are unsupportive of their independence and self-sufficiency (La Greca et al., 1995; Martin et al., 1998).

Developmental Tasks and Illness

Many psychologists use a developmental approach in order to understand how an individual grows and changes psychologically throughout his or her life span. Early psychodynamic theorists, such as Sigmund Freud, proposed that development is confined to childhood. The theorist Erik Erikson argued, however, that each life stage presents a variety of tasks to be mastered before an individual can move on to the next psychological stage (Erikson, 1963). According to Erikson, development progresses from the "trust vs. mistrust" stage in infancy through "ego integrity vs. despair" in late adulthood (see Table 12.1 for a summary of all stages). This formulation is particularly relevant to the understanding of illness. Because of certain uncontrollable life events, such as illness, a person might fail to master the psychological tasks necessary at each stage of development. Erikson's theory holds that competence at each stage is necessary in order to move on and meet the challenges of the next stages and that adaptation to illness or disability depends a great deal upon the stage at which it first appears. A particular limitation may have a huge impact at one stage of development but a much smaller impact at another; the accomplishments of the previous stage can make adjustment more or less

TABLE 12.1   Erikson's Stages of Psychosocial Development

Stage	Age	Developmental Task
Trust vs. mistrust	Birth to 12-18 mos.	Form trusting relationship with caregiver
Autonomy vs. shame/doubt	18 mos. to 3 years	Learn self-control, bodily control
Initiative vs. guilt	3 to 6 years	Learn independence, assertiveness
Industry vs. inferiority	6 to 12 years	Gain social and academic skills
Identity vs. role confusion	Adolescence	Achieve personal sense of identity, including gender roles, occupational choice, values, and goals
Intimacy vs. isolation	Young adulthood	Develop intimate relationship
Generativity vs. stagnation	Middle adulthood	Contribute to the next generation
Ego integrity vs. despair	Late adulthood	See one's life as having had purpose; feel that one has accomplished something meaningful to the world

possible when illness or disability appear. The patient's developmental level will also affect the number and type of demands he or she places on family members, and within a family the developmental levels of the various other members may affect their reactions and adjustments to the patient's limitations.

Briefly, Erikson described the major task of infancy as the attainment of a sense of basic trust, which comes from perceiving the caretaker as consistent and reliable. Serious illness at this stage can interfere with such attainment because illness may require separation from parents and the frustration of basic needs. In early childhood, the main task is to strive for autonomy, particularly in controlling bodily functions. Successful toilet training is a source of pride for the young child who feels that he or she has accomplished something important, and illness and disability can bring considerable restriction in activity and the curtailment of efforts toward independence. Chronically ill children under age 4 often react with willfulness and attempt to test the boundaries of the control their parents exert over them. School-age children (age 5 to puberty) typically attempt to develop a sense of industry and competence, as well as the capacity for sustained effort. Adolescents need opportunities for unique self-expression, independence, and close and loving relationships with those their own age. Illness or disability during adolescence may not only interfere with these pursuits but may, when independent action becomes impossible, threaten what was accomplished at earlier stages of development. It can be difficult for the parent of an ill or disabled adolescent to provide the required physical care and at the same time devise an environment in which the adolescent can express his or her individuality, receive needed emancipation from parental control, establish rewarding peer relationships, and develop values that are independent of parents.

Box 12.3 examines some of the difficult issues that should be addressed when a child must be hospitalized and suggests what can be done to support the child so that the experience is not as traumatic.

BOX **12.3**

Hot Topic

Children in the Hospital

An individual's developmental stage is an important determinant of how he or she reacts to illness and hospitalization. For a child, hospitalization can be particularly terrifying and associated with high levels of anxiety (Bossert, 1994; Lizasoain & Polaino, 1995). Frequently, young children are not able to understand what is happening to them and are likely to become more frightened than older children. Uncertainty and confusion about the illness experience is stressful for most people regardless of their age, but children are more susceptible to this stress because they have limited awareness of the causes of illness and they normally receive little information to help them comprehend their feelings. Some interpret "feeling bad" as a punishment for having behaved badly; some think they are sick or hurt because their family members did not protect them. In a hospital, they may feel abandoned by their parents and left alone to face a confusing array of health professionals and strange, uncomfortable medical procedures. Children who are hospitalized often experience anger, humiliation, and considerable anxiety. Some respond by regressing to babyish behavior. Some even lose their recent gains, such as toilet training or the ability to dress themselves or brush their teeth. Others, out of panic, carry on with temper tantrums.

Several decades ago, few (if any) hospitals would allow a parent to stay with a hospitalized child. This rule was adhered to, despite the tremendous difficulties encountered by toddlers and young children in being separated from their parents. Now, most hospitals permit parents to "room-in" with their sick children and even to participate in delivering their care. Older children and adolescents are given the opportunity to reduce their separation and loneliness with opportunities for peer contact. Many hospitals have programs to provide parents and children with adequate information and preparation for what will be experienced. Such interventions may include reviewing what has happened, talking about the child's beliefs about *why* it happened, helping parents control their own emotional expressions so as not to upset the child, and explaining what is going to be done by the medical professional (Bronfman et al., 1998). It is important that explanations be given in language that children can understand. Children are found to be more likely to comply with treatment regimens when given a chance to participate in their own care and to take some control. One child for example, was able to tolerate painful bone marrow aspirations when the physician followed the child's orders to first count to ten. Another was able to tolerate an uncomfortable diagnostic examination when she was able to choose whether she would sit up or lie down for the procedure. Children do best when they are given the opportunity to verbalize their feelings and to exert some control over what is happening to them (Koocher, 1985).

Hospitalized children can also benefit from relaxation techniques and cognitive-behavioral approaches that help them to relax when feeling anxious (Lizasoain & Polaino, 1995). For instance, children may feel better if they are allowed to listen to happy or relaxing music, hold a familiar stuffed animal, or talk with a parent about a pleasurable outing that the family enjoyed together. A medical procedure might be made into a sort of game, with the child's patience or endurance being rewarded with something he or she values. Or, guided imagery might be used to harness the child's imagination and make experiences in the hospital less threatening.

Impaired Social Relationships with Peers and Siblings

The difficulties of illness do not stop with the chronically ill child. Peers and siblings both affect and are affected by the psychological and social concomitants of illness and disability. Because of the limitations placed on the entire family, siblings of a chronically ill child may be deprived of a family atmosphere that is suitable to their own development (e.g., Bluebond-Langner, 1996). They may become jealous of the increased attention and special privileges given to the ill child (Derouin & Jessee, 1996). The ill sibling who receives medications and special diets may appear to be overindulged. Siblings may experience decreased parental tolerance for them, increased parental expectations for their maturity and independence, and a lack of positive emotional expression toward them. The ill sibling may have significantly diminished energy, making normal sibling interactions impossible. Many siblings of chronically ill children experience confusion and anxiety from a lack of information about what is happening to their sibling. They experience loneliness from decreased parental involvement, feelings of parental rejection, sadness at the loss of former family interactions, embarrassment about and unwillingness to express their own negative reactions, and even survivor guilt at witnessing the ill child's physical deterioration and pain as they themselves remain healthy. Siblings of ill children experience fears of loss: loss of the sibling whom they love, as well as loss of one or both parents who are often separated physically and/or emotionally from the rest of the family while caring for the ill and sometimes hospitalized child. As a result, siblings may develop behavioral problems at home and in school (Shapiro & Brack, 1994; Stawski et al., 1997).

Although there are several factors that threaten the adjustment and well-being of siblings of chronically ill children, many children with a chronically ill sibling are themselves well-adjusted and happy. In fact, reviews of the literature indicate that only about 60 percent of studies show that siblings of chronically ill children are at increased risk for social and emotional problems. The remainder of studies show either no increased risk or a mixture of negative and positive outcomes (Williams, 1997). Research suggests that the problematic effects of having a chronically ill child in the family may be limited if certain factors are dealt with effectively (Drotar & Crawford, 1985; Faux, 1993; Williams, 1997). The ways in which individual family dynamics and unique characteristics interact are very complex, and it is difficult to predict which siblings will be more likely to experience problems. For example, if a sibling is naturally shy, social difficulties may be exacerbated if he or she must stay home to help care for the chronically ill child. Opportunities to refine social skills may not then be available. Alternatively, qualities like compassion, conscientiousness, and responsibility might be fostered in children who have a chronically ill sibling. It has been suggested that rather than focusing on the vulnerabilities of children who have chronically ill siblings, researchers should focus on the factors that make many of these children particularly mature and resilient (Leonard, 1991).

The connections between peer relationships and social functioning in children with chronic illness is a complex and important issue. Peers exert an important influence on children, whether or not they are ill. Peers may have a tendency to reject children with chronic illnesses, and because of difficulties gaining peer acceptance, chronically ill children often experience loneliness (Krulik, 1987). "Being different" can expose them to ridicule. Among school-age children, acceptance and popularity often depend upon physical appearance and demeanor, and so the degree of rejection experienced is usually influenced by how much the condition interferes with normal classroom and play activities, how noticeable the defect is, and the level of cognitive development and maturity of the ill child's peers (Roberts, 1986). Efforts to help peers (for example, members of a child's class) to understand his or her condition and to deal with their own fears and anxieties regarding their friend's illness can help peers to be supportive of the ill child instead of rejecting.

In a study of adolescents with cystic fibrosis, it was found that there are three typically used techniques for reducing the feeling of being "different" from peers: (1) keeping things secret, (2) hiding as many visible differences as possible, and (3) setting new baselines (that is, creating new definitions for "normal" abilities and viewing their own strengths differently). Having a close friend also helped these chronically ill adolescents to minimize the impact that their differences had on their lives (Christian & D'Auria, 1997). In terms of providing social support, friends of chronically ill adolescents have actually been found to provide significantly more companionship support than do families, while both friends and families provide emotional support (La Greca, 1992).

Children with chronic illnesses have many experiences that have the potential to impede their social development. Friendships may be difficult to maintain because of interruptions by illness crises and treatment. Children who are chronically ill sometimes develop characteristics that separate them from other people, such as shyness and avoidance stemming from embarrassment about their symptoms and treatments. Despite all of this, some children maintain normal, or even exceptional, levels of adjustment and social functioning. For example, one recent empirical study compared 76 children (ages 8–15) with cancer who were receiving chemotherapy with a control group of 76 classroom peers. The children with cancer were not different from the healthy children on measures of depression, anxiety, loneliness, or self-concept. Further, their parents did not perceive that they had more behavior problems or that they had lower social functioning or psychological well-being than other children. In fact, they were actually rated by their teachers and/or peers as being more sociable, less aggressive, and having more social acceptance than the control group (Noll et al., 1999). This does not mean, of course, that the chronically ill child doesn't face unique obstacles and challenges. This research does highlight, however, the strong spirit that many of these children exhibit daily.

Various programs exist to help children who are chronically ill or disabled in some way to cope with their illness and to thrive in spite of it. For example, since the early 1980s, special summer camps have been available for children and adolescents who have been severely burned (Biggs et al., 1997). The goal of the camps is for the children to interact with peers in an enjoyable setting and thereby increase their self-esteem. Although not all campers experience an increase in self-esteem as a result of going to camp, over one-third do so. This is just one example of an integrative technique that fosters children's adjustment to life-changing injury or illness.

The Emotional and Physical Adjustment of the Family

There is no single pattern of stress faced by families with children who have long-term chronic illnesses. Rather, the quantity and the quality of stress depend upon the type and extent of the child's limitations (Holroyd & Guthrie, 1986). For example, some children may be wheelchair-bound or even totally dependent upon their parents for physical care. Their capacities may slowly deteriorate over time. Others may experience periods of poor functioning that alternate with relatively active and healthy periods during which they can develop normally. Inconsistencies in, and uncertainties about, the child's abilities may be particularly difficult to deal with, since patients and their families must adapt to conditions that are continually changing. For example, just when they become accustomed to the child's good health, there may be yet another exacerbation of the disease, causing tensions to mount again. Partly because of the tremendous stress placed on the entire family, compliance with recommended treatments may become very difficult. In one study of children with cancer, for example, it was found that 67 percent had stopped taking their medication before they were told to do so by their physicians (Roberts, 1986). Some ill or disabled children become passive, dependent, and overprotected by their parents and do not learn to take responsibility for their care. Others resent the restrictions placed on them and rebel, becoming excessively independent and even daring to risk serious medical consequences. When family members are distressed in trying to cope with a child's chronic illness, they may not be functioning in an optimal way to support adherence to the treatment regimen (Manne et al., 1993).

The type of disability the child experiences is also an important factor in family adjustment. Limitations in intellectual and cognitive development, such as that which may accompany neuromuscular disease, tend to be more difficult to cope with than physical difficulties alone. Of course, even when there is no effect on the child's mind, the physical limitations and financial pressures of many chronic conditions (renal disease, for example) can seriously affect a family's ability to cope. Many aspects of day-to-day life may be altered because of the requirements of the ill child's care. Much attention may be required by the schedules of medical visits and the timing of exercise, meals, and travel. The desires of the other children in the family (for example, to have a pet) may be thwarted by requirements for the ill child's care (Wilson-Pessano & McNabb, 1985). Some parents of chronically ill children report interference with their jobs, effects on their own relationships, considerable psychological distress, and a home life characterized by high conflict and emotional disconnection from one another (Mastroyannopoulou et al., 1997).

Psychologists do not yet have enough information about why some families rise to the challenge of a crisis of illness or disability while others fall apart. Certainly the strength of the family bonds, including the viability of the marriage, are important factors, as are the degree of adjustment and emotional health enjoyed by the individual parents. When parents are emotionally healthy themselves and feel that their child's illness is controllable, the child's own ability to cope seems to be assisted (Timko et al., 1992).

Interestingly, mothers seem to be particularly important in this process. One researcher found that maternal psychological and physical adjustment correlated highly with overall family response to a handicapped child (Shapiro, 1986). If the mother was depressed or ill herself, the family was often seriously disrupted by the presence of the child's illness. Under these circumstances, the family members tended to have angry or prolonged negative feelings toward the chronically ill child or to perceive him or her to be a burden. On the other hand, mothers who were able to seek emotional support from a variety of sources, who felt in control of the problem, who were not depressed, and who were themselves in good health had families who adjusted better to the chronic illness of one of the children (Shapiro, 1986).

Finally, in this research, mothers who tried to normalize family life as much as possible (for example, matter-of-factly giving the ill child's medication at the same time the other children take their vitamins) achieved higher levels of functioning in their families. Alternatively, those who avoided facing their feelings about their child's illness and who blamed themselves were depressed, had poorer health, had lower levels of personal functioning, and had families that experienced poorer adjustment. It is important to remember, of course, that it is quite difficult to decide which factor causes which, because causal inference is not possible in this research (Shapiro, 1986). Did the mother's good health and emotional stability cause good family adjustment, or vice versa?

Although mothers seem to play a pivotal role in the dynamics of families with chronically ill children, the relationship between the mother and ill child may be the one at highest risk. Researchers reviewed the literature on the effects of pediatric chronic illness on families and found that the mother-child dyads were more likely to experience adjustment problems than were mothers and children in healthy families. As we have seen before, however, there was a great deal of individual variation. Not every mother and child was destined to experience problems, and many did very well (Wallander & Varni, 1998)!

In general, clinicians have noted that more negative family and individual outcomes are likely to result if family members have difficulty resolving conflicts and cannot talk openly about the child's condition (Manne et al., 1993; Shapiro, 1986). Destructive coping mechanisms such as denial might be chosen, making communication about the illness among family members impossible. Feelings of self-blame, which parents may find preferable to facing the often random tragedies of illness, may cause further harm by alienating family members from one another (Shapiro, 1986).

As we saw above, the entire family environment can be affected by the limitations that accompany the illness or disability of one child. Because of this, medical practitioners now recognize that they must work with the family as a whole unit whenever they treat a child (Drotar & Crawford, 1985; Williams, 1997). They must focus on interaction patterns and the ability of family members to communicate with one another and to express and deal with their feelings (Drotar & Crawford, 1985).

With the support of their health professionals, parents of chronically ill children can do a great deal to help them develop as normally as possible. For example, parents can work within the family to minimize the differences between the chronically ill

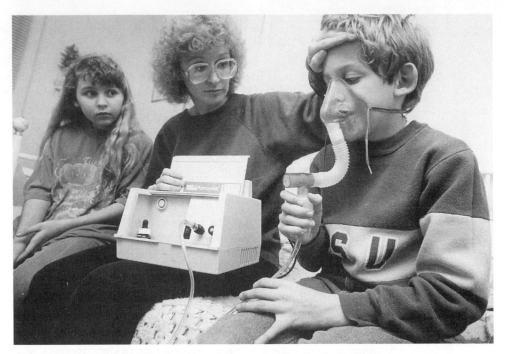

Chronic illness, such as childhood asthma, can strongly affect family dynamics.

child and his or her peers and siblings. Within the bounds of the required treatment regimens, parents can provide the child with opportunities for normal peer contacts and with help to avoid social isolation (Krulik, 1987). Extra effort on the part of the parent may be required to find activities in which the child can successfully participate. Parents can help the child to solidify sibling relationships by avoiding overprotection, overindulgence, permissiveness, and any hints of favoritism (Boone & Hartman, 1972).

Parents can also help their chronically ill child by communicating honestly and focusing on the child's feelings. Some parents may try to avoid answering their child's questions about the illness, or they may be willing to discuss only day-to-day care but not the child's feelings about being ill. The child may learn that certain topics are taboo and may become isolated in his or her own private fears. Because the experience of chronic illness increases the risk of experiencing psychological problems, it has been suggested that psychologists should be involved in the care of such children from the time of diagnosis (Elander & Midence, 1997). Although not every child will need extensive psychological treatment, an early assessment would help to insure that children who are in need of extra help receive it as early as possible in their illness experience. Treatments such as psychotherapy can be extremely beneficial in helping some children to understand and find meaning in their illness, as well as to learn more effective ways to adapt and grow (Stauffer, 1998). There may be many problems to overcome, but the demands of chronic illness and disability can be incorporated into a rewarding family life. See Figure 12.2 for an example of the complex psychosocial effects of a complication of diabetes.

Chronic Illness in Adulthood

Many adults suffer from chronic diseases. In fact, three-fourths of the eventual deaths of U.S. adults age 25 to 64 are due to a chronic disease (NCHS, 1998). Chronic disease in adulthood presents its own unique set of challenges. For those who have been ill since childhood, there may be residual effects from the early years in addition to the current physical limitations inherent in the illness itself. For example, some individuals who have been chronically ill since childhood may not have developed in social maturity as effectively as their healthy peers (Kokkonen, 1995). For those who become chronically ill in adulthood, the challenge may be to learn to adapt to what is sometimes a drastically different lifestyle than that to which the individual was accustomed. In the following sections we will look at how chronic illness affects the lives of young and middle-aged adults, along with their families.

Patient's Physiological Response to Hypoglycemia

Brain
Headache,
aphasia,
twitching,
dizziness,
depression,
blurred vision,
drowsiness,
loss of consciousness,
convulsions

Heart
Hypotension,
tachycardia

Stomach
Vomiting,
hunger,
nausea

Adrenal gland
Increased epinephrine
secretion causes sweating,
shakiness, trembling,
weakness, anxiety, pallor,
increased respirations

Family Response

- Additional responsibility
- Anxiety over medical emergencies
- Guilt
- Fear of long-term consequences to child
- Confusion over steps to take for effective diabetes management

FIGURE 12.2 Patient and family response to hypoglycemia (low blood sugar)—a complication of diabetes management.

Chronic Illness in Young Adulthood

Illness and disability can have a profound impact upon young adults and can significantly affect the people in the patient's **family of origin** (parents, siblings), **family of commitment** (spouse and children), and **close social network** (extended family and close friends). Social and emotional development do not stop in adolescence but continue throughout the life span. At all ages, illness and disability can interfere.

During early adulthood (roughly ages 20–39), an individual usually strives both to develop a career and to initiate an intimate relationship with another person (Erikson, 1963; see Table 12.1). Chronic illness and disability can significantly interfere with these goals. Preferred career choices may become unavailable to the patient, and alternative plans must be developed. Physical limitations can alter the patient's ability to relate to an intimate partner. For example, a young couple may be starting their life together when one of them is suddenly propelled by the dependency of illness to an earlier stage of development. The demands of illness may cause the couple to lose the autonomy they had just begun to develop. The spouse or partner of the ill or disabled patient may not have developed enough emotionally to be able to withstand the stresses of chronic illness. Limitations in maturity may challenge his or her commitment to stay with the partner. The patient's physical limitations can also limit a couple's sexual expression. Illness, bodily disfigurement, disability, or medications may bring certain physiological changes that make sexual functioning difficult or impossible (e.g., Dailey, 1998; El-Rufaie et al., 1997). Psychological factors such as changes in body image and alterations in social environment may bring a lowered self-concept for the patient and may restrict opportunities for and comfort with intimacy (Glueckauf & Quittner, 1984).

During young adulthood, chronic illness may place close relationships in serious jeopardy. After the onset of illness or disability, a young couple may need to renegotiate the terms of their relationship. The able-bodied spouse may have had to take on new pressures that were never expected when the commitment took place. Very often, the patient has gone through experiences that the spouse cannot understand. Sometimes the partners have become so alienated from one another emotionally that parting is the only alternative (Ireys & Burr, 1984). In all cases, young adults whose lives have been changed by chronic illness must struggle to redefine their roles and relationships with regard to one another. Many young adults who do not have partners are forced by their disabilities to move back to their family of origin (Ireys & Burr, 1984). Such a move often has a negative effect on the patient's self-image. Parents, who may have already reached their retirement years, are placed back into the role of providing care for their young adult child. In addition, individuals who have had a chronic illness since childhood are less likely to get married and are more likely to be living at home with their parents than healthy individuals of the same age (Kokkonen, 1995). For the parents of chronically ill young adults, parenting must continue.

When a young adult who has lived on his or her own for a time before the disability is forced to return to the family of origin, certain tasks must be undertaken and certain important goals achieved. Parents and siblings must maintain the opportunity to continue with their own developmental tasks. New patterns of relating must be developed that do not simply repeat the old patterns that existed in the family at an earlier time. For example, siblings in the household may need to abandon certain aspects of the relationships they had as children and develop new adult patterns of interaction.

Chronic Illness in Middle Age

Chronic illness can bring serious problems even among middle-aged patients (roughly ages 40–65) who have strong family ties and considerable emotional support. A significant alteration in roles and lifestyles within the family may occur, and this is understandably stressful for everyone (Compas et al., 1996). A spouse may have to accept total responsibility for the financial support of the family as well as for all domestic chores and care of the children. The chronically ill adult who was once a nurturer may become the one who needs nurturing (Rustad, 1984). Chronic illness and disability can challenge the financial stability of the family. Workers whose employment involves physical strain may be unable to continue in their jobs and as a result lose their health insurance and retirement and disability benefits. Such financial constraints can significantly limit the opportunities afforded other family members (such as the ability to take a vacation or go to a college) and can challenge the ill person's conception of him- or herself as an active contributor to the family.

Illness interferes with many of the normal tasks of midlife, such as helping teenage children to grow into responsible and happy adults, developing adult leisure time activities, and caring for aged parents. By the time they have reached their 40s and 50s, many people have gained a sense of mastery over their lives. They may have developed more equal relationships with their spouses than they had in the earlier years of their marriage. Unfortunately, illness and disability may once again bring the need for more rigid roles, even ones that are quite different from what the family was previously accustomed to. For example, when a wife is disabled, her husband may be thrust into the role of nurturer and caretaker, a role he may never have played before. Likewise, when a husband is disabled, a wife who was once dependent in the realm of financial matters may be required to learn about financial management.

Typically, chronic illness causes a change in the couple's sexual relationship. They may even cease sexual relations altogether (e.g., Dailey, 1998; El-Rufaie et al., 1997). Sexual activity may be particularly problematic if there is anxiety that sex might jeopardize the patient's condition (for example, if the individual has had a heart attack). By interfering with sexual expression, chronic illness may jeopardize the couple's opportunities for emotional intimacy. This issue is examined further in Box 12.4.

The Effect on the Patient's Children

The children of a chronically ill or disabled patient are likely to be affected in significant ways. If alternative methods are not found for a parent to fulfill the children's needs, the long-term effects of such illness or disability may be quite profound. Illness and disability may interfere with two important roles that a parent plays with respect to his or her child, namely that of teacher and protector. Because of limitations in a parent's physical condition, for example, a child may not have appropriate controls and

BOX **12.4**

Research Close-up

Sex and Chronic Illness

Among patients with chronic illness and disability, the pleasures of sexual expression may be severely threatened. There is considerable research evidence that sexual behavior often becomes limited or nonexistent among those who suffer from various chronic medical conditions (e.g., Badeau, 1995; El-Rufaie et al., 1997). Some patients become impotent or nonorgasmic; others lose interest in sex or become fearful of it. Even after they have their disease under control and are doing well in many other areas of their lives, patients may avoid sexual activity.

The sexual problems experienced by those with chronic illnesses can be related directly or indirectly to the disease or disability (Anderson et al., 1997). For instance, surgery or chemotherapy can interfere with physical functioning so that sexual behavior is not possible. This would be a direct effect. Or, the disease or disability may result in anxiety and depression that, in turn, diminish sexual appetite (an indirect effect). Problems with sexual dysfunction are particularly common when the disease or injury involves the sexual structures of the body (such as prostate cancer and gynecologic cancers) (Moyer & Salovey, 1996).

Certainly patients with serious medical difficulties have problems that, at the time, seem much more important than sex. They may be concerned about surviving and avoiding long-term disablility. At some point, however, when survival is likely and control of the condition possible, threats to sexuality can begin to affect other dimensions of their lives. These include their feelings of attractiveness, their self-esteem, their feelings of physical and emotional support from a partner, and even the stability of their primary relationship with that partner. The illness or disability may frustrate or even threaten the relationship. While some individuals and couples may be comfortable forgoing sexual activity altogether, many very much want to regain the ability to enjoy this means of closeness.

Medical professionals can do a great deal to help patients and their partners by providing them with essential information about the impact of their medical condition on sexuality. Many patients may be embarrassed to bring up the issue of sex. Health professionals should, therefore, be comfortable introducing the topic and asking patients sensitively if they would like to discuss it. There are currently many methods available to help individuals overcome a variety of sexual problems. For example, the drug sildenafil citrate (Viagra) is an effective way to treat erectile dysfunction in men (whether it stems from chronic illness, a drug side effect, or a psychological factor). There is some indication that Viagra might be a useful tool in treating sexual dysfunction in women, as well, although evidence is not conclusive (Kaplan et al., 1999).

Unfortunately, health professionals often fail to provide even the most rudimentary information about sex to their patients. Enlightened medical professionals would provide this as a matter of course and would be careful to deal with individual patient differences, such as the existing medical condition, potential side effects of treatments for that condition, the patient's and partner's attitudes, comfort level, and satisfaction (Viera et al., 1999). Sensitivity and attention to patients' sexual difficulties can foster recovery on emotional and social dimensions.

boundaries placed on his or her behavior. Or, the child may perceive the disabled parent as unable to protect him or her, leaving the child with feelings of insecurity. The period after onset of illness and disability is likely to be particularly stressful and children may feel exceptionally vulnerable and in need of support. In addition, hospitalization may deprive them of much-needed contact with their parents. However, both the ill and the caretaking parent may become so absorbed in physical care and in their own adjustment that they remain emotionally unavailable to the children. Younger children may experience considerable anxiety that is fueled by their fears and fantasies of losing the parent and being abandoned. Older children who have a better understanding of the situation may experience more realistic, but no less terrifying, fears.

When children are forced to care for their disabled parents (for example, staying at home when they should be establishing autonomy), their own development can be disrupted. Children with a disabled parent may be thrust into a situation that is well beyond their current developmental stage. Concern for the physical care of a parent is normally part of middle-age adult development (in the 40s and 50s), not of development in the adolescent and young adult years. Offspring in their late teens and early 20s who are old enough to leave the family to make their own lives may feel conflict between their own desire for freedom and independence and parental demands (expressed or implicit) for physical and emotional support.

Of course, the difficulties of parental chronic illness can be overcome, and alternative ways for parent and child to interact can be found. Intervention by psychologists and other medical professionals can help to prevent or to solve many of the difficulties faced by the children of chronically ill parents.

How Families Cope

As we have noted, families cope with chronic illness in many different ways, depending upon the nature and timing of the illness, its limitations, and a host of other factors. Some families are brought closer together as a result of their open expression of feelings. Others develop considerable resentment and the patient becomes a source of chronic stress and a burden to the family. The character of family adjustment prior to the illness can be a very important factor in post-illness coping. The pressures of illness and disability can cause a basically stable family unit to mobilize resources to deal with the crisis and to adjust to the long-term effects of the illness. In a well-functioning family system, individuals adjust their roles with respect to one another and cope with the difficulties that illness and disability can bring.

Box 12.5 examines the effectiveness of "psychoeducational care" for patients with a variety of chronic diseases. Psychoeducational programs not only provide chronically ill patients with information, but they also use a variety of approaches to help patients and their families cope with what are often complex and demanding treatment regimens.

BOX **12.5**
Research Close-up

Psychoeducational Care for Chronic Diseases: Meta-analysis Shows That It Works!

Today, mortality from chronic conditions, such as cardiovascular and pulmonary disease, is significantly lower than it was just a few decades ago. The likely reason for this reduction is a combination of better acute care and better rehabilitation. Much of the recent focus of rehabilitation has been on enhancing primary health habits such as physical activity, fitness, and a healthy diet, as well as on avoiding or quitting smoking and reducing stress. Patients with chronic disease are encouraged to live as normal and as satisfying a life as they can. In order to do so, many need to undergo a formal retraining of their habits and to be taught how to initiate and maintain changes in their lifestyles. As we saw in Chapter 6, health information is not enough to change behavior, and more comprehensive health promotion programs (which combine affective, behavioral, cognitive, and educational interventions) result in the highest levels of patient adherence to treatment.

Several important reports from the area of patient counseling and health education show that the method of "psychoeducational care" does well in promoting adherence to treatment for at-risk and chronic conditions. Psychoeducational care involves education, behavioral change, and psychosocial support. In the realm of treating chronic obstructive pulmonary disease such as emphysema, for example, psychoeducational care programs include pulmonary rehabilitation, exercise training, and a variety of educational and supportive interventions. Such programs can be expensive, however, and so it is vitally important to assess their effectiveness in improving health and reducing medical problems.

Studies assessing the effectiveness of psychoeducational care rely on "meta-analysis," a methodology we first introduced in Chapter 1. Meta-analysis statistically combines the results from a number of research studies in order to yield an overall answer to a specific research question. A meta-analysis by Devine and Pearcy (1996), for example, has shown that among studies of psychoeducational care for patients with chronic obstructive pulmonary disease, 30 percent more patients had better physical functioning if they participated in psychoeducational care than if they did not (based on eight studies), and 27 percent more patients had better oxygen volume levels (based on five studies). In a meta-analysis of studies of patients with asthma, psychoeducational care was found to reduce asthma attacks (27% difference based on eleven studies) and to increase patient adherence (36% difference based on seven studies) (Devine, 1996). Among hypertensive patients, psychoeducational care lowered blood pressure (28% difference based on seventy-six studies) and improved medication compliance (34% difference based on seventeen studies) (Devine & Reifschneider, 1995). In a meta-analysis of nineteen studies of psychoeducational care for back problems (sometimes called "back school"), there was improved strength and spinal mobility and considerably reduced pain (14% difference) (DiFabio, 1995).

Let's look more intensively at psychoeducational care programs for patients who have had a heart attack. These programs focus on stress management and on health education and behavior change (supporting patients to alter their diets, increase their physical activity, and stop smoking). Using the meta-analysis methodology, Dusseldorp and colleagues analyzed thirty-seven studies that provided information on the outcomes of these programs for heart attack victims (Dusseldorp et al., 1999). Overall, the data suggest that with psychoeducational care, deaths from heart attack were reduced by approximately 34 percent and subsequent heart attack rates were reduced by 29 percent. Furthermore, these patients had lower blood pressure, better cholesterol levels, and they smoked less, exercised more, and had better eating habits than heart attack patients who did not have psychoeducational care.

The effects of psychoeducational care on health in the control of chronic disease are significant. Providing patients with information and helping them to make needed behavioral changes can significantly improve their health and functioning and may even lengthen their lives. Obviously, the patients themselves need to make and follow through with the commitment to alter their health behaviors, but psychoeducational care can offer them a pathway as well as support and motivation for change.

Chronic Illness and the Aged

Kate Quinton is an 80-year-old widow who lives in Brooklyn, New York, with Claire, one of her two daughters. Claire Quinton is unmarried, in her 50s, and has cared for her aging mother for many years. Kate's other daughter, Barbara, lives in New Jersey with her husband and is in conspicuous conflict with Claire about how their mother should be cared for. From her vantage point in the suburbs, uninvolved with her mother's day-to-day life and emotionally distant from her mother and sister, Barbara believes that her mother belongs in a nursing home. But Claire, who cares for all of her mother's needs despite her own extensive spine problems, believes that her mother should remain at home where she can maintain her spirits and live a fairly independent life.

The Quintons are a real family, described in a book by Susan Sheehan called *Kate Quinton's Days* (Sheehan, 1997). This book clearly describes the plight of many elderly people and their families and the huge burden that can be placed upon the caregivers of the elderly. The story of the Quintons also demonstrates how difficult it can be for an elderly, chronically ill person to avoid being committed to a nursing home. One incident in the winter of 1982 started the process that brought Kate to the brink of being put into a nursing home and began Claire's struggles to care adequately for her mother. Kate had severe abdominal pain and, unable to reach their family physician, Claire called a physician service that sent a doctor to make a house call. The doctor visited, charged $40, and recommended that Kate be taken to the emergency room of the hospital. He recommended an ambulance service, for which Claire paid $90. Kate and Claire were then living on only $271.10 per month, which constituted Kate's monthly Social Security benefit (Claire was unemployed). Thus, this single incident cost them roughly half of their monthly subsistence. In the hospital, Medicare paid the bill. But, the elderly Kate was subjected to extensive testing even after the source of her problem, a urinary tract infection, was identified and treated. The doctors tested her to check for malignancies, even though Kate, at 80 years old, might not have even wanted to be treated for cancer if it were found. Kate was considerably weakened and debilitated by these tests, and within a few weeks the doctors and nurses suggested that she be transferred to a nursing home. They told Claire that the nursing home care would be temporary, "to regain her strength," but, as Sheehan noted, many older people who go to a nursing home stay there permanently.

Claire considered the nursing home, because she herself had a severe, painful back problem after having had several unsuccessful back surgeries. She eventually rejected the nursing home offer, however, and was glad to learn that her mother was eligible for a home care program sponsored by New York City. This program was one designed to help loved ones care for their aged relatives at home. The program involved home attendants who could clean up the house and care for Kate, lifting her when necessary and generally doing things that Claire could not do. In practice, however, Claire found the program lacking in many ways. The home care attendants messed up the house more than they cleaned it, and they were not careful to prevent the aged Mrs. Quinton from being injured. Paid minimum wage by the city, these attendants arrived late, left early, and quit after only a few weeks. Medicare paid Kate's medical bills because she was over 65 and qualified for government healthcare assistance. Yet without supplemental insurance the care was inadequate. She needed special shoes because of her severe arthritis, but she had to wait a long time to get them. Claire spent weeks trying to find an optometrist who would take the reduced payments from Medicare so that her mother could have glasses, and several more weeks finding a dentist who would make Kate's dentures for the Medicare payment. Claire persisted in caring for her mother, although her own life was severely restricted. She was constantly fearful that her mother would have another medical crisis. Her one enjoyable weekend in years was spent when a friend came to visit her and they went to the movies twice in the same weekend. Faced with the option of institutionalizing a mother whose intellectual faculties were quite intact, Claire chose the difficult route of home care, with great cost to herself.

There are many myths about those over age 65, individuals whom many term "the elderly." Perhaps one of the most prevalent of those myths is that most old people are shut off in nursing homes, alone and uncared for by their families. This is far from the truth, however. As we will see in this section, although many older people do have certain physical, social, and financial limitations, many are also able to live gratifying, independent lives. Furthermore, their loved ones, particularly their spouses and children, do a great deal to care for most elderly. Sometimes, as we see in the case of Claire Quinton, above, these loved ones deliver such care at great personal sacrifice.

Losses of Old Age

One of the major tasks of old age is adapting to the many losses that accompany the last decades of life. In 1995, 32 percent of women and 24 percent of men who were over the age of 70 and not institutionalized reported having some difficulty in performing **activities of daily living (ADL)**, such as getting up from the bed or a chair, bathing, dressing, using the toilet, and eating (NCHS, 1998). Between 12 and 15 percent of these people had to have help from others in order to accomplish at least one of their ADLs. As we saw earlier, the major developmental task of late adulthood is establishing a sense of ego integrity (a feeling that one's life has been worthwhile) instead of despair. The losses typical of late adulthood, particularly if one has not yet accomplished all that one desires, may interfere with feelings of ego integrity, and thus contribute to despair. The necessity of relinquishing certain responsibilities is often difficult and may make an older person feel that he or she is "losing" some of the things that were accomplished in life.

The uncertainty that is associated with chronic illness is often greater for older people than it is for those who are younger. It is difficult to relinquish one's independence at any age, and most elderly people face this task at some point, particularly after a serious event like a stroke. A recent study examined the beliefs that older people had about their prognosis following a stroke and found that they tended to assume that if they just focused enough energy and effort, their recovery was bound to happen. They often received ambiguous responses from their medical care providers regarding their likely outcomes, and this helped to fuel their expectations for recovery. What they were not told tended to affect their expectations about recovery just as much as what they were told. These stroke patients were much more likely to be disappointed when their anticipated recovery did not occur or was not as complete as they had imagined it would be (Becker & Kaufman, 1995).

Socially, the elderly are sometimes hampered by the negative stereotypes held about them by members of the younger generations (e.g., Burggraf & Barry, 1998; Slotterback & Saarnio, 1996). Younger people often see the elderly as very different from themselves. Certain stereotypes about what the elderly can and cannot do may significantly limit their employment possibilities and interfere with their interpersonal relationships. Stereotypes can even affect caregivers such as physicians, nurses, counselors, and therapists. Less may be expected of the elderly than of younger people, and the concerns of elderly patients may be downplayed or ignored.

Health psychologists like to use the following brief conversation to illustrate a point about the interactions among doctors and elderly patients.

> **MRS. JONES:** Doctor, my right leg hurts and I can't walk on it any more.
> **DOCTOR:** Well, what do you expect Mrs. Jones? You're 80 years old!
> **MRS. JONES:** But Doctor, my left leg is also 80 years old, and it feels fine.

The concerns of many elderly patients are not taken seriously by many health providers, who hold stereotyped beliefs that suffering and limitations are a part of aging.

Many elderly people face financial difficulties. Those who are not affluent may be forced to live on fixed incomes from social security. Many have no pensions. With no private health insurance to supplement it, many must rely solely on Medicare, a federal healthcare reimbursement system that provides them with coverage of their healthcare costs but severely limits the services available. Many elderly meet with the frustrations described above in the story of the Quintons, including long waits for sometimes inadequate services.

Many elderly also must cope with such emotional losses as the deaths of their spouses and friends. Some have very limited contact with their children, who may have moved away to live their own independent lives. Because of a narrowing of their social networks, many elderly people are lonely. In fact, research has found that about a quarter of the elderly describe themselves as severely lonely (Hendrick et al., 1982; Revenson, 1986). Depression is also a common symptom in the aged. Depression in

Nursing home care typically involves the provision of all aspects of care for the elderly client. For example, he or she is bathed, dressed, and fed. But, provision of these services may not always be to the benefit of the elderly person. For example, someone who can maintain independence by dressing, washing, and self-feeding may cease to attempt such activities when these are carried out for him or her. In such an atmosphere of complete care, the elderly person may learn to become helpless and depressed.

Research indicates that people in nursing homes generally wish that they had more choices than they actually have (Jirovec & Maxwell, 1993). In addition, people adjust better to moving to a nursing home if they feel that they have some choice in where they go; if the components of the move are predictable, social support is available, and the move is seen as challenging rather than as a threat (Armer, 1993). Dependency and depression can be minimized or avoided when the elderly person is able to exert some control over his or her environment and carry out responsible actions.

A sense of control for a nursing home patient can be achieved relatively simply; one interesting and classic study examined the effects of control on the morale and health of the institutionalized elderly (Langer & Rodin, 1976). Patients on one floor of a nursing home (the experimental group patients) were given a plant to care for and were asked to choose when they would like to participate in some of the activities available to them in the nursing home. Patients on another floor (the comparison group patients) were also given a plant but were told that the staff would take care of it for them. They participated in the same activities as the first group, but were not allowed to choose when they would do so. Several weeks later, nurses rated the moods and activity levels of the patients. Those patients who had experienced the intervention were rated as more active and as having greater psychological well-being than were the control group patients. A year later, patients who had been given control in the experiment were still healthier than their counterparts both physically and mentally, and more of them were still alive (Rodin & Langer, 1977).

Further research evidence shows that the *possibility of control* must remain in effect in order for a successful outcome to be maintained. If nursing home patients are first given a chance to control their environment and then that control is taken away, they may be worse off than before they were given control (Schulz, 1976).

The desire for successful aging, rather than simple preservation of life, is probably universal. A recent review indicates that people who are able to adapt to changes, who have someone they can talk to about important issues, and who feel that there is a deeper purpose to life than just survival are those who age most successfully (Solomon & Peterson, 1994). Further, because older age is, almost without exception, associated with increasing levels of dependence, it has been suggested that dependence be viewed not as an indicator of deterioration but instead as a developmental change that allows for emotional growth and reciprocity for both the caregiver and care receiver (Motenko & Greenberg, 1995). That is, the elderly person and caregiver may have the chance to grow closer and to spend meaningful time together. This is an opportunity for the caregiver to experience the fulfillment of giving back something to a loved one, and the recipient's acceptance of such help may be an important component in making the exchange satisfying for both parties.

In this chapter, we have examined chronic illness across the life span. We have considered how chronic illness affects people at many different stages of their development. We have seen that the strength and character of the impact of chronic illness on the individual's life depends, to a great extent, upon the point in development that the illness is manifested. We have also noted that the patient is rarely the only person affected by his or her chronic illness. Friends and particularly family members often suffer a great deal. The conduct of their lives is altered; their plans for the future are threatened; and their empathy for the patient can make the illness almost as frightening and emotionally painful for them as it is for the victim. We have also seen how illness can affect parents, siblings, and children of the victim, and we have examined how individuals cope with chronic illness in old age. Finally, we considered the factors that affect institutionalization of the elderly and the role of environmental control on the elderly person's adjustment in a nursing home.

Summary

1. Chronic conditions involve disease or impairments in structure and/or functioning; limitations are common, and control but not cure is possible.

   - Chronic conditions are very common; over 22 million Americans suffer such limitations; they vary greatly by age.
   - Symptom control is a major challenge for the chronically ill individual.
   - Nonadherence to treatment regimens is a common problem; regimens may be complex and time-consuming.
   - Self-help groups can provide social support as well as practical tips.
   - The uncertainty of symptom progression can be challenging.

2. Maintaining social ties is a major task for the chronically ill; members of the social network can become alienated. Once adjustments to the illness are made, fulfilling relationships may be deepened by illness or disability.

3. Planning for the future can be a major hurdle. Those who develop contingency plans fare better than those who have only a single plan.

   - Those with more flexibility in their coping styles tend to adjust better.

4. Issues related to chronic illness for children and adolescents are unique.

   - Illness in infancy may interfere with the development of trust and secure attachment for the child.
   - In early childhood, illness may impede autonomy and independence.
   - Self image and personal competence are important developmental issues for school-age children, and illness may interfere with these.
   - Adolescents may experience difficulties in uniquely expressing themselves, forming close peer bonds, and moving away from parental control when they are chronically ill.

- For all children and adolescents, peer social relationships are influenced by illness; having a close friend helps children and adolescents to minimize the negative impact of their illness.
- Families vary a great deal in their ability to deal effectively with a chronically ill child. Openly discussing the child's condition and making the tasks of care a normal part of everyday life are important predictors of success.

5. Chronic illness in adulthood requires unique coping skills.

- For adults who have been chronically ill or disabled since childhood, there may be deficits in social functioning.
- For young adults, career development and creating an intimate partnership are prime developmental issues that can be interfered with by chronic illness and disability.
- For middle-aged adults, chronic illness brings a shift in roles and responsibilities, requiring substantial adjustment.
- Children who must care for their disabled or chronically ill parent may assume roles for which they are not ready.

6. Although stereotypes of the elderly portray them as lonely and uncared for, this is not often the case; loss is an important component of aging.

- Socially, older adults are sometimes hampered by the negative stereotypes held about them by younger people, even their own health professionals.
- Many elderly individuals may face their own physical incapacities and those of their spouse. Emotional losses associated with the deaths of friends, or of the spouse, make coping more difficult.
- Family members can help to ease the strain associated with the losses of aging, both through physical care and through emotional support.
- In a nursing home, individuals who feel some control and independence fare better than those who do not.

THINKING CRITICALLY

1. Imagine the life of a 22-year-old who suffers from cerebral palsy and who has been confined to a wheelchair since childhood. Compare this to the life of a 22-year-old who was in a boating accident a year before and is now confined to a wheelchair. How might the perspectives of these two individuals differ? How does your analysis involve the issue of developmental opportunities as described by Erikson?

2. What are the unique challenges faced by a person who is chronically ill but who has an "invisible" illness—one that is not obvious

to other people? Clearly, there are some ways in which being able to hide illness is easier than dealing with an obvious condition. On the other hand, can you think of reasons why invisibility might make illness or disability even more difficult to deal with?

3. What can a parent do to maximize opportunities for a chronically ill child to have a "normal life"? How can this parent maintain a positive environment for the ill child's siblings?

4. Given what you know about independence and a sense of control for the elderly, how would you structure a nursing home to

maintain the highest levels of functioning and quality of life for its residents? Since most residents are unlikely to say that they actually *like* living in a residential care facility, how would you know if you had truly created a positive living environment?

GLOSSARY

Accommodative coping: Coping by setting goals but being flexible.

Activities of daily living (ADL): Activities that are carried out as a part of everyday life, such as getting up, walking, bathing, dressing, cooking, and eating.

Assimilative coping: Coping by setting goals and persistently pursuing them in an unaltered form; potentially problematic if continuing to strive unrealistically.

Bronchial asthma: A respiratory condition marked by swelling of and spasm in the bronchial passages, making it difficult to expel carbon dioxide and take in oxygen.

Chronic condition: Impairment or deviation from normal physical structure and functioning that remains permanent; usually accompanied by residual disability.

Close social network: An individual's extended family and close friends.

Epilepsy: A disease that affects the nervous system, causing seizures that range from barely noticeable to severely incapacitating.

Family of commitment: An individual's spouse and children.

Family of origin: An individual's parents (and stepparents) and siblings.

Identity spread: Overgeneralization from an individual's actual limitations to additional expected limitations.

Insulin dependent diabetes mellitus (IDDM): Type I diabetes; a chronic metabolic disorder. It affects about 150,000 children and their families and is treatable but not curable; it requires careful adherence to a complex treatment regimen.

Multiple sclerosis (MS): A disease in which cellular changes in the brain and spinal cord disrupt proper nerve transmission; affects about 350,000 Americans. MS is a major cause of chronic disability in young adults.

Myelin: Material essential to the synaptic transmission of nerve impulses; destruction of myelin such as in MS can cause neurological symptoms that are in some cases transient, in others chronic, and in others severely degenerative.

Normalizing: The process of hiding symptoms as much as possible so that they remain unnoticed by others. Sometimes arrangements to normalize must be ingenious and elaborate.

Passing: Efforts by an ill or impaired individual to find ways to hide symptoms and limitations and to live a relatively independent life.

Peritoneal dialysis: Dialysis involves the process of cleansing the blood of impurities, a task carried out by the kidneys unless they have been damaged in some way. Peritoneal dialysis involves the installation of a solution in the abdominal cavity overnight.

Work of worrying: The process of rehearsing various alternative plans and courses of action when faced with a life change or stressful life event.

Facing Death

The possibility of death hangs over everyone, but death is particularly salient to those who are ill. Any illness or injury that carries more than a negligible chance of mortality brings a terrifying confrontation with the fact that one's life may soon be over. In some cases, death can be almost a certain outcome. Facing his or her own death is probably the most difficult task of an individual's development. Death brings the loss of everyone and everything that a person loves. Every aspect of life that one may have taken for granted suddenly seems intensely valuable; the certainty of its loss is acutely painful (Kübler-Ross, 1969).

One's feelings about death depend partly upon how one conceives of death in the first place, and particularly upon how much one fears it. Those with a strong religious orientation are often very much at peace in the last days of their lives because their world view holds that there is an afterlife during which they will be happy. Often, fear of death reflects an individual's difficulty in facing the incompleteness of his or her life. Death may seem like a premature and unfair revoking of one's potential (Kübler-Ross, 1969).

A young surgeon, stricken with Hodgkin's disease and facing the possibility of a premature death, was grief-stricken at the idea that he may not have a chance to see how his life would turn out. He found that the thought of being absent from the important milestones in the lives of his wife and children made him immensely sad (Shlain, 1979).

Uncertainty

For those who are in remission from a fatal disease and who do feel relatively (albeit temporarily) well, there are different problems. The physical tortures may give way to the psychological ones. People are plagued by massive uncertainty about the most important of issues, their own survival. A 31-year-old poet, dying of leukemia, wrote: ". . . in the year of my death, this year, month unknown . . ." (Rosenthal, 1970). How should one spend time in the face of this uncertainty? Should one go back to work, seeing one's children only during the evenings and weekends, or quit work and take them to the park, the mountains, and the ocean? Almost invariably there are differing opinions from doctors about when one is likely to die. There are no certainties. The patient "plays the odds" and takes risk with the remaining time, not knowing how much of it there really is. A patient whose cancer was in remission, possibly soon to recur, or possibly gone forever, noted how difficult it was for him to be living on "two tracks." The chances were good that he was going to survive, but he also felt a certain caution to work less and spend time with his family, ". . . take many vacations and try to live a quality life, and God knows that's hard enough to do" (Shlain, 1979, p. 182).

The Patient's Experience of Dying

Suppose you knew for sure that you had six months to live. Most likely you would try to spend the time in a way that was enjoyable and meaningful for you. You might quit school and take a trip around the world, pay off old debts, or even run up new ones.

You might do things you had always been afraid to try. This, of course, is an abstract consideration because it assumes that your physical condition allows you to carry out your plans. By its very nature, however, terminal illness causes patients to become weak and sick and to require a great deal of medical and nursing care. They are often prevented from spending their remaining time in the ways they wish. Attempts to "buy more time" with treatments may keep them ill and in the hospital. Healthy, enjoyable time between diagnosis and the end of life may be limited and precious.

In most cases, death does not come unexpectedly; there is time to think about it and to prepare for it. Until fairly recently, however, the psychological reactions of the terminally ill were virtually ignored by medical professionals in the United States. Even when a patient's condition was obviously hopeless, most physicians would act as if the issue of dying was irrelevant. They would continue to fight the disease long past the point of any hope for recovery. At best, the family might be told to get the patient's affairs in order. The patient would face a conspiracy of silence, however, and be denied the truth and a chance to choose the way that he or she preferred to spend the final days of life. While this is still true in some countries, in the United States things have changed.

The pioneering work of psychiatrist Dr. Elizabeth Kübler-Ross influenced this process a great deal (Kübler-Ross, 1969). She clearly demonstrated that most dying patients were already well aware that they were terminally ill, even though no one had explicitly told them. They knew that they were not getting better, and they received many clues from the behavior of others toward them. Their physicians would avoid their questions and spend very little time with them. Their family members would try to smile but have tears in their eyes. Kübler-Ross found that not only were dying people able to hear the truth, they desperately wanted to talk about their feelings about dying.

Thanks to the work of Dr. Kübler-Ross, attitudes toward dying patients have changed dramatically over the past several decades. Now, almost all physicians tell patients the truth about their medical conditions. They tell them the likely prognosis as well as the best and the worst that can be expected and try to do so in a compassionate and supportive manner. Nurses and other medical professionals, such as psychologists and social workers, are often available to help terminally ill patients and their families accept and deal emotionally with the prognosis.

Stages of Dying

Researchers in the field of **thanatology** (the study of death and dying) have learned a great deal about how people react psychologically to terminal illness (Kastenbaum, 1977; Kastenbaum & Aisenberg, 1972; Kübler-Ross, 1969). Initially, many people attempt to deny the facts they have learned or else to deny the meaning of those facts. A patient may be told that he or she is suffering a recurrence of leukemia and that the chances of experiencing another remission (temporary arresting of the disease) are very low. The day after hearing the news, he or she may ask the doctor when it will be permissible to leave the hospital and go back to work. When questioned, the patient might remember nothing of what he or she has been told. When told again, the patient may laugh as if hearing a joke. The patient might then explain to the doctor that there's been a mix-up of charts and that it is really someone else who is dying. The patient may make commitments to do things many months or years in the future. Denial stems from tremendous anxiety and represents an attempt to keep the threatening facts from entering consciousness. (The patient who knows and acknowledges the truth, but prefers to put it out of mind while trying to do everything possible to improve the chances of survival, is not exhibiting denial, however; such a patient is taking positive action.) The patient's immersion in denial may change from time to time. A patient might gradually allow into consciousness the threatening details of the condition and the meaning of those details, and as time passes come to accept the information and succeed in incorporating it into his or her emotional life.

Some patients become extremely angry when they receive a diagnosis of terminal illness, as they become overwhelmed with anxiety. The angry terminally ill patient may threaten to sue the physician, make accusations of incompetence, or seek many medical opinions. Such anger can have both good and bad consequences. The angry patient might be motivated to find the most modern and effective treatment for his or her condition, or to find health professionals who are the most knowledgeable and experienced with his or her particular disease. Such active involvement in getting the things that are needed might actually help the patient to survive longer and with a better quality of life than a patient who is passive (Molassiotis et al., 1997). Anger can be a manifestation of the will to live and to fight for life. Expressions of anger toward others, however, can alienate those close to the patient and reduce the chances of social support. The patient might cause loved ones to withdraw emotionally at a time when he or she needs considerable emotional support.

Some patients engage in "bargaining" in an effort to survive. A patient might volunteer to participate in a research project and serve as a subject to test a new drug or treatment. The patient assumes the role of a test subject in an effort to achieve a cure. This kind of behavior can be quite rational, for it may vastly increase the patient's chances of surviving. Other forms of bargaining might have a less direct effect. The religious patient might promise to be a better person and lead a perfect life if only given another chance. Such thoughts might make the patient feel better emotionally, but they could prevent him or her from also taking certain practical actions necessary to increase the chances of survival (see Figure 13.1).

Depression is a common response to a terminal prognosis and can occur immediately or after some delay. Depression often results after many failed efforts to change the course of the illness, or it can be the reaction of a patient who has given up without a fight. Some mental health professionals argue that depression is an inevitable, and perhaps even necessary, state for the terminally ill patient to experience while disengaging from life. Depression involves giving up, however, and no longer fighting for survival; the person might miss opportunities to battle the disease or to live any remaining time in satisfying and enjoyable ways.

Some patients do arrive at acceptance of the inevitability of death in a peaceful manner and strive to understand and come to terms with the meaning of their own lives. The patient who has accepted death gradually withdraws physically and emotionally from the surrounding world and becomes less and less involved in life's activities. There is some evidence that acceptance of death, although it is related to better *planning* for death, is also associated with greater hopelessness and even shorter survival

FIGURE 13.1   **The uncertainty inherent in life.**

times (Griffin & Rabkin, 1998; Molassiotis et al., 1997). Certainly, after experiencing considerable pain and exhaustion fighting for life, the patient might finally come to see death as a welcome relief.

The five reactions examined above—denial, anger, bargaining, depression, and acceptance—are exhibited by many, although by no means all, dying patients. Dr. Kübler-Ross originally proposed the reactions as stages, although others who have followed her in the study of death and dying have modified her theory in recognition of the fact that a stage model cannot always account for the transitions that patients undergo (Schulz & Aderman, 1974). Clinical observation has shown that some patients experience these five reactions in the order that they are described, but many patients do not. The order of reactions, and indeed whether they appear at all, can be influenced by the characteristics of the terminal disease or condition among other things. Remission might, for example, return a patient who has accepted death as inevitable back to the stage of denial that he has a serious disease at all. Even Dr. Kübler-Ross did not argue that all stages must occur in a particular order. She recognized that dying is an extremely complex and personal process, affected by a variety of circumstances too vast to be packaged neatly into a set of stages. Nonetheless, healthcare professionals sometimes expect that patients will follow the pattern as it has been presented in Kübler-Ross's writings (Silver & Wortman, 1980). They may become frustrated with the unpredictability of patients who do not experience the stages as they "should" and may try to pressure patients to follow the stages.

Anxiety and Loneliness

Anxiety, although not included as one of Kübler-Ross's stages, is a very common response to finding out that one has a terminal illness. Anxiety often remains, at least to some degree, until death occurs. Many things related to terminal illness are highly anxiety provoking: the fear of sudden death during surgery; the fear of being constantly sick, weak, nauseated, or in severe pain due to the illness or its treatment; and the fear of slowly losing faculties, until there is little quality left in one's life. Kübler-Ross once pointed out that of all the fears that dying patients have, the greatest one is the fear of being left alone and abandoned. Social isolation and loneliness are indeed major problems for the terminally ill. Those who are dying are often afraid to talk with their loved ones about what is foremost on their minds; they may be afraid to burden their family and friends, or to "break down" emotionally. Terminally ill people sometimes have difficulty maintaining normal social relationships because they have a very distressing identity: that of a "dying person" whose presence reminds others of their own mortality.

Choosing Death

Terminal or chronic debilitating illnesses may cause a person's quality of life to diminish to such a degree that life seems to be no longer worth living. Certain conditions are truly "worse than death" for some patients. When patients are in a great deal of pain, have no hope for the future, and can no longer do any of the things in life that bring them happiness, they may see death as a less threatening option than the struggle of life (Ditto et al., 1996). Consider the reactions of a patient who weighed his options and decided that death was more suitable than life.

> Brent was only 28 when he was diagnosed with Lou Gehrig's disease, a debilitating illness in which paralysis gradually takes over the body. Death is eventually due to choking or asphyxiation. Brent had a loving family to take care of him, and he was able to enjoy many things over the three years of his illness. By the time he was 31, however, he had very little functioning left, and his condition continued to worsen. He talked candidly with his physician about what his final months would be like. He was already unable to move and had to be fed pureed foods because he could barely chew or swallow. He was weak and in a good deal of pain. His physician explained to him that there were things that could be done to keep him alive for quite some time, but that eventually his paralysis would stop him from breathing, and he would die by suffocation.
>
> Brent also learned that he could allow himself to die more peacefully by refusing to eat or even to drink. By not being fed intravenously and taking only enough water or ice chips to satisfy his thirst, he could slowly slip into unconsciousness and death. This decision may have been easier for him because he had no wife or children. He preferred to say goodbye to his parents and sisters while he could still mumble a few words of speech, and then fade peacefully.

The Patient Self-Determination Act, which was passed into law in 1990, requires medical facilities that treat Medicare and Medicaid patients to have written policies regarding patient options for life-sustaining treatments such as artificial breathing apparatus and intravenous feeding. Patients may choose whether they wish to have heroic measures taken in the event of a medical crisis, such as a heart attack. Some patients choose to create a "living will," which is a written statement of their wishes regarding life-sustaining measures. This document allows families and physicians to legally carry out the patient's wishes in the event that he or she is incapacitated. Even for patients who have a living will, however, there is no assurance that their wishes will be honored. Some physicians consider it their duty to preserve life at all costs and act in direct contradiction of the patient's wishes in order to keep patients from dying (Seneff et al., 1995). Box 13.1 examines the controversial issue of physician-assisted suicide and the man who brought this issue to the forefront, Dr. Jack Kevorkian.

BOX **13.1**

Hot Topic

Doctor Death

Dr. Jack Kevorkian, born in 1928 in Pontiac, Michigan, is a retired pathologist who has been known since the 1950s in certain circles as "Dr. Death"; it is said that this name reflected his early fascination with photographing the eyes of dying patients. In the late 1950s he gained some notoriety by presenting a paper at a professional meeting in which he advocated medical experiments on consenting convicts during their executions. In the 1980s he began writing about **euthanasia** (the process of acting to hasten the death of a terminally ill person) and outlining his ideas for "suicide clinics" in which individuals suffering from terminal illnesses could choose how and when to die.

On June 4, 1990, Dr. Kevorkian assisted his first suicide, a 54-year-old woman named Jane Adkins who was suffering from Alzheimer's disease. The suicide was accomplished with an injection of potassium chloride, using a machine (called the "mercitron") that Kevorkian made himself for about $30. Although he was charged with murder in that case, the charge was dismissed six months later. Since then he has helped at least 130 other people to end their lives, using a variety of different methods. In 1995 he opened a suicide clinic in Michigan, but was evicted soon after aiding the death of his first patient. Throughout the 1990s, he appeared in court often, but was always acquitted (three times) or had a mistrial (once). That is, until April 1999.

The case of Thomas Youk, a man suffering from Lou Gehrig's disease, was different. This patient was severely incapacitated and in pain, and he requested the help of Dr. Kevorkian to end his life. His family supported his decision and was in favor of the hastening of his death. Dr. Kevorkian, however, in his crusade for the right to die, had decided to videotape the assisted suicide, which occurred in September 1998. In November 1998, the videotape aired nationwide on CBS's "60 Minutes" television show, sparking an instant and ferocious controversy. Three days later Kevorkian was charged with first-degree murder.

In April of the following year, Kevorkian was convicted of second-degree murder and sentenced to 10 to 25 years in prison. The judge who heard the case stated that the "trial was not

(continued)

BOX **13.1**   (Continued)

about the political or moral correctness of euthanasia. . . . It was about lawlessness. It was about disrespect for a society that exists because of the strength of the legal system. No one, sir, is above the law. No one." Kevorkian, who acted as his own attorney, argued that in order to have a crime there must be vicious will and a vicious act, neither of which he had. Some acts, he said, "by sheer common sense are not crimes." Dr. Kevorkian plans to appeal.

Dr. Kevorkian's views are not without support in the medical community. A 1995 survey of physicians' attitudes toward assisted suicide showed that, under some circumstances, a large number of physicians do support assisted suicide. Much of the controversy seems to surround the criteria for establishing the "right to die." Many are worried that assisted suicide will be used disproportionately by, or against, the poor and underprivileged, or that it will be abused by family members who no longer want the burden of caring for their ill relative. Dr. Kevorkian has many supporters among the general public, as well. Particularly vocal are those who have watched a loved one suffer a protracted and painful death. They argue that death with dignity is something to which all human beings are entitled, and many view Kevorkian as a crusader and even a saint.

Caring for Terminally Ill Patients

Although the importance of open communication with patients regarding their prospects for survival is usually recognized, this knowledge does not always translate smoothly into the care that terminally ill patients actually receive. For instance, a recent study of the communication between 130 adults with advanced cancer and their doctors showed that almost 10 percent of them were unaware of their cancer diagnosis! One-fourth of those who did know their diagnosis said that the information had not been given to them in a caring and clearly understandable fashion. One-third of the patients did not understand their prognosis, and their pain was severely underestimated (by as much as 89%) by their physicians (Chan & Woodruff, 1997).

Hospitals are busy places, and hospital staff are not always able to provide the kind of emotional care that dying patients so desperately need. Patients at home have difficulties, too, as their families struggle with bills, additional family chores, and their own emotional trauma. There are, however, specific things that caregivers can do to understand terminally ill patients and help make their experiences more comfortable.

Children and Adolescents

Before age 5, children do not have a good understanding of what death is all about, and they are typically not afraid of it. Usually, they are unconcerned, or even curious, about death itself, but highly affected by the more concrete aspects of their illness. Young children are likely to be quite intimidated by the vast technical equipment found in the hospital, by the many strangers that come and go, and by the needles they must frequently endure and the distasteful concoctions they often have to swallow.

Children cope better when they are told what to expect (in simple terms), and when they have a parent close by so that they do not feel abandoned. The sensitivity and caring manner of health professionals are also extremely important. The "white coat phenomenon" that tends to hold for adults does not reliably translate to children, however. This refers to a situation in which the presence of a physician in a white coat results in anxiety and physiological arousal (namely higher blood pressure) in the adult patient (Stergiou et al., 1998; Verdecchia, 1999). Although some studies have demonstrated that some children do become somewhat more anxious in the presence of a formally clad physician (Hornsby et al., 1991), there is substantial evidence that children and even teens are not intimidated simply by a doctor wearing a white coat (as opposed to less formal street clothes), and in fact they may actually prefer the white coat (Matsui et al., 1998; McCarthy et al., 1999). Children do strongly prefer a smiling physician, and one who provides a pleasant treatment environment (McCarthy et al., 1999). Above all, it is the kindness, warmth, and understanding of health professionals, particularly in the face of the somberness of serious illness, that matter most to young patients and can make a great deal of difference in the provision of effective, humane care.

At some point between the ages of 5 and 10, children develop the concept of death and are generally afraid of it. Terminally ill children at this age fear what will happen to them after they die and may believe that "something" will come to take them away. Depending on the level of cognitive development of a particular child, more or less detail may be used in explaining the process of death, but research shows that it is not useful to try to hide a child's condition from him or her. Children who are dying often know much more about their condition than the adults around them realize (Bluebond-Langner, 1977; Spinetta, 1982). Also, there is some indication that terminally ill children (especially when they are very near death) have an unusually sophisticated understanding of the finality of death (O'Halloran & Altmaier, 1996). These

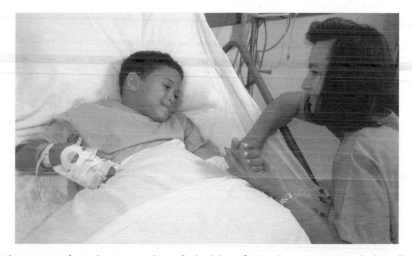

The kindness, warmth, and understanding of a health professional matter a great deal to all patients, especially children.

children must not be shortchanged, but must have their concerns addressed in a forth-right manner. Many times, parents use religious beliefs to soothe the child and to let him or her know that death is not scary but part of a natural progression, and that sep-aration from loved ones is only temporary.

Children may also find acceptance and understanding easier if they are allowed to participate in rituals that memorialize death in some way. For example, 6-year-old Andy who suffered from leukemia, was constantly preoccupied with what would hap-pen to him after he was dead. Where would he be put? Would his mom cry? Explana-tions about the funeral and heaven seemed to do little good, however, so his parents decided to hold a special funeral just for Andy. They and Andy planned it together. It was held in the family living room one Sunday afternoon, and several extended family members, as well as one school friend, were there. Andy chose the hymns that he liked best, and these were played on the stereo. Each of Andy's parents gave a short speech about how much they loved him, how they would miss him, and how they were anx-ious to see him again in heaven. Andy then gave his own speech about how he would miss his friends, his family, and his cats. He asked everyone to be sure to find him as soon as they got to heaven because he wanted to give them a tour. Then, everyone placed flowers in a beautiful box and went into the back yard for a BBQ with all of Andy's favorite foods. The "funeral" was not elaborate, and Andy's parents admitted that it was emotionally difficult. But, it clearly eased Andy's mind and aided his accep-tance of his own death, and for this reason they were very glad to have done it.

Adolescence is a time of struggle even for the healthy individual. Addressing one's own mortality at this early stage of life is uniquely traumatic (Carr-Gregg et al., 1997). Adolescents are likely to feel robbed of life. They will never have a career, a spouse, their own children, or many of the other things that typical adolescents take for granted. The emotional and physical availability of parents to their terminally ill ado-lescents is essential. Counseling of the patient with parents or other family members may suggest ways to best meet the needs of the patient and help everyone deal with the tremendous emotional stresses of impending loss.

Adults

For young through middle-aged adults, dealing with a terminal illness may be espe-cially difficult because it often means leaving behind one's spouse and children. Parents experience severely the loss associated with being unable to see their children grow up. This pain is particularly sharp if the children are very young, and terminally ill parents worry about their children's welfare. There is often the concern of leaving one's spouse to raise the children on his or her own. A supportive extended family network can help ease these concerns, letting the patient know that his or her children will be cared for.

Although dying is never easy, it may be somewhat less difficult for older adults than for younger ones. When a person has lived a "full life" there may be less of a sense that death is robbing one of opportunities. There is more chance for reflection on accomplishments rather than lamentations about what might have been. In addition, older adults may have had more experience with death, perhaps having seen some of their friends die or having lost their own parents. The prospect of dying may not be quite as shocking as it is for a younger person. For adults at all ages, putting one's life into perspective is important. It often makes people feel better to know that when they are gone they will not be forgotten. Leaving behind a legacy, whether it is children, books, works of art, or lives that have been touched, can make a great deal of difference in one's ability to accept death (Lifton, 1977).

There are some obvious ways in which counseling a terminally ill patient is very different from counseling a healthy individual, or even someone who is ill but expects to recover. In the latter cases, long-term plans can be made, and the focus of counseling tends to be on the future. In cases of terminal illness, the counseling relationship is likely to be cut short by the patient's condition, and it is impossible to focus on long-term goals. Instead, issues center around completing "unfinished business" and coming to view one's life as having been worthwhile. Patients may find it hard to view their lives as meaningful if there are things in their lives left undone, or if they have failed to accomplish tasks that are important to them. The therapist's work involves helping the patient to see the value in his or her life and accomplishments. One framework for caring for terminally ill patients proposes eight important elements, which are framed as "8 Cs" (Pusari, 1998). They are described in detail in Table 13.1. These elements are proposed to be essential for anyone who is attempting to provide holistic care to a dying individual—care that takes into account not just the person's physical needs, but also his or her emotional, spiritual, and cultural needs.

Hospice and Home Care

Earlier in this century, most terminally ill people died at home amidst their family members and friends, close to the day-to-day routines they enjoyed and with which they were familiar. Opportunities presented themselves constantly for loved ones to visit, express their deep feelings, and say goodbye. Children naturally learned the

---

TABLE 13.1 Elements of Care for the Terminally Ill Patient

1. *Compassion*: Having a deep sense of caring for the terminally ill individual and keeping his or her best interests at the forefront.

2. *Competence*: Utilizing appropriate methods of care and conducting them efficiently.

3. *Confidence*: Having a belief in oneself as an effective caretaker and a belief in the meaningfulness of the patient.

4. *Conscience*: Embodying a sense of integrity when dealing with the patient.

5. *Commitment*: Demonstrating that one will be there over the course of the illness and that one will not flee from difficulties brought about by the process of dying.

6. *Courage*: Having the strength to face head-on the difficult issues related to the patient's condition.

7. *Culture*: Taking social and cultural factors related to the process of dying into account.

8. *Communication*: Dealing openly with the patient regarding his or her illness and prognosis; being a good listener as well as an honest respondent.

Source: Pusari, 1998.

meaning of death and watched the transition of grandparents and other people they loved through old age to final peace. Since the advent of technological medicine (roughly the 1950s), however, the process of dying has become hidden away in acute care hospitals where there may be little if any acknowledgement that a patient's death is soon to come. Efforts are undertaken to resuscitate patients who will never get well. Death occurs amidst machines and strangers.

In 1975 in the United States, a powerful grassroots movement began that argued for and helped to promote an alternative to aggressive hospital care for the terminally ill. This alternative is called **hospice.** The number of hospices in the United States has now grown to several thousand, and they provide care not only for the dying patient but also for his or her family. The focus is not on cure but on alleviation of symptoms, particularly pain (Wall et al., 1993). The atmosphere is homelike and patients have considerable autonomy in making decisions about their care. Attention is given not only to the requirements for physical care but also to the emotional, social, and spiritual needs of the patient and family.

Hospice care is available in this country in inpatient settings as well as in home care (which involves visits from the staff daily or several times a week). Multidisciplinary teams of physicians, nurses, social workers, psychiatrists, psychologists, and physical therapists provide hospice services. Many hospices also provide some bereavement intervention, in preparation for the death as well as after the death, in an effort to promote adjustment among loved ones of the deceased. In all hospices, a great deal of attention is paid to the quality of the patient's life. Family members are encouraged to speak openly with the terminally ill loved one. There is an effort, in a supportive atmosphere, to promote closeness and expressions of love while the opportunity still exists to do so. Although the technical level of care is comparable, the hospice environment is much less stressful for the patient than is a traditional hospital (Adkins, 1984; Kane et al., 1985). While home care can be emotionally the most satisfying for the patient, studies do show that even with help from a home-based hospice program, home care can place tremendous stress on the other members of the family (Aneshensel et al., 1993). Hospices, which combine a family-like feeling with the support of a hospital or skilled nursing facility may, for many, be the best choice for palliative care.

Bereavement and Grieving

The death of a loved one can be emotionally devastating and one of the most stressful life events a person can experience. Recovery may be long and painful. Understanding the effects of death on survivors is essential if medical professionals are to intervene in an effective manner to help survivors cope. Healthcare professionals are typically involved in the process of death, either through the care they provide during terminal illness or through resuscitation attempts. They also typically inform the family in the case of accidents or sudden deaths. The extent of a health professional's contributions in helping survivors cope, of course, depends upon the nature of his or her relationship to the patient's family members and other loved ones. Health professionals, including psychologists, can provide information, education, and emotional support. They can help recognize clinically abnormal patterns of reactions and adjustment in those who have suffered a loss so that individuals who need help can get it. During a patient's terminal illness, healthcare staff can effectively establish themselves as resource persons for the family and friends of the patient and much can be done during the period of terminal illness to facilitate the adjustment of those to be left behind. Clarification of the patient's physical situation, accurate information about the cause of the condition, as well as ongoing updates of the patient's care, can be extremely important. Physicians can arrange for extended visiting hours so that patient and family can have privacy to talk openly with one another. Thus, it is important for healthcare professionals to understand the experience of survivors as well as to learn ways to help them cope with their own physical and emotional reactions.

Before examining the grief experience in more detail, let us define some important terms that we will be using in this section. **Bereavement** is the fact of loss through death. A person who survives the death of a loved one is bereaved. **Bereavement reactions** are psychological, physical, or behavioral responses to bereavement. **Grief** is the feeling or affective state associated with the condition of bereavement.

Grief Experiences

Sharon Myers sat and stared at the carpet in the air-conditioned coolness of the fluorescent-lit waiting room. She did not cry as she listened to her husband's doctor tell of their efforts to save him on the operating table. This was to have been a routine surgery, but her husband Pete was dead. What she was experiencing seemed completely unreal, and she felt that it simply couldn't be true. She must have said something to the doctor that made sense, because the doctor said again and again how sorry she was for Sharon's loss, and then she left. Sharon was alone in the waiting room for only a few minutes when the hospital chaplain came in and offered her a box of tissues. When he first asked her, she couldn't think of anyone to call, but then she remembered that her son and his wife were on their way to the hospital. She lay on the couch in the family room, clutching a pillow when her son and daughter-in-law arrived. She felt that she was in a dream, which she hoped would end soon.

Over the next few weeks, Sharon could hardly sleep. She usually spent the hours from 1 AM until 7 AM in front of the television, staring blankly at infomercials and old reruns. She wasn't hungry, but made it a point to eat at least something every day. She still went to church and talked to people, but when she came home she couldn't remember what she'd said, or what anyone might have said to her. She felt numb and dazed and experienced waves of sadness and a feeling of incredible emptiness. Sometimes she would start to make lunch or a pot of coffee for herself and Pete, and then remember that he was dead. She would start to ask him if he was ready for bed, then realize that she was alone in the living room. When she did sleep, she often had very vivid dreams that he was still alive, or that he was talking to her from the grave. She usually awoke from these with goosebumps and was unable to stop herself from sobbing.

The manner in which physicians break bad news to patients can affect grieving.

The grief reaction can be overwhelming to a person, both psychologically and physically. Not only is a person's mind affected, but his or her biological homeostasis is interrupted as well. Researchers have systematically observed and measured changes in emotions, thought patterns, and behaviors during grief. They have witnessed intense physical and psychological reactions. Although there is substantial individual variation in grief reactions, there are also many commonalties (Parkes & Weiss, 1983; Schuchter & Zisook, 1993). One of the most frequent responses following death of a loved one is shock, numbness, and a sense of disbelief. This tends to be true regardless of whether the loss was anticipated. Initially, those left behind feel as though things around them are unreal. They may express no emotion and appear to be holding up quite well. Illusions and misperceptions appear often in this early stage. There may be dreams in which the deceased person is still alive, and visual and auditory hallucinations of the dead person may even occur (Grimby, 1998). Once the bereaved comes to an emotional acceptance that the deceased person is really gone, however, these illusions usually diminish in frequency and eventually cease. The grieving person may experience difficulty concentrating, as well as feelings of anger, guilt, irritability, restlessness, extreme sadness, and/or a severely depressed mood.

During the period of acute grief, the bereaved person's movements are often slowed down, and he or she may have a slumped posture. Sometimes there is alternating agitation, restlessness, and increased motor activity. During periods of despair, the bereaved person may give up favorite activities and avoid socializing. Some may engage in excessive smoking and drinking and other health-compromising behaviors, particularly if they had been users of such substances before the death. These and other risk-taking behaviors likely represent an attempt to defend against the painful feelings of grief rather than to accept and work through them. It is important to note that although grief and depression may appear similar in terms of the individual's behavior, they are quite different in an important way. Both involve sadness and "vegetative" signs such as appetite and sleep disturbances, but depression usually also involves feelings of unworthiness or worthlessness, negative beliefs and thoughts about the self, and withdrawal from social networks.

Acute grief symptoms often come in waves of distress lasting several minutes and including agitation, crying, aimless activity, preoccupation with an image of the deceased, and sighing respirations. Chronic disturbances lasting anywhere from weeks to months include decreased concentration, anxiety, altered food intake, changes in body weight, sleep disturbances, and muscular weakness (Clayton, 1974; Lindemann, 1944; Parkes, 1972). Like many other severe stressors, grief frequently leads to changes in the endocrine, immune, nervous, and cardiovascular systems. There is evidence of higher adrenocortical activity, more catecholamine (stress hormone) secretion, changes in growth hormones, and increased prolactin activity for many who are bereaved (e.g., Calabrese et al., 1987; Kim & Jacobs, 1993; Syvalahti, 1987). Clearly, the process of bereavement upsets bodily homeostasis and places increased stress on the body. Bereavement has been associated with reduced natural killer (NK) cell activity, as well as increased levels of cortisol and lower levels of lymphocyte stimulation (Goodkin et al., 1996; Irwin et al., 1988; Schleifer et al., 1983). Thus, immunity seems to be significantly reduced. This may be true because bereavement is associated with increased levels of neuropeptides that activate the sympathetic nervous system. Some researchers suggest that this is the mechanism by which cellular immunity is moderated following a loss (Irwin & Pike, 1993). Those who become depressed following the death of a loved one are at greatest risk for impaired immune functioning (Zisook et al., 1994). On the other hand, in a study of asymptomatic, HIV-seropositive men followed over a 6-month period, those with an active coping style demonstrated better immune functioning than did those with a passive style. The authors suggest that support groups for the bereaved might not only help bereaved individuals deal more actively with their grief but also promote better physical health via immunologic pathways (Goodkin et al., 1996).

Several large-scale studies have demonstrated that mortality rates are significantly higher among the bereaved, particularly during the first year after their loss (e.g., Kaprio et al., 1987; Schaefer et al., 1995). Longitudinal studies have shown consistent causal patterns, showing that the death of a loved one is indeed a factor in the death of the bereaved. Researchers find that higher mortality rates tend to result from cancer, accidents, sudden cardiac death, and suicide, and that grief brings a higher incidence of such problems as cardiac arrhythmias, myocardial infarction, and congestive heart failure. Cardiac problems are thought to be accounted for by disturbances in autonomic cardiovascular regulation and in circulating catecholamines (such as adrenaline) that may exaggerate cardiac risk in patients who have preexisting cardiovascular regulation problems (of which they may even be unaware). As we saw in Chapter 9, psychological stress produces physiological reactions and it is understandable that a severe stressor, such as the loss of a loved one, could result in serious physical changes. Patients with heart conditions and hypertension are particularly prone to exacerbation of their conditions in response to threatened or actual loss of a human relationship (Osterweis et al., 1984).

The process of grieving sometimes results in outcomes that threaten the bereaved individual's sense of stability and forestall his or her recovery. For example, a person who has been bereaved may express psychological pain through physical symptoms. Acute grief is often associated with physical complaints including pain, gastrointestinal disturbances, and vegetative symptoms such as loss of energy, and sleep and appetite disturbances. Beyond these expected physical complaints, some bereaved individuals identify with the deceased by also taking on the symptoms that contributed to the loved one's death. One study found that 15 percent of bereaved persons reported feeling "just like" the person who died, 8 percent had acquired habits of the deceased, 12 percent felt they had the same illness, and 9 percent had pains in the same area of the body as the person who died (Zisook et al., 1982). Such physical symptoms may arise almost immediately, or many years after the death, and may reflect unresolved feelings of grief. When and if the grief is resolved, the symptoms usually disappear. See Figure 13.2 for an examination of the biopsychosocial effects of bereavement and grieving.

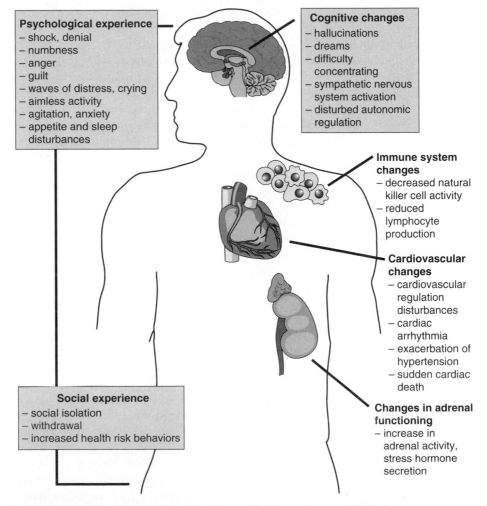

FIGURE 13.2   The biopsychsocial effects of bereavement and grieving.

Anniversary reactions can be particularly troubling. The feelings and symptoms triggered by bereavement can recur around birthdays, anniversaries, and holidays. In vulnerable persons, anniversaries can be more than just reminders of the deceased; they can trigger serious emotional reactions such as severe depression (Pollock, 1982). Reinvestment in new relationships, particularly a new marriage, might appear to signal acceptance of and adjustment to the death but although such apparent social adaptation has occurred, emotional adaptation may still be far behind. Many widowed men seemingly recover socially and even remarry well before they have recovered emotionally from their loss; women tend to delay social reinvestment, avoiding dating and remarriage until they have healed emotionally (Parkes & Weiss, 1983).

The character of the relationship that the bereaved person had with the deceased is one of the best predictors of bereavement adjustment (Parkes & Weiss, 1983; Zisook & DeVaul, 1985). If the bereaved had felt a significant amount of hostility toward the deceased, there is often a sense of remorse when the loved one dies; conflicted, ambivalent, or overly dependent relationships are less likely to be resolved successfully than unconflicted ones. Those who had been in relationships with a high level of marital conflict were found, in one study, to be twice as likely as those in low conflict relationships to be depressed, anxious, guilty, in poor health, and yearning for their deceased spouses as long as two to four years after the death (Parkes & Weiss, 1983).

The process of grieving involves development from a state of disbelief to one of gradual acceptance, although not usually in a straightforward fashion. The grieving person may go back and forth many times from avoidance of thinking about the deceased to cultivation of the person's memory, from acceptance of the loss, to immersion in a world of fantasies and dreams in which the deceased person is still alive. It may take a bereaved person months, or even years, to control depression and mood swings, to become settled emotionally, and to accept the death. Eventually, the grieving person is able to recall the deceased without being overwhelmed by sadness or emotions, and he or she may feel ready to reinvest in the world. Recovery may often take as long as two and a half years in the normal process of bereavement adjustment (Shlain, 1979).

Bereavement, of course, can bring changes in a person's social status, such as from being married to being widowed or from being a parent to being childless. The bereaved person may have had opportunities to socialize while part of a couple, but find fewer such opportunities as a single person. If friendships were tied up with the person who is deceased, making new friends may be very difficult. Although not a complete explanation, reduced (or complete lack of) social contact and support has been suggested as the link between increased mortality risk and bereavement (Stroebe, 1994). Widows typically have more social support available to them than do widowers, so this may partially explain the fact that men who lose their spouses are at higher mortality risk than women who lose their spouses (Stroebe et al., 1999).

The end of the grieving process can be called **recovery** or **adaptation**. Although the sense of loss may never be completely overcome, the bereaved person may develop a renewed hopefulness, the capacity to experience gratification, and adaptation to new roles. The completion of grieving can even have positive, growth-producing effects such as increased creativity and productivity (Pollock, 1982). Some older women who have been in traditional marriages and become widowed may find themselves with the time and opportunity to develop their full potential, assume responsibility for their own lives, and carry out activities, such as going back to school or traveling, that they had never been able to do before.

Cultural Influences on Grieving

Bereavement is a sociocultural phenomenon in that it typically affects not just one individual but an entire group of persons. While this may have been even more true in the past, when societies were organized with great emphasis on kinship, the death of an individual today can affect an entire extended family and community and bring people from diverse locations to share in common grief. **Mourning** is the social expression of grief; in every society there are mourning rituals and associated behaviors, such as the wearing of black by the bereaved. Partly because ethnic and religious ties today are weaker than they were several decades ago, there tend to be fewer social prescriptions regarding grieving and mourning. Rituals are no less important, however. The wake and funeral, for example, can help in adjustment to and recovery from the loss and can help families to express their grief. Mourning rituals such as the funeral bring together those who knew the deceased to confirm and validate the death and to facilitate expressions of support for those closest to the deceased. These rituals initiate transitions to new stages of personal identity (for example, from wife to widow) and provide for public articulation of private distress and reassertion of values such as family and friendship. Rituals help to re-moralize, through the expression of support from others, those who have been demoralized by loss. Grief responses tend to vary significantly by culture (Braun & Nicholas, 1997; Oltjenbruns, 1998), and sometimes it can be difficult to separate individual grief from culturally prescribed mourning (Rosenblatt, 1993). Cultural differences in grieving rituals within the family (for instance, by in-laws who do not share the same cultural norms) may create additional tensions and those who try to conform to the grieving norms of a culture other than their own may have difficulty coming to terms with the death. Box 13.2 examines cultural variations in the ritual of the funeral.

BOX 13.2

Across Cultures

Can You Spot the Funeral?

The young man came in a little bit late and found that the party was already well underway. He smiled when he heard the music—his father's favorite song. He arrived at a good time! He made his way to the end of the room, to a long table piled high with delicious food. He stopped to chat with a group of his friends who were talking animatedly. After he filled his plate, he went to sit with his father. He hugged him tightly and looked deep into the shining eyes that had loved him since his birth. "I'm glad you made it," his father chided, and then chuckled as he saw that he had embarrassed his son. "Your uncle has a story that you've got to hear!"

Another young man entered a dim chapel and immediately heard the organ music. It was a familiar hymn, one that his father had loved, and the sound of it brought tears to his eyes. As he made his way to the front pew, several friends reached out to rub his shoulder or pat his arm. When he looked at them he saw their sadness, and it made him feel both comforted and alone. He found a spot next to his mother, sat down, and after gathering his courage he looked at his father's peaceful face.

Which of these scenarios describes a death ceremony? You may have already guessed it— they both do. In all cultures, death is a significant event for the person who dies, as well as for those who are left behind. The differences between these two scenarios dramatically illustrate just how wide cultural variations in attitudes toward death can be! The "funeral" for the first young man's father took place long ago in an Eskimo tribe (Freuchen, 1961). "But," you may be thinking, "the father wasn't even dead! " In this particular tribe, the death ceremony is a special event where villagers and family members alike gather to help the elderly person make his or her way to the afterlife. The ceremony is very festive, with lots of food, music, and dancing. Even the person who is about to die is cheerful. When everyone has had a good time, and the celebration has neared its end, the elderly person chooses the individual who will help him die (usually the oldest son or the favorite child). After saying goodbye, a special rope is placed around the elderly person's neck and the rope is pulled over a beam in the roof. Because it is a great honor to help someone go to the afterlife, other partygoers might help by adding their weight to the rope.

The second "funeral" you read about is probably much more familiar. It is a traditional, North American, Christian ceremony with an open casket held in a church. You may have been to such a ceremony and have almost certainly seen one on the television or in a movie. The predominant emotion at this ceremony was grief, which is in stark contrast to the great happiness expressed at the Eskimo ceremony. Of course, there are many cultural variations both in the way death is approached and in the death ceremony itself. These differences are largely determined by what is believed in the culture to happen after death (Pickett, 1993). Some cultures (such as the traditional Japanese) view death as simply a transition to another state of being, or a different world. Such beliefs may help the living to accept the death and may also make it easier for a person to accept his or her own death. When death is seen as final, with no afterlife and no continuation of the soul, acceptance may be more difficult.

Health psychologists and other healthcare providers need to be aware of cultural norms regarding death when they work with dying patients and their families (Pickett, 1993). An "appropriate death" occurs when caregivers, family members, and the dying person are able to collaborate and communicate about the process of dying and about the rituals that they would like followed. Although there are certain expectations for the death process that most cultures share (such as dignity and respect), there are many differences in how death is viewed (Waters, 1999). Being aware of and accepting the death-related attitudes and traditions of many cultures can be particularly challenging, though extremely important, in a multicultural environment such as the United States.

Pathological Grief

There is little agreement about what constitutes "normal" versus "pathological" grief. Over the years, the norms regarding appropriate periods of grieving have changed considerably and the "accepted" length of the grieving period has generally been lengthened. There is also recognition that for a significant number of otherwise normal individuals, certain aspects of grieving may never be finished (Schuchter & Zisook, 1993). Clinicians and researchers have found that some people do persist in the intensity of their grief reactions despite the passage of a great deal of time. They become "stuck" in the grieving process, unable to diminish the intensity of their relationship with the deceased. Some experience excessive anger, guilt, self-blame, and depression for greatly extended periods of time. A person experiencing long-term, chronic grief may feel there is nothing left to look forward to and may still be grieving his or her loss after many years. Many widowed individuals never completely accept the death of their spouses (Stroebe & Stroebe, 1987; Zisook & Schuchter, 1985).

Complete lack of emotional involvement in the death is a related problematic pattern for some bereaved persons, and some individuals may even experience a total absence of feeling in response to their loss. They face neither distress nor the typical symptoms of grief. They deny their feelings and may even prevent other people from making references to the loss. They "fend off" threatening emotions that are too painful to bear. Typically, those who struggle with chronic grief feel too weak to undertake the tremendous emotional work of grieving. Instead, they may develop persistent symptoms of depression, sometimes masked for several years by a multitude of physical complaints (Baur, 1988).

Pathological grief, then, can be any grief that is greatly out of line with the "norm." If we think of the demonstration of grief as normally distributed, behavior at the extremes may be considered abnormal (Middleton et al., 1993). It has been suggested that the following categories of pathological grief exist:

1. Delayed (the grief experience is typical, but simply delayed)
2. Absent (there seems to be denial, with no overt expression of grief)
3. Chronic (prolonged grieving, with no indication of improvement, and involving high levels of guilt and distress)
4. Unresolved (prolonged, but with some indication of improvement)
5. Inhibited (in which the individual is completely unable to talk about the loss) (Middleton et al., 1993).

Contrary to typical psychological advice (which is to focus on and work through emotionally painful topics), some researchers have found that when dealing with the death of a loved one, it may be better to avoid too much thinking about the death and constant attempts to try to make sense of it (Bonanno et al., 1995). This may be particularly true in cases where the person who died was young, and the death is especially difficult to understand. As we noted in Chapter 10 regarding the topic of coping, in many difficult situations taking action to improve reality—and dealing with a problem rather than avoiding it—is often the best approach. Loss through death is a very different situation, however, because nothing can be done to bring the deceased back. In the case of bereavement, some individuals may find it easier to adjust to their circumstances if they do not allow themselves to spend too much time ruminating over their loss.

Anticipatory Grieving versus Sudden Death

Is it easier to cope with a death that has been anticipated or one that has happened suddenly? There is disagreement among experts about whether emotional responses to the impending death of a loved one are comparable to grief and therefore allow the individual to gradually adjust to the impending loss. Some researchers argue that

anticipatory grieving follows the same patterns of post-death reactions. They note that during this anticipatory period, the person who will be left behind has a chance to disengage emotionally from the dying individual (Brown & Stoudemire, 1983). Other researchers have found, however, that individuals threatened with loss sometimes develop even more intense attachments to their dying loved ones than ever before, making it even more difficult to separate later (Parkes & Weiss, 1983). This difference may depend partly on the age of the bereaved. Research on spousal death shows, for example, that for younger people, sudden death (with less than two weeks warning) is extremely traumatic and difficult to adjust to and that adjustment is better with some time to become accustomed to the idea of the loss. For children and adolescents, parental death tends to be very traumatic regardless of its timing (Saldinger et al., 1999). Elderly persons, many of whom are accustomed to the death of friends and relatives, sometimes do adjust better to the sudden death of their spouses than to prolonged death, possibly because prolonged death can leave older survivors drained physically, financially, and emotionally from caring for their aged spouses (Parkes & Weiss, 1983). One study did find, however, that with support older caregivers were able to adjust to and prepare for the eventuality of widowhood (Wells & Kendig, 1997).

Deaths in the Family

The experience of loss is somewhat different, depending on *who* has died. Although there are some similarities in the experiences, the effects of specific losses at specific times in life can vary considerably.

Death of a Parent

Losing a parent to death is a common phenomenon. At any given time, approximately 5 percent of the U. S. adult population has suffered the death of a parent within the previous year. Losing a parent can affect some people quite intensely. In one study, half of the 75 adults who committed suicide in West Sussex, Great Britain, had experienced maternal bereavement in the previous three years (Bunch et al., 1971). Single men were found to be at highest risk for suicide following deaths of their mothers. This may be because men are more likely to "act out" their distress, whereas women more often seek medical and psychiatric help following the death of a parent. In addition, single men might rely on their mothers more for emotional support than do married men who rely on their wives. Although there has been little systematic research on the subject, clinicians agree that the death of a parent is a serious life event that leads, in many cases, to measurable distress (Horowitz et al., 1981). It is noted by clinicians that the death of a mother is often harder to sustain than the death of a father, possibly because of the mother's early role as nurturer. This may also be because, in 75 percent of couples, the husband dies first. The bereaved children may be most upset with the second loss because both parents are then deceased.

Bereavement during childhood or adolescence can be an important factor in later emotional and personality development. As we have seen, a child's understanding of the meaning of death varies with age, and a full understanding of death may not be arrived at until roughly age 9. Therefore, the precise effect that bereavement has on a child depends upon his or her level of development, degree of understanding of the loss, the closeness of the relationship, the degree of disruption in the child's day-to-day life, and the emotional reactions of others, including the continued ability of remaining loved ones to provide emotional support. Early research that showed devastating effects of parental loss had focused on children who were separated from their parents and placed in institutions (e.g., Bowlby, 1961). Such losses were multiple, including loss of familiar persons, removal from the home environment, and immersion in unfamiliar, sometimes chaotic, circumstances of institutional placement. Subsequent research has suggested that the effects of loss need not be devastating and that problematic effects can be minimized (e.g., Hurd, 1999). One interesting study followed children in the year following a parent's death and found that these children developed an "inner construction" of their deceased parent. They maintained an active image of this parent in their minds and continued a relationship with this inner image (Silverman et al., 1992). This relationship with the dead parent seemed to help them cope with their loss and with the alterations in their lives as a result of the death.

Children typically experience a wide range of emotions and behaviors following the death of parents, siblings, or grandparents who were involved in their lives. After such losses, young children often become sad, angry, and fearful. They experience appetite and sleep disturbances, difficulty concentrating, withdrawal, dependency, restlessness, aggressiveness, learning difficulties, and/or regression to an earlier stage of development. There is often a marked effect on their school performance and athletic interest, and bereaved youth have more behavior problems, psychological problems, and delinquency than do their nonbereaved peers (Thompson et al., 1998). Interestingly, new research indicates that there is a gender difference in the effects of parental versus sibling loss. Boys seem most affected by the loss of a parent, while girls are most affected by the loss of a sibling, particularly a sister (Worden et al., 1999).

In order to understand the effects of loss on a child's behavior, it is important to understand the grieving process for children. One major research project studied children whose fathers had died. During the first year these children typically experienced tremendous pain, sadness and anger; depending upon their developmental level, some tried to explore the implications of the loss and understand the concept of death. During the second year, many showed significant anxiety, demanding and aggressive behavior, restlessness, and difficulties with discipline. In subsequent years, they manifested considerable overdependency on their mothers, with 39 percent of the formerly well-adjusted sample showing signs of continued emotional distress four years after their fathers' deaths (Elizur & Kaffman, 1983). Some children try to identify with the deceased, taking on his or her characteristics. A boy whose father has died may try to become the "man of the house" and even begin to behave in an authoritarian way. The identification may result from the child's defending against normal feelings of grief, and such powerful identification with adult behavior may cause the child to be rejected by his or her peer group.

Interesting new research shows that the loss of a parent during childhood can have long-lasting effects on a person's body and physical functioning. One study compared university students who had lost a parent prior to the age of 16 with a group of students who had not suffered such a loss. Those who had lost a parent had higher blood pressure and increased cortisol output in response to stressful tasks even though, in many cases, the loss was in the distant past. The students who had lost a parent were more vulnerable to stress than those who had not (Luecken, 1998). These findings raise important questions about the ways in which children deal with parental death and the long-term health implications of the loss.

It is important to recognize that children who are bereaved often exhibit emotional expressions that can be frightening or distressing to adults. Children may become angry, anxious, clinging, and obstinate; the world may seem unpredictable and unsafe, and the child may need considerable help to rebuild trust in relationships. Sometimes, the child idealizes the lost parent in fantasy and projects hostility onto the surviving parent, who might even be accused of causing the death or not preventing it. Healthy mourning in childhood seems to be predicted by positive relationships with both parents, adequate emotional support from the remaining parent, and open and honest communication about death (Hurd, 1999). Most bereaved children have the following three questions in their minds, although they may not articulate them: Did I cause this to happen? Will it happen to me? Who will take care of me now? Someone close to the child (the surviving parent if the child is parentally bereaved, or both parents if the child has lost a sibling) must answer these questions in a careful and loving way. What the child understands must be carefully checked to be sure that there are no misconceptions that can cause harm. Because of their developmental stages and more "primitive" defenses (particularly the use of denial and regression), children often have more difficulty coping with their grief than do adults. The continued fantasy that the dead parent really is still alive and waiting somewhere is an example of a primitive defense that can prevent the child from coming to grips with the loss. Adults need to know what to expect when children display their grief. Children often want to keep photographs and clothing of the deceased to remember and represent the relationship; they may work through their understanding of a death by playing "funeral" or "undertaker." Children may tell strangers and relatives over and over again about the death and appear to have a light attitude about the loss. This behavior can unnerve adults who may also be suffering intensely.

Although the death of one's parents during one's adulthood may be preferable to such a loss during one's childhood, the death of a parent can still be quite difficult to cope with. Such a death may mean the loss of the only person in the world who accepts one unconditionally. Such a death may be perceived as a developmental push to the next stage of adulthood in which one becomes a member of the oldest generation in the family (Osterweis et al., 1984).

In Box 13.3, the death of a beloved grandparent is considered through the personal experience of one of your book's authors (L.M.).

Death of a Sibling

The loss of a sibling is an event that creates an intense grief experience (e.g., Robinson & Mahon, 1997). Surprisingly little data exists, however, regarding adults' reactions to

BOX **13.3**

Hot Topic

When Protecting a Child Really Hurts

Some of my earliest childhood memories are of my paternal grandmother. I was born just a few blocks from her house, and in my early childhood saw her almost daily. When we moved to another town, I still saw her every weekend and spent more extensive periods of time with her during school vacations. There was order and routine in her house—something that I craved as a child. She was poised, eloquent, smart, and everything that I wanted to be. She was also very proud of me, and I sometimes think that I lived my childhood years to please her.

During my eighth grade year I remember that she sometimes seemed to have a backache, and I believe she may have even mentioned the pain once or twice. But she was still the same grandma, so I didn't think much of it. Then, just a few weeks before my graduation, she was taken to the hospital in extreme pain, and the next thing we knew she was in surgery, having a cancerous tumor almost the size of a basketball removed from her abdomen.

I saw her once, the day after her surgery. She looked tired, but otherwise seemed the same, and she had a smile for me and told me everything would be all right. I believed her. I expected her to come home from the hospital soon, and the realization that her condition was really serious (that she might not be coming home) was slow in coming. She remained in the hospital for a several weeks. As I heard my parents talking in the living room late at night, and as I saw their somber expressions, I felt a sense of panic. I was old enough to know what death was, and I could feel it coming. I desperately wanted

to visit my grandma and to have a few moments of communion with her. When I asked, however, I was told that she didn't want me to see her "in her condition" and that I should stay home. I was an obedient child; I did not argue.

My grandma didn't make it to my eighth grade graduation. She died a few days before I marched down that aisle, and it's almost as if I missed the graduation, too. Of course, I know I was there because I have photographs to prove it. But my heart was not there. It took me many years to accept her death, and to deal with the fact that she and I never said goodbye. I know that she, and the rest of my family, were just trying to protect me from something that they thought would be too traumatic. They were making a loving decision, with my best interests in the forefront of their minds. But that decision was wrong.

Every child is unique, and there is no prescription for dealing with the death of a grandparent, or other loved one, that will work for all children. But care should be taken to fully examine the wishes and needs of the individual child when dealing with death-related issues. Children, particularly if they are not very young, may be the best judges of what they can handle, and what they need in order to cope with the loss. The questions of, "Should we allow him to see his grandpa when grandpa is so sick?" and "Is it a good idea to let her go to the funeral?" cannot be answered simply. Open communication of needs between parents and children (and perhaps a health care professional) will facilitate good decision making.

---

the death of a brother or sister (Worden et al., 1999). In many cases, the empathy that siblings develop for one another in childhood continues into adulthood, and the loss can be quite devastating. Sibling relationships tend to assume greater importance in older age as many elderly siblings live together or at least maintain close contact

(Osterweis et al., 1984). Loss of a sibling also tends to increase an individual's fears of mortality.

It can be particularly difficult to explain the death of a sibling to a child (Corr & Corr, 1985). The child may expect his or her sibling to return later or may feel abandoned; some children have been found to exhibit guilt reactions most likely because they fear that their rivalrous feelings and aggressive wishes toward the sibling have actually come true (Sourkes, 1980). Many children have prolonged or "anniversary" identifications with the prominent symptoms of the dead sibling (Cain et al., 1964), and many children exhibit emotional and behavioral problems including low self-esteem (Pettle-Michael & Lansdown, 1986). As children attempt to deal with the loss of a brother or sister, they may try to serve as a replacement for a deceased sibling, taking on the sibling's characteristics and suppressing their own personalities and interests. Sometimes they are unconsciously reinforced for this by family members who are anxious to regain their own equilibrium and who rely on the child as a substitute for the one who passed away (Krell & Rabkin, 1979). A number of studies highlight the importance of open communication within families, both prior to and after the death, which helps to create an environment that fosters recovery from the loss (Birenbaum, 1989; Finke et al., 1994; Gibbons, 1992).

Death of a Child

The death of any loved one is difficult to deal with, but researchers and clinicians agree that the death of one's child is by far the most painful. These days, people expect that their children will live to adulthood. Nevertheless, about 96 children out of every 100,000 die before the age of 15 (Hodge et al., 1995). Further, as more and more parents live to very old age, the experience of premature death of their middle-aged children is becoming more common. When a person outlives his or her child, the loss of a major investment in the life and happiness of another person of the next generation must be faced. Consciously or not, people have dreams, wishes, and hopes for their children's futures. Their feelings of guilt and self-blame are also very prominent, as people feel responsible for keeping their children well and safe and protecting them from harm (Videka-Sherman, 1982). Let us consider the deaths of children at different ages, for they typically bring different reactions in parents.

Death before Birth.   A **stillbirth**, in which a fetus either dies in utero or during labor and delivery, can be an extremely painful emotional experience for young parents. Typically, the mother, and in many cases both parents, have bonded closely to the baby and the loss can be very traumatic. The grieving process for those who have experienced stillbirth can sometimes seem like a "conspiracy of silence" (Osterweis et al., 1984). Until very recently, medical professionals believed that it was better for parents not to discuss their loss. In fact, many physicians sedated the mother so much that she could not feel anything emotionally, and she was not even allowed to see her baby. Recent research has shown, however, that the silence surrounding a bereaved mother intensifies her feelings of guilt and makes the death "unspeakable," confirming, in a sense, that it is too terrible to talk about (Stringham et al., 1982). Mothers who have lost babies confirm the loneliness they feel because they alone have known the baby intimately. They feel guilt that they may have been responsible, and a loss of self-esteem that they could not produce a healthy baby. Recently, medical professionals have learned that it is best if parents have visual and physical contact with the dead infant to facilitate the process of grieving. It is even helpful for them to take pictures of and gather locks of hair from the infant, to remind themselves later that the baby really existed as a member of their family.

Miscarriage (death of the fetus in the earlier months of pregnancy, before it can be expected to live outside the mother's body) presents a variation of the loss from still-birth. Although the parents may have had less time to become attached to the baby, the reactions they have after such a loss are usually quite intense. Fetal loss, even as early as six or eight weeks of gestation, can have a significant emotional impact. As soon as the pregnancy is confirmed, there is investment in the future and in fantasies of the new life. Miscarriage involves lost hope for a particular future and loss of a potential family member.

Perinatal Death.   Unlike stillborns, babies who live for a few days or weeks are accorded personhood, given names, held, talked to, talked about, and visited by members of the extended family. Such a death can be quite traumatic for parents, who may need to be involved in complex decisions about care during the perinatal period. They may be required to approve interventions that have only a small chance of saving their baby. Although there may be somewhat more support for parents who experience perinatal death than for those who suffer after a stillbirth, many people in the parents' social network may ignore the death and try to avoid discussing it. The parents are left alone to deal with their complex emotions of guilt, anger, sadness, and relief.

Crib Death.   Crib death (**Sudden Infant Death Syndrome or SIDS**) is the most common cause of death in the first year of an infant's life, after the perinatal period. SIDS accounts for one-third of all deaths of infants between one week and one year of age, and it occurs in two to three babies per 1,000 in the United States. Nearly 10,000 babies die of SIDS each year. The peak incidence of death is between 2 and 4 months of age, and almost all SIDS deaths occur before 6 months of age. Babies with SIDS die in their sleep with no forewarning and no audible noise. Babies have died with an adult right near them in the room, unaware that anything was happening; parents report that their baby was perfectly fine just moments before the death. Although early theories about the cause of SIDS have ranged from the type of feeding (breast versus bottle) to the type of bedclothes used and the temperature of the room, all such theories have been overthrown by empirical data. Currently researchers believe that the cause of SIDS is a problem with the brain mechanism that controls breathing and sleep. Although autopsies of these infants show pulmonary congestion and swelling, there has been no established connection with a viral or bacterial agent. Fortunately, the incidence of SIDS in the United States has recently decreased significantly with the recommendation that babies not be put to sleep on their stomachs, but instead placed on their sides or backs (David, 1997).

The family that loses a baby to SIDS suffers a tremendous tragedy. The parents usually feel responsible for the death, and emergency personnel, neighbors, and even the police and news media may add to parents' feelings of blame by questioning the circumstances that surround the death. Parents are helped most by those who recognize the SIDS condition and are careful to tell them clearly that there was nothing they could have done to prevent the death. Without action to forestall their feelings of responsibility, parents may suffer tremendously. Studies of the longer-term reactions of parents to the loss of a child to SIDS indicate that even several years after the loss, parents may be severely affected by the death (e.g., Carroll & Shaefer, 1994).

Death of Older Children. Among older children, accidents are the most frequent cause of death (45%) followed by leukemia and other cancers (18%). Children and adolescents who die have well-formed personalities and leave a large store of memories. Not surprisingly, a commonly expressed emotion among bereaved parents is anger. The loss of a child, compared with loss of other family members, results in more intense grief reactions of the somatic type, as well as more feelings of depression and despair. Bizarre responses and suicidal thoughts have been found to be common. Parents report feeling totally vulnerable and having suffered a blow from which they believe they may never recover. The course of bereavement for parents can be considerably longer than for those otherwise bereaved. Grief sometimes intensifies rather than diminishes over time, and may last for many years (Osterweis et al., 1984).

Parents of terminally ill children seem to start the grieving process early, often at the time of the diagnosis, and recovery appears to be better among parents who feel they have participated actively in the care of their terminally ill child (Eiser, 1996). Research has shown somewhat less difficult adaptation among parents whose children have died at home rather than at a hospital; such parents tend to experience less marital strain (Lauer et al., 1983). Of course, the determining factor may not have been the hospital versus the home environment at all, but preexisting personality characteristics and attitudes that have influenced parental choice of home versus hospital care for their children.

Parents generally experience significant problems in grieving for a child. Even the best grief scenario (called "uncomplicated grief") involves considerable sadness and remorse but does not include self-blame or rejection of their concept of God. It employs a good social network to aid in the process (Oliver & Fallat, 1995). Much more common, however, is what these researchers call "pathologic" grieving in which parents have little support network beyond the family, avoid the grieving process, view God as distant and punitive, and reject spiritual support.

The death of a child often has a devastating effect on marriage (Osterweis et al., 1984). A good marriage with strong communication can become stronger with the terminal illness or sudden death of a child. It is not uncommon, however, for marriages to break down under the strain of the death of a child. Marital discord and divorce occur in 50 to 70 percent of families in which a child dies of cancer. One reason for the discord may be the fact that the two parents often have different styles of grieving, and the spouses may not understand one another. In general, mothers exhibit more of the typical outward signs of grief than do fathers (Moriarty et al., 1996; Schwab, 1996).

Mothers tend to express signs of sorrow such as crying and appearing depressed, whereas fathers express more anger, fear, and loss of control and try to hide their feelings. In doing so, however, they may appear to their wives as cold and unsupportive and as unaffected by the loss of the child. Medical and psychological professionals can do a great deal to help bereaved parents understand their own and one another's emotional reactions to their loss.

Being Widowed

Of all the conditions of bereavement, widowhood has received the most research attention; this research has looked not only at the special emotional difficulties of widowhood but also at the physical outcomes of bereavement. Researchers have found that, next to the loss of a child, the death of one's spouse is considered by most people to be the most stressful of life events (Holmes & Rahe, 1967). Such a change in one's life is thought to bring tremendous difficulties and to require significant adjustment of life circumstances and expectations (Holmes & Masuda, 1974). Why is the death of a spouse so stressful? The reason probably has to do with how intertwined the lives of married people often become (Parkes, 1993). Spouses are co-managers of home and family. They jointly set family policy and either participate together in all aspects of running the family or divide the tasks so that each person is primarily responsible for certain things such as finances, home maintenance, and child rearing. Spouses are sexual partners and, if the relationship is close, they are best friends and emotionally supportive of one another. Spouses are also fellow members of larger social units such as the extended family, the community of parents in their children's school, their circle of friends, and perhaps their church or community organizations. Because of these social connections, the death of a spouse sometimes leaves the widowed person feeling abandoned and left to function alone without the help and companionship of the partner. Responsibilities that were once shared become the sole responsibility of the survivor. In many cases, the individual left behind is not prepared to take over certain jobs because he or she may know nothing about how to do them. Widowed parents are often overwhelmed with their children's demands for attention and understanding. The widowed parent sometimes must subordinate his or her own grief reactions in order to help children deal with their own feelings at having lost a parent. The death of the spouse can alter a person's social role, leaving him or her excluded from the social activities of couples and causing significant social isolation.

Although many studies have methodological limitations (such as being retrospective or lacking a perfectly comparable control group), the evidence is quite strong that people are at increased risk for mortality after the death of their spouse. This has been demonstrated in a number of different countries (M.S. Stroebe & W. Stroebe, 1993). One of the earliest studies on this topic examined death records and found that among people of younger ages (20s and 30s), the mortality rate of widowed individuals was strikingly higher than that of married people. The gap narrowed with increasing age of the widowed person, until in old age there was little difference between those married and those widowed in terms of how likely they were to die (Kraus & Lilienfeld, 1959). For those under age 45, however, mortality of the widowed was found to be at least seven times higher than mortality for those who were married. Further, mortality rates for widowed males were significantly higher than for widowed females. Widowed men were most likely to die of heart conditions such as arteriosclerosis and myocardial degeneration, stroke, and respiratory diseases such as tuberculosis and pneumonia. Death from cardiovascular disease was ten times greater in widowed men than in married men of the same age.

In one two-year-long study of bereavement in young widows and widowers, about one-third did not show much sign of recovery over the entire course of the study. Men who confronted their loss seemed to benefit, but higher socioeconomic status and more social support did not have the buffering effects that were expected (W. Stroebe & M.S. Stroebe, 1993). No matter how many friends or how much money people had, their losses were still equally devastating. A major prospective study of almost 92,000 persons was conducted in Maryland from 1963 to 1975. Individuals who became widowed during that time were matched to a married, nonwidowed group on race, sex, age and many other factors such as geographic location of residence (Helsing et al., 1981). Particularly among younger and middle-aged men, there was significantly greater mortality in the widowed group; this effect did not occur among those widowed after age 75. The risk of death was also found to be greatest in the first year of widowhood, and in the first six months of bereavement rates of suicide were 2.5 times higher among widowed than among married men. In the second and third years of bereavement, suicide rates were 1.5 times higher among widowed men, and suicide among the widowed was higher in men than women. (In Box 13.4, the complicated and troubling issue of suicide, and the possibility of its prevention, are considered in detail.) An extensive review of the literature has been very helpful in sorting out the complicated effects of bereavement on mortality. Generally, widowers experience a greater increase in mortality risk than do widows, and age may interact with this gender difference, putting younger men who have lost their wives at the highest risk, particularly during the first six months of widowhood (M.S. Stroebe & W. Stroebe, 1993). Patterns have been found to be less consistent for women, although increased risk of mortality does exist in the first two to three years of widowhood. Widowers who remarried decreased their risks, but widows who remarried did not. For widowers under the age of 65, mortality risk was highest if their wife's death was sudden and unexpected. For widows under 50 this same effect was found, but for widows age 50 to 64 the highest risk followed spousal death at the end of a chronic illness (Smith & Zick, 1996). These gender, age, and mode-of-death differences were found to be consistent with theories of social roles and social support.

Depression, decreased psychological well-being, lower levels of social support, and decreases in morale are all associated with bereavement for both men and women (Bennett, 1996; Lichtenstein et al., 1996; Thuen et al., 1997). Widowhood is more likely to bring about depression in men than in women, however (Lee et al., 1998). It has been hypothesized that this effect may be partly explained by the fact that women typically outlive men, so widowhood is a more expected, normal part of life for women than it is for men. It is also possible that women's relatively stronger social support systems, and societal acceptance of emotional grief expressions, may help them to more effectively combat depression. Although symptoms of depression and distress generally

BOX 13.4
Research Close-up

Suicide

The loss of a close friend or family member is certainly very painful, but it can be even more so when the death was caused by suicide. More than 27,000 people commit suicide in the United States every year. This is a conservative estimate, of course, because many deaths of an ambiguous nature, such as accidents, could easily have been suicides that were not labeled as such. Among young people, there are many risk factors including drug and alcohol use, mood disorders, anxiety disorders, and problematic home environments (Gould et al., 1998; Vannatta, 1996). Among the elderly, medical illness plays a large role in contributing to suicide, as do anxiety, social isolation, and depression (Hendin, 1999; Mireault & de Man, 1996). Men who are 75 years old and older have the highest rate of suicides in almost all industrialized countries (Pearson et al., 1997).

After a suicide, survivors are left to deal with some very complex feelings and are typically at greater risk for physical and mental health problems than are those bereaved in a nonsuicidal fashion (Gallagher-Thompson et al., 1993). Survivors of a loved one's suicide often display exaggerated bereavement reactions such as blaming themselves for not preventing the death. Sometimes those who commit suicide leave notes or other communications that even directly blame survivors, who experience considerable guilt and distress. Survivors often fear that they are vulnerable and that their own death will eventually be caused by suicide. Feelings of inevitability are typically unconscious, and for children of suicide victims these feelings often arise as they approach the age at which their parent died. The fact that someone close used suicide as a solution to overwhelming problems may legitimize it as a choice. Survivors of suicide often need professional help. In addition to the loss itself, they must deal with the social stigma of suicide (Osterweis et al., 1984). Unless the suicide was straightforwardly ascribed to an outside cause (such as the victim's

terminal illness), professional psychotherapeutic intervention may be needed to help survivors to resolve their own conflicting and sometimes terrifying feelings about what the deceased has chosen to do (Osterweis et al., 1984).

Some suicides can actually be prevented if surrounding loved ones know what to look for. Researchers have been working to understand people who commit (or try to commit) suicide in order to learn why they do it and at what point they might have been stopped (Shneidman, 1985). These findings are based on information left behind (notes, diaries) by people who have been successful at committing suicide, on interviews with those who tried to kill themselves but survived, and on interviews with the bereaved. Suicide is not a bizarre or incomprehensible act of self-destruction. Suicidal people have a particular style of thinking that brings them to the conclusion that death is the only answer to their problems. Steps can be taken to stop a suicide if one knows how and when to intervene. There are ten common characteristics of a suicidal person (Shneidman, 1985). People who commit suicide often experience:

1. *Unendurable psychological pain.* The immediate goal of a person attempting to prevent the suicide is to reduce that pain in whatever way possible, even just a little.
2. *Frustrated psychological needs.* The inner life of the suicidal person is desperately in need of something such as security, achievement, trust, love, or friendship. The helper must find out what that is and help the person to see a way to get it.
3. *The need for a solution.* The suicidal person really thinks that death is the only way out of a problem or crisis.
4. *A desire to end consciousness.* Suicide is a move to stop awareness of a painful existence.

5. *Helplessness and hopelessness.* Underlying all the negative emotions felt by the individual is a sense of powerlessness and a belief that nobody can help.
6. *Constriction of options.* The suicidal person does not look for several ways to solve his or her problems; dying is seen as the only method.
7. *Ambivalence.* The suicidal person both wants and does not want to die. That is, at the same time the person is taking or planning to take his or her life, a cry for help is likely to be going out.
8. *Communication of intent.* About 80 percent of suicidal people give friends and family very clear clues that they intend to kill themselves. Many essentially say goodbye, put their affairs in order, even state that they can no longer endure their pain and intend to die. There is often a clear chance for intervention, particularly by preventing the person from obtaining the means to destroy him- or herself.
9. *Departure.* Suicidal people express a desire to escape. A helper can aid them to distinguish between the need to get away from everything (e.g., leave a marriage, leave school) and the desire to die.
10. *Lifelong coping pattern.* People who commit suicide often have a style of problem solving known as "cut and run." They end marriages by walking out and end jobs by quitting. Such actions suggest a need for control, which may be at the heart of the decision to commit suicide.

With information about why a person would choose to end his or her life, others may be able to help him or her to try a different approach to getting what is wanted and needed emotionally.

---

decrease to "normal" within about two and one-half years of the death of one's spouse, other reactions, such as yearning and loss-related distress, typically go on beyond this time (Thompson et al., 1998).

The process of bereavement and adjustment to widowhood is characterized by feelings of loneliness, difficulties with new roles and responsibilities, feelings of depression, challenges to a sense of personal identity, and physical health problems. The experience does not seem to follow a linear pattern of stages, but rather may be more like the experience of a "roller coaster," with some gradual improvement interspersed with periods of poor adjustment (Lund et al., 1993). While there are somewhat higher rates of depression and use of counseling services, particularly among the younger bereaved compared with persons of similar age who are not bereaved (Parkes & Brown, 1972), there is little evidence to link bereavement with subsequent psychiatric illness (Osterweis et al., 1984). It is estimated that approximately 15 percent of the bereaved still have a constellation of depressive symptoms a year after the death. Because loss of a spouse is a tremendous life stressor, depression is likely to be precipitated in those who are predisposed to it by virtue of family history or personality (Clayton, 1979).

Studies of the effects of bereavement on illness behavior document somewhat less immediate physical expressions of distress than one might expect. The young widowed tend to have more anxiety than do those who are married, resulting in a somewhat greater focus on some physical symptoms. There seem, however, to be no major changes among the bereaved in their use of healthcare services or in complaints for which no organic basis can be found (Osterweis et al., 1984). Certain existing physical problems such as hypertension and congestive heart failure can be seriously affected by the emotional stresses of bereavement (Osterweis et al., 1984). Increases in illness and death among the bereaved can be accounted for in many cases by a significant increase in poor health habits, such as failing to take necessary medications, smoking heavily, and drinking considerable amounts of alcohol (Aiken & Marx, 1982).

Individuals who form new romantic attachments and/or are remarried tend to have significantly higher well-being than those who do not, although it is not clear whether remarriage brings about better adjustment or vice versa (Schneider et al., 1996). Men are much more likely to make this kind of transition, and women are more likely to have negative feelings about forming bonds with new people, especially a new spouse (Schneider et al., 1996; Wu, 1995).

Summary

1. The prospect of death can cause a great deal of emotional turmoil for the terminally ill person and his or her family. The individual may initially struggle with whether to go on with life as usual, or prepare for death. Plans for the future become uncertain and difficult, and unique challenges must be faced.

2. When it becomes clear that death is likely in the near future, individuals must cope emotionally. Dr. Kübler-Ross outlined five stages that many, although not all, dying individuals go through. These stages do not occur in any particular order, and the patient may experience a shifting back and forth between stages.

   ■ The first stage is denial, in which the person simply refuses to accept that his or her illness is terminal.
   ■ The second stage is anger, and the individual may lash out at anyone from doctors to family to God.
   ■ The third stage is bargaining, in which the person tries to "buy" his or her health, either by working out an elaborate framework through which death can be cheated, or by begging higher powers for healing.
   ■ The fourth stage is depression, typified by withdrawal and resignation to the fate of death.
   ■ The fifth and final stage is acceptance, in which the person no longer tries to fight against the inevitable, but is not depressed or angry.
   ■ Another reaction that most terminally ill individuals experience is anxiety, although this is not one of Kübler-Ross's stages of dying.

3. Sometimes when the pain is too great, or future prospects too dim, individuals may choose to limit the length of their lives in one way or another. Some may request that heroic measures *not* be taken to save their lives. Others may desire a more active role and request that they be assisted in ending their lives. The latter is very controversial in the United States.

4. Caring for terminally ill patients always requires compassion, but the issues related to death tend to be somewhat different at various ages.

   ■ Young children do not understand the concept of death and although they should be told the truth, explanations must necessarily be simple.
   ■ Adolescents who are just embarking on the voyage of self-discovery may have a particularly difficult time coping with the prospect of death.

- Young parents mourn their inability to see their children grow up.
- Older adults face the prospect of ending deep, long-term relationships.

5. Until recently it was common to hide impending death from terminally ill patients, but this is no longer a common practice.

6. Hospice care may provide terminally ill patients with comfort and pain relief during their last days. Hospices have trained professionals available at all times, at the patients' home or in a hospital or skilled nursing facility.

7. The grief experience varies widely from person to person, although there are some consistencies. Most people experience a period of shock and denial followed by a range of reactions such as anger, restlessness, and intense sadness. Ultimately, some form of resolution and acceptance is usually achieved.

8. Cultural norms for grieving and rituals for mourning can help survivors come to terms with their pain, receive validation of their loss, and receive social support.

9. Although many individuals go through the culturally and socially prescribed grief behaviors and then resume "normal" functioning, some do not. "Pathological grief" is difficult to define because the grief experience is so personal. Generally, pathological grief involves the extremes of the distribution of grieving behavior.

10. Many researchers and clinicians believe that the mourning process and emotional adjustment can begin prior to an anticipated death. Knowledge of impending death sometimes creates even more intense emotional attachments between the dying individual and family members, impeding survivors' acceptance of the death.

11. The experiences of losing a parent, sibling, child, and spouse have unique characteristics. Knowledge of these differences is important to facilitate coping.

THINKING CRITICALLY

1. How is the experience of dying likely to be different for very young children compared with adolescents? How would a psychologist need to tailor his or her interactions with the child in contrast to those with the adolescent?

2. Think about the "funeral" that Andy's parents had for him. Do you think you would feel able to participate in such a service for your own child or for a younger sibling? If you were terminally ill, would you want to have some sort of ceremony prior to your death? Why or why not?

3. Think about the norms for grieving here in the United States. What are our rituals? How do the rituals in your culture of origin differ? (Consider the culture of origin of someone you know well, or a culture with which you are familiar, if you prefer.) Which rituals do you think serve the most useful purposes? What are these purposes?

4. If you had only about one year to live, would you want to know now? Why or why not? Based on what you know about the literature on anticipatory grieving, would you want others to know? If a loved one had only a year to live, would you want to know?

5. What are the ethical issues surrounding information regarding terminal illness? If a 10-year-old is terminally ill and his or her parents want it kept a secret, is this ethical? If a doctor knows that a patient is terminally ill, and that death might be hastened if the person is told (because the patient will likely become depressed and lose the will to live), should the patient be told anyway?

GLOSSARY

Anticipatory grieving: The process by which, when death is expected, a survivor begins the grieving process prior to the actual death of the loved one.

Bereavement: The fact of loss through death.

Bereavement reactions: Psychological, physical, or behavioral responses to bereavement.

Euthanasia: The process of acting to hasten the death of a terminally ill individual, often someone who is suffering from severe pain.

Grief: The feeling or affective state associated with the condition of bereavement.

Hospice care: Care that is meant to make the patient comfortable and pain-free (rather than to cure him or her) and seeks to provide psychological comfort to both patient and family.

Miscarriage: Fetal loss; even as early as 6 or 8 weeks of gestation, miscarriage can have a significant emotional impact on parents, involving diminishment of hope for a particular future and loss of a potential family member.

Mourning: The social expression of grief.

Recovery or **adaptation**: The end of the grieving process.

Stillbirth: Death of a fetus in utero or during labor and delivery.

Sudden Infant Death Syndrome (SIDS): Also known as crib death; the most common cause of death in the first year of an infant's life after the perinatal period; occurs in 2 to 3 babies per thousand in the United States; peak incidence of death is 2 to 4 months of age. Babies with SIDS die in their sleep, with no forewarning, and no audible noise.

Thanatology: The study of death and dying.

14 The Future of Health Psychology

The demand for health psychologists, both in clinical and academic positions, has increased dramatically over the past two decades. For example, in the early 1980s, on average 27 health psychology positions were advertised each month in the *American Psychological Association Monitor* (Altman & Cahn, 1987). In the months of late 1999 and early 2000, we found on average 89 positions advertised for psychologists with health-related expertise. In this final chapter we will examine the professional opportunities available to health psychologists, as well as what we believe will be the major trends in health psychology research and application over the next decades. In Box 14.1 you will find information that will be useful to you if you are considering an advanced degree and career in health psychology.

One of the first issues that we addressed in this book was the changing nature of the disease profile in this country, and, in fact, in the world. Infectious disease was once the cause of most deaths. Now, however, the majority of infections can be easily controlled, and most deaths occur from chronic diseases such as cardiovascular conditions and cancer. Biomedical and social science research has therefore turned attention to these ailments. Because infectious disorders no longer claim the lives of many young

people, and because improved nutrition and medical care have resulted in healthier aging, a larger proportion of adults than ever before live to much older ages. Because people do live longer, many must contend with the limitations of chronic health problems. Further, issues of cost containment in medicine have become increasingly significant. Health psychologists have many opportunities to study the changes in Americans and their lifestyles in response to the maladies they struggle with, as well as the dilem-

BOX 14.1
Hot Topic

Graduate Training and Careers in Health Psychology

Many students majoring in psychology look forward to attending graduate school. After finishing college, one might consider obtaining a Master's degree, a PhD, or a PsyD. Combined with clinical training and supervised experience, a Master's degree can be preparation for licensing in Marriage, Family, and Child Counseling (MFCC). The PhD is a research degree requiring a dissertation project and can be preparation for a university teaching and/or research position or, combined with clinical training and supervised experience, as preparation for delivering clinical care. The PsyD is a doctoral degree specifically focused on preparation for clinical work and does not require dissertation research.

To be a successful applicant to graduate school in psychology, one must take the Graduate Record Exam (GRE) late in the junior year or early in the senior year of college. This test is similar in format to the SAT taken for entrance to college. Early on in college, one should try to find a supportive faculty member who can offer research experience and mentorship and eventually a letter of recommendation. Most graduate schools expect applicants to have had some psychology research experience during their college years. In addition to providing excellent experience, working as a research assistant allows a student to contribute to the field and to determine which areas of psychology he or she is most interested in.

It is important for prospective graduate students to consider the type of work that they would ultimately like to do with their education. Will it be clinical work directly with patients, teaching, research and writing, or some combination of these? What kind of clinical work is of interest—that concerned primarily with mental health or with medical treatment, or both? The answers to each of these questions point to particular areas of training in psychology.

Below is a list of the graduate programs that currently offer training in the field of health psychology. If this area of study is of interest to you, perhaps this list will be helpful. For further information about graduate study in psychology, consult the following books published by the American Psychological Association in Washington, DC: *Graduate Study in Psychology: 2000 edition* and *Career Paths in Psychology* (1997; written by Robert J. Sternberg). Both books, and additional information about the field of psychology, can be obtained at APA's website: http://www.apa.org

A Listing of U.S. and Canadian Graduate Programs for Prospective Health Psychologists

Antioch University, Seattle (MA)
Appalachian State University (MA)
Arizona State University (PhD)
Bowling Green State University (PhD)
California School of Professional Psychology, Alameda (PhD, PsyD)
California School of Professional Psychology, Los Angeles (PhD, PsyD)

California School of Professional
Psychology, San Diego (PhD, PsyD)

Case Western Reserve University,
Cleveland, Ohio (PhD)

Claremont Graduate School (PhD)

Connecticut College (MA)

Dalhousie University (PhD)

Duke University (PhD)

Finch University of Health Sciences,
Chicago Medical School (PhD)

Georgia State University (PhD)

Illinois School of Professional Psychology,
Chicago Campus (PsyD)

Indiana State University (MA, MS)

Iowa State University (PhD)

Lesley College (MA)

Loma Linda University (PhD, PsyD/DrPH)

Loyola College (MA, MS)

McGill University, Montreal (PhD)

Northern Arizona University (MA)

Northwestern University Medical School
(PhD)

Ohio State University (PhD)

Ohio University (PhD)

Rutgers: The State University of New
Jersey, New Brunswick (PhD)

Saint Joseph's University (MS)

Stanford University (MA, PhD)

State University of New York, Stony Brook
(PhD)

Syracuse University (PhD)

Uniformed Services University of the
Health Sciences (PhD)

University of British Columbia (MA, PhD)

University of Calgary (MSc, PhD)

University of California, Irvine (MA, PhD)

University of California, Los Angeles (PhD)

University of California, Riverside (PhD)

University of Florida, Miami (PhD)

University of Illinois, Chicago (PhD)

University of Iowa (PhD)

University of Kansas (PhD)

University of Kentucky (PhD)

University of Manitoba (PhD)

University of Memphis (PhD)

University of North Texas (PhD)

University of Utah (PhD)

University of Vermont (PhD)

University of Washington (PhD)

Virginia Polytechnic Institute and State
University (PhD)

Washington State University (PhD)

Yale University (MS, PhD)

Yeshiva University (PhD)

---

mas of how best to offer and pay for treatment of these conditions. These are some of the issues to which health psychologists apply their research in real-life settings.

Health psychology has done much to promote the biopsychosocial model of healthcare (Belar, 1997). The biopsychosocial model not only emphasizes the interactive nature of biological and psychological processes, but also focuses significant attention on prevention as a primary technique for health maintenance. Psychologists, and particularly health psychologists, are increasingly moving into broadly defined roles as health professionals, rather than focusing solely on the realm of mental health (VandenBos et al., 1991). Psychologists and physicians often work together in both inpatient and outpatient settings. More and more hospitals are placing psychologists throughout their facilities instead of restricting their work to departments of psychiatry (Matarazzo, 1994; Siegel, 1995).

Morbidity versus Mortality

Historically, medicine has focused more attention on issues of mortality (death) and morbidity (disease) than on functioning and quality of life. Certainly, the promotion of long and disease-free life is an important goal, but health-related quality of life is also extremely important. Further, while the curing of disease is vital, the greatest benefit to people may be achieved by preventing disease from developing in the first place. One way of doing this, of course, is to focus considerable attention at the individual and the societal levels on health promotion and disease prevention activities, instead of attending solely to interventions that occur after someone is already ill. This trend has already begun, and we believe that it will continue and grow even stronger. In recent years, a great deal of media attention has been devoted to public health issues such as exercise, proper diet, and quitting smoking (or never starting in the first place). Although people sometimes have a hard time altering their lifestyles to meet their goals, most do realize that healthy habits are important. Changes are slowly being made. Many individuals receive encouragement from their families, employers, doctors, and Health Maintenance Organizations. Sometimes they are given specific incentives to improve their health, such as lower insurance deductibles for maintaining their weight in a healthy range or a financial bonus for exercising regularly. Some companies provide on-site gyms or walking trails to make exercising easier for their employees, and others take steps to make preventive care convenient, such as having influenza vaccines or nutritional counseling available at the office. Health psychologists are often instrumental in designing such health promotion programs to be both cost-efficient and effective in helping people to eliminate harmful habits and create new, healthy ones.

One of the best ways of promoting good health is to prevent the development of bad habits in the first place. Health psychologists play an important role in this endeavor by identifying, through their research and clinical practice, the best methods for controlling health-related behaviors. They study, for example, the best ways to encourage safer sex (or abstinence) and the avoidance of alcohol, drugs, and smoking. Many of these interventions are best applied with children and adolescents in the school setting, and health psychologists are involved there, too, working to minimize students' initial participation in risky and sometimes addictive behaviors.

Cost Containment and Care Equalization

Healthcare expenses in the United States have increased more rapidly than other elements of the cost of living, and U.S. healthcare spending is higher than anywhere else in the world (Whitney, 1993). Without controls, it is projected that by the year 2005, U.S. healthcare costs could account for nearly 20 percent of the Gross Domestic Product (Anderson & Poullier, 1999). Despite this, however, life expectancy in the United States is not higher than in other first-world countries, and our infant mortality rate is not the lowest. Why? There are two major reasons. First, not all of our healthcare dollars are actually spent on healthcare. Because our healthcare and health insurance systems are very complex (private and public hospitals, private and public insurance companies, HMOS and PPOs, government-funded healthcare plans, many types of specialists), a lot of bureaucracy and paperwork is required to keep it all afloat. Thus, administrative expenditures add substantially to the cost of medical care without contributing any actual health benefit (Weitz, 1996). Second, there is a wide range of

FIGURE 14.1 The disadvantages of cost containment.

living conditions in the United States, which differentially affect certain members of society. Although these are largely driven by political and socioeconomic factors, they nonetheless have a profound effect on physical health (Adler et al., 1993; Taylor et al., 1997). For example, a child who is poor and lives in a noisy, high-crime neighborhood likely experiences more stress than a middle-class child who lives in a quiet and safe neighborhood. As we saw in Chapter 9, stress can play a major role in both cardiovascular and immune system functioning.

One important task for health psychologists in the coming decades will be to aid in cost containment and the equalization of care for all Americans. By increasing both the number and effectiveness of disease prevention programs, healthcare costs can be reduced substantially. In addition, healthcare systems could be streamlined to decrease the administrative burden and its associated costs. Many other countries have employed effective strategies to control healthcare costs, such as instituting government control of hospital construction, the purchase of technological equipment, and the number of "specialists" (Weitz, 1996). Although these countries have fewer specialists and less access to medical technology, everyone has access to healthcare, and the system for obtaining care is relatively simple. Furthermore, because it is easier to obtain primary care, including preventive medicine, there is less need for expensive, high-tech treatments. Of course, many of these goals can also be achieved through free-market enterprise in managed health care. In the next decades, many changes in the delivery of healthcare will take place, and the delivery of healthcare in the United

States is expected to evolve in important ways that will affect the health and well-being of most Americans. The basic tenets, those of the biopsychosocial model, remain.

A related endeavor for health psychologists is to clarify the links between conditions of the social environment and physical health outcomes. We know that situations that are high stress, or that teach people that they are powerless, can damage the cardiovascular and immune systems and lead to persistent psychological disorders such as chronic anxiety and depression. In turn, these psychological disorders can threaten physical health. Thus, poverty and social class are not only political and civil rights issues, but are also issues of public health. Psychologists can make convincing arguments in this regard and can shed light on the ways in which these factors exert their sometimes subtle influences on well-being.

Women's Health

Another important role that health psychologists fulfill is that of encouraging research on underrepresented groups, the largest of which is women (Matthews et al., 1997). Over the years empirical studies in medicine have typically focused on men as research subjects. It has been assumed that whatever has been found to be true for men (for instance, about heart attacks) is also true for women. This is often not the case, however. For example, women seem to be more susceptible to harm from cigarette smoking than are men (Taubes, 1993). Why has research on women, until recently, been largely ignored? Part of the answer lies in the social norms that have shaped medical research. We have been, and to some degree remain, a male-dominated society. The tendency to overlook research on women has not been intentional, but instead is usually based on deeply ingrained sociocultural biases. Because women have not been studied as extensively as men, however, we still do not know whether the risk factors for many major diseases are equivalent across genders. Health psychologists can contribute to changing the face of medical research and care by continuing to support both biomedical and biopsychosocial research that includes women, as well as underrepresented minority groups. Their research can be influential by seeking to understand gender and cultural/ethnic differences in areas such as cardiovascular reactivity and responses to stress, normative social networks, psychoneuroimmunology, health promotion and disease prevention, physician-patient communication, patient adherence to treatment, and many other topics that affect health.

Health issues that are unique to women (such as breast cancer) have received a good deal of research attention. Some new trends also exist in research on conditions that are unique to women such as premenstrual syndrome (PMS) and menopause. As women's roles in society have changed, their buying power and vocalization about their needs have both increased. One thing that has been found from research is that the common assumptions about PMS may be much too simple and this syndrome is actually quite controversial. Some researchers view it as largely culturally determined, while others view it as a serious and pervasive medical problem (Halbreich, 1995; Rodin, 1992). Because PMS involves emotional and mood issues, as well as physiological effects, health psychologists have been instrumental in conducting research in this area.

The population of the United States is aging, and there is a good deal of public attention focused on menopause. As the "baby boomers" approach later adulthood, healthcare providers and pharmaceutical companies are recognizing that there is a large and growing market for remedies that can alleviate some of the uncomfortable symptoms of menopause, including hot flashes, irritability, and joint pain. Health psychologists bring expertise to this area as well, and their research is an important component in devising effective medical treatments that can enhance women's health and quality of life. For example, hormone replacement therapy may not only play a regulatory role for more minor symptoms such as hot flashes and mood swings, but may also guard women against the rather significant increases in risk for coronary heart disease and osteoporosis that occur with menopause (Matthews et al., 1996).

Healthy Aging

Research in health psychology has tended to focus primarily on risk factors for various diseases and ways of minimizing these risks. Although such a focus is important, the reverse approach—that of studying positive factors that predict increased health and longevity—has received less attention. The same has been true of the field of psychology in general. Psychologists have typically studied predictors of mental health problems, rather than devoting resources to learning what makes people emotionally healthy and happy. A new movement called "positive psychology" is currently afoot with Drs. Martin Seligman and Ed Diener at the forefront. This approach promotes research attention to positive psychological factors, quality of life, and well-being. And the same trend is starting in health psychology, as researchers increasingly focus on factors that may decrease people's risks for developing certain diseases and disorders and improve their health (Ryff & Singer, 1996).

Genetics and Health

One of the most significant research projects of the past decade has been *The Human Genome Project*, which has mapped human chromosomes and identified roughly 35,000 genes in the human genome. The project began in 1990 and was carried out with the collaboration of many individual researchers and research laboratories around the world. Although most diseases have both a genetic (biological) and an environmental component, the ability to identify particular genes will greatly advance the detection and eventual treatment of physical abnormalities and diseases. Unlike twin studies, which somewhat crudely sort out genetic and environmental influences on behavior, new research on gene markers and DNA structure can pinpoint genetic contributions precisely. For example, a form of the gene called Apo-E4 appears to more than triple an individual's risk for developing Alzheimer's disease (Plomin, 1998). A full understanding of the physiological and psychosocial aspects of Alzheimer's disease would be incomplete without examination of the implications of this genetic marker. Genetics research has also made it possible to assess an individual's potential for diseases long

Health psychologists can be very helpful in examining long-term impact on families of decisions about genetic testing.

before they actually occur—even before birth. This ability brings with it a host of ethical issues, such as if and when it is appropriate to abort a fetus. Certain medical problems, such as trisomy 21 (Down syndrome), can even now be identified before a child is born, and these issues are already being dealt with on a small scale. When there exist even better technologies to detect diseases and deformities of all types, however, the moral and ethical issues will become even more complex.

What is the role of health psychology in dealing with the advances of genetic research? This research is conducted by geneticists, and ". . . although few health psychologists will join the hunt for genes, it is crucial for the field that we be prepared to use genes as they are found" (Plomin, 1998, p. 54). Because of their expertise on psychosocial issues, health psychologists may be uniquely suited to viewing the long-term impact of decisions about genetic issues on individuals and on family units. Important will be questions such as, "What is this individual's or this family's social support network like?" "Will help and a supportive, loving environment be available if a child is born with medical problems?" "What are the religious views of this individual, and to what degree is his or her self-concept influenced by them?" "Is this individual prone to depression, anxiety, or other disorders that might be exacerbated by the medical choices that are made?" "What kinds of socioemotional interventions will this individual need in order to adjust to the aftermath of medical decisions?"

Health psychologists also play important roles in identifying the ways in which genetics and environment interact to produce harmful behaviors such as substance use, and drug or alcohol addiction. Research has recently found, for example, that the dopamine D4 receptor gene actually moderates the relationship between depression and cigarette smoking (Lerman et al., 1998). Smokers with this genetic marker were more likely to be depressed and to use their habit as a form of self-medication. This finding is important because efforts to help these individuals to quit smoking must address the physiological basis of their need for nicotine (and perhaps provide nicotine replacement) as well as address the underlying depression that they try to self-medicate.

Addiction was once thought to be simply the result of a person not having enough willpower to overcome his or her weakness. Now we know that there are genetic factors that predispose individuals to addictions of all sorts. This does not mean, of course, that if a person is born with a particular gene, he or she is doomed to be an addict. Nor does it imply that once one is addicted, one can never overcome that addiction. What it does indicate, however, is that biological factors do play a role in addiction, and that treatment strategies must include an understanding of genetic predisposition. Health psychologists have made major contributions to scientific knowledge in this area. They provide a crucial link between science and practice as they design successful interventions that integrate biological and social factors to treat substance abuse problems.

There may be countless opportunities for using DNA research to supplement traditional health psychology. Perhaps one day, for example, individual differences in the pain experience will be explained by genes, or individuals under acute stress who do not succumb to illness will be found to have a particular gene that facilitates their cognitive adaptation. It is difficult to fully imagine the impact that new genetic research will have on health psychology, but it is exciting to try!

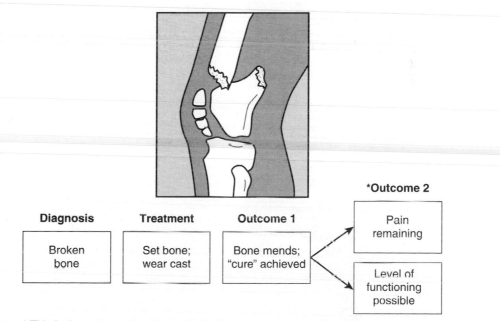

* This is the outcome health psychologists are concerned with.

FIGURE 14.2   Analysis of outcomes of treatment of fracture.

Outcomes Research

Health psychology, because of its focus on the whole person, has generally geared itself toward measuring not objective physical criteria but rather a person's health-related quality of life. This is consistent with a biopsychosocial approach, but it is quite different from the more narrow focus of the traditional biomedical model. According to this biomedical model, diseases cause symptoms, and when symptoms are understood, a diagnosis can be made. The disease can then be treated, and when it is gone, a "cure" is achieved. The biopsychosocial model, on the other hand, recognizes that objective "cure" does not necessarily correspond to a functional "cure." For example, a recent television advertisement touted the ability of a certain heartburn medication to reduce stomach acidity for 12 full hours. In small print at the bottom of the screen was a statement that acid reduction was "not correlated with symptoms relief." This provides an excellent example of a physiological "cure" being achieved, but the functional quality-of-life outcome being less than satisfactory. As another example, imagine that you have broken your arm, endured wearing a cast for eight weeks, and have now been declared to have a perfectly healed arm. You disagree, however. You feel more pain than you think you should and cannot seem to use your arm as you once could. Perhaps you also

Health psychology is concerned with health-related quality of life and functioning, not just objective physical outcomes.

feel very cautious because you are afraid of rebreaking it, and you worry that your arm may be too weak to do certain things. Thus, while you have been pronounced cured, you have not returned to your "prebreak" functional status (see Figure 14.2).

In both of the examples above—of stomach acid and a broken arm—the wrong outcome is being emphasized. Instead of focusing on the ultimate result of functioning, an intermediate endpoint has been designated (reduction of acid; knitting of bone), measured, and declared achieved. In both these cases, the recipient of the "cure" is likely to be dissatisfied. Health psychologists recognize the importance of functional outcomes for patients and are readily able to incorporate psychosocial and behavioral techniques into treatment regimens in order to achieve optimal outcomes. Of course, physicians and other healthcare providers want their patients to be as healthy and satisfied as possible, but they may not have the type of training that enables them to easily see the alternative avenues for achieving these goals. By working in collaboration with healthcare providers, psychologists can effect more positive outcomes for patients, making healthcare delivery more successful, efficient, and rewarding for all involved.

Health psychologists can also contribute their expertise to the care of patients who have physical health symptoms that are exacerbated by psychological factors. The care of such patients can be very costly to the healthcare system because they often require extensive testing and the trial of various treatments that may be only minimally, if at all, effective. Such patients often receive inappropriate treatment because the true basis of their problems would be more adequately addressed by psychotherapeutic than by purely medical means (Kaplan, 1991). As in so many areas, health psychologists can contribute a great deal to research on these issues and to the design of healthcare procedures to appropriately diagnose, treat, and educate medical professionals about psychologically related conditions, toward the ultimate goal of improving patients' health-related quality of life.

Summary

1. Health psychologists are increasingly moving into broadly defined roles as healthcare professionals, rather than simply focusing on mental health.

   - They often function as part of a medical team, along with doctors, nurses, physical therapists, nutritionists, and so on.
   - Promoting high quality of life, not just quantity, is at the heart of their mission. Often this can be achieved through preventive medicine routes.
   - Another important goal for health psychologists is to aid in cost containment and equalization of care.

2. Some of the exciting areas of research and intervention that are now emerging are those of women's health, healthy aging, and genetic factors in health. Health psychologists have played key roles in each of these areas.

3. Health psychology research has generally been outcomes-focused. As mainline medicine moves toward outcomes research, health psychologists are in a strong position to be able to share knowledge gained over the past forty years.

THINKING CRITICALLY

1. What do you think will be the healthcare issue that defines the next decade? What role will health psychologists play in it?

2. Some argue that, as more research focus is aimed at women, men are being left behind and that there is now a "reverse discrimination" of sorts. Do you agree with this? Why or why not?

3. Think about your own physical health from a biopsychosocial perspective. What areas of your life contribute to good health (and remember that *health* is an inclusive term)? What areas may be detrimental to your health? What can you do to improve and maintain health and quality of life?

A — The Human Body

The human body is a complex structure. It consists of organs in organ systems supported by a framework of muscle and bone, enclosed in an external covering of skin. A *cell* is the smallest unit of life. Specialized cells, similar in structure and function, are assembled together into a mass called *tissue*. Different kinds of tissues have varying characteristics according to their function (such as connective tissue, muscular tissue, nervous tissue, and epithelial tissue, which forms the outer surface of skin and linings of organs). Various tissues combine to form *organs* of the body, such as the heart, lungs, liver, and kidneys. Although they act as units, organs do not work independently. Several organs combine to form a *system* in order to perform a specific, complicated function. For example, the respiratory system is involved in taking oxygen into the lungs and excreting carbon dioxide, and the urinary system filters waste from the blood and eliminates it from the body. Although the systems of the body are conceptualized as distinct from each other, they are actually quite interdependent.

Let us examine several of these systems briefly. The student who wishes more detailed information is referred to the classic textbook of anatomy and physiology by Guyton (1985) and to the text of biological principles by Nelson (1984).

The Skeletal and Muscular Systems

The skeleton is the framework of the human body, made up of over 200 bones and pieces of cartilage that give the body its shape and support it. The skeleton allows for the attachment of tendons, muscles, and ligaments and makes body movement possible. The skeleton also affords protection to various vital organs, such as the heart and lungs (see Figure A.1).

A joint is a structure that holds separate bones together with ligaments of connective tissue. The study of bones is called *osteology*; the study of joints is called *arthrology*.

Muscle is tissue composed of long slender cells called *fibers*. These fibers are able to contract and thus produce movement of the body and its organs. All human activity (whether voluntary or involuntary) is carried on by muscles, of which about 500 are large enough to be seen with the naked eye and thousands of others are so small that they can be seen only through a microscope. The form of a person's body is due largely to the muscles covering the bones, and an individual's posture is due to the

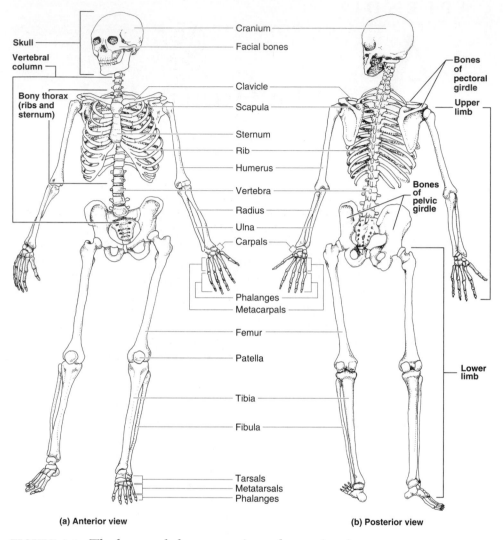

FIGURE A.1   The human skeleton: anterior and posterior views.

development of certain muscles of the trunk of the body. Muscles make up many of the internal organs such as the heart, uterus, lungs, and intestines (see Figure A.2).

Muscles are attached to bones with strong, fibrous white bands called *tendons*. *Fascia* hold together muscle bundles and *ligaments* hold together bones and keep organs in place. The motor nerve for any particular muscle causes that muscle to move.

Muscles are divided into three types: *voluntary* or skeletal muscles (striated), which compose about 40 percent of human body weight; *involuntary* (unstriated or smooth), such as found in the walls of the stomach, intestines, blood vessels, glands, and eyes; and *cardiac* or *heart muscle*.

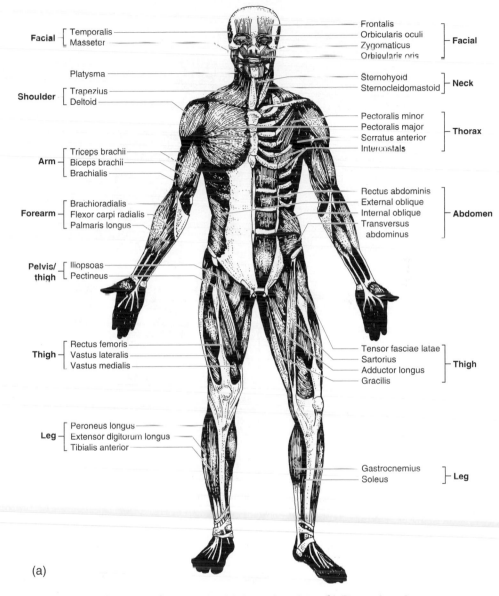

Facial — Temporalis
          Masseter

Shoulder Platysma
            Trapezius
            Deltoid

Arm — Triceps brachii
         Biceps brachii
         Brachialis

Forearm — Brachioradialis
             Flexor carpi radialis
             Palmaris longus

Pelvis/ thigh — Iliopsoas
                   Pectineus

Thigh — Rectus femoris
           Vastus lateralis
           Vastus medialis

Leg — Peroneus longus
         Extensor digitorum longus
         Tibialis anterior

Frontalis
Orbicularis oculi
Zygomaticus
Orbicularis oris — **Facial**

Sternohyoid
Sternocleidomastoid — **Neck**

Pectoralis minor
Pectoralis major
Serratus anterior
Intercostals — **Thorax**

Rectus abdominis
External oblique
Internal oblique
Transversus
abdominus — **Abdomen**

Tensor fasciae latae
Sartorius
Adductor longus
Gracilis — **Thigh**

Gastrocnemius
Soleus — **Leg**

(a)

FIGURE A.2   The muscular system. (a) Anterior view. (b) Posterior view.

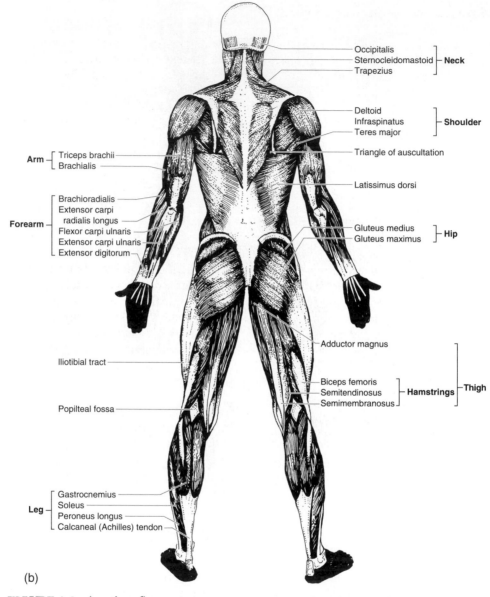

(b)

FIGURE A.2 (*continued*)

The Cardiovascular System

The cardiovascular system (see Figure A.3) consists of the heart, arteries, veins, capillaries, and blood. The *heart*, a hollow muscular pump about the size of a clenched fist, furnishes the force to propel and circulate blood through the body. The heart is enclosed in a membranous fluid-filled sac called the *pericardium*. The middle muscular layer of the heart wall is called the *myocardium*. The heart is lined internally by the *endocardium* and externally by the *epicardium*. The heart beats over 100,000 times a day from the beginning of life until death. After leaving the heart, it takes about one minute for the blood to make a complete circuit of the body and return.

Arteries carry blood from the heart to the rest of the body and *veins* carry blood to the heart from the rest of the body. Blood travelling toward the lungs is laden with carbon dioxide, whereas blood travelling away from the lungs is oxygen rich (carbon dioxide has been expelled).

The heart is divided into four chambers. The top two are called the *right atrium* and *left atrium*, and the bottom two are called the *right* and *left ventricles*. Carbon dioxide rich blood enters the heart at the right atrium and passes through a valve to the right ventricle. From the right ventricle, blood is pumped to the lungs, where it is oxygenated. Then it travels to the left atrium of the heart and passes to the left ventricle, which pumps it out into the body throughout a large vessel called the *aorta*. The blood is pumped by means of rhythmic contractions of the myocardium.

Blood is the fluid pumped by the heart through miles of blood vessels in the body. Blood carries nutrients, oxygen, and water to all the cells of the body and returns carbon dioxide to the lungs for disposal. Blood carries hormones to the cells of the tissues and serves as a temperature regulator of the body. Blood also acts to protect the body against disease and infection because it contains certain complex chemical substances (such as antibodies) that are the basis of defense against injurious agents. The blood also carries away waste products that are harmful to life. The kidneys and liver, though not part of the cardiovascular system, are particularly important elements in this latter function. The kidneys receive blood and cleanse it of waste products, passing the wastes on to be eliminated in the urine. The liver receives blood both from the circulation system and from the intestinal tract. The liver cleanses the blood of bacteria and also removes and stores nutrients such as sugars and amino acids.

Blood pressure is the force of the blood pushing through the body. It is also the force exerted on the artery walls as blood is pumped through the closed circulatory system. When the heart is at rest between contractions, it fills with blood. The blood pressure in this closed system measured at this rest point is called the *diastolic pressure*. When the heart pumps the blood out and through the body, the maximum force in the arteries is called the *systolic pressure*. The measurement of blood pressure is expressed as two numbers, the systolic over the diastolic. Systolic pressure is the highest because it is caused by contraction, or systole, of the heart. Diastolic pressure is the lowest because it is present during relaxation, or diastole, of the heart. Normal blood pressure

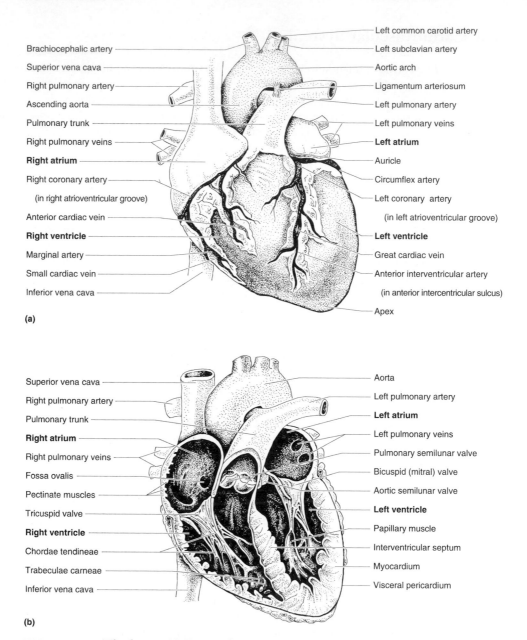

Left common carotid artery

Brachiocephalic artery

Left subclavian artery

Superior vena cava

Aortic arch

Right pulmonary artery

Ligamentum arteriosum

Ascending aorta

Left pulmonary artery

Pulmonary trunk

Left pulmonary veins

Right pulmonary veins

Left atrium

Right atrium

Auricle

Right coronary artery

Circumflex artery

(in right atrioventricular groove)

Left coronary artery

Anterior cardiac vein

(in left atrioventricular groove)

Right ventricle

Left ventricle

Marginal artery

Great cardiac vein

Small cardiac vein

Anterior interventricular artery

Inferior vena cava

(in anterior intercentricular sulcus)

Apex

(a)

Superior vena cava

Aorta

Right pulmonary artery

Left pulmonary artery

Pulmonary trunk

Left atrium

Right atrium

Left pulmonary veins

Right pulmonary veins

Pulmonary semilunar valve

Fossa ovalis

Bicuspid (mitral) valve

Pectinate muscles

Aortic semilunar valve

Tricuspid valve

Left ventricle

Right ventricle

Papillary muscle

Chordae tendineae

Interventricular septum

Trabeculae carneae

Myocardium

Inferior vena cava

Visceral pericardium

(b)

FIGURE A.3   The heart. (a) External anterior view. (b) Frontal section.

in a young adult is about 120 mm Hg systolic and 70 to 90 mm Hg (diastolic). Hypertension is a condition in which blood pressure is elevated. Any individual whose blood pressure is over 140 mm Hg systolic and/or 90 mm Hg diastolic is considered to have high blood pressure, or *hypertension*.

Blood pressure is affected by several factors. Activity level tends to increase blood pressure—for example, during exercise and for a period of time thereafter. Posture affects blood pressure so that when we go from sitting or lying down to standing, blood flow to the heart slows down causing a drop in *cardiac output* (the volume of blood being pumped per minute through the heart). There is then a reduction in blood flow to the brain and the individual may feel dizzy. Temperature can affect blood pressure. In high temperatures blood pressure falls, making us feel sluggish and drowsy. In low temperatures, blood pressure rises. Finally, emotional distress and emotional arousal (such as stress, anxiety, anger) can increase cardiac output and thereby raise both systolic and diastolic blood pressure (James et al., 1986). Very high systolic blood pressure (over 200 Hg) can cause constant strain on arteries and eventually may result in the rupture of a blood vessel, particularly one in the brain, causing a very serious condition called a *stroke*. Stroke can cause paralysis, loss of speech, and even death.

Blood pressure is higher among people who are overweight than among people who are of normal weight. Blood pressure also tends to be higher in males than in females, and higher in blacks than in whites. High blood pressure can be hereditary, but diet may also play a role in blood pressure. Hypertension is a "silent killer" because many people do not know they have it. High blood pressure is an asymptomatic condition that can be very dangerous.

The composition of blood is an important issue in health. Because these days we hear a great deal about "cholesterol" in the blood and its effects on health, it may be helpful to examine cholesterol and other elements of the blood. Blood is composed of "formed elements" and of plasma. Formed elements of blood comprise less than 50 percent of it. These include *red blood cells* that are formed in the bone marrow and contain *hemoglobin*, a protein that transports oxygen to body cells and tissue. They also include *leukocytes*, which are white blood cells that protect the body by destroying bacteria, as well as *platelets* that are produced by the bone marrow and aid in the clotting of blood. Hemophilia is a disease in which platelets do not function effectively and jeopardize the clotting of blood, leaving the individual open to possibly bleeding to death. In the plasma portion of the blood are *plasma protein* (which thickens the blood) and various organic and inorganic elements. In plasma are found nutrients from digestion such as vitamins, minerals, amino acids, and fatty materials. Fatty materials make up the class of substances called *lipids*. Cholesterol is a blood lipid.

Cholesterol is a fatty substance that collects on the walls of an artery and narrows the opening through which blood can flow. Cholesterol is manufactured by the body, but some comes from an individual's diet. A diet high in saturated fats tends to increase the level of cholesterol in the blood. Thus, while some people may have high cholesterol levels regardless of what they eat (because of hereditary factors, for example), the amount of cholesterol in one's blood can be at least partly determined by behavioral factors such as the kinds of food chosen. When cholesterol builds up on the walls of an artery (in patches called *plaques*), a condition called *atherosclerosis* occurs. The walls of the artery harden because of these plaques and "hardening of the arteries" or *arteriosclerosis* results. Arteriosclerosis can cause high blood pressure. Also, when an artery becomes blocked due to atherosclerosis, blood, and hence oxygen, cannot get to the heart muscle and some of the heart muscle tissue can die as a result.

The death of a portion of heart muscle tissue is called a *myocardial infarction* or a "heart attack." *Angina pectoris* is a condition marked by pain and a sense of tightness in the chest. It occurs when the heart muscle is not getting enough oxygen because plaques obstruct an artery. As noted above, one kind of stroke (rupture of a cerebral artery) can be caused by very high blood pressure. But another kind of stroke is related to atherosclerosis. A blood clot, or *thrombosis*, becomes lodged in a cerebral blood vessel and can damage the brain by depriving it of oxygenated blood.

The Respiratory System

The respiratory system (Figure A.4) consists of the *nose*, *mouth*, *pharynx* (airway between nasal chambers, mouth, and larynx), *larynx* (voice box), *trachea* (windpipe), *bronchial tubes*, and *lungs*. The bronchial tubes divide into smaller branches called *bronchioles* inside the lungs and end in millions of tiny air sacs called *alveoli*. Each air sac consists of a thin membrane through which passes oxygen, carbon dioxide, and other gasses.

Respiration is the process by which the body takes in oxygen that is required by all cells and releases carbon dioxide as a waste product. There are three components of the cycle of respiration. The process involves inhalation (inspiration) of oxygen and exhalation (or expiration) of carbon dioxide, as well as the interval between inspiration and expiration. Oxygen is absorbed by the lungs, passed into the bloodstream, combined with hemoglobin (the oxygen-carrying part of the blood) and carried to the tissues and cells of the body. Carbon dioxide is constantly formed in the body and carried by the blood back to the lungs for expiration. The respiratory center of the brain controls the rhythmic movements of respiration via the nerves that pass down to the chest wall and diaphragm. Chemical changes in the blood also stimulate the respiratory center. When excessive carbon dioxide accumulates in the blood, messages from the respiratory center in the brain cause respiration to become faster in order to rid the system of carbon dioxide. The muscles of respiration act automatically under normal circumstances. Under conditions of emotional distress, respiration can be altered and shallow breathing can result.

When foreign particles and microorganisms enter the respiratory tract, protective mechanisms are put into operation. Sneezing clears irritating particles from the nasal passages and coughing clears the lower parts of the respiratory system.

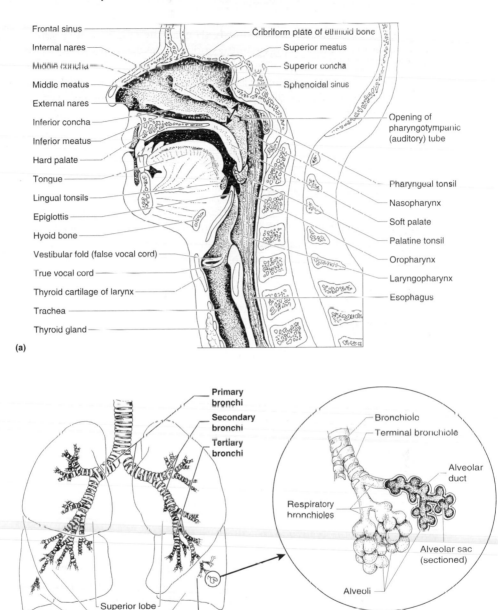

FIGURE A.4 The respiratory system. (a) The upper respiratory tract. (b) The lower respiratory tract, lungs and bronchial structure.

Cigarette smoking can seriously damage the respiratory system. *Emphysema*, a disease strongly linked with cigarette smoking, destroys the walls between the alveoli and decreases the surface within the lung that can be used to exchange gasses. Emphysema also decreases the elasticity of lung tissue. *Chronic bronchitis*, another smoking-related disorder, is a condition in which the bronchial tubes become inflamed and produce excess mucus. *Lung cancer* is a disease characterized by the uncontrolled growth of cells in the tissues that line the bronchial tubes. Eighty percent of lung cancers are caused by cigarette smoking.

The Gastrointestinal System

The gastrointestinal (or digestive) system (see Figure A.5) is responsible for taking in food, using nutrients, and eliminating waste products. Nutrients are absorbed from food into the bloodstream and transported to all cells of the body. Nutrients provide energy and contribute to the body's growth and repair.

The digestive system consists of the alimentary canal plus some accessory organs such as the salivary glands, liver, pancreas, and gallbladder. The *alimentary canal* extends from the mouth through the body to the anus and is about 30 feet long. The alimentary canal includes the esophagus, the stomach, and the small and large intestines. As food passes through the alimentary canal, the process of digestion extracts nutrients and carries waste material for elimination.

Food is broken down by the grinding action of chewing as well as by enzymes in the mouth and stomach. *Enzymes* are substances that speed up chemical reactions. Some of the enzymes that digest different types of food are sucrase, which helps to break down sucrose or sugar, and lactase, which helps to break down the lactose in milk. Many individuals have a deficiency of lactase, particularly as they grow older, and as a result are unable effectively to digest the lactose in dairy products. They are "lactose-intolerant" and may experience severe gastrointestinal symptoms whenever they eat dairy products. There are enzymes in saliva that start the process of breaking down starches in the mouth. The smell and appearance of food can cause neural impulses originating in the brainstem to stimulate the release of saliva in the mouth (Nelson, 1984).

Food passes from the mouth to the *esophagus*, a tube that pushes food down to the stomach using the action of muscle contractions called *peristalsis*. In the stomach, hydrochloric acid and pepsin break down the food into liquid that passes into the small intestine. There, further digestion, particularly of fats, takes place. Through the process of *absorption*, nutrients are absorbed through the small intestine into the bloodstream. Food material then passes into the large intestine, also called the colon, where some further absorption takes place and the material is converted through the action of bacteria into feces that are then eliminated from the body.

As we see in Chapter 9, emotional stress can affect the gastrointestinal system. This occurs chiefly in the formation of *ulcers*, which are sores in the lining of the stomach or intestine. These sores are partially caused by excess gastric juices that erode the lining of the stomach and duodenum (the beginning section of the small intestine).

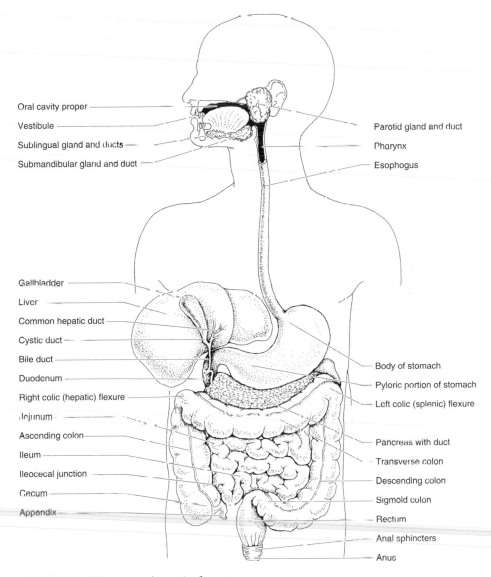

Oral cavity proper
Vestibule
Sublingual gland and ducts
Submandibular gland and duct

Parotid gland and duct
Pharynx
Esophogus

Gallbladder
Liver
Common hepatic duct
Cystic duct
Bile duct
Duodenum
Right colic (hepatic) flexure
Jejunum
Ascending colon
Ileum
Ileocecal junction
Cecum
Appendix

Body of stomach
Pyloric portion of stomach
Left colic (splenic) flexure
Pancreas with duct
Transverse colon
Descending colon
Sigmoid colon
Rectum
Anal sphincters
Anus

FIGURE A.5   The gastrointestinal system.

The *liver* is an essential organ that is situated in the upper right part of the abdomen. The liver produces bile, which converts sugar into glycogen. The liver also stores glycogen. The effective functioning of the liver can be seriously jeopardized by forms of *hepatitis*, a viral disease in which the liver becomes inflamed. Hepatitis A, or infectious hepatitis, is transmitted through contaminated food and water. Hepatitis B, or serum hepatitis, is transmitted through the transfusion of infected blood as well as through the sharing of needles by intravenous drug users and by vaginal or anal intercourse. Hepatitis, particularly Hepatitis B, can lead to permanent liver damage.

The Nervous System

The human body is governed by a central mechanism that serves to control and to meet all of its required functions. This is the *nervous system*.

The brain relays messages to the body by way of the spinal cord through nerve fibers that radiate to every structure in the body. The cells of the nervous system are called *neurons*. They exist in the billions in an intricate network throughout the body. Neurons vary in character depending upon their function, but generally they consist of a *cell body*, an axon, and branches called *dendrites*. Dendrites receive messages from adjacent neurons. These messages are passed through the neuron's long projection called the *axon*. This electrical message travels along the axon, which then splits into branches that have small swellings called synaptic knobs that lie close to the dendrites of adjacent neurons. A neural message in the form of a chemical signal, or neurotransmitter, crosses the gap between neurons, called the *synapse*, to the adjacent neuron. There are many different types of neurotransmitters, some of which excite and some of which inhibit the adjacent neurons.

Neurons are able to carry impulses rapidly for considerable distance. *Myelin*, a white fatty substance, surrounds the axons of most neurons and increases the speed of nerve impulses. The disease of *multiple sclerosis* involves a degeneration of these myelin sheaths and causes muscle weakness, loss of coordination, and spastic movements.

The nervous system can be divided into the *central nervous system* and the *peripheral nervous system*. The peripheral nervous system can be further divided into the *somatic* and the *autonomic nervous systems*. The central nervous system includes the brain and the spinal cord; the peripheral nervous system is composed of the nerves outside the brain and spinal cord.

The Central Nervous System

The brain comprises about 98 percent of the central nervous system (see Figure A.6). The brain lies in the protection of the skull and consists of three main parts: the forebrain, the midbrain, and the hindbrain.

The midbrain and hindbrain can be viewed as outgrowths of the spinal cord. In humans, the hindbrain serves primarily as a reflex and relay center. The *brainstem* is the lowest part of the brain and is found at the top of the spinal cord. All ascending and descending nerve tracts connect the brain with the spinal cord through the brainstem. The *midbrain* is the topmost structure of the brainstem. The midbrain relays messages from the spinal cord to the hypothalamus. Also in the brainstem is the *reticular system*, a network of neurons through the brainstem extending into the thalamus. The reticular system controls sleep as well as various stages of arousal. The *pons* is involved in facial expressions and eye movements. The *medulla* is found at the bottom of the brain-

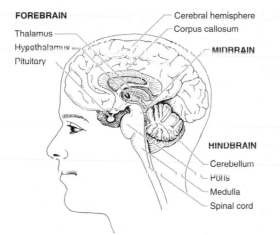

FOREBRAIN
Thalamus
Hypothalamus
Pituitary
Cerebral hemisphere
Corpus callosum
MIDBRAIN
HINDBRAIN
Cerebellum
Pons
Medulla
Spinal cord

FIGURE A.6   The brain. A view of the brain, split from top to bottom.

stem and controls breathing, heart rate, and blood pressure. Several conditions can affect the brainstem and threaten life. The virus *poliomyelitis*, which can be virtually eradicated with effective immunization, can attack and damage the medulla and threaten life because of the central role that the medulla plays in regulating vital functions. *Epilepsy*, a condition that brings periodic convulsions and loss of consciousness, is believed to result from abnormalities in the reticular system. *Parkinson's disease* is linked to degeneration of the midbrain. Parkinson's typically strikes older persons and can cause motor tremors as well as tremendous stiffness and rigidity in posture.

The *spinal cord* extends down from the brainstem and lies inside the spinal column. The spinal cord conveys sensory impulses to the brain and carries motor impulses from the brain to the peripheral parts of the body. *Sensory*, or *afferent, neurons* conduct impulses from the sense organs to the spinal cord and brain. *Motor*, or *efferent, neurons* convey impulses from the brain and spinal cord to the muscles and glands of the body. If the spinal cord is severed in an accident, the parts of the body below the point at which the cord is severed become paralyzed.

The *cerebellum* at the back of the brain is a structure that maintains the body's balance and coordination by connecting to both motor and sensory centers. Injury to this part of the brain can cause jerky, uncoordinated movement called *ataxia*.

The *forebrain* is the highest part of the brain and it consists of two parts: the *diencephalon* and the *telencephalon*.

Above the brainstem is the diencephalon, consisting of the *thalamus* and the *hypothalamus*. The thalamus is a kind of relay station for sensory messages to various parts of the cerebrum in the telencephalon as well as for motor messages to the skeletal muscles from the motor cortex of the cerebrum. The hypothalamus controls eating, drinking, and sexual activity and maintains the temperature homeostasis of the body. The hypothalamus plays an important role in the recognition of pain, temperature, touch, and pressure.

The telencephalon consists of the *limbic system* and the *cerebrum*. The limbic system lies next to the diencephalon and plays an important role in the expression of emotions. The limbic system appears to be the seat of arousing emotions such as anger, fear, and excitement.

The most highly developed part of the brain is the cerebrum, the surface of which is composed of billions of cells that form a gray layer called the cerebral cortex. The cerebrum is divided into motor areas that control muscular movement throughout the body, sensory areas that interpret sensory signals, and association areas that are concerned with emotional and intellectual processes. The cerebrum has two hemispheres, right and left, which are responsible for different types of processes. The motor cortex of each hemisphere controls movement on the opposite side of the body. The left hemisphere generally controls language processes including speech and writing while the right hemisphere controls visual imagery and the perception of music. Each hemisphere has a frontal lobe, a parietal lobe, an occipital lobe, and a temporal lobe. The *frontal lobes* are involved in motor activities as well as the association of ideas, self-awareness, and emotion. Damage to the frontal lobes, such as in a "frontal lobotomy," a surgery once done to reduce the symptoms of dangerous psychosis, can cause major alterations in personality and emotional reactions. The *temporal lobes* are sites of hearing and are involved in vision and memory. The *occipital lobes* contain the visual centers of the brain. Damage to them can cause blindness. The *parietal lobes* are involved in the perception of touch as well as other bodily sensations such as pain, cold, and heat.

The Peripheral Nervous System

The *peripheral nervous system* conveys messages from the central nervous system to the muscles and glands and is divided into the somatic and the autonomic nervous systems. The *somatic nervous system* involves *afferent neurons* that carry messages to the spinal cord from sensory organs and *efferent neurons* that carry messages to skeletal muscles to initiate and sustain movement.

The *autonomic nervous system* controls internal organs such as the glands and smooth muscles of the heart, lungs, blood vessels, lining of the stomach, and intestines. The autonomic nervous system is divided into the *sympathetic* and *parasympathetic* nervous systems. Under stress, the sympathetic nervous system dominates bodily functioning and speeds up heart rate, increases blood supply to the muscles, releases glucose, and dilates the bronchi of the lungs for increased oxygen consumption. The parasympathetic nervous system acts in opposition to the sympathetic to calm or quiet arousal responses. The parasympathetic nervous system is dominant during times of relaxation and functions to maintain the body in a condition of rest. It is also active in the digestion of food.

The Endocrine System

The *endocrine system* involves glands that are controlled by the autonomic nervous system. The glands in the endocrine system send messages to various parts of the body by releasing chemical substances called *hormones* directly into the bloodstream.

The nervous and endocrine systems are linked by connections between the hypothalamus and the *pituitary gland*. The pituitary gland releases hormones into the blood. These pituitary hormones stimulate other glands to secrete their own hormones, which in turn affect physical and psychological functioning. For example, when the sympathetic nervous system becomes aroused in response to an emergency, the hypothalamus chemically stimulates the pituitary to release ACTH (adrenocorticotropic hormone) into the blood.

ACTH stimulates the release of other hormones in response to stress. For example, the *adrenal glands*, located on top of the kidneys, are stimulated to produce *epinephrine* and *norepinephrine* (adrenaline and noradrenaline), which speed up the heart and respiration and increase the liver's output of sugar to the muscles. *Cortisol* is also released by the adrenal glands during perceived emergencies to help control swelling should injury occur. In Chapter 9, where stress responses are considered in more detail, we see that these adrenal hormones can remain in the bloodstream long after the sympathetic nervous system response has quieted and they can be harmful to the body.

There are other glands in the endocrine system as well. These include the *thyroid* gland, which produces hormones that regulate general activity and growth. The thyroid gland is located in the neck. An excess of hormone results in *hyperthyroidism*, a condition characterized by insomnia, high activity levels, tremors, and weight loss. Hyperthyroidism is sometimes misdiagnosed as anxiety! A deficiency of thyroid hormone results in *hypothyroidism*, characterized by low levels of activity and the gaining of weight. The *thymus* gland is located in the chest and plays an important role in immunity. The thymus gland is where T-lymphocyte cells mature. Finally, the *pancreas*, located below the stomach, regulates the body's blood sugar levels. *Diabetes mellitus* is a condition in which the pancreas does not produce enough insulin. Diabetes can be controlled through diet and daily medication or by the injection of insulin.

The Immune System

The *immune system* is the body's means of warding off foreign invaders such as bacteria, fungi, protozoa, viruses, and carcinogenic substances. A general term for these foreign invaders is antigens. Until recently, not much was known about the immune system, and most people took it for granted. With the appearance of the acquired immunodeficiency syndrome (AIDS) there has been a burgeoning interest in research on how the immune system functions and what role it plays in keeping us healthy.

The lymphatic organs are primarily involved in immune responses. The lymphatic organs include bone marrow, the thymus gland, lymph nodes, lymph vessels, and spleen. *Lymphocytes* are white blood cells that are critical in defending the body against antigens or foreign substances. They originate in the bone marrow, deep within the core of the bones. *Lymph nodes* are nodes of spongy tissue that are located in various parts of the body including the neck, armpits, abdomen, and groin. Lymph nodes capture antigens and house lymphocytes and other white blood cells. The *spleen*, located in the upper left side of the abdomen, filters out antigens and worn red blood cells from the blood. The spleen also houses white blood cells.

Nonspecific immune response involves a process called *phagocytosis* in which *phago-cytes*, scavengers of the immune system, engulf and destroy antigens. The two types of phagocytes are *macrophages*, which remain attached to tissue and *monocytes*, which freely circulate in the blood. Phagocytes are nonspecific in their action. They'll consume anything!

On the other hand, *specific immune responses* involve two types of immunological reactions: *humoral* and *cell-mediated* reactions. *Humoral immunity*, or antibody-mediated immunity, occurs when B-lymphocytes differentiate into plasma cells that produce antibodies to fight a foreign invader. *Antibodies* are protein molecules that attach to the surface of invading substances and help to arrange for their destruction by other elements of the immune system. They slow down an invader so that phagocytes can destroy it. They also form a memory for the invader so that another like it in the future can be recognized and defended against more quickly. Finally, antibodies help to destroy the membrane of the offending microorganism. *Cell-mediated immunity* involves T-lymphocytes from the thymus gland and is slower acting than humoral immunity. *T-cells* are infection-fighting white blood cells that have matured in the thymus gland. Their level of activity (along with lymphocyte activity) is a key element in immune system functioning. Instead of releasing antibodies into the blood, cell mediated immunity depends directly upon T-cells. Killer T-cells directly invade tissue that is recognized as foreign, cancerous cells and cells that have been invaded by antigens. Memory T-cells enable the body to defend itself against invaders that have been experienced in the past by holding a memory for the invader. Helper T-cells stimulate lymphocytes to reproduce and attack invaders, and suppressor T-cells slow down or stop cell-mediated and humoral immunity when the antigen has been destroyed (Jemmot & Locke, 1984).

B Measurement Tools for Research in Health Psychology

Subjective Well-Being

Affect Intensity Measure

Larsen, R.J. (1983). *Manual for the Affect Intensity Measure*. Unpublished manuscript, Department of Psychology, Purdue University, West Lafayette, IN.

Affectometer 2

Kammann, R., & Flett, R. (1983). Affectometer 2: A scale to measure current level of general happiness. *Australian Journal of Psychology, 35*, 259–265.

Affect Scales: Positive Affect, Negative Affect, Affect Balance

Bradburn, N. (1969). The structure of psychological well-being. Chicago: Aldine.

Andrews and Withey's Life Satisfaction Measure

Andrews, F.M., & Withey, S.V. (1976). *Social indicators of well-being*. New York: Plenum Press.

Bradbum's Subjective Well-Being Scale

Bradbum, N.M. (1969). *The structure of psychological well-being*. Chicago: Aldine.

General Well-Being Schedule

Fazio, A.F. (1977). A concurrent validation study of the NCH1 General Well-Being Schedule. (Dept. of HEW Publ. No. HRA-78-1347) Hyattsville, MD: National Center for Health Statistics.

Index of Happiness

Fordyce, M.W. (1977). The happiness measures. Unpublished paper available from the author at Edison Community College, Fort Myers, FL.

Index of Well-Being, Index of General Affect

Campbell, A., Converse, P.E., & Rodgers, W.L. (1976). *The quality of American life: Perceptions, evaluation and satisfaction*. New York: Russell Sage.

Life 3 Scale

Andrews, F.M., & Withey, S.B. (1976). *Social indicators of well-being*. New York: Plenum.

Life Satisfaction Scale

Neugarten, B.L., Havighurst, R.J., & Tobin, S. (1961). The measurement of life satisfaction. *Journal of Gerontology, 16*, 134–143.

Memorial University of Newfoundland Scale of Happiness

Kozma, A., & Stones, M.J. (1980). The measurement of happiness: Development of the Memorial University of Newfoundland Scale of Happiness (MUNSH). *Journal of Gerontology, 35*, 906–912.

PGC Morale Scale (Revised)

Lawton, M.P. (1975). The Philadelphia Geriatric Center Morale Scale: A revision. *Journal of Gerontology, 30*, 85–89.

The PSYCHAP Inventory

Fordyce, M. (1986). The PSYCHAP Inventory: A multi-item test to measure happiness and its concomitants. *Social Indicators Research, 18*, 1–33.

Satisfaction With Life Scale

Diener, E., Emmons, A., Larsen, R.J., & Griffin, S. (1985). The Satisfaction With Life Scale: A measure of life satisfactions. *Journal of Personality Assessment, 49*, 71–75.

Sematic Differential Scale

Campbell, A., Converse, P.E., & Rodgers, W.L. (1976). *The quality of American life*. New York: Russell Sage Foundation.

Self-Esteem Scales

The Body-Esteem Scale

Franzoi, S.L., & Shields, S.A. (1984). The Body Self-Esteem Scale: Multidemensional structure and sex differences in a college population. *Journal of Personality Assessment, 48*, 173–178.

The Feelings of Inadequacy Scale

Janis, I.L., & Field, P.B. (1959). Sex differences and factors relation to persuasibility. In C.I. Hovland & I.L. Janis (Eds.), *Personality and persuasibility*. New Haven, CT: Yale University Press.

Personal Evaluation Inventory

Information can be obtained by writing Dr. Sidney Shrauger, Psychology Department, Park Hall, State University of New York at Buffalo, Buffalo, New York 14260.

Piers-Harris Children's Self-Concept Scale

The scale is copyrighted and available through Western Psychological Services, 12031 Wilshire Blvd., Los Angeles, California 90025.

The Revised Janis-Field Scale

Brockner, J. (1988). *Self-esteem at work: Research, theory and practice*. Lenington, MA: D.C. Health.

Self-Description Questionnaire

The scale is copyrighted and available through the Psychological Corporation, 555 Academic Court, San Antonio, Texas 78204-2498.

The Self-Esteem Inventory

Coopersmith, S. (1967). The antecedents of self-esteem. San Fransico: W.H. Freeman. Items for Form B are identified in Coopersmith, S. (1975). Self-concept, race, and education. In C.K. Verma & C. Bagley (Eds.), *Race and education across cultures*. London: Heinemann.

The Self-Esteem Scale

Rosenberg, M. (1965). *Society and the adolescent self-image*. Princeton, NJ: Princeton University Press.

Self Perception Profile for Children

The scales are available from Dr. Susan Harter at the Psychology Department, University of Denver, Denver, Colorado 80208-0204.

Social Self-Esteem

Ziller, R.C., Hagey, J., Smith, M.D., & Long, B. (1969). Self-esteem: A self-social construct. *Journal of Consulting and Clinical Psychology, 33,* 84 95.

Tennessee Self-Concept Scale

The TSCS is copyrighted and available through Western Psychological Services, 12031 Wilshire Blvd., Los Angeles, California 90025.

Texas Social Behavior Inventory

Helmreich, R., & Stapp, J. (1974). Short forms of the Texas Social Behavior Inventory (TSBI), an objective measure of self-esteem. *Bulletin of the Psychonomic Society, 4,* 473–475.

Social Anxiety Scales

Embarrassability Scale

Modigliani, A. (1966). *Embarrassment and social influence*. Unpublished doctoral dissertation, University of Michigan, Ann Arbor.

Fear of Negative Evaluation Scale (FNE)

Original 30-item scale: Watson, D., & Friend, R. (1969). Measurement of social-evaluative anxiety. *Journal of Consulting and Clinical Psychology, 33,* 448–457.

Revised 12-item scale: Leary, M.R. (1983). A brief version of the Fear of Negative Evaluation Scale. *Personality and Social Psychology Bulletin, 9,* 371–375.

Hospital Anxicty and Depression Scale (HAD)

Zigmund, A.S., Snaith, R.P. (1983). The Hospital Anxiety and Depression Scale. *Acta Psychiatrica Scandinavia, 67,* 361–370.

Interaction Anxiousness Scale

Leary, M.R. (1983). Social anxiousness: The construct and its measurement. *Journal of Personality Assessment, 47,* 66–75.

Personal Report of Communication Apprehension (PRCA-24)

McCroskey, J.C. (1982) *An introduction to rhetorical communication* (4th ed.). Englewood Cliffs, NJ: Prentice-Hall.

Personal Report of Confidence as a Speaker

Paul, F.L. (1966). *Insight vs. desensitization in psychotherapy*. Stanford, CA: Stanford University Press.

Shyness Scale

Cheek, J.M., & Buss, A.H. (1981). Shyness and sociability. *Journal of Personality and Social Psychology, 41,* 330–339.

Social Anxiety Scale for Children

La Greca, A.M., Dandes, S.K., Wick, P., Shaw, K., & Stone, W.L. 1988). Development of the Social Anxiety Scale for Children: Reliability and concurrent validity. *Journal of Clinical Child Psychology, 17,* 84–91.

Social Anxiety Subscale of the Self-Consciousness Scale

Original Scale: Renigstein, A., Scheier, M.F., & Buss, A.H. (1975). Public and private self-consciousness: Assessment and theory. *Journal of Consulting and Clinical Psychology, 43,* 522–527.

Revised scale for non-college populations: Scheier, M.F., & Carver, C.S. (1985). The Self-Consciousness Scale: A revised version for use with general populations. *Journal of Applied Social Psychology, 15,* 687–699.

Social Avoidance and Distress Scale (SAD)

Watson, D., & Friend, R. (1969). Measurement of social evaluative anxiety. *Journal of Consulting and Clinical Psychology, 33,* 448–457.

Social Reticence Scale

Jones, W.H., & Briggs, S.R. (1986). *Manual for the Social Reticence Scale.* Palo Alto, CA: Consulting Psychologists Press.

Depression and Loneliness Scales

Academic Attributional Style Questionnaire

Peterson, C. & Barrett, L.C. (1987). Explanatory style and academic performance among university freshman. *Journal of Personality and Social Psychology, 53,* 603–607.

Attributional Style Questionnaire

Peterson, C., Semmel, A., von Baeyer, C., Abramson, L.Y., Metalsky, G.I., & Seligman, M.E.P. (1982). The Attributional Style Questionnaire. *Cognitive Therapy and Research, 6,* 287–300.

Attributional Style Questionnaire

Peterson, C., & Villanova, P. (1988). An expanded Attributional Style Questionnaire. *Journal of Abnormal Psychology, 97,* 87–89.

The Automatic Thoughts Questionnaire

Hollon, S.D., & Kendall, P.C. (1980). Cognitive self-statements in depression: Development of an Automatic Thoughts Questionnaire. *Cognitive Therapy and Research, 4,* 383–395.

Beck Depression Inventory

Original 21-item scale: Beck, A.T. (1967). *Depression: Causes and treatment.* Philadelphia: University of Pennsylvania Press.

Revised 21-item scale: Beckham, E.E., & Leber, W.R. (Eds.) (1985). *Handbook of depression: Treatment, assessment, and research (Appendix 3).* Homewood, IL: Dorsey.

Short form (13 items): Beck, A.T., & Beck, R.W. (1972). Screening depressed patients in family practice: A rapid technic. *Postgraduate Medicine, 52,* 81–85.

Carroll Rating Scale for Depression

Carroll, B.J., Feinberg, M., Smouse, P.E., Rawson, S.G., & Greden, J.F. (1981). The Carroll Rating Scale for depression: I. Development, reliability and validation. *British Journal of Psychiatry, 138,* 205–209.

Center for Epidemiologic Studies Depression Scale

Radloff, L.S. (1977). The CES-D scale: A self-report depression scale for research in the general population. *Applied Psychological Measurement, 1,* 385–401.

Children's Depression Inventory

Kovacs, M. (1980/1981). Rating scales to assess depression in school-aged children. *Acta Paedopsychiatry, 46*, 305–315.

Children's Loneliness Scale

Asher, S.R., Hymel, S., & Renshaw, P.D. (1984). Loneliness in children. *Child Development, 55*, 1456–1464.

The Cognitive Bias Questionnaire

Krantz, S., & Hammen, C. (1979). Assessment of cognitive bias in depression. *Journal of Abnormal Psychology, 88*, 611–619.

Depression Adjective Checklist

Lubin, B. (1965). Adjective checklists for measurement of depression. *Archives of General Psychiatry, 12*, 57–62.

Depressive Experience Questionnaire

Blatt, S.J., D'Afflitti, J.P., & Quinlan, D.M. (1976b). Experiences of depression in normal young adults. *Journal of Abnormal Psychology, 85*, 383–389.

Instructions can be obtained from Dr. Sydney Blatt, Yale University School of Medicine, 25 Park Street, New Haven, CT 06519.

Differential Loneliness Scale

Schmidt, N., & Sermat, V. (1983). Measuring loneliness in different relationships. *Journal of Personality and Social Psychology, 44*, 1038–1047.

Emotional-Social Loneliness Inventory

Vincenzi, H., & Grabosky, F. (1987). Measuring the emotional/social aspects of loneliness and isolation. *Journal of Social Behavior and Personality, 2* (2, Part 2), 257–270.

Emotional versus Social Loneliness Scales

Russell, D. Cutrona, C.E., Rose, J., & Yurko, K. (1984). Social and emotional loneliness: An examination of Weiss's typology of loneliness. *Journal of Personality and Social Psychology, 46*, 1313–1321.

The Geriatric Depression Scale

Brink, T.L., Yesavage, J.A., Lum, O., Heersema, P.H., Adey, M., & Rose, T.L. (1982). Screening tests for geriatric depression. *Clinical Gerontologist, 1*, 37–43.

Loneliness Rating Scale

de Jong-Gierveld, J., & van Tilburg, T. (1990). *Manual of the Loneliness Scale.* Vrije Universiteit Amsterdam Koningtslaan 22–24, 1075 AD Amsterdam, The Netherlands.

POMS

McNair, D.M., Lorr, M.J., & Droppleman, L.F. (1971). *Profile of Mood States.* San Diego, CA: EDITS

Self Rating Depression Scale

Zung, W.W.K. (1965). A self-rating depression scale. *Archives of General Psychiatry, 12*, 63–70.

State Versus Trait Loneliness Scales

Gerson, A.C., & Perlman, D. (1979). Loneliness and expressive communication. *Journal of Abnormal Psychology, 88*, 258–261.

UCLA Loneliness Scale (Versions 2 & 3)

Original scale: Russell, D., Peplau, L.A., & Ferguson, M.L. (1978). Developing a measure of loneliness. *Journal of Personality Assessment, 42*, 290–294.

Version 2: Russell, D., Peplau, L.A., & Cutrona, C.E. (1980). The revised UCLA Loneliness Scale: Concurrent and discriminant validity evidence. *Journal of Personality and Social Psychology, 39,* 472–480.

History, review, and scale: Russell, D. (1982). The measurement of loneliness. In L.A. Peplau & D. Perlman (Eds.), *Loneliness: A sourcebook of current theory, research, and therapy* (pp. 81–104). New York: Wiley (Interscience).

Version 3: Russell, D.W., & Cutrona, C.E. (1988). *Development and evolution of the UCLA Loneliness Scale.* Unpublished manuscript, Center for Health Services Research, College of Medicine, University of Iowa.

Sense of Coherence

Meaninglessness Scale

Neal, A., & Groat, H.T. (1974). Social class correlates of stability and change in levels of alienation. *Sociological Quarterly, 15,* 548–558.

Orientation to Life

Antonovsky, A. (1987). *Unraveling the mystery of health.* San Francisco: Jossey-Bass.

The Purpose in Life Test

Crumbaugh, J. (1968). Cross-validation of a purpose in life test based on Frankl's concepts. *Journal of Individual Psychology, 24,* 74–81.

Locus of Control

Adult Nowicki-Strickland Internal-External Control Scale

Nowicki, S., & Duke, M.P. (1983). The Nowicki-Strickland life span locus of control scales: Construct validation. In H.M. Lefcourt (Ed.) *Research with the locus of control construct* (Vol. 2, pp. 9–43). New York: Academic Press.

The Desired Control Scale

Reid, D.W., & Ziegler, M. (1981). The Desired Control Measure and adjustment among the elderly. In H.M. Lefcourt (Ed.), *Research with the locus of control contruct* (Vol. 1, pp. 127–157). New York: Academic Press.

Drinking-Related Locus of Control Scale

Donovan, D.M., & O'Leary, M.R. (1978). The Drinking-Related Locus of Control Scale. *Journal of Studies on Alcohol, 39,* 759–784.

Dyadic Sexual Regulation Scale

Catania, J.A., McDermott, L.V., & Wood, J.A. (1984). Assessment of locus of control: Situational specificity in the sexual context. *Journal of Sex Research, 20,* 310–324.

Intellectual Achievement Responsibility Questionnaire

Crandall, V.V., Katkovsky, W., & Crandall, V.J. (1965). Children's beliefs in their own control of reinforcements in intellectual-academic achievement situations. *Child Development, 36,* 91–109.

Internal-External Locus of Control Scale

Rotter, J.B. (1966). Generalized expectancies for internal versus external control of reinforcement. *Psychological MonogrAphs, 80,* (1, Whole No. 609).

Internality, Powerful Others, and Chance Scales

Levenson, H. (1981). Differentiating among internality, powerful others, and chance. In H.M. Lefcourt (Ed.), *Research with the locus of control construct* (Vol. 1, pp. 15–63). New York: Academic Press.

Levenson Locus of Control Scale

Levenson, H. (1974). Activism and powerful others: Distinctions within the concept of internal–external control. *Journal of Personality Assessment, 38*, 377–383.

The Marital Locus of Control Scale

Miller, P.C., Lefcourt, H.M., & Ware, E.E. (1983). The construction and development of the Miller Marital Locus of Control Scale. *Canadian Journal of Behavioural Science, 15*, 266–279.

Mental Health Locus of Control Scale

Hill, D.J., & Bale, R.M. (1980). Development of the Mental Health Locus of Control and Mental Health Locus of Origin Scales. *Journal of Personality Assessment, 44*, 148–156.

Multidimensional Health Locus of Control Scale

Wallston, K.A., Wallston, B.S., & DeVellis, R. (1978). Development of the Multidimensional Health Locus of Control Scales. *Health Education Monographs, 6*, 161–170.

Multidimensional Measure of Children's Perceptions of Control

Connell, J.P. (1985). A new multidimensional measure of children's perceptions of control. *Child Development, 56*, 1018–1041.

The Multidimensional-Multiattributional Causality Scale

Lefcourt, H.M., Van Baeyer, C.L., Ware, E.E., & Cox, D.J. (1979). The Multidimensional-Multiattributional Causality Scales. *Canadian Journal of Behavioural Science, 11*, 286–304.

Nowicki-Strickland Internal-External Control Scale for Children

Nowicki, S., Jr., & Strickland, B.R. (1973). A locus of control scale for children. *Journal of Consulting and Clinical Psychology, 10*, 148–154.

Parenting Locus of Control Scale

Campis, L.K., Lyman, R.D., & Prentice-Dunn, S. (1986). The parental locus of control scale: Development and validation. *Journal of Clinical Psychology, 15*, 260–267.

Spheres of Control

Paulhus, D. (1983). Sphere-specific measures of perceived control. *Journal of Personality and Social Psychology, 44*, 1253–1265.

The Weight Locus of Control Scale

Saltzer, E.B. (1981). Cognitive moderators of the relationship between behavioral intentions and behavior. *Journal of Personality and Social Psychology, 41*, 260–271.

Authoritarianism

Attitude Toward Authority Scales

Ray, J.J. (1971). An "attitude toward authority" scale. *Australian Psychologist, 6*, 31–50.

Authoritarianism-Rebellion Scale (A-R)

Kohn, P.M. (1972). The Authoritarianism-Rebellion scale: A balanced F scale with left-wing reversals. *Sociometry, 35*, 176–189.

Buss-Durkee Hostility Inventory

Buss, A.J., & Durkee, A. (1957). An inventory for assessing different kinds of hostility. *Journal of Consulting Psychology, 21*, 343–349.

Dogmatism (D) Scale

Rokeach, M. (1956). Political and religious dogmatism: An alternative to the authoritarian personality. *Psychological Monographs, 70* (Whole No. 425).

Fascist Attitudes Scale

Stagner, R. (1936). Fascist attitudes: An exploratory study. *Journal of Social Psychology, 6,* 309–319.

Framingham Type A Scale

Haynes, S.G., Feinleib, M., & Kannel, W.B. (1980). The relationships of psychosocial factors to coronary heart disease in the Framingham Study: Eight-year incidence of coronary heart disease. *American Journal of Epidemiology, 111,* 37–58.

Jenkins Activity Survey of Type A

Jenkins, C.D., Zyzanski, S.J., & Rosenman, R.H. (1974). Prediction of clinical coronary heart disease by a test for the coronary prone behavior pattern. *New England Journal of Medicine, 23,* 1271–1275.

Naysaying Low F Scale

Couch, A., & Keniston, K. (1960). Yeasayers and naysayers: Agreeing response set as a personality variable. *Journal of Abnormal and Social Psychology, 60,* 151–174.

Political-Economic Progressivism (P.E.P.) Scale

Newcomb, T.M. (1943). *Personality and social change.* New York: Dryden.

Right-Wing Authoritarianism (RWA)

Altemeyer, B. (1981). *Right-wing authoritarianism.* Winnipeg: University of Manitoba.

Type A Structured Interview

Rosenman, R.H. (1978). The interview method of assessment of the coronary-prone behavior pattern. In T.M. Dembroski, S.M. Weiss, J.L. Shields, S.G. Haynes, & M. Feinleib (Eds.), *Coronary-prone behavior* (p. 55–70). New York: Springer-Verlag.

Unlabeled Fascist Attitudes

Edwards, A.L. (1941). Unlabeled fascist attitudes. *Journal of Abnormal and Social Psychology, 36,* 579–582.

Miscellaneous

CEC Scale

Watson, M., & Greer, S. (1983). Development of a questionnaire measure of emotional control. *Journal of Psychosomatic Research, 27,* 299–305.

Content Analysis of Verbatim Explanations

Peterson, C., Schulman, P., Castellon, C., & Seligman, M.E.P. (1992). CAVE: Content Analysis of Verbatim Explanations. In C.P. Smith (Ed.), *Motivation and personality: Handbook of thematic content analysis* (pp. 383–392). New York: Cambridge University Press.

Coping Strategies Questionnaire (CSQ)

Gil, K.M., Abrams, M.R., Phillips, G., & Keefe, F.J. (1989). Sickle cell disease pain: Relation of coping strategies to adjustment. *Journal of Consulting and Clinical Psychology, 57,* 725–731.

Eysenck Personality Questionnaire

Eysenck, H.J., & Eysenck, S.B.G. (1975). *Manual for the Eysenck Personality Questionnaire.* San Diego, CA: Educational and Industrial Testing Service.

Eysenck's Revised Personality Inventory

Eysenck, S.B.G., Eysenck, H.J., & Barrett, P. (1985). A revised version of the Psychoticism Scale. *Personality and Individual Differences, 6,* 21–29.

Hardiness Test

Maddi, S.R. (1987). Hardiness training at Illinois Bell Telephone. In J.P. Opatz (Ed.), *Health promotion evaluation.* Stevens Point, WI: National Wellness Institute.

Heart Patients Psychological Questionnaire

Erdman, R.A. (1982). *HPPQ: Heart Patients Psychological Questionnaire.* Lisse, Netherlands: Swets & Zeitlinger.

Life Orientation Test

Scheier, M.F. & Carver, C.S. (1985). Optimism, coping and health: Assessment and implication of generalized outcome expectancies. *Health Psychology, 4,* 219–247.

Manifest Anxiety Scale

Taylor, J.A. (1953). A personality scale of manifest anxiety. *Journal of Abnormal and Social Psychology, 48,* 285–290.

NEO PI-R

Costa, P.T. Jr., & McCraie, R.R. (1987a). *The Revised NEO Personality Inventory professional manual.* Odessa, FL · PAR

State-Trait Anxiety Inventory

Spielberger, C.D., Gorsuch, R.L., & Lushene, R.E. (1970). *Manual for the State-Trait Anxiety Inventory.* Palo Alto, CA: Consulting Psychologists Press.

Twenty-Item Toronto Alexithymia Scale

Bagby, R.M., Taylor, G.J., & Parker, J.D.A. (1994). The Twenty-Item Toronto Alexithymia Scale-II: Convergent, discriminant, and concurrent validity. *Journal of Social psychology, 136,* 49–56.

Ways of Coping Scale

Lazarus, R.S., & Folkman, S. (1984). *Stress, appraisal and coping.* New York: Springer.

REFERENCES

Aalto, A.M., Uutela, A., & Aro, A.R. (1997). Health-related quality of life among insulin-dependent diabetics: Disease-related and psychosocial correlates. *Patient Education and Counseling, 30,* 215–225.

Abraido-Lanza, A.F., Guier, C., & Revenson, T.A. (1996). Coping and social support resources among Latinas with arthritis. *Arthritis Care and Research, 9,* 501–508.

Adelman, R.D., Fields, S.D., & Jutagir, R. (1992). Geriatric education, part II: The effect of well elderly program on medical student attitudes toward geriatric patients. *Journal of the American Geriatric Society, 40,* 970–973.

Ader, R. (Ed.). (1981). *Psychoneuroimmunology.* New York: Academic Press.

Ader, R., & Cohen, N. (1985). CNS-immune system interactions: Conditioning phenomena. *Behavioral and Brain Sciences, 8,* 379–395.

Ader, R., Felton, D.L., & Cohen, N. (Eds.) (1991). *Psychoneuroimmunology.* San Diego, CA: Academic Press.

Adewuyi-Dalton, R., Ziebland, S., Grunfeld, E., & Hall, A. (1998). Patients' views of routine hospital follow-up: A qualitative study of women with breast cancer in remission. *Psychooncology, 7,* 436–439.

Adkins, L. (1984). Hospice care for terminally ill children. *Child Welfare, 63,* 559–562.

Adler, M.L. (1972). Kidney transplantation and coping mechanisms. *Psychosomatics, 13,* 337–341.

Adler, N., & Matthews, K.A. (1994). Health and psychology: Why do some people get sick and some stay well? *Annual Review of Psychology, 45,* 229–259.

Adler, N.E., Boyce, W.T., Chesney, M.A., Folkman, S., & Syme, L. (1993). Socioeconomic inequalities in health: No easy solution. *Journal of the American Medical Association, 269,* 3140–3145.

Agran, P.F. (1981). Motor vehicle occupant injuries in noncrash event. *Pediatrics, 67,* 838–840.

Agras, W.S., Berkowitz, R.I., Arnow, B.A., Telch, C.F., Marnell, M., Henderson, J., Morris, Y, & Wilfley, D.E. (1996). Maintenance following a very-low-calorie diet. *Journal of Consulting & Clinical Psychology, 64,* 610–613.

Ahles, T.A., Cassens, H.L., & Stalling, R.B. (1987). Private body consciousness, anxiety and the perception of pain. *Journal of Behavior Therapy and Experimental Psychiatry, 18,* 215–222.

Aiken, L.H. (1983). Nurses. In D. Mechanic (Ed.), *Handbook of health, health care, and the health professions.* New York: Free Press.

Aiken, L.H., & Marx, M.M. (1982). Hospices: Perspectives on the public policy debate. *American Psychologist, 37,* 1271–1279.

Ajzen, I. (1985). From intentions to actions: A theory of planned behavior. In J. Kuhland & J. Beckman (Eds.), *Action-control: From cognitions to behavior* (pp. 11–39). Heidelberg, Germany: Springer.

Ajzen, I., & Fishbein, M. (1977). Attitude-behavior relations: A theoretical analysis and review of empirical research. *Psychological Bulletin, 84,* 888–918.

Ajzen, I., & Fishbein, M. (1980). *Understanding attitudes and predicting social behavior.* Englewood Cliffs, NJ: Prentice-Hall.

Akil, H., Watson, S.J., Young, E., Lewis, M.E., Khachaturian, H., & Walker, J.M. (1984). Endogenous opioids: Biology and function. *Annual Review of Neuroscience, 7,* 223–255.

Alberman, E. (1986). Prevention and health promotion. *British Medical Bulletin, 42,* 212–216.

Alexander, F. (1950). *Psychosomatic medicine.* New York: Norton.

Allman, R.M., Steinberg, E.P. Keruly, J.C. & Dans, P.E. (1985). Physician tolerance for uncertainty: Use of liver-spleen scans to detect metastases. *Journal of the American Medical Association, 254,* 246–248.

Allport, G.W. (1935). Attitudes. In C. Murchinson (Ed.), *A handbook of social psychology* (pp. 798–844). Worcester, MA: Clark University Press.

Alon, G., Kantor, G., & Smith, G.V. (1999). Peripheral nerve excitation and plantar flexion force elicited by electrical stimulation in males and females. *Journal of Orthopedic Sports Physical Therapy, 29,* 208–214.

Altman, D.G., & Cahn, J. (1987). Employment options for health psychologists. In G.C. Stone, S.M. Weiss, J.D. Matarazzo, N.E. Miller, J. Rodin, C.D. Belar, M.J. Follick, & J.E. Singer (Eds.), *Health psychology: A discipline and a profession.* Chicago, IL: University of Chicago Press.

American Cancer Society (ACS). (2000). Colon and rectum cancer: Detection and symptoms. In *Colorectal cancer* [online]. Available: http://www3.cancer.org.

American Diabetes Association. (1976). *What you need to know about diabetes*. New York: Author.

American Heart Association (1984). *Heart facts*. Dallas, TX: Author.

Anand, K.J.S., & Craig, K.D. (1996). New perspectives on the definition of pain. *Pain, 67*, 3–6.

Anda, R.F., Remington, P.L., Sienko, D.G., & Davis, R.M. (1987). Are physicians advising smokers to quit? The patient's perspective. *Journal of the American Medical Association, 257*, 1916–1919.

Andersen, R.E., Walden, T.A., Bartlett, S.J., Zemel, B., Verde, T.J., & Franckowiak, S.C. (1999). Effects of lifestyle activity vs. structured aerobic exercise in obese women: A randomized trial. *Journal of the American Medical Association, 281*, 335–340.

Anderson, G.F., Hurst, J., Hussey, P.S., & Jee-Hughes, M. (2000). Health spending and outcomes: Trends in OECD countries, 1960-1998. *Health Affairs, 19*, 150–157.

Anderson, G.F., & Poullier, J.P. (1999). Health spending, access, and outcomes: Trends in industrialized countries. *Health Affairs, 18*, 178–192.

Anderson, K.O., & Masur, F.T. (1983). Psychological preparation for invasive medical and dental procedures. *Journal of Behavioral Medicine, 6*, 1–40.

Anderson, R.M., Funnell, M.M, Butler, P.M., Arnold, M.S., Firsgerald, J.T., & Feste, C.C. (1995). Patient empowerment: Results of a randomized controlled trial. *Diabetes Care, 18*, 943–949.

Anderson, R.N., Kochanek, K.D., & Murphy, S.L. (1997). Report of final mortality statistics, 1995. *Monthly Vital Statistics Report, 45*, 23–32 suppl.

Aneshensel, C.S., Pearlin, L.I., & Schuler, R.H. (1993). Stress, role captivity, and the cessation of caregiving. *Journal of Health & Social Behavior, 34*, 54–70.

Anthony, J. (1991). Psychologic aspects of exercise. *Clinical Sports Medicine, 10*, 171–180.

Anton, R.F., Kranzler, H.R., & Meyer, R.E. (1995). Neurobehavioral aspects of the pharmacotherapy of alcohol dependence. *Clinical Neuroscience, 3*, 145–154.

Antoni, M.H. (1987). Neuroendocrine influences in psychoimmunology and neoplasia: A review. *Psychology and Health, 1*, 3–24.

Antonovsky, A. (1979). *Health, stress, and coping: New perspectives on mental and physical well-being*. San Francisco, CA: Jossey-Bass.

Antonovsky, A. (1987). *Unraveling the mystery of health: How people manage stress and stay well*. San Francisco, CA: Jossey-Bass.

Antonovsky, A. (1998). The sense of coherence: An historical and future perspective. In H.I. McCubbin, E.A. Thompson, et al. (Eds.), *Stress, coping, and health in families: Sense of coherence and resiliency* (pp. 3–20). Thousand Oaks, Ca: Sage.

Arango, M.A., & Cano, P.O. (1998). A potential moderation role of stress in the association of disease activity and psychological status among patients with rheumatoid arthritis. *Psychological Reports, 83*, 147–157.

Arborelius, E. (1996). Using doctor-patient communication to affect patients' lifestyles. Theoretical and practical implications. *Psychology & Health, 11*, 845–855.

Armer, J.M. (1993). Elderly relocation to a congregate setting: Factors influencing adjustment. *Issues in Mental Health Nursing, 14*, 157–172.

Arntz, A., & de Jong, P. (1993). Anxiety, attention and pain. *Journal of Psychosomatic Research, 37*, 423–431.

Arntz, A., Dreessen, L., & Merckelbach, H. (1991). Attention, not anxiety, influences pain. *Behavior Research and Therapy, 29*, 41–50.

Arntz, A., & Hopmans, M. (1998). Underpredicted pain disrupts more than correctly predicted pain, but does not hurt more. *Behaviour Research and Therapy, 36*, 1121–1129.

Aronoff, G.M., Wagner, J.M., & Spangler, A.S. (1986). Chemical interventions for pain. *Journal of Consulting and Clinical Psychology, 54*, 769–775.

Asefzadeh, S. (1997). Patient flow analysis in a children's clinic. *International Journal of Quality Health Care, 9*, 143–147.

Ashenden, R., Silagy, C., & Weller, D. (1997). A systematic review of the effectiveness of promoting lifestyle change in general practice. *Family Practice, 14*, 160–175.

Asmundson, G.J., Norton, G.R., & Allerdings, M.D. (1997). Fear and avoidance in dysfunctional chronic back pain patients. *Pain, 69*, 231–236.

Asmundson, G.J., & Taylor, S. (1996). Role of anxiety sensitivity in pain-related fear and avoidance. *Journal of Behavioral Medicine, 19*, 577–586.

Aspinwall, L.G., & Taylor, S.E. (1997). A stitch in time: Self-regulation and proactive coping. *Psychological Bulletin, 121*, 417–436.

Astin, J.A. (1998). Why patients use alternative medicine: Results of a national study. *Journal of the American Medical Association, 279*, 1548–1553.

Atkins, C.J. (1981, April). *Improving exercise compliance among chronic lung patients: A comparison of cognitive and behavioral approaches*. Paper presented at the meeting of the Western Psychological Association, Los Angeles, CA.

Atlanti, L., Carael, M., Brunt, J., Frasca, T., & Chaika, N. (2000). Social change and HIV in the former USSR: The making of a new epidemic. *Social Science & Medicine, 50*, 1547–1556.

Audrain, J.E., Klesges, R.C., & Klesges, L.M. (1995). Relationship between obesity and the metabolic effects of smoking in women. *Health Psychology, 14*, 116–123.

Awbrey, B.J. (1985). Reflections on medical education: Concerns of the student. *Journal of Medical Education, 60*, 98–105.

Badeau, D. (1995). Illness, disability and sex in aging. *Sexuality & Disability, 13*, 219–237.

Bain, D.J.G. (1976). Doctor-patient communication in general practice consultations. *Medical Education, 10*, 125–131.

Bakal, D. (1999). *Minding the body: Clinical uses of somatic awareness*. New York: Guilford Press.

Baker, L.C. (1996). Differences in earnings between male and female physicians. *New England Journal of Medicine, 334*, 960–964.

Baker, L.M., & Connor, J.J. (1994). Physician-patient communication from the perspective of library and information science. *Bulletin of the Medical Library Association, 82*, 37–42.

Baldwin, D.C., Jr., Hughes, P.H., Conard, S.E., Storr, C.L., & Sheehan, D.V. (1991). Substance use among senior medical students: A survey of 23 medical schools. *Journal of the American Medical Association, 265*, 2074–2078.

Baldwin, P.J., Dodd, M., & Wrate, R.W. (1997). Young doctors' health – I, II. *Social Science & Medicine, 45*, 35–44.

Balint, M. (1957). *The doctor, his patient, and the illness.* New York: International Universities Press.

Ballard-Reisch, D.S. (1990). A model of participative decision making for physician-patient interaction. *Health Communication, 2*, 91–104.

Baltrusch, H.J., Stangel, W., & Titze, I. (1991). Stress, cancer, and immunity. *Acta Neurologica, 13*, 315–327.

Bandura, A. (1969). *Principles of behavior modification.* New York: Holt, Rinehart, and Winston.

Bandura, A. (1977). Self-efficacy: Toward a unifying theory of behavioral change. *Psychological Review, 84*, 191–215.

Bandura, A. (1986). *Social foundations of thought and action: A social cognitive theory.* Englewood Cliffs, NJ: Prentice-Hall.

Bandura, A. (1997). *Self-efficacy: The exercise of control.* New York: Freeman.

Barbee, R.A., & Feldman, S.E. (1970). A three-year longitudinal study of the medical interview and its relationship to student performance in clinical medicine. *Journal of Medical Education, 45*, 770–776.

Barber, J. (1982). Hypnosuggestive procedures in the treatment of clinical pain: Implications for theories of hypnosis and suggestive therapy. In T. Millon, C.J. Green, & R.B. Meagher, Jr. (Eds.), *Handbook of Clinical Health Psychology.* New York: Plenum Press.

Barber, J. (1986). Hypnotic analgesia. In A.D. Holzman & D.C. Turk (Eds.), *Pain management: A handbook of psychological treatment approaches.* New York: Pergamon.

Barefoot, J.C., Dahlstrom, W.G., & Williams, R.B. (1983). Hostility, CHD incidence, and total mortality: A 25-year follow-up study of 255 physicians. *Psychosomatic Medicine, 45*, 59–63.

Barefoot, J.C., Siegler, J.C., Nowlin, J.B., Peterson, B.L., Haney, T.L., Williams, R.B. (1987). Suspiciousness, health, and mortality: A follow-up study of 500 older adults. *Psychosomatic Medicine, 49*, 450–457.

Barling, N.R., & Lehmann, M. (1999). Young men's awareness, attitudes and practice of testicular self-examination: A health action process approach. *Psychology, Health, and Medicine, 4*, 255–263.

Barnes, V., Schneider, R., Alexander, C., & Staggers, F. (1997). Stress, stress reduction, and hypertension in African Americans: An updated review. *Journal of the National Medical Association, 464–476*, 464–476.

Barnlund, D.C. (1976). The mystification of meaning: Doctor-patient encounter. *Journal of Medical Education, 51*, 716–725.

Barsky, A.J. (1988). The paradox of health. *New England Journal of Medicine, 318*, 414–418.

Barsky, A.J., Ahern, D.K., Bailey, E.D., & Delamater, B.A. (1996). Predictors of persistent palpitations and continued medical utilization. *Journal of Family Practice, 42*, 465–472.

Barsky, A.J., & Borus, J.F. (1995). Somatization and medicalization in the era of managed care. *Journal of the American Medical Association, 274*, 1931–1934.

Barsky, A.J., & Borus, J.F. (1999). Functional somatic syndromes. *Annals of Internal Medicine, 130*, 910–921.

Barsky, A.J., Fama, J.M., Bailey, E.D., & Ahern, D.K. (1998a). A prospective 4- to 5-year study of DSM-III-R hypochondriasis. *Archives of General Psychiatry, 55*, 737–744.

Barsky, A.J., Orav, J.E., Delamater, B.A., Clancy, S.A., & Hartley, L.H. (1998b). Cardiorespiratory symptoms in response to physiological arousal. *Psychosomatic Medicine, 60*, 604–609.

Bart, P.B. (1968). Social structure and vocabularies of discomfort: What happened to female hysteria? *Journal of Health and Social Behavior, 9*, 188–193.

Basara, L.A.R. (1995). The impact of direct-to-consumer advertising of prescription medications on new prescription volume and consumer information search behavior. *Dissertation Abstracts International, 56-06B*, 3144.

Bates, M.S., Rankin-Hill, L., & Sanchez-Ayendez, M. (1997). The effects of the cultural context of health care on treatment of and response to chronic pain and illness. *Social Science & Medicine, 45*, 1433–1447.

Battista, R.N., & Fletcher, S.W. (1988). Making recommendations on preventive practices: Methodological issues. In R.N. Battista & R.S. Lawrence (Eds.), *Implementing preventive services* (pp. 53–67). New York: Oxford University Press.

Battle, E.K., & Brownell, K.D. (1996). Confronting a rising tide of eating disorders and obesity: Treatment vs. prevention and policy. *Addictive Behavior, 21*, 755–765.

Baum, A., Herberman, H., & Cohen, L. (1995). Managing stress and managing illness: Survival and quality of life in chronic disease. *Journal of Clinical Psychology in Medical Settings, 2*, 309–333.

Baum, A., & Posluszny, D.M. (1999). Health psychology: Mapping biobehavioral contributions to health and illness. *Annual Review of Psychology, 50*, 137–163.

Baumann, B. (1961). Diversities of conceptions of health and physical fitness. *Journal of Health and Human Behavior, 2*, 39–46.

Baur, S. (1988). *Hypochondria.* Berkeley, CA: University of California Press.

Beck, K.H., & Frankel, A. (1981). A conceptualization of threat communications and protective health behavior. *Social Psychology Quarterly, 44*, 204–217.

Becker, E.S., Rinck, M., Roth, W.T., & Margraf, J. (1998). Don't worry and beware of white bears: Thought suppression in anxiety patients. *Journal of Anxiety Disorders, 12*, 39–55.

Becker, G., & Kaufman, S.R. (1995). Managing an uncertain illness trajectory in old age: Patients' and physicians' views of stroke. *Medical Anthropology Quarterly, 9*, 165–187.

Becker, H.S., & Geer, B. (1958). The fate of idealism in medical school. *American Sociological Review, 23,* 50–56.

Becker, M.H., & Joseph, J.G. (1988). AIDS and behavioral change to reduce risk: A review. *American Journal of Public Health, 78,* 394–410.

Becker, M.H., & Maiman, L.A. (1980). Strategies for enhancing patient compliance. *Journal of Community Health, 6,* 113–135.

Beecher, H.K. (1956). Relationship of significance of wound to pain experienced. *Journal of the American Medical Association, 161,* 1609–1613.

Beecher, H.K. (1959). *Measurement of subjective responses.* New York: Oxford University Press.

Beecher, H.K. (1972). The placebo effect as a non-specific force surrounding disease and the treatment of disease. In R. Janzen, W.D. Keidel, A. Herz, C. Steichele, J.P. Payne, & R.A.P. Burt (Eds.), *Pain: Basic principles, pharmacology, therapy.* Stuttgart, West Germany: George Thieme.

Beisecker, A.E., & Beisecker, T.D. (1990). Patient information-seeking behaviors when communicating with doctors. *Medical Care, 28,* 19–28.

Belar, C.D. (1997). Clinical health psychology: A specialty for the 21st century. *Health Psychology, 16,* 411–416.

Belgrave, F.Z. (1998). Psychosocial aspects of chronic illness and disability among African Americans. Westport, CT: Auburn House/Greenwood Publishing Group.

Benbassat, J., Pilpel, D., & Tidhar, M. (1998). Patients' preferences for participation in clinical decision making: A review of published surveys. *Behavioral Medicine, 24,* 81–88.

Bendtsen, L., Norregaard, J., Jensen, R., & Olesen, J. (1997). Evidence of qualitatively altered nociception in patients with fibromyalgia. *Arthritis and Rheumatism, 40,* 98–102.

Benedict, A. (1995). Attributions of causes for chronic illness among aged persons. *Activities, Adaptation, & Aging, 19,* 49–59.

Bennett, K.M. (1996). A longitudinal study of wellbeing in widowed women. *International Journal of Geriatric Psychiatry, 11,* 1005–1010.

Benoliel, J.Q. (1975). Childhood diabetes: The commonplace in living becomes uncommon. In A.L. Strauss (Ed.), *Chronic illness and the quality of life* (pp. 89–98). St. Louis, MO: C.V. Mosby.

Benschop, R.J., Geenen, R., Mills, P.J., Naliboff, B.D., et al. (1998). Cardiovascular and immune responses to acute psychological stress in young and old women: A meta-analysis. *Psychosomatic Medicine, 60,* 290–296.

Bensing, J.M., Kerssens, J.J., & van der Pasch, M. (1995). Patient-directed gaze as a tool for discovering and handling psychosocial problems in general practice. *Journal of Nonverbal Behavior, 19,* 223–242.

Ben-Sira, Z. (1980). Affective and instrumental components of the physician-patient relationship: An additional dimension of interaction theory. *Journal of Health and Social Behavior, 21,* 170–180.

Benson, H. (1974). Your innate asset for combatting stress. *Harvard Business Review, 52,* 49–60.

Benson, H., Beary, J.F., & Carol, M.P. (1974). The relaxation response. *Psychiatry, 37,* 37–46.

Benson, R.C. (Ed.). (1984). *Current obstetrical and gynecologic diagnosis and treatment.* (5th ed.). Los Altos, CA: Lange Medical Publications.

Benyamini, Y., Leventhal, E.A., & Leventhal, H. (1997). Attributions and health. In A. Baum, S. Newman, J. Weinman, R. West, & C. McManus (Eds.), *Cambridge handbook of psychology, health, and medicine.* Cambridge, UK: Cambridge University Press.

Berg, J.A., & Lipson, J.G. (1999). Information sources, menopause beliefs, and health complaints of midlife Filipinas. *Health Care for Women International, 20,* 81–92.

Berger, K., & Bostwick, J. III (1984). A woman's decision: Breast care, treatment, and reconstruction. New York: Ballantine.

Berkley, K.J. (1997). Sex differences in pain. *Behavioral & Brain Sciences, 20,* 371–380.

Berman, B.M., Singh, B.B., Lao, L., Langenberg, P., Li, H., Hadhazy, V., Bareta, J., & Hochberg, M. (1999). A randomized trial of acupuncture as an adjunctive therapy in osteoarthritis of the knee. *Rheumatology Oxford, 38,* 346–354.

Berman, M., Feldman, S., Alter, M., Zilber, N., & Kahana, E. (1981). Acute transverse myelitis: Incidence and etiologic considerations. *Neurology, 31,* 966–971.

Bernabei, R., Gambassi, G., Lapane, K., Landi, F., Gatsonis, C., Dunlop, R., Lipsitz, L., Steel, K., & Mor, V. (1998). Management of pain in elderly patients with cancer. *Journal of the American Medical Association, 279,* 1877–1882.

Bernieri, F.J., & Rosenthal, R. (1991). Interpersonal coordination: Behavior matching and interactional synchrony. In R.S. Feldman, & B. Rime (Eds.), *Fundamentals of nonverbal behavior.* London: Cambridge University Press.

Bernstein, L., & Bernstein, R.S. (1980). Interviewing: A guide for health professionals (3rd ed.). New York: Appleton-Century-Crofts.

Berrey, A.L., & White, K.R. (2000). Search for the new medicine: Patients increasingly forgo high-tech treatments for less conventional ones. *American Journal of Nursing, 100,* 45.

Berry, D.C., Mihas, I.C., Gillie, T., & Forster, M. (1997). What do patients want to know about their medicines, and what do doctors want to tell them? A comparative study. *Psychology & Health, 12,* 467–480.

Berry, D.S., & Pennebaker, J.W. (1993). Nonverbal and verbal emotional expression and health. *Psychotherapy and Psychosomatics, 59,* 11–19.

Bertakis, K.D., Helms, L.J., Callahan, E.J., Azari, R., & Robbins, J.A. (1995). The influence of gender on physician practice style. *Medical Care, 33,* 407–416.

Bertman, S., & Krant, M.J. (1977). To know of suffering and the teaching of empathy. *Social Science and Medicine, 11,* 639–644.

Bertolotti, G., & Carone, M. (1994). From mechanical ventilation to home-care: The psychological approach. *Monaldi Archives for Chest Disease, 49,* 537–540.

Biggs, K.S., Heinrich, J.J., Jekel, J.F., & Cuono, C.B. (1997). The burn camp experience: Variables that influence the enhancement of self-esteem. *Journal of Burn Care Rehabilitation, 18*, 93–98.

Billings, A.C., & Moos, R.H. (1981). The role of coping responses and social resources in attenuating the stress of life events. *Journal of Behavioral Medicine, 4*, 139–158.

Billings, A.C., & Moos, R.H. (1982). Social support and functioning among community and clinical groups: A panel model. *Journal of Behavioral Medicine, 5*, 295–312.

Biondi, M., & Zannino, L. (1997). Psychological stress, neuroimmunomodulation, and susceptibility to infectious diseases in animals and man: A review. *Psychotherapy and Psychosomatics, 66*, 3–26.

Birenbaum, L.K. (1989). The relationship between parent-sibling communication and coping of siblings with death experiences. *Journal of Pediatric Oncological Nursing, 6*, 86–91.

Blachly, P.H., Disher, W., & Roduner, G. (1968). Suicide by physicians. *Bulletin of Suicidology, 1*–18.

Blackhall, L.J., Murphy, S.T., Frank, G., Michel, V., & Azen, S. (1995). Ethnicity and attitudes toward patient autonomy. *Journal of the American Medical Association, 274*, 820–825.

Blair, S.N., Kohl, H.W., III, Paffenbarger, R.S., Jr., Clark, D.G., Cooper, K.H., & Gibbons, L.W. (1989). Physical fitness and all-cause mortality: A prospective study of healthy men and women. *Journal of American Medicine, 262*, 2395–2436.

Blanchard, E.B., & Andrasik, F. (1985). *Management of chronic headaches: A psychological approach*. New York: Peragamon Press.

Blanchard, E.B., Andrasik, F., Applebaum, K.A., Evans, D.D., Myers, P., & Barron, K.D. (1986). Three studies of the psychologic changes in chronic headache patients associated with biofeedback and relaxation therapies. *Psychosomatic Medicine, 48*, 73–83.

Blanchard, E.B., Andrasik, F., Neff, D.F., Teders, S.J., Pallmeyer, T.P., Arena, J.G., Jurish, S.E., Saunders, N.L., Ahles, T.A., & Rodichok, L.D. (1982). Sequential comparisons of relaxation training and biofeedback in the treatment of three kinds of chronic headache or, the machines may be necessary some of the time. *Behavior Research Therapy, 20*, 469–481.

Blanchard, E.B., & Epstein, L.H., (1977). The clinical usefulness of biofeedback. In M. Hersen, R.M. Eisler, & P.M. Miller (Eds.), *Progress in behavior modification* (Vol. 4). New York: Academic Press.

Block, L.G., & Keller, P.A. (1998). Beyond protection motivation: An integrative theory of health appeals. *Journal of Applied Social Psychology, 28*, 1584–1608

Blondis, M.N., & Jackson, B.E. (1977). *Nonverbal communication with patients*. New York: John Wiley & Sons.

Bloom, S.W. (1963). *The doctor and his patient: A sociological interpretation*. New York, NY: Russell Sage Foundation.

Bluebond-Langner, M. (1977). Meanings of death to children. In H. Feifel (Ed.), *New meanings of death*. New York: McGraw-Hill.

Bluebond-Langner, M. (1996). *In the shadow of illness: Parents and siblings of the chronically ill child*. Princeton, NJ: Princeton University Press.

Blumenthal, J.A., & McCubbin, J.A. (1987). Physical exercise as stress management. In A. Baum & J.E. Singer (Eds.), *Handbook of psychology and health* (vol. 5). Hillsdale, NJ: Erlbaum.

Bok, S. (1978). *Lying: Moral choice in public and private life*. New York: Random House.

Bonanno, G.A., Keltner, D., Holen, A., & Horowitz, M.J. (1995). When avoiding unpleasant emotions might not be such a bad thing: Verbal-autonomic response dissociation and midlife conjugal bereavement. *Journal of Personality and Social Psychology, 69*, 957–989.

Bond, G.G., Aiken, L.S., & Somerville, S.C. (1992). The health belief model and adolescents with insulin-dependent diabetes mellitus. *Health Psychology, 11*, 190–198.

Bonfanti, P., Capetti, A., & Rizzardini, G. (1999). HIV disease treatment in the era of HAART. *Biomedical Pharmacotherapy, 53*, 93–105.

Bonica, J.J. (1990). Definitions and taxonomy of pain. In J.J. Bonica (Ed.), *The management of pain* (2nd ed.). Malvern, PA: Lea & Febiger.

Bonica, J.J. (1992). Pain research and therapy. Past and current status and future goals. In C.E. Short & A. van Posnik (Eds.), *Animal pain: Proceedings of the symposium on animal pain and its control*. New York: Churchill-Livingston.

Boone, D.R., & Hartman, B.H. (1972). The benevolent over-reaction. A well-intentioned but malignant influence on the handicapped child. *Clinical Pediatrics, 11*, 268–271.

Booth-Kewley, S., & Friedman, H.S. (1987). Psychological predictors of heart disease: A quantitative review. *Psychological Bulletin, 101*, 343–362.

Borawski, E.A., Kinney, J.M., & Kahana, E. (1996). The meaning of older adults' health appraisals: Congruence with health status and determinant of mortality. *Journal of Gerontology: Series B: Psychological Sciences & Social Sciences, 51B*, S157–S170.

Borysenko, J. (1984). Stress, coping, and the immune system. In J.D. Matarazzo, S.M. Weiss, J.A. Herd, N.E. Miller, & S.M. Weiss (Eds.), *Behavioral health: A handbook of health enhancement and disease prevention*. New York: Wiley.

Borysenko, M., & Borysenko, J. (1982). Stress, behavior, and immunity: Animal models and mediating mechanisms. *General Hospital Psychiatry, 4*, 59–67.

Borzo, G. (1994). Message system sends patients results by phone. *American Medical News, 37*, 5–6.

Bossert, E. (1994). Stress appraisals of hospitalized school-age children. *Children's Health Care, 23*, 33–49.

Boutin, P.D., Buchwald, D., Robinson, L., & Collier, A.C. (2000). Use of and attitudes about alternative and complementary therapies among outpatients and physicians at a municipal hospital. *Journal of Alternative and Complementary Medicine, 6*, 335–343.

Bower, J.E., Kemeny, M.E., Taylor, S.E., & Fahey, J.L. (1998). Cognitive processing, discovery of meaning, CD4 decline, and AIDS-related mortality among bereaved HIV-seropositive men. *Journal of Consulting & Clinical Psychology, 66,* 979–986.

Bowlby, J. (1961). Childhood mourning and its implications for psychiatry. *American Journal of Psychiatry, 118,* 481–498.

Bradshaw, P.W., Ley, P., Kincey, J.A., & Bradshaw, J. (1975). Recall of medical advice: Comprehensibility and specificity. *British Journal of Social and Clinical Psychology, 14,* 55–62.

Branden, N. (1971). *The disowned self.* Los Angeles, CA: Nash.

Braun, K.L., & Nicholas, R. (1997). Death and dying in four Asian American cultures: a descriptive study. *Death Study, 21,* 327–359.

Bray, G.A. (1992). Pathophysiology of obesity. *American Journal of Clinical Nutrition, 55,* 488–494 suppl.

Brayne, C., Do, K.-A., Green, L., & Green, A.C. (1998). Is health protective behavior in adolescents related to personality? A study of sun protective behavior and Eysenck Personality Questionnaire (junior version) in Queensland. *Personality & Individual Differences, 25,* 889–895.

Brecht, M.L., Dracup, K., Moser, D.K., & Riegel, B. (1994). The relationship of marital quality and psychosocial adjustment to heart disease. *Journal of Cardiovascular Nursing, 9,* 74–85.

Brenner, N.D., & Collins, J.L. (1998). Co-occurrence of health-risk behaviors among adolescents in the United States. *Journal of Adolescent Health, 22,* 209–213.

Bressler, L.R., Geraci, M.C., & Schatz, B.S. (1991). Misperceptions and inadequate pain management in cancer patients. DICP: The Annals of Pharmacotherapy, 25, 1225–1230.

Brodland, G.A., & Andreasen, N.J.C. (1974). Adjustment problems of the family of the burned patient. *Social Casework, 55,* 13–18.

Brody, B.A. (1997). When are placebo-controlled trials no longer appropriate? *Controlled Clinical Trials, 18,* 661–666.

Brody, B.A. (2000). *The placebo response,* New York: HarperCollins.

Brody, E.M. (1985). Patient care as a normative family stress. *The Gerontologist, 25,* 19–29.

Brody, H. (1982). The lie that heals: The ethics of giving placebos. *Annals of Internal Medicine, 97,* 112–118.

Broe, G.A., Jorm, A.F., Creasey, H.; Grayson, D., et al. (1998). Impact of chronic systemic and neurological disorders on disability, depression and life satisfaction. *International Journal of Geriatric Psychiatry, 13,* 667–673.

Bromet, E.J., Dew, M.A., Parkinson, D.K., Cohen, S., & Schwartz, J.E. (1992). Effects of occupational stress on the physical and psychological health of women in a microelectronics plant. *Social Science and Medicine, 34,* 1377–1383.

Bronfman, E.T., Biron-Campis, L., & Koocher, G.P. (1998). Helping children to cope: Clinical issues for acutely injured and medically traumatized children. *Professional Psychology: Research and Practice, 29,* 574–581.

Brown, G.W. (1974). Meaning, measurement, and stress of life events. In B.S. Dohrenwend & B.P. Dohrenwend (Eds.), *Stressful life events: Their nature and effects* (pp. 217–244). New York: Wiley.

Brown, J.B. (1992). Female family doctors: Their work and well-being. *Family Medicine, 24,* 591–595.

Brown, J.T., & Stoudemire, G.A. (1983). Normal and pathological grief. *Journal of the American Medical Association, 250,* 378–382.

Brown, K.W., & Moskowitz, D.S. (1997). Does unhappiness make you sick? The role of affect and neuroticism in the experience of common physical symptoms. *Journal of Personality and Social Psychology, 72,* 907–917.

Brown, R. S., Ramirez, D.E., & Taub, J.M. (1978). The prescription of exercise for depression. *The Physician and Sports Medicine, 6,* 34–45.

Brownell, K.D., & Cohen, L.R. (1995). Adherence to dietary regimens 2: Components of effective interventions. *Behavioral Medicine, 20,* 155–164.

Brownell, K.D., Marlatt, G.A., Lichtenstein, E., & Wilson, G.T. (1986). Understanding and preventing relapse. *American Psychologist, 41,* 765–782.

Brownell, K.D., & Stunkard, A.J. (1980). Exercise in the development and treatment of obesity. In A.J. Stunkard (Ed.), *Obesity.* Philadelphia: Saunders.

Bruijnzeels, M.A., Foets, M., van der Wouden, J.C., van den Heuvel, W.J., & Prins, A. (1998). Everyday symptoms in childhood: Occurrence and general practitioner consultation rates. *British Journal of General Practice, 48,* 880–884.

Bryan, W.V. (1999). *Multicultural aspects of disabilities: A guide to understanding and assisting minorities in the rehabilitation process.* Springfield, IL: Charles C. Thomas Publisher.

Buchsbaum, D.G. (1986). Reassurance reconsidered. *Social Science and Medicine, 23,* 423–427.

Buck, J.A. (1984). Effects of the community mental health centers program on the growth of mental health facilities in nonmetropolitan areas. *American Journal of Community Psychology, 12,* 609–622.

Buck, M., & Paice, J.A. (1994). Pharmacologic management of acute pain in the orthopaedic patient. *Orthopaedic Nursing, 13,* 14–23.

Bulman, J.R., & Wortman, C.B. (1977). Attributions of blame and coping in the "real world": Severe accident victims react to their lot. *Journal of Personality, 35,* 351–363.

Bunch, J., Barraclough, B., Nelson, B., & Sainsbury, P. (1971). Suicide following death of parents. *Social Psychiatry, 6,* 193–199.

Burack, J.H., Barrett, D.C., Stall, R.D., Chesney, M.A., Ekstrand, M.L., & Coates, T.J. (1993). Depressive symptoms and CD4 lymphocyte decline among HIV-infected men. *Journal of the American Medical Association, 270,* 2568–2573.

Burckhardt, C.S., Clark, S.R., O'Reilly, C.A., & Bennett (1997). Pain-coping strategies of women with fibromyalgia: Relationship to pain, fatigue, and quality of life. *Journal of Musculoskeletal Pain, 5,* 5–21.

Burgess, E.S., & Haaga, D.A.F. (1998). Appraisals, coping resonses, and attributions as predictors of individual differences in negative emotions among pediatric cancer patients. *Cognitive Therapy and Research, 22,* 547–573.

Burggraaf, V., & Barry, R.J. (1998). Older? Who me? Growing old should not mean giving up. *Journal of Gerontological Nursing, 24,* 5–7.

Burner, S.T., & Waldo, D.R. (1995). National health expenditure projections, 1994–2005. *Health Care Financial Review, 16,* 221–242.

Burns, J.W. (2000). Repression predicts outcome following multidisciplinary treatment of chronic pain. *Health Psychology, 19,* 75–84.

Burns, J.W., Johnson, B.J., Mahoney, N., Devine, J., et al. (1998). Cognitive and physical capacity process variables predict long-term outcome after treatment of chronic pain. *Journal of Consulting and Clinical Psychology, 66,* 434–439.

Burns, R.B., Freund, K.M., Moskowitz, M.A., Kasten, L., Feldman, H., & McKinlay, J.B. (1997). Physician characteristics: Do they influence the valuation and treatment of breast cancer in older women? *American Journal of Medicine, 103,* 263–269.

Bush, C., Ditto, B., & Feurstein, M. (1985). A controlled evaluation of paraspinal EMG biofeedback in the treatment of chronic low back pain. *Health Psychology, 4,* 307–321.

Bush, J.P. (1987). Pain in children: A review of the literature from a developmental perspective. *Psychology and Health, 1,* 215–236.

Bush, J.P., Melamed, B.G., Sheras, P.L., & Greenbaum, P.E. (1986). Mother-child patterns of coping with anticipatory medical stress. *Health Psychology, 5,* 137–157.

Butler, C.C., Pill, R., & Stott, N.C. (1998). Qualitative study of patients' perceptions of doctors' advice to quit smoking: Implications for opportunistic health promotion. *Behavioral Medicine Journal, 316,* 1878–1881.

Butt, H.R. (1977). A method for better physician-patient communication. *Annals of Internal Medicine, 86,* 478–480.

Cady, L.D., Gertler, M.M., Gotsch, L.D., & Woodbury, M.A. (1961). The factor structure concerned with coronary artery disease. *Behavioral Science, 6,* 37–41.

Cain, A., Fast, I., & Erickson, M. (1964). Childrens' disturbed reactions to the death of a sibling. *American Journal of Orthopsychiatry, 34,* 741–752.

Calabrese, J.R., Kling, M.A., & Gold, P.W. (1987). Alterations in immunocompetence during stress, bereavement, and depression: Focus on neuroendocrine regulation. *The American Journal of Psychiatry, 144,* 9.

Calfras, K.J., Sallis, J.F., Oldenburg, B., & French, M. (1997). Mediators of change in physical activity following an intervention in primary care: PACE. *Preventive Medicine: An International Journal Devoted to Practice and Theory, 26,* 297–304.

Cameron, L., Leventhal, E.A., & Leventhal, H. (1995). Seeking medical care in response to symptoms and life stress. *Psychosomatic Medicine, 57,* 1–11.

Cameron, L.D., & Nicholls, G. (1998). Expression of stressful experiences through writing: Effects of a self-regulation manipulation for pessimists and optimists. *Health Psychology, 17,* 84–92.

Campbell, C., Guy, A., & Banim, M. (1999). Assessing surgical patients' expectations and subsequent perceptions of pain in the context of exploring the effects of preparatory information: Raising issues of gender and status. *European Journal of Pain, 3,* 211–219.

Cannell, C.F., Oksenberg, L., & Converse, J.M. (1977). Striving for response accuracy: Experiments in new interviewing techniques. *Journal of Marketing Research, 14,* 306–315.

Cannon, W.B. (1932). *The wisdom of the body.* New York: Norton.

Cape, J.D. (1996). Psychological treatment of emotional problems by general practitioners. *British Journal of Medical Psychology, 69,* 85–99.

Caplan, R. (1979). Patient, provider, and organization: Hypothesized determinants of adherence. In S.J. Cohen (Ed.), *New directions in patient compliance.* Lexington, MA: D.C. Heath.

Carmel, S., & Glick, S.M. (1996). Compassionate-empathic physicians: Personality traits and social-organizational factors that enhance or inhibit this behavior pattern. *Social Science and Medicine, 43,* 1253–1262.

Carpenter, P.J. (1992). Perceived control as a predictor of distress in children undergoing invasive medical procedures. *Journal of Pediatric Psychology, 17,* 757–773.

Carr-Gregg, M.R., Sawyer, S.M., Clarke, C.F., & Bowes, G. (1997). Caring for the terminally ill adolescent. *Medical Journal of Aust, 166,* 255–258.

Carroll, R.M., & Shaefer, S. (1994). Similarities and differences in spouses coping with SIDS. Omega: *Journal of Death & Dying, 28,* 273–284.

Cartwright, L.K. (1977). Personality changes in a sample of young woman physicians. *Journal of Medical Education, 52,* 467–474.

Cartwright, L.K. (1978). Career satisfaction and role harmony in a sample of young woman physicians. *Journal of Vocational Behavior, 12,* 184–196.

Carver, C.S., Pozo-Kaderman, C., Harris, S.D., Noriega, V., Scheier, M.F., Robinson, D.S., Ketcham, A.S., Moffat, F.L., Jr., & Clark, K.C. (1994). Optimism versus pessimism predicts the quality of women's adjustment to early stage breast cancer. *Cancer, 73,* 1213–1220.

Carver, C.S., Pozo-Kaderman, C., Price, A.A., Noriega, V., Harris, S.D., Derhagopian, R.P., Robinson, D.S., & Moffat, F.L., Jr. (1998). Concern about aspects of body image and adjustment to early stage breast cancer. *Psychosomatic Medicine, 60,* 168–174.

Caspi, A., Bolger, N., & Eckenrode, J. (1987). Linking person and context in the daily stress process. *Journal of Personality and Social Psychology, 52,* 184–195.

Cassata, D.M. (1978). Health communication theory and research: An overview of the communication specialist interface. In D. Nimmo (Ed.), *Communication Yearbook II.* Austin, TX: International Communication Association.

Cassell, E.J. (1985a). *Talking with patients: Volume 1: The theory of doctor-patient communication.* Cambridge, MA: The M.I.T. Press.

Cassell, E.J. (1985b). *Talking with patients: Volume 2: Clinical technique.* Cambridge, MA: The M.I.T. Press.

Catalano, R., Dooley, D., Wilson, G., & Hough, R. (1993). Job loss and alcohol abuse: A test using data from the Epidemiologic Catchment Area Project. *Journal of Health & Social Behavior, 34,* 215–225.

Cates, J.R., & Cates, W., Jr. (1999). STD prevention in the United States: Lessons from history for the new millennium. *American Journal of Preventive Medicine, 16,* 75–77.

Catz, S.L., Kelly, J.A., Bogart, L.M., Benotsch, E.G., & McAuliffe, T.L. (2000). Patterns, correlates, and barriers to medication adherence among persons prescribed new treatments for HIV disease. *Health Psychology, 19,* 124–133.

Cavill, N. (1998). National campaigns to promote physical activity: Can they make a difference? *International Journal of Obesity and Related Metabolic Disorders, 22,* S48–S51.

Ceniceros, S., & Brown, G.R. (1998). Acupuncture: A review of its history, theories, and indications. *Southern Medical Journal, 91,* 1121–1125.

Centers for Disease Control. (2000). A glance at the HIV epidemic. CDC Update, December 2000. Available: http://www.cdc.giv/hiv/pubs.htm.

Chabal, C., Fishbain, D.A., Weaver, M., & Heine, L.W. (1998). Long-term transcutaneous electrical nerve stimulation (TENS) use: Impact on medication utilization and physical therapy costs. *Clinical Journal of Pain, 14,* 66–73.

Chakour, M.C., Gibson, S.J., Bradbeer, M., & Helme, R.D. (1996). The effect of age on A delta- and C-fibre thermal pain perception. *Pain, 64,* 143–152.

Chan, A., & Woodruff, R.K. (1997). Communicating with patients with advanced cancer. *Journal of Palliative Care, 13,* 29–33.

Chapman, C.R. (1984). New directions in the understanding and management of pain. *Social Science and Medicine, 19,* 1261–1277.

Chapman, C.R., Casey, K.L., Dubner, R., Foley, K.M., Gracely, R.H., & Reading, A.E. (1985). Pain measurement: An overview. *Pain, 22,* 1–31.

Chapman, G.B., Bergus, G.R., & Elstein, A.S. (1996). Order of information affects clinical judgment. *Journal of Behavioral Decision Making, 9,* 201–211.

Chapman-Smith, D. (2000). *The chiropractic profession.* WDM, IA: NCMIC Group.

Charles, S.T., Gatz, M., Pedersen, N.L., & Dahlberg, L. (1999). Genetic and behavioral risk factors for self-reported joint pain among a population-based sample of Swedish twins. *Health Psychology, 18,* 644–654.

Charmaz, K. (1995). The body, identity, and self: Adapting to impairment. *Sociologial Quarterly, 36,* 657–680.

Chaves, J.F., & Dworkin, S.F. (1997). Hypnotic control of pain: Historical perspectives and future prospects. *International Journal of Clinical and Experimental Hypnosis, 45,* 356–376.

Chesney, M.A., Frautschi, N.M., & Rosenman, R.H. (1985). Modifying Type A behavior. In J.C. Rosen & L.J. Solomon (Eds.), Prevention in health psychology. Hanover, NH: University Press of New England.

Chesney, M.A., & Rosenman, R.H. (1985). *Anger and hostility in cardiovascular and behavioral disorders.* New York: Hemisphere.

Chesney, M.A., & Shelton, J.L. (1976). A comparison of muscle relaxation and electromyogram biofeedback treatment for muscle contraction headache. *Journal of Behavior Therapy and Experimental Psychiatry, 7,* 221–225.

Christian, B.J., & D'Auria, J.P. (1997). The child's eye: Memories of growing up with cystic fibrosis. *Journal of Pediatric Nursing,12,* 3–12.

Christman, N.J., McConnell, E.A., Pfeiffer, C., Webster, K.K., Schmitt, M., & Ries, J. (1988). Uncertainty, coping, and distress following myocardial infarction: Transition from hospital to home. *Research in Nursing and Health, 11,* 71–82.

Christy, N.P. (1979). English is our second language. *New England Journal of Medicine, 300,* 979–981.

Chung, K.C., Hamill, J.B., Kim, H.M., Walters, M.R., & Wilkins, E.G. (1999). Predictors fo patient satisfaction in an outpatient plastic surgery clinic. *Annals of Plastic Surgery, 42,* 56–60.

Churgin, P.G. (1995). Computerized patient records: The patients' response. *HMO Practice, 9,* 182–185.

Chwalisz, K., & Kisler, V. (1995). Perceived stress: A better measure of caregiver burden. *Measurement and Evaluation in Counseling and Development, 28,* 88–98.

Ciccone, D.A., & Grzesiak, R.C. (1984). Cognitive dimensions of chronic pain. *Social Science Medicine, 19,* 1339–1345.

Cipher, D.J., & Fernandez, E. (1997). Expectancy variables predicting tolerance and avoidance of pain in chronic pain patients. *Behaviour Research and Therapy, 35,* 437–444.

Citron, M.L., Johnston-Early, A., Boyer, M., Krasnow, S.H., Hood, M., & Cohen, M.H. (1986). Patient-controlled analgesia for severe cancer pain. *Archives of Internal Medicine, 146,* 734–736.

Clark, C.R. (1997). Creating information messages for reducing patient distress during health care procedures. *Patient Education & Counseling, 30,* 247–255.

Clark, L.M., & Hartman, M. (1996). Effects of hardiness and appraisal on the psychological distress and physical health of caregivers to elderly relatives. *Research on Aging, 18,* 379–401.

Clark, N.M., & Dodge, J.A. (1999). Exploring self-efficacy as a predictor of disease management. *Health Education and Behavior, 26,* 72–89.

Clark, N.M., Gong, M., Schork, M.A., Evans, D., Roloff, D., Hurwitz, M., Maiman, L., & Mellins, R.B. (1998). Impact of education for physicians on patient outcomes. *Pediatrics, 101,* 831–836.

Clarke, T.A., Maniscalco, W.M., Taylor-Brown, S., Roghmann, K.J., Shapiro, D.L. & Hannon-Johnson, C. (1984). Job satisfaction and stress among neonatologists. *Pediatrics, 74,* 52–57.

Classen, C., Sephton, S.E., Diamond, S., & Spiegel, D. (1998). Studies of life-extending psychosocial interventions. In J.C. Holland (Ed.), *Psycho-oncology.* New York: Oxford University Press.

Clavel, F., Benhamou, S., & Flamant, R. (1987). Nicotine dependence and secondary effects of smoking cessation. *Journal of Behavioral Medicine, 10,* 555–558.

Clayton, P.J. (1974). Mortality and morbidity in the first year of widowhood. *Archives of General Psychiatry, 30,* 747–750.

Clayton, P.J. (1979). The sequelae and nonsequelae of conjugal bereavement. *American Journal of Psychiatry,136,* 1530–1543.

Cloninger, C.R. (1987). Neurogenetic adaptive mechanisms in alcoholism. *Science, 236,* 410–416.

Cobb, B. (1954). Why do people detour to quacks? *The Psychiatric Bulletin, 3,* 66–69.

Cobb, J.M.T., & Steptoe, A. (1996). Psychosocial stress and susceptibility to upper respiratory tract illness in an adult population sample. *Psychosomatic Medicine, 58,* 404–412.

Cobb, S. (1976). Social support as a moderator of life stress. *Psychosomatic Medicine, 38,* 300–314.

Cobb, S., & Rose, R.M. (1973). Hypertension, peptic ulcer, and diabetes in air traffic controllers. *Journal of the American Medical Association, 224,* 489–492.

Coderre, T.J., Katz, J., Vaccarino, A.L., & Melzack, R. (1993). Contribution of central neuroplasticity to pathological pain: Review of clinical evidence. *Pain, 52,* 259–285.

Cody, J., & Robinson, A. (1977). The effect of low-cost maintenance medication on the relationships of schizophrenic outpatients. *American Journal of Psychiatry, 134,* 73–76.

Cofrancesco, J., Whalen, J.J., & Dobs, A.S. (1997). Testosterone replacement treatment options for HIV-infected men. *Journal of Acquired Immune Deficiency Syndrome and Human Retrovirology, 16,* 254–265.

Coggan, P.G., Macdonald, S.C., Camacho, Z., Carline, J., & Taylor, T. (1985). An analysis of the magnitude of clinical reasoning deficiencies in one class. *Journal of Medical Education, 60,* 293–301.

Cohen, F., & Lazarus, R.S. (1979). Coping with the stress of illness. In G.C. Stone, F. Cohen, & N.E. Adler (Eds.), *Health psychology: A handbook* (pp. 217–254). San Francisco, CA: Jossey-Bass.

Cohen, F., & Lazarus, R.S. (1983). Coping and adaptation in health and illness. In D. Mechanic (Ed.), *Handbook of health, health care, and the health profession.* New York: Free Press.

Cohen, S. (1980). Aftereffects of stress on human performance and social behavior: A review of research and theory. *Psychological Bulletin, 88,* 82–108.

Cohen, S. (1996). Psychological stress, immunity, and upper respiratory infections. *Current Directions in Psychological Science, 5,* 86–90.

Cohen, S., & Herbert, T.B. (1996). Health psychology: Psychological factors and physical disease from the perspective of human psychoneuroimmunology. *Annual Review of Psychology, 47,* 113–142.

Cohen, S., & McKay, G. (1983). Social support, stress, and the buffering hypothesis: A theoretical analysis. In A. Baum, S.E. Taylor, & J. Singer (Eds.), *Handbook of psychology and health* (vol. 4). Hillsdale, N.J: Erlbaum.

Cohen, S., & Wills, T.A. (1985). Stress, social support, and the buffering hypothesis. *Psychological Bulletin, 98,* 310–357.

Cohen, S., Frank, E., Doyle, W.J., Skoner, D.P., et al. (1998). Types of stressors that increase susceptibility to the common cold in healthy adults. *Health Psychology, 17,* 214–223.

Cohen, S., Tyrrell, D.A.J., & Smith, A.P. (1993). Negative life events, perceived stress, negative affect, and susceptibility to the common cold. *Journal of Personality and Social Psychology, 64,* 131–140.

Cole, S.W., Kemeny, M.E., & Taylor, S.E. (1997). Social identity and physical health: Accelerated HIV progression in rejection-sensitive gay men. *Journal of Personality and Social Psychology, 72,* 320–335.

Collins, R.L., Taylor, S.E., & Skokan, L.A. (1990). A better world or a shattered vision? Changes in perspectives following victimization. *Social Cognition, 8,* 263–285.

Colliver, J.A., Willis, M.S., Robs, R.S., Cohen, D.S., et al. (1998). Assessment of empathy in a standardized-patient examination. *Teaching and Learning in Medicine, 10,* 8–11.

Comarow, A. (1998). Going outside the medical mainstream. Can 42 percent of Americans be wrong? *U.S. News & World Report, 125,* 83.

Compas, B.E., Worsham, N.L., Ey, S., & Howell, D.C. (1996). When mom or dad has cancer: II. *Health Psychology, 15,* 167–175.

Compton, A.B., & Purviance, M. (1992). Emotional distress in chronic medical illness: Treatment with time-limited group psychotherapy. *Military Medicine, 157,* 533–535.

Condon, W.S., & Ogston, W.D. (1967). A segmentation of behavior. *Journal of Psychiatric Research, 5,* 221.

Conn, V.S. (1998). Older adults and exercise: Path analysis of self-efficacy related constructs. *Nursing Research, 47,* 180–189.

Connelly, J.E., Smith, G.R., Philbrick, J.T., & Kaiser, D.L. (1991). Healthy patients who perceive poor health and their use of primary care services. *Journal of General Internal Medicine, 6,* 47–51.

Cook, A.J., & Thomas, M.R. (1994). Pain and the use of health services among the elderly. *Journal of Aging and Health, 6,* 155–172.

Cook, T., & Flay, B. (1978). The temporal persistence of experimentally induced attitude change: An evaluative review. In L. Berkowitz (Ed.), *Advances in experimental social psychology* (vol. 11). New York: Academic Press.

Cooper, M.L., Frone, M.R., Russel, M., & Mundar, P. (1995). Drinking to regulate positive and negative emotions: A motivational model of alcohol use. *Journal of Personality and Social Psychology, 69,* 990–1005.

Cormier, L.S., Cormier, W.H., & Weisser, R.J. (1984). *Interviewing and helping skills for health professionals.* Belmont, CA: Wadsworth.

Corr, C.A., & Corr, D.M. (1985). Situations involving children: A challenge for the hospice movement. *The Hospice Journal, 1,* 63–77.

Costa, P.T., Jr., & McCrae, R.R. (1987). Neuroticism, somatic complaints, and disease: Is the bark worse than the bite? *Journal of Personality, 55,* 299–316.

Cottington, E.M., & House, J.S. (1987). Occupational stress and health: A multivariate relationship. In A. Baum & J.E. Singer (Eds.), *Handbook of psychological and health* (vol. 5).

Cottington, E.M., Matthews, K.A., Talbott, E., & Kuller, L.H. (1986). Occupational stress, suppressed anger, and hypertension. *Psychosomatic Medicine, 48,* 249–260.

Coughlin, A.M., Badura, A.S., Fleischer, T.D., & Guck, T.P. (2000). Multidisciplinary treatment of chronic pain patients: Its efficacy in changing patient locus of control. *Archives of Physical Medicine and Rehabilitation, 81,* 739–840.

Cousins, N. (1976). Anatomy of an illness (as perceived by the patient). *New England Journal of Medicine, 295,* 1458–1463.

Cousins, N. (1979). *Anatomy of an illness.* New York: Norton.

Cousins, N. (1983). *The healing heart: Antidotes to panic and helplessness.* New York: W.W. Norton & Co.

Cowley, G., King, P., Hager, M., & Rosenberg, D. (1995). Going mainstream. *Newsweek, 125,* 56–57.

Coyne, J.C., Aldwin, C., & Lazarus, R.S. (1981). Depression and coping in stressful episodes. *Journal of Abnormal Psychology, 90,* 439–447.

Coyne, J.C., & Holroyd, K. (1982). Stress, coping, and illness: A transactional perspective. In T. Millon, C. Green, & R. Meagher (Eds.), *Handbook of clinical health psychology.* New York: Plenum.

Craig, K.D. (1992). The facial expression of pain: Better than a thousand words? American Pain Society Journal, 1, 153–162.

Craig, K.D., Hadjistavropoulos, H.D., Grunau, R.V.E., & Whitfield, M.F. (1994). A comparison of two measures of facial activity during pain in the newborn child. *Journal of Pediatric Psychology, 19,* 305–318.

Craig, K.D., Prkachin, K.M., & Grunau, R.V.E. (1992). The facial expression of pain. In C. Turk & R. Melzack (Eds.), *Handbook of pain assessment* (pp. 255–274). NewYork: Guilford Press.

Croen, L.G., Woesner, M., Herman, M., & Reichgott, M. (1997). A longitudinal study of substance use and abuse in a single class of medical students. *Academic Medicine, 72,* 376–381.

Crombez, G., Eccleston, C., Baeyens, F., & Eelen, P. (1996). The disruptive nature of pain: An experimental investigation. *Behavior Research Therapy, 34,* 911–918.

Cronan, T.A., Shaw, W.S., Gallagher, R.A., & Weismen, M. (1995). Predicting health care use among older osteoarthritis patients in an HMO. *Arthritis Care and Research, 8,* 66–72.

Crow, R., Gage, H., Hampson, S., Hart, J., Kimber, A., & Thomas, H. (1999). The role of expectancies in the placebo effect and their use in the delivery of health care: A systematic review. *Health Technology Assessment, 3,* 1-96.

Cruess, D.G., Antoni, M.H., Schneiderman, N., Ironson, G., McCabe, P., Fernandez, J.B., Cruess, S.E., Klimas, N., & Kumar, M. (2000). Cognitive-behavioral stress management increases free testosterone and decreases psychological distress in HIV-seropositive men. *Health Psychology, 19,* 12–20.

Cummings, N.A. (1996). The new structure of health care and a role for psychology. In R.J. Resnick & R.H. Rozensky (Eds.), *Health psychology through the life span: Practice and research opportunities.* Washington, DC: APA.

Cunnington, J.P.W., Turnbull, J.M., Regher, G., Marriott, M., et al. (1997). The effect of presentation in order in clinical decision making. *Academic Medicine, 72,* S40-S42.

Dackman, L. (1987). Sex and the single-breasted woman. *Vogue,* 420–436.

Dailey, D.M. (1998). Understanding and affirming the sexual/relationship realities of end-stage renal disease patients and their significant others. *Advances in Renal Replacement Therapy, 5,* 81–88.

Daugherty, S.R., & Baldwin, D.C. Jr. (1996). Sleep deprivation in senior medical students and first-year residents. *Academic Medicine, 71,* S93–S95.

David, C.M. (1997). Sudden infant death syndrome: A hypothesis. *Medical Hypotheses, 49,* 61–67.

Davidhizar, R. (1992). Interpersonal communication: A review of eye contact. *Infection Control in Hospital Epidemiology, 13,* 222–225.

Davidson, K., MacGregor, M.W., Stuhr, J., Dixon, K., & MacLean, D. (2000). Constructive anger verbal behavior predicts blood pressure in a population-based sample. *Health Psychology, 19,* 55–64.

Davidson, K., & Prkachin, K. (1997). Optimism and unrealistic optimism have an interacting impact on health-promoting behavior and knowledge changes. *Personality and Social Psychology Bulletin, 23,* 617–625.

Davis, C.G., Lehman, D.R., Silver, R.C., Wortman, C.B., et al. (1996). Self-blame following a traumatic event: The role of perceived avoidability. *Personality and Social Psychology Bulletin, 22,* 557–567.

Davis, F. (1960). Uncertainty in medical prognosis: Clinical and functional. *American Journal of Sociology, 66,* 41–47.

Davis, M.S. (1971). Variations in patients' compliance with doctors' orders: Medical practice and doctor-patient interaction. *Psychiatry in Medicine, 2,* 31–54.

Decina, L.E., & Knoebel, K.Y. (1997). Child safety seat misuse patterns in four states. *Accident Analysis and Prevention, 29,* 125–132.

Deckard, G., Meterko, M., & Field, D. (1994). Physician burnout: An examination of personal, professional, and organizational relationships. *Medical Care, 32,* 745–754.

Deinzer, R., & Schueller, N. (1998). Dynamics of stress-related decrease of salivary immunoglobulin A (sIgA): Relationship to symptoms of the common cold and studying behavior. *Behavioral Medicine, 23,* 161–169.

Delahanty, D.L., Wang, T., Maravich, C., Forlenza, M., & Baum, A. (2000). Time-of-day effects on response of natural killer cells to acute stress in men and women. *Health Psychology, 19,* 39–45.

DeLeon, P.H., VandenBos, G.R., & Bulatao, E.Q. (1991). Managed mental health care: A history of the federal policy initiative. *Professional Psychology: Research & Practice, 22,* 15–25.

Del Mar, C.B., Green, A.C., & Battistutta, D. (1997). Do public medic campaigns designed to increase skin cancer awareness result in increased skin excision rates? *Australia and New Zealand Journal of Public Health, 21,* 751–754.

DeLongis, A., Coyne, J.C., Dakof, G., Folkman, S., & Lazarus, R.S. (1982). Relationship of daily hassles, uplifts, and major life events to health status. *Health Psychology, 1,* 119–136.

Dement, W.C., & Vaughn, C. (1999). *The promise of sleep: A pioneer in sleep medicine explores the vital connection between health, happiness, and a good night's sleep.* New York: Dell.

Derouin, D., & Jessee, P.O. (1996). Impact of a chronic illness in childhood: Siblings' perceptions. *Issues in Comprehensive Pediatric Nursing, 19,* 135–147.

De Valle, M.N., & Norman, P. (1992). Causal attributions, health locus of control beliefs and lifestyle changes among pre-operative coronary patients. *Psychology & Health, 7,* 201–211.

Devine, E.C. (1996). Meta-analysis of the effects of psychoeducational care in adults with asthma. *Research in Nursing and Health, 19,* 367–376.

Devine, E.C., & Pearcy, J. (1996). Meta analysis of the effects of psychoeducational care in adults with chronic obstructive pulmonary disease. *Patient Education and Counseling, 29,* 167–178.

Devine, E.C., & Reifschneider, E. (1995). A meta-analysis of the effects of psychoeducational care in adults with hypertension. *Nursing Research, 44,* 237–245.

Diamond, E.L. (1982). The role of anger and hostility in essential hypertension and coronary heart disease. *Psychological Bulletin, 92,* 410–433.

DiClemente, R.J. (1998). Preventing sexually transmitted infections among adolescents. *Journal of the American Medical Association, 279,* 1574–1575.

DiFabio, R.P. (1995). Efficacy of comprehensive rehabilitation programs and back school for patients with low back pain: A meta-analysis. *Physical Therapy, 75,* 865–878.

DiLorenzo, T.M., Bargman, E.P., Stucky-Ropp, R., Brassington, G.S., French, P.A., & La Fontaine, T. (1999). Long term effects of aerobic exercise on psychological outcomes. *Preventive Medicine, 28,* 75–85.

DiMatteo, M.R. (1979). A social-psychological analysis of physician-patient rapport: Toward a science of the art of medicine. *Journal of Social Issues, 35,* 12 33.

DiMatteo, M.R. (1985). Physician-patient communication: Promoting a positive health care setting. In J.C. Rosen & L.J. Solomon (Eds.), *Prevention in health psychology.* Hanover, NH: University Press of New England.

DiMatteo, M.R. (1993). Expectations in the physician-patient relationship: Implications for patient adherence to medical treatment recommendations. In P.D. Blanck et al. (Eds.), *Interpersonal expectations: Theory, research, and applications. Studies in emotion and social interaction* (pp. 296 315). New York: Cambridge University Press.

DiMatteo, M.R. (1994). Enhancing patient adherence to medical recommendations. *Journal of the American Medical Association, 271,* 79–83.

DiMatteo, M.R., & DiNicola, D.D. (1982). *Achieving patient compliance: The psychology of the medical practitioner's role.* Elmsford, NY: Pergamon Press.

DiMatteo, M.R., & Hays, R. (1980). The significance of patients' perceptions of physician conduct: A study of patient satisfaction in a family practice center. *Journal of Community Health, 6,* 18–34.

DiMatteo, M.R., Hays, R., & Prince, L.M. (1986). Relationship of physicians' nonverbal communication skill to patient satisfaction, appointment noncompliance, and physician workload. *Health Psychology, 5,* 581–594.

DiMatteo, M.R., & Lepper, H.S. (1998). Promoting adherence to courses of treatment: Mutual collaboration in the physician-patient relationship. In L.D. Jackson & B.K. Duffy (Eds.), *Health communication research: A guide to developments and directions.* Westport, CT: Greenwood Press.

DiMatteo, M.R., Lepper, H.S., & Croghan, T.W. (2000). Depression is a risk factor for noncompliance with medical treatment: A meta-analysis of the effects of anxiety and depression on patient adherence. *Archives of Internal Medicine, 160,* 2101–2107.

DiMatteo, M.R., Linn, L.S., Chang, B.L., & Cope, D.W. (1985). Affect and neutrality in physician behavior. *Journal of Behavioral Medicine, 8,* 397–409.

DiMatteo, M.R., Reiter, R.C., & Gambone, J.C. (1994). Enhancing medication adherence through communication and informed collaborative choice. *Health Communication, 6,* 253–265.

DiMatteo, M.R., & Taranta, A. (1979). Nonverbal communication and physician-patient rapport: an empirical study. *Professional Psychology, 10,* 540–547.

DiMatteo, M.R., Taranta, A., Friedman, H.S., & Prince, L.M. (1980). Predicting patient satisfaction from physicians' nonverbal communication skills. *Medical Care, 18,* 376–387.

Dimsdale, J.E., Alpert, B.S., & Schneiderman, N. (1986). Exercise as a modulator of cardiovascular reactivity. In K.A. Matthews, S.M. Weiss, T. Detre, T.M. Dembroski, B. Falkner, S.B. Manuck, & R.B. Williams (Eds.), *Handbook of stress, reactivity, and cardiovascular disease.* New York: Wiley.

Dinh, K.T., Sarason, I.G., Peterson, A.V., & Onstad, L.E. (1995). Children's perceptions of smokers and nonsmokers: A longitudinal study. *Health Psychology, 14,* 32–40.

Dishman, R.K., & Buckworth, J. (1997). Adherence to physical activity. In W.P. Morgan (Ed.), *Physical activity and mental health.* Washington, DC: Taylor & Francis.

Ditto, P.H., Druley, J.A., Moore, K.A., Danks, H.J., & Smucker, W.D. (1996). Fates worse than death: The role of valued life activities in health-state evaluations. *Health Psychology, 15,* 332–343.

Doan, B.T., Plante, T.G., Digregorio, M.P., & Manuel, G.M. (1995). Influence of aerobic exercise activity and relaxation training in coping with test-taking anxiety. *Anxiety, Stress & Coping: An International Journal, 8,* 101–111.

Doll, J., & Orth, B. (1993). The Fishbein and Ajzen theory of reasoned action applied to contraceptive behavior: Model variants and meaningfulness. *Journal of Applied Social Psychology, 23*, 335–341.

Dorgan, C., & Editue, A. (1995). *Statistical record of health and medicine: 1995*. Detroit, MI: Orale Research.

Dorland's Illustrated Medical Dictionary (26th ed.) (1994). Philadelphia, PA: Saunders.

Dorpat, T.L. (1992). Doctor abuse and the interactional dynamics of graduate-medical training. *International Journal of Communicative Psychoanalysis & Psychotherapy, 7*, 39–40.

Doyle, A.C. (1984). *The illustrated Sherlock Holmes treasury*. New York: Avenel Books & Crown Publishers.

Doyle, B.J., & Ware, J.E. (1977). Physician conduct and other factors that affect consumer satisfaction with medical care. *Journal of Medical Education, 52*, 793–801.

Dracup, K., & Moser, D.K. (1997). Beyond sociodemographics: Factors influencing the decision to seek treatment for symptoms of acute myocardial infarction. *Heart and Lung, 26*, 253–262.

Drewnowsky, A. (1995). Energy intake and sensory properties of food. *American Journal of Clinical Nutrition, 62*, 1081S–1085S.

Drewry, B., & Chu, R. (1995). What do people want from dentistry? An action research approach. *Probe, 29*, 202–208.

Drotar, D. (1981). Psychological perspectives in chronic childhood illness. *Journal of Pediatric Psychology, 6*, 211–228.

Drotar, D., & Crawford, P. (1985). Psychological adaptation of siblings of chronically ill children: research and practice implications. *J. Dev Behav Pediatr, 6*, 355–362.

Druss, B.G., & Rosenheck, R.A. (1999). Association between use of unconventional therapies and conventional medical services. *Journal of the American Medical Association, 282*, 651–656.

Dryson, E.W., Scragg, R.K.R., Metcalf, P.A., & Baker, J.R. (1996). Stress at work: An evaluation of occupational stressors as reported by a multicultural New Zealand workforce. *International Journal of Occupational and Environmental Health, 2*, 18–25.

Dua, J.K. (1994). Comparative predictive value of attributional style, negative affect, and positive affect in predicting self-reported physical health and psychological health. *Journal of Psychosomatic Research, 38*, 669–680.

Dudley-Brown, S. (1996). Living with ulcerative colitis. *Gastroenterology Nursing, 19*, 60–64.

Duitsman, D.M., & Cychosz, C.M. (1994). Psychosocial similarities and differences among employed and unemployed heart transplant recipients. *Journal of Heart Lung Transplant, 13*, 108–115.

Dunbar, F. (1943). *Psychosomatic diagnosis*. New York: Hoeber.

Dunham, C.S. (1978). Social-sexual relationships. In R.M. Goldenson, J.R. Dunham & C.S. Dunham (Eds.), *Disability and rehabilitation handbook* (pp. 28–35). New York: McGraw-Hill.

Dunn, A.L., Marcus, B.H., Kampert, J.B., Garcia, M.E., Kohl, H.W., III, & Blair, S.N. (1999). Comparison of lifestyle and structured interventions to increase physical activity and cardiorespiratory fitness: A random-

ized trial. *Journal of the American Medical Association, 281*, 327–334.

du Pre, A., & Beck, C.S. (1997). "How can I put this?" Exaggerated self-disparagement as alignment strategy during problematic disclosures by patients to doctors. *Qualitative Health Research, 7*, 487–503.

Dusseldorp, E., van Elderen, T., Maes, S., Meulman, J., & Kraaij, V. (1999). A meta-analysis of psychoeducational programs for coronary heart disease patients. *Health Psychology, 18*, 506–519.

Dworkin, S.F. (1994). Somatization, distress, and chronic pain. *Quality of Life Research, 3*, S77–S83.

Dykema, J., Bergbower, K., & Peterson, C. (1995). Pessimistic explanatory style, stress, and illness. *Journal of Social and Clinical Psychology, 14*, 357–371.

D'Zurilla, T.J., & Nezu, A.M. (1990). Development and preliminary evaluation of the Social Problem-Solving Inventory. *Psychological Assessment, 2*, 156–163.

Earman, W.A., Andersson, G.B., Leavitt, F., McNeill, T.W., et al. (1996). Factors influencing the costs of chronic low back injuries: An analysis of data from independent medical examinations. *Journal of Occupational Rehabilitation, 6*, 5–16.

Eccleston, C. (1995). The attentional control of pain: methodological and theoretical concerns. *Pain, 63*, 3–10.

Eccleston, C., Crombez, G., Aldrich, S., & Stannard, C. (1997). Attention and somatic awareness in chronic pain. *Pain, 72*, 209–215.

Eckhardt, M.J., Harford, T.C., Kaelber, C.T., Parker, E.S., Rosenthal, L.S., Ryback, R.S., Salmoiraghi, G.C., Vanderveen, E., & Warren, K.R. (1981). Health hazards associated with alcohol consumption. *Journal of the American Medical Association, 246*, 648–666.

Eddy, D.M. (1982). Probabilistic reasoning in clinical medicine: Problems and opportunities. In D. Kahneman & A. Tversky (Eds.), *Judgment under uncertainty: Heuristics and biases* (pp. 249–267). New York: Cambridge University Press.

Edelwich, J., & Brodsky, A. (1980). *Burnout: Stages of disillusionment in the helping professions*. New York: Human Sciences Press.

Egbert, L.D., Battit, G.E., Turndorf, H. & Beecher, H.K. (1963). Value of preoperative visit by anesthetist: Study of doctor-patient rapport. *Journal of the American Medical Association, 185*, 553–555.

Egbert, L.D., Battit, G.E., Welch, C.E., & Bartlett, M.K. (1964). Reduction of post-operative pain by encouragement and instruction of patients: A study of doctor-patient rapport. *New England Journal of Medicine, 270*, 825–827.

Eisenberg, C. (1989). Sounding board: Medicine is no longer a man's profession or When the men's club goes coed, it's time to change the regs. *New England Journal of Medicine, 321*, 1542–1544.

Eisenberg, D.M., Davis, R.B., Ettner, S.L., Appel, S., Wilkey, S., Van Rompay, M., & Kessler, R.C. (1998). Trends in alternative medicine use in the United States, 1990–1997: Results of a follow-up national survey. *Journal of the American Medical Association, 280*, 1569–1575.

Eisenberg, D.M., Kessler, R.C., Foster, C., Norlock, F.E., et al. (1993). Unconventional medicine in the United States: Prevalence, costs, and patterns of use. *New England Journal of Medicine, 328*, 246–252.

Eisenthal, S., & Stoeckle, J.D. (1998). Medical residents evaluate their medical school training in psychosocial care. *Psychological Reports, 82*, 1375–1386.

Eiser, C. (1996). Comprehensive care of the child with cancer: Obstacles to the provision of psychological support in pediatric oncology: A comment. *Psychology, Health and Medicine, 1*, 145–157.

Eiser, J.R., & Gentle, P. (1988). Health behavior as goal-directed action. *Journal of Behavioral Medicine, 11*, 523–336.

Eiser, J.R., & van der Plight, J. (1986). Smoking cessation and smokers' perception of their addiction. *Journal of Social and Clinical Psychology, 4*, 60–70.

Ekman, P. & Friesen, W.V. (1974). Detecting deception from the body or face. *Journal of Personality and Social Psychology, 29*, 288–298.

Ekstrand, M.L., & Coates, T.J. (1990). Maintenance of safer sexual behaviors and predictors of risky sex: The San Francisco Men's Health Study. *American Journal of Public Health, 80*, 973–977.

Elander, J., & Midence, K. (1997). Children with chronic illness. *Psychologist, 10*, 211–215.

Elderkin-Thompson, V., Silver, R.C., & Waitzkin, H. (1998). Narratives of somatizing and non-somatizing patients in a primary care setting. *Journal of Health Psychology, 3*, 407–428.

Elias, W.S., & Murphy, R.J. (1986). The case for health promotion programs containing health care costs: a review of the literature. *American Journal of Occupational Therapy, 40*, 759–763.

Elizur, E., & Kaffman, M. (1983). Children's bereavement reactions following death of the father: II. *Journal of the American Academy of Child Psychiatry, 21*, 474–480.

Ellis, A. (1962). *Reason and emotion in psychotherapy*. New York: Lyle Stuart.

Ellis, A. (1977). The basic clinical theory of rational-emotional therapy. In A. Ellis & R. Grieger (Eds.), *Handbook of rational-emotive therapy*. New York: Springer.

Ellsworth, P., Friedman, H., Perlick, D., & Hoyt, M. (1978). Some effects of gaze on subjects motivated to seek or to avoid social comparison. *Journal of Experimental Social Psychology, 14*, 69–87.

Elovainio, M., & Kivimaki, M. (1998). Work and strain on physicians in Finland. *Scandanavian Journal of Social Medicine, 26*, 26–33.

El-Rufaie, O.E.F., Bener, A., Abuzeid, M., & Ali, T.A. (1997). Sexual dysfunction among type II diabetic men: A controlled study. *Journal of Psychosomatic Research, 43*, 605–612.

Engel, C.C., von Korff, M., & Katon, W.J. (1996). Back pain in primary care: Predictors of high health-care costs. *Pain, 65*, 197–204.

Engel, G.L. (1977). The need for a new medical model: The challenge for biomedicine. *Science, 196*, 129–136.

Engel, G.L. (1980). The clinical application of the biopsychosocial model. *American Journal of Psychiatry, 137*, 535–544.

Engel, G.L. (1997). From biomedical to biopsychosocial: Being scientific in the human domain. *Psychosomatics, 38*, 521–528.

English, E.H., & Baker, T.B. (1983). Relaxation training and cardiovascular response to experimental stressors. *Health Psychology, 2*, 239–259.

Ennett, S.T., & Bauman, K.E. (1991). Mediators in the relationship between parental and peer characteristics and beer drinking by early adolescents. *Journal of Applied Social Psychology, 21*, 1699–1711.

Epping-Jordan, J.E., Campos, B.E., Osowiecki, D.M., Oppedisano, G., Gerhardt, C., Primo, K., & Krag, D.N. (1999). Psychological adjustment in breast cancer: Processes of emotional distress. *Health Psychology, 18*, 315–326.

Epstein, L., Miller, G.J., Stitt, F.W., & Morris, J.N. (1976). Vigorous exercise in leisure time, coronary risk factors, and resting electrocardiogram in middle-aged civil servants. *British Heart Journal, 38*, 403.

Epstein, L.H. (1984). The direct effects of compliance on health outcome. *Health Psychology, 3*, 385–393.

Epstein, L.H., & Clauss, P.A. (1982). A behavioral medicine perspective on adherence to long-term medical regimens. *Journal of Consulting Clinical Psychology, 50*, 950–971.

Epstein, L.H., & Wing, R.R. (1980). Behavioral approaches to exercise habits and athletic performance. In J.M. Ferguson & C.B. Taylor (Eds.), *The comprehensive handbook of behavioral medicine: Vol. 1.1—Systems interventions* (pp. 125–137). New York: S.P. Medical & Scientific Books.

Epstein, R.M., Quill, T.E., & McWhinney, I.R. (1999). Somatization reconsidered: Incorporating the patient's experience of illness. *Archives of Internal Medicine, 159*, 215–222.

Eraker, S.A., & Politser, P. (1982). How decisions are reached: Physician and patient. *Annals of Internal Medicine, 97*, 262–268.

Erdelyi, M.H. (1985). *Psychoanalysis: Freud's cognitive psychology*. New York: W.H. Freeman.

Erikson, E.H. (1963). *Childhood and society* (2nd ed). New York: W.W. Norton.

Ernst, E., Resch, K.L., & White, A.R. (1995). Complementary medicine: What physicians think of it: A meta-analysis. *Archives of Internal Medicine, 155*, 2405–2408.

Ernst, E., & White, A.R. (1998). Acupuncture for back pain: A meta-analysis of randomized controlled trials. *Archives of Internal Medicine, 158*, 2235–2241.

Esterling, B.A., Antoni, M.H., Kumar, M., & Schneiderman, N. (1990). Emotional repression, stress disclosure responses, and Epstein-viral caspid antigen titers. *Psychosomatic Medicine, 52*, 397–410.

Esterling, B.A., Kiecolt-Glaser, J.K., Bodnar, J.C., & Glaser, R. (1994). Chronic stress, social support, and persistent alterations in the natural killer cell response to cytokines in older adults. *Health Psychology, 13*, 291–298.

Evans, E. (1926). *A psychological study of cancer*. New York: Dodd, Mead, & Co.

Evans, G.L., & Whitney, F.W. (1998). The role of medical conditions and depression in the functional outcome of stroke survivors: A review and pilot study. *Topics in Stroke Rehabilitation, 5,* 30–50.

Evans, L. (1990). Restraint effectiveness, occupant ejection from cars, and fatality reductions. *Accident Analysis and Prevention, 22,* 167–175.

Evans, L. (1996). Safety-belt effectiveness: The influence of crash severity and selective recruitment. *Accident Analysis and Prevention, 28,* 423–433.

Evans, R.I., Smith, C.K., & Raines, B.E. (1984). Deterring cigarette smoking in adolescents: A psychosocial-behavioral analysis of an intervention strategy. In A. Baum, S.E. Taylor, & J.E. Singer (Eds.), *Handbook of psychology and health (vol. 4): Social psychological aspects of health.* Hillsdale, NJ: Erlbaum.

Everson, R.B., & Fraumeni, J.F. (1975). Mortality among medical students and young physicians. *Journal of Medical Education, 50,* 809–811.

Facione, N.C., Dodd, M.J., Holzemer, W., & Meleis, A.I. (1997). Helpseeking for self-discovered breast symptoms: Implications for early detection. *Cancer Practice, 5,* 220–227.

Falk, I.S. (1964). Medical care: Its social and organizational aspects. *New England Journal of Medicine, 270,* 22–28.

Falvo, D.R. (1999). *Medical and psychosocial aspects of chronic illness and disability* (2nd ed.). Gaithersburg, MD: Aspen Publishers.

Faux, S.A. (1993). Siblings of children with chronic physical and cognitive disabilities. *Journal of Pediatric Nursing, 8,* 305–317.

Fearon, I., McGrath, P.J., & Achat, H. (1996). "Boo-boos": The study of everyday pain among young children. *Pain, 68,* 55–62.

Feighny, K.M., Monaco, M., & Arnold, L. (1995). Empathy training to improve physician-patient communication skills. *Academic Medicine, 70,* 435–436.

Feldenkreis, M. (1981). *The elusive obvious.* Cupertino, CA: Meta Publications.

Feller, B.A. (1979). *Characteristics of general internists and the content of care of their patients.* Washington, DC: U.S. Department of Health, Education, and Welfare, HRA-79-652.

Felton, G.M., Parsons, M.A., & Bartoces, M.G. (1997). Demographic factors: Interaction effects on health-promoting behavior and health related factors. *Public Health Nursing, 14,* 361–367.

Ferguson, R.J., & Ahles, T.A. (1998). Private body consciousness, anxiety and pain symptom reports of chronic pain patients. *Behavior Research and Therapy, 36,* 527–35.

Fernandez, E. (1986). A classification system of cognitive coping strategies for pain. *Pain, 26,* 141–151.

Fernandez, E., & Milburn, T.W. (1994). Sensory and affective predictors of overall pain and emotions associated with affective pain. *Clinical Journal of Pain, 10,* 3–9.

Fernandez, E., & Sheffield, J. (1996). Relative contribution of life events versus daily hassles to the frequency and intensity of headaches. *Headache, 36,* 595–602.

Fernandez, E., & Turk, D.C. (1989). The utility of cognitive coping strategies for altering pain perceptions: A meta-analysis. *Pain, 38,* 123–135.

Feuerstein, M., Papciak, A.S., & Hoon, P.E. (1987). Biobehavioral mechanisms of chronic low back pain. *Clinical Psychology Review, 7,* 243–273.

Fichera, L.V., & Andreassi, J.L. (1998). Stress and personality as factors in women's cardiovascular reactivity. *International Journal of Psychophysiology, 28,* 143–155.

Field, D., & Lennox, A. (1996). Gender in medicine: The views of first and fifth year medical students. *Medical Education, 30,* 246–252

Field, T.M. (1996). Touch therapies for pain management and stress reduction. In R.J. Resnick & R.H. Rozensky (Eds.), *Health psychology through the life span: Practice and research opportunities.* Washington, DC: APA.

Fife, B.L. (1995). The measurement of meaning in illness. *Social Science & Medicine, 40,* 1021–1028.

Fine, C. (1981). *Married to medicine: An intimate portrait of doctors' wives.* New York: Atheneum.

Finke, L.M., Birenbaum, L.K., & Chand, N. (1994). Two weeks post-death report by parents of siblings' grieving experience. *Journal of Child & Adolescent Psychiatric Nursing, 7,* 17–25.

Finney, J.W., & Moos, R.H. (1991). The long-term course of treated alcoholism, I: Mortality, relapse, and remission rates and comparisons with community controls. *Journal of Studies on Alcoholism, 52,* 44–54.

Firth-Cozens, J., & Greenhalgh, J. (1997). Doctors' perceptions of the links between stress and lowered clinical care. *Social Science and Medicine, 44,* 1017–1022.

Fischer, R. (1976). I can't remember what I said last night, but it must have been good. *Psychology Today, 10,* 68–72.

Fischer, R., & Landon, G. (1972). On the arousal state-dependent recall of "subconscious" experience: State-boundness. *British Journal of Psychiatry, 120,* 159–172.

Fishbein, M. (1980). A theory of reasoned action: Some applications and implications. In M.M. Page (Ed.), *1979 Nebraska Symposium on Motivation.* Lincoln: University of Nebraska Press.

Fishbein, M., & Ajzen, I. (1975). *Belief, attitude, intention, and behavior: An introduction to theory and research.* Reading, MA: Addison-Wesley.

Fisher, E.B., & Rost, K. (1986). Smoking cessation: A practical guide for the physician. *Clinics in Chest Medicine, 7,* 551–565.

Fisher, E.S., & Welch, H.G. (1999). Avoiding the unintended consequences of growth in medical care: How might more be worse? *Journal of the American Medical Association, 281,* 446–453.

Fisher, K., & Johnston, M. (1998). Emotional distress and control cognitions as mediators of the impact of chronic pain on disability. *British Journal of Health Psychology, 3,* 225–236.

Fisher, S. (1986). *In the patient's best interest: Women and the politics of medical decisions* (pp. 29–58). New Brunswick, NJ: Rutgers University Press.

Fisher, W.A., Fisher, J.D., & Rye, B.J. (1995). Understanding and promoting AIDS-preventive behavior:

Insights from the theory of reasoned action. *Health Psychology, 14,* 255–264.

Flaherty, J.A., & Richman, J.A. (1993). Substance use and addiction among medical students, residents, and physicians. *Psychiatry Clinics of North America, 16,* 189–197.

Fleming, I., Baum, A., Davidson, L.M., Rectanus, E., & McArdle, S. (1987). Chronic stress as a factor in physiologic reactivity to challenge. *Health Psychology, 6,* 221–237.

Focht, B.C., & Koltyn, K.F. (1999). Influence of resistance exercise of different intensities on state anxiety and blood pressure. *Medical Science & Sports Exercise, 31,* 456–463.

Folkman, S. (1993). Psychosocial effects of HIV infection. In L. Goldberger & S. Breznitz (Eds.), Handbook of stress: Theoretical and clinical aspects (2nd ed.). New York: Free Press.

Folkman, S., & Lazarus, R.S. (1980). An analysis of coping in a middle-aged community sample. *Journal of Health and Social Behavior, 21,* 219–239.

Follette, W., & Cummings, N.A. (1967). Psychiatric services and medical utilization in a prepaid health plan setting. *Medical Care, 5,* 25–35.

Ford, C.V. (1995). Dimensions of somatization and hypochondriasis. *Neurologic Clinics, 13,* 241–253.

Fordyce, W.E. (1976). *Behavioral methods for chronic pain and illness.* St. Louis, MO: C.V. Mosby.

Fordyce, W.E. (1985). Back pain, compensation, and public policy. In J.C. Rosen & L.J. Solomon (Eds.). *Prevention in health psychology* (pp. 390–400). Hanover, NH: University Press of New England.

Fordyce, W.E. (1988). Pain and suffering: A reappraisal. *American Psychologist, 43,* 276–283.

Fordyce, W.E., & Steger, J.C. (1979). Behavioral management of chronic pain. In O.F. Pomerleau & J.P. Brady (Ed.), *Behavioral medicine: Theory and practice.* Baltimore, MD: Williams & Wilkins.

Forrow, L., & Wolf, M.L. (1998). Deals in action: The U.S. Schweitzer Fellows Programs. *Academic Medicine, 73,* 658–661.

Foster, G.D., Wadden, T.A., Kendall, P.C., Stunkard, A.J., & Vogt, R.A. (1996). Psychological effects of weight loss and regain: A prospective evaluation. *Journal of Consulting and Clinical Psychology, 64,* 752–757.

Fournier, P.E., Stalder, J., Mermillod, B., & Chantraine, A. (1997). Effects of a 110 kilometers ultra-marathon race on plasma hormone levels. *International Journal of Sports Medicine, 18,* 252–256.

Francis, M.E., & Pennebaker, J.W. (1992). Putting stress into words: The impact of writing on physiological, absentee, and self-reported emotional well being measures. *American Journal of Health Promotion, 6,* 280–287.

Frank, E., & Harvey, L.K. (1996). Prevention advice rates of women and men physicians. *Archives of Family Medicine, 5,* 215–219.

Frankel, R.M. (1995). Emotion and the physician-patient relationship. *Motivation and Emotion, 19,* 163–173.

Frankenhaeuser, M. (1975). Sympathetic-adrenomedullary activity behavior and the psychosocial environment. In

P.H. Venables & M.J. Christie (Eds.), *Research in psychophysiology.* New York: Wiley.

Frankenhaeuser, M. (1986). A psychobiological framework for research on human stress and coping. In M.H. Appley & R. Trumbull (Eds.), *Dynamics of stress: Physiological, psychological, and social perspectives.* New York: Plenum.

Franks, P., Culpepper, L., & Dickinson, J. (1982). Psychobiologic bias in the diagnosis of obesity. *Journal of Family Practice, 14,* 745–750.

Fraser, R.T., & Clemmons, D.C. (Eds.). (2000). *Traumatic brain injury rehabilitation: Practical vocational, neuropsychological, and psychotherapy interventions.* Boca Raton, FL: CRC Press, Inc.

Frederikson, L.G. (1995). Exploring information-exchange in consultation: The patients' view of performance and outcomes. *Patient Education & Counseling, 25,* 237–246.

Frederikson, L.G., & Bull, P.E. (1995). Evaluation of a patient education leaflet designed to improve communication in medical consultations. *Patient Education & Counseling, 25,* 51–57.

Freemon, B., Negrete, V.F., Davis, M., & Korsch, B.M. (1971). Gaps in doctor-patient communication: Doctor-patient interaction analysis. *Pediatric Research, 5,* 298–311.

Freeth, D., & Nicol, M. (1998). Learning clinical skills: An interprofessional approach. *Nurse Education Today, 18,* 455–461.

Freidson, E. (1970). *Profession of medicine.* New York: Dodd-Mead.

French, S.A., Hennrikus, D.J., & Jeffery, R.W. (1996). Smoking status, dietary intake, and physical activity in a sample of working adults. *Health Psychology, 15,* 448–454.

Freuchen, P. (1961). *Book of the Eskimo.* Greenwich, CT: Fawcett.

Freud, S. (1924). The dynamics of transference. In *Collected papers (vol. 2.).* London: Institute of Psychoanalysis and Hogarth Press.

Fried, M. (1982). Endemic stress: The psychology of resignation and the politics of scarcity. *American Journal of Orthopsychiatry, 52,* 4–19.

Fried, R.G., Friedman, S., Paradis, C., Hatch, M., Lynfield, Y., Duncanson, C., & Shalita, A. (1995). Trivial or terrible? The psychosocial impact of psoriasis. *International Journal of Dermatology, 34,* 101–105.

Fried, T.R., Pollack, D.M., & Tinetti, M.E. (1998). Factors associated with six-month mortality in recipients of community-based long-term care. *Journal of the American Geriatrics Society, 46,* 193–197.

Friedman, H.S. (1982). Nonverbal communication in medical interaction. In H.S. Friedman & M.R. DiMatteo (Eds.), *Interpersonal issues in health care.* New York: Academic Press.

Friedman, H.S., & Booth-Kewley, S. (1987). The "disease-prone personality" A meta-analytic view of the construct. *American Psychologist, 42,* 539–555.

Friedman, H.S., Hall, J.A., & Harris, M.J. (1985). Type A behavior, nonverbal expressive style, and health. *Journal of Personality and Social Psychology, 48,* 1299–1315.

Friedman, H.S., Harris, M.J., & Hall, J.A., (1984). Nonverbal expressions of emotion: Healthy charisma or coronary-prone behavior? In C. Van Dyke, L. Temoshok, & L.S. Zegans (Eds.), *Emotions in health and illness: Applications to clinical practice* (pp. 151–165). San Diego, CA: Grune & Stratton.

Friedman, H.S., & Martin, L.R. (May, 1999). *Heck with the surgeon general: A new approach to health promotion.* Address to the annual convention of the Western Psychological Association, Irvine, CA.

Friedman, H.S., Tucker, J.S., Schwartz, J.E., Martin, L.R., Tomlinson-Keasey, C., Wingard, D.L., & Criqui, M.H. (1995). Childhood conscientiousness and longevity: Health behaviors and cause of death. *Journal of Personality and Social Psychology, 68,* 696–703.

Friedman, H.S., Tucker, J.S., Tomlinson-Keasey, C., Schwartz, J.E., Wingard, D.L., & Criqui, M.H. (1993). Does childhood personality predict longevity? *Journal of Personality and Social Psychology, 65,* 176–185.

Friedman, M., & Rosenman, R.H. (1974). *Type A behavior and your heart.* New York: Alfred A. Knopf.

Friedman, M., & Ulmer, D. (1984). *Treating Type A behavior and your heart.* New York: Knopf.

Friedman, M.H., Connell, K.J., Olthoff, A.J., Sinacore, J.M., et al. (1998). Medical student errors in making a diagnosis. *Academic Medicine, 73,* S19–S21.

Friedman, R., Sobel, D., Myers, P., Caudill, M., & Benson, H. (1995). Behavioral medicine, clinical health psychology, and cost offset. *Health Psychology, 14,* 509–518.

Friend, R., Hatchett, L., Schneider, M.S., & Wadhwa, N.K. (1997). A comparison of attributions, health beliefs, and negative emotions as predictors of fluid adherence in renal dialysis patients: A prospective analysis. *Annals of Behavioral Medicine, 19,* 344–347.

Frost, H., Lamb, S.E., Moffett, J.A.K., Fairbank, J.C.T., et al. (1998). A fitness programme for patients with chronic low back pain: 2-year follow-up of a randomised controlled trial. *Pain, 75,* 273–279.

Fuchs, R. (1996). Causal models of physical exercise participation: Testing the predictive power of the construct "pressure to change." *Journal of Applied Social Psychology, 26,* 1931–1960.

Fukunishi, I. (1999). Relationship of cosmetic disfigurement to the severity of posttraumatic stress disorder in burn injury or digital amputation. *Psychotherapy and Psychosomatics, 68,* 82–86.

Fukunishi, I., Akimoto, M., Horikawa, N., Shirasaka, K., et al. (1998). Stress coping and social support in glucose tolerance abnormality. *Journal of Psychosomatic Research, 45,* 361–369.

Fuller, T.D., Edwards, J.N., Sermsri, S., & Vorakitphokatorn, S. (1993). Gender and health: Some Asian evidence. *Journal of Health and Social Behavior, 34,* 252–271.

Funk, M., & Griffey, K.A. (1994). Relation of gender to the use of cardiac procedures in acute myocardial infarction. *American Journal of Cardiology, 74,* 1170–1173.

Funk, S.C. (1992). Hardiness: A review of theory and research. *Health Psychology, 11,* 335–345.

Gaillard, A.W. (1993). Comparing the concepts of mental load and stress. *Ergonomics, 36,* 991–1005.

Gal, R., & Lazarus, R.S. (1975). The role of activity in anticipating and confronting stressful situations. *Journal of Human Stress, 1,* 4–20.

Gallagher, E.J., Viscoli, C.M., & Horowitz, R.I. (1993). The relationship of treatment adherence to the risk of death after myocardial infarction in women. *Journal of the American Medical Association, 270,* 742–743.

Gallagher-Thompson, D. Futterman, A., Farberow, N., Thompson, L.W., & Peterson, J. (1993). The impact of spousal bereavement on older widows and widowers. In M.S. Stroebe, W. Stroebe, & R.O. Hansson (Eds.), *Handbook of bereavement.* New York: Cambridge University Press.

Gallant, M.P., & Connell, C.M. (1998). The stress process among dementia spouse caregivers: Are caregivers at risk for negative health behavior change? *Research on Aging, 20,* 267–297.

Gallo, A.M., & Knafl, K.A. (1998). Parents' reports of "tricks of the trade" for managing childhood chronic illness. *Journal of the Society of Pediatric Nurses, 3,* 93–100.

Gallo, J.J. (1990). The effect of social support on depression in caregivers of the elderly. *Journal of Family Practice, 30,* 430–436.

Gambone, J.C., & Reiter, R.C. (1991). Quality improvement in health care. *Current Problems in Obstetrics, Gynecology, & Fertility, 14,* 169–175.

Gandy, G.L., Martin, E.D., Jr., & Hardy, R.E. (Eds.). (1999). *Counseling in the rehabilitation process: Community services for mental and physical disabilities* (2nd ed.). Springfield, IL: Charles C. Thomas Publisher.

Gapen, P. (1980). Stress: Medical school's perilous rites of passage. *New Physician, 29,* 18–22.

Garbutt, J.C., West, S.L., Carey, T.S., Lohr, K.N., & Crews, F.T. (1999). Pharmacological treatment of alcohol dependence: A review of evidence. *Journal of the American Medical Association, 281,* 1318–1325.

Gardner, W., Kelleher, K.J., Wasserman, R., Childs, G., Nutting, P., Lillienfeld, H., & Pajer, K. (2000). Primary care treatment of pediatric psychosocial problems: A study from pediatric research in office settings and ambulatory sentinel practice network. *Pediatrics, 106,* E44.

Garland, A.F., & Ziegler, E.F. (1994). Psychological correlates of help-seeking attitudes among children and adolescents. *American Journal of Orthopsychiatry, 64,* 586–593.

Garrity, T.F., & Marx, M.B. (1979). Critical life events and coronary disease. In W.D. Gentry & R.B. Williams (Eds.), *Psychological aspects of myocardial infarction and coronary care* (2nd ed.). St. Louis, MO: C.V. Mosby.

Geiss, A., Varadi, E., Steinbach, K., Bauer, H.W., & Anton, F. (1997). Psychoneuroimmunological correlates of persisting sciatic pain in patients who underwent discectomy. *Neuroscience Letters, 237,* 65–68.

Gelfand, D.M. (1978). Social withdrawal and negative emotional states: Behavior therapy. In B.B. Wolman, J. Egan, & A.O. Ross (Eds.), *Handbook of treatment of mental disorders in childhood and adolescence*. Englewood Cliffs, NJ: Prentice-Hall.

George, S.A. (2000). Barriers to breast cancer screening: An integrative review. *Health Care of Women International, 21,* 53–65.

Gerrard, M., Gibbons, F.X., Benthin, A.C., & Hessling, R.M. (1996). A longitudinal study of the reciprocal nature of risk behaviors and cognitions in adolescents: What you do shapes what you think, and vice versa. *Health Psychology, 15,* 344–354.

Gibbons, M.B. (1992). A child dies, a child survives: The impact of sibling loss. *Journal of Pediatric Health Care, 6,* 65–72.

Gilbertson, T.A., Fontenot, D.T., Liu, L., Zhang, H., & Monroe, W.T. (1997). Fatty acid modulation of K⁺ channels in taste receptor cells: Gustatory cues for dietary fat. *American Journal of Physiology, 272,* C1203–C1210.

Gilden, J.L., Hendryx, M.S., Clar, S., Casia, C., & Singh, S.P. (1992). Diabetes support groups improve health care of older diabetic patients. *Journal of the American Geriatric Society, 40,*147–150.

Gill, V.T. (1998). Doing attributions in medical interaction: Patients' explanations for illness and doctors' responses. *Social Psychology Quarterly, 61,* 342–360.

Glenn, S.W., Parsons, O.A., & Stevens, L. (1989). Effects of alcohol abuse and familiar alcoholism on physical health in men and women. *Health Psychology, 8,* 325–341.

Glinder, J.G., & Campos, B.E. (1999). Self-blame attributions in women with newly diagnosed breast cancer: A prospective study of psychological adjustment. *Health Psychology, 18,* 475–481.

Glueckauf, R.L., & Quittner, A.L. (1984). Facing physical disability as a young adult: Psychological issues and approaches. In M.G. Eisenberg, L.C. Sutkin, & M.A. Jansen (Eds.), *Chronic illness and disability through the life span: Effects on self and family* (pp. 167–183). New York: Springer.

Godin, G., & Kok, G. (1996). The theory of planned behavior: A review of its applications to health-related behaviors. *American Journal of Health Promotion, 11,* 87–98.

Goff, D.C., Jr., Sellers, D.E., McGovern, P.G., Meischke, H., Goldberg, R.J., Bittner, V., Hedges, J.R., Allender, P.S., & Nichaman, M.Z. (1998). Knowledge of heart attack symptoms in a population survey in the United States: The REACT Trial, Rapid Early Action for Coronary Treatment. *Archives of Internal Medicine, 158,* 2329–2338.

Goffman, E. (1963). *Stigma*. Englewood Cliffs, NJ: Prentice-Hall.

Goldbeck, R. (1997). Denial in physical illness. *Journal of Psychosomatic Research, 43,* 575–593.

Goldberg, M.A., & Katz, B. (1990). The effect of nonreciprocated and reciprocated touch on power/dominance perception. *Journal of Social Behavior & Personality, 5,* 379–386.

Goldberg, R.J., O'Donnell, C., Yarzebski, J., Bigelow, C., Savageau, J., & Gore, J.M. (1998). Sex differences in symptom presentation associated with acute myocardial infarction: A population-based perspective. *American Heart Journal, 136,* 189–195.

Goldenson, R.M. (1978a). Dimensions of the field. In R.M. Goldenson, J.R. Dunham, & C.S. Dunham (Eds.), *Disability and rehabilitation handbook* (pp. 3–11). New York: McGraw-Hill.

Goldenson, R.M. (1978b). Independent living: Ways and means. In R.M. Goldenson, J.R. Dunham, & C.S. Dunham (Eds.), *Disability and rehabilitation handbook* (pp. 36–52). New York: McGraw-Hill.

Goldstein, A.P. (1980). Relationship-enhancement methods. In F.H. Kanfer & A.P. Goldstein (Eds.), *Helping people change* (2nd ed., pp. 18-57). New York: Pergamon.

Goldstein, A.P., & Kanfer, F.H. (Eds.) (1979). *Maximizing treatment gains: Transfer enhancement in psychotherapy*. New York: Academic Press.

Goldstein, M.J. (1973). Individual differences in response to stress. *American Journal of Community Psychology, 1,* 113–137.

Golin, C.E., DiMatteo, M.R., & Gelberg, L. (1996). The role of patient participation in the doctor visit. Implications for adherence to diabetes care. *Diabetes Care, 19,* 1153–64.

Goodall, T.A., & Halford, W.K. (1991). Self-management of diabetes mellitus: A critical review. *Health Psychology, 10,* 1–8.

Goodkin, K., Feaster, D.J., Tuttle, R., Blaney, N.T., Kumar, M., Baum, M.K., Shapshak, P., & Fletcher, M.A. (1996). Bereavement is associated with time-dependent decrements in cellular immune function in asymptomatic human immunodeficiency virus type 1-seropositive homosexual men. *Clinical Diagnosis and Laboratory Immunology, 3,* 109–118.

Goodwin, J.S., Goodwin, J.M., & Vogel, A.V. (1979). Knowledge and use of placebos by house officers and nurses. *Annals of Internal Medicine, 91,* 106–110.

Gordon, T., & Doyle, J.T. (1987). Drinking and mortality: The Albany Study. *American Journal of Epidemiology, 125,* 263–270.

Gordon, T., & Kannel, W.B. (1984). Drinking and mortality: The Framingham Study. *American Journal of Epidemiology, 120,* 97–107.

Gottlieb, B.H. (1997). *Coping with chronic stress*. New York: Plenum.

Gottlieb, D.J., Parenti, C.M., Peterson, C.A., & Lofgren, R.P. (1991). Effect of a change in house staff work schedule on resource utilization and patient care. *Archives of Internal Medicine, 151,* 2065–2070.

Gould, M.S., King, R., Greenwald, S., Fisher, P., et al. (1998). Psychopathology associated with suicidal ideation and attempts among children and adolescents. *Journal of the American Academy of Child and Adolescent Psychiatry, 37,* 915–923.

Graham, D.T. (1972). Psychosomatic medicine. In N.S. Greenfield & R.A. Sternbach (Eds.), *Handbook of psychophysiology*. New York: Holt, Rinehart, & Winston.

Graham, N.M. (1998). Studies of antiretroviral therapy in the Multicenter AIDS Cohort Study. *Journal of Acquired Immune Deficiency Syndromes and Human Retrovirology, 17,* S9–S12.

Graveley, E.A., & Oseasohn, C.S. (1991). Multiple drug regimens: Medication compliance among veterans 65 years and older. *Research in Nursing and Health, 14,* 51–58.

Gray, P.G. & Cartwright, A. (1953). Choosing and changing doctors. *Lancet, 19,* 1308.

Greenberg, E.S., & Grunberg, L. (1995). Work alienation and problem alcohol behavior. *Journal of Health & Social Behavior, 36,* 83–102.

Greene, M.G., & Adelman, R.D. (1996). Psychosocial factors in older patients' medical encounters. *Research on Aging, 18,* 84–102.

Greene, M.G., Majerovitz, S.D., Adelman, R.D., & Rizzo, C. (1994). The effects of the presence of a third person on the physician-older patient medical interview. *Journal of the American Geriatric Society, 42,* 413–419.

Greenfield, S., Kaplan, S.H., Ware, J.E., Jr., Yano, E.M., & Frank, H.J.L. (1988). Patients' participation in medical care: Effects on blood sugar control and quality of life in diabetes. *Journal of General Internal Medicine, 3,* 448–457.

Greenwald, B.D., & Narcessian, E.J. (1999). Opioids for managing patients with chronic pain: Community pharmacists' perspectives and concerns. *Journal of Pain Symptom Management, 17,* 369–375.

Griffin, K.W., & Rabkin, J.G. (1998). Perceived control over illness, realistic acceptance, and psychological adjustment in people with AIDS. *Journal of Social and Clinical Psychology, 17,* 407–424.

Griffith, C.H., Haist, S.A., Wilson, J.F., & Rich, E.C. (1996). Housestaff social history knowledge. *Evaluation Health Professional, 19,* 81–90.

Griffith, C.H., Rich, E.C., & Wilson, J.F. (1995). Housestaff's knowledge of their patients' social histories. *Academic Medicine, 70,* 64–66.

Grilli, R., Freemantle, N., Minozzi, S., Domenighetti, G., & Finer, D. (1998). Impact of mass media on the use of health services: A systematic review of the literature. *Epidemiology and Prevention, 22,* 103–110.

Grimby, A. (1998). Hallucinations following the loss of a spouse: Common and normal events among the elderly. *Journal of Clinical Geropsychology, 4,* 65–74.

Gross, D.A., Zyzanski, S.J., Borawski, E.A., Cebul, R.D., et al. (1998). Patient satisfaction with time spent with their physician. *Journal of Family Practice, 47,* 133–137.

Gross, E.B. (1992). Gender differences in physician stress. *Journal of the American Medical Women's Association, 47,* 107–112.

Gross, E.B. (1998). Gender differences in physician stress: Why the discrepant findings? *Women & Health, 26,* 1–14.

Grunau, R.V.E. Johnston, C.C., & Craig, K.D. (1990). Neonatal facial and cry responses to invasive and non-invasive procedures. *Pain, 42,* 295–305.

Guttman, N. (1993). Patient-practitioner information exchange as an asymmetrical social encounter: Do patients actually know what their practitioners think they know? In J.R. Schement & B. Ruben (Eds.), *Between communication and information.* New Brunswick, NJ: Transaction Books.

Guyll, M., & Contrada, R.J. (1998). Trait hostility and ambulatory cardiovascular activity: Responses to social interaction. *Health Psychology, 17,* 30–39.

Guyton, A.C. (1985). *Anatomy and physiology.* Philadelphia: Saunders.

Hackett, G.F., & Horan, J.J. (1978). Focused smoking: An equivocally safe alternative to rapid smoking. *Journal of Drug Education, 8,* 261–265.

Hadlow, J., & Pitts, M. (1991). The understanding of common health terms by doctors, nurses, and patients. *Social Science & Medicine, 32,* 193–196.

Hagenzieker, M.P., Bijleveld, F.D., & Davidse, R.J. (1997). Effects of incentive programs to stimulate safety belt use: A meta-analysis. *Accident Analysis Prevention, 29,* 759–777.

Halberstadt, A.G. (1985). Race, socioeconomic status and nonverbal behavior. In A.W. Siegman & S. Feldstein (Eds.), *Multichannel integrations of nonverbal behavior* (pp. 227–266). Hillsdale, NJ: Erlbaum.

Halbreich, U. (1995). Menstrually related disorders: What we do know, what we only believe that we know, and what we know that we do not know. *Critical Review of Neurobiology, 9,* 163–175.

Hall, H.I., May, D.S., Lew, R.A.., Koh, H.K., & Nadel, M. (1997). Sun protection behaviors of the U.S. White population. *Preventive Medicine, 26,* 401–407.

Hall, J.A., Epstein, A.M., DeCiantis, M.L., & McNeil, B.J. (1993). Physicians' liking for their patients: More evidence for the role of affect in medical care. *Health Psychology, 12,* 140–146.

Hall, J.A., Harrigan, J.A., & Rosenthal, R. (1995). Nonverbal behavior in clinician-patient interaction. *Applied & Preventive Psychology, 4,* 21–37.

Hall, J.A., Irish, J.T., Roter, D.L., Ehrlich, C.M., & Miller, L.H. (1994). Gender in medical encounters: An analysis of physician and patient communication in a primary care setting. *Health Psychology, 13,* 384–392.

Hall, J.A., Roter, D.L., & Katz, N.R. (1988). Meta-analysis of correlates of provider behavior in medical encounters. *Medical Care, 26,* 1–19.

Hall, J.A., Roter, D.L., & Rand, C.S. (1981). Communication of affect between patient and physician. *Journal of Health and Social Behavior, 22,* 18–30.

Hallett, J.D., Zasler, N.D., Maurer, P., & Cash, S. (1994). Role change after traumatic brain injury in adults. *American Journal of Occupational Therapy, 48,* 241–246.

Halpern, J. (1993). Empathy: Using resonance emotions in the service of curiosity. In H. Spiro, M.G.M. Curnen, E. Peschel & D. St. James (Eds.). *Empathy and the practice of medicine* (pp. 160–173). New Haven: Yale University Press.

Hamberger, K. & Lohr, J. (1984). *Stress and stress management: Research and applications.* New York: Springer.

Hamburg, D.A., Hamburg, B., & DeGoza, S. (1953). Adaptive problems and mechanisms in severely burned patients. *Psychiatry, 16,* 1–20.

Hamilton, M.A., Rouse, R.A., & Rouse, J. (1994). Dentist communication and patient utilization of dental services: Anxiety inhibition and competence enhancement effects. *Health Communication, 6,* 137–158.

Hampson, S.E., Glasgow, R.E., & Toobert, D.J. (1990). Personal models of diabetes and their relations to self-care activities. *Health Psychology, 9,* 632–646.

Handron, D.S. (1993). Denial and serious chronic illness—a personal perspective. *Perspectives in Psychiatric Care, 29,* 29–33.

Harburg, E., Erfurt, J.C., Hauenstein, L.S., Chape, C., Schull, W.J., & Schork, M.A. (1973). Socio-ecological stress, suppressed hostility, skin color, and black-white male blood pressure: Detroit. *Psychosomatic Medicine, 35,* 276–296.

Hardison, J.E. (1986). The house officer's changing world. *New England Journal of Medicine, 314,* 1713–1715.

Hare, B.D., & Milano, R.A. (1985). Chronic pain: Perspectives on physical assessment and treatment. *Annals of Behavioral Medicine, 7,* 6–10.

Harkins, S.W., & Chapman, C.R. (1976). Detection and decision factors in pain [perception in young and elderly men. *Pain, 2,* 253–264.

Harkins, S.W., Price, D.D., & Martelli, M. (1986). Effects of age on pain perception: Thermonociception. *Journal of Gerontology, 41,* 58–63.

Harper, F.D. (1978). Outcomes of jogging: Implication for counseling. *Personnel and Guidance Journal, 57,* 74–78.

Harrigan, J.A., Oxman, T., & Rosenthal, R.R. (1985). Rapport expressed through nonverbal behavior. *Journal of Nonverbal Behavior, 9,* 95–110.

Harris, M.B. (1981). Runner's perceptions of the benefits of running. *Perceptual and Motor Skill, 52,* 153–154.

Harrison, C.J. (1995). Rational selection of antimicrobials for pediatric upper respiratory infections. *Pediatric Infectious Disease Journal, 14,* S121–129.

Harrison, K.F. (1986). The use of non-essential drugs, alcohol, and cigarettes during pregnancy. *Irish Medical Journal, 79,* 338–341.

Harte, J.L., Eifert, G.H., & Smith, R. (1995). The effects of running and meditation on beta-endorphin, corticotropin-releasing hormone and cortisol in plasma, and on mood. *Biological Psychology, 40,* 251–265.

Hashemi, L., Webster, B.S., & Clancy, E.A. (1998). Trends in disability duration and cost of workers' compensation low back pain claims (1988–1996). *Journal of Occupational and Environmental Medicine, 40,* 1110–1119.

Haug, M. & Lavin, B. (1983). *Consumerism in medicine: Challenging physician authority.* Beverly Hills, CA.: Sage Publications.

Hausenblas, H.A., Carron, A.V., & Mack, D.E. (1997). Application of the theories of reasoned action and planned behavior to exercise behavior: A meta-analysis. *Journal of Sport and Exercise Psychology, 19,* 36–51.

Hawkins, M.R., Vichick, D.A., Silsby, H.D., Kruzich, D.J., & Butler, R. (1985). Sleep and nutritional deprivation and performance of house officers. *Journal of Medical Education, 60,* 530–535.

Hayes-Bautista, D.E., Hsu, P., Hayes-Bautista, M., Stein, R.M., Dowling, P., Beltran, R., & Villagomez, J. (2000). Latino physician supply in California: Sources, locations, and projections. *Academic Medicine, 75,* 727–736.

Haynes, R.B. (1979). Strategies to improve compliance with referrals, appointments, and prescribed medical regimens. In R.B. Haynes, D.W. Taylor, & D.L. Sackett (Eds.), *Compliance in health care* (pp. 121–143). Baltimore, MD: Johns Hopkins University Press.

Haynes, R.B., McKibbon, K.A., & Kanani, R. (1996). Systematic review of randomised controlled trials of the effects on patient adherence and outcomes of interventions to assist patients to follow prescriptions for medications. *The Cochrane Library, 2,* 1–26.

Haynes, S.G., Levine, S., Scotch, N., Feinleib, M., & Kannel, W.B. (1978). The relationship of psychosocial factors to coronary heart disease in the Framingham Study: I. Methods and risk factors. *American Journal of Epidemiology, 107,* 362–383.

Hays, L.R., Cheever, T., & Patel, P. (1996). Medical student suicide, 1989–1994. *American Journal of Psychiatry, 153,* 553–555.

Hays, R.D., Stacy, A.W., & DiMatteo, M.R. (1984). Cocariation among health related behaviors. *Addictive Behaviors, 9,* 315–318.

Haythornthwaite, J.A., Menefee, L.A., Quatrano-Piacentini, A.L., & Pappagallo, M. (1998). Outcome of chronic opioid therapy for non-cancer pain. *Journal of Pain and Symptom Management, 15,* 185–194.

Healy, B. (1991). Women's health, public welfare. *Journal of the American Medical Association, 266,* 566–568.

Heath, C. (1984). Participation in the medical consultation: The coordination of verbal and nonverbal behavior between the doctor and patient. *Sociology of Health & Illness, 6,* 311–338.

Hedges, J.R., Mann, N.C., Meischke, H., Robbins, M., Goldberg, R., & Zapka, J. (1998). Assessment of chest pain onset and out-of-hospital delay using standardized interview questions: The REACT Pilot Study, Rapid Early Action for Coronary Treatment (REACT) Study Group. *Academic Emergency Medicine, 5,* 773–780.

Heffer, R.W., Worchel-Prevatt, R., Rae, W.A., Lopez, M.A., et al. (1997). The effects of oral versus written instructions on parents' recall and satisfaction after pediatric appointments. *Journal of Developmental & Behavioral Pediatrics, 18,* 377–382.

Heft, M.W., Cooper, B.Y., O'Brien, K.K., Hemp, E., & O'Brien, R. (1996). Aging effects on the perception of noxious and non-noxious thermal stimuli applied to the face. *Aging, 8,* 35–41.

Heinrich, R.L., Cohen, M.J., Naliboff, B.D., Collins, G.A., & Bonnebakker, A.D. (1985). Comparing physical and behavior therapy for chronic low back pain on physical abilities, psychological distress, and patients' perceptions. *Journal of Behavioral Medicine, 8,* 61–78.

Heitkamp, H.C., Huber, W., & Scheib, K. (1996). Beta-endorphin and adrenocorticotrophin after incremental exercise and marathon running—female responses. *European Journal of Applied Physiology, 72,* 417–424.

Heitkamp, H.C., Schulz, H., Rocker, K., & Dickhuth, H.H. (1998). Endurance training in females: Changes in beta-endorphin and ACTH. *International Journal of Sports Medicine, 19,* 260–264.

Helfer, R.E. (1970). An objective comparison of the pediatric interviewing skills of freshman and senior medical student. *Pediatrics, 45,* 623–627.

Helfer, R.E., & Ealy, K.F. (1972). Observations of pediatric interviewing skills: A longitudinal and cross-sectional study. *American Journal of Diseases of Children, 123,* 556–560.

Hellerstein, D. (1986). *Battles of life and death.* New York: Houghton Mifflin, Co.

Helsing, K.J., Szklo, M., & Comstock, G.W. (1981). Factors associated with mortality after widowhood. *American Journal of Public Health, 71,* 802–809.

Hendin, H. (1999). Suicide, assisted suicide, and medical illness. *Journal of Clinical Psychiatry, 60,* 46–50.

Hendrick, C., Wells, K.S., & Faletti, M.V. (1982). Social and emotional effects of geographical relocation on elderly retirees. *Journal of Personality and Social Psychology, 41,* 951–962.

Henley, N.M. (1977). *Body politics.* Englewood Cliffs, NJ: Prentice Hall.

Hennrikus, D., Girgis, A., Redman, S., & Sanson-Fisher, R.W. (1991). A community study of delay in presenting with signs of melanoma to medical practitioners. *Archives of Dermatology, 127,* 356–361.

Henson, R.H. (1997). Analysis of the concept of mutuality. *IMAGE: Journal of Nursing Scholarship, 29,* 77–81.

Herbert, T.B., & Cohen, S. (1993). Depression and immunity: A meta-analytic review. *Psychological Bulletin, 113,* 472–486.

Herman, M. (1972). The poor: Their medical needs and the health services available to them. *Annals of the American Academy of Political and Social Sciences, 399,* 12–21.

Heron, E. (1987). *Intensive care: The story of a nurse.* New York: Ballantine.

Hewitt, J.P. (1979). *Self and society: A symbolic interactionist social psychology* (2nd ed.). Boston: Allyn & Bacon.

Hilgard, E.R. (1978). Hypnosis and pain. In R.A. Sternbach (Ed.), *The psychology of pain.* New York: Raven Press.

Hilgard, E.R., & Hilgard, J.R. (1975). *Hypnosis in the relief of pain.* Los Altos, CA: Kaufman.

Hill, J.O., & Peters, J.C. (1998). Environmental contributions to the obesity epidemic. *Science, 280,* 1371–1374.

Hillhouse, J.J., Stair, A.W., III, & Adler, C.M. (1996). Predictors of sunbathing and sunscreen use in college undergraduates. *Journal of Behavioral Medicine, 19,* 543–561.

Hinkle, L.E., Jr. (1973). The concept of "stress" in the biological and social sciences. *Science, Medicine, and Man, 1,* 31–48.

Hippocrates. (1923 translation). *Volume II: On decorum and the physician* (W.H.S. Jones, Trans.). London: William Heinemann.

Hirsch, M.S., & Liebert, R.M. (1998). The physical and psychological experience of pain: The effects of labeling and cold pressor temperature on three pain measures in college women. *Pain, 77,* 41–48.

Hobson, C.J., Kamen, J., Szostek, J., Nethercut, C.M., et al. (1998). Stressful life events: A revision and update of the Social Readjustment Rating Scale. *International Journal of Stress Management, 5,* 1–23.

Hodge, M.J., Dougherty, G.E., & Pless, I.B. (1995). Pediatric mortality and hospital use in Canada and the United States, 1971 through 1987. *American Journal of Public Health, 85,* 1276–1279.

Hoffman, C., Rice, D., & Sung, H.Y. (1996). Persons with chronic conditions: Their prevalence and costs. *Journal of the American Medical Association, 276,* 1473–1479.

Hogeweg, J.A., Kuis, W., Oostendorp, R.A., & Helders, P.J. (1996). The influence of site of stimulation, age, and gender on pain threshold in healthy children. *Physical Therapy, 76,* 1331–1339.

Hojat, M., Brigham, T.P., Gottheil, E., Xu, T., et al. (1998). Medical students' personal values and their career choices a quarter-century later. *Psychological Reports, 83,* 243–248.

Hojat, M., Gonnella, J.S., & Xu, G. (1995). Gender comparisons of young physicians' perceptions of their medical education, professional life, and practice: A follow-up study of Jefferson Medical College graduates. *Academic Medicine, 70,* 305–312.

Holmberg, S.D. (1996). The estimated prevalence and incidence of HIV in 96 large U.S. metropolitan areas. *American Journal of Public Health, 86,* 642–654.

Holmes, T.H. & Masuda, M. (1974). Life change and illness susceptibility. In B.S. Dohrenwend & B.P. Dohrenwend (Eds.), *Stressful life events: Their nature and effects* (pp. 45–72). New York: Wiley.

Holmes, T.H., & Rahe, R.H. (1967). The Social Readjustment Rating Scale. *Journal of Psychosomatic Research, 11,* 213–218.

Holroyd, J., & Guthrie, D. (1986). Family stress with chronic childhood illness: Cystic fibrosis, neuromuscular disease, and renal disease. *Journal of Clinical Psychology, 42,* 552–561.

Holroyd, K.A., & Penzien, D.B. (1990). Pharmacological versus non-pharmacological prophylaxis of recurrent migraine headache: A meta-analytic review of clinical trials. *Pain, 42,* 1–13.

Holzemer, W.L., Corless, I.B., Nokes, K.M., Turner, J.G., Brown, M.A., Powell-Cope, G.M., Inouye, J., Henry, S.B., Nicholas, P.K., & Portillo, C.J. (1999). Predictors of self-reported adherence in persons living with HIV disease. *Aids Patient Care STDS, 13,*185–197.

Horner, K.L. (1998). Individuality in vulnerability: Influences on physical health. *Journal of Health Psychology, 3,* 71–85.

Hornsby, J.L., Mongan, P.F., Taylor, A.T., & Treiber, F.A. (1991). "White coat" hypertension in children. *Journal of Family Practice, 33,* 617–23.

Horowitz, M.J., Krupnick, J., Kaltreider, N., Wilner, N., Leong, A., & Marmar, C. (1981). Initial psychological response to parental death. *Archives of General Psychiatry, 38,* 316–323.

Horowitz, R.I., Viscoli, C.M., Berkman, L., Donaldson, R.M., Horowitz, S.M., Murray, C.J., Ransohoff, D.F., & Sindelar, J. (1990). Treatment adherence and risk of death after a myocardial infarction. *Lancet, 336,* 542–545.

Hoskins, C.N. (1995). Patterns of adjustment among women with breast cancer and their partners. *Psychological Reports*, 77, 1017–1018.

Hotopf, M., Mayou, R., Wadsworth, M., & Wessely, S. (1999). Psychosocial and developmental antecedents of chest pain in young adults. *Psychosomatic Medicine*, 61, 861–867.

Houldin, A.D., Jacobsen, B., & Lowery, B.J. (1996). Self-blame and adjustment to breast cancer. *Oncological Nursing Forum*, 23, 75–79.

House, J.A. (1981). *Work stress and social support*. Reading, MA: Addison-Wesley.

House, J.S., Robbins, C., & Metzner, H.L. (1982). The association of social relationships and activities with mortality: Prospective evidence from the Tecumseh Community Health Study. *American Journal of Epidemiology*, 116, 123–140.

Houts, P.S., Bachrach, R., Witmer, J.T., Tringali, C.A., et al. (1998). Using pictographs to enhance recall of spoken medical instructions. *Patient Education & Counseling*, 35, 83–88.

Hovland, C.I. (1959). Reconciling conflicting results derived from experimental and survey studies of attitude change. *American Psychologist*, 14, 8–17.

Hovland, C.I., Janis, I.L., & Kelley, H.H. (1953). *Communication and persuasion*. New Haven, CT: Yale University Press.

Hughes, J.R. (1993). Pharmacotherapy for smoking cessation: Unvalidated assumptions, anomalies and suggestions for future research. *Journal of Consulting and Clinical Psychology*, 61, 751–760.

Hughes, P.H., Brandenburg, R., Baldwin, D.C., Jr., Storr, C.L., Williams, K.M., Anthony, J.C., & Sheehan, D.V. (1992). Prevalence of substance use among U.S. physicians. *Journal of the American Medical Association*, 267, 2333–2339.

Hull, J.G. (1981). A self-awareness model of the cause and effects of alcohol consumption. *Journal of Abnormal Psychology*, 90, 586–600.

Humphries, S.A, Johnson, M.H., & Long, N.R. (1996). An investigation of the gate control theory of pain using the experimental pain stimulus of potassium ion tophoresis. *Perception and Psychophysics*, 58, 693–703.

Hunt, D.K., Lowenstein, S.R., Badgett, R.G., & Steiner, J.F. (1995). Safety belt nonuse by internal medicine patients: A missed opportunity in clinical preventive medicine. *American Journal of Medicine*, 98, 343–348.

Hunt, L.M., Pugh, J., & Valenzuela, M. (1998). How patients adapt diabetes self-care recommendations in everyday life. *Journal of Family Practice*, 46, 207–215.

Hunt, W.A., Barnett, L.W., Branch, L.G. (1971). Relapse rates in addiction programs. *Journal of Clinical Psychology*, 27, 455–456.

Hunter, R.C.A., Lohrenz, J.G., & Schwartzman, A.E. (1964). Nosophobia and hypochondriasis in medical students. *Journal of Nervous and Mental Disease*, 139, 147–152.

Hurd, R.C. (1999). Adults view their childhood bereavement experiences. *Death Studies*, 23, 17–41.

Ice, R. (1985). Long term compliance. *Physical Therapy*, 65, 1832–1839.

Imboden, J.B., Canter, A. & Cluff, E. (1961). Convalescence from influenza: A study of the psychological and clinical determinants. *Archives of Internal Medicine*, 108, 393–399.

Ireys, H.T., & Burr, C.K. (1984). Apart and a part: Family issues for young adults with chronic illness and disability. In M.G. Eisenberg, L.C. Sutkin, & M.A. Jansen (Eds.), *Chronic illness and disability through the life span: Effects on self and family* (pp. 184–206). New York: Springer.

Irish, J.T., & Hall, J.A. (1995). Interruptive patterns in medical visits: The effects of role, status, and gender. *Social Science & Medicine*, 41, 873–881.

Ironson, G., Wynings, C., Shneiderman, N., Baum, A., Rodriguez, M., Greenwood, D., Benight, C., Antoni, M., LaPerriere, A., Huang, H.S., Klimas, N., & Fletcher, M.A. (1997). Post-traumatic stress symptoms, intrusive thoughts, loss, and immune function after Hurricane Andrew. *Psychosomatic Medicine*, 59, 493–498.

Irvine, J., Baker, B., Smith, J., Jandciu, S., Paquette., M., Cairns, J., Connolly, S., Roberts, R., Gent, M., & Dorian, P. (1999). Poor adherence to placebo or Amiodarone Therapy predicts mortality: Results from the CAMIAT study. *Psychosomatic Medicine*, 61, 566–575.

Irwin, M., Daniels, M, Bloom, E.T., Smith, T.L., & Weiner, H. (1987). Life events, depressive symptoms, and immune function. *American Journal of Psychiatry*, 144, 437–441.

Irwin, M., Daniels, M, Risch, S.C., Bloom, E., & Weiner, H. (1988). Plasma cortisol and natural killer cell activity during bereavement. *Biological Psychiatry*, 24, 173–8.

Irwin, M., & Pike, J. (1993). Bereavement, depressive symptoms, and immune function. In M.S. Stroebe, W. Stroebe, & R.O. Hansson (Eds.), *Handbook of bereavement: Theory, research, and intervention* (pp. 160–171). New York: Cambridge University Press.

Ishigami, T. (1919). The influence of psychic acts on the progress of pulmonary tuberculosis. *American Review of Tuberculosis*, 2, 470–484.

Izard, C.E. (1977). *Human emotions*. New York: Plenum Press.

Jacknow, D.S., Tschann, J.M., Link, M.P, & Boyce, W.T. (1994). Hypnosis in the prevention of chemotherapy-related nausea and vomiting in children: A prospective study. *Journal of Developmental and Behavioral Pediatrics*, 15, 258–264.

Jackson, L.D. (1992). Information complexity and medical communication: The effects of technical language and amount of information in a medical message. *Health Communication*, 4, 197–210.

Jackson, T., Iezzi, A., & Lafreniere, K. (1996). The differential effects of employment status on chronic pain and health comparison groups. *International Journal of Behavioral Medicine*, 3, 354–369.

Jacobsen, P.B., & Hann, D.M. (1998). Cognitive-behavioral interventions. In J.C. Holland (Ed.), *Psycho-oncology*. New York: Oxford University Press.

Jacobson, P.D., Bovbjerg, D.H., Schwartz, M.D., Hudis, C.A., Gilewski, T.A., & Norton, L. (1995). Conditioned emotional distress in women receiving chemotherapy for breast cancer. *Journal of Consulting & Clinical Psychology*, 63, 108–114.

Jacques, C.H., Lynch, J.C., & Samkoff, J.S. (1990). The effect of sleep loss on cognitive performance of resident physicians. *Journal of Family Practice, 30,* 223–229.

Jamerson, P.A., Scheibmeir, M., Bott, M.J., Crighton, F., Hinter, R.H., & Cobb, A.K. (1996). The experiences of families with a relative in the intensive care unit. *Heart & Lung, 25,* 467–474.

James, G.D., Yee, L.S., Harshfield, G.A., Blank, S.G., & Pickering, T.G. (1986). The influence of happiness, anger, and anxiety on the blood-pressure of borderline hypertensives. *Psychosomatic Medicine, 48,* 502–508.

Jamison, R.N., Anderson, K.O., Peeters-Asdourian, C., & Ferrante, F.M. (1994). Survey of opioid use in chronic nonmalignant pain patients. *Reg Anesthesiology, 19,* 225–230.

Janet, P. (1929). *The major symptoms of hysteria: Fifteen lectures given in the medical school of Harvard University.* New York: Hafner.

Janis, I.L. (1958). *Psychological stress.* New York: Wiley.

Jarvinen, K.A. (1955). Can ward rounds be a danger to patients with myocardial infarction? *British Medical Journal, 1,* 318–320.

Jay, S., Litt, I.F., & Durant, R.H. (1984). Compliance with therapeutic regimens. *Journal of Adolescent Health Care, 5,* 124–136.

Jeffery, D.R., Mandler, R.N., & Davis, L.E. (1993). Transverse myelitis. Retrospective analysis of 33 cases, with differentiation of cases associated with multiple sclerosis and parainfectious events. *Archives of Neurology, 50,* 532–535.

Jelicic, M., & Kempen, G.I.J.M. (1997). Cognitive function in community-dwelling elderly with chronic medical conditions. *International Journal of Geriatric Psychiatry, 12,* 1039–1041.

Jemmot, J.B., & Locke, S.E. (1984). Psychosocial factors, immunological mediation, and human susceptibility to infectious diseases: How much do we know? *Psychological Bulletin, 95,* 78–108.

Jennings, G., Nelson, L., Nestel, P., Esler, M., Korner, P., Burton, D., & Bazelmans, J. (1986). The effects of changes in physical activity on major cardiovascular risk factors,

Jessor, R., Turbin, M.S., & Frances, M. (1998). Protective factors in adolescent health behavior. *Journal of Personality & Social Psychology, 75,* 788–800.

Jirovec, M.M., & Maxwell, B.A. (1993). Nursing home residents' functional ability and perceptions of choice. *Journal of Gerontology Nursing, 19,* 10–14.

Johansson, E.E., Hamberg, K., Westman, G., & Lindgren, G. (1999). The meanings of pain: An exploration of women's descriptions of symptoms. *Social Science and Medicine, 48,* 1791–1802.

Johnson, B.A., & Ait-Daoud, N. (2000). Neuropharmacological treatments for alcoholism: Scientific background and clinical findings. *Psychopharmacology, 149,* 327–344.

Johnson, D.W., & Matross, R.P. (1975). Attitude modification methods. In F.H. Kanfer & A.P. Goldstein (Eds.), *Helping people change* (pp. 51–88). New York: Pergamon.

Johnson, J.C., Jayadevappa, R., Taylor, L., Askew, A., Williams, B., & Johnson, B. (1998). Extending the pipeline for minority physicians: A comprehensive program for minority faculty development. *Academic Medicine, 73,* 237–244.

Johnson, J.H. (1986). *Life events as stressors in childhood and adolescence.* Newbury Park, CA: Sage.

Johnson, J.H., Sarason, I.G., & Siegel, J.M. (1979). Arousal seeking as a moderator of life stress. *Perceptual and Motor Skills, 49,* 665–666.

Johnson, M.H., & Petrie, S.M. (1997). The effects of distraction on exercise and cold pressor tolerance for chronic low back pain sufferers. *Pain, 69,* 43–48.

Johnson, S.B., Kelly, M., Henretta, J.C., Cunningham, W.R., Tomer, A., & Silverstein, J.H. (1992). A longitudinal analysis of adherence and health status in childhood diabetes mellitus. *Journal of Pediatric Psychology, 17,* 537–553.

Johnson, S.K., Craft, M., Titler, M., Halm, M., et al. (1995). Perceived changes in adult family members' roles and responsibilities during critical illness. *IMAGE: Journal of Nursing Scholarship, 27,* 238–243.

Johnson, S.M., Kurtz, M.E., Tomlinson, T., & Howe, K.R. (1986). Students' stereotypes of patients as barriers to clinical decision-making. *Journal of Medical Education, 61,* 727–735.

Johnston, C.C., Stevens, B., Craig, K.D., & Grunau, R.V.E. (1993). Developmental changes in pain expression in premature, full-term, two- and four-month old infants. *Pain, 52,* 201–208.

Jones, J.W. (1981). Diagnosing and treating staff burnout among health professionals. In J.W. Jones (Ed.), *The burnout syndrome.* Park Ridge, IL.: London House Management Press.

Julian, D.G. (1996). If I woke with central chest pain . . . *Lancet, 348,* S29–S31.

Kabat-Zinn, J., Lipworth, L., & Burney, R. (1985). The clinical use of mindfulness meditation for the self-regulation of chronic pain. *Journal of Behavioral Medicine, 8,* 163–190.

Kamen-Siegel, L., Rodin, J., Seligman, M.E., & Dwyer, J. (1991). Explanatory style and cell-mediated immunity in elderly men and women. *Health Psychology, 10,* 229–235.

Kane, R.L., Klein, S.J., Bernstein, L., Rothenberg, R., & Wales, J. (1985). Hospice role in alleviating the emotional stress of terminal patients and their families. *Medical Care, 23,* 189–197.

Kang, D., Coe, C.L., Karaszewski, J., & McCarthy, D.O. (1998). Relationship of social support to stress responses and immune function in healthy and asthmatic adolescents. *Research in Nursing & Health, 21,* 117–128.

Kanner, A., Coyne, J.C., Schaefer, C., & Lazarus, R.S. (1981). Comparison of two modes of stress measurement: Daily hassles and uplifts versus major life events. *Journal of Behavioral Medicine, 4,* 1–39.

Kanner, R. (1986). Pain management. *Journal of the American Medical Association, 256,* 2110–2114.

Kaplan, B.H., Cassel, J.C., & Gore, S. (1977). Social support and health. *Medical Care, 15,* 47–58.

Kaplan, R.M. (1991). Health-related quality of life in patient decision making. *Journal of Social Issues, 47,* 69–90.

Kaplan, S.A., Reis, R.B., Kohn, I.J., Ikeguchi, E.F., Laor, E., Te, A.E., & Martins, A.C. (1999). Safety and efficacy of sildenafil in postmenopausal women with sexual dysfunction. *Urology, 53,* 481–486.

Kaprio, J., Koskenvuo, M., & Rita, H. (1987). Mortality after bereavement: A prospective study of 95,647 widowed persons. *American Journal of Public Health, 77,* 283–7.

Karoly, P. (1980). Operant methods. In F.H. Kanfer & A.P. Goldstein (Eds.), Helping people change (2nd ed.). New York: Pergamon Press.

Karoly, P., & Ruehlman, L.S. (1996). Motivational implications of pain: Chronicity, psychological distress, and work global construal in a national sample of adults. *Health Psychology, 15,* 383–390.

Kasl, S.V. (1975). Issues in patient adherence to health care regimens. *Journal of Human Stress, 1,* 5–17.

Kasl, S., & Cobb, S. (1966). Health behavior, illness behavior, and sick role behavior. I. Health and illness behavior. *Archives of Environmental Health, 12,* 246–266.

Kassebaum, D.G., & Cutler, E.R. (1998). On the culture of student abuse in medical school. *Academic Medicine, 73,* 1149–1158.

Kastenbaum, R. (1977). Death and development through the lifespan. In H. Feifel (Ed), *New meanings of death.* New York: McGraw-Hill.

Kastenbaum, R. & Aisenberg, R.B. (1972). *The psychology of death.* New York: Springer.

Katon, W.J., & Walker, E.A. (1998). Medically unexplained symptoms in primary care. *Journal of Clinical Psychiatry, 59,* 15–21.

Katz, D.L. (2000). Conventional medical care and unconventional therapies. *Journal of the American Medical Association, 283,* 56–57.

Katz, J. (1984). *The silent world of doctor and patient.* New York: Free Press.

Katz, R.C., Meyers, K., & Walls, J. (1995). Cancer awareness and self-examination practices in young men and women. *Journal of Behavioral Medicine, 18,* 377–384.

Katz, R.C., & Zlutnick, S. (1975). *Behavior therapy and health care: Principles and applications.* New York: Pergamon Press.

Keefe, F.J., Lefebvre, J.C., Maixner, W., Salley, A.N., et al. (1997). Self-efficacy for arthritis pain: Relationship to perception of thermal laboratory pain stimuli. *Arthritis Care and Research, 10,* 177–184.

Keesling, B., & Friedman, H.S. (1987). Psychosocial influences on immunity. Health Psychology, 6, 477–493.

Kellner, R. (1986). *Somatization and hypochondriasis* New York: Praeger.

Kelly, J.A., Otto-Salaj, L.L., Sikkema, K.J., Pinkerton, S.D., & Bloom, F.R. (1998). Implications of HIV treatment advances for behavioral research on AIDS: Progress and new challenges in HIV secondary prevention. *Health Psychology, 17,* 310–319.

Kemeny, M.E., Solomon, G.F., Morley, J.E., & Herbert, T.L. (1992). Psychoneuroimmunology. In C.B. Nemeroff (Ed.), *Neuroendocrinology.* Boca Raton, FL: CRC Press.

Kenshalo, D.R., Sr. (1986). Somesthetic sensitivity in young and elderly humans. *Journal of Gerontology, 41,* 732–742.

Kerns, R.D., Turk, D.C., & Rudy, T.E. (1985). The West Haven-Yale Multidimensional Pain Inventory (WHYMPI). *Pain, 23,* 345–356.

Kerssens, J.J., Bensing, J.M., & Andela, M.G. (1997). Patient preference for genders of health professionals. *Social Science and Medicine, 44,* 1531–1540.

Kiecolt-Glaser, J.K., Fisher, L.D., Ogrocki, P., Stout, J.C., Speicher, C.E., & Glaser, R. (1987). Marital quality, marital disruption, and immune function. *Psychosomatic Medicine, 49,* 13–34.

Kiecolt-Glaser, J.K., Garner, W., Speicher, C., Penn, G.M., Holliday, J., & Glaser, R. (1984). Psychosocial modifiers of immunocompetence in medical students. *Psychosomatic Medicine, 46,* 7–14.

Kiecolt-Glaser, J.K., & Glaser, R. (1986). Psychological influences on immunity. *Psychosomatics, 27,* 621–624.

Kiecolt-Glaser, J.K., Glaser, R., Cacioppo, J.T., & Malarkey, W.B. (1998). Marital stress: Immunologic, neurendocrine, and autonomic correlates. *Annals of the New York Academy of Sciences, 840,* 656–663.

Kiecolt-Glaser, J.K., Marucha, P.T., Malarkey, W.B., Mercado, A.M., & Glaser, R. (1995). Slowing of wound healing by psychological stress. *Lancet, 346,* 1194–1196.

Kiecolt-Glaser, J.K., Stephens, R.E., Lipetz, P.D., Speicher, C.E., & Glaser, R. (1985). Distress and DNA repair in human lymphocytes. *Journal of Behavioral Medicine, 8,* 311–320.

Kiesler, C.A., & Sakamura, J.A. (1966). A test of a model for commitment and dissonance. *Journal of Personality and Social Psychology, 3,* 349–353.

Kikano, G.E., Goodwin, M.A., & Stange, K.C. (1998). Physician employment status and practice patterns. *Journal of Family Practice, 46,* 499–505.

Kim, K., & Jacobs, S. (1993). Neuroendocrine changes following bereavement. In M.S. Stroebe, W. Stroebe, & R.O. Hansson (Eds.), *Handbook of bereavement: Theory, research, and intervention.* New York: Cambridge University Press.

Kimball, C.P. (1977). Psychological responses to the experience of open heart surgery. In R.H. Moos (Ed.), *Coping with physical illness* (pp. 113–133). New York: Plenum.

King, D.W., King, L.A., Gudanowski, D.M., & Vreven, D.L. (1995). Alternative representations of war zone stressors: Relationships to post traumatic stress disorder in male and female Vietnam veterans. *Journal of Abnormal Psychology, 104,* 184–196.

Kinney, W.B., & Coyle, C.P. (1992). Predicting life satisfaction among adults with physical disabilities. *Archives of Physical Medical Rehabilitation, 73(9),* 863–869.

Kisely, W., Goldberg, D., & Simon, G. (1997). A comparison between somatic symptoms with and without clear organic cause: Results of an international study. *Psychological Medicine, 27,* 1011–1019.

Kizer, K.W., & Trent, R.B. (1991). Safety belts and public health. The role of medical practitioners. *Western Journal of Medicine, 154,* 303–306.

Klapper, J.T. (1960). *The effects of mass communication.* Glencoe, IL: The Free Press.

Klass, P. (1987a). *A not entirely benign procedure: Four years as a medical student.* New York: G.P. Putnam.

Klass, P. (1987b). Sick jokes. *Discover, 8,* 30–35.

Kleck, R. (1968). Physical stigma and nonverbal cues emitted in face-to-face interaction. *Human Relations, 21,* 119–128.

Kleiber, D.A., Brock, S.C., Lee, Y., Dattilo, J., et al. (1995). The relevance of leisure in an illness experience: Realities of spinal cord injury. *Journal of Leisure Research, 27,* 283–299.

Klein, D.F. (1993). False suffocation alarms, spontaneous panics, and related conditions: An integrative hypothesis. *Archives of General Psychiatry, 50,* 306–317.

Kleinman, A. (1988). *The illness narratives: Suffering, healing, and the human condition.* New York: Basic Books.

Kliszcz, J., & Rembowski, J. (1998). Emotional and cognitive empathy in medical schools. *Academic Medicine, 73,* 541.

Klohn, L.S., & Rogers, R.W. (1991). Dimensions of the severity of a health threat: The persuasive effects of visibility, time of onset, and rate of onset on young women's intentions to prevent osteoporosis. *Health Psychology, 10,* 323–329.

Klonoff, E.A., & Landrine, H. (1992). Sex roles, occupational roles, and symptom-reporting: A test of competing hypotheses on sex differences. *Journal of Behavioral Medicine, 15,* 355–364.

Kobasa, S.C. (1979). Stressful life events, personality and health: An inquiry into hardiness. *Journal of Personality and Social Psychology, 37,* 1–11.

Kobasa, S.C. (1982). The hardy personality: Toward a social psychology of stress and health. In G.S. Sanders & J. Suls (Eds.), *Social psychology of health and illness* (pp. 3–32) Hillsdale, NY: Erlbaum Associates.

Kobasa, S.C., Maddi, S.R. & Puccetti, M.C. (1982). Personality and exercise as buffers in the stress-illness relationship. *Journal of Behavioral Medicine, 5,* 391–403.

Kobasa, S.C., Maddi, S.R., Puccetti, M.C., & Zola, M.A. (1994). Effectiveness of hardiness, exercise and social support as resources against illness. In A. Steptoe, J. Wardle, et al. (Eds.), *Psychosocial Processes and Health: A Reader* (pp. 247–260). Cambridge, England: Cambridge University Press.

Koenig, H.G., & George, L.K. (1998). Depression and physical disability outcomes in depressed medically ill hospitalized older adults. *American Journal of Geriatric Psychiatry, 6,* 230–247.

Koh, H.K., Bak, S.M., Geller, A.C., Mangione, T.W., Hingson, R.W., Levenson, S.M., Miller, D.R., Lew, R.A., & Howland, J. (1997). Sunbathing habits and sunscreen use among White adults: Results of a national survey. *American Journal of Public Health, 87,* 1214–1217.

Kohli, N., & Dalal, A.K. (1998). Culture as a factor in causal understanding of illness: A study of cancer patients. *Psychology and Developing Societies, 10,* 115–129.

Kohlmann, C.W., Weidner, G., Dotzauer, E., & Burns, L.R. (1997). Gender differences in health behaviors: The role of avoidant coping. *European Review of Applied Psychology, 47,* 115–129.

Kokkonen, J. (1995). The social effects in adult life chronic physical illness since childhood. *European Journal of Pediatrics, 154,* 676–81.

Koocher, G.P. (1985). Promoting coping with illness in childhood. In J.C. Rosen & L.J. Solomon (Eds.), *Prevention in health psychology* (pp. 311–327). Hanover, NH: University Press of New England.

Korsch, B.M., Gozzi, E.K., & Francis, V. (1968). Gaps in doctor-patient communication. I. Doctor-patient interaction and patient satisfaction. *Pediatrics, 42,* 855–871.

Korsch, B.M., & Negrete, V.F. (1972). Doctor-patient communication. *Scientific American, 227,* 66–74.

Kosa, J, & Robertson, L. (1975). The social aspects of health and illness. In J. Kosa et. al. (Eds.), *Poverty and health: A sociological analysis.* Cambridge, MA: Harvard University Press.

Koss, T., & Rosenthal, R. (1997). Interactional synchrony, positivity and patient satisfaction in the physician-patient relationship. *Medical Care, 35,* 1158–1163.

Kraemer, R.R., Dzewaltowski, D.A., Blair, M.S., Rinehardt, K.F., & Castracane, V.D. (1990). Mood alteration from treadmill running and its relationship to beta-endorphin, corticotropin, and growth hormone. *Journal of Sports Medicine and Physical Fitness, 30,* 241–246.

Krakowski, A.J. (1982). Stress and the practice of medicine: II. Stressors, stresses, and strains. *Psychotherapy and Psychosomatics, 38,* 11–23.

Krantz, D.S., Baum, A., & Singer, J.E. (Eds.). (1983). *Handbook of psychology and health (vol. 3): Cardiovascular disorders and behavior.* Hillsdale, NJ: Erlbaum.

Krantz, D.S., Baum, A. & Wideman, M.V. (1980). Assessment of preferences for self-treatment and information in health care. *Journal of Personality and Social Psychology, 39,* 977–990.

Krantz, D.S., & Deckel, A.W. (1983). Coping with coronary heart disease and stroke. In T.G. Burish & L.A. Bradley (Eds.), *Coping with chronic disease: Research and applications.* New York: Academic Press.

Kraus, A.S. & Lilienfeld, A.M. (1959). Some epidemiological aspects of the high mortality rate in the young widowed group. *Journal of Chronic Disease, 10,* 207–217.

Krell, R., & Rabkin, L. (1979). The effects of sibling death on the surviving child: A family perspective. *Family Process, 18,* 471–7.

Kreps, G.L., (1988). The pervasive role of information in health care: Implications for health communication policy. In J. Anderson (Ed.), *Communication yearbook 11.* Newbury Park, CA: Sage.

Krige, J.E., Isaacs, S., Hudson, D.A., King, H.S., Strover, R.M., & Johnson, C.A. (1991). Delay in the diagnosis of cutaneous malignant melanoma: A prospective study in 250 patients. *Cancer, 68,* 2064–2068.

Krishnan, S.P. (1996). Health education at family planning clinics: Strategies for improving information about contraception and sexually transmitted diseases for low-income women. *Health Communication, 8,* 353–366.

Krol, D., Morris, V., Betz, J., & Cadman, E. (1998). Factors influencing the career choices of physicians trained at Yale New Haven Hospital from 1929 through 1994. *Academic Medicine, 73,* 313–317.

Kronfol, Z., Silva, J., Greden, J., Dembinski, S., Gardner, R., & Carroll, B. (1983). Impaired lymphocyte function in depressive illness. *Life Sciences, 33,* 241–247.

Krulik, T. (1987). Loneliness and social isolation in school-age children with chronic life-threatening illness. In T. Krulik, B. Holaday, & I.M. Martinson (Eds.), *The child and family facing life-threatening illness* (pp. 133–161). New York: Lippincott.

Krupat, E., Irish, J.T., Kasten, L.E., Freund, K.M., Burns, R.B., Moskowitz, M.A., & McKinlay, J.B. (1999). Patient assertiveness and physician decision-making among older breast cancer patients. *Social Science and Medicine, 49,* 449–457.

Kübler-Ross, E. (1969). *On death and dying.* New York: Macmillan.

Kuiper, N.A., Martin, R.A., & Olinger, L.J. (1993). Coping humor, stress, and cognitive appraisals. *Canadian Journal of Behavioural Science, 25,* 81–96.

Kulik, J.A., & Carlino, P. (1987). The effect of verbal communication and treatment choice on medication compliance in a pediatric setting. *Journal of Behavioral Medicine, 10,* 367–376.

Kulik, J.A., Moore, P.J., & Mahler, H.I. (1993). Stress and affiliation: Hospital roommate effects on preoperative anxiety and social interaction. *Health Psychology, 12,* 118–124.

Kuzel, A.J., Schwartz, R.H., Luxenberg, M.G., Lewis, D.C., & Kyriazi, N.C. (1991). A survey of drinking patterns during medical school. *Southern Medical Journal, 84,* 9–12.

LaCrosse, M.B. (1975). Nonverbal behavior and perceived counselor attractiveness.

La Greca, A.M. (1992). Peer influences in pediatric chronic illness: An update. *Journal of Pediatric Psychology, 17,* 775–84.

La Greca, A.M., Auslander, W.F., Greco, P., Spetter, D., et al. (1995). I get by with a little help from my family and friends: Adolescents' support for diabetes care. *Journal of Pediatric Psychology, 20,* 449–476.

Lander, J., & Fowler-Kerry, S. (1991). Age differences in children's pain. *Perceptual and Motor Skills, 73,* 415–418.

Landrine, H., & Klonoff, E.A. (1994). Cultural diversity in causal attributions for illness: The role of the supernatural. *Journal of Behavioral Medicine, 17,* 181–194.

Lang, E.V., Benotsch, E.G., Fick, L.J., Lutgendorf, S., Berbaum, M.L., Berbaum, A., Logan, H., & Spiegel, D. (2000). Adjunctive non-pharmacological analgesia for invasive medical procedures: A randomised trial. *Lancet, 355,* 1486–1490.

Lange, J.E., & Voas, R.B. (1990). Nighttime observations of safety belt use: An evaluation of California's primary law. *American Journal of Public Health, 88,* 1718–1720.

Langer, E.J., Janis, I.L., & Wolfer, J.A. (1975). Reduction of psychological stress in surgical patients. *Journal of Experimental Social Psychology, 11,* 155–165.

Langer, E.J., & Rodin, J. (1976). The effects of choice and enhanced personal responsibility for the aged: A field experiment in an institutional setting. *Journal of Personality and Social Psychology, 34,* 191–198.

Langewitz, W.A., Eich, P., Kiss, A., & Woeessmer, B. (1998). Improving communication skills—A randomized controlled behaviorally oriented intervention study for residents in internal medicine. *Psychosomatic Medicine, 60,* 268–276.

Lantz, P.M., House, J.S., Lepkowski, J.M., Williams, D.R., et al. (1998). Socioeconomic factors, health behaviors, and mortality: Results from a nationally respresentative prospective study of U.S. adults. *Journal of the American Medical Association, 279,* 1703–1708.

Larsen, K.M., & Smith, C.K. (1981). Assessment of nonverbal communication in the patient-physician interview. *Journal of Family Practice, 12,* 481–488.

Larson, E.B., & Bruce, R.A. (1987). Health benefits of exercise in an aging society. *Archives of Internal Medicine, 147,* 353–356.

Larson, R., & Sutker, S. (1966). Value differences and value consensus by socio-economic levels. *Social Forces, 44,* 563–569.

Larsson, U.S., Saljo, R., & Aronsson, K. (1987). Patient-doctor communication on smoking and drinking: Lifestyle in medical consultation. *Social Sciences & Medicine, 25,* 1129–1137.

Lau, R.R., Hartman, K.A., & Ware, J.E. Jr. (1986). Health as a value: Methodological and theoretical considerations. *Health Psychology, 5,* 25–43.

Lau, R.R., Kane, R., Berry, S., Ware, J.E., Jr., & Roy, D. (1980). Channeling health: A review of televised health campaigns. *Health Education Quarterly, 7,* 56–89.

Lauer, M., Mulhern, R., Wallskog, J., & Camitta, B. (1983). A comparison study of parental adaptation following a child's death at home or in the hospital. *Pediatrics, 71,* 101–111.

Lautenbacher, S., & Strain, F. (1991). Similarities in age differences in heat pain perception and thermal sensitivity. *Functional Neurology, 6,* 129–135.

Lauver, S.C., & Johnson, J.L. (1997). The role of neuroticism and social support in older adults with chronic pain behavior. *Personality and Individual Differences, 23,* 165–167.

Lavey, R.S. & Taylor, C.B. (1985). The nature of relaxation therapy. In S.R. Burchfield, (Ed.), *Stress: Psychological and physiological interactions.* Washington, DC: Hemisphere.

Lazarus, R.S. (1983). The costs and benefits of denial. In S. Bresnitz (Ed.), *Denial of stress* (pp. 1–30). New York: International Universities Press.

Lazarus, R.S. (1984). Puzzles in the study of daily hassles. *Journal of Behavioral Medicine, 7,* 375–389.

Lazarus, R.S. (1985). The trivialization of distress. In J.C. Rosen & L.J. Solomon (Eds.), *Prevention in health psychology* (pp. 279–298). Hanover, NH: University Press of New England.

Lazarus, R.S. (1999). *Fifty years of the research and theory of R.S. Lazarus: An analysis of historical and perennial issues.* Mahwah, NJ: Erlbaum.

Lazarus, R.S. & Cohen, J.B. (1979). Environmental stress. In I. Altman & J.E. Wohlwill (Eds.), *Human behavior and the environment* (vol. 2). New York: Plenum.

Lazarus, R.S., & Folkman, S. (1984). *Stress, appraisal, and coping.* New York: Springer.

Lazarus, R.S., & Launier, R. (1978). Stress-related transactions between person and environment. In L.A. Pervin & M. Lewis (Eds.), *Internal and external determinants of behavior.* New York: Plenum.

Lebenthal, A., Kaiserman, I., & Lernau, O. (1996). Student abuse in medical school: A comparison of students' and faculty's perceptions. *Israeli Journal of Medical Science, 32,* 229–238.

Lebovits, A.H., Florence, I., Bathina, R., Hunko, V., et al. (1997). Pain knowledge and attitudes of healthcare providers: Practice characteristic differences. *Clinical Journal of Pain, 13,* 237–243.

Lederer, H. (1952). How the sick view their world. *Journal of Social Issues, 8,* 4–16.

Lee, G.R., Willetts, M.C., & Seccombe, K. (1998). Widowhood and depression: Gender differences. *Research on Aging, 20,* 611–630.

Lee, J.A. (1997). Declining effect of latitude on melanoma mortality rates in the United States: A preliminary study. *American Journal of Epidemiology, 146,* 413–417.

Leigh, H., & Reiser, M.F. (1980). *The patient: Biological, psychological, and social dimensions of medical practice.* New York: Plenum.

Leigh, J.P., Markowitz, S.B., Fahs, M., Shin, C., & Landrigan, P.J. (1997). Occupational injury and illness in the United States: Estimates of costs, morbidity, and mortality. *Archives of Internal Medicine, 157,* 1557–1568.

Leist, J.C., & Konen, J.C. (1996). Four factors of clinical decision making: A teaching model. *Academic Medicine, 71,* 644–646.

Lenderking, W.R., Nackley, J.F., Anderson, R.B., & Testa, M.A. (1996). A review of the quality-of-life aspects of urinary urge incontinence. *Pharmacoeconomics, 9,* 11–23.

Leng, G. (1999). A year of acupuncture in palliative care. *Palliative Medicine, 13,* 163–164.

Leonard, B.J. (1991). Siblings of chronically ill children: A question of vulnerability versus resilience. Pediatrics *Annals, 20,* 505–6.

Lepper, H.S., DiMatteo, M.R., & Tinsley, B.J. (1994). Postpartum depression: How much do obstetric nurses and obstetricians know? *Birth, 21,* 149–154.

Lerman, C., Caporaso, N., Main, D., Audrain, J., Boyd, N.R., Bowman, E.D., & Shields, P.G. (1998). Depression and self-medication with nicotine: The modifying influence of the dopamine D4 receptor gene. *Health Psychology, 17,* 56–62.

Lerman, C., Daly, M., Walsh, W.P., Resch, N., Seay, J., Barsevick, A., Birenbaum, L., Heggan, T., Martin, G. (1993). Communication between patients with breast cancer and health care providers. Determinants and implications. *Cancer, 72,* 2612–2620.

Lerner, M. (1980). *The belief in a just world: A fundamental delusion.* New York: Plenum.

Lesch, O.M., & Walter, H. (1996). Subtypes of alcoholism and their role in therapy. *Alcohol, Suppl. 1,* 63–67.

Leserman, J., Petitto, J.M., Perkins, D.O., Folds, J.D., et al. (1997). Severe stress, depressive symptoms, and changes in lymphocyte subsets in human immunodeficiency virus-infected men. A 2-year follow-up study. *Archives of General Psychiatry, 54,* 279–285.

LeShan, L.L., & Worthington, R.E. (1956). Personality as a factor in the pathogenesis of cancer: Review of literature. *British Journal of Medical Psychology, 29,* 49–6.

Leung, L., & Becker, C.E. (1992). Sleep deprivation and house staff performance: Update 1984–1991. *Journal of Occupational Medicine, 34,* 1153–1160.

Levenson, J.L., & Bemis, C. (1991). The role of psychological factors in cancer onset and progression. *Psychosomatics, 32,* 124–132.

Levenson, J.L., Hamer, R.M., & Rossiter, L.F. (1990). Relation of psychopathology in general medical inpatients to use and cost of services. *American Journal of Psychiatry, 147,* 1498–1503.

Levenstein, S. (1998). Stress and peptic ulcer: Life beyond Helicobacter. *Behavioral Medicine Journal, 316,* 538–541.

Levenstein, S., Ackerman, S., Kiecolt-Glaser, J.K., & Dubois, A. (1999). Stress and peptic ulcer disease. *Journal of the American Medical Association, 281,* 10–11.

Leventhal, H., & Cleary, P.D. (1980). The smoking problem: A review of the research and theory in behavioral risk modification. *Psychological Bulletin, 88,* 370–405.

Leventhal, H., & Diefenbach, M. (1991). The active side of illness cognition. In J.A. Skelton & R.T. Croyle (Eds.), *Mental representation in health and illness.* New York: Springer-Verlag.

Levi, L. (1965). The urinary output of adrenalin and noradrenalin during pleasant and unpleasant emotional stress. *Psychosomatic Medicine, 27,* 80–85.

Levin, M.L., Berry, J.I., & Leiter, J. (1998). Management of pain in terminally ill patients: Physicians reports of knowledge, attitudes and behavior. *Journal of Pain and Symptom Management, 15,* 27–40.

Levine, J., Rudy, T., & Kerns, R. (1994). A two factor model of denial of illness: A confirmatory factor analysis. *Journal of Psychosomatic Research, 38,* 99–110.

Levinson, W., Roter, D.L., Mullooly, J.P., Dull, V.T., & Frankel, R.M. (1997). Physician-patient communication: The relationship with malpractice claims among primary care physicians and surgeons. *Journal of the American Medical Association, 277,* 553–559.

Levy, S.M. (1985a). *Behavior and cancer.* San Francisco: Jossey-Bass.

Levy, S.M. (1985b). Emotional response to disease and its treatment. In J.C. Rosen & L.J. Solomon (Eds.), *Prevention in health psychology* (pp. 299–310). Hanover, NH: University Press of New England.

Lewis, J.M., Nace, E.P., Barnhart, F.D., Carson, D.I., & Howard, B.L. (1994). The lives of female physicians. *Texas Medicine, 90,* 56–61.

Ley, P. (1979). Memory for medical information. *British Journal of Social and Clinical Psychology, 18,* 245–255.

Ley, P. (1998). The use and improvement of written communication in mental health care and promotion. *Psychology, Health & Medicine, 3,* 19–53.

Ley, P., & Spelman, M.S. (1965). Communication in an outpatient setting. *British Journal of Social and Clinical Psychology, 4,* 114–116.

Li, L., & Moore, D. (1998). Acceptance of disability and its correlates. *Journal of Social Psychology, 138,* 13–25.

Lichtenstein, E. (1982). The smoking problem: A behavioral perspective. *Journal of Consulting and Clinical Psychology, 50,* 804–819.

Lichtenstein, E., & Glasgow, R.E. (1992). Smoking cessation: What have we learned over the past decade? *Journal of Consulting and Clinical Psychology, 60,* 518–527.

Lichtenstein, E., & Glasgow, R.E. (1997). A pragmatic framework for smoking cessation: Implications for clinical and public health programs. *Psychology of Addictive Behaviors, 11,* 142–151.

Lichtenstein, P., Garz, M., Pedersen, N.L., Berge, S., et al. (1996). A co-twin control study of response to widowhood. *Journals of Gerontology: Series B: Psychological Sciences and Social Sciences, 51,* 279–289.

Lichtman, R.R. (1982). *Close relationships after breast cancer.* Unpublished doctoral dissertation, University of California, Los Angeles.

Liddell, A., & Locker, D. (1997). Gender and age differences in attitudes to dental pain and dental control. *Community Dental and Oral Epidemiology, 25,* 314–318.

Lieberman, M.A. (1982). The effects of social supports on responses to stress. In L. Goldberger & L. Breznitz (Eds.), *Handbook of stress.* New York: Free Press.

Lifton, R.J. (1977). The sense of immortality: On death and the continuity of life. In H. Feifel (Ed.), *New meanings of death.* New York: McGraw Hill.

Like, R., & Zyzanski, S.J. (1987). Patient satisfaction with the clinical encounter: Social pyschological determinants. *Social Science Medicine, 24,* 351–357.

Lillemoe, K.D., Ahrendt, G.M., Yeo, C.J., Herlong, H.F., & Cameron, J.L. (1994). Surgery—still an "old boys' club"? *Surgery, 116,* 255–259.

Lin, W.C., & Ball, C. (1997). Factors affecting the decision of nursing students in Taiwan to be vaccinated against hepatitis B infection. *Journal of Advances in Nursing, 25,* 709–718.

Linde, K., Clausius, N., Ramirez, G., Melchart, D., Eitel, F., Hedges, L.V., & Jonas, W.B. (1990). Are the clinical effects of homeopathy placebo effects? A meta-analysis of placebo-controlled trials. *Lancet, 350,* 834–843.

Lindeman, C. (1984). Nursing and health education. In J.D. Matarazzo, S. Weiss, J.A. Herd, N.E. Miller, & S.M. Weiss (Eds.), *Behavioral health,* (pp. 1214–1217). New York: Wiley.

Lindemann, E. (1944). The symptomatology and management of acute grief. *American Journal of Psychiatry, 101,* 141–148.

Linder, M. (1995). Playing chicken with people: The occupational safety and health consequences of throughput uber alles. *International Journal of Health Services, 25,* 633–666.

Linn, B.S. & Zeppa, R. (1984). Stress in junior medical students: Relationship to personality and performance. *Journal of Medical Education, 59,* 7–12.

Linn, L.S., & DiMatteo, M.R. (1983). Humor and other communication preferences in physician-patient encounters. *Medical Care, 21,* 1223–1231.

Linn, L.S., Yager, J., Cope, D., & Leake, B. (1985). Health status, job satisfaction, job stress, and life satisfaction among academic and clinical faculty. *Journal of the American Medical Association, 254,* 2775–2782.

Linn, L.S., Yager, J., Cope, D.W., & Leake, B. (1986). Factors associated with life satisfaction among practicing internists. *Medical Care, 24,* 830–837.

Linton, S.J., & Buer, N. (1995). Working despite pain: Factors associated with work attendance versus dysfunction. *International Journal of Behavioral Medicine, 2,* 252–262.

Lipton, R.B., Losey, L.M., Giachello, A., Mendez, J., & Girotti, M.H. (1998). Attitudes and issues in treating Latino patients with type 2 diabetes: Views of healthcare providers. *Diabetes Education, 24,* 67–71.

Littrell, J. (1996). How psychological states affect the immune system: Implications for interventions in the context of HIV. *Health & Social Work, 21,* 287–295.

Liu, W.T. (1986). Culture and social support. *Research on Aging, 8,* 57–83.

Lizasoain, O., & Polaino, A. (1995). Reduction of anxiety in pediatric patients: Effects of a psychopedagogical intervention programme. *Patient Education and Counseling, 25,* 17–22.

Lloyd, C., & Gartrell, N.K. (1983). A further assessment of medical school stress. *Journal of Medical Education, 58,* 964–967.

Locke, S.E., Kraus, L., Leserman, J., Hurst, M.W., Heisel, J.S., & Williams, R.M. (1984). Life change stress, psychiatric symptoms, and natural killer cell activity. *Psychosomatic Medicine, 46,* 441–453.

Logan, H.L., Lutgendorf, S., Hartwig, A., Lilly, J., & Berberich S.L. (1998). Immune, stress, and mood markers related to recurrent oral herpes outbreaks. *Oral Surgery, Oral Medicine, Oral Pathology, Oral Radiology and Endodontics, 86,* 48–54.

Long, B.C. (1984). Aerobic conditioning and stress inoculation: A comparison of stress-management interventions. *Cognitive Therapy and Research, 8,* 517–541.

Long, L., Paradise, L.V., & Long, T.J. (1981). *Questioning: Skills for the helping process.* Monterey, CA: Brooks/Cole.

Lorber, J. (1975). Good patients and problem patients: Conformity and deviance in a general hospital. *Journal of Health and Social Behavior, 16,* 213–225.

Lorenz, J., & Bromm, B. (1997). Event-related potential correlates of interference between cognitive performance and tonic experimental pain. *Psychophysiology, 34,* 436–445.

Lown, B. (1983). Introduction. In N. Cousins, *The healing heart: Antidotes to panic and helplessness.* New York: W.W. Norton.

Lown, B. (1996). *The lost art of healing.* Boston: Houghton-Mifflin.

Ludman, L, & Spitz, L. (1996). Coping strategies of children with faecal incontinence. *Journal of Pediatric Surgery, 31,* 563–7.

Luecken, L.J. (1998). Childhood attachment and loss experiences affect adult cardiovascular and cortisol function. *Psychosomatic Medical, 60,* 765–72.

Lumsden, D.P. (1981). Is the concept of "stress" of any use, any more? In D. Randall (Ed.), *Contributions to primary prevention in mental health: Working papers.* Toronto: Toronto National Office of the Canadian Mental Health Association.

Lund, D.A., Caserta, M.S., & Dimond, M.F. (1993). The course of spousal bereavement in later life. In M.S. Stroebe, W. Stroebe, & R.O. Hansson (Eds.), *Handbook of bereavement: Theory, research, and intervention.* New York: Cambridge University Press.

Lupton, D. (1997). Consumerism, reflexivity and the medical encounter. *Social Science & Medicine, 45,* 373–381.

Lurie, N., Rand, B., Parenti, C., Woolley, T., & Snoke, W. (1989). How do house officers spend their nights? A time study of internal medicine staff on call. *New England Journal of Medicine, 320,* 1673–1677.

Lyketsos, C.G., Hoover, D.R., Guccione, M., Senterfitt, W., Dew, M.A., et al. (1993). Depressive symptoms as predictors of medical outcomes in HIV infection. *Journal of the American Medical Association, 270,* 2563–2567.

Lykken, D.T. (1987). Psychophysiology. In R.J. Corsini (Ed.), *Concise encyclopedia of psychology.* New York: Wiley.

Lynch, J.J., Thomas, S.A., Mills, M.E., Malinow, K., & Katcher, A.H. (1974). The effects of human contact on cardiac arrhythmia in coronary care patients. *Journal of Nervous and Mental Disease, 158,* 88–99.

Macgregor, F.C. (1990). Facial disfigurement: Problems and management of social interaction and implications for mental health. *Aesthetic Plastic Surgery,14,* 249–257.

Maddi, S.R., Kahn, S., & Maddi, K.L. (1998). The effectiveness of hardiness training. *Consulting Psychology Journal: Practice and Research, 50,* 78–86.

Madlem, L.L. (1997). The PPO advantage. *Health Care Innovations, 7,* 24–26.

Mages, N.L., & Mendelsohn, G.A. (1979). Effects of cancer on patients' lives: A personological approach. In G.C. Stone, F. Cohen, & N.E. Adler (Eds.), *Health psychology: A handbook* (pp. 255–284). San Francisco, CA: Jossey-Bass.

Maheux, B., Dufort, F., Beland, F., Jacques, A., & Levesque, A. (1990). Female medical practitioners: More preventive and patient-oriented. *Medical Care, 28,* 87–92.

Mahoney, M.J., & Thoreson, C.E. (1974). *Self-control: Power to the person.* Monterey, CA: Brooks/Cole.

Maier, S.F., & Seligman, M.E.P. (1976). Learned helplessness: Theory and evidence. *Journal of Experimental Psychology: General, 105,* 3–46.

Major, B., & Heslin, R. (1982). Perceptions of same-sex and cross-sex touching: It's better to give than to receive. *Journal of Nonverbal Behavior, 6,* 148–162.

Maly, R.C., Bourque, L.B., & Engelhardt, R.F. (1999). A randomized controlled trial of facilitating information given to patients with chronic medical conditions: Effects on outcomes of care. *Journal of Family Practice, 48,* 356–63.

Manne, S., & Miller, D. (1998). Social support, social conflict, and adjustment among adolescents with cancer. *Journal of Pediatric Psychology, 23,* 121–130.

Manne, S.L., Jacobsen, P.B., Gorfinkle, K., Gerstein, F., & Redd, W.H. (1993). Treatment adherence difficulties among children with cancer: The role of parenting style. *Journal of Pediatric Psychology, 18,* 47–62.

Manne, S.L., & Zautra, A.J. (1990). Couples coping with chronic illness: Women with rheumatoid arthritis and their healthy husbands. *Journal of Behavioral Medicine, 13,* 327–342.

Manusov, V. (1993). "It depends on your perspective": Effects of stance and beliefs about intent on person perception. *Western Journal of Communication, 57,* 27–41.

Manyande, A., & Salmon, P. (1998). Effects of pre-operative relaxation on post-operative analgesia: Immediate increase and delayed reduction. *British Journal of Health Psychology, 3,* 215–224.

Margalith, I., & Shapiro, A. (1997). Anxiety and patient participation in clinical decision making: The case of patients with ureteral calculi. *Social Science & Medicine, 45,* 419–427.

Margittai, K.J., Moscarello, R., & Rossi, M.F. (1996). Forensic aspects of medical student abuse: A Canadian perspective. *Bulletin of the American Academy of Psychiatry and Law, 24,* 377–385.

Margolis, C.G. (1997). Hypnotic trance: The old and the new. *Primary Care, 24,* 809–823.

Marlatt, G.A. (1982). Relapse prevention: A self-control program for the treatment of addictive behaviors. In R.B. Stuart (Ed.), *Adherence, compliance, and generalization in behavioral medicine.* New York: Brunner/Mazel.

Marlatt, G.A., Larimer, M.E., Baer, J.S., & Quigley, L.A. (1993). Harm reduction for alcohol problems: Moving beyond the controlled drinking controversy. *Behavior Therapy, 24,* 461–504.

Marlatt, G.A., & Rohsenow, D.J. (1980). Cognitive processes in alcohol use: Expectancy and the balanced placebo design. In N. Mello (Ed.), *Advances in substance abuse: Behavioral and biological research.* Greenwich, CT: JAI Press.

Marquis, K.H. (1970). Effects of social reinforcement on health reporting in the household interview. *Sociometry. 33,* 203–215.

Marsland, D.W., Wood, M.B., & Mayo, F. (1976). The databank for patient care, curriculum and research in family practice: 526,196 patient problems. *Journal of Family Practice, 3,* 25–28.

Martin, D. (1996). Pre-operative visits to reduce patient anxiety: A study. *Nursing Standards, 28*, 33–38.

Martin, J.A., & Bjerknes, L.K. (1996). The legal and ethical implications of gag clauses in physician contracts. *American Journal of Law & Medicine, 22*, 433–476.

Martin, J.B., Ahles, T.A., & Jeffery, R. (1991). The role of private body consciousness and anxiety in the report of somatic symptoms during magnetic resonance imaging. *Journal of Behavior Therapy and experimental Psychiatry, 22*, 3–7.

Martin, L.R., Friedman, H.S., Tucker, J.S., Tomlinson-Keasey, C., Criqui, M.H., & Schwartz, J.E. (in press). A life course perspective on childhood cheerfulness and its relation to mortality risk.

Martin, M.T., Miller-Johnson, S., Kitzmann, K.M., & Emery, R.E. (1998). Parent-child relationships and insulin-dependent diabetes mellitus: Observational ratings of clinically relevant dimensions. *Journal of Family Psychology, 12*, 102–111.

Marucha, P.T., Kiecolt-Glaser, J.K., & Favagehi, M. (1998). Mucosal wound healing is impaired by examination stress. *Psychosomatic Medicine, 60*, 362–365.

Maslach, C. (1976). Burned-out. *Human Behavior, 5*, 16–22.

Maslach, C. (1982). *Burnout: The cost of caring*. Englewood Cliffs, NJ: Prentice Hall.

Mason, J.L., Barkley, S.E., Kappelman, M.M., Carter, D.E., & Beachy, W.V. (1988). Evaluation of a self-instructional method for improving doctor patient communication. *Journal of Medical Education, 63*, 629–635.

Mason, J.W. (1975). A historical view of the stress field. *Journal of Human Stress, 1*, 22–36.

Mason, J.W., Giller, E.L., & Kosten, T.R. (1988). Serum testosterone differences between patients with schizophrenia and those with affective disorder. *Biological Psychiatry, 23*, 357–366.

Mason, J.W., Kosten, T.R., Southwick, S.M., & Giller, E.L., Jr. (1990). The use of psychoendocrine strategies in post traumatic stress disorder. *Journal of Applied Social Psychology, 20*, 1822–1846.

Mastroyannopoulou, K., Stallard, P., Lewis, M., & Lenton, S. (1997). The impact of childhood non-malignant life-threatening illness on parents: Gender differences and predictors of parental adjustment. *Journal of Child Psychology and Psychiatry and Allied Disciplines, 38*, 823–829.

Matarazzo, J.D. (1980). Behavioral health and behavioral medicine: Frontiers for a new health psychology. *American Psychologist, 35*, 807–817.

Matarazzo, J.D. (1994). Health and behavior. The coming together of science and practice in psychology and medicine after a century of benign neglect. *Journal of Clinical Psychology in Medical Settings, 1*, 7–39.

Matsui, D., Cho, M., & Rieder, M.J. (1998). Physicians' attire as perceived by young children and their parents: The myth of the white coat syndrome. *Pediatric Emergency Care, 14*, 198–201.

Matt, G.E., & Dean, A. (1993). Social support from friends and psychological distress among elderly persons: Moderator effects of age. *Journal of Health & Social Behavior, 34*, 187–200.

Matthews, D., & Hingson, R. (1977). Improving patient compliance. A guide for physicians. *Medical Clinics of North America, 61*, 879–889.

Matthews, J.J. (1983). The communication process in clinical settings. *Social Science and Medicine, 17*, 1371–78.

Matthews, K.A., Kuller, L.H., Wing, R.R., Meilahn, E.N., & Plantinga, P. (1996). Prior to use of estrogen replacement therapy, are users healthier than non-users? *American Journal of Epidemiology, 143*, 971–978.

Matthews, K.A., Schumaker, S.A., Bowen, D.J., Langer, R.D., Hunt, J.R., Kaplan, R.M., Klesges, R.C., & Ritenbaugh, C. (1997). Women's health initiative: Why now? What is it? What's new? *American Psychologist, 52*, 101–116.

May, H.J., & Revicki, D.A. (1985). Professional stress among family physicians. *Journal of Family Practice, 20*, 165–171.

Mayer-Oakes, S.A., Atchison, K.A., Mattias, R.E., De Jong, F.J., et al. (1996). Mammography use in older women with regular physicians: What are the predictors? *American Journal of Preventive Medicine, 12*, 44–50.

Mayerson, E.W. (1976). *Putting the ill at ease*. New York: Harper & Row.

Maynard, C., Litwin, P.E., Martin, J.S., & Weaver, W.D. (1992). Gender differences in the treatment and outcome of acute myocardial infarction: Results of the Myocardial Infarction Triage and Intervention Registry. *Archives of Internal Medicine, 152*, 972–976.

McArthur, D.B. (1998). Heart healthy eating behaviors of children following school-based intervention: A meta-analysis. *Issues in Comprehensive Pediatric Nursing, 21*, 35–48.

McAuliffe, W.E., Rohman, M., Breer, P., Wyshak, G., Santangelo, S., & Magnuson, E. (1991). Alcohol use and abuse in random samples of physicians and medical students. *American Journal of Public Health, 81*, 177–182.

McBride, C.M., French, S.A., Pirie, P.L., & Jeffery, R.W. (1996). Changes over time in weight concerns among women smokers engaged in the cessation process. *Annals of Behavioral Medicine, 18*, 273–279.

McCann, I.L., & Holmes, D.S. (1984). Influence of aerobic exercise on depression. *Journal of Personality and Social Psychology, 46*, 1142–1147.

McCann, S., & Weinman, J. (1996). Encouraging patient participation in general practice consultations: Effect on consultation length and content, patient satisfaction and health. *Psychology & Health, 11*, 857–869.

McCarthy, J.J., McCarthy, M.C., & Eilert, R.E. (1999). Children's and parents' visual perception of physicians. *Clinical Pediatrics, 38*, 145–52.

McClelland, D.C., & Cheriff, A.D. (1997). The immunoenhancing effects of humor on secretory IgA and resistance to respiratory infections. *Psychology and Health, 12*, 329–344.

McCracken, L.M., Goetsch, V.L., & Semenchuk, E.M. (1998). Coping with pain produced by physical activity in persons with chronic low back pain: Immediate assessment following a specific pain event. *Behavioral Medicine, 24,* 29–34.

McCue, J.D. (1982). The effects of stress on physicians and their medical practice. *New England Journal Medicine, 306,* 458–463.

McCue, J.D. (1985). The distress of internship: Cause and prevention. New *England Journal of Medicine, 312,* 449–452.

McDaniel, S.H. (1995). Collaboration between psychologists and family physicians: Implementing the biopsychosocial model. *Professional Psychology: Research & Practice, 26,* 117–122.

McEldowney, R.P., & Berry, A. (1995). Physician supply and distribution in the USA. *Journal of Management in Medicine, 9,* 68–74.

McFarland, K.F., & Rhoades, D.R. (1998). Gender-related values and medical specialty choice. *Academic Psychiatry, 22,* 236–239.

McGaughey, J., & Harrisson, S. (1994). Understanding the pre-operative information needs of patients and their relatives in intensive care units. *Intensive Critical Care Nursing, 10,* 186–194.

McGee, D.S., & Cegala, D.J. (1998). Patient communication skills training for improved communication competence in the primary care medical consultation. *Journal of Applied Communication Research, 26,* 4112–430.

McGuire, L.C. (1996). Remembering what the doctor said: Organizations and adults' memory for medical information. *Experimental Aging Research, 22,* 403–428.

McGuire, W.J. (1969). The nature of attitudes and attitude change. In G. Lindzey & E. Aronson (Eds.), *Handbook of social psychology* (vol. 3; pp. 136–314). Reading, MA: Addison-Wesley.

McKinlay, J.B., Potter, D.A., & Feldman, H.A. (1996). Non-medical influences on medical decision making. *Social Science & Medicine, 42,* 769–776.

McNeil, B.J., Stephen, G., Pauker, M.D., Sox, H.C., Jr., & Tversky, A. (1982). Special articles on the elicitation of preferences for alternative therapies. *New England Journal of Medicine, 306,* 1259–1262.

Meagher, M.W. (in press). Clinical implications of animal pain research. In M.E. Carroll & J.B. Overmier (Eds.) *Linking animal research and human psychological health.* Washington, DC: American Psychological Association.

Meagher, M.W., McLemore, S., King, T.E., Sieve, A.N., Crown, E.D., & Grau, J.W. (in review). The generality of stress-induced hyperalgesia.

Mechanic, D. (1968). *Medical sociology: A selective view.* New York: The Free Press.

Mechanic, D. (1972). Social psychological factors affecting the presentation of bodily complaints. *The New England Journal of Medicine, 286,* 1132–1139.

Mechanic, D. (1978). Effects of phychological distress on perceptions of physical health and use of medical psychiatric facilities. *Journal of Human Stress, 4,* 26–32.

Mechanic, D. (1979). The stability of health and illness behavior: Results from a 16-year follow-up. *American Journal of Public Health, 69,* 1142–1145.

Mechanic, D. (1997). Managed care as a target of distrust. *Journal of the American Medical Association, 277,* 1810–1811.

Mechanic, D., & Schlesinger, M. (1996). The impact of managed care on patients' trust in medical care and their physicians. *Journal of the American Medical Association, 275,* 1693–1697.

Mechanic, D. & Volkart, E.H. (1961). Stress, illness behavior, and the sick role. *American Sociological Review, 26,* 51–58.

Mehrabian, A. (1972). *Nonverbal communication.* Chicago, IL: Aldine-Atherton.

Meichenbaum, D.H. (1985). *Stress inoculation training.* New York: Pergamon Press.

Meichenbaum, D.H., & Cameron, R. (1983). Stress inoculation training: Toward a general paradigm for training coping skills. In D. Meichenbaum & M.E. Jaremko (Eds.), *Stress reduction and prevention.* New York: Plenum.

Meinl, E. (1999). Concepts of viral pathogenesis of multiple sclerosis. *Current Opinions in Neurology, 12,* 303–307.

Meischke, H., Ho, M.T., Eisenberg, M.S., Schaeffer, S.M., & Larsen, M.P. (1995). Reasons patients with chest pain delay or do not call 911. *Annals of Emergency Medicine, 25,* 193–197.

Melamed, S., Kushnir, T., Strauss, E., & Vigiser, D. (1997). Negative association between reported life events and cardiovascular disease risk factors in employed men: The Cordis study. *Journal of Psychosomatic Research, 43,* 247–258.

Melnick, S.L., Sherer, R., Louis, T.A., Hillman, D., Rodriguez, E.M., Lackman, C., Capps, L., Brown, L.S., Jr., Carlyn, M., Korvick, J.A., et al. (1994). Survival and disease progression according to gender of patients with HIV infection: The Terry Beirn Community Programs for Clinical Research on AIDS. *Journal of the American Medical Association, 272,* 1915–1921.

Melzack, R. (1973). *The puzzle of pain.* New York: Basic Books.

Melzack, R. (Ed.) (1983). *Pain measurement and assessment.* New York: Raven.

Melzack, R. (1989). Labat lecture: Phantom limbs. *Regional Anesthesiology, 14,* 208–211.

Melzack, R. (1993). Pain: Past and future. *Canadian Journal of Experimental Psychology, 47,* 615–629.

Melzack, R. (1995). Phantom-limb and the brain. In B. Bromm, J.E. Desmedt, et al. (Eds.), *Pain and the brain: From nociception to cognition. Advances in pain research and therapy (vol. 22).* New York: Raven Press.

Melzack, R. (1999). From the gate to the neuromatrix. *Pain, Suppl 6,* 121–126.

Melzack, R., & Torgerson, W.S. (1971). On the language of pain. *Anesthesiology, 34,* 50–59.

Melzack, R., & Wall, P.D. (1965). Pain mechanisms: A theory. *Science, 150,* 971–979.

Melzack, R., & Wall, P.D. (1982). *The challenge of pain.* New York: Basic Books.

Mercadante, S., Casuccio, A., & Genovese, G. (1998). Ineffectiveness of dextromethorphan in cancer pain. *Journal of Pain Symptom Management, 16,* 317–322.

Mermelstein, R., Cohen, S., Lichtenstein, E., Baer, J.S., & Kamarck, T. (1986). Social support and smoking cessation and maintenance. *Journal of Consulting and Clinical Psychology, 54,* 447–453.

Merriam-Webster's Medical Dictionary Disk (MWMDD). (1996). Springfield, MA: Merriam-Webster.

Meyer, D., Leventhal, H., & Gutman, M. (1985). Commonsense models of illness: The example of hypertension. *Health Psychology, 4,* 115–135.

Meyerowitz, B.E. (1983). Postmastectomy coping strategies and quality of life. *Health Psychology, 2,* 117–132.

Meza, J.P. (1998). Patient waiting times in a physician's office. *American Journal of Managed Care, 4,* 703–712.

Michie, S., Rosebert, C., Heaversedge, J., Madden, S., et al. (1996). The effects of different kinds of information on women attending an out-patient breast clinic. *Psychology, Health, & Medicine, 1,* 285–296.

Middleton, W., Raphael, B., Martinek, N., & Misso, V. (1993). Pathological grief reactions. In M.S. Stroebe, W. Stroebe, & R.O. Hansson (Eds.), *Handbook of bereavement: Theory, research, and intervention.* New York: Cambridge University Press.

Miller, A.H. (1998). Neuroendocrine and immune system interactions in stress and depression. *Psychiatric Clinics of North America, 21,* 443–463.

Miller, C.A. (1994). What's a woman doing in a place like this? *Surgical Neurology, 42,* 171–176.

Miller, G.E., Kemeny, M.E., Taylor, S.E., Cole, S.W., et al. (1997). Social relationships and immune processes in HIV seropositive gay and bisexual men. *Annals of Behavioral Medicine, 19,* 139–151.

Miller, S.M., & Mangan, C.E. (1983). Interacting effects of information and coping style in adapting to gynecologic stress: Should the doctor tell all? *Journal of Personality and Social Psychology, 45,* 223–236.

Miller, W.C., Koceja, D.M., & Hamilton, E.J. (1997). A meta-analysis of the past 25 years of weight loss research using diet, exercise, or diet plus exercise intervention. *International Journal of Obesity Related Metabolic Disorders, 21,* 941–947.

Milligan, R.A.K., Burke, V., Beilin, L.J., Richards, J., Dunbar, D., Spencer, M. Balde, E., & Gracey, M.P. (1997). Health-related behaviors and psycho-social charactistics of 18-year-old Australians. *Social Science & Medicine, 45,* 1549–1562.

Milmoe, S., Rosenthal, R., Blane, H.T., Chafetz, M.L., & Wolf, I. (1967). The doctor's voice: Postdictor of successful referral of alcoholic patients. *Journal of Abnormal Psychology, 72,* 78–84.

Mintzer, J.E., Rubert, M.P., Loewenstein, D., Gamez, E., Millor, A., Quinteros, R., Flores, L., Miller, M., Rainerman, A., & Eisdorfer, C. (1992). Daughters' caregiving for Hispanic and non-Hispanic Alzheimer patients: Does ethnicity make a difference? *Community Mental Health Journal, 28,* 293–303.

Mireault, M., & de Man, A.F. (1996). Suicidal ideation among the elderly: Personal variables, stress and social support. *Social Behavior and Personality, 24,* 385–392.

Mizrahi, T. (1984). Managing medical mistakes: Ideology, insularity and accountability among internists-in-training. *Social Science and Medicine, 19,* 135–146.

Mizrahi, T. (1985). Getting rid of patients: Contradictions in the socialisation of internists to the doctor-patient relationship. *Sociology of Health and Illness, 7,* 214–235.

Molassiotis, A., Van Den Akker, O.B.A., Milligan, D.W., & Goldman, J.M. (1997). Symptom distress, coping style and biological variables as predictors of survival after bone marrow transplantation. *Journal of Psychosomatic Research, 42,* 275–285.

Montagu, A. (1978). *Touching.* New York: Harper & Row.

Montano, D.E., & Taplin, S.H. (1991). A test of an expanded theory of reasoned action to predict mammography participation. *Social Science & Medicine, 32,* 733–741.

Montgomery, G.H., Tomoyasu, N., Bovbjerg, D.H., Andrykowski, M.A., et al. (1998). Patients' pretreatment expectations of chemotherapy-related nausea are an independent predictor of anticipatory nausea. *Annals of Behavioral Medicine, 20,* 104–108.

Moos, R.H., & Finney, J.W. (1983). The expanding scope of alcoholism treatment evaluation. *American Psychologist, 38,* 1036–1044.

Moos, R.H. & Tsu, V.D. (1977). The crisis of physical illness: An overview. In R.H. Moos (Ed.), *Coping with physical illness* (pp. 3–21). New York: Plenum.

Moriarty, H.J., Carrol, R., & Cotroneo, M. (1996). Differences in bereavement reactions within couples following death of a child. *Research in Nursing and Health, 19,* 461–469.

Morley, S., & Pallin, V. (1995). Scaling the affective domain of pain: A study of the dimensionality of verbal descriptors. *Pain, 62,* 39–49.

Moscarello, R., Margittai, K.J., & Rossi, M. (1994). Differences in abuse reported by female and male Canadian medical students. *Canadian Medical Association Journal, 150,* 357–363.

Moses, R., & Cividali, M. (1966). Differential levels of awareness of illness: Their relation to some salient features in cancer patients. *Annals of the New York Academy of Sciences, 125,* 984–994.

Motenko, A.K., & Greenberg, S. (1995). Reframing dependence in old age: A positive transition for families. *Social Work, 40,* 382–90.

Mountcastle, V.B. (1974). Pain and temperature sensibilities. In V.B. Mountcastle (Ed), *Medical physiology.* St. Louis, MO: C.V. Mosby.

Moyer, A. (1997). Psychosocial outcomes of breast-conserving surgery versus mastectomy: A meta-analytic review. *Health Psychology, 16,* 284–298.

Moyer, A., & Salovey, P. (1996). Psychosocial sequelae of breast cancer and its treatment. *Annals of Behavioral Medicine, 18,* 110–125.

Mullan, F. (1983). *Vital signs: A young doctor's struggle with cancer.* New York: Farrar, Straus, Giroux.

Mullen, P.D., Simons-Morton, D.G., Ramirez, G., Frankowski, R.F., Green, L.W., & Mains, D.A. (1997). A meta-analysis of trials and evaluating patient education and counseling for three groups of preventive health behaviors. *Patient Education & Counseling, 32,* 157–173.

Mullins, L.L., Chaney, J.M., Pace, T.M., & Hartman, V.L. (1997). Illness uncertainty, attributional style, and psychological adjustment in older adolescents and young adults with asthma. *Journal of Pediatric Psychology, 22,* 871–880.

Mundinger, M.O., Kane, R.L., Lenz, E.R., Totten, A.M., Tsai, W., Cleary, P.D., Friedewald, W.T., Siu, A.L., & Shelanski, M.L. (2000). Primary care outcomes in patients treated by nurse practitioners or physicians. *Journal of the American Medical Association, 283,* 59–68.

Munstedt, K., Manthey, N., Sachsse, S., & Vahrson, H. (1997). Changes in self-concept and body image during alopecia induced cancer chemotherapy. *Support Care Cancer, 5,* 139–143.

Murphy, H., Dickens, C., Creed, F., & Bernstein, R. (1999). Depression, illness perception, and coping in rheumatoid arthritis. *Journal of Psychosomatic Research, 46,* 155–164.

Murphy, J.M., Nadelson, C.C., & Notman, M.T. (1984). Factors influencing first-year medical students' perceptions of stress. *Journal of Human Stress, 10,* 165–173.

Murphy, P.L., & Volinn, E. (1999). Is occupational low back pain on the rise? *Spine, 24,* 691–697.

Murphy, S.M. (Ed.) (1995). *Sport psychology interventions.* Champaign, IL: Human Kinetics Publishers.

Murray, M.T. (1994). *Natural alternatives to over-the-counter and prescription drugs.* New York: William & Morrow.

Muzzin, L.J., Anderson, N.J., Figueredo, A.T., & Gudelis, S.O. (1994). The experience of cancer. *Social Science & Medicine, 38,* 1201–1208.

Myers, L.B., & Midence, K. (Eds.) (1998). *Adherence to treatment in medical conditions.* Amsterdam: Harwood.

Myrtek, M. (1995). Type A behavior pattern, personality factors, disease, and physiological reactivity: A meta-analytic update. *Personality and Individual Differences, 18,* 491–502.

Naber, S.J., Halstead, L.K., Broome, M.E., & Rehwaldt, M. (1995). Communication and control: Parent, child, and health care professional interactions during painful procedures. *Issues in Comprehensive Pediatric Nursing, 18,* 79–90.

Naliboff, B.D., Benton, D., Solomon, G.F., Morley, J.E., Fahey, J.L., Bloom, E.T., Makinodan, T., & Gilmore, S.L. (1991). Immunological changes in young and old adults during brief laboratory stress. *Psychosomatic Medicine, 53,* 121–132.

Nathanson, C. (1977). Sex, illness, and medical care. *Social Science and Medicine, 11,* 13–15.

National Center for Health Statistics (NCHS). (1997). *Healthy People 2000, Review, 1997.* Hyattsville, MD: Public Health Service.

National Center for Health Statistics (NCHS). (1998). *Health, United States, 1997.* Hyattsville, MD: Public Health Service.

National Center for Health Statistics (NCHS). (1998). *Health, United States, 1998 with socioeconomic status and health chartbook.* Hyattsville, MD: Public Health Service.

National Institute of Alcoholism and Alcohol Abuse (NIAAA). (1981). *First statistical compendium on alcohol and health* (U.S. Department of Health and Human Services Publication No. 81-115). Washington, DC: U.S. Government Printing Office.

Neitzert, C.S., Davis, C., & Kennedy, S.H. (1997). Personality factors related to the prevalence of somatic symptoms and medical complaints in a healthy student population. *British Journal of Medical Psychology, 70,* 93–101.

Nelson, D.E., Bolen, J., & Kresnow, M. (1998). Trends in safety belt use by demographics and by type of state safety belt law, 1987 through 1993. *American Journal of Public Health, 88,* 245–249.

Nelson, D.S. (1992). Humor in the pediatric emergency department: A 20-year retrospective. *Pediatrics, 89,* 1089–1090.

Nelson, E.S., Karr, K.M., & Coleman, P.K. (1995). Relationships among daily hassles, optimism, and reported physical symptoms. *Journal of College Student Psychotherapy, 10,* 11–26.

Nelson, G.E. (1984). *Biological principles with human perspectives* (2nd ed). New York: Wiley.

Nemiah, J.C. (1961). *Foundations of psychopathology.* New York: Oxford University Press.

Nerenz, D.R., & Leventhal, H. (1983). Self-regulation theory in chronic illness. In T.G. Burish & L.A. Bradley (Eds.), *Coping with chronic disease: Research and applications.* New York: Academic Press.

Neumann, W., Kugler, J., Seelbach, H., & Kruskemper, G.M. (1997). Effects of nondirective suggestions on pain tolerance, pain threshold, and pain intensity perception. *Perceptual and Motor Skills, 84,* 963–966.

Neumark-Sztainer, D., Story, M., Toporoff, E., Himes, J.H., Resnick, M.D., & Blum, R.W. (1997). Covariations of eating behaviors with other health-related behaviors among adolescents. *Journal of Adolescent Health, 20,* 450–458.

Newacheck, P.W., & Halfon, N. (1998). Prevalence and impact of disabling chronic conditions in childhood. *American Journal of Public Health, 88,* 610–617.

Newman, J. (1997). Early detection techniques in breast cancer management. *Radiology Technology, 68,* 309–324.

Newman, R., & Reed, G.M. (1996). Psychology as a health care profession: Its evolution and future directions. In R.J. Resnick & R.H. Rozensky (Eds.), *Health psychology through the life span: Practice and research opportunities.* Washington, DC: APA.

Newman, R.I., & Seres, J. (1986). The interdisciplinary pain center: An approach to the management of chronic pain. In A.D. Holzman & D.C. Turk (Eds.), *Pain management: A handbook of psychological treatment approaches.* New York: Pergamon.

Nezu, A.M., & Nezu, C.M. (Eds.). (1983). *Clinical decision making in behavior therapy: A problem-solving perspective*. Champaign, IL: Research Press.

Niemi, P.M., & Vainiomaeki, P.T. (1999). Medical students' academic distress, coping, and achievement strategies during the preclinical years. *Teaching and Learning in Medicine, 11*, 125–134.

Nilsson, N. (1995). The prevalence of cervicogenic headache in a random population sample of 20–59 year olds. *Spine, 20*, 1884–1888.

Nilsson, N., & Bove, G. (2000). Evidence that tension-type headache and cervicogenic headache are distinct disorders. *Journal of Manipulative and Physiological Therapeutics, 23*, 288–289.

Nilsson, N., Christensen, H.W., & Hartvigsen, J. (1997). The effect of spinal manipulation in the treatment of cervicogenic headache. *Journal of Manipulative and Physiological Therapeutics, 20*, 326–330.

Nolen-Hoeksema, S. (1990). *Sex differences in depression*. Stanford, CA: Stanford University Press.

Noll, R.B., Gartstein, M.A., Vannatta, K., Correll, J., Bukowski, W.M., & Davies, W.H. (1999). Social, emotional, and behavioral functioning of children with cancer. *Pediatrics, 103*, 71–78.

Norman, R.M., & Malla, A.K. (1994). A prospective study of daily stressors and symptomatology in schizophrenic patients. *Social Psychiatry & Psychiatric Epidemiology, 29*, 244–259.

Northouse, P.G., & Northouse, L.L. (1985). *Health communication: A handbook for health professionals*. Englewood Cliffs, NJ: Prentice Hall.

Noseworthy, J.H. (1999). Progress in determining the causes and treatment of multiple sclerosis. *Nature, 399*, A40–A47.

O'Brien, C.P. (1994). Treatment of alcoholism as a chronic disorder. *Alcohol, 11*, 433–437.

O'Brien, M.K. (1997). Compliance among health professionals. In A. Baum, S. Newman, J. Weinman, R. West, & C. McManus (Eds.), *Cambridge handbook of psychology, health and medicine*. Cambridge, UK: Cambridge University Press.

Ogden, J., & Mitandabari, T. (1997). Examination stress and changes in mood and health related behaviours. *Psychology and Health, 12*, 288–299.

Ogden-Niemeyer, L. & Jacobs, K. (1989). *Work-hardening state of the art*. Thorofare, NJ: Slack.

O'Halloran, C.M., & Altmaier, E.M. (1996). Awareness of death among children: Does a life-threatening illness alter the process of discovery? *Journal of Counseling and Development, 74*, 259–266.

Older, J. (1984). Teaching touch at medical school. *Journal of the American Medical Association, 252*, 931–933.

Oliver, R.C., & Fallat, M.E. (1995). Traumatic childhood death: How well do parents cope? *Journal of Trauma, 39*, 303–307.

Olson, J., & Hanchett, E. (1997). Nurse-expressed empathy, patient outcomes, and development of a middle-range theory. *IMAGE: Journal of Nursing Scholarship, 29*, 71–76.

Oltjenbruns, K.A. (1998). Ethnicity and the grief response. Mexican American versus Anglo American college students. *Death Studies, 22*, 141–155.

O'Malley, S.S. (1996). Opioid antagonists in the treatment of alcohol dependence: Clinical efficacy and prevention of relapse. *Alcohol, Suppl. 1*, 77–81.

Orne, M.T. (1989). On the construct of hypnosis: How its definition affects research and its clinical application. In G.D. Burrows & L. Dennerstein (Eds.), *Handbook of hypnosis and psychosomatic medicine*. Amsterdam: Elsevier.

Orr, S.P., Lasko, N.B., Shalev, A.Y., & Pitman, R.K. (1995). Physiologic responses to loud tones in Vietnam veterans with posttraumatic stress disorder. *Journal of Abnormal Psychology, 104*, 75–82.

Osler, Sir W. (1899). Lecture to medical students. *Albany Medical Annals, 20*, 307.

Osler, Sir W. (1904). The master word in medicine. In *Aequanimitas, with other addresses to medical students, nurses, and practitioners of medicine* (pp. 369–371). Philadelphia: Blakiston.

Osterweis, M., Solomon, F. & Green, M. (Eds.). (1984). *Bereavement, Reactions, consequences, and care*, Washington, DC: National Academy of Sciences Press.

Ow, R., & Katz, D. (1999). Family secrets and the disclosure of distressful information in Chinese families. *Families in Society, 80*, 620–628.

Owen, H., & Plummer, J. (1997). Patient-controlled analgesia: Current concepts in acute pain management. *CNS Drugs, 8*, 203–218.

Paffenbarger, R.S., & Hale, W.E. (1975). Work activity and coronary heart mortality. *New England Journal of Medicine, 292*, 545.

Paffenbarger, R.S., Wing, A.L., & Hyde, R.T. (1978). Physical activity as an index of heart risk in college alumni. *American Journal of Epidemiology, 108*, 161–175.

Pagani, M., & Lucini, D. (1999). Chronic fatigue syndrome: A hypothesis focusing on the autonomic nervous system. *Clinical Science, 96*, 117–125.

Page, G.G., & Ben-Eliyahu, S. (1997). The immune-suppressive nature of pain. *Seminars in Oncology Nursing, 13*, 10–15.

Page-Shafer, K., Delorenze, G.N., Satariano, W.A., & Winkelstein W. Jr. (1996). Comorbidity and survival in HIV-infected men in the San Francisco Men's Health Survey. *Annals of Epidemiology, 6*, 420–430.

Paice, J.A., Toy, C., & Shott, S. (1998). Barriers to cancer pain relief: Fear of tolerance and addiction. *Journal of Pain Symptom Management, 16*, 1–9.

Panzarino, P.J., Jr. (1998). The costs of depression: Direct and indirect; treatment versus nontreatment. *Journal of Clinical Psychiatry, 59*, 11–14.

Parkes, C.M. (1972). *Bereavement: Studies of grief in adult life*. London: Tavistock.

Parkes, C.M. (1993). Bereavement as a psychosocial transition: Processes of adaptation to change. In M.S. Stroebe, W. Stroebe, & R.O. Hansson (Eds.), *Handbook of bereavement: Theory, research, and intervention*. New York: Cambridge University Press.

Parkes, C.M., & Brown, R. (1972). Health after bereavement: A controlled study of young Boston widows and widowers. *Psychosomatic Medicine, 34,* 449–461.

Parkes, C.M., & Weiss, R.S. (1983). *Recovery from bereavement.* New York: Basic Books.

Parrott, R. (1994). Exploring family practitioners' and patients' information exchange about prescribed medications: Implications for practitioners' interviewing and patients' understanding. *Health Communication, 6,* 267–280.

Parsons, T. (1951). *The social system* (pp. 428–479). Glencoe, IL: The Free Press.

Parsons, T. (1975). The sick role and the role of the physician reconsidered. *Millbank Memorial Fund Quarterly, 53,* 257–278.

Pasnau, R.O., & Stoessel, P. (1994). Mental health service for medical students. *Medical Education, 28,* 33–39.

Pate, R.R., Pratt, M., Blair, S.N., Haskell, W.L., Macera, C.A., Bouchard, C., Buchner, D., Ettinger, W., Heath, G.W., King, A.C., Kriska, A., Leon, A.S., Marcus, B.H., Morris, J., Paffenbarger, R.S. Jr., Patrick, K., Pollock, M.L., Rippe, J.M., Sallis, J., & Wilmore, J.H. (1995). Physical activity and public health. *Journal of the American Medical Association, 273,* 402–407.

Paterson, B.L., Thorne, S., & Dewis, M. (1998). Adapting to and managing diabetes. *Image Journal of Nursing Schools, 30,* 57–62.

Patterson, M.L. (1983). *Nonverbal behavior: A functional perspective.* New York: Springer-Verlag.

Patterson, T.L., Semple, S.J., Temoshok, L.R., Atkinson, J.H., McCutchan, J.A., Straits-Troster, K., Chandler, J.L., & Grant I. (1995). Stress and depressive symptoms prospectively predict immune change among HIV-seropositive men: HIV Neurobehavioral Research Center Group. *Psychiatry, 58,* 299–312.

Pauker, S.G. & Kassirer, J.P. (1987). Medical progress decision analysis. *New England Journal of Medicine, 316,* 250–257.

Pavlov, I.P. (1927). *Conditioned reflexes.* New York: Dover.

Payer, L. (1988). *Medicine and culture.* New York: Henry Holt.

Payer, L. (1992). *Disease mongers.* New York: Wiley.

Pearlin, L.I., & Schooler, C. (1978). The structure of coping. *Journal of Health and Social Behavior, 19,* 2–21.

Pearson, J.L., Conwell, Y., Lindesay, J., Takahashi, Y., et al. (1997). Elderly suicide: A multi-national view. *Aging and Mental Health, 1,* 107–111.

Peay, M.Y., & Peay, E.R. (1998). The evaluation of medical symptoms by patients and doctors. *Journal of Behavioral Medicine, 21,* 57–81.

Pederson, L.L., Bull, S.B., Ashley, M.J., & MacDonald, J.K. (1996). Quitting smoking: Why, how, and what might help. *Tobacco Control, 5,* 209–214.

Penkower, L., Dew, M.A., Kingsley, L., Becker, J.T., Satz, P., Schaerf, F.W., & Sheridan, K. (1991). Behavioral, health and psychosocial factors and risk for HIV infection among homosexual men: The Multicenter AIDS Cohort Study. *American Journal of Public Health, 81,* 194–196.

Pennebaker, J.W. (1982). *The psychology of physical complaints.* New York: Springer-Verlag.

Pennebaker, J.W. (1983). Accuracy of symptom perception. In A. Baum, S.E. Taylor, & J. Singer (Eds.), *Handbook of psychology and health* (vol. 4). Hillsdale, NJ: Erlbaum.

Pennebaker, J.W. (1995). *Emotion, disclosure, and health* (Edited). Washington, DC: American Psychological Association.

Pennebaker, J.W. (1997). *Opening up: The healing power of expressing emotions* (rev. ed.). New York: Guilford Press.

Pennebaker, J.W., Burnam, M.A., Schaeffer, M.A., & Harper, D.C. (1977). Lack of control as a determinant of perceived physical symptoms. *Journal of Personality and Social Psychology, 35,* 167–174.

Pennebaker, J.W., & Susman, J. R. (1988). Disclosure of traumas and psychosomatic processes. *Social Science and Medicine, 26,* 327–332.

Pennebaker, J.W., & Watson, D. (1991). The psychology of somatic symptoms. In L.J. Kirmayer & J.M. Robbins (Eds.) *Current concepts of somatization: Research and clinical perspectives* (pp. 21–35). Washington, DC: American Psychiatric Press.

Penninx, B.W.J.H., van Tilburg, T., Boeke, A.J.P., Deeg, D.J.H., et al. (1998). Effects of social support and personal coping resources on depressive symptoms: Different for various chronic diseases? *Health Psychology, 17,* 551–558.

Peter, R., Alfredsson, L., Hammar, N., Siegrist, J., et al. (1998). High effort, low reward, and cardiovascular risk factors in employed Swedish men and women: Baseline results from the WOLF study. *Journal of Epidemiology & Community Health, 52,* 540–547.

Peter, R., & Siegrist, J. (1997). Chronic work stress, sickness absence and hypertension in middle managers: General or specific sociological explanations? *Social Science & Medicine, 45,* 1111–1120.

Peters, K.D., Kochanek, K.D., & Murphy, S.L. (1998). Deaths: Final data for 1996. *National Vital Statistics Reports, 47,* 1–100.

Peters, M.L., Godaert, G.L., Ballieux, R.E., van Vliet, M., et al. (1998). Cardiovascular and endocrine responses to experimental stress: Effects of mental effort and controllability. *Psychoneuroendocrinology, 23,* 1–17.

Peterson, C. & Seligman, M.E.P. (1987). Explanatory style and illness. *Journal of Personality, 55,* 237–265.

Peterson, C., Seligman, M.E.P., & Vaillant, G.E. (1988). Pessimistic explanatory style is a risk factor for physical illness: A thirty-five-year longitudinal study. *Journal of Personality and Social Psychology, 55,* 23–27.

Peterson, C., Seligman, M.E.P., Yurko, K.H., Martin, L.R., & Friedman, H.S. (1998). Catastrophizing and untimely death. *Psychological Science, 9,* 127–130.

Petrie, K.J., Booth, R.J., & Pennebaker, J.W. (1998). The immunological effects of thought suppression. *Journal of Personality & Social Psychology, 75,* 1264–1272.

Petrie, K.J., Booth, R.J., Pennebaker, J.W., Davison, K.P., et al. (1995). Disclosure of trauma and immune response to a hepatitis B vaccination program. *Journal of Consulting and Clinical Psychology, 63,* 787–792.

Pettle-Michael, S.A., & Lansdown, R.G. (1986). Adjustment to the death of a sibling. *Archives of Disease in Childhood, 61,* 278–283.

Pfeiffer, C., Madray, H., Ardolino, A., & Willms, J. (1998). The rise and fall of students' skill in obtaining a medical history. *Medical Education, 32,* 283–288.

Pfeiffer, R.J. (1983). Early-adult development in the medical student. *Mayo Clinic Proceedings, 58,* 127–134.

Phillips, A.N., Antunes, F., Stergious, G., Ranki, A., Jensen, G.F., Bentwich, Z., Sachs, T., Pedersen, C., Lundgren, J.D., & Johnson, A.M. (1994). A sex comparison of rates of new AIDS-defining disease and death in 2554 AIDS cases: AIDS in Europe Study Group. *AIDS, 8,* 831–835.

Phillips, D. (1996). Medical professional dominance and client dissatisfactions. A study of doctor-patient interaction and reported dissatisfaction with medical care among female patients at four hospitals in Trinidad and Tobago. *Social Science & Medicine, 42,* 1419–1425.

Piccinelli, M., & Simon, G. (1997). Gender and cross-cultural differences in somatic symptoms associated with emotional distress: An international study in primary care. *Psychological Medicine, 27,* 433–444.

Pickett, M. (1993). Cultural awareness in the context of terminal illness. *Cancer Nursing, 16,* 102–106.

Pinkerton, S.S., Hughes, H., & Wenrich, W.W. (1982). *Behavioral medicine: Clinical applications.* New York: Wiley Interscience.

Pinkston, M., & Linsk, N.L. (1984). *Care of the elderly: A family approach.* New York: Pergamon.

Pitts, F.N., Schuller, A.B., Rich, C.L., & Pitts, A.F. (1979). Suicide among U.S. women physicians, 1967–1972. *American Journal of Psychiatry, 136,* 694–696.

Plomin, R. (1998). Using DNA in Health Psychology. *Health Psychology, 17,* 53–55.

Pollock, G.H. (1982). The mourning-liberation process and creativity: The case of Kathe Kollwitz. *The Annual of Psychoanalysis, 10,* 333–354.

Pomeroy, V.M., Conroy, M.C., & Coleman, P.G. (1997). Setting handicap goals with elderly people: A pilot study of the Life Strengths Interview. *Clinical Rehabilitation, 11,* 156–161.

Pratt, L. (1976). *Family structure and effective health behavior: The energized family.* Boston, MA: Houghton-Mifflin.

Pratt, M. (1999). Benefits of lifestyle activity vs. structured exercise. *Journal of the American Medical Association, 281,* 375–376.

Pratt, O.E. (1982). Alcohol and the developing fetus. *British Medical Bulletin, 38,* 48–52.

Presti, D.E., Ary, D.V., & Lichtenstein, E. (1992). The context of smoking initiation and maintenance: Findings from interviews with youths. *Journal of Substance Abuse, 4,* 35–45.

Prkachin, K.M., & Craig, K.D. (1995). Expressing pain: The communication and interpretation of facial pain signals. *Journal of Nonverbal Behavior, 19,* 191–205.

Probst, J.C., Greenhouse, D.L., & Selassie A.W. (1997). Patient and physician satisfaction with an outpatient care visit. *Journal of Family Practice, 45,* 418–425.

Prochaska, J.O., & DiClemente, C.C. (1984). *The transtheoretical approach: Crossing traditional boundaries of therapy.* Chicago: Dow Jones/Irwin.

Prochaska, J.O., & Velicer, W.F. (1997). The transtheoretical model of health behavior change. *American Journal of Health Promotion, 12,* 38–48.

Professional Guide to Diseases (PGD). (1982). Springhouse, PA: Springhouse.

Professional Guide to Diseases (PGD). (1998). Springhouse, PA: Springhouse.

Pusari, N.D. (1998). Eight "Cs" of caring: A holistic framework for nursing terminally ill patients. *Contemporary Nurse, 7,* 156–160.

Putnam, S.M., & Stiles, W.B. (1993). Verbal exchanges in medical interviews: Implications and innovations. *Social Science & Medicine, 36,* 1597–1604.

Putnam, S.M., Stiles, W.B., Jacob, M.C., & James, S.A. (1985). Patient exposition and physician explanation in initial medical interviews and outcomes of clinic visits. *Medical Care, 23,* 74–83.

Quick, J.C., & Quick, J.D. (1984). *Organizational stress and preventive management.* New York: McGraw-Hill.

Rabin, D.L., & Bush, P.J. (1975). Who's using medicines? *Journal of Community Health, 1,* 106–117.

Rahe, R.H., Mahan, J.L., & Arthur, R.J. (1970). Prediction of near-future health change from subjects' preceding life changes. *Journal of Psychosomatic Research, 14,* 401–406.

Rainville, P., Carrier, B., Hofbauer, R.K., Bushnell, M.C., & Duncan, G.H. (1999). Dissociation of sensory and affective dimensions of pain using hypnotic modulation. *Pain, 82,* 159–171.

Ramritu, P.L., & Croft, G. (1999). Needs of parents of the child hospitalised with acquired brain damage. *International Journal of Nursing Studies, 36,* 209–216.

Rao, G.G. (1998). Risk factors for the spread of antibiotic-resistant bacteria. *Drugs, 55,* 323–330.

Rathore, S.S., Lenert, L.A., Weinfurt, K.P., Tinoco, A., Taleghani, C.K., Harless, W., & Schulman, K.A. (2000). The effects of patient sex and race on medical students' ratings of quality of life. *American Journal of Medicine, 108,* 561–566.

Raveis, V.H., Siegel, K., & Gorey, E. (1998). Factors associated with HIV-infected women's delay in seeking medical care. *AIDS Care, 10,* 549–562.

Ray, E.B., & Ray, G.B. (1990). The relationship of paralinguistic cues to impression formation and the recall of medical messages. *Health Communication, 2,* 47–57.

Reagan, M.D. (1992). *Curing the crisis: Options for America's health care.* San Francisco: Westview Press.

Reed, G.M., Kemeny, M.E., Taylor, S.E., & Visscher, B.R. (1999). Negative HIV-specific expectancies and AIDS-related bereavement as predictors of onset in asymptomatic HIV-positive gay men. *Health Psychology, 18,* 354–363.

Reich, W. (1942). *Character-analysis* (3rd ed.). New York: Noonday Press.

Reidenberg, M.M. & Lowenthal, D.T. (1968). Adverse non-drug reactions. *New England Journal of Medicine, 279,* 678–679.

Reifman, A. (1995). Social relationships, recovery from illness, and survival: A literature review. *Annals of Behavioral Medicine, 17,* 124–131.

Repetti, R.L. (1993). Short-term effects of occupational stressors on daily mood and health complaints. *Health Psychology, 12,* 125–131.

Resnick, R.J., & Rozensky, R.H. (Eds.). (1996). *Health psychology through the life span: Practice and research opportunities.* Washington, DC: APA.

Reuben, D.B. (1985). Depressive symptoms in medical house officers. *Archives of Internal Medicine, 145,* 286–288.

Reuben, D.B., & Noble, S. (1990). House officer responses to impaired physicians. *Journal of the American Medical Association, 263,* 958–960.

Revenson, T.A. (1986). Debunking the myth of loneliness in late life. In E. Seidman & J. Rappaport (Eds.), *Redefining social problems* (pp. 115–135). New York: Plenum.

Revicki, D.A., Wu, A.W., & Murray, M.I. (1995). Change in clinical status, health status, and health utility outcomes in HIV-infected patients. *Medical Care, 33,* AS173–182.

Reynolds, F. (1997). Coping with chronic illness and disability through creative needlecraft. *British Journal of Occupational Therapy, 60,* 352–356.

Richardsen, A.M., & Burke, R.J. (1991). Occupational stress and job satisfaction among physicians: Sex differences. *Social Science and Medicine, 33,* 1179–1187.

Richardsen, A.M., & Burke, R.J. (1993). Occupational stress and work satisfaction among Canadian women physicians. *Psychological Reports, 72,* 811–821.

Richardsen, D.A., Becker, M., Frank, R.R., & Sokol, R.J. (1997). Assessing medical students' perceptions of mistreatment in their second and third years. *Academic Medicine, 72,* 728–730.

Richardson, G.S., Wyatt, J.K., Sullivan, J.P., Orav, E.J., Ward, A.E., Wolf, M.A., & Czeisler, C.A. (1996). Objective assessment of sleep and alertness in medical house staff and the impact of protected time for sleep. *Sleep, 19,* 718–726.

Richman, J.A., & Flaherty, J.A. (1986). Sex differences in drinking among medical students: Patterns and psychosocial correlates. *Journal of Studies in Alcohol, 47,* 283–289.

Richman, J.A., & Flaherty, J.A. (1990). Gender differences in medical student distress: contributions of prior socialization and current role-related stress. *Social Science and Medicine, 30,* 777–787.

Richman, J.A., Flaherty, J.A., Rospenda, K.M., & Christensen, M.L. (1992). Mental health consequences and correlates of reported medical student abuse. *Journal of the American Medical Association, 267,* 692–694.

Riggio, R.E,. & Friedman, H.S. (1983). Individual differences and cues to deception. *Journal of Personality and Social Psychology, 45,* 899–915.

Rimm, D.C., & Masters, J.C. (1979). *Behavior therapy: Techniques and empirical findings* (2nd ed.). New York: McGraw-Hill.

Rizzo, J.A. (1993). Physician uncertainty and the art of persuasion. *Social Science and Medicine, 37,* 1451–1459.

Rizzo, J.A., Abbott, T.A., III, & Berger, M.L. (1998). The labor productivity effects of chronic backache in the United States. *Medical Care, 36,* 1471–1488.

Roberts, A.H. (1986). The operant approach to the management of pain and excess disability. In A.D. Holzman & D.C. Turk (Eds.), *Pain management: A handbook of psychological treatment approaches.* New York: Pergamon.

Robin, E.D. (1984). *Matters of life and death: Risks versus benefits of medical care.* New York: W.H. Freeman.

Robinson, C.A. (1993). Managing life with a chronic condition: The story of normalization. *Quality Health Research, 3,* 6–28.

Robinson, D. (1971). *The process of becoming ill.* London: Routledge & Kegan Paul.

Robinson, D. (1973). Ten noted doctors answer ten tough questions. *Parade,* July 15.

Robinson, J.D. (1998). Getting down to business: Talk, gaze, and body orientation during openings of doctor-patient consultations. *Human Communication Research, 25,* 97–123.

Robinson, L., & Mahon, M.M. (1997). Sibling bereavement: A concept analysis. *Death Studies, 21,* 477–499.

Robinson-Whelen, S., & Kiecolt-Glaser, J. (1997). Spousal caregiving: Does it matter if you have a choice? *Journal of Clinical Geropsychology, 3,* 283–289.

Rodin, J., & Langer, E.J. (1977). Long-term effects of a control-relevant intervention with the institutionalized aged. *Journal of Personality and Social Psychology, 35,* 897–902.

Rodin, M. (1992). The social construction of premenstrual syndrome. *Social Science and Medicine, 35,* 49–56.

Rodrigue, J.R. (1996). Promoting healthier behaviors, attitudes, and beliefs toward sun exposure in parents of young children. *Journal of Consulting & Clinical Psychology, 64,* 1431–1436.

Roessler, R., Reed, C., & Brown, P. (1998). Coping with chronic illness at work: Case studies of five successful employees. *Journal of Vocational Rehabilitation, 10,* 261–269.

Roger, V.L., Farkouh, M.E., Weston, S.A., Reeder, G.S., Jacobsen, S.J., Zinmeister, A.R., Yawn, B.P., Kopecky, S.L., & Gabriel, S.E. (2000). Sex differences in evaluation and outcome of unstable angina. *Journal of the American Medical Association, 283,* 646–652.

Rogers, C.R. (1951). *Client-centered therapy.* Boston: Houghton Mifflin.

Rogers, C.R. (1957). The necessary and sufficient conditions of therapeutic personality change. *Journal of Consulting Psychology, 21,* 95–103.

Rokeach, M. (1973). *The nature of human values.* New York: The Free Press.

Ronis, D.L. (1992). Conditional health threats: Health beliefs, decisions, and behaviors among adults. *Health Psychology, 11,* 127–134.

Rose, K.D., & Rosow, I. (1973). Physicians who kill themselves. *Archives of General Psychiatry, 29,* 800–805.

Rose, R.J., & Chesney, M.A. (1986). Cardiovascular stress reactivity: A behavior-genetic perspective. *Behavior Therapy, 17,* 314–323.

Rosenberg, D.A., & Silver, H.K. (1984). Medical student abuse an unnecessary and preventable cause of stress. *Journal of the American Medical Association, 251,* 739–741.

Rosenberg, M.J., & Hovland, C.I. (1960). Cognitive, affective, and behavioral components of attitudes. In C.I. Hovland & M.J. Rosenberg (Eds.), *Attitude organization and change.* New Haven, CT: Yale University Press.

Rosenblatt, P.C. (1993). Grief: The social context of private feelings. In M.S. Stroebe, W. Stroebe, & R.O. Hansson (Eds.), *Handbook of bereavement: Theory, research, and intervention.* New York: Cambridge University Press.

Rosenstock, I.M. (1974). Historical origins of the health belief model. *Health Education Monographs, 2,* 328–335.

Rosenstock, I.M. (1985). Understanding and enhancing patient compliance with diabetic regimens. *Diabetes Care, 8,* 610–616.

Rosenthal, R. (1969). Interpersonal expectations: Effects of the experimenter's hypothesis. In R. Rosenthal & R.L. Rosnow (Eds.), *Artifacts in behavioral research.* New York: Academic Press.

Rosenthal, R., Hall, J.A., DiMatteo, M.R., Rogers, P.L., & Archer, D. (1974). Body talk and tone of voice: The language without words. *Psychology Today, 8,* 64–68.

Rosenthal, T. (1970). *How could I not be among you?* Berkeley, CA: Benchmark Films.

Roseveare, C., Seavell, C., Patel, P., Criswell, J., Kimble, J., Jones, C., & Shepherd, H. (1998). Patient-controlled sedation and analgesia, using propofol and alfentanil, during colonoscopy: A prospective randomized controlled trial. *Endoscopy, 30,* 768–773.

Ross, M. (1971). Suicide among physicians. *Psychiatry in Medicine, 2,* 189–198.

Rostad, F.G., & Long, B.C. (1996). Exercise as a coping strategy for stress: A review. *International Journal of Sports Psychology, 27,* 197–222.

Roter, D., Lipkin, M., & Korsgaard, A. (1991). Sex differences in patients' and physicians' communication during primary care medical visits. *Medical Care, 29,* 1083–1093.

Roter, D.L. (1984). Patient question asking in physician-patient interaction. *Health Psychology, 3,* 395–410.

Roter, D.L., & Hall, J.A. (1992). *Doctors talking with patients/patients talking with doctors.* Westport, CT: Auburn House.

Roter, D.L., Hall, J.A., Merisca, R., Nordstrom, B., Cretin, D., & Svarstad, B. (1998). Effectiveness of interventions to improve patient compliance: A meta-analysis. *Medical Care, 36,* 1138–1161.

Roter, D.L., Rosenbaum, J., de Negri, B., Renaud, D., et al. (1998). The effects of a continuing medical education programme in interpersonal communication skills on doctor practice and patient satisfaction in Trinidad and Tobago. *Medical Education, 32,* 181–189.

Roter, D.L., Stewart, M., Putnam, S.M., Lipkin, M., Jr., Stiles, W.B., & Inui, J. (1997). Communication patterns of primary care physicians. *Journal of the American Medical Association, 277,* 350–356.

Roth, B., & Creaser, T. (1997). Mindfulness meditation-based stress reduction: Experience with a bilingual inner-city program, *Nurse Practitioner, 22,* 150–152.

Roth, J.A. (1972). The necessity and control of hospitalization. *Social Science and Medicine, 6,* 426–448.

Rothman, A.J., Salovey, P., Turvey, C., & Fishkin, S. (1993). Attributions of responsibility and persuasion: Increasing mammography utilization among women over 40 with an internally oriented message. *Health Psychology, 12,* 39–47.

Rounds, J.B., & Zevon, M.A. (1993). Cancer stereotypes: A multidimensional scaling analysis. *Journal of Behavioral Medicine, 16,* 485–496.

Rout, U. (1996). Stress among general practitioners and their spouses: A qualitative study. *British Journal of General Practice, 46,* 157–160.

Rowe, P.C., & Calkins, H. (1998). Neurally mediated hypotension and chronic fatigue syndrome. *American Journal of Medicine, 105,* 15S–21S.

Rubin, R., Orris, P., Lau, S.L., Hryhorczuk, D.O., Furner, S., & Letz, R. (1991). Neurobehavioral effects of the on-call experience in housestaff physicians. *Journal of Occupational Medicine, 33,* 13–18.

Rudberg, M.A., Sager, M.A., & Zhang, J. (1996). Risk factors for nursing home use after hospitalizations for medical illness. *Journals of Gerontology, 51,* 189–194.

Rudolph, U., & Steins, G. (1998). Causal versus existential attributions: Different perspectives on highly negative events. *Basic & Applied Social Psychology, 20,* 191–205.

Ruffin, C.L. (1993). Stress and health: Little hassles vs. major life events. *Australian Psychologist, 28,* 201–208.

Rundall, T.G., & Wheeler, J.R.C. (1979). The effect of income on use of preventive care: An evaluation of alternative explanations. *Journal of Health & Social Behavior, 20,* 397–406.

Rushton, A., Clayton, J., & Calnan, M. (1998). Patients' action during their cardiac event: Qualitative study exploring differences in modifiable factors. *Behavioral Medicine Journal, 316,* 1060–1064.

Rustad, L.C. (1984). Family adjustment to chronic illness and disability in mid-life. In M.G. Eisenberg, L.C. Sutkin, & M.A. Jansen (Eds.), *Chronic illness and disability through the life span: Effects on self and family* (pp. 222–242). New York: Springer.

Rutter, D.R., Iconomou, T., & Quine, L. (1996). Doctor-patient communication and outcome in cancer patients: An intervention. *Psychology and Health, 12,* 57–71.

Ryan, W. (1971). *Blaming the victim.* New York: Random House

Ryff, C.D., & Singer, B. (1996). Psychological well-being: Meaning, measurement, and implications for psychotherapy research. *Psychotherapy and Psychosomatics, 65,* 14–23.

Sackett, D.L., & Snow, J.C. (1979). The magnitude of compliance and noncompliance. In R.B. Haynes, D.W. Taylor, Y.D.L. Sackett (Eds.), *Compliance in health care* (pp. 11–22). Baltimore, MD: Johns Hopkins University Press.

Sadava, S.W., & Pak, A.W. (1994). Problem drinking and close relationships during the third decade of life. *Psychology of Addictive Behaviors, 8*, 251–258.

Safer, M.A., Tharps, Q.J., Jackson, T.C., & Leventhal, H. (1979). Determinants of three stages of delay in seeking care at a medical care clinic. *Medical Care, 17*, 11–29.

Safran, C. (1977). I don't intend to die this year. In R.H. Moos (Ed.), *Coping with physical illness* (pp. 403–411). New York: Plenum.

Saldinger, A., Caine, A., Kalter, N., & Lohnes, K. (1999). Anticipating parental death in families with young children. *American Journal of Orthopsychiatry, 69*, 39–48.

Samkoff, J.S., & Jacques, C.H. (1991). A review of studies concerning effects of sleep deprivation and fatigue on residents' performance. *Academic Medicine, 66*, 687–693.

Samora, J., Saunders, L., & Larson, R.F. (1961). Medical vocabulary knowledge among hospital patients. *Journal of Health and Human Behavior, 2*, 83–89.

Sander, R.W., Holloway, R.L., Eliason, B.C., Marbella, A.M., et al. (1996). Patient-initiated prevention of discussions: Two interventions to stimulate patients to initiate prevention discussions. *Journal of Family Practice, 43*, 468–474.

Sanders, S.H. (1996). Operant conditioning with chronic pain: Back to basics. In R.J. Gatchel, & D.C. Turk (Eds.), *Psychological approaches to pain management: A practitioner's handbook* (pp. 112–130). New York: Guilford Press.

Sands, T., Archer, J. Jr., & Puleo, S. (1998). Prevention of health-risk behaviors in college students: Evaluating seven variables. *Journal of College Student Development, 39*, 331–342.

Sangster, L.M., & McGuire, D.P. (1999). Perceived role of primary care physicians in Nova Scotia's reformed health care system. *Canadian Family Physician, 45*, 94–101.

Sarnoff, R., & Rundall, T. (1998). Meta-analysis of effectiveness of interventions to increase influenza immunization rates among high-risk population groups. *Medical Care Research & Review, 55*, 432–456.

Sartory, G., Mueller, B., Metsch, J., & Pothmann, R. (1998). A comparison of psychological and pharmacological treatment of pediatric migraine. *Behavior Research and Therapy, 36*, 1155–1170.

Sato, T., Takeichi, M., Shirahama, M., Fukui, T., & Gude, J.K. (1995). Doctor-shopping patients and users of alternative medicine amongst Japanese primary care patients. *General Hospital Psychiatry, 17*, 115–125.

Sausen, K.P., Lovallo, W.R., Pincomb, G.A., & Wilson, M.F. (1992). Cardiovascular responses to occupational stress in male medical students: A paradigm for ambulatory monitoring studies. *Health Psychology, 11*, 55–60.

Sawyer, T. (1966). Measurement and prediction: Clinical and statistical. *Psychological Bulletin, 66*, 178–200.

Scarpaci, J.L. (1988). Help-seeking behavior, use, and satisfaction among frequent primary care users in Santiago de Chile. *Journal of Health and Social Behavior, 29*, 199–213.

Schachter, S. (1980). Urinary pH and the psychology of nicotine addiction. In P.O. Davidson & S.M. Davidson (Eds.), *Behavioral medicine: Changing lifestyles*. New York: Brunner/Mazel.

Schachter, S. (1982). Recidivism and self-cure of smoking and obesity. *American Psychologist, 37*, 436–444.

Schaefer, C., Quesenberry C.P. Jr., & Wi, S. (1995). Mortality following conjugal bereavement and the effects of a shared environment. *American Journal of Epidemiology, 141*, 1142–1152.

Schechter, N.L., Bernstein, B.A., Beck, A., Hart, L., & Scherzer, L. (1991). Individual differences in children's response to pain: Role of temperament and parental characteristics. *Pediatrics, 87*, 171–177.

Schedlowski, M., Jacobs, R., Alker, J., Proehl, F., et al. (1993). Psychophysiological, neuroendocrine and cellular immune reactions under psychological stress. *Neuropsychobiology, 28*, 87–90.

Scheier, M.F., & Carver, C.S. (1987). Dispositional optimism and physical well-being: The influence of generalized outcome expectancies on health. *Journal of Personality, 55*, 169–210.

Scheier, M.F., & Carver, C.S. (1992). Effects of optimism on psychological and physical well-being: Theoretical overview and empirical update. *Cognitive Therapy and Research, 16*, 201–228.

Scheier, M.F., Matthews, K.A., Owens, J., Magovern, G.J., Sr., Lefebvre, R.C., Abbott, R.A., & Carver, C.S. (1989). Dispositional optimism and recovery from coronary artery bypass surgery: The beneficial effects on physical and psychological well-being. *Journal of Personality and Social Psychology, 57*, 1024–1040.

Scheier, M.F., Matthews, K.A., Owens, J.F., Schulz, R., Bridges, M.W., Magovern, G.J., & Carver, C.S. (1999). Optimism and rehospitalization after coronary artery bypass graft surgery. *Archives of Internal Medicine, 159*, 829–835.

Scherck, K.A., (1997). Recognizing a heart attack: The process of determining illness. *American Journal of Critical Care, 6*, 267–273.

Schiaffino, K.M., Shawaryn, M.A., Blum, D. (1998). Examining the impact of illness representations on psychological adjustment to chronic illnesses. *Health Psychology, 17*, 262–268.

Schiffman, H.R. (1976). *Sensation and perception: An integrated approach*. New York: Wiley.

Schiffman, S.S. (1997). Taste and smell losses in normal aging and disease. *Journal of the American Medical Association, 278*, 1357–1362.

Schleifer, S.J., Keller, S.E., Camerino, M., Thornton, J.C., & Stein, M. (1983). Suppression of lymphocyte stimulation following bereavement. *Journal of the American Medical Association, 250*, 374–377.

Schmitz, U., Saile, H., & Nilges, P. (1996). Coping with chronic pain: Flexible goal adjustment as an interactive buffer against pain-related distress. *Pain, 67*, 41–51.

Schneider, D.S., Sledfe, P.A., Shuchter, S.R., & Zisook, S. (1996). Dating and remarriage over the first two years of widowhood. *Annals of Clinical Psychiatry, 8*, 51–57.

Schnitzer, T.J. (1998). Non-NSAID pharmacologic treatment options for the management of chronic pain. *American Journal of Medicine, 105,* 45S–52S.

Schuchert, M.K. (1998). The relationship between verbal abuse of medical students and their confidence in their clinical abilities. *Academic Medicine, 73,* 907–909.

Schuchter, S.R., & Zisook, S. (1993). The course of normal grief. In M.S. Stroebe & W. Stroebe (Eds.), *Handbook of bereavement: Theory, research, and intervention* (pp. 23–43). New York: Cambridge University Press.

Schug, S.A., Merry, A.F., & Acland, R.H. (1991). Treatment principles for the use of opioids in pain of non-malignant origin. *Drugs, 42,* 228–239.

Schulman, K.A., Berlin, J.A., Harless, W., Kerner, J.F., Sistrunk, S., Gersh, B.J., Dube, R., Taleghani, C.K., Burke, J.E., Williams, S., Eisenberg, J.M., & Escarce, J.J. (1999). The effect of race and sex on physicians' recommendations for cardiac catheterization. *New England Journal of Medicine, 340,* 618–626.

Schulz, R. (1976). Effects of control and predictability on the physical and psychological well-being of the institutionalzed aged. *Journal of Personality and Social Psychology, 33,* 563–573.

Schulz, R., & Aderman, D. (1974). Clinical research and the stages of dying. *Omega, 5,* 137–143.

Schulz, R., Newsom, J., Mittelmark, M., Burton, L., et al. (1997). Health effects of caregiving: The caregiver health effects study: An ancillary study of the Cardiovascular Health Study. *Annals of Behavioral Medicine, 19,* 110–116.

Schulz, R., O'Brien, A.T., Bookwala, J., & Fleissner, K. (1995). Psychiatric and physical morbidity effects of dementia caregiving: Prevalence correlates, and causes. *Gerontologist, 35,* 771–791.

Schulz, R., Visintainer, P., & Williamson, G.M. (1990). Psychiatric and physical morbidity effects of caregiving. *Journal of Gerontology, 45,* 181–191.

Schumaker, S.A., Schron, E.B., Ockene, J.K., & McBee, W.L. (Eds.) (1998). *The handbook of health behavior change* (2nd ed.). New York: Springer.

Schuter, R. (1977). A field study of non-verbal communication in Germany, Italy and the United States. *Communication Monographs, 44,* 298–305.

Schwab, R. (1996). Gender differences in parental grief. *Death Studies, 20,* 103–113.

Schwartz, G.E., & Weiss, S.M. (1977). *Yale conference on behavioral medicine.* Washington, DC: Department of Health, Education, and Welfare; National Heart, Lung, and Blood Institute.

Schwartz, R.H., Lewis, D.C., Hoffmann, N.G., & Kyriazi, N.C. (1990). Cocaine and marijuana use by medical students before and during medical school. *Archives of Internal Medicine, 150,* 883–886.

Schwarzer, R., & Weiner, B. (1991). Stigma controlability and coping as predictors of emotions and social support. *Journal of Social & Personal Relationships, 8,* 133–140.

Seale, C., & Addington-Hall, J. (1994). Euthanasia: Why people want to die earlier. *Social Science and Medicine, 39,* 647–654.

Seeman, M. & Evans, J.W. (1961a). Stratification and hospital care. Part 1: The performance of the medical intern. *American Sociological Review, 26,* 67–80.

Seeman, M., & Evans, J.W. (1961b). Stratification and hospital care: Part 2: The objective criterion of performance. *American Sociological Review, 26,* 193–204.

Seeman, M., Seeman, A.Z., & Budros, A. (1988). Powerlessness, work, and community: A longitudinal study of alienation and alcohol use. *Journal of Health and Social Behavior, 29,* 185–198.

Segal, S.P., Egley, L., Watson, M.A., Miller, I., et al. (1995). Factors in the quality of patient evaluations in general hospital psychiatric emergency services. *Psychiatric Services, 46,* 1144–1148.

Segerstrom, S.C., Taylor, S.E., Kemeny, M.E., Reed, G.M., et al. (1996). Causal attributions predict rate of immune decline in HIV-seropositive gay men. *Health Psychology, 15,* 485–493.

Seligman, M.E.P. (1975). *Helplessness: On depression, development and death.* San Francisco, CA: Freeman.

Sellick, S.M., & Zaza, C. (1998). Critical review of 5 non-pharmacologic strategies for managing cancer pain. *Cancer Prevention and Control, 2,* 7–14.

Selye, H. (1956). The stress of life. New York: McGraw-Hill.

Selye, H. (1976). The stress of life (rev. ed). New York: McGraw-Hill.

Selye, H. (1993). History of the stress concept. In L. Goldberger, & S. Breznitz (Eds.), *Handbook of stress: Theoretical and clinical aspects* (2nd ed.) New York: Free Press.

Seneff, M.G., Wagner, D.P., Wagner, R.P., Zimmerman, J.E., & Knaus, W.A. (1995). Hospital and 1-year survival of patients admitted to intensive care units with acute exacerbation of chronic obstructive pulmonary disease. *Journal of the American Medical Association, 274,* 1852–1857.

Sensky, T. (1997). Causal attributions of physical illness. *Journal of Psychosomatic Research, 43,* 565–573.

Shafer, R.W., & Vuitton, D.A. (1999). Highly active antiretroviral therapy (HAART) for the treatment of infection with human immunodeficiency virus type 1. *Biomedical Pharmacotherapy, 53,* 73–86.

Shankar, J., & Famuyiwa, O.O. (1991). Stress among factory workers in a developing country. *Journal of Psychometric Research, 35,* 163–171.

Shapiro, A. (1960). A contribution to a history of the placebo effect. *Behavioral Science, 5,* 109–135.

Shapiro, A.K., & Shapiro, E. (1997). The placebo: Is it much ado about nothing? In A. Harrington (Ed.), *The placebo effect: An interdisciplinary exploration.* Cambridge, MA: Harvard University Press.

Shapiro, D., & Goldstein, I.B. (1982). Biobehavioral perspectives on hypertension. *Journal of Consulting and Clinical Psychology, 50,* 841–858.

Shapiro, D.E., Boggs, S.R., Melamed, B.G., & Graham-Pole, J. (1992). The effect of varied physician affect on recall, anxiety, and perceptions in women with breast cancer: An analogue study. *Health Psychology, 11,* 61–66.

Shapiro, D.H. (1985). Meditation and behavioral medicine:Application of a self-regulation strategy to the clinical management of stress. In S.R. Burchfield (Ed.), *Stress: Psychological and physiological interactions*. Washington, DC: Hemisphere.

Shapiro, J. (1986). Assessment of family coping with illness. *Psychosomatics, 27*, 262–271.

Shapiro, M., & Brack, G. (1994). Psychosocial aspects of siblings' experiences of pediatric cancer. *Elementary School Guidance and Counseling, 28*, 264–273.

Shattuck, F.C. (1907). The science and art of medicine in some of their aspects. *Boston Medical and Surgical Journal, 157*, 63–67.

Sheehan, K.H., Sheehan, D.V., White, K., Leibowitz, A., & Baldwin, D.C., Jr. (1990). A pilot study of medical student "abuse": Student perceptions of mistreatment and misconduct in medical school. *Journal of the American Medical Association, 263*, 533–537.

Sheehan, S.S. (1997). *Kate Quinton's day*. Boston: Houghton Mifflin.

Shekelle, PG., Adams, A.H., Chassin, M.R., Hurwitz, E.L., & Brook, R.H. (1992). Spinal manipulation for low-back pain. *Annals of Internal Medicine, 117*, 590–598.

Shekelle, R.B., Gayle, M., Ostfeld, A.M., & Paul, O. (1983). Hostility, risk of coronary heart disease, and mortality. *Psychosomatic Medicine, 45*, 109–114.

Shen, J., & Wenger, N.S. (1998). Fee-for-service versus capitated medical care: Are there differences in physicians' treatment decisions and perceived conflict? *Association for Health Services Research, 15*, 132–133.

Sher, K.J., & Levenson, R.W. (1982). Risk for alcoholism and individual differences in the stress-response-dampening effect of alcohol. *Journal of Abnormal Psychology, 91*, 350–367.

Sherbourne, C.D., & Stewart, A.L. (1991). The MOS social support survey. *Social Science and Medicine, 32*, 705–714.

Shiffman, S. (1982). Relapse following smoking cessation: A situational analysis. *Journal of Consulting and Clinical Psychology, 50*, 71–86.

Shlain, L. (1979). Cancer is not a four-letter word. In C.A. Garfield (Ed.), *Stress and survival: The emotional realities of life-threatening illness*. St. Louis, MO: C.V. Mosby.

Shlay, J.C., Chaloner, K., Max, M.B., Flaws, B., et al. (1998). *Journal of the American Medical Association, 280*, 1590–1595.

Shneidman, E. (1985). *Definition of suicide*. New York: Wiley.

Shore, B.E., & Franks, P. (1986). Physician satisfaction with patient encounters. *Medical Care, 24*, 580–589.

Shumaker, S.A., & Grunberg, N.E. (Eds) (1986). Proceedings of the National Working Conference on Smoking Relapse. *Health Psychology, 5* (Supplement), 1–99.

Shuy, R.W. (1976). The medical interview: problems in communication. *Primary Care, 3*, 365–386.

Siegel, K., Schrimshaw, E.W., & Dean, L. (1999). Symptom interpretation: Implications for delay in HIV testing and care among HIV-infected late middle-aged and older adults. *AIDS Care, 11*, 525–535.

Siegel, L.J. (1995). What will be the role of psychology in health care settings of the future? *Professional Psychology: Research & Practice, 26*, 341–365.

Sife, W. (Ed.). (1998). After stroke: Enhancing quality of life. New York: The Haworth Press.

Sifneos, P.E. (1996) Alexithymia: Past and present. *American Journal of Psychiatry, 153*, 137–142

Signorielli, N. (1998). Health images on television. In L.D. Jackson, B.K. Duffy, et al. (Eds.). *Health communication research: A guide to developments and directions* (pp. 163–179). Westport, CT: Greenwood Press/Greenwood Publishing Group, Inc.

Silver, E.J., Bawnan, L.J., & Ireys, H.T. (1995). Relationships of self-esteem and efficacy to psychological distress in mothers of children with chronic physical illnesses. *Health Psychology, 14*, 333–340.

Silver, H.K., & Glicken, A.D. (1990). Medical student abuse, incidence, severity and significance. *Journal of the American Medical Association, 263*, 527–533.

Silver, R.L., & Wortman, C.B. (1980). Coping with undesirable life events. In J. Garber & M.E.P. Seligman (Eds.), *Human helplessness: Theory and applications*. New York: Academic Press.

Silverman, P.R., Nickman, S., & Worden, J.W. (1992). Detachment revisited: The child's reconstruction of a dead parent. *American Journal of Orthopsychiatry, 62*, 494–503.

Simon, G.E., VonKorff, M., Piccinelli, M., Fullerton, C., Ormel, J. (1999). An international study of the relation between somatic symptoms and depression. *New England Journal of Medicine, 341*, 1329–1335.

Simons-Morton, B.G., Donohew, L.C., & Aria, D. (1997). Health communication in the prevention of alcohol, tobacco, and drug use. *Health Education and Behavior, 24*, 544–554.

Sist, T., Florio, G.A., Miner, M.F., Lema, M.J., et al. (1998). The relationship between depression and pain language in cancer and chronic non-cancer pain patients. *Journal of Pain and Symptom Management, 15*, 350–358.

Skinner, B.F. (1938). *The behaviors of organisms: An experimental analysis*. New York: Appleton-Century-Crofts.

Slotterback, C.S., & Saarnio, D.A. (1996). Attitudes toward older adults reported by young adults: Variation based on attitudinal task and attribute categories. *Psychology of Aging, 11*, 563–571.

Smelser, N.J., & Baltes, P.B. (Eds.). (in press). *International encyclopedia of the social and behavioral sciences*. London: Elsevier.

Smith, D.L. (1989). Compliance packaging: A patient education tool. *American Pharmacy, NS29*, 42–53.

Smith, J.W., Denny, W.F., & Witzke, D.B. (1986). Emotional impairment in internal medicine house staff: Results of a national survey. *Journal of the American Medical Association, 255*, 1155–1158.

Smith, K.R., & Zick, C.D. (1996). Risk of mortality following widowhood: Safe and sex differences by mode of death. *Social Biology, 43*, 59–71.

Smith, R.C., Lyles, J.S., Mettler, J.A., Marshall, A.A., et al (1995). A strategy for improving patient satisfaction by the intensive training of residents in psychosocial medicine: A controlled, randomized study. *Academic Medicine, 70*, 729–732.

Smith-Coggins, R., Roseking, M.R., Buccino, K.R., Dinger, D.F., & Moser, R.P. (1997). Rotating shift-work schedules: Can we enhance physician adaptation to night shifts? *Academic Emergency Medicine, 4*, 951–961.

Snipe, R.M. (1979). Rapport as a factor in the diagnosis and treatment of physical illness. *Journal of the National Medical Association, 71*, 1142–1144.

Snyder, S.H. (1977). Opiate receptors and internal opiates. *Scientific American, 236*, 44–56.

Solomon, R., & Peterson, M. (1994). Successful aging: How to help your patients cope with change. *Geriatrics, 49*, 41–47.

Sonstroem, R.J. (1984). Exercise and self-esteem. *Exercise and Sports Science Review, 12*, 123–155.

Sourkes, B.M. (1980). Siblings of the pediatric cancer patient. In J Kellerman (Ed.), *Psychological aspects of childhood cancer*. Springfield, IL: Thomas.

Sourkes, B.M. (1996). The broken heart: Antipatory grief in the child facing death. *Journal of Palliative Care, 12*, 56–59.

Spaide, R. (1983). Patientspeak. The New Physician, 5, 5–6.

Speedling, E.J., & Rose, D.N. (1985). Building an effective doctor-patient relationship participation. *Social Science and Medicine, 15E*, 215–222.

Spencer, S.M., Lehman, J.M., Wynings, C., Arena, P., Carver, C.S., Antoni, M.H., Derhagopian, R.P., Ironson, G., & Love, N. (1999). Concerns about breast cancer and relations to psychosocial well-being in a multiethnic sample of early stage patients. *Health Psychology, 18*, 159–168.

Spiegel, D., Bloom, J.R., Kraemer, H.C., & Gottheil, F. (1989). Effect of psychosocial treatment on survival of patients with metastatic breast cancer. *Lancet, 2*, 888–891.

Spiegel, D., & Kato, P. (1996). Psychosocial influences on cancer incidence and progression. *Harvard Review of Psychiatry, 4*, 10–26.

Spiegel, D.A., Smolen, R.C., & Hopfensperger, K.A. (1986). Medical student stress and clerkship performance. *Journal of Medical Education, 61*, 929–931.

Spiegel, P., & Machotka, P. (1974). Messages of the body. New York: Free Press.

Spinetta, J.J. (1982). Behavioral and psychological research in childhood cancer: An overview. *Cancer, 50* (Suppl.), 1939–1943.

Spirig, R. (1998). Support groups for people living with HIV/AIDS: A review of literature. *Journal of Association of Nurses AIDS Care, 9*, 43–55.

Spragins, E. (1996). Does your HMO stack up? *Newsweek, June 24*, 56–63.

Stabler, B. (1993). On the role of patient. *Journal of Pediatric Psychology, 18*, 301–312.

Stang, D.J., & Wrightsman, L.S. (1981). *Dictionary of social behavior and social research methods*. Monterey, CA: Brooks/Cole.

Starfield, B., Steinwachs, D., Morris, I., Bause, G., Siebert, S., & Westin, C. (1979). Patient-doctor agreement about problems needing follow-up visit. *Journal of the American Medical Association, 242*, 344–246.

Starfield, B., Wray, C., Hess, K., Gross, R., Birk, P.S., & D'Lugoff, B.C. (1981). The influence of patient-practitioner agreement on outcome of care. *American Journal of Public Health, 71*, 127–131.

Stauffer, M.H. (1998). A long-term psychotherapy group for children with chronic medical illneess. *Bulletin of the Menninger Clinic, 63*, 15–32.

Stawski, M., Auerbach, J.G., Barasch, M., Lerner, Y., et al. (1997). Behavioural problems of children with chronic physical illness and their siblings. *European Child and Adolescent Psychiatry, 6*, 20–25.

Stedman's Medical Dictionary (26th ed.) (1995). Baltimore, MD: Williams & Wilkins.

Steers, W.N., Elliot, E., Nemiro, J., Ditman, D., et al. (1996). Health beliefs as predictors of HIV-preventive behavior and ethnic differences in prediction. *Journal of Social Psychology, 136*, 99–110.

Stein, P.N., Gordon, W.A., Hibbard, M.R., & Sliwinski, M.J. (1992). An examination of depression in the spouses of stroke patients. *Rehabilitation Psychology, 37*, 121–130.

Steptoe, A., Lipsey, Z., & Wardle, J. (1998). Stress, hassles, and variations in alcohol consumption, food choice, and physical exercise: A diary study. *British Journal of Health Psychology, 3*, 51–63.

Srergiou, G.S., Zourbaki, A.S., Skeva, I.I., & Mountokalakis, T.D. (1998). White coat effect detected using self-monitoring of blood pressure at home: Comparison with ambulatory blood pressure. *American Journal of Hypertension, 11*, 820–827.

Sterling, R.C., Gottheil, E., Weinstein, S.P., Lundy, A., & Serota, R.D. (1996). Learned helplessness and cocaine dependence: An investigation. *Journal of Addictive Disorders, 15*, 13–24.

Stern, D.T. (1998). In search of the informal curriculum: When and where professional values are taught. *Academic Medicine, 73*, S28–S30.

Sternbach, R.A. (1968). *Pain, a psychophysiological analysis*. New York: Academic Press.

Sternbach, R.A. (1974). *Pain patients: Traits and treatments*. New York: Academic Press.

Stevens, B., & Johnston, C.C. (1993). Pain in the infant: Theoretical and conceptual issues. *Maternal–Child Nursing Journal, 21*, 3–14.

Stevens, V.M., Hatcher, J.W., & Bruce, B.K. (1994). How compliant is compliant? Evaluating adherence with breast self-exam positions. *Journal of Behavioral Medicine, 17*, 523–535.

Stewart, M.A. (1995). Effective physician-patient communication and health outcomes: A review. *Canadian Medical Association Journal, 152*, 1423–1433.

Stewart, S.M., Betson, C., Lam, T.H., Marshall, I.B., et al. (1997). Predicting stress in first year medical students: A longitudinal study. *Medical Education, 31,* 163–168.

Stiles, W.B. (1996). Stability of the verbal exchange structure of medical consultations. *Psychology and Health, 11,* 773–785.

Stiles, W.B., Putnam, S.M., & Jacob, M.C. (1982). Verbal exchange structure of initial medical interviews. *Health Psychology, 1,* 315–336.

Stiles, W.B., Putnam, S.M., Wolf, M.H. & James, S.A. (1979). Interaction exchange structure and patient satisfaction with medical interviews. *Medical Care, 17,* 667–681.

Stockhorst, U., Klosterhalfen, S., & Steingrueber, H.J. (1998a). Conditioned nausea and further side-effects in cancer chemotherapy: A review. *Journal of Psychophysiology, 12,* 14–33.

Stockhorst, U., Wiener, J.A., Klosterhalfen, S., Klosterhalfen, W., et al. (1998b). Effects of overshadowing on conditioned nausea in cancer patients: An experimental study. *Physiology and Behavior, 64,* 743–753.

Stoller, E.P. (1984). Self-assessments of health by the elderly: The impact of informal assistance. *Journal of Health and Social Behavior, 25,* 260–270.

Stoller, E.P., & Forster, L.E. (1994). The impact of symptom interpretation on physician utilization. *Journal of Aging & Health, 6,* 507–534.

Stone, A.A., Neale, J.M., Cox, D.S., Napoli, A., Valdimarsdottir, H., & Kennedy-Moore, E. (1994). Daily events are associated with a secretory immune response to an oral antigen in men. *Health Psychology, 13,* 440–446.

Stone, G.C. (1979). Patient compliance and the role of the expert. *Journal of Social Issues, 35,* 34–59.

Stone, R., Cafferata, G.L., & Sangl, J. (1987). Caregiving of the frail elderly: A national profile. *The Gerontologist, 27,* 616–629.

Strasser, S., Aharony, L., & Greenberger, D. (1993). The patient satisfactions process: Moving toward a comprehensive model. *Medical Care Review, 50,* 219–248.

Strathman, A., Gleicher, F., Boninger, D.S., & Edwards, C.S. (1994). The consideration of future consequences: Weighing immediate and distant outcomes of behavior. *Journal of Personality & Social Psychology, 66,* 742–752.

Strauss, A.L. (1975). *Chronic illness and the quality of life.* St. Louis, MO: Mosby.

Straw, M.K. (1983). Coping with obesity. In T.G. Burish & L.A. Bradley (Eds.), *Coping with chronic disease: Research and application.* New York: Academic Press.

Strecher, V.J., Seijts, G.H., Kok, G.J., Latham, G.P., et al. (1995). Goal setting as a strategy for health behavior change. *Health Education Quarterly, 22,* 190–200.

Street, R.L. (1991). Information-giving in medical consultations: The influence of patients' communicative styles and personal characteristics. *Social Science & Medicine, 32,* 541–548.

Street, R.L. (1992). Communicative styles and adaptations in physician/parent consultations. *Social Science & Medicine, 34,* 1155–1163.

Street, R.L., & Buller, D.B. (1987). Nonverbal response patterns in physician/patient interactions: A functional analysis. *Journal of Nonverbal Behavior, 11,* 234–253.

Stringham, J., Riley, J.H., & Ross, A. (1982). Silent birth: Mourning a stillborn baby. *Social Work, 27,* 322–327.

Stroebe, M.S. (1994). The broken heart phenomenon: An examination of the mortality of bereavement. *Journal of Community and Applied Social Psychology, 4,* 47–61.

Stroebe, M.S., & Stroebe, W. (1993). The mortality of bereavement: A review. In M.S. Stroebe, W. Stroebe, & R.O. Hansson (Eds.), *Handbook of bereavement: Theory, research, and intervention.* New York: Cambridge University Press.

Stroebe, W., Stroebe, M., & Abakoumikin, G. (1999). Does differential social support cause sex differences in bereavement outcome? *Journal of Community and Applied Social Psychology, 9,* 1–12.

Stroebe, W., & Stroebe, M.S. (1987). *Bereavement and health: The psychological and physical consequences of partner loss.* New York: Cambridge University Press.

Stroebe, W., & Stroebe, M.S. (1993). Determinants of adjustment to bereavement in younger widows and widowers. In M.S. Stroebe, W. Stroebe, & R.O. Hansson (Eds.), *Handbook of bereavement: Theory, research, and intervention.* New York: Cambridge University Press.

Stroman, C.A. (2000). Explaining illness to African Americans: Employing cultural concerns with strategies. In B.B. Whaley (Ed.) *Explaining illness: Research, theory, and strategies* (pp. 299–316). Mahwah, NJ: Erlbaum.

Struckman-Johnson, D. & Struckman-Johnson, C. (1996). Can you say condom? It makes a difference in fear-arousing AIDS prevention public service announcements. *Journal of Applied Social Psychology, 26,* 1068–1083.

Stuart, R.B., & Davis, B. (1972). *Slim chance in a fat world: Behavioral control of obesity.* Champaign, IL: Research Press.

Stunkard, A.J. (1979). Behavioral medicine and beyond: The example of obesity. In O.F. Pomerleau & J.P. Brady (Eds.), *Behavioral medicine: Theory and practice.* Baltimore, MD: Williams & Wilkins.

Sullivan, P., & Buske, L. (1998). Results from CMA's huge 1998 physician survey point to a dispirited profession. *Canadian Medical Association Journal, 159,* 525–528.

Suls, J. (1982). Social support, interpersonal relations, and health: Benefits and liabilities. In G.S. Sanders & J. Suls (Eds.), *Social psychology of health and illness.* Hillsdale, NJ: Erlbaum.

Sumartojo, E. (1993). When tuberculosis treatment fails. *American Review of Respiratory Diseases, 147,* 1311–1320.

Surgeon General. (1964). *Smoking and health.* Washington, DC: USDHEW Public Health Service.

Surgeon General (1979). *Healthy people: The surgeon general's report on health promotion and disease prevention.* Washington, DC: USDHEW Public Health Service.

Svarstad, B. (1976). Physician-patient communication and patient conformity with medical advice. In D. Mechanic (Ed.), *The growth of bureaucratic medicine* (pp. 220–238). New York: John Wiley & Sons.

Swanson, V., Power, K., & Simpson, R. (1996). A comparison of stress and job satisfaction in female and male GPs and consultants. *Stress Medicine, 12*, 17–26.

Syvalahti, E. (1987). Endocrine and immune adaptation in stress. *Annual Clinical Research, 19*, 70–77.

Szasz, T.S. & Hollender, M.H. (1956). A contribution to the philosophy of medicine: The basic models of the doctor-patient relationship. *Archives of Internal Medicine, 97*, 585–592.

Taira, D., Safran, D.G., Seto, T.B., Rogers, W.H., et al. (1997). The relationship between patient income and physician discussion of health risk behaviors. *Journal of the American Medican Association, 278*, 1412–1417.

Tan, S.Y., & Leucht, C.A. (1997). Cognitive-behavioral therapy for clinical pain control: A 15-year update and its relationship to hypnosis. *International Journal of Clinical and Experimental Hypnosis, 45*, 396–416.

Tasker, R.A., Choiniere, M., Libman, S.M., & Melzack, R. (1987). Analgesia produced by injection of lidocaine into the lateral hypothalamus. *Pain, 31*, 237–248.

Taubes, G. (1993). Claim of higher risk for women smokers attacked. *Science, 262*, 1375.

Taylor, C.E. (1994). International experience and idealism in medical education. *Academic Medicine, 69*, 631–634.

Taylor, N., Hall, G.M., & Salmon, P. (1996). Is patient-controlled analgesia controlled by the patient? *Social Science and Medicine, 43*, 1137–1143.

Taylor, S.E. (1979). Hospital patient behavior: Reactance, helplessness, or control? *Journal of Social Issues, 35*, 156–184.

Taylor, S.E. (1982). Hospital patient behavior: Reactance, helplessness, or control? In H.S. Friedman & M.R. DiMatteo (Eds.), *Interpersonal issues in health care* (pp. 201–231). New York: Academic Press

Taylor, S.E. (1989). *Positive illusions: Creative self deception and the healthy mind.* New York: Basic Books.

Taylor, S.E., Lichtman, R.R., & Wood, J.V. (1984). Attributions, beliefs about control, and adjustment to breast cancer. *Journal of Personality and Social Psychology, 46*, 489–502.

Taylor, S.E., Lichtman, R.R., Wood, J.V., Bluming, A.Z., Dosik, G.M., & Leibowitz, R.L. (1985). Illness related and treatment related factors in psychological adjustment to breast cancer. *Cancer, 55*, 2506–2513.

Taylor, S.E., Repetti, R.L., & Seeman, T. (1997). Health psychology: What is an unhealthy environment and how does it get under the skin? *Annual Review of Psychology, 48*, 411–447.

Temoshok, L. (1987). Personality, coping style, emotion and cancer: Towards an integrative model. *Cancer Surveys, 6*, 545–567.

Temoshok, L., DiClemente, R.J., Sweet, D.M., Blois, M.S., & Sagebiel, R.W. (1984). Factors related to patient delay in seeking medical attention for cutaneous malignant melanoma. *Cancer, 54*, 3048–3053.

Tennen, H., & Affleck, G. (1987). The costs and benefits of optimistic explanations and dispositional optimism. *Journal of Personality, 55*, 376–393.

Tepper, B.J., & Nurse, R.J. (1997). Fat perception is related to PROP taster status. *Physiology and Behavior, 61*, 949–954.

Theorell, T. (1974). Life events before and after the onset of a premature myocardial infraction. In B.S. Dohrenwend & B.P. Dohrenwend (Eds.), *Stressful life events: Their nature and effects.* New York: Wiley.

Theorell T., & Rahe, R.H. (1975). Life change events, ballistocardiography, and coronary death. *Journal of Human Stress, 1*, 18–24.

Thomas, L. (1979). *The medusa and the snail.* New York: Viking.

Thomas, P.D., Goodwin, J.M., & Goodwin, J.S. (1985). Effect of social support on stress-related changes in cholesterol level, uric acid, and immune function in an elderly sample. *American Journal of Psychiatry, 124*, 735–737.

Thompson, C.L., & Pledger, L.M. (1993). Doctor-patient communication: Is patient knowledge of medical terminology improving? *Health Communication, 5*, 89–97.

Thompson, H.C., III, & Weiser, M.A. (1999). Support programs for minority students at Ohio University College of Osteopathic Medicine. *Academic Medicine, 74*, 390–392.

Thompson, M.P., Kaslow, N.J., Kingree, J.B., King, M., et al. (1998). Psychological symptomatology following parental death in a predominantly minority sample of children and adolescents. Journal *of Clinical Child Psychology, 27*, 434–441.

Thompson, S.C. (1981). Will it hurt less if I can control it? A complex answer to a simple question. *Psychological Bulletin, 90*, 89–101.

Thoreson, C.E., & Mahoney, M.J. (1974). *Behavioral self-control.* New York: Holt, Rinehart, & Winston.

Thuen, F., Reime, M.H., & Skrautvoll, K. (1997). The effect of widowhood on psychological wellbeing and social support in the oldest group of the elderly. *Journal of Mental Health, 6*, 265–274.

Tickle-Degnen, L., & Rosenthal, R. (1990). The nature of rapport and its nonverbal correlates. *Psychological Inquiry, 1*, 285.

Timko, C., Stovel, K.W., Moor, R.H., & Miller, J.J., III (1992). A longitudinal study of risk and resistance factors among children with juvenile rheumatic disease. *Journal of Clinical Child Psychology, 21*, 132–142.

Timmerman, I.G.H., Emmelkamp, P.M.G., & Sanderman, R. (1998). The effects of a stress-management training program in individuals at risk in the community at large. *Behavior Research and Therapy, 36*, 863–875.

Timmons, B.H. (1994). Breathing-related issues in therapy. In B.H.Timmons & R. Ley (Eds.), *Behavioral and psychological approaches to breathing disorders* (pp. 261–292). New York: Plenum Press.

Tinsley, J.A., Finlayson, R.E., & Morse, R.M. (1998). Developments in the treatment of alcoholism. *Mayo Clinic Proceedings, 73*, 857–863.

Tomaka, J., Blascovich, J., Kibler, J., & Ernst, J.M. (1997). Cognitive and physiological antecedents of threat and challenge appraisal. *Journal of Personality & Social Psychology, 73,* 63–72.

Torrens, P.R. (1978). The American health care system. St. Louis, MO: Mosby.

Trevisan, M., Krogh, V., Freudanheim, J., Blake, A., Muti, P., Panico, S., Farinaro, E., Mancini, M., Menotti, A., & Ricci, G. (1990). Consumption of olive oil, butter, and vegetable oils and coronary heart disease risk factors. *Journal of the American Medical Association, 263,* 688–692.

Triandis, H.C. (1977). *Interpersonal behavior.* Monterey, CA: Brooks Cole.

Trostle, J.A. (1997). Patient compliance as an ideology. In D.S. Gochman (Ed.), *Handbook of health behavior research II: Provider determinants.* New York: Plenum.

Tsai, G., Gastfriend, D.R., & Coyle, J.T. (1995). The glutamatergic basis of human alcoholism. *American Journal of Psychiatry, 152,* 332–340.

Tucker, C. (1990). Acute pain and substance abuse in surgical patients. *Journal of Neuroscience Nursing, 22,* 339–349.

Tucker, L.A. (1985). Physical, psychological, social, and lifestyle differences among adolescents classified according to cigarette smoking intention status. *Journal of School Health, 55,* 127–131.

Tucker, M.A., Andrew, M.F., Ogle, S.J., & Davison, J.G. (1989). Age-associated change in pain threshold measured by transcutaneous neuronal electrical stimulation. *Age and Ageing, 18,* 241–246.

Turk, D.C., & Meichenbaum, D. (1991). Adherence to self-care regimens: The patient's perspective. In R.H. Rozensky, J.J. Sweet, & S.M. Tovian (Eds.), *Handbook of clinical psychology in medical settings.* New York: Plenum.

Turk, D.C., Meichenbaum, D., & Genest, M. (1983). *Pain and behavioral medicine: A cognitive-behavioral perspective.* New York: Guilford.

Turk, D.C., & Okifuji, A. (1997). What factors affect physicians' decisions to prescribe opioids for chronic noncancer pain patients? *Clinical Journal of Pain, 13,* 330–336.

Turk, D.C., & Rudy, T.E., (1986). Assessment of cognitive factors in chronic pain: A worthwhile enterprise? *Journal of Consulting and Clinical Psychology, 54,* 760–768.

Turk, D.C., Sist, T.C., Okifuji, A., Miner, M.F., et al. (1998). Adaptation to metastatic cancer pain, regional/local cancer pain and non-cancer pain: Role of psychological and behavioral factors. *Pain, 74,* 247–256.

Turk, D.C., Wack, J.T., & Kerns, R.D. (1985). An empirical examination of the "pain-behavior" construct. *Journal of Behavioral Medicine, 8,* 119–130.

Tursky, B., & Sternbach, R.A. (1967). Further physiolgical correlates of ethnic differences in response to shock. *Psychophysiology, 4,* 67–74.

Tversky, A., & Kahneman, D. (1974). Judgement under certainty: Heuristics and biases. *Science, 185,* 1124–1131.

Tyc, V.L., Mulhern, R.K., & Bieberich, A.A. (1997). Anticipatory nausea and vomiting in pediatric cancer patients: An analysis of conditioning and coping variables. *Journal of Developmental and Behavioral Pediatrics, 18,* 27–33.

Tyson, T.R. (2000). The internet: Tomorrow's portal to non-traditional health care services. *Journal of Ambulatory Care Management, 23,* 1–7.

Uchino, B.N., Cacioppo, J.T., & Keicolt-Glaser, J.K. (1996). The relationship between social support and physiological processes: A review with emphasis on underlying mechanisms and implications for health. *Psychological Bulletin, 119,* 488–531.

Uhari, M., Kokkonen, J., Nuutinen, M., Vainionpaa, L., Rantala, H., Lautala, P., & Vayrynen, M. (1994). Medical student abuse: An international phenomenon. *Journal of the American Medical Association, 271,* 1049–1051.

Uhlenberg, P., & Cooney, T.M. (1990). Male and female physicians: Family and career comparisons. *Social Science Medicine, 30,* 373–378.

Ulmer, J.F. (1997). An exploratory study of pain, coping, and depressed mood following burn injury. *Journal of Pain and Symptom Management, 13,* 148–157.

U.S. Bureau of the Census (USBC). (1998). *Statistical abstract of the United States: 1998* (118th ed.). Washington, DC: Bureau of the Census.

U.S. Department of Health, Education, & Welfare & U.S. Public Health Service, Centers for Disease Control. (1964). *Smoking and health: Report of the advisory committee of the Surgeon General of the Public Health Service* (Publication No. PHS 1103). Washington, DC: U.S. Government Printing Office.

U.S. Department of Health and Human Services (USD-HHS). (1981). *Alcohol and health.* Rockville, MD: National Institute of Alcohol Abuse and Alcoholism.

U.S. Department of Health and Human Services (USD-HHS). (1996). *Physical activity and health: A report of the Surgeon General.* Atlanta, GA: CDC.

U.S. Department of Health and Human Services (USD-HHS). (1998a). *Health, United States, 1998.* Washington, DC: U.S. Government Printing Office.

U.S. Department of Health and Human Services (USD-HHS). (1998b). *Healthy people 2010 objectives: Draft for public comment.* Washington, DC: U.S. Government Printing Office.

Vaccarino, A.L., & Melzack, R. (1992). Temporal processes of formalin pain: Differential role of the cingulum bundle, fornix pathway and medial bulboreticular formation. *Pain, 49,* 257–271.

Vaccarino, J.M. (1977). Malpractice: The problem in perspective. *Journal of the American Medical Association, 238,* 861–863.

Valdimarsdottir, H.B., & Bovbjerg, D.H. (1997). Positive and negative mood: Association with natural killer cell activity. *Psychology and Health, 12,* 319–327.

Valdiserri, R.O., Tama, G.M., & Ho, M. (1988). A survey of AIDS patients regarding their experiences with physicians. *Journal of Medical Education, 63,* 726–728.

Valentino, L., Pillay, K.V., & Walker, J. (1998). Managing chronic nonmalignant pain with continuous intrathecal morphine. *Journal of Neuroscience Nursing, 30,* 243–244.

Valko, R.J., & Clayton, P.J. (1975). Depression in the internship. *Diseases of the Nervous Systems, 36,* 26–29.

VandenBos, G.R. (1993). U.S. mental health policy: Proactive evolution in the midst of health care reform. *American Psychologist, 48,* 283–290.

VandenBos, G.R., DeLeon, P.H., & Belar, C.D. (1991). How many psychologists are needed? It's too early to know! *Professional Psychology: Research & Practice, 22,* 441–448.

Van Der Merwe, J.V. (1995). Physician-patient communication using ancestral spirits to achieve holistic healing. *American Journal of Obstetrics and Gynecology, 172,* 1080–1087.

van Dulmen, A.M., Verhaak, R.F.M., & Bilio, H.J.G. (1997). Shifts in doctor-patient communication during a series of outpatient consultations in non-insulin-dependent diabetes mellitus. *Patient Education & Counseling, 30,* 227–237.

van Heck, G.L. (1997). Personality and physical health: Toward an ecological approach to health-related personality research. *European Journal of Personality, 11,* 415–443.

van Komen, R.W., & Redd, W.H. (1985). Personality factors associated with anticipatory nausea and vomiting in patients receiving cancer chemotherapy. *Health Psychology, 4,* 189–202.

Van Lankveld, W., Naring, G., Van der Staak, C., Van Pad Bosch, P., & Van de Putte, L. (1993). Stress caused by rheumatoid arthritis: Relation among subjective stressors of the disease, disease status, and well-being. *Journal of Behavioral Medicine, 16,* 309–322.

Vannatta, R.A. (1996). Risk factors related to suicidal behavior among male and female adolescents. *Journal of Youth and Adolescence, 25,* 149–160.

van Ryn, M., Lytle, L.A., & Kirscht, J.P. (1996). A test of the theory of planned behavior for two health-related practices. *Journal of Applied Social Psychology, 26,* 871–883.

van Wijk, C.M., & Kolk, A.M. (1997). Sex differences in physical symptoms: The contribution of symptom perception theory. *Social Science and Medicine, 45,* 231–246.

Ventura, S.J., Anderson, R.N., Martin, J.A., & Smith, B.L. (1998). Births and deaths: Preliminary data for 1997. *National Vital Statistics Reports, 47,* 1–41.

Verdecchia, P. (1999). White-coat hypertension in adults and children. *Blood Pressure Monitor, 4,* 175–179.

Vessey, J.A., Carlson, K.L., & McGill, J. (1994). Use of distraction with children during an acute pain experience. *Nursing Research, 43,* 369–372.

Viano, D.C. (1995). Restraint effectiveness, availability and use in fatal crashes: Implications to injury control. *Journal of Trauma, 38,* 538–546.

Videka-Sherman, L. (1982). Coping with the death of a child: A study over time. *American Journal of Orthopsychiatry, 52,* 688–698.

Viera, A.J., Clenney, T.L., Shenenberger, D.W., & Green, G.F. (1999). Newer pharmacologic alternatives for erectile dysfunction. *American Family Physician, 60,* 1159–1166.

Vilhjalmsson, R. (1998). Direct and indirect effects of chronic physical conditions on depression: A preliminary investigation. *Social Science and Medicine, 47,* 603–611.

Vincent, R. (1996). Advances in early diagnosis and management of acute myocardial infarction. *Journal of Accident and Emergency Medicine, 13,* 74–79.

Voll, R., & Poustka, F. (1994). Coping with illness and coping with handicap during the vocational rehabilitation of physically handicapped adolescents and young adults. *International Journal of Rehabilitation Research, 17,* 305–318.

Volmink, J., Lancaster, T., Gray, S., & Silagy, C. (1996). Treatments for postherpetic neuralgia—a systematic review of randomized controlled trials. *Family Practice, 13,* 84–91.

Voytovich, A.E., Rippey, R.M., & Suffredini, A. (1985). Premature conclusions in diagnostic reasoning. *Journal of Medical Education, 60,* 302–307.

Wachter, R.M., Cooke, M., Hopewell, P.C., & Luce, J.M. (1988). Attitudes of medical residents regarding intensive care for patients with the Acquired Immunodeticiena Syndrome. *Archives of Internal Medicine, 148,* 149–152.

Wagner, E.R. (1989). Types of managed health care organizations. In P.R. Kongstvedt (Ed.), *The managed care health care handbook.* Aspen, CO: Aspen Publishers.

Waid, W.M., Wilson, S.K., & Orne, M.T. (1981). Cross-modal physiological effects of electrodermal lability in the detection of deception. *Journal of Personality Social Psychology, 40,* 1118–1125.

Waitzkin, H. (1984). Doctor-patient communication: Clinical implications of social scientific research. *Journal of the American Medical Association, 252,* 2441–2446.

Waitzkin, H. (1985). Information giving in medical care. *Journal of Health and Social Behavior, 26,* 81–101.

Waitzkin, H., & Britt, T. (1993). Processing narratives of self-destructive behavior in routine medical encounters: Health promotion, disease prevention, and the discourse of health care. *Social Science & Medicine, 36,* 1121–1136.

Waitzkin, H., Cabrera, A., Arroyo de Cabrera, E., Radlow, M., et al. (1996). Patient-doctor communication in cross-national perspective. *Medical Care, 34,* 641–671.

Waitzkin, H., & Stoeckle, J.D. (1976). Information control and the micropolitics of health care: Summary of an ongoing research project. *Social Science and Medicine, 10,* 263–276.

Waldron, I. (1997). Changing gender roles and gender differences in health behavior. In D.S. Gochman (Ed.), *Handbook of health behavior research I: Personal and social determinants.* New York: Plenum Press.

Walker, J.S., & Carmody, J.J. (1998). Experimental pain in healthy human subjects: Gender differences in nociception and in response to ibuprofen. *Anesthesiology and Analgesia, 86,* 1257–1262.

Wall, E., Rodriguez, G., & Saultz, J. (1993). A retrospective study of patient care needs on admission to an inpatient hospice facility. *Journal of the American Board of Family Practice, 6,* 233–238.

Wallston, K.A., & Wallston, B.S. (1983). Who is responsible for your health? The construct of health locus of

control. In G. Saunders & J. Suls (Eds.), *Social psychology of health and illness.* Hillsdale, NJ: Erlbaum.

Wallander, J.L., & Varni, W.(1998). Effects of pediatric chronic physical disorders on child and family adjustment. *Journal of Child Psychology and Psychiatry & Allied Disciplines, 39,* 29–46.

Waltz, M. (1986). Marital context and post-infarction quality of life: Is it social support or something more? *Social Science & Medicine, 22,* 791–805.

Wanberg, K.W., & Horn, J.L. (1983). Assessment of alcohol use with multidimensional concepts and measures. *American Psychologist, 38,* 1055–1069.

Wang, C.Y., & Abbott, L.J. (1998). Development of a community based diabetes and hypertension preventive program. *Public Health Nursing, 15,* 406–414.

Warburg, M.M., Cleary, P.D., Rohman, M., Barnes, H.N., Aronson, M., & Delbanco, T.L. (1987). Residents' attitudes, knowledge, and behavior regarding diagnosis and treatment of alcoholism. *Journal of Medical Education, 62,* 497–503.

Warde, C., Allen, W., & Gelberg, L. (1996). Physician role conflict and resulting career changes: Gender and generational differences. *Journal of General Internal Medicine, 11,* 729–235.

Ware, J.E., & Young, J. (1979). Issues in the conceptualization and measurement of value placed on health. In S.J. Mushkin & D.W. Dunlop (Eds.), *Health: What is it worth?* (pp. 141–166). New York: Pergamon.

Warwick, Z.S., & Schiffman, S.S. (1992). Role of dietary fat in calorie intake and weight gain. *Neuroscience and Biobehavioral Reviews, 16,* 585–596.

Waters, C.M. (1999). Professional nursing support for culturally diverse family members of critically ill adults. *Research in Nursing and Health, 22,* 107–117.

Watson, O.M. (1970). *Proxemic behavior: A cross-cultural study.* The Hague: Mouton.

Webb, W.B. (Ed.) (1982). *Biological rhythms, sleep, and performance.* New York: Wiley.

Wegner, D.M. (1990). *White bears and other unwanted thoughts: Suppression, obsession, and the psychology of mental control.* New York: Penguin Books.

Wegner, D.M., & Pennebaker, J.W. (1993). Changing our minds: An introduction to mental control. In D.M. Wegner & J.W. Pennebaker (Eds.), *Handbook of mental control* (pp. 1–12). Englewood Cliffs, NJ: Prentice Hall.

Wegner, D.M., Schneider, D.J., Knutson, B., & McMahon, S.R. (1991). Polluting the stream of consciousness: The effect of thought suppression on the mind's environment. *Cognitive Therapy and Research, 15,* 141–152.

Weidner, G., Connor, S.L., Chesney, M.A., Burns, J.W., Connor, W.E., Matarazzo, J.D., & Mendell, N.R. (1991). Sex differences in high density lipoprotein cholesterol among low-level alcohol consumers. *Circulation, 83,* 176–180.

Weidner, G., Friend, R., Ficarrotto, T.J., & Mendell, N.R. (1989). Hostility and cardiovascular reactivity to stress in women and men. *Psychosomatic Medicine, 51,* 36–45.

Weidner, G., Sexton, G., McLellarn, R., Connor, S.L., & Matarazzo, J.D. (1987). The role of the Type A behavior and hostility in an elevation of plasma lipids in adult women and men. *Psychosomatic Medicine, 49,* 450–457.

Weil, A. (1997). *Eight weeks to optimum health.* New York: Knopf.

Weil, A. (1998). *Natural health, natural medicine.* Boston: Houghton Mifflin.

Weinstein, H.M. (1983). A committee on well-being of medical students and house staff. *Journal of Medical Education, 58,* 373–381.

Weisenberg, M. (1977). Pain and pain control. *Psychological Bulletin, 84,* 1008–1044.

Weisenberg, M. (1987). Psychological intervention for the control of pain. *Behaviour Research and Therapy, 25,* 301–312.

Weisenberg, M., Schwarzwald, J., & Tepper, I. (1996). The influence of warning signal timing and cognitive preparation on the aversiveness of cold-pressor pain. *Pain, 64,* 379–385.

Weisman, C.S., & Teitelbaum, M.A. (1985). Physician gender and the physician-patient relationship: Recent evidence and relevant questions. *Social Science and Medicine, 20,* 1119–1127.

Weiss, G.L., Larsen, D.L., & Baker, W.K. (1996). The development of health protective behaviors among college students. *Journal of Behavioral Medicine, 19,* 143–161.

Weitz, R. (1996). *The sociology of health, illness, and health care: A critical approach.* Belmont, CA: Wadsworth.

Wells, A. (1991). Effects of dispositional self-focus, appraisal and attention instructions on responses to a threatening stimulus. *Anxiety Research, 3,* 291–301.

Wells, Y.D., & Kendig, H.L. (1997). Health and well-being of spouse caregivers and the widowed. *Gerontologist, 37,* 666–674.

Wertlieb, D., Hauser, S.T., & Jacobson, A.M. (1986). Adaptation to diabetes: Behavior symptoms and family context. *Journal of Pediatric Psychology, 11,* 463–479.

Wessely, S., Nimnuan, C., & Sharpe, M. (1999). Functional somatic syndromes: One or many? *Lancet, 354,* 936–939.

West, C. (1983). "Ask me no questions . . .": An analysis of queries and replies in physician-patient dialogues. In S. Fisher & A.D. Todd (Eds.), *The social organization of doctor-patient communication* (pp. 75–106). Washington, DC: Center for Applied Linguistics.

West, C. (1984). *Routine complications: Troubles with talk between doctors and patients.* Bloomington: Indiana University Press.

Wheaton, B. (1983). Stress, personal coping resources, and psychiatric symptoms: An investigation of interactive models. *Journal of Health and Social Behavior, 24,* 208–229.

Wheaton, B. (1994). Sampling the stress universe. In W.R. Avison & I.H. Gotlib (Eds.). *Stress and mental health* (pp. 77–223). New York: Plenum.

White, A.R., & Ernst, E. (1999). A systematic review of randomized controlled trials of acupuncture for neck pain. *Rheumatology Oxford, 38,* 143–147.

White, J., Levinson, W., & Roter, D. (1994). "Oh, by the way . . .": The closing moments of the medical visit. *Journal of General Internal Medicine, 9,* 24–28.

White, J.C., Rosson, C., Christensen, J., Hart, R., et al. (1997). Wrapping things up: A qualitative analysis of the closing moments of the medical visit. *Patient Education &Counseling, 30,* 155–165.

White, J.C., & Sweet, W.H. (1969). *Pain and the neurosurgeon: A forty-year experience.* Springfield, IL: Charles C. Thomas.

White, K.L., Williams, T.F., & Greenberg, B.G. (1961). The ecology of medical care. *New England Journal of Medicine, 265,* 885–892.

White, L.L. (1960). *The unconscious before Freud.* New York: Basic Books.

Whiteside, T.L., & Friberg, D. (1998). Natural killer cells and natural killer cell activity in chronic fatigue syndrome. *American Journal of Medicine, 105,* 27S–34S.

Whitney, C.R. (1993). Coverage for all, with choices. *New York Times,* November 14.

Wickersham, B.A. (1984). The exercise program. In G.K. Riggs & E.P. Gall (Eds.), *Rheumatic diseases: Rehabilitation and managment.* Boston: Butterworth.

Wiggs, J.S., & Elam, C.L. (2000). Recruitment and retention: The development of an action plan for African-American health professions students. *Journal of the National Medical Association, 92,* 125–130.

Wilkins, K, & Beaudet, M.P. (1998). Work stress and health. *Health Reports, 10,* 47–62.

Williams, A.C., Richardson, P.H., Nicholas, M.K., Pither, C.E., et al. (1996). Inpatient vs. outpatient pain management: Results of a randomised controlled trial. *Pain, 66,* 13–22.

Williams, A.W., Ware, J.E., Jr., & Donald, C.A. (1981). A model of mental health, life events, and social supports applicable to general populations. *Journal of Health and Social Behavior, 22,* 324–336.

Williams, B. (1999). Women in medicine: Still a long way to go, baby. *Tennessee Medicine, 92,* 327–330.

Williams, D.A., Feuerstein, M., Durbin, D., & Pezzullo, J. (1998). Health care and indemnity costs across the natural history of disability in occupational low back pain. *Spine, 23,* 2329–2336.

Williams, J.M., & Getty, D. (1986). Effects of levels of exercise on psychological mood states, physical fitness, and plasma beta-endorphin. *Perceptual and Motor Skills, 63,* 1099–1105.

Williams, P.D. (1997). Siblings and pediatric chronic illness: A review of the literature. *International Journal of Nursing Studies, 34,* 312–323.

Williamson, D.F. (1993). Descriptive epidemiology of body weight and weight change in U.S. adults. *Annals of Internal Medicine, 119,* 106–112.

Williamson, G.M. (1998). The central role of restricted normal activities in adjustment to illness and disability: A model of depressed affect. *Rehabilitation Psychology, 43,* 327–347.

Wills, T.A. (1984). Supportive functions of interpersonal relationships. In S. Cohen & L. Syme (Eds.), *Social support and health.* New York: Academic Press.

Wilson, E.J., & Sherrell, D.L. (1993). Source effects in communication and persuasion research: A meta-analysis of effect size. *Journal of the Academy of Marketing Science, 21,* 101–112.

Wilson, G.T. (1980). Cognitive factors in lifestyle changes: A social learning perspective. In P.O. Davidson & S.M. Davidson (Eds.), *Behavioral medicine: Changing health lifestyles.* New York: Brunner-Mazel.

Wilson-Barnett, J. (1998). Psychological reactions to medical procedures. In G.A. Fava, H. Freyberger (Eds.), *Handbook of psychosomatic medicine* (pp. 501–516). Madison, WI: International Universities Press.

Wilson-Pessano, S.R., & McNabb, W.L. (1985). The role of patient education in the management of childhood asthma. *Preventive Medicine, 14,* 670–687.

Wilters, J.H. (1998). Stress, burnout and physician productivity. *Medical Group Management Journal, 45,* 32–24, 36–37.

Winters, R. (1985). Behavioral approaches to pain. In N. Schneiderman & J.T. Tapp (Eds.), *Behavioral medicine: The biopsychosocial approach.* Hillsdale, NJ: Erlbaum.

Wipf, J.E., Pinsky, L.E., & Burke, W. (1995). Turning interns into senior residents: Preparing residents for their teaching and leadership roles. *Academic Medicine, 70,* 591–596.

Wittkower, E. (1953). Psychological aspects of tuberculosis. *American Review of Tuberculosis, 67,* 869–873.

Wolf, S.M. (1988). Conflict between doctor and patient. *Law, Medicine, & Health Care, 16,* 197–203.

Wolf, T.M. (1997). Perceived mistreatment and psychosocial well-being of graduating medical students. *Psychology, Health & Medicine, 2,* 273–284.

Wolf, T.M., Scurria, P.L., & Webster, M.G. (1998). A four year study of anxiety, depression, loneliness, social support, and perceived mistreatment in medical students. *Journal of Health Psychology, 3,* 125–136.

Wood, C. (1998). The misplace of litigation in medical practice. *Australian and New Zealand Journal of Obstetrics and Gynaecology, 38,* 365–376.

Wood, M.M., Ashby, M.A., Somogyi, A.A., Fleming, B.G. (1998). Neuropsychological and pharmacokinetic assessment of hospice inpatients receiving morphine. *Journal of Pain and Symptom Management, 16,* 112–120.

Woodward, C.A., Hutchinson, B.G., Abelson, J., & Norman, G. (1996). Do female primary care physicians practise preventive care differently from their male colleagues? *Canadian Family Physician, 42,* 2370–2379.

Worchel, F.F, Prevatt, B.C., Miner, J., Allen, M., et al. (1995). Pediatrician's communication style: Relationship to parent's perceptions and behaviors. *Journal of Pediatric Psychology, 20,* 633–644.

Worden, J.W., Davies, B., & McCown, D. (1999). Comparing parent loss with sibling loss. *Death Studies, 23,* 1–15.

World Health Organization. (1946). *Official Record, Vol. 2* (p. 100). Geneva, Switzerland: Author.

World Health Organization. (1948). *Constitution of the World Health Organization.* Geneva, Switzerland: Author.

Wortman, C.B., & Dunkel-Schetter, C. (1979). Interpersonal relationships and cancer: A theoretical analysis. *Journal of Social Issues, 35,* 120–155.

Wortman, C.B., & Dunkel-Schetter, C. (1987). Conceptual and methodological issues in the study of social support. In A. Baum & J.E. Singer (Eds.), *Handbook of psychology and health* (vol. 5). Hillsdale, NJ: Erlbaum.

Wu, K.K., & Lam, D.J. (1993). The relationship between daily stress and health: Replicating and extending previous findings. *Psychology & Health, 8,* 329–344.

Wu, Z. (1995). Remarriage after widowhood: A marital history study of older Canadians. *Canadian Journal on Aging, 14,* 719–736.

Wyshak, G., & Barsky, A. (1995). Satisfaction with and effectiveness of medical care in relation to anxiety and depression. Patient and physician ratings compared. *General Hospital Psychiatry, 17,* 108–114.

Yates, A.J., & Thain, J. (1985). Self-efficacy as a predictor of relapse following voluntary cessation of smoking. *Addictive Behaviors, 10,* 291–298.

Yeater, R.A., & Ullrich, I.H. (1985). The role of physical activity in disease prevention and treatment. *The West Virginia Medical Journal, 81,* 35–39.

Young, M., & Klingle, R.S. (1996). Silent partners in medical care: A cross-cultural study of patient participation. *Health Communication, 8,* 29–53.

Zajonc, R.B. (1968). Attitudinal effects of mere exposure. *Journal of Personality and Social Psychology (monograph supplement), 9,* 1–27.

Zarit, S.H. & Zarit, J.M. (1984). Psychological approaches to families of the elderly. In M.G. Eisenberg, L.C. Sutkin, & M.A. Jansen (Eds). *Chronic illness and disability through the life span: Effects on self and family* (pp. 269–288). New York: Springer.

Zastowny, T.R., Kirschenbaum, D.S., & Meng, A.L. (1986). Coping skills training for children: Effects on distress before, during, and after hospitalization for surgery. *Health Psychology, 5,* 231–247.

Zborowski, M. (1952). Cultural components in responses to pain. *Journal of Social Issues, 8,* 16–30.

Zborowski, M. (1969). *People in pain.* San Franciso: Jossey-Bass.

Zelinski, E.M., Crimmins, E., Reynolds, S., Seeman, T. (1998). Do medical conditions affect cognition in older adults? *Health Psychology, 17,* 504–512.

Zenz, M., Strumpf, M., & Tryba, M. (1992). Long-term oral opioid therapy in patients with chronic nonmalignant pain. *Journal of Pain Symptom Management, 7,* 69–77.

Ziegler, J.L., Kansas, N., Strull, W.M., & Bennet, N.E. (1984). A stress discussion group for medical interns. *Journal of Medical Education, 59,* 205–207.

Zimbardo, P.G., Ebbesen, E.B., & Maslach, C. (1977). *Influencing attitudes and changing behavior* (2nd ed.). Reading, MA: Addison-Wesley.

Zinn, W. (1993). The empathic physician. *Archives of Internal Medicine, 153,* 306–312.

Zisook, S., Devand, R.A., & Click, M.A. (1982). Measuring symptoms of grief and bereavement. *American Journal of Psychiatry, 139,* 1590–1593.

Zisook, S., & DeVaul, R. (1985). Unresolved grief. *American Journal of Psychoanalysis, 45,* 370–379.

Zisook, S., & Schuchter, S.R. (1985). Time course of spousal bereavement. *General Hospital Psychiatry, 7,* 95–100.

Zisook, S., Schuchter, S.R., Irwin, M., Darko, D.F., Sledge, P., & Resovsky, K. (1994). Bereavement, depression, and immune function. *Psychiatry Research, 52,* 1–10.

Zlatin, D.M. (1995). Life themes: A method to understand terminal illness. *Omega: Journal of Death and Dying, 31,* 189–206.

Zola, I.K. (1973). Pathways to the doctor—from person to patient. *Social Science and Medicine, 7,* 677–689.

Zucker, R.A., & Gomberg, E.S.L. (1986). Etiology of alcoholism reconsidered: The case for a biopsychosocial process. *American Psychologist, 41,* 783–793.

Zuckerman, M. (Ed.) (1983). *Biological bases of sensation seeking, impulsivity, and anxiety.* Hillsdale, NJ: Erlbaum.

Zuckerman, M., DePaulo, B.M., & Rosenthal, R. (1981). Verbal and nonverbal communication of deception. In L. Berkowitz, (Ed.), *Advances in experimental social psychology (vol. 14).* New York: Academic Press.

INDEX

Photo credits: Corbis Digital Stock, p. 1; Penny Tweedie/Stone, p. 7; Dennis MacDonald/Photo Edit, p. 14; Michael Newman/Photo Edit, p. 17; Leslie R. Martin, pp. 25, 54, 77, 103, 163, 323, 356, 377, 393, 425, 499, 508; Jose Pelaez/Corbis Stock Market, pp. 36, 241; Chronis Jons/Stone, p. 43; Will & Deni McIntyre/Photo Researchers, p. 65; George Bellerose/Stock Boston, p. 70; Cindy Karp/Black Star Publishing/PictureQuest, p. 90; Cindy Charles/Photo Edit, p. 113; Michelle Del Guerico/Photo Researchers, p. 121; David Wells/The Image Works, p. 126; Mark Harmel/Stone, p. 133; Stewart Cohen/Stone, p. 147; Spencer Grant/Photo Edit, p. 172; Spencer Grant/Stock Boston, p. 192; David Young/Wolff/Photo Edit, pp. 198, 208; Tony Freeman/Photo Edit, p. 203; Dan Bosler/Stone, p. 217; Jim Cummins/Corbis Stock Market, p. 226; Michael Newman/Photo Edit, p. 234; Ken Cavanagh/Photo Researchers, p. 247; Chris Baker/Stone, p. 259; Bob Daemmrich/The Image Works, p. 270; Pearson Education/PH College, p. 276; Tom Stewart/Corbis Stock Market, p. 291; Bonnie Kamin/Photo Edit, p. 307; Susan Van Etten Lawson/Photo Edit, p. 317; Myrleen Ferguson Cate/Photo Edit, p. 332; David Madison/Stone, p. 341; Christopher Bissell/Stone, p. 348; Kevin R. Morris/Corbis, p. 383; Bob Daemmrich/Stock Boston, p. 386; Angela Wyant/Stone, p. 414; CC Studio/Science Photo Laboratory/Photo Researchers, p. 421; Tim Barnwell/Stock Boston, p. 436; Jerry Berndt/Stock Boston, p. 448; Myrleen Cate/Stone, p. 458; Mark Richards/Photo Edit, p. 464; Larry Mulvehill/Photo Edit, p. 473; Charles Gupton/Stock Boston, p. 478; Bruce Ayres/Stone, p. 506.